MONEY LAUNDERIN
LAW AND REGULATIC

A Practical Guide

MONEY LAUNDERING LAW AND REGULATION

A Practical Guide

ROBIN BOOTH
Partner, BCL Burton Copeland

SIMON FARRELL QC
Barrister, 3 Raymond Buildings

GUY BASTABLE
Partner, BCL Burton Copeland

NICHOLAS YEO
Barrister, 3 Raymond Buildings

OXFORD
UNIVERSITY PRESS

OXFORD

UNIVERSITY PRESS

Great Clarendon Street, Oxford OX2 6DP

Oxford University Press is a department of the University of Oxford.
It furthers the University's objective of excellence in research, scholarship,
and education by publishing worldwide in

Oxford New York

Auckland Cape Town Dar es Salaam Hong Kong Karachi
Kuala Lumpur Madrid Melbourne Mexico City Nairobi
New Delhi Shanghai Taipei Toronto

With offices in

Argentina Austria Brazil Chile Czech Republic France Greece
Guatemala Hungary Italy Japan Poland Portugal Singapore
South Korea Switzerland Thailand Turkey Ukraine Vietnam

Oxford is a registered trade mark of Oxford University Press
in the UK and in certain other countries

Published in the United States
by Oxford University Press Inc., New York

British Library Cataloguing-in-Publication Data
Data available

Library of Congress Control Number 2011920660

Typeset by Glyph International, Bangalore, India

Printed in Great Britain   by
Ashford Colour Press Ltd,
Gosport, Hampshire

ISBN 978-0-19-954303-8

PREFACE

They have but few laws, and such is their constitution, that they need not many. They do very much condemn other nations, whose laws, together with the commentaries on them, swell up to so many volumes; for they think it an unreasonable thing to oblige men to obey a body of laws, that are both of such a bulk, and so dark, that they cannot be read or understood by every one of the subjects.

Utopia by Sir Thomas More, 1516 (in the translation by Bishop Gilbert Burnet).

The Proceeds of Crime Act 2002 consists mainly of provisions for the recovery of the proceeds of crime, measures aimed at stripping criminals of their ill-gotten gains. Most of the books on proceeds of crime reflect this emphasis: they deal primarily with restraint and confiscation in criminal proceedings and with civil recovery of criminal assets.

This book has a different emphasis and is more concerned with the activity of money laundering and the law intended to combat money laundering. It deals with the three serious and widely defined criminal offences of money laundering and with the considerable impact of these offences (whose mental element is, in practice, no more than suspicion) on ordinary law-abiding citizens. The money laundering offence under the Terrorism Act 2000 and the other terrorist property offences are also covered, both as substantive criminal offences and in the context of the disclosure provisions that are broadly equivalent to those in the Proceeds of Crime Act.

New or greatly extended powers of investigation and widely drawn offences, together with a much more proactive approach to tackling crime through the suspected proceeds of crime, have enormously increased the scale and frequency with which law enforcement activity impacts on individuals and businesses innocent of any criminal activity or intention. Any person carrying out a financial or property transaction, whether in a personal capacity or by way of business or professional services, may come to suspect that the property in question is criminal property. From the time that the suspicion arises, that person may well be committing an offence of money laundering and may need to make a consent report in order to escape from criminal liability.

The book also deals with the direct impact of current anti-money laundering measures on the many people who work in banks and financial services or in other businesses and professions now regulated for money laundering purposes and who are, therefore, subject to the regulatory requirements and restrictions intended to prevent and detect money laundering.

Accordingly, this book aims to provide detailed treatment of the law and regulation relating to money laundering: the criminal offences of money laundering, the disclosure regime and related disclosure offences, and the customer due diligence and other obligations created by the Money Laundering Regulations 2007. It does not cover the law relating to the recovery of the proceeds of crime through confiscation, civil asset recovery and other means such as taxation. It does, however, also deal with cash declaration and with the seizure, detention and forfeiture of cash, for the reasons noted below. The final chapter of the book, through a detailed scenario and commentary, considers how the new anti-money laundering law works out in practice.

A secondary purpose of the book is to cover those aspects of anti-money laundering law which may, at any time, suddenly and adversely affect companies and individuals (mainly, but not exclusively, those in the regulated sector), when they are carrying on their ordinary business, e.g. through the action of a bank in effectively freezing a bank account after making a consent report or through the exercise by a police or customs officer or border agency officer of the power to seize and detain cash. For this reason, cash seizure powers are included in the book and restraint orders are dealt with in the context of the scenario in the final chapter.

Strictly speaking, the book deals with the law of England and Wales, but the criminal law and other provisions in Part 7 of the Proceeds of Crime Act 2002 apply throughout the United Kingdom. The Terrorism Act 2000 (insofar as it is relevant to the subject matter of this book—mainly Part III of the Act) and the Money Laundering Regulations 2007 also apply throughout the United Kingdom. We have tried to state the law as at 1 November 2010.

A E Housman, a classical scholar as well as a poet, said that '… accuracy is a duty and not a virtue…'. If that is true with regard to the editing of a Latin author such as Manilius, it is surely no less true of a book that aims to set out the current state of a difficult and contentious area of law. Despite our efforts to comply with the duty of accuracy, however, it is all too possible that some errors may have escaped detection and correction; for any errors that remain, the authors must accept responsibility.

Robin Booth, Simon Farrell QC,
Guy Bastable, Nicholas Yeo
23 November 2010

ACKNOWLEDGEMENTS

This book is the work of four practitioners and would never have seen the light of day without much help from others. We wish particularly to record our grateful thanks for the contributions and ready assistance given by two lawyers at BCL Burton Copeland, Shaul Brazil and John Binns, and to Peter de Verneuil Smith, a barrister at 3 Verulam Buildings.

Selected sections of Chapter 4 of this work have been taken from the looseleaf *Smith, Owen and Bodnar on Asset Recovery, Criminal Confiscation, and Civil Recovery*, edited by Ian Smith, Tim Owen QC, and Andrew Bodnar (© Oxford University Press, 2007). The Third EU Money Laundering Directive is reproduced by kind permission of the Publications Office of the European Union (© European Union, 1995–2010, source: <http://eur-lex.europa.eu>). The FATF 40 Recommendations and FATF 9 Special Recommendations are reproduced by kind permission of the Financial Action Task Force (© FATF/OECD. All rights reserved). Every effort has been made to contact the copyright holders of the material reproduced here. However, the Publisher will be delighted to rectify any omission upon reprinting of this book.

The authors have good reason to be grateful to the publishers for their forbearance over the long period of gestation. We wish to thank all of the team at Oxford University Press for their help throughout the period from the time of the initial proposal to publication. We would like particularly to thank Faye Judges, whose persistence, patience and encouragement (plus editorial pressure when needed) eventually brought the project to a conclusion, and Ela Kotkowska whose tact and determination at the production stage turned the finished work into a book.

Finally, the authors would like to thank Claire Rice at BCL Burton Copeland for her skilful assistance and continued good humour throughout the writing of this book, for co-ordinating the work of the authors, and for bringing order to the whole process.

BCL Burton Copeland   **3 Raymond Buildings**

Robin Booth   Simon Farrell QC
Guy Bastable   Nicholas Yeo

CONTENTS

APPENDICES

TABLE OF CASES

TABLE OF LEGISLATION

LIST OF TABLES

LIST OF ABBREVIATIONS

AML	anti-money laundering
ATCSA 2001	Anti-Terrorism, Crime and Security Act 2001
BBA	British Bankers' Association
BIS	Department for Business, Innovation and Skills

[Note that BIS also stands for the Bank for International Settlements - see Appendix 8, Useful Websites.]

CCAB	Consultative Committee of Accountancy Bodies
CCRC	Criminal Cases Review Commission
CDD	customer due diligence
CJA	Criminal Justice Act 1988
CPS	Crown Prosecution Service
CTF	counter terrorist financing
CTED	Counter Terrorism Committee Executive Directorate
DETI	Department of Enterprise, Trade and Investment
DNFBPs	Designated Non-Financial Businesses and Professions
ECHR	European Convention on Human Rights
EEA	European Economic Area
FATF	Financial Action Task Force
FIU	Financial Intelligence Unit
FSA	Financial Services Authority
HMRC	Her Majesty's Revenue and Customs
HMT	Her Majesty's Treasury
HO	Home Office
HVD	high-value dealer
ICAEW	Institute of Chartered Accountants in England and Wales
JMLSG	Joint Money Laundering Steering Group
LPP	legal professional privilege
LEA	law enforcement authority

MLD3	Third Money Laundering Directive
MLAC	Money Laundering Advisory Committee
MLR 2007	Money Laundering Regulations 2007
MLRO	money laundering reporting officer
MSB	money service business
NCCTs	non-co-operative countries and territories
NCIS	National Criminal Intelligence Service
OFT	Office of Fair Trading
PEP	politically exposed person
PIU	Performance and Innovation Unit
POAC	Proscribed Organizations Appeal Commission
POCA	Proceeds of Crime Act 2002
SAR	suspicious activity report
SFO	Serious Fraud Office
SOCA	Serious Organised Crime Agency
SOCPA	Serious Organised Crime and Police Act 2005
STR	suspicious transaction report
TA 2000	Terrorism Act 2000
TCSP	trust or company service provider

1

THE BACKGROUND TO ANTI-MONEY LAUNDERING LAW AND REGULATION

A. Introduction

The term money laundering describes graphically the process by which dirty money, money **1.01** obtained through crime, is cleaned so that it is, or at least appears to be, legitimate money with no taint of its criminal origin.

Money laundering as a legal concept and legislation to combat money laundering are barely **1.02** 25 years old, but most countries in the world now have legislation that criminalizes money laundering and facilitates the recovery of the proceeds of crime. Criminal law has traditionally been the sovereign preserve of individual states and the rapid global development of anti-money laundering measures, including new criminal offences, in line with agreed international standards has been a remarkable development.[1]

1.03 The anti-money laundering law and regulation which are now a part of the law and practice of most countries in the world have a number of distinctive features.

- There is a common core of anti-money laundering measures in each jurisdiction which is largely derived from and implements the 40 Recommendations of the Financial Action Task Force (FATF) on how to combat money laundering. Increasingly, too, the 9 Special Recommendations designed to combat terrorist financing have supplemented the anti-money laundering measures. International agreements, such as the UN Conventions of Vienna and Palermo, and the setting of standards by an international body, the Financial Action Task Force, have been ratified or adopted by governments throughout the world and have, to a considerable degree, given a global consistency to attempts to combat money laundering.

- This common core of anti-money laundering measures uses not only the criminal law, but also civil law and the regulation of relevant businesses and professions in order to combat money laundering at every stage through measures that aim to prevent and detect money laundering, to investigate and prosecute money launderers, and to recover the money or other property being laundered, whether through criminal confiscation proceedings or in civil proceedings.

- Legislation, regulation and the enforcement of anti-money laundering law form only a part of the overall effort to combat money laundering. At both national and international levels, a range of public and private sector bodies contribute to this anti-money laundering effort through the setting of standards and the issuing of guidance, as well as through supervision, monitoring and inspection. At an international level, bodies such as the Basel Committee on Banking Supervision and the Wolfsberg Group, as well as major institutions such as the IMF and the World Bank, contribute to the setting of industry-specific standards and to establishing and monitoring good anti-money laundering practice. Within countries, representative industry and professional bodies have an important role in providing detailed guidance on compliance and in anti-money laundering training.

1.04 The anti-money laundering measures that are now applied in most countries bring with them another feature: that is, the extent to which large sections of the public, individuals and institutions, are—through the requirements of anti-money laundering regulatory regimes—enrolled in the anti-money laundering effort and required to play a significant part in support of law enforcement.

---

[1] International efforts to tackle corruption are developing in a similar way, following on from the OECD Convention on Combating Bribery of Foreign Public Officials in International Business Transactions, 18 September 2001 and the UN Convention against Corruption, 31 October 2003.

B. Money Laundering Defined

The Financial Action Task Force, which has set international standards for anti-money laun- **1.05**
dering measures since it first issued its 40 Recommendations in 1990, answers the question
'what is money laundering?' in this way:

> The goal of a large number of criminal acts is to generate a profit for the individual or group
> that carries out the act. Money laundering is the processing of these criminal proceeds to
> disguise their illegal origin. This process is of critical importance, as it enables the criminal to
> enjoy these profits without jeopardising their source.

In his book *The Laundrymen*,[2] Jeffrey Robinson says that: 'Money laundering is called what **1.06**
it is because that perfectly describes what takes place—illegal, or dirty, money is put through
a cycle of transactions, or washed, so that it comes out the other end as legal, or clean, money.
In other words, the source of illegally obtained funds is obscured through a succession of
transfers and deals in order that those same funds can eventually be made to reappear as
legitimate income.'

Money laundering as a legal concept and as a criminal offence is variously defined in different **1.07**
jurisdictions. The popular understanding of money laundering as the deliberate washing
clean of dirty money accords quite closely with the nature of the money laundering offence
that FATF recommends countries to incorporate in their criminal law. The wording of that
offence is derived from the UN Conventions of Vienna and Palermo (see paragraphs 1.41
(re Vienna) and 1.43 (re Palermo) below).

C. The Process of Money Laundering

The term 'money laundering' and criminal offences of money laundering may be relatively **1.08**
new, but there is nothing new in dirty money and other proceeds of crime being concealed or
disguised and converted so that the assets can be used by criminals as freely as if it were legitimate money or other property. The way that money is laundered is conventionally described,
by FATF and others, as a three-stage process: placement, layering, and integration.

Placement. This describes the process of introducing large cash proceeds of crime into the **1.09**
banking and financial system. Over the years, this has become more necessary because the
use of cash for large purchases is increasingly difficult and regarded with suspicion in many
countries. It has also become harder to introduce large amounts of cash because banks have
become more vigilant about money laundering and more wary of large cash deposits.
Smurfing, that is making a series of deposits below reporting thresholds, carries increasing
risks of detection, so that introducing large amounts of cash into the banking system now
generally requires deception and disguise, such as the use of cash-generating businesses as
cover.

Layering. This may take many forms, but the motive and purpose are always the same: to **1.10**
obscure the criminal origin of the money and, as far as possible, to distance the funds and the

---

[2] Simon & Schuster UK Ltd (revised edition 1998), p 3.

beneficial owner of those funds from their source, and to make it difficult for an investigator to trace the funds back to that source. Layering may be done in part through repeated transfers of money between accounts with financial institutions in different jurisdictions, especially ones with a low level of anti-money laundering compliance and poor law enforcement co-operation with other countries, and may involve the use of a variety of transactions and the use of corporate structures as cover and to hide details of beneficial ownership. Whatever techniques are used, layering is central to the process and purpose of money laundering. With each transfer or transaction, the intention is that the dirty money is washed cleaner and the taint of crime becomes fainter.

1.11 *Integration.* This stage completes the process of money laundering by moving the now apparently clean funds into reputable banks and financial institutions from which funds can be drawn by the criminal or criminals in order to invest and use the criminal proceeds freely within the legitimate economy.

1.12 This conventional way of describing the process of money laundering has explanatory value, but money laundering is not a rigid and defined process. A complex series of conversions and transactions to obscure the true source of criminal proceeds is only necessary and practicable where large sums are involved. The placement stage may be necessary for the cash proceeds of drug trafficking or people trafficking, but will not generally be necessary for fraudsters perpetrating financial scams, where the proceeds of crime may be received by transfer directly into the fraudster's bank account.

1.13 The particular methods by which money laundering is carried out are changing all the time. Increasingly sophisticated anti-money laundering measures may prevent some money laundering and detect instances of money laundering, but it is likely that it often merely displaces money laundering activity, leading criminals and those who assist them in the cleaning of dirty money to find and exploit new ways of doing so.

D. The Rise of Global Anti-money Laundering Measures

1.14 The years 1988 to 1991 laid the foundation for the current global anti-money laundering measures. The primary concern that generated international action during this period was a concern about the immense profits being made by drug cartels in South America and elsewhere. If there is a single starting point that one can identify in the international effort to tackle the laundering of the proceeds of serious crime, it would be the United Nations Conference for the Adoption of a Convention against Illicit Traffic in Narcotic Drugs and Psychotropic Substances which met at the Neue Hofburg in Vienna from 25 November to 20 December 1988.

1.15 The Vienna Convention of 1988 was specifically concerned with drugs, but in Article 3 it produced a template for money laundering offences that was later adopted by FATF. Creating offences of laundering the proceeds of drug trafficking was seen as providing a new and potentially powerful means of tackling drug trafficking.

1.16 The 1990s saw a widening of the focus of concern from drug money to the profits derived from other serious crime such as fraud, corruption and people trafficking. There seemed to be no good reason to restrict to the proceeds of drug trafficking anti-money laundering measures that could prove equally useful against the laundering of the proceeds of other kinds of serious acquisitive crime.

The Financial Action Task Force was established at the G7 meeting in Paris in 1989. In the **1.17** following year FATF issued its 40 Recommendations on money laundering (recommending, inter alia, that states introduce money laundering offences, make provisions for the freezing, seizure, and confiscation of assets, and establish a regulatory regime for banks and other financial institutions in order to prevent and detect money laundering). These Recommendations, which were updated in 1996 and thoroughly reviewed and revised in 2003, remain the international standard for anti-money laundering measures. In October 2001 the original 40 Recommendations were supplemented by 8 Special Recommendations on terrorist financing, with a 9th Special Recommendation added in October 2004. Although FATF has no executive powers, its 'recommendations' are treated as authoritative by governments and intergovernmental bodies throughout the world.

For the UK and other member states of the EU, the *recommendations* of FATF were largely **1.18** translated into the *requirements* of the First Money Laundering Directive of 1991 ('First Money Laundering Directive').[3] Revisions of the 40 Recommendations and the 9 Special Recommendations on terrorist financing have since been incorporated in the Second Money Laundering Directive of 2001 ('Second Money Laundering Directive')[4] and the Third Money Laundering Directive of 2005 ('Third Money Laundering Directive').[5]

After the 40 Recommendations were issued by FATF and—in the European Union—the **1.19** First Money Laundering Directive was issued, anti-money laundering measures became increasingly part of the legal and regulatory framework in countries throughout the world. Alongside the continuing concern about money laundering there was increasing international concern about terrorism and the financing of terrorism, leading to the UN Convention on the Suppression of the Financing of Terrorism in 1999. Although terrorist financing is significantly different from money laundering, it was seen by governments and by FATF to be susceptible to a very similar legal and regulatory approach:[6] counter terrorist financing (CTF[7]) joined anti-money laundering and, since 9 September 2001, they have become two parts of a single legal and regulatory regime.

Money laundering, like drug trafficking and fraud, is international in character and uses **1.20** cross-border movements of currency as part of the layering process. Money launderers may also indulge in their own version of 'forum shopping'—carrying out financial and property transactions where they perceive anti-money laundering measures to be weak and the chances of detection lowest. Money laundering, therefore, needs an international response.

---

[3] Council Directive 92/308/EEC of 10 June 1991 on prevention of the use of the financial system for the purpose of money laundering.

[4] Council Directive 2001/97/EC of 4 December 2001 amending Council Directive 92/308/EEC of 10 June 1991 on prevention of the use of the financial system for the purpose of money laundering.

[5] Council Directive 2005/60/EC of 26 October 2005 on the prevention of the use of the financial system for the purpose of money laundering and terrorist financing.

[6] Proliferation financing is now being viewed in this way: see the FATF Proliferation Financing Report of 18 June 2008 and the SOCA Guidelines for Counter Proliferation Financing Reporting of November 2008.

[7] AML is the standard abbreviation for anti-money laundering. CTF is the abbreviation generally used in the UK for counter-terrorist financing, but CFT is often used.

Table 1.1 Anti-money laundering measures: Chronology of key events and documents (to 1999)

Europe & International		UK
	1986	Drug Trafficking Offences Act
The Vienna Convention	1988	Criminal Justice Act
Financial Action Task Force (FATF) established	1989	
FATF 40 Recommendations on money laundering	1990	Criminal Justice (International Co-operation) Act
The Strasbourg Convention	1990	
First Money Laundering Directive	1991	
	1993	Criminal Justice Act
	1993	Money Laundering Regulations
	1994	Drug Trafficking Act
The Egmont Group of Financial Intelligence Units formed	1995	Proceeds of Crime Act
FATF 40 Recommendations revised	1996	
UN Convention on the Suppression of the Financing of Terrorism	1999	

1.21 The capacity for international co-operation in criminal intelligence, with particular reference to money laundering and terrorist financing, was enhanced by the creation in 1995 of the Egmont Group of Financial Intelligence Units which now has over 100 members. The Egmont Group provides a forum to enhance mutual co-operation and to share information useful in detecting and combating money laundering and terrorist financing. The broader development of the international response from 1988 onwards is reflected in the chronologies above in Table 1.1 and below in Table 1.2.

Anti-money laundering developments: 2000 onwards

1.22 The first few years of the new millennium saw another period of great change and substantial development in global anti-money laundering measures. In particular, this period saw the concern with the proceeds of all serious crime, and the measures to address them, incorporated in international instruments such as the Palermo Convention of 2000, where the primary focus was on serious transnational crime, and, in the extended anti-money laundering legal and regulatory requirements of the Second Money Laundering Directive, as well as in the FATF 8 Special Recommendations on terrorist financing.

1.23 Since 2004, FATF and its associated bodies[8] have kept up the pressure to make its anti-money laundering and counter-terrorist financing standards not just a global phenomenon, but the universal norm. FATF has also begun to develop constructive relationships with the private sector bodies whose members carry substantial responsibilities and make an important contribution to the prevention and detection of money laundering.

---

[8] FATF has 36 members (34 countries and territories and two regional organizations), as well as associate members such as the Asia/Pacific Group on Money Laundering.

Table 1.2 Anti-money laundering measures: Chronology of key events and documents (from 2000)

Europe & International		UK
The Palermo Convention	2000	The PIU Report on Recovering the Proceeds of Crime
The Wolfsberg Anti-money Laundering Principles for Private Banking	2000	Terrorism Act
Second Money Laundering Directive	2001	Money Laundering Regulations
FATF 8 Special Recommendations on terrorist financing	2001	Anti-Terrorism, Crime and Security Act
The Patriot Act (USA)	2001	
	2002	Proceeds of Crime Act
FATF 40 Recommendations revised	2003	Money Laundering Regulations
	2003	KPMG Report on on the SARs Regime
FATF 8 Special Recommendations on terrorist financing updated and a 9th Special Recommendation added	2004	Her Majesty's Chief Inspector of Constabulary Report—'Payback Time'
Third Money Laundering Directive	2005	The Lander Report—Review of the SARs regime
	2005	Serious Organised Crime and Police Act
	2006	Establishment of the Serious Organised Crime Agency and transfer of the UK FIU from NCIS to SOCA.
	2007	Money Laundering Regulations
	2007	The Terrorism Act 2000 and Proceeds of Crime Act 2002 (Amendment) Regulations 2007
	2008	Counter-Terrorism Act

By 2005, the current international framework for anti-money laundering and counter-terrorist financing, within which countries operate, was largely in place, and, in Europe, the Third Money Laundering Directive incorporated these developments. **1.24**

In the UK, changes in anti-money laundering and counter-terrorist financing law and regulation since 2005 have implemented the requirements of the Third Money Laundering Directive and amended the Proceeds of Crime Act 2002 (POCA) and the Terrorism Act 2000 (TA 2000). **1.25**

E. The Role of the Financial Action Task Force

Established in 1989 and based in Paris, FATF is not a permanent international body but a task force of the OECD (Organisation for Economic Co-operation and Development) whose current mandate expires in 2012. Its primary role has been to set the international standard for anti-money laundering measures through its 'recommendations', which now also include counter-terrorist financing measures. FATF is a policy-making body that makes its recommendations to governments throughout the world. In the introduction to its **1.26**

40 Recommendations,[9] FATF '. . . calls upon all countries to take the necessary steps to bring their national systems for combating money laundering and terrorist financing into compliance with the new FATF Recommendations, and to effectively implement these measures'.

1.27 The aims of these anti-money laundering measures, as expressed in Task Force documents, are:

- to prevent criminals from laundering the proceeds of their crimes;
- to prevent others from deliberately assisting in the laundering of criminal funds;
- to prevent criminals and money launderers from being able to misuse the legitimate services of banks, accountants, lawyers, and others to launder criminal funds.

1.28 In the view of FATF, these anti-money laundering measures, if successfully implemented, should help, firstly, to deprive criminals of their ill-gotten gains and, secondly, to deter others from acquisitive or financial crime and so to prevent or reduce the incidence of crime. FATF notes that, as an additional benefit of anti-money laundering measures, financial transaction reports often provide an audit trail that yields evidence not only against money launderers, but also against the criminals from whose crimes the criminal funds are ultimately derived.

1.29 The extent to which countries have effectively implemented the Recommendations is monitored by a process of mutual evaluations conducted by FATF and FATF-style regional bodies. Another important aspect of FATF's work is to identify and study methods and trends in money laundering and terrorist financing. FATF issues typologies and other guidance material to assist regulated sector institutions, in particular, to recognize and respond to attempts to misuse their services.

1.30 The burden of compliance with the FATF Recommendations falls most heavily on the private sector. In recent years FATF has developed a dialogue with the private sector, firstly with financial institutions and, latterly, with other regulated businesses and professions. A practical outcome of this has been the joint FATF/private sector project which has produced, in 2008, a series of sector-specific guidance papers. This guidance is intended to assist both public authorities and regulated businesses and professions to apply a risk-based approach to combating money laundering and terrorist financing.

1.31 The current text of the 40 Recommendations on the FATF website is that of October 2003 ('incorporating all subsequent amendments until October 2004'). There are also the Special Recommendations: the first eight were issued in October 2001 and the ninth was issued in October 2004. In 2010, FATF announced that it was conducting a review of the 40 + 9 Recommendations 'to ensure that they remain up-to-date and relevant and to benefit from lessons learnt from implementing and evaluating the current standards'.

---

[9] The 20th anniversary of the FATF Recommendations was celebrated at the FATF Plenary meeting at Amsterdam in June 2010. For the FATF Annual Report for 2009/10 see: <http://www.fatf-gafi.org/dataoecd/50/53/45712700.pdf>.

The 40 Recommendations on money laundering

The 40 Recommendations start with the recommendation to criminalize money laundering, **1.32** but they cover a wide range of measures designed to prevent and detect money laundering, to make it more difficult for criminals to launder money through banks and financial institutions or through other financial and property transactions, and to facilitate the investigation and prosecution of money laundering and the recovery of the proceeds of crime.

The main elements of the 40 Recommendations are: **1.33**

- Law
  The recommendations include legal measures relating to:
  — criminalization of money laundering;
  — 'seizure and freezing' of assets;
  — confiscation of the proceeds of crime;
  — investigative powers to identify and trace assets.
- Regulation
  The recommendations include measures for the regulation and supervision of financial institutions and designated non-financial business and professions. These measures require the regulated sector, which now comprises all banks and financial institutions and various professions and businesses considered to be vulnerable to money laundering:
  — to carry out customer due diligence (CDD) checks and keep transaction records;
  — to have internal systems and controls to detect and prevent money laundering;
  — to increase awareness by anti-money laundering training;
  — to report suspicious transactions and not to tip off customers and others about suspicious transaction reports.
- The creation of a national financial intelligence unit to receive, analyse and disseminate information from suspicious transaction reports.
- The provision of specialist investigative bodies, adequately resourced and with appropriate powers, to deal with cases of suspected money laundering and with recovery of assets.
- The provision of an appropriate legal framework and the necessary resources to facilitate international co-operation, mutual legal assistance, and extradition, and to provide effective co-operation between 'competent authorities' in different countries.

The recommendation to create criminal offences of money laundering

In Recommendation 1 the Task Force calls for the creation of a criminal offence[10] that con- **1.34** sists of the laundering of money or property derived from other criminal offences. Recommendation 1 states that countries should criminalize money laundering on the basis of two United Nations Conventions: the Vienna Convention of 1988 and the Palermo Convention of 2000. These Conventions contain three draft offences which together comprise the crime of money laundering.

FATF recommends that 'Countries should apply the crime of money laundering **1.35** to all serious offences with a view to including the widest range of predicate offences.'

---

[10] A largely new, if not quite unprecedented, criminal offence at the time when the original 40 Recommendations were issued in 1990.

The Recommendation requires that each country should 'at a minimum' include a range of designated[11] categories of serious crime, such as:

- organized crime and racketeering;
- terrorism, including terrorist financing;
- trafficking in human beings;
- drug trafficking;
- corruption.

1.36 From the Vienna Convention of 1988 to the Palermo Convention of 2000 and beyond, the justification for strong measures against money laundering is expressed in terms of serious and organized crime and its harmful effect on society. The criminalization of money laundering is seen as a significant additional means of combating serious and organized crime.

F. The Origins of the Money Laundering Offences in International Law

1.37 In the 1980s, the wealth and power of the major drug cartels created the serious concerns reflected in the Preamble to the United Nations Convention against Illicit Traffic in Narcotic Drugs and Psychotropic Substances ('the Vienna Convention'), which was adopted on 19 December 1988.

The Vienna Convention

1.38 The Vienna Convention was about drug trafficking, but the Preamble—in the paragraphs set out below—clearly expresses the rationale for the money laundering offences in Article 3 and recognizes the links between drug trafficking and other serious and organized crime which led to the scope of the money laundering offences being widened in the Palermo Convention of 2000:

> The Parties to this Convention,
>
> Deeply concerned by the magnitude of and rising trend in the illicit production of, demand for and traffic in narcotic drugs and psychotropic substances, which pose a serious threat to the health and welfare of human beings and adversely affect the economic, cultural and political foundations of society,
>
> . . .
>
> Recognizing the links between illicit traffic [in narcotic drugs and psychotropic substances] and other related organized criminal activities which undermine the legitimate economies and threaten the stability, security and sovereignty of State,
>
> Recognizing also that illicit traffic is an international criminal activity, the suppression of which demands urgent attention and the highest priority,

1.39 The drugs offences under Article 3 cover drug trafficking in its broadest sense, including not only the production, selling and distribution of drugs, and related activities, but also the 'organisation, management or financing' of any of the other drugs offences.

---

[11] The 20 designated categories of serious crime are listed in the Glossary that forms an appendix to the 40 Recommendations.

The concern about the threat that drug trafficking poses to society and to the economy is reflected in an equal concern about the power to do harm which the proceeds of such 'illicit traffic' gives to organized criminals. The Preamble continues: **1.40**

> Aware that illicit traffic generates large financial profits and wealth enabling transnational criminal organizations to penetrate, contaminate and corrupt the structures of government, legitimate commercial and financial business, and society at all its levels,
>
> Determined to deprive persons engaged in illicit traffic of the proceeds of their criminal activities and thereby eliminate their main incentive for so doing. . .

Responding to the concern about the proceeds of drug trafficking, the second part of Article 3 required the parties to introduce criminal offences of laundering property obtained through the illicit traffic in drugs. The three laundering offences,[12] briefly summarized, are: **1.41**

- The intentional conversion or transfer of property derived from drug trafficking to conceal or disguise the illicit origin of the property or assist a drug trafficker to evade the law.
- The concealment or disguise of the true nature, source, location, etc, of property, knowing it to be derived from drug trafficking.
- The acquisition, possession or use of property knowing it to be derived from drug trafficking.

The Palermo Convention

The criminal offences of money laundering in the Palermo Convention 2000 are, in substance, the same as the offences under Article 3 of the Vienna Convention. The scope of the money laundering offences, however, is greatly extended: whereas the money laundering offences under the Vienna Convention related to the laundering of the proceeds of drug trafficking offences, the Palermo Convention applies them to the proceeds of serious crime.[13] **1.42**

These offences are set out in Article 6: **1.43**

> *Criminalization of the laundering of proceeds of crime*
> 1. Each State Party shall adopt, in accordance with fundamental principles of its domestic law, such legislative and other measures as may be necessary to establish as criminal offences, when committed intentionally:
>   (a) (i) The conversion or transfer of property, knowing that such property is the proceeds of crime, for the purpose of concealing or disguising the illicit origin of the property or of helping any person who is involved in the commission of the predicate offence to evade the legal consequences of his or her action;
>   (ii) The concealment or disguise of the true nature, source, location, disposition, movement or ownership of or rights with respect to property, knowing that such property is the proceeds of crime;
>   (b) Subject to the basic concepts of its legal system:
>   (i) The acquisition, possession or use of property, knowing, at the time of receipt, that such property is the proceeds of crime;

---

[12] See paras 1.87–1.89 below.

[13] Art 6.1 itself refers simply to the 'proceeds of crime', as defined in Art 2(e), but the application of money laundering offences to serious crime under the Palermo Convention requires reference to Art 6.2(a) and (b), and is subject to the terms of Art 2(b), where 'serious crime' is defined, and to Art 3.1.

1.44 The money laundering offences set out in Article 6 of the Palermo Convention are, in all essential respects, the criminal offences which are required today by international standards (through Recommendation 1 of the FATF 40 Recommendations and, in the European context, through Article 1 of the Third Money Laundering Directive).

1.45 In addition, the Palermo Convention, in Article 7, required parties to introduce other measures to combat money laundering, effectively endorsing the FATF Recommendations for a regulatory and supervisory regime for financial institutions and other businesses particularly vulnerable to money laundering.

The money laundering offences in the Third Money Laundering Directive

1.46 The Recommendations of FATF are directed at 'countries', and throughout the world most governments have responded to those Recommendations, implementing them as they see fit through national legislation. Within the European Union, member states are subject to directives which seek largely to follow the FATF Recommendations, but which have their own legal status and compelling authority. One of the aims of the three Money Laundering Directives was to promote consistency within the European community in anti-money laundering and counter-terrorist financing measures.[14]

1.47 Paragraph (5) of the Preamble makes it clear that the Third Money Laundering Directive is intended to follow the Recommendations of FATF:

> The Community action should continue to take particular account of the Recommendations of the Financial Action Task Force (hereinafter referred to as the FATF), which constitutes the foremost international body active in the fight against money laundering and terrorist financing. Since the FATF Recommendations were substantially revised and expanded in 2003, this Directive should be in line with that new international standard.

1.48 So far as the criminal offences of money laundering are concerned, the Third Money Laundering Directive is drafted in accordance with FATF Recommendation 1 which states that countries should criminalize money laundering on the basis of the UN Conventions of Vienna (1988) and Palermo (2000). In reality, this means on the basis of the Palermo Convention which extended the scope of the offences to the proceeds of all serious crime. Although the directives derive the wording of the money laundering offences specifically from the UN Conventions, the member states of the Council of Europe had agreed in 1990, in Article 6(1) of the Strasbourg Convention,[15] on money laundering offences based on the Vienna Convention, but broadened to cover the proceeds of all criminal offences.

G. Terrorist Financing

1.49 The shock of 9/11 led quickly to the widening of FATF's remit and to the development by FATF of Special Recommendations to counter terrorist financing. The Special Recommendations bring to terrorist financing a similar approach to that of the 40 Recommendations on money laundering. They cover criminalization of the financing of terrorism and associated money laundering, the freezing and confiscation of terrorist assets,

---

[14] See the Preamble to the Third Money Laundering Directive, paras 3–5 inclusive.
[15] Convention on Laundering, Search, Seizure and Confiscation of the Proceeds from Crime, Council of Europe, Strasbourg 8 November 1990.

and the reporting of suspicious transactions related to terrorism. There are also provisions to enhance international co-operation, and specific Recommendations on alternative remittance systems, wire transfers and the abuse of non-profit organizations.

Money laundering and terrorist financing compared

Terrorist financing is very different from money laundering and the differences make it harder to detect. Money laundering is essentially about the cleaning of dirty money, turning the proceeds of crime into apparently legitimate money and assets which can be freely used and traded in the normal way. Terrorist offences, however, are not crimes committed for the purpose of financial gain, and the motivation of terrorists, ideological rather than material, is very different from that of drug dealers and fraudsters. Terrorist financing is about the misuse of clean—or dirty—money for terrorist purposes. The aim of counter-terrorist financing measures is, as far as possible, to cut off 'the lifeblood of terrorism'. **1.50**

Terrorism is not necessarily an expensive enterprise. Maintaining a terrorist organization over time requires significant funds, but individual acts of terrorism may cost little. The cost of the terrorist attacks in London on 7 July 2005 has been estimated at only about £7,235.[16] The monetary cost bore no relation to the cost in human suffering that the terrorists inflicted. The terrorist attacks on the United States on 11 September 2001 required more elaborate and lengthy preparation, but the report of The National Commission on Terrorist Attacks Upon the United States[17] concluded that: 'Bin Ladin and his aides did not need a very large sum to finance their planned attack on America. The 9/11 plotters eventually spent somewhere between $400,000 and $500,000 to plan and conduct their attack.' **1.51**

Although terrorist organizations often rely partly on criminal activity to generate funds for their activities, much terrorist financing involves legitimate funds that can be transferred and used through the banking system and normal channels in amounts that do not give rise to suspicion and in ways that are otherwise normal. **1.52**

Similar measures to those designed to combat money laundering are now applied to counter terrorist property and terrorist money laundering.[18] Terrorist financing covers a wide range of proscribed activities (in TA 2000, sections 15 to 17 inclusive) relating to the funding of terrorism and the use and possession of terrorist property, as well as terrorist money laundering (in section 18). **1.53**

Terrorist offences are not offences by which, other than incidentally, property is obtained. The money laundering offence in section 18 of TA 2000 may appear to be very similar to the arrangement offence in section 328 of POCA, but in reality it is quite different because terrorist property[19] is mainly about resources likely to be used for terrorist purposes, not about proceeds of crime. **1.54**

---

[16] See Simon Dilloway, *7/7 Attack—London Bombings* (at <http://www.lophamconsultancy.co.uk>).
[17] See <http://www.9-11commission.gov/>.
[18] Similar measures but with many differences in the detailed provisions.
[19] Terrorist property is defined in TA 2000, s 14.

H. Anti-money Laundering Law and Regulation in the UK

1.55 Although the UK has enacted legislation to implement the provisions of the Vienna Convention and of each of the three Money Laundering Directives, there are significant differences between the drafting of the money laundering offences in UK law and money laundering offences drafted in accordance with FATF Recommendation 1 or with the requirements of the three Money Laundering Directives. (See section I, below, on the mental element in money laundering offences.)

1.56 UK anti-money laundering law goes back to section 24 of the Drug Trafficking Offences Act 1986, which created an offence of assisting another to retain the benefit of drug trafficking and also contained a disclosure defence:

> 24.— Assisting another to retain the benefit of drug trafficking
>
> (1) Subject to subsection (3) below, if a person enters into or is otherwise concerned in an arrangement whereby—
>   (a) the retention or control by or on behalf of another (call him "A") of A's proceeds of drug trafficking is facilitated (whether by concealment, removal from the jurisdiction, transfer to nominees or otherwise), or
>   (b) A's proceeds of drug trafficking—
>   (i) are used to secure that funds are placed at A's disposal, or
>   (ii) are used for A's benefit to acquire property by way of investment,
>   knowing or suspecting that A is a person who carries on or has carried on drug trafficking or has benefited from drug trafficking, he is guilty of an offence.
> (2) In this section, references to any person's proceeds of drug trafficking include a reference to any property which in whole or in part directly or indirectly represented in his hands his proceeds of drug trafficking.

1.57 The money laundering offence, like the more widely drawn money laundering offences under Part 7 of POCA, carried a maximum penalty of 14 years' imprisonment.

1.58 The inclusion of this money laundering provision in the 1986 Act, preceding the Vienna Convention by two years, shows the UK developing its anti-money laundering law independently and the drafting of that new offence of money laundering perhaps helps to explain how far the UK's anti-money laundering law diverges from the international norm.

1.59 There were defences of lack of relevant knowledge or suspicion, and a defence of intending to disclose (under subsection (3), see below), but having a reasonable excuse for not doing so.

Disclosure and consent

1.60 Section 24(3) introduced a new type of provision as an exception or defence to the money laundering offence: disclosure to a constable and consent to do an act that would otherwise be an act of money laundering:

> (3) Where a person discloses to a constable a suspicion or belief that any funds or investments are derived from or used in connection with drug trafficking or any matter on which such a suspicion or belief is based—
>   (a) the disclosure shall not be treated as a breach of any restriction upon the disclosure of information imposed by contract, and

(b) if he does any act in contravention of subsection (1) above and the disclosure relates to the arrangement concerned, he does not commit an offence under this section if the disclosure is made in accordance with this paragraph, that is—

    (i) it is made before he does the act concerned, being an act done with the consent of the constable, or

    (ii) it is made after he does the act, but is made on his initiative and as soon as it is reasonable for him to make it.

1.61 The disclosure and consent defence in section 24(3), when combined in legislation with the disclosure requirements on the regulated sector derived from the three Money Laundering Directives, has led to the creation of two distinct reporting regimes that complicate UK anti-money laundering law.[20]

The Criminal Justice (International Co-operation) Act 1990

1.62 The Criminal Justice (International Co-operation) Act 1990 was enacted partly to enable the United Kingdom to implement the Vienna Convention. Section 14 was accompanied by the sidenote 'Concealing or transferring proceeds of drug trafficking'. The first three subsections of section 14 of the 1990 Act were in these terms:

(1) A person is guilty of an offence if he—
    (a) conceals or disguises any property which is, or in whole or in part directly or indirectly represents, his proceeds of drug trafficking; or
    (b) converts or transfers that property or removes it from the jurisdiction, for the purpose of avoiding prosecution for a drug trafficking offence or the making or enforcement in his case of a confiscation order.

(2) person is guilty of an offence if, knowing[21] or having reasonable grounds to suspect that any property is, or in whole or in part directly or indirectly represents, another person's proceeds of drug trafficking, he—
    (a) conceals or disguises that property; or
    (b) converts or transfers that property or removes it from the jurisdiction, for the purpose of assisting any person to avoid prosecution for a drug trafficking offence or the making or enforcement of a confiscation order.

(3) A person is guilty of an offence if, knowing or having reasonable grounds to suspect that any property is, or in whole or in part directly or indirectly represents, another person's proceeds of drug trafficking, he acquires that property for no, or for inadequate, consideration.

1.63 The wording of these money laundering offences differs materially from the drafting of the offences in Article 3 of the Vienna Convention, particularly with regard to the mental element in the offences where the implementing legislation has no requirement for actual knowledge that the relevant property is the proceeds of crime and introduces, in subsections (2) and (3), 'having reasonable grounds to suspect' as an alternative to knowledge.

The development of UK anti-money laundering law

1.64 In the UK there have been two periods in which anti-money laundering measures have been substantially revised and enhanced: the first period was roughly from 1993 to 1994 and the second from 2000 to 2003.

---

[20] See Chapter 5 below at paras 5.19 *et seq*.
[21] Under Art 3.3 of the Convention, 'Knowledge, intent or purpose required as an element of an offence. . . may be inferred from objective factual circumstances.'

1.65   The UK first had a reasonably comprehensive set of anti-money laundering measures after the developments in 1993/1994: criminal laws against the laundering of the proceeds of drug trafficking and of other serious crime, together with Money Laundering Regulations that applied to banks and the financial services sector. The criminal law was not, however, consolidated and there were two separate but parallel sets of money laundering offences, the first dealing with the proceeds of drug trafficking offences and the second dealing with the proceeds of other serious crimes.

1.66   The creation of a regulated sector for anti-money laundering purposes, comprising banks and financial services firms (but not, at that stage, including money service businesses), was brought about by the Money Laundering Regulations 1993, which came into force on 1 April 1994.

1.67   The second period of major reform of anti-money laundering law began with the publication in 2000 of the Performance and Innovation Unit (PIU) report on Recovering the Proceeds of Crime. This carried a foreword by the Prime Minister Tony Blair in which he said:

> This Government is determined to create a fair and just society in which crime does not pay. That is why I asked the PIU to carry out a study into how we could attack crime through its financial lifeblood. For too long, we paid insufficient attention to the financial aspects of crime. We must remember that many criminals are motivated by money and profit.

1.68   The Prime Minister ended his Foreword to the PIU report with a statement of the government's aims:

> The conclusions of this report represent agreed Government policy. Through implementing the recommendations in this report, we shall help turn the tide against criminals. We will deter people from crime by ensuring that criminals do not hang on to their unlawful gains. We will enhance confidence in the law by demonstrating that nobody is beyond its reach. We will make it easier for courts to recover the proceeds of crime from convicted criminals. And we will return to society the assets that have been unlawfully taken. All this will need to be achieved in a way that respects civil liberties; we will ensure that is the case.

1.69   This report led directly to the Proceeds of Crime Bill which was in the course of its passage through Parliament when the events of 9/11 occurred. The Proceeds of Crime Act, which received the royal assent on 24 July 2002, reformed the law on money laundering, bringing unity to the money laundering offences[22] in respect of the proceeds of drugs offences and other criminal offences. Part 7 of the Proceeds of Crime Act 2002, which consolidated and significantly amended the money laundering offences contained in previous legislation, has greatly extended the reach of the criminal offences of money laundering and of the offences arising from the obligation, direct or indirect, to disclose knowledge or suspicion of money laundering. Part 7 also substantially revised the requirements placed on the regulated sector to make suspicious activity reports.

1.70   Counter-terrorist financing measures were revised and enhanced by the Terrorism Act 2000, as amended by the ATCSA 2001, and by the Counter-Terrorism Act 2008.

1.71   On the regulatory side, the Money Laundering Regulations 2001 brought money service businesses into the regulated sector. More wide-ranging changes were made in the Money Laundering Regulations 2003, which implemented the Second Money Laundering Directive

---

[22] In ss 327–9.

and greatly widened the regulated sector, bringing into it a mixed bag of businesses and professions including casino operators, estate agents, high-value dealers, accountants, and lawyers.[23] The common feature was that they were all perceived to be vulnerable to the misuse by money launderers of their products and services.

By the time that the Money Laundering Regulations 2003 came into force on 1 March 2004, **1.72** a further Money Laundering Directive was already taking shape. The Third Money Laundering Directive was intended both to consolidate the first two directives and to strengthen the anti-money laundering provisions; it also extended the scope of the measures to cover terrorist financing, taking into account the FATF Special Recommendations on Terrorist Financing.

Amendments, in some cases substantial, have been made to Part 7 of POCA, partly to **1.73** attempt to deal with the concerns of the private sector about the operation of the Act and partly in response to further international obligations under the Third Money Laundering Directive. These changes have resolved some problems, but have also greatly complicated the provisions of Part 7.

The current UK money laundering offences

In the three money laundering offences[24] under POCA, the acts or activities that amount to **1.74** money laundering are described in much wider terms than in the FATF 40 Recommendations or other international instruments. The reach of the offences is further extended by the way in which 'criminal conduct' and 'criminal property' are defined.[25] As Brooke LJ noted in the case of *Bowman v Fels*[26], '. . . Parliament has given a much wider meaning to the phrases "criminal conduct" and "criminal property" than was required by the relevant Money Laundering Directive'. The detailed interpretation provisions—in section 340(2) to (11) inclusive—are, therefore, the key to understanding just how broad is the ambit of these offences.

Criminal property can be or represent, directly or indirectly, not only the actual proceeds but **1.75** even the notional proceeds of or benefit from any criminal offence in the UK, or (with some exceptions) of conduct abroad that would be an offence in the UK; also, there is no requirement for criminal intent and the requirement for a mental element is satisfied by mere suspicion. These features, together with the very wide definition of criminal property, extend the range of the offences far beyond that envisaged in the relevant provisions of the Vienna and Palermo UN Conventions, the 40 Recommendations, and the EC Money Laundering Directives.

The scope of the offences is so broad that a great many 'prohibited acts', which give rise to the **1.76** need to make an authorised disclosure and seek consent, do not amount to 'money laundering' either as understood by FATF or in any meaningful sense; they are acts that could not reasonably be regarded as seriously wrongful—and in some cases, are merely technical.

---

[23] In FATF parlance, these are the Designated Non-Financial Businesses and Professions (DNFBPs). They were brought into the regulated sector through the expanded definition of 'relevant business' in the Money Laundering Regulations 2003, Reg 2(2)(f)–(n) inclusive.

[24] Subs (1) of each of ss 327, 328, and 329 of the Proceeds of Crime Act 2002.

[25] See the discussion of these terms in Chapter 2 on the key concepts of money laundering.

[26] *Bowman v Fels* [2005] EWCA Civ 226.

1.77 The three sections create offences that apply to criminals laundering massive proceeds of drug trafficking or other serious crime as well as to those knowingly and deliberately assisting them. They apply equally to otherwise law-abiding people carrying out a variety of commercial transactions and professional services, such as bankers, accountants, lawyers, and estate agents. For them, a failure to disclose is treated as the same offence as serious and deliberate money laundering.

1.78 The contrast between money laundering under UK law and money laundering according to international standards is clearest in relation to the mental element of the offences. Comparison of the provisions in the relevant international treaties (the UN Conventions of Vienna and Palermo) and the three Money Laundering Directives demonstrates both the consistency of the international approach to the mental element of the offences and the extent to which UK law diverges from this approach.

1.79 In a number of significant respects, the UK's current money laundering offences differ from and go beyond both the recommendations of the Financial Action Task Force and the requirements of the Money Laundering Directives. The UK has taken full advantage of Article 5 of the Third Money Laundering Directive[27] which states that: 'The Member States may adopt or retain in force stricter provisions in the field covered by this Directive to prevent money laundering and terrorist financing.' In *Bowman v Fels* (at paragraph 19 of the judgment), the Court of Appeal recognized that the legislation originated from the requirements of the Money Laundering Directives of 1991 and 2001, but Brooke LJ went on to say that: 'From the outset we must take note of the fact that Part 7 of the 2002 Act includes more stringent provisions than were required by the second of these Directives.'

1.80 The drafting of these provisions in the Proceeds of Crime Bill reflected the frustration of the government and of law enforcement agencies in the UK arising from the perceived ineffectiveness of the previous money laundering law. In the House of Commons on 17 January 2002, Bob Ainsworth, Parliamentary Under Secretary of State at the Home Office, said: 'We are highly dissatisfied with the way in which matters operate currently. We want a sea change in how we deal with money laundering in this country.'

1.81 Part 7 of the Act has produced such a 'sea change', but whether it has produced money laundering laws that are clear and proportionate to the harm that they seek to combat may be open to question. The enormously wide scope of sections 327 to 329 of the Act takes UK law a long way from the original or core idea of what money laundering is (i.e. the changing, disguising, cleaning, and legitimizing of dirty money or, as the Task Force describes it, the processing of criminal proceeds to disguise their illegal origin).

1.82 The main features of Part 7 of the Act that diverge from and go beyond the Recommendations and beyond the requirements of the Money Laundering Directives are:[28]

- The three money laundering offences have been widely drafted so that they criminalize a broad range of acts or activities with no requirement for criminal intent and with suspicion being a sufficient mental element.

---

[27] And, previously, of the similar provision in Art 15 of the First Money Laundering Directive.

[28] The scope of the money laundering offences under POCA is also greater because predicate criminal activity is not limited to serious crimes.

- The scope of the three money laundering offences is further widened through the breadth and uncertainty of the definition of 'criminal property' contained in section 340 subsections (3) to (10) inclusive.
- In the three money laundering offences, the defence of making a money laundering disclosure, which in most cases is the only effective defence, creates a need to disclose equivalent to an indirect reporting requirement that applies equally to those outside as to those inside the regulated sector.

At national and international level, politicians have argued that the justification for strong **1.83** anti-money laundering legislation was the need to tackle serious acquisitive crime and to combat the serious harm to society and the economy that was said to result from the laundering of the proceeds of such crime.[29] In the UK, the objectives of anti-money laundering measures have been widened, combined with an extension of the money laundering disclosure regime, and aligned with other law enforcement objectives.

I. Offences of Money Laundering: the Mental Element

The critical difference between the money laundering offences in UK law and the money **1.84** laundering offences in the relevant international documents lies in the mental element of the offences. The position in Recommendation 1 of the FATF 40 Recommendations (in which the wording of the offence is derived from the Vienna and Palermo Conventions) and the very similar wording in the Third Money Laundering Directive is compared below with the position in UK law—Part 7 of POCA.

The money laundering offences proposed in the UN Conventions and adopted by FATF

The first of FATF's 40 Recommendations is that countries should criminalize money laun- **1.85** dering on the basis of the offences as worded in the Vienna and Palermo Conventions. Recommendation 2 deals specifically with the mental element in the offence of money laundering and states that countries should ensure that 'the intent and knowledge required to prove the offence of money laundering is consistent with the standards set forth in the Vienna and Palermo UN Conventions'.

In practice, what constitutes the criminal offence of money laundering varies from jurisdiction **1.86** to jurisdiction. Countries that follow closely the terms of the FATF Recommendations or, if in the European Union, the terms of Article 1 of the Third Money Laundering Directive, will have a criminal offence of deliberate money laundering that recognizably deals with money laundering as generally described and understood. In UK law, however, money laundering is defined so widely[30] that many criminal acts of money laundering, that is 'prohibited acts' under sections 327 to 329 of POCA, bear little relation to this conception of money laundering.

---

[29] See Peter Alldridge, *Money Laundering Law: Forfeiture, Confiscation, Civil Recovery, Criminal Laundering and Taxation of the Proceeds of Crime*, 2003, Hart Publishing. This book, published in January 2003, remains the best critical examination of the new anti-money laundering law under POCA. On the economic aspects of money laundering see, in particular, Peter Reuter and Edwin M Truman, *Chasing Dirty Money: The Fight Against Money Laundering*, 2005, Institute for International Economics, US.
[30] POCA, s 340(11).

The Vienna Convention

1.87   The proposed offences of money laundering under Article 3 of the Vienna Convention are framed in terms of *intentional* dealings with the proceeds of certain serious criminal offences (mainly drug trafficking) by a person who *knows* that relevant property is derived from such an offence or offences.

1.88   In addition:

(1) The first offence, of converting or transferring such property, is only committed by a person whose actions are done '*for the purpose of concealing or disguising* the illicit origin of the property'.

(2) The second offence of '*concealment or disguise*' contains—implicit within that phrase—the same requirement for a criminal intent.

1.89   Both of these offences require knowledge of the criminal origin of the property. They are what might be termed classic money laundering offences, typically committed by a person who may well have had no involvement in the drug trafficking or other predicate offences but who is aware of the source of the money or property and who assists serious criminals to conceal or disguise, or otherwise launder, the cash or other proceeds derived from their crimes:

(3) The third proposed money laundering offence criminalizes acquisition, possession or use of property where a person *knows, at the time of receipt*, the criminal origin of the property.

The Palermo Convention

1.90   Whereas the Vienna Convention was primarily about drugs, the focus of the Palermo Convention was on transnational organized crime. In this context, Article 6 of the Convention restated the money laundering offences in wider terms:

Article 6
1. Each State Party shall adopt, in accordance with fundamental principles of its domestic law, such legislative and other measures as may be necessary to establish as criminal offences, *when committed intentionally*:
   (a) (i) The conversion or transfer of property, *knowing* that such property is the proceeds of crime, *for the purpose of concealing or disguising* the illicit origin of the property or of helping any person who is involved in the commission of the predicate offence to evade the legal consequences of his or her action;
       (ii) The *concealment or disguise* of the true nature, source, location, disposition, movement or ownership of or rights with respect to property, *knowing* that such property is the proceeds of crime;
   (b) Subject to the basic concepts of its legal system:
       (i) The acquisition, possession or use of property, *knowing, at the time of receipt*, that such property is the proceeds of crime;
       . . .
   (f) *Knowledge, intent or purpose* required as an element of an offence set forth in paragraph 1 of this article may be inferred from objective factual circumstances. [Emphasis added.]

The Third Money Laundering Directive

1.91   The three Money Laundering Directives (1991, 2001, and 2005) have closely followed the FATF Recommendations in the drafting of the money laundering offences:[31]

---

[31] See the Third Money Laundering Directive, Art 1.

Article 1

1. Member States shall ensure that money laundering and terrorist financing are prohibited.
2. For the purposes of this Directive, the following conduct, *when committed intentionally*, shall be regarded as money laundering:
   (a) the conversion or transfer of property, *knowing* that such property is derived from criminal activity or from an act of participation in such activity, *for the purpose of concealing or disguising* the illicit origin of the property or of assisting any person who is involved in the commission of such activity to *evade the legal consequences of his action*;
   (b) the *concealment or disguise* of the true nature, source, location, disposition, movement, rights with respect to, or ownership of property, *knowing* that such property is derived from criminal activity or from an act of participation in such activity;
   (c) the acquisition, possession or use of property, *knowing, at the time of receipt*, that such property was derived from criminal activity or from an act of participation in such activity;

   . . .

5. *Knowledge, intent or purpose required as an element of the activities* mentioned in paragraphs 2 and 4 *may be inferred from objective factual circumstances.* [Emphasis added.]

Comparison of the provisions relating to the criminal offence of money laundering in the FATF 40 Recommendations, the two UN Conventions and the three Money Laundering Directives demonstrates a consistent approach to the definition of the offence and the state of mind required for the offence to be committed. **1.92**

The three money laundering offences in Part 7 of POCA

Sections 327 to 329 of POCA create offences of dealing in various ways with 'criminal property'. They are more widely drawn than the offences of money laundering in Article 6 of the Palermo Convention. The drafting of the offences is unusual in that the main mental element, common to each of the offences, is absent from the offence-creating sections, but is contained in the definition of criminal property in section 340: **1.93**

340 Interpretation

. . .

(3) Property is criminal property if—
(a) it constitutes a person's benefit from criminal conduct or it represents such a benefit (in whole or part and whether directly or indirectly), and
(b) the *alleged offender knows or suspects* that it constitutes or represents such a benefit. [Emphasis added.]

Section 327 makes it an offence to conceal, disguise, convert, or transfer criminal property or remove it from the jurisdiction. Two of the five ways in which this offence can be committed—'*disguise*' and '*conceal*'—import an element of intention into the offence; otherwise, the operative words are neutral. **1.94**

Section 328, which concerns arrangements to launder, does contain a mental element in addition to that contained in 'criminal property', that is the requirement that for the offence to be committed the person must have the relevant knowledge or suspicion about the effect of the arrangement: **1.95**

328 Arrangements

(1) A person commits an offence if he enters into or becomes concerned in an arrangement which he *knows or suspects* facilitates (by whatever means) the acquisition, retention, use or control of criminal property by or on behalf of another person. [Emphasis added.]

1.96 Section 329 contains no mental element in the offence itself.

1.97 Because they do not require any criminal intent and because of their wide drafting, these criminal offences are not specifically directed against those deliberately laundering the proceeds of crime, whether their own or someone else's. The money laundering offence conditions will apply to those in the regulated sector whose work involves dealing, on behalf of a third party, with 'criminal property',[32] that is property which they suspect may be the proceeds of criminal conduct, actual or notional. The defence of authorised disclosure combined with obtaining consent to do a prohibited act, which will usually be the only available defence, creates a need to disclose equivalent to a reporting obligation.

1.98 These are situations commonly met in the ordinary course of business by those working in the regulated sector, particularly those in banks and financial institutions and lawyers dealing with transactional work. They will apply in many cases where nothing is being done that would ordinarily be described as money laundering. They apply, therefore, in many cases to a section of the community consisting essentially of responsible people going about their normal daily work in a variety of legitimate businesses and professions. The principal money laundering offences are thus used to extend and enforce the anti-money laundering reporting regime through the authorised disclosure and consent defence.

J. Implementation of the New Money Laundering Law and Regulation

1.99 The anti-money laundering law and the money laundering reporting requirements of POCA were not new, nor were the regulatory requirements such as customer due diligence, but both law and regulation had been greatly changed and their scope expanded in 2002 and 2003.

1.100 The new law was not simply a set of new or revised criminal provisions and related regulations, but created a complex anti-money laundering regime. Implementation proved to be far from straightforward and nowhere was this more evident than in relation to the anti-money laundering reporting regime, the area which necessarily involves the greatest degree of interaction between the public and the private sector.

1.101 The enhanced reporting obligations under POCA gave rise to a number of problems and concerns shared by banks and financial services institutions, lawyers, accountants, and others in the private sector. There were concerns about whether the Financial Intelligence Unit (FIU) of the National Criminal Intelligence Service (NCIS) had the necessary resources and skills[33] to fulfil its central role in the operation of the consent regime, the quality of decision-making in consent cases, the difficulty of obtaining quick decisions in urgent cases, and the lack of feedback from NCIS and the law enforcement authorities. There was also real concern about the number of cases in which the confidentiality[34] of suspicious activity

---

[32] It may, of course, turn out that the property is not in fact the proceeds of crime, but to avoid potential liability for a money laundering offence a person who suspects that property is the proceeds of crime needs to make a report.

[33] On the question of resources, see the KPMG report: Review of the Regime for Handling Suspicious Activity Reports, 1 July 2003.

[34] On the confidentiality of SARs, see the Lander Review 2006 (paras 35 and 62 to 70 inclusive) <http://www.soca.gov.uk/about-soca/the-uk-financial-intelligence-unit/ukfiu-publication>, and the HO Circular on the Confidentiality of SARs. *Confidentiality of SARs—Home Office Circular 53/2005.*

reports (SARs) was breached, with consequent risks to those who had made money laundering reports, and the absence of any rules or guidelines on the confidentiality of SARs[35] for NCIS staff and law enforcement officers.

There were practical problems of implementation where the requirements of POCA seemed **1.102** to conflict with other statutory obligations: for instance, in the interaction of the new anti-money laundering law and the Data Protection Act 1998.[36] There was uncertainty about how an organization holding data on an individual should respond to a request by an individual for access to his personal data, a 'subject access request', in circumstances where providing the data might amount to an offence of 'tipping off'.

Practical problems of implementation arose, too, from difficulties in interpreting the new **1.103** provisions in Part 7 of POCA. Uncertainty over the meaning and scope of criminal property, both actual and notional property, led to uncertainty about the effect on a customer's bank account or accounts of the introduction of even a small amount of criminal property[37] (and the practical question of whether banks should be making more consent reports before processing regular payments on accounts). Other problematical aspects of the new law concerned the effect of the—originally unqualified—foreign conduct provision[38] in the money laundering offences and whether, as appeared to be the case, legal professional privilege did not apply in relation to the three offences of money laundering.[39]

Whatever the impact on criminals may have been, the impact on law-abiding citizens, mainly **1.104** but not exclusively in the regulated sector, and on the conduct of legitimate business was considerable. In the first years after Part 7 of POCA came into force, the most serious practical result of the new powers was that refusals of consent following authorised disclosures led to the disruption both of ordinary commercial activity and of litigation and the business of the courts.

As the President of the Family Division, Dame Elizabeth Butler-Sloss, observed in giving **1.105** judgment, in October 2003, in the case of *P v P*:[40] 'The coming into force of this Act in February has caused immense confusion and disruption in family proceedings. . .'. The hastily arranged hearing in the case of *P v P* and the subsequent judgment led to some clarification of the conflicting duties of lawyers engaged in litigation, but left other issues unresolved. In the later case of *Bowman v Fels*, the Court of Appeal heard full argument (including argument on the critical question of the applicability of legal professional privilege to sections 327 to 329 of POCA) and set out an '. . .approach to the construction of the statute [which] will, we hope, remove most of the difficulties which have impeded the orderly conduct of litigation ever since section 328 became law'.

---

[35] See, now, the HO Circular (above) and on the issue of disclosure of SARs and public interest immunity, see *Chemists (a firm) v The Commissioners for Her Majesty's Revenue and Customs* [2009] UKTFF 66 (TC).

[36] See the Guidance Notes for the Financial Sector issued by HM Treasury in April 2002: *The UK's Anti-Money Laundering Legislation and the Data Protection Act 1998*.

[37] See the letter from the BBA (British Bankers' Association) to HM Treasury dated 18 December 2009 with its submission in response to the review of the MLR 2007.

[38] Amended by the Serious Organised Crime and Police Act 2005, s 102(2).

[39] An issue not resolved until *Bowman v Fels*.

[40] *P v P* [2003] EWHC Fam 2260. The hearing in the High Court took place on 15 to 17 July 2003; judgment was given on 8 October 2003.

1.106 POCA and the Money Laundering Regulations 2003 had created the formal structure through which the government hoped to achieve its policy aims of combating money laundering and recovering from criminals the proceeds of their crimes in order to 'attack crime through its financial lifeblood'. The early years of implementation showed, particularly in the critical area of the SARs regime, that the infrastructure was lacking and that, for reasons that went beyond issues of resourcing, the NCIS FIU and the law enforcement authorities were not ready and prepared to make proper use of the new level of criminal intelligence from SARs or to respond to the demands of the consent regime.

1.107 As importantly, it became clear that the new anti-money laundering measures, but particularly the SARs regime, would only work effectively if the public and private sector bodies involved, with very different aims and perspectives on the regime, worked constructively together.[41] At the start, there was no adequate provision for co-ordination and co-operation in order to make the provisions work as a coherent system.

1.108 Government responsibility for the anti-money laundering regime was divided between the Home Office and HM Treasury. HM Treasury had responsibility for financial regulation and for the implementation of the three Money Laundering Directives as well as a wide responsibility for financial crime. The Home Office had responsibility for the criminal law, criminal justice and law enforcement aspects of money laundering, as well as for the effective implementation of the Proceeds of Crime Act, including the SARs regime.

1.109 To respond to the concerns of the private sector, the Home Office set up working groups involving private and public sector representatives, but progress was slow in the absence of any real shared understanding of objectives and the best means of achieving them. The government had, however, already set up a high-level advisory group that was broadly representative of the various public and private sector bodies involved in the anti-money laundering regime: the Money Laundering Advisory Committee.

The Money Laundering Advisory Committee

1.110 In 2001, the Treasury had suggested the idea of establishing an advisory committee on UK money laundering policy. From this idea was born the government's Money Laundering Advisory Committee. The first meeting of MLAC took place on 5 May 2002. In a discussion paper on the terms of reference of the new committee, the Treasury said: 'It had been noted that it would be useful to have a strategic-level forum in which those with an interest in the UK's anti-money laundering regime could discuss topical issues and pass the views of those they represent to government. In this way, the Treasury would be able to canvas opinion from a broad range of interested parties before formulating policy advice to Ministers.'

1.111 Against this background, the membership of MLAC was '. . .determined in order to maximise the range of views and interests represented, including those of law enforcement, government, industry, industry regulators and consumers'. MLAC was chaired by HM Treasury and the topic at the head of the agenda when MLAC got underway was the implementation in the UK of the requirements of the Second Money Laundering Directive. This led to the

---

[41] The simple model on which the legislation appeared to be constructed—proscription, prescription, and compliance enforced by criminal penalties—was not only inadequate but counter-productive. On the subsequent development of the risk-based approach to money laundering regulation, see Chapter 9 at paras 9.23 *et seq.*

replacement of the 1993 and 2001 Money Laundering Regulations by the Money Laundering Regulations 2003.

MLAC provided a forum in which different perspectives on the new law and regulations **1.112** could be discussed constructively and through which the government developed its anti-money laundering strategy. The Terms of Reference of MLAC,[42] as revised in March 2008, begin with a statement of the overall aim of MLAC: 'To ensure that the UK's anti-money laundering regime is fair, effective and proportionate to the risks involved and responds flexibly to change by providing a forum for discussing the views of all relevant stakeholders and coordinating action across the regime.'

The first two of the objectives set out in MLAC's Terms of Reference are: **1.113**

- overseeing the implementation of the 2007 Financial Crime Strategy and reviewing the effectiveness of the UK's anti-money laundering policies, taking into account the potential costs and benefits, whilst balancing the risks involved; and
- enabling better co-ordination and coherence of the UK's anti-money laundering regime.

The division of responsibility for anti-money laundering measures between HM Treasury **1.114** and the Home Office proved increasingly unhelpful and, from June 2005, MLAC has been alternately chaired by HM Treasury and the Home Office. The former Home Office working groups were reconstituted as sub-groups of MLAC and, other sub-groups were formed, where necessary to address specific issues, such as customer identification.

The composition of MLAC, and the number and variety of public and private sector bodies **1.115** represented, illustrates the complex nature of the regime created and of the interactions between different players required to achieve results. Some of the main participants are:

Government:

- HM Treasury
- Home Office
- Foreign and Commonwealth Office

Law enforcement, criminal intelligence, and prosecution:

- Police (Association of Chief Police Officers, Metropolitan Police, City of London Police)
- HM Revenue & Customs
- Serious Organised Crime Agency (including the Financial Intelligence Unit)
- Crown Prosecution Service

Regulators and trade/professional bodies:

The wide range of bodies in the regulated sector is represented by a number of both trade and professional bodies and regulators, including the following:

- The Financial Services Authority
- British Bankers Association and Joint Money Laundering Steering Group
- The Law Society

---

[42] The MLAC Revised Terms of Reference are available on MLAC website at <http://www.hm-treasury.gov.uk/d/mlac_meeting_revisedtor180308.pdf>.

- Institute of Chartered Accountants in England and Wales and the Consultative Committee of Accountancy Bodies
- Royal Institution of Chartered Surveyors
- National Association of Estate Agents
- The Gambling Commission

1.116 MLAC has proved a useful forum for discussion and the gradual development of a shared understanding of how the government's anti-money laundering and counter-terrorist financing strategy can best be put into practice. Outside MLAC, there are other joint bodies that provide a forum for discussion and co-ordination in relation to particular anti-money laundering measures or bring together groups with similar or shared responsibilities such as the Regulators' Forum, the SARs Regime Committee, and the SOCA Vetted Group.

The UK government's anti-money laundering strategy

1.117 The new anti-money laundering law contained in Part 7 of the Proceeds of Crime Act 2002, which came into force on 24 February 2003, embodied the policy recommendations of the Performance and Innovation Unit Report of 2000 and preceded the development by the government of a wider anti-money laundering strategy. The government first published a money laundering strategy document, to which the members of MLAC had contributed, in 2004. The strategy was revised and re-launched in February 2007 in *The Financial Challenge to Crime and Terrorism*.[43]

1.118 The government's objectives are summarized in the extract below from the 2007 strategy document:

> The Government's over-riding goal is to protect its citizens and reduce the harm caused by crime and terrorism. Whilst finance is the lifeblood of criminal and terrorist networks, it is also one of their greatest vulnerabilities. The Government's objectives are to use financial measures to:
>
> - **deter** crime and terrorism in the first place—by increasing the risk and lowering the reward faced by perpetrators;
> - **detect** the criminal or terrorist abuse of the financial system; and
> - **disrupt** criminal and terrorist activity—to save lives and hold the guilty to account.
>
> In order to deliver these objectives successfully, action in this area must be underpinned by the three key organising principles that were first set out in the 2004 Anti-Money Laundering Strategy:
>
> - **effectiveness**—making maximum impact on the criminal and terrorist threat;
> - **proportionality**—so that the benefits of intervention are justified and that they outweigh the costs; and
> - **engagement**—so that all stakeholders in government and the private sector, at home and abroad, work collaboratively in partnership.

1.119 Part 7 of POCA shows clearly the concern of the government to achieve 'effectiveness' in the new anti-money laundering law, but makes no concessions to 'proportionality' or 'engagement' that might stand in the way of the drive for effectiveness pursued through the use of

---

[43] Published by HMSO for HM Treasury (and available on the HM Treasury website: <http://www.hm-treasury.gov.uk>).

the criminal law. There were, nevertheless, good reasons to develop a more balanced and inclusive approach to tackling money laundering, and one which better reflected both the complexity of the regime and the contribution which law-abiding citizens could make in support of law enforcement objectives.

The 47 articles of the Third Money Laundering Directive are preceded by a preamble **1.120** containing 48 paragraphs, the very first of which reads: 'Massive flows of dirty money can damage the stability and reputation of the financial sector and threaten the single market, and terrorism shakes the very foundations of our society. *In addition to the criminal law approach*, a preventive effort via the financial system can produce results' (emphasis added).

Under UK law, every requirement placed on the regulated sector by the Money Laundering **1.121** Regulations 2007 (MLR 2007) and everything that those who work in the regulated sector are obliged to do or not to do by the primary legislation, in POCA and TA 2000, is part of 'the criminal law approach' and is backed by criminal sanctions and the threat of imprisonment. It is arguable that this approach to regulation is counter-productive: criminal sanctions against individuals, especially front-line staff, create a fear culture, and encourage a defensive, tick-box approach to compliance. They inhibit the development of a risk-based approach and of a culture of active involvement and co-operation in tackling financial crime and money laundering.

Both the 40 Recommendations of FATF and the Third Money Laundering Directive suggest **1.122** an approach to ensuring compliance by the regulated sector that is more proportionate and does not rely so heavily on criminal sanctions. FATF Recommendation 17 recognizes the need for sanctions, the range of possible sanctions and the importance of proportionality, but it is not prescriptive about the means.[44] 'Countries should ensure that effective, proportionate and dissuasive sanctions, whether criminal, civil or administrative, are available to deal with natural or legal persons covered by these Recommendations that fail to comply with anti-money laundering or terrorist financing requirements.'

The legislation, both POCA 2002 and the Money Laundering Regulations 2003, preceded **1.123** the anti-money laundering strategy and it could scarcely be said that it was underpinned by any organizing principle other than effectiveness. The second and third of the three 'key organizing principles', if applied in practice, are very important for the large number of people and institutions, mainly in the regulated sector (but not confined to it) for whom the legislation creates significant responsibilities and heavy financial commitments.

Since the publication of the strategy in 2004, there has been a greater recognition that the **1.124** anti-money laundering regime created by Part 7 of POCA and the Money Laundering Regulations 2003 requires a wide variety of very different public and private bodies to work together.

The private sector and the regulated sector

The private sector, mainly but not exclusively those working in businesses regulated for anti- **1.125** money laundering purposes, has a significant role in the prevention and detection of money

---

[44] Whether the heavy reliance on criminal sanctions in UK law is proportionate must be in doubt; whether the disproportionate use of criminal sanctions makes the UK's anti-money laundering regime more effective is open to question.

laundering and terrorist financing: in the exercise of its customer due diligence responsibilities, in ensuring that its staff are well-trained and informed about money laundering, and in recognizing and reporting suspected money laundering.

1.126 The enhanced money laundering reporting provisions in Part 7 of POCA enlarged the anti-money laundering responsibilities of the regulated sector and increased the financial costs needed to fulfil those responsibilities. The full impact of the changes on the regulated sector came when the Money Laundering Regulations 2003 were brought into force in 1 March 2004, widening the regulated sector to include businesses and professions such as casino operators, high-value dealers, accountants, and lawyers. The Money Laundering Regulations 2007 have since added to the responsibilities of the regulated sector.

1.127 The regulated sector consists of 'relevant persons', that is persons acting in the course of business of the kinds specified in Regulation 3(1) of MLR 2007. Although it is only the regulated sector which has to comply with the regulations and with the reporting requirements of sections 330 and 331 of POCA, many others in the private sector have put into place similar anti-money laundering systems and procedures. Businesses outside the regulated sector need to be aware of money laundering risks and money laundering law, particularly in relation to SARs: they may not be subject to any obligation to report money laundering, but they still may need to make reports on occasions, under the authorised disclosure and consent regime, in order to avoid potential criminal liability for one of the principal money laundering offences.[45]

1.128 Regulated businesses could contribute to anti-money laundering practice simply through compliance with the regulations, but they are able to make a more effective and growing contribution if working as a responsible partner in co-operation with the SOCA FIU and law enforcement. Both prevention and detection are likely to be improved if the knowledge and understanding that regulated sector staff have of money laundering and terrorist financing is increased by up-to-date information on money laundering trends and typologies. Data-sharing between the public and private sectors has grown, and this includes the provision by SOCA to regulators and regulated bodies of 'alerts', which give information about specific current threats and kinds of criminal activity.

Regulators and supervisors

1.129 Regulators and supervisors have an important role in raising and maintaining anti-money laundering standards, and they have a range of rule-making, investigatory, and enforcement powers. They are likely to be well informed about compliance issues and will necessarily have a better knowledge and understanding of the industry or profession that they regulate than the police or the CPS can have. They also have available to them a wider spectrum of sanctions that can be used against firms as well as individuals.

1.130 Even after the extension of anti-money laundering regulation to a number of other businesses and professions, the banks and financial services firms form the major part of the regulated sector and the Financial Services Authority (FSA) is the leading regulator. One of the four statutory objectives of the FSA (under the Financial Services and Markets Act 2000)

---

[45] Note the obligation to report placed on Money Laudering Reporting Officers, including those outside the regulated sector, by POCA, s 332.

is: '. . .the reduction of financial crime: reducing the extent to which it is possible for a business to be used for a purpose connected with financial crime'.

In pursuing this objective, the FSA has emphasized the need for commitment from the **1.131** senior management of firms to tackling money laundering and financial crime by creating and maintaining effective anti-money laundering systems and processes.[46] The FSA has played an important part in raising anti-money laundering standards and in promoting, across the whole regulated sector, a responsible, risk-based approach rather than bare compliance with rules. At the same time, the FSA has not been slow to use its powers, especially financial sanctions, against banks and other financial institutions where there have been serious failures in compliance with the requirements of the Money Laundering Regulations and of its own rules.

Most of the businesses and professions now in the regulated sector were already regulated for **1.132** purposes other than money laundering and their regulators have widened their role to incorporate the oversight of anti-money laundering compliance by those they regulate. Where this was not the case, the government has intervened to ensure UK compliance with the FATF and Third Money Laundering Directive requirement for supervision. HM Revenue & Customs now acts as the supervisory authority for these purposes of money service businesses, high-value dealers and trust and company service providers.

Representative industry and professional organizations

Representative industry and professional organizations, as well as regulators, have an impor- **1.133** tant part to play both in helping their members comply fully with anti-money laundering requirements, but also in bringing to the attention of government concerns about the anti-money laundering regime and proposals for reform of the legislation. If the 'key organising principles' of *proportionality* and *engagement* are to be given due weight alongside *effectiveness*, representative organizations must have a significant continuing role in the implementation of the government's anti-money laundering strategy.

Representative organizations will usually be able to give particular assistance to the industry **1.134** or profession they represent by:

- raising awareness of money laundering and terrorist financing (through their website, newsletters, articles in trade journals, etc) and of what their members can do to help prevent and detect them;
- providing or facilitating anti-money laundering training; and
- providing detailed anti-money laundering guidance which is designed to help their members comply with the law and regulations and is related to the nature of their work and their particular needs.

Anti-money laundering guidance

The law and the regulations are complicated but they have to be applied and complied with **1.135** by all those who work in the regulated sector, most of whom have no legal training and no particular expertise in the area of financial crime. Helpful guidance to the legal and regulatory requirements is therefore essential.

---

[46] The FSA Manual: SYSC 6.3.

1.136 Most anti-money laundering guidance is produced by representative industry or professional bodies. Where such bodies exist and possess the necessary authority they will generally be best placed to draft guidance because they can bring to the task the experience and expertise required to deal with the specific issues and concerns that relate to the work of their members. In some cases, however, guidance is provided by the regulator or supervisor. After it became a supervisor for money laundering purposes, HM Revenue & Customs issued guidance for the businesses that it supervised in Public Notice MLR8: *Preventing Money Laundering and Terrorist Financing*. In 2010, MLR8 was replaced by detailed sector-specific guidance on its website for money service businesses, high-value dealers, and trust or company service providers (<http://www.hmrc.gov.uk)>.

1.137 The foremost industry guidance is that produced by the Joint Money Laundering Steering Group (JMLSG), which is made up of the leading UK trade associations in the financial service industry. Its stated aim is: '. . .to promulgate good practice in countering money laundering and to give practical assistance in interpreting the UK Money Laundering Regulations. This is primarily achieved by the publication of industry guidance.' JMLSG has been producing money laundering guidance for the financial sector since 1990, well before the bringing into force of the first Money Laundering Regulations (1993).

1.138 The JMLSG guidance, which is approved by HM Treasury and regularly updated, makes an important and influential contribution to anti-money laundering practice. It is addressed to and geared to the needs of financial services firms, but as the JMLSG modestly observes, regulated firms outside the financial sector: '. . .may also find this guidance helpful'.

1.139 Industry-specific anti-money laundering guidance has also been produced for other businesses and professions, including detailed guidance for the two main professional groups brought into the regulated sector by the Money Laundering Regulations 2003: accountants (the money laundering guidance issued by the Consultative Committee of Accountancy Bodies) and lawyers (the Anti-Money Laundering Practice Note issued by the Law Society).

The SARs regime

1.140 If the requirement for customer due diligence is something of a blunt instrument, resource-intensive and of uncertain value in combating money laundering, the SARs regime is the sharp end of anti-money laundering and the FIU is the point of intersection between the private sector and the law enforcement agencies. In 2005, continuing problems with the operation of the money laundering reporting regime and with the capacity of the NCIS FIU to process SARs and of law enforcement agencies to make use of them led the government to set up the Lander review of the SARs regime.[47] The Lander review team consulted widely and listened to the views and concerns of all those involved in the public and private sector. Its report,[48] which reflected the concerns expressed and the thoroughness of its consultation, faced the issues with refreshing directness.

1.141 It recognized that the operation of the SARs regime involved three participants with very different responsibilities and interests—the private sector, the FIU, and law enforcement agencies—and that the first and the last of these consisted of a large number of different organizations. It concluded that collaboration between the participants in the

---

[47] See also the KMPG report: Review of the Regime for Handing Suspicious Activity Reports, 1 July 2003.
[48] Review of the Suspicious Activity Report Regime (The SARs Review), Sir Stephen Lander, March 2006.

regime was essential and noted that such collaboration had not previously been apparent. For collaboration to be real and effective there had to be good communication, shared objectives, and—as the Lander review team had recognized—a degree of trust which was little in evidence at first and had to be built up slowly and against the tenor of the legislation.

The report made a series of practical recommendations which were adopted by the new **1.142** Serious Organised Crime Agency (SOCA) when it took over responsibility for the FIU from NCIS in April 2006. The key recommendation, specifically welcomed by the government,[49] was Recommendation 1: 'SOCA should take overall responsibility for the effective functioning of the SARs regime.'

The implementation of the Lander report recommendations on a tight timescale signifi- **1.143** cantly improved the operation of the SARs regime and went a long way to resolving outstanding private sector concerns, but perhaps more importantly it changed the atmosphere in which the SARs regime operated from one of compulsion to one of real consultation and co-operation. This change in one part, albeit a critical part, of the anti-money laundering regime has contributed significantly to promoting a partnership approach right across the anti-money laundering regime in line with the government's strategy.

K. Conclusion

The UK's anti-money laundering regime is still developing and continues to improve. There **1.144** remain a number of practical problems yet to be resolved[50] and underlying the specific issues are serious questions about the proportionality, fairness, and cost-effectiveness of the regime as a whole. But, some seven or so years after POCA and the 2003 Money Laundering Regulations came into force, the UK does have a functioning anti-money laundering and counter-terrorist financing regime and one that was judged to be largely compliant with international standards in the Mutual Evaluation conducted by FATF in late 2007, as supplemented by its follow-up report in October 2009.[51]

---

[49] See the Foreword to the report signed by Charles Clarke and Gordon Brown.
[50] See Chapter 12 on anti-money laundering law in practice and some of the difficulties associated with it.
[51] For the Mutual Evaluation see <http://www.fatf-gafi.org/dataoecd/55/29/39064399.pdf> and for the follow-up report, see <http://www.fatf-gafi.org/dataoecd/44/8/44048060.pdf>.

2

THE KEY CONCEPTS IN MONEY LAUNDERING LAW

A. Introduction

2.01 This chapter introduces the concepts of criminal property and criminal conduct. These terms are central to the definitions of offences in the Proceeds of Crime Act 2002 (POCA). The definitions are broad and have given rise to controversy. Their scope and application is explored below. Particular regard is given to the nature, location, and timing of the 'predicate offence'—the underlying criminal conduct which renders the property *criminal* property. The mental element in money laundering offences, which can be either knowledge or suspicion that the property is the proceeds of criminal conduct, is considered in detail.

B. Criminal Property

Defined

2.02 At the heart of the money laundering regime is the concept of criminal property. Property is criminal if it constitutes a benefit of the defendant (D) from criminal conduct. It must be both the proceeds of crime and known or suspected to be such proceeds by D. As the definition depends in part on D's state of mind, a particular piece of property may be criminal property in the hands of one person, but not in the hands of another. Whatever D's state of mind the prosecution must prove that property is *in fact* the proceeds of criminal conduct. In this sense money laundering is not a thought crime.[1]

On the face of POCA the definition of property as criminal is so wide that it catches almost **2.03** any property/pecuniary advantage tainted in whole or in part by criminal conduct. There must however be some predicate or underlying criminal conduct before a money laundering crime can be committed.

This reflects both Article 2(h) of the UN Convention Against Transactional Organized **2.04** Crime (the Palermo Convention of 15 November 2000) and Article 1(2)(c) of the Third EC Money Laundering Directive, which define 'acquisition, use or possession' to include *knowing at the time of receipt* that such property was derived from criminal activity.

Criminal property is defined in section 340 of the Act: **2.05**

> 340 . . .
> (3) Property is criminal property if—
> (a) it constitutes a person's benefit from criminal conduct or it represents such a benefit (in whole or part and whether directly or indirectly), and
> (b) the alleged offender knows or suspects that it constitutes or represents such a benefit.
> . . .
> (5) A person benefits from conduct if he obtains property as a result of or in connection with the conduct.
> . . .
> (8) If a person benefits from conduct his benefit is the property obtained as a result of or in connection with the conduct.

Criminal conduct is, in turn, a term of art defined in the Act and explained at paragraph 2.23 below.

The objective element in criminal property

The Crown must prove that that the property is in fact the proceeds of criminal conduct, as well **2.06** as that the alleged offender knew or suspected it to so be. In *Montilla*[2] it was held that this was also the case under the old law. The House of Lords referred to POCA in the following way:[3]

> The language that [Parliament] has chosen to use in the 2002 Act is different from that in the enactments which are in issue in this case. There is no room for any ambiguity. The property that is being dealt with in each case must be shown to have been criminal property. But it would be surprising if the intention was to reduce the scope of these offences. The problem of money laundering has not gone away. The fact that these offences have been designed on the assumption that proof that the property being dealt with was in fact criminal property fits into the pattern which was set by the international instruments and which the wording of the subsections themselves . . . indicates.

The subjective element in criminal property

Property which constitutes the benefit of criminal conduct is not criminal property **2.07** unless the alleged offender knows or suspects that it constitutes or represents such a benefit.

---

[1] *R v Montilla* [2004] UKHL 50.
[2] Ibid.
[3] Ibid, para 41.

Whether or not property is criminal is a function both of the derivation of the property itself, and of the state of knowledge of the person dealing with it. Property may be criminal property in the hands of the criminal, but is not criminal property in the hands of, for example, the bank dealing with it, until such time as the latter's suspicions are aroused.

2.08　The property must be criminal property at the time of the money laundering transaction by virtue of a previous criminal offence. It is not sufficient that the property becomes criminal property by virtue of the laundering itself.

2.09　Knowledge means actual knowledge that the relevant facts exist (see below). Suspicion means thinking that there is a possibility, which is more than fanciful, that the relevant facts exist (see below).

The form of property

2.10　Property is defined broadly in a similar way to the definition to be found in the Theft Act 1968:[4]

> 340
>> (9) Property is all property wherever situated and includes—
>>> (a) money;
>>> (b) all forms of property, real or personal, heritable or moveable;
>>> (c) things in action and other intangible or incorporeal property.
>> (10) The following rules apply in relation to property—
>>> (a) property is obtained by a person if he obtains an interest in it;
>>> (b) references to an interest, in relation to land in England and Wales or Northern Ireland, are to any legal estate or equitable interest or power;
>>> (c) references to an interest, in relation to land in Scotland, are to any estate, interest, servitude or other heritable right in or over land, including a heritable security;
>>> (d) references to an interest, in relation to property other than land, include references to a right (including a right to possession).

The definition of criminal property is therefore very wide.

Pecuniary advantage

2.11　Where a pecuniary advantage is obtained in connection with criminal conduct it is to be treated as an obtaining of criminal property of an equal value:

> 340
>> (6) If a person obtains a pecuniary advantage as a result of or in connection with conduct, he is to be taken to obtain as a result of or in connection with the conduct a sum of money equal to the value of the pecuniary advantage.

Whether and in what circumstances a pecuniary advantage has been obtained 'in connection with' offending has been considered in a number of criminal confiscation cases under Part 2 of POCA 2002. This is because section 76(5) states that 'if a person obtains a pecuniary advantage as a result of or in connection with conduct, he is to be taken to obtain as a result of or in connection with the conduct a sum of money equal to the value of the pecuniary advantage'.

---

[4] Theft Act 1968, s 4(1): ' "Property" includes money and all other property, real or personal, including things in action and other intangible property.'

A defendant benefits from conduct if he obtains property as a result of or in connection with **2.12** that conduct (section 76(4)). The case law prior to the House of Lords decision in *R v May, Jennings and Green*[5] supported the proposition that as long as there was 'more than de minimis' connection (or causal link) between the conduct in question and the benefit obtained such would be sufficient to permit the court to determine that it had been obtained as a result of that conduct. This de minimis test was rejected by the House of Lords in *May* who concluded that the court considering confiscation must apply ordinary common law principles to the facts as found.

The Court of Appeal in an earlier case considered with care the need for a sufficient causal **2.13** connection between the offending and the benefit said to have been obtained by the defendant. In *R v Rigby and Bailey*[6] the defendants had been convicted of offences contrary to the Financial Services and Markets Act 2000. They had misled the London stock market as to the inclusion of revenue in a market report. As a result of the misleading statements the share price of the defendants' company increased and the defendants retained their employment for far longer than would otherwise have been the case. The FSA argued that had the true position been known the defendants would have lost their employment and the share price would have been much lower. It followed that the increase in share price and the wages paid were a benefit received in connection with the commission of the offending. This line of reasoning was rejected by the Court of Appeal on the basis that there was insufficient causal connection between the offending and the receipt of wages and the increase in the share price. The share price went down and the defendants had not realized any profit/gain as the shares had not been sold. Their salaries were not received as a result of the offending but were received despite it. However in other cases the Court of Appeal has found that wages legitimately earned may be the proceeds of crime, for example where D is an illegal immigrant and has obtained employment by deception. In such cases D's criminal conduct, of obtaining a pecuniary advantage by deception, has been held to have a sufficient nexus with the wages earned[7] so that they are deemed to be the proceeds of crime. It follows that wages earned may be criminal property.[8]

There are other considerations. In *Cadman Smith*[9] the House of Lords decided when exam- **2.14** ining the similarly worded confiscation provisions that a defendant who evaded duty by smuggling contraband into the UK did obtain a pecuniary advantage equal to the amount of the duty evaded. Such a defendant guilty of offences, contrary to section 170 of Customs and Excise Management Act 1979 (CEMA), may also be guilty of a money laundering offence, namely acquiring criminal property which includes a pecuniary advantage (in this case the duty evaded).

Aspects of the definition

Mixed property

Where property is derived partly from the proceeds of criminal conduct and partly from **2.15** legitimate sources, the whole of the property is criminal property as the whole of the property

---

[5] [2008] UKHL 28, 29, 30.
[6] [2006] 1 WLR 3067.
[7] *R v Carter, Kulish and Denis Lyashov* [2006] EWCA Crim 416; *R v Paulet* [2009] EWCA Crim 288.
[8] *CPS v Paulet* [2009] EWCA Crim 1573, [2009] EWCA Crim 288.
[9] [2001] UKHL 68.

constitutes, in part, a person's benefit from criminal conduct. Section 340(7) gives further effect to this:

340

(7) References to property or a pecuniary advantage obtained in connection with conduct include references to property or a pecuniary advantage obtained in both that connection and some other.

2.16 Section 93C(1) of the Criminal Justice Act (CJA) 1988 created an offence of concealing or transferring the proceeds of criminal conduct. It was an offence to conceal etc any property which is 'or in whole or in part directly or indirectly represents his proceeds of criminal conduct'. This was expressed in materially similar terms to the definition of criminal property in POCA. That section was considered in the case of *R v Causey*[10] in which Otton LJ said:

> The expression 'proceeds of criminal conduct' even without consideration of the preceding words 'in whole or in part directly or indirectly' is broad and appears to cover property or financial advantage obtained partly in connection with criminal conduct. The preceding words in section 93C(1) 'in whole or in part directly or indirectly' expand the definition of 'through proceeds of criminal conduct'. Thus . . . if one penny or one penny's worth of the property dealt with is the proceeds of criminal conduct then the section is satisfied and fundamentally that 'directly or indirectly' must include property which comes the defendant's way and/or is available to him to be dealt with because he is in receipt elsewhere in his estate of property traceable to the criminal conduct.

Although the Court of Appeal quashed the conviction in the *Causey* case on the grounds that the trial judge had, erroneously, told the jury that the defendant had earlier been convicted of a conspiracy, the case has been taken to be authority for the proposition that criminal property includes property available to a person because of receipt elsewhere of money traceable to criminal conduct. *Causey* is a short judgment and there was little reference to authority. Its importance should not be overstated. Nevertheless the conclusion arguably follows necessarily from the wording of the Act.

2.17 The *Causey* principle, if taken too far, could lead to money laundering cases in which it would be clearly oppressive and an abuse of the process for the Crown to proceed on a money laundering charge. In the confiscation case *R v Shabir*[11] a pharmacist was convicted of obtaining £179,000 by deception which he had received in several monthly payments. He had inflated the claims but the Crown accepted he was entitled to all but £464 of the total obtained. The Court of Appeal had to consider what his benefit was within the meaning of section 76(4) of POCA. In addition the lifestyle provisions had been triggered because the offending amounted to more than £5,000 and an order was made for £212,000. The court ruled that although the defendant had benefitted within the meaning of section 76 of POCA in the amount of £179,000 it was oppressive and an abuse of the process for the Crown to seek a confiscation order when in any ordinary language his claims were dishonestly inflated by only a few hundred pounds and when the statutory assumptions were unfairly triggered.

---

[10] 98/7879/WC 18 October 1999, CA, Otton LJ, Potts J and the recorder of Liverpool HHJ David Clarke.

[11] [2008] EWCA Crim 1809.

What if Shabir had been charged with money laundering on the grounds that the whole **2.18** of the £179,000 was criminal property even though D was entitled to all but £464 of it? Leaving aside difficulties for the prosecution as to whether there is a predicate offence it would surely have been oppressive to charge D with a money laundering offence in respect of £179,000.

The CPS Guidance to Prosecutors as to when it may be oppressive to seek confiscation[12] **2.19** published in May 2009 reflects the decision in *Shabir*. The Guidance states that such cases call for 'the most careful consideration by prosecutors' because the application of the relevant statute may lead the court to conclude that money obtained for the most part legitimately must be treated as the benefit of criminal conduct. Such cases, however, 'will be rare' and confined to cases of 'true oppression'.

Indirect criminal property

Where the benefit of criminal conduct has been converted into new property through a **2.20** process of laundering (for example, the proceeds of a robbery passed through a number of accounts before being used to buy the property in question), that new property may be criminal property: the property represents indirectly a person's benefit from criminal conduct. So assets that can be traced back to crime are criminal property.

The person whose benefit is under consideration may be the alleged offender or another **2.21** person. 'It is immaterial who carried out the conduct and who benefited from it.'[13] In cases where the prosecution can only prove that property is illicit, by circumstantial evidence as to how the property is handled for instance, the person holding it may have stolen it himself, or may be dealing with it on behalf of another criminal.[14] Either scenario would equally be money laundering in law. The Explanatory Notes to POCA (paragraph 469) make it clear that the money laundering offences apply to the offender laundering the proceeds of his own crime as well as those of a crime committed by another. As discussed elsewhere in this chapter there must be predicate or underlying criminal conduct before money laundering can occur. The CPS issued Guidelines to prosecutors[15] as to when a money laundering offence should be charged. These make clear that 'careful prosecutorial discretion' is required and that 'money laundering activities should not be seen as "part and parcel" of the underlying criminality'.

Property obtained in connection with criminal conduct

The definition of criminal property includes both property obtained as a result of criminal **2.22** conduct, that is to say the proceeds of crime, and property *obtained in connection with criminal conduct*.[16]

---

[12] <http://www.cps.gov.uk>: 'Guidance for Prosecutors on the Discretion to Instigate Confiscation Proceedings', 28 May 2009.

[13] s 340(4).

[14] See the comments in Chapter 3 contrasting handling and money laundering.

[15] Crown Prosecution Service Legal Guidance: 'Money Laundering', updated 6 May 2010 (available at <http://www.cps.gov.uk>).

[16] s 340(3).

C. Criminal Conduct

Defined

2.23   *Criminal conduct* is defined for the purposes of Part 7 of POCA as follows.

> **340**
>
> (2) Criminal conduct is conduct which—
>> (a) constitutes an offence in any part of the United Kingdom, or
>> (b) would constitute an offence in any part of the United Kingdom if it occurred there.
>
> . . .
>
> (4) It is immaterial—
>> (a) who carried out the conduct;
>> (b) who benefited from it;
>> (c) whether the conduct occurred before or after the passing of this Act.

2.24   The underlying criminal conduct which gives rise to the criminal property is called the predicate offence. Although the Crown are not obliged to prove the type of predicate offence in every money laundering case they are, in such a case, under an obligation to give detailed particulars as to why property must be criminal. There must be a predicate or underlying offence before money laundering can occur. Although D can launder the proceeds of his own crime generally there must be separate conduct from it for a money laundering offence to be committed. For example, where D obtains a loan by deception it is wrong to charge him with 'acquiring criminal property' contrary to section 329(1)(a) of POCA as there is no predicate offence. The fraudulent obtaining of the loan happens at the same time as the property is 'acquired'.[17]

2.25   Section 329 also creates different ways of committing the offence namely by 'using' (section 329(1)(b)) and having possession of criminal property (section 329(1)(c)). It is arguable that these ways of committing the offence are continuing. If D steals a bicycle and rides it around he is 'using' criminal property which he has stolen.

2.26   In one case discussed below D1 said of D2, who owned a bureau de change, 'he's as sound as a pound. He cleaned millions for us last year.' The bureau de change had holes in its records, false documentation and had converted substantial amounts of cash. In such a case although the Crown cannot prove the type of predicate offence it would be a strange result if the conduct proved did not amount to money laundering. However, where the predicate offence is unknown, the circumstances in which the property is handled must be sufficiently strong so that the only irresistible inference is that the property must derive from crime. This in practice may place a heavy burden on the Crown. The defendant must know in sufficient detail the case that he meets otherwise the law potentially falls foul of the 'certainty test' in Article 7 ECHR.

Identifying the kind or kinds of predicate offence

2.27   There is no requirement for the prosecution to plead or to prove the kind or kinds of the underlying offence or offences. This issue was considered in the case of *Anwoir*,[18] in which Latham LJ stated:

---

[17] *R v Kausar* (CA, 30 July 2009).
[18] *R v Anwoir and others* [2009] 1 WLR 980.

We consider that in the present case the Crown are correct in their submission that there are two ways in which the Crown can prove the property derives from crime, a) by showing that it derives from conduct of a specific kind or kinds and that conduct of that kind or those kinds is unlawful, or b) by evidence of the circumstances in which the property is handled which are such as to give rise to the irresistible inference that it can only be derived from crime.

In that case, the court was considering two apparently conflicting authorities: **2.28**

In *NW*[19] the court had appeared to hold that for the purposes of a prosecution under section 328 of POCA the prosecution, whilst it did not have to establish precisely what crime or crimes had generated the property in question, did have to establish at least the class or type of criminal conduct involved. Laws LJ said at paragraph 6:

> To establish guilt under section 327 or 328, must the Crown prove what particular criminal conduct, or at least what type of criminal conduct, has generated the benefit which the alleged criminal property represents? Or is it enough if they can show, no doubt by reference to the large sums involved and the defendant's want of any means of substance (as well as any other relevant evidence), that the money in question can have had no lawful origin even if they have no lawful evidence of the crime or class of crime involved?

In seeking to answer that question, Laws LJ reviewed the two main authorities on the court's **2.29** approach in relation to the civil enforcement provisions contained in Part 5 of POCA, the decision of Sullivan J in *Green*[20] and the decision of the Court of Appeal, Civil Division, in *Szepietowski.*[21] In *Green* Sullivan J held that the Crown in such proceedings was required to give at least some particulars of what the criminal conduct in question was said to be. A wholly unparticularized allegation of 'unlawful conduct' was not sufficient. In *Szepietowski*, the Court of Appeal expressly agreed, holding that the statute had deliberately steered a careful course between requiring the Director to prove the commission of a specific criminal offence and allowing the Director to make wholly unparticularized allegations of 'unlawful conduct' of the kind which would require a respondent to justify his lifestyle: see paragraph 102 of the judgment of Moore-Bick LJ. Laws LJ also said in paragraph 16 that 'we did not understand the defendants to submit that there could never be a case in which the Crown might properly invite the jury to infer from the available facts that criminal activity was the only reasonable and non fanciful explanation for the presence of the relevant property in the hands of the defendants, even though there was nothing to show what class of crime was involved. We would in any event reject so general and unqualified a position. Everything of course depends on the facts. The protection for the defendants is that such an inference can only properly be drawn if it meets the criminal standard of proof, and the jury must of course be so directed.'

In *Craig*[22] (which was not drawn to the attention of the court in *NW*), a different approach **2.30** was taken. Gage LJ cited a passage from the decision of Butterfield J in *Kelly* (unreported) in which the judge said:

> Whilst the prosecution must prove that the property is 'criminal property' within the meaning of the statutory definition, there is nothing in the wording of the section which imports

---

[19] *R v W, SW, RC and CC* [2009] 1 WLR 965.
[20] *Director of the Assets Recovery Agency v Green* [2005] EWHC Admin 3168.
[21] *Director of the Assets Recovery Agency v Szepietowski* [2007] EWCA Civ 766.
[22] *R v Craig* [2007] EWCA Crim 2913.

any further requirement that the property emanated from a particular crime or any specific type of criminal conduct.

Gage LJ at paragraph 29 of his judgment said:

> We accept this is a correct statement of principle, although it was given in a case where the point was not raised in the way in which it has been today.

2.31   In *Anwoir* the court resolved the apparent conflict between the cases, in favour of *Craig*. The prosecution do not have to identify the kind or kinds of offending from which the property derives, provided they can prove it to be criminal in origin.

2.32   This approach was confirmed in *F & B*.[23]

Tax fraud: the case of Gabriel

2.33   In *Gabriel*[24] the Court of Appeal held that a failure to declare, to the Inland Revenue or the Department for Work and Pensions, profits made from trading in legitimate goods did not convert those profits into criminal property. In *IK*[25] that court held that the decision in *Gabriel* did not mean that the fact that undeclared takings were derived from a legitimate business meant those takings could not amount to criminal property. Whilst profits made from a legitimate business without declaring them for tax purposes did not become criminal property simply by reason of the failure to declare the profits, they were capable of doing so where there was a *prima facie* case of the offence of cheat.[26]

The 'all crimes' approach

2.34   Any crime no matter how minor may be the subject of money laundering under UK law. A narrower approach has been taken internationally. For instance, the Second Money Laundering Directive applied to the proceeds of 'criminal activity' which includes drug offences, organized crime, fraud, corruption, and any 'offence which may generate substantial proceeds and which is punishable by a severe sentence of imprisonment in accordance with the penal law of the Member State'.[27] However member states may voluntarily 'designate any other offence as a criminal activity for the purposes of this Directive'.[28]

2.35   Under the Third Money Laundering Directive 'criminal activity' has been re-defined to include any involvement in 'serious crimes', which now includes 'all offences which are punishable by deprivation of liberty or a detention order for a maximum of more than one year'.

The timing of the predicate conduct

2.36   It is immaterial whether the predicate criminal conduct occurred before or after the passing of the Act.[29] So the conduct which gives rise to the benefit may have occurred at any time in the past. This does not affect the fact that the conduct constituting the money laundering itself (the dealing with criminal property) must have happened after the commencement of the Act. As with all criminal statutes, the Act is not retroactive.

---

[23] *R v F and B* [2008] EWCA Crim 1868.
[24] *R v IK* [2007] 1 WLR 2272.
[25] *R v IK* [2007] 1 WLR 2262.
[26] See [2007] Crim LR 645.
[27] Art 1 as amended.
[28] Ibid.
[29] POCA, s 340(4)(c).

The conduct which *constitutes the money laundering offence* must occur after the commence-   **2.37**
ment of the Act. The conduct which *gave rise to the benefit* that is the subject of the laundering
may have occurred at any time.

Example

A luxury car salesman receives a visit from a man who he instantly recognizes as a notorious   **2.38**
robber—who had just completed a 20-year sentence for his part in a number of high-profile
robberies. The man asks to buy a £50,000 sports car and asks what discount is available for
cash. Given the fact that the man has only just been released, the salesman suspects that this
money must have come from his criminal past, but he knows the robberies took place in
1980—long before the money laundering laws came into being. Nevertheless, if the salesman sells the car to the robber he is guilty of a money laundering offence. The proceeds of
those robberies are the benefit of criminal conduct and the salesman suspects this to be the
case. Therefore the money is criminal property.[30]

The location of the predicate offence

The location of the conduct is immaterial to the question of whether it is criminal conduct.   **2.39**
The question is: would the conduct in question constitute an offence in any part of the UK
if it occurred there? This question requires the consideration of a number of criminal regimes,
most notably the criminal law of England and Wales, and the criminal law of Scotland. If the
predicate offence is said to be a theft in a foreign country, there is no need for the English
court to enquire into the theft laws of that country. It must rather ask itself whether the conduct would amount to theft under the English Theft Act 1968 or an equivalent Scottish
offence.

Criminal conduct is conduct anywhere in the world which would be a criminal offence had   **2.40**
it occurred anywhere in the UK.

As much of criminal law is derived from internationally shared social norms, it is likely that   **2.41**
conduct which is an offence in the UK is also an offence where it occurred, and vice versa,
but not invariably so. It is worth considering three special cases, which are dealt with
below:

- conduct which is an offence in the UK but not in the country where it was committed;
- conduct which is an offence in the country where it was committed but not in the UK;
- conduct which is only an offence in the UK because of something peculiar to the UK.

Special cases relating to the location of the predicate offence

*Conduct which is an offence in the UK but not in the country where it was committed—the
overseas conduct exception*

Each of the principal money laundering offences contains a clause in the following terms:[31]   **2.42**

> But a person does not commit an offence if —
> (a) he knows, or believes on reasonable grounds, that the relevant criminal conduct occurred
>   in a particular country or territory outside the United Kingdom, and

---

[30] The car salesman may have a defence to acquiring criminal property if he gives adequate consideration
(see Chapter 3).
[31] ss 327(2A)(b)(ii), 328(3)(b)(ii), and 329(2A)(b)(ii).

(b) the relevant criminal conduct—

    (i) was not, at the time it occurred, unlawful under the criminal law then applying in that country or territory, and

    (ii) is not of a description prescribed by an order made by the Secretary of State.

The Proceeds of Crime Act 2002 (Money Laundering Exceptions to Overseas Conduct Defence) Order 2006[32] prescribes for these purposes all conduct which would carry a maximum term of over 12 months in any part of the United Kingdom:

2.

(1) Relevant criminal conduct of a description falling within paragraph (2) is prescribed for the purposes of sections 327(2A)(b)(ii), 328(3)(b)(ii) and 329(2A)(b)(ii) of the Proceeds of Crime Act 2002 (exceptions to defence where overseas conduct is legal under local law).

(2) Such relevant criminal conduct is conduct which would constitute an offence punishable by imprisonment for a maximum term in excess of 12 months in any part of the United Kingdom if it occurred there other than—

    (a) an offence under the Gaming Act 1968;

    (b) an offence under the Lotteries and Amusements Act 1976, or

    (c) an offence under section 23 or 25 of the Financial Services and Markets Act 2000.

2.43 The combined effect of these two legislative measures is that conduct overseas which is not criminal in the country where it occurs, is exempt from money laundering offences, provided it carries 12 months imprisonment or under in the UK, except for each of the offences listed in (a), (b), and (c) above.

2.44 **Example 1: bullfighting**   Bullfighting is both lawful and popular in Spain; the top matadors earn salaries akin to those of top soccer players. If a top matador wishes to invest his money in the London stock market, would it be money laundering to allow him to do so? The conduct of bullfighting incorporates what in the UK would be offences relating to animal fights, carrying 6 months' weeks imprisonment.[33] Because the test of what is criminal property asks whether the conduct would be criminal in the UK, the matador's income from bull fighting is criminal property. But because bullfighting is legal in Spain and the maximum sentence for it here would not be more than 12 months, his investments will not involve money laundering offences.

2.45 **Example 2: cannabis dealing**   A Dutch entrepreneur A operates a chain of retail outlets in Amsterdam. These sell cannabis for smoking, on the one hand, and tulip bulbs on the other. He is looking to expand the bulb business into London, and negotiates to buy a shop from D. A tells D that the money comes from his business empire at large, including the cannabis café part of it. Should D accept payment for the shop? The question does not involve a consideration of whether the cannabis cafés are lawful in Amsterdam, or merely tolerated, but rather whether the supply of cannabis is an offence in any part of the United Kingdom. It is. The money is criminal property, and D knows it. The proceeds of cannabis dealing, or being concerned in the management of premises where cannabis is smoked, would carry up to 14 years' imprisonment if committed in the UK and are not exempt. If D accepted the payment he could be committing a money laundering offence.[34]

---

[32] SI 2006/1070.

[33] E.g. Animal Welfare Act 2006, s 8.

[34] Note that provided D gives fair value, he could avail himself of the adequate consideration defence to the s 329 offence.

Conduct which is criminal in the country where it was committed but not in the UK

Conduct which is criminal in the country where it was committed but not in the UK is not **2.46** 'criminal conduct' within the meaning of the Act.

Often, the prosecution seek to prove that property is the proceeds of criminal conduct not **2.47** by direct evidence of the conduct itself, but by inference from the furtive manner in which the property has been treated. Care must be taken with this approach when the property which is alleged to be the proceeds of criminal conduct comes from a foreign jurisdiction. The property may be treated in an unusual or furtive manner because of its illegality in that jurisdiction, but that does not necessarily make it criminal in the UK.

Example: exchange controls   Exchange controls are often enforced by criminal sanctions **2.48** in foreign jurisdictions, but this is not the case in the UK. The Exchange Control Act 1947 which criminalized breaches of UK exchange controls was repealed by the Finance Act 1987. Therefore the breach of a country's exchange controls is not criminal conduct within the meaning of the Act, and dealing with the proceeds of such breaches will not be money laundering under POCA. A person breaching local exchange controls may well treat the proceeds in a furtive manner so as to avoid detection by that country's authorities. That furtive conduct should not be treated as evidence that the property is criminal property in the UK.

Conduct which is only an offence in the UK because of something peculiar
to the United Kingdom

Some offences are defined in terms of UK institutions or processes. Where equivalent con- **2.49** duct is carried out in a foreign jurisdiction, the UK institution is missing, so the offence is not made out and the conduct is not criminal conduct within the meaning of the Act.

Example 1: fraudulent trading   Fraudulent trading is defined, under the Companies Act **2.50** 2006 as:

> **1 Companies**
> (1) In the Companies Acts, unless the context otherwise requires—
>   "company" means a company formed and registered under this Act
>   . . .
> **993 Offence of fraudulent trading**
> (1) If any business of a company is carried on with intent to defraud creditors of the company
>   or creditors of any other person, or for any fraudulent purpose, every person who is know-
>   ingly a party to the carrying on of the business in that manner commits an offence.

Plainly, it is impossible to commit the offence with respect to a business other than one that has been registered under the Act.[35] This requires registration through Companies House. A foreign business may have an equivalent status to a UK limited company, but because it is not registered under the UK Companies Act, it could not be the subject of a fraudulent trading offence. So the proceeds of conduct akin to fraudulent trading with respect to the foreign equivalent of a limited company are not criminal property within the meaning of the Act.

Example 2: tax fraud   It is arguable that tax fraud and cheating the public revenue fall **2.51** within this category. The offences are defined in terms of the Inland Revenue and the Crown, each of which are UK institutions. The underlying rules as to how much tax is to be paid by

---

[35] Though there is now a wider offence of fraudulent business under the Fraud Act 2006.

whom under what circumstances are peculiar to the UK. So arguably the proceeds of foreign tax fraud do not fall within the definition of criminal property.

2.52 It is certainly the case that resolving such cases can be enormously complex. If a particular payment is made to a Russian company in breach of that country's tax laws, would it also be an offence under the UK regime?

2.53 **Alternative offences** It should be noted, that there are often multiple ways of criminalizing the same conduct. The charge of false accounting[36] which relates to falsifying 'any account or any record or document made or required for any accounting purpose', is very wide. Also, conspiracy to defraud applies where there is an agreement dishonestly to prejudice another's right. Often tax frauds and the like involve other criminal conduct in their execution.

D. The Mental Element: Knowledge, Belief, and Suspicion

Proving states of knowledge

2.54 At the heart of the POCA penal regime are offences which are defined in terms of various actual/implied states of knowledge of the alleged offender:

- knowledge;
- suspicion;
- reasonable grounds for knowing or suspecting.

2.55 Except where there is a confession by the defendant, the defendant's state of knowledge or suspicion must be inferred from the surrounding facts. It is a requirement of the money laundering directives that 'knowledge, intent or purpose required as an element of the [money laundering offences] may be inferred from objective factual circumstances'.[37] In English law this happens by default. The jury is routinely invited, by the judge at the conclusion of any criminal trial, to 'draw inferences: that is come to common sense conclusions based on the evidence which you accept'.[38]

2.56 In the context of the money laundering offences, the defendant's state of knowledge must be inferred from the evidence surrounding the transaction or the dealing with property. A transaction may have no apparent commercial purpose. The defendant may have acted in an unusual or furtive manner. The defendant may have failed to ask obvious questions. In relation to a person's state of knowledge, Lord Bridge said, in *Westminster City Council v Croyalgrange Ltd*:[39]

> . . . it is always open to the tribunal of fact . . . to base a finding of knowledge on evidence that the defendant had deliberately shut his eyes to the obvious or refrained from inquiry because he suspected the truth but did not wish to have his suspicion confirmed.

---

[36] Theft Act 1968, s 17.
[37] First, Second and Third Money Laundering Directives, Art 1 and Council of Europe Convention on Laundering, Art 6.2c.
[38] JSB direction on 'Functions of Judge and Jury' (Crown Court Bench Book, July 2007).
[39] (1986) 83 Cr App R 155, at 164.

Example: proving the defendant's knowledge

In *Loizou*,[40] £87,010 of cash was passed between two motor vehicles parked in the car park **2.57** of a Holiday Inn. Those who were party to the exchange were prosecuted under section 327 for the transfer of criminal property, namely the cash. The facts upon which the prosecution relied to prove their assertion as to knowledge (and the fact that the cash was criminal property) included the defendants' anti-surveillance tactics, the co-ordinated movement of vehicles from each location to the final destination, the contemporaneity of mobile phone messages to Loizou which explained the purpose behind the hand-over, and the fact that no person had come forward to claim the money.

Knowledge

The definition of criminal property requires that 'the alleged offender knows or suspects' that **2.58** the property constitutes or represents the benefit of a person's criminal conduct. It is plain that knowledge is a higher level of certainty in the hierarchy of mental states than belief and suspicion. It is an ordinary word and is unlikely to need any definition.[41]

Knowledge is to be distinguished from belief and suspicion. In *Hall*,[42] in the context of **2.59** handling, Boreham J said:[43]

> A man may be said to know that goods are stolen when he is told by someone with first hand knowledge (someone such as the thief or the burglar) that such is the case. Belief, of course, is something short of knowledge. It may be said to be the state of mind of a person who says to himself: 'I cannot say I know for certain that these goods are stolen, but there can be no other reasonable conclusion in the light of all the circumstances, in the light of all that I have heard and seen.' Either of those two states of mind is enough to satisfy the words of the [the Theft Act]. The second is enough (that is, belief) even if the defendant says to himself: 'Despite all that I have seen and all that I have heard, I refuse to believe what my brain tells me is obvious'. What is not enough, of course, is mere suspicion. 'I suspect that these goods may be stolen, but it may be on the other hand that they are not.' That state of mind, of course, does not fall within the words 'knowing or believing'.

The Joint Money Laundering Steering Group Guidance states:[44] **2.60**

> Having knowledge means actually knowing something to be true. In a criminal court, it must be proved that the individual in fact knew that [fact]. That said, knowledge can be inferred from the surrounding circumstances; so, for example, a failure to ask obvious questions may be relied upon by a jury to imply knowledge.

This accords with the view of the editors of *Archbold*,[45] that mental states short of actual knowledge, such as wilful blindness (see below) are insufficient to amount to knowledge in the criminal law. Rather, they are evidence from which knowledge can be inferred.[46]

---

[40] *R v L, G, Q, and M (Loizou)* [2005] EWCA Crim 1579.
[41] *R v Harris* (1986) 84 Cr App Rep 75.
[42] *R v Hall* (1985) 81 Cr App R 260.
[43] At 264.
[44] At para 7.8.
[45] Para 17-49 Archbold 2011.
[46] See *Westminster City Council v Croyalgrange* above.

Contrasted with imputed knowledge

2.61   The meaning of 'knowledge' in the criminal law is to be contrasted with the usage in certain contexts within civil law. In breach of trust cases, knowledge has been given a wide meaning to include knowledge which may be imputed to the fiduciary. It has been said the requirement of knowledge would be satisfied if there was:[47]

- actual knowledge;
- a wilful shutting of one's eyes to the obvious;
- a wilful and reckless failure to make inquiries that an honest and reasonable man would have made;
- knowledge of circumstances which would have indicated the facts to an honest and reasonable man; or
- knowledge of circumstances which would have put an honest and reasonable man on inquiry.

Only actual knowledge satisfies the requirement in the criminal law.

Suspicion

2.62   The Court of Appeal, in the case *R v Da Silva*,[48] has given guidance as to how the jury should be directed on 'suspicion', where it is necessary to do so:

> To have a suspicion means to think that there is a possibility, which is more than fanciful, that the relevant facts exist.

2.63   In *Da Silva* the Court of Appeal considered the meaning of 'suspecting' in section 93A(1)(a) of the Criminal Justice Act 1988 which applied, inter alia, to those who entered into an arrangement, whereby the control of another's proceeds of criminal conduct is facilitated, 'knowing or suspecting' that that other has been engaged in criminal conduct. It was said:[49]

> What then does the word 'suspecting' mean in its particular context in the 1988 Act? It seems to us that the essential element in the word 'suspect' and its affiliates, in this context, is that the defendant must think that there is a possibility, which is more than fanciful, that the relevant facts exist. A vague feeling of unease would not suffice. . . . We consider therefore that, for the purpose of a conviction under section 93A(1)(a) of the 1988 Act, the prosecution must prove that the defendant's acts of facilitating another person's retention or control of the proceeds of criminal conduct were done by a defendant who thought that there was a possibility, which was more than fanciful, that the other person was or had been engaged in or had benefited from criminal conduct. We consider that, if a judge feels it appropriate to assist the jury with the word 'suspecting', a direction along these lines will be adequate and accurate.

Although *Da Silva* was a case under the 1988 Act, there is no reason to suppose any different definition would apply to a charge under POCA. *In K Ltd v Natwest Bank*[50] the Court of Appeal Civil Division applied the definition in *Da Silva* to POCA.

2.64   An earlier definition, taken from the civil courts, remains pertinent. That is that given in *Hussien v Chang Fook Kam*,[51] in which the Privy Council was considering the state of mind

---

[47]   *Baden Delvaux v Société Générale* [1993] 1 WLR 509.
[48]   [2007] 1 WLR 303.
[49]   At para 16.
[50]   [2006] EWCA 1039.
[51]   [1970] AC 942.

necessary for a law enforcement officer to trigger the power of arrest. The committee made it plain that reasonable suspicion was not the same as prima facie proof, and Lord Devlin said:[52]

> Suspicion in its ordinary meaning is a state of conjecture or surmise where proof is lacking: 'I suspect but I cannot prove'. Suspicion arises at or near the starting point of an investigation of which the obtaining of prima facie proof is the end.

The Joint Money Laundering Steering Group guidance states:[53]   **2.65**

> Suspicion is more subjective [than knowledge] and falls short of proof based on firm evidence. Suspicion has been defined by the courts as being beyond mere speculation and based on some foundation, for example:
>
> 'A degree of satisfaction and not necessarily amounting to belief but at least extending beyond speculation as to whether an event has occurred or not'; and
>
> 'Although the creation of suspicion requires a lesser factual basis than the creation of a belief, it must nonetheless be built upon some foundation.'

The former definition is taken from the case of *Corporate Affairs Cmr v Guardian Investments*.[54] The latter is from *Walsh v Loughman*.[55]

Suspicion as distinct from an 'inkling'

The trouble with leaving 'suspicion' as a term for the jury to interpret is that the word   **2.66** gives rise to a spectrum of meaning. In *Manifest Shipping Co Ltd v Uni-Polaris Insurance Co Ltd ('The Star Sea')*[56] the House of Lords considered the word in a civil context, and Lord Scott said:[57]

> Suspicion is a word that can be used to describe a state-of-mind that may, at one extreme, be no more than a vague feeling of unease and, at the other extreme, reflect a firm belief in the existence of the relevant facts.

He went on to conclude that, in the context then under consideration, suspicion must be firmly grounded and targeted on specific facts. Lord Scott's view of the breadth of meaning is confirmed by the Chambers Dictionary which defines 'suspicion' as:

> act of suspecting . . . the imagining of something without evidence or on slender evidence: inkling: mistrust.[58]

The 'inkling' referred to in Chambers and the 'vague feeling of unease' referred to in the *Manifest Shipping* case is insufficient to found a suspicion in POCA cases. In *Da Silva* the Court of Appeal disapproved a direction by the judge that had referred the jury to the Chambers definition and had continued 'therefore, any inkling or fleeting thought that the money being paid into her account . . . might be the proceeds of criminal conduct will suffice for the offence against her to be proved'. The Court of Appeal said that if a judge feels

---

[52] At p 948.
[53] Para 7.9.
[54] [1984] VR 1019.
[55] [1991] 2 VR 351.
[56] [2001] UKHL 1, [2003] 1 AC 469.
[57] At para 116.
[58] *Chambers English Dictionary* (Cambridge, 1988).

it appropriate to assist the jury with the word 'suspecting', a direction along the lines of the definition given above (see paragraph 2.63) will be adequate and accurate.

2.67 At the time of *Da Silva* and *K Ltd v Nat West*, the then current edition of the textbook *Mitchell, Taylor and Talbot on Confiscation and Proceeds of Crime* stated:

> Thus any inkling or fleeting thought that the property might be [criminal property] will suffice.[59]

However in *K Ltd v Nat West,* in which the author of that work appeared as an advocate for the intervening parties, the court noted that he had 'expressed unease at the definition used in his important work'.[60]

Suspicion as distinct from reasonable suspicion

2.68 Suspicion is a subjective concept. There is no requirement in the definition of criminal property in the Act that the suspicion need be a reasonable one. Elsewhere in the Act, where reasonable grounds are sufficient, overt reference is made to having 'reasonable grounds for . . . suspecting'.[61] Hence, it can be assumed that where there is no reference Parliament did not intend that reasonableness be implied. In *Da Silva* the court said:[62]

> This court could not, even if it wished to, imply a word such as 'reasonable' into this statutory provision. To do so would be to make a material change in the statutory provision for which there is no warrant.

In *Holtham v MPC*[63] it was said 'suspicion may or may not be based upon reasonable grounds but it still remains suspicion and nothing more'.

Suspicion as a settled state

2.69 The suspicion must be one that the person has settled upon, not one which occurs transiently before it is dismissed.

2.70 Comments of the Minister of State whilst POCA was passing through Parliament tended to suggest that a fleeting suspicion would be enough. Bob Ainsworth said 'In the event of suspicion, *no matter how fleeting*, all that the person must do is report it—make a disclosure— and he relieves himself of any doubt about any consequences.'[64]

2.71 However, in *Da Silva* the court gave a definition of suspicion and followed it with a possible qualification:[65]

> The only possible qualification to this conclusion, is whether, in an appropriate case, a jury should also be directed that the suspicion must be of a settled nature; a case might, for example, arise in which a defendant did entertain a suspicion in the above sense but, on further thought, honestly dismissed it from his or her mind as being unworthy or as contrary to such evidence as existed or as being outweighed by other considerations. In such a case a careful

---

[59] Volume II, section VIII 008-009.
[60] At para 15.
[61] s 330(2).
[62] At para 8.
[63] *The Times,* 28 Nov 1987.
[64] Bob Ainsworth, Minister of State, SC B (Proceeds of Crime Bill), Hansard HC (series 6), vol 377, col 983 (17 January 2002).
[65] At para 16.

direction to the jury might be required. But, in our view, before such a direction was necessary there would have to be some reason to suppose that the defendant went through some such thought process as set above. The present case was not a case where any such direction could be thought to be necessary.

Or, as it was put In *K Ltd v Nat West,* the definition 'is subject, in an appropriate case, to the further requirement that the suspicion so formed should be of a settled nature'.[66]

It is submitted, that the scheme of the money laundering legislation at large supports the **2.72** view that the suspicion must be a settled one. The JMLSG Guidance encourages financial institutions to use a risk-based approach to the prevention of money laundering, that is to say identifying indicators of the risk of a transaction involving money laundering and targeting prevention efforts towards those which present the greater risk. So, a bank teller receiving an unusually large cash deposit may have suspicions, based upon his training that such deposits are susceptible to use by money launderers, but that suspicion may be allayed by the teller informing himself from bank records that the customer is in a cash-based business. The teller has formed a suspicion but on balance concluded that that suspicion is allayed.

Reasonable grounds for knowing or suspecting

Section 330 applies to a person in the regulated sector who knows or suspects, *or has reason-* **2.73** *able grounds for knowing or suspecting*, that another person is engaged in money laundering.

An objective test?

Having 'reasonable grounds for knowing or suspecting' is an objective concept. All that is **2.74** required is that the defendant has knowledge of the circumstances which objectively give reasonable grounds for knowing or suspecting. The case of *Griffiths and Pattison*[67] is an example of a case in which the jury made a distinction between 'knowing or suspecting' and 'having reasonable grounds for knowing or suspecting'. The defendant was acquitted of a principal money laundering offence but convicted of the section 330 failure to disclose offence, hence the jury must have convicted on the understanding that he did not actually know or suspect, but did have reasonable grounds to do so.

This approach to the law would accord with the purpose behind the regime. The money **2.75** laundering regulations ensure that financial institutions have in place appropriate measures to prevent money laundering. The requirement for training ensures that those in the regulated sector will have been trained in what is likely to amount to reasonable grounds for knowing or suspecting that another is involved in money laundering. However there is an alternative view.

An alternative view

Surprisingly, to have 'reasonable grounds to suspect' has been held to be a part subjective test; **2.76** the person must actually suspect, as well as having reasonable grounds to do so. In effect 'reasonable grounds to suspect' means to suspect on reasonable grounds.

In *O'Hara v Chief Constable of the Royal Ulster Constabulary*,[68] where the issue related to the **2.77** test in section 12(1) of the Prevention of Terrorism (Temporary Provisions) Act 1984 which

---

[66] Ibid.
[67] [2006] EWCA Crim 2155.
[68] [1997] AC 286.

gave power to a constable to arrest a person without warrant if he had reasonable grounds for suspecting that he was concerned in acts of terrorism, Lord Hope said:[69]

> In part it is a subjective test, because he must have formed a genuine suspicion in his own mind that the person has been concerned in acts of terrorism. In part also it is an objective one, because there must also be reasonable grounds for the suspicion which he has formed. But the application of the objective test does not require the court to look beyond what was in the mind of the arresting officer. It is the grounds which were in his mind at the time which must be found to be reasonable grounds for the suspicion which he has formed.

2.78 In *Saik* Lord Hope applied this approach to section 93C[70] of the Criminal Justice Act 1988:[71]

> . . . The subjective test—actual suspicion—is not enough. The objective test—that there were reasonable grounds for it—must be satisfied too.
>
> . . . The subsection assumes that a person who is proved to have had reasonable grounds to suspect that the property had a criminal origin did in fact suspect that this was so when he proceeded to deal with it. A person who has reasonable grounds to suspect is on notice that he is at the same risk of being prosecuted under the subsection as someone who knows. It is not necessary to prove actual knowledge, which is a subjective requirement. The prosecutor can rely instead on suspicion. But if this alternative is adopted, proof of suspicion is not enough. It must be proved that there were reasonable grounds for the suspicion. In other words, . . . [the] requirement contains both a subjective part—that the person suspects— and an objective part—that there are reasonable grounds for the suspicion.

See also the judgment of Lord Brown.[72]

2.79 In his commentary on the case, Professor Ormerod describes this aspect as 'one of the more surprising aspects of the decision'. He goes on to state:[73]

> The assumption that the term 'reasonable grounds to suspect' was in this context a purely objective one is supported by the use of that term as a form of *mens rea* in some POCA offences (cf. Lord Brown at [110]). For example in s.330 of the 2002 Act it is a sufficient *mens rea* either that the defendant suspected, or that he had reasonable grounds to suspect the relevant facts. On their Lordships' analysis, proof of the latter will necessarily involve proof of the former. 'Reasonable grounds to suspect' would then seem to be a redundant alternative because no prosecutor is likely to take the more onerous route. It may be that the practical reality is that there is little difference—Lord Hope commented that 'the subsection [93C(2)] assumes that a person who is proved to have had reasonable grounds to suspect that the property had a criminal origin did in fact suspect that this was so' (at [53]).

2.80 It may be that the distinction between 'reasonable grounds *to* suspect' in the old legislation and 'reasonable grounds *for* . . . suspecting', in section 330 is sufficient to distinguish section 330 from the reasoning applied to 93C Criminal Justice Act 1988 in *Saik*.

---

[69] At 298.
[70] s 93C(2): 'A person is guilty of an offence if, knowing or having reasonable grounds to suspect that any property is, or in whole or in part directly or indirectly represents, another person's proceeds of criminal conduct, he—(a) conceals or disguises that property . . .'
[71] At para 52.
[72] At para 108.
[73] *Saik* [2006] Crim LR 998.

Knowledge and conspiracy: *Saik*

To prove a conspiracy to commit a money laundering offence, it is not sufficient for the **2.81** prosecution to prove that the offender suspected that the property that he was dealing with was criminal property.

A higher *mens rea* is required: **2.82**

- Where the property which is the subject of the offending has not been identified when the conspiracy agreement is reached, the prosecution must prove that the offender *intended* that the property would be criminal property.
- Where the property is identified when the conspiracy agreement is reached, the prosecution must prove that the alleged offender *knew* that the property was criminal property.

This is the effect of section 340 of POCA taken together with the statutory offence of conspiracy as enacted by section 1 of the Criminal Law Act 1977, and in particular subsection 1(2).[74]

Section 1(2) of the Criminal Law Act 1977 states that: **2.83**

> where any liability for any offence may be incurred without knowledge on the part of the person committing it of any particular fact or circumstance necessary for the commission of the offence, a person shall nevertheless not be guilty of conspiracy to commit the offence by virtue of subsection (1) above unless he and at least one other party to the agreement intend or know that that fact or circumstance shall or will exist at the time when the conduct constituting the offence is to take place.

Under the previous money laundering regimes, it was held that, although it was not explic- **2.84** itly stated in the legislation, the Crown had to prove that property was derived from crime as a matter of fact, as well as that the defendant knew or suspected that to be the case. This was decided by the Court of Appeal in *R v Liaquat Ali, Akhtar Hussain, Mohsin Khan and Shaid Bhatti*[75] and the House of Lords in *R v Montilla*.[76] Under POCA the definition of criminal property makes it plain that this remains so.[77]

That the property is derived from crime is a fact or circumstance necessary for the commis- **2.85** sion of the offence. Hence from section 1(2), a person shall not be guilty of conspiracy to commit the offence unless he and at least one other party to the agreement intend or know that the fact or circumstance shall or will exist at the time of the conduct, i.e. that the property is derived from crime.

The above is the law as decided by the House of Lords in *Saik*. Prior to that case it had been **2.86** widely assumed that suspicion was a sufficient *mens rea* for conspiracy to money launder. Many juries had been directed and many defendants convicted on the basis of that assumption.

---

[74] *Saik* [2006] UKHL 18.
[75] [2006] QB 322.
[76] [2004] UKHL 50.
[77] s 340(3).

The fallout from Saik

2.87 *Saik* led to a number of appeals. In the case of *Ramzan*,[78] the Court of Appeal dealt with a number of joined appeals in cases where juries had been given the wrong direction in conspiracy to money launder cases. Where applications were made for leave to appeal out of time, the court refused them in the light of the practice of the Court of Appeal not to grant leave to appeal out of time where the conviction was entirely proper under the law as it stood at the time of trial unless substantial injustice would otherwise be done to the applicant.[79] Some cases were before the court upon a reference by the Criminal Case Review Commission (CCRC) and these were allowed[80] because, pursuant to section 9(2) of the Criminal Appeal Act 1995, 'a reference stands as if leave has been granted' and the court had no option but to consider the safety of the conviction. In these cases, where the court allowed the appeal, it ordered a retrial.

2.88 Following this further references were made by the CCRC. The Director of Revenue and Customs Prosecutions challenged the decision of the CCRC to refer cases, arguing that the CCRC should adopt the same practice as the Court of Appeal in change of law cases. The challenge to the reference failed,[81] the administrative court stating that the CCRC 'was under no obligation to have regard to, still less to implement, a practice of the CACD which operates at a stage [the leave stage] with which the Commission is not concerned'.

2.89 Ultimately, the further appeals by way of reference by the CCRC were allowed by the Court of Appeal in *El Kurd and others*.[82]

2.90 Section 42 of the Criminal Justice and Immigration Act 2008 grants the Court of Appeal the power to dismiss appeals following references by the CCRC in the circumstances which arose in that case, by inserting a new section 16C into the Criminal Appeal Act 1968. The section has effect from 14 July 2008.

---

[78] [2006] EWCA Crim 1974.

[79] At [30].

[80] At [41].

[81] *R (Director of Revenue and Customs Prosecutions) v Criminal Cases Review Commission* [2008] 1 All ER 383 (Admin).

[82] [2007] 1 WLR 3190.

3

MONEY LAUNDERING OFFENCES UNDER THE PROCEEDS OF CRIME ACT 2002

A. Introduction

This chapter sets out an overview of the money laundering offences followed by a detailed **3.01** description of the offences under sections 327, 328, and 329 of POCA. In addition relevant case law is discussed and the sentencing provisions are set out, as are sample counts and indictments. The chapter also deals with the exceptions or limitations and the defences available for these offences.

B. Overview of Offences

Under POCA, it is a money laundering offence to deal, in one of three broad ways, with a **3.02** person's benefit from criminal conduct, knowing or suspecting that it is such a benefit. The various international definitions of money laundering are discussed in Chapter 1. Notably, however, money laundering law in the UK is significantly different from the international definitions insofar as it covers not only processes designed to disguise the illegal origin of criminal property,[1] but in practice any act of dealing with criminal property, including simply possessing criminal property.

3.03 There are five elements to the money laundering offences:

- *criminal conduct* giving rise to the benefit being laundered;
- property that is objectively *criminal property*; that is to say it constitutes the benefit of criminal conduct (or is derived from it);
- property that is subjectively *criminal property*; that is to say the defendant *knows or suspects* that it is such property;
- a dealing with the property in one of the ways described in the Act ('the prohibited acts'); that is to say *concealing, disguising, converting, transferring* criminal property, or *removing it from the jurisdiction* (under section 327), *entering into or becoming concerned in an arrangement which facilitates the retention, use or control* of criminal property (under section 328), or *acquiring, using or possessing* criminal property (under section 329);
- a failure to disclose to the authorities that the property is criminal property prior to the prohibited act, and seek appropriate consent ('the authorised disclosure exception') along with the inapplicability of the other exceptions.

Strictly speaking, a failure to make an authorised disclosure and the other exceptions are not elements of the money laundering offences. Rather, they are specified qualifications to the offences, which will fall to be proved only if the offence would otherwise have been committed and if raised as an issue by the defendant.

3.04 'Criminal conduct' and 'criminal property' have been discussed in Chapter 2. This chapter deals with the money laundering offences. Authorised disclosures and appropriate consent are dealt with in Chapters 5 and 6.

C. The Concealing etc. Offence (Section 327)

The offence

3.05 Section 327 of the Proceeds of Crime Act 2002 states:

> **327 Concealing etc**
> (1) A person commits an offence if he—
>   (a) conceals criminal property;
>   (b) disguises criminal property;
>   (c) converts criminal property;
>   (d) transfers criminal property;
>   (e) removes criminal property from England and Wales or from Scotland or from Northern Ireland.
>   . . .
> (3) Concealing or disguising criminal property includes concealing or disguising its nature, source, location, disposition, movement or ownership or any rights with respect to it.

---

[1] See, for example, the definition provided by the Financial Action Task Force, Chapter 1, para 1.43.

The section applies to conduct which commenced on or after 24 February 2003. It does not **3.06** have effect where the conduct constituting the offence began before that date (and ended on or after that date).[2] However, it is permissible to charge an offence under POCA beginning on 24 February 2003 where the conduct could be said to be a part of a course of conduct commencing before that date.[3]

Section 49 of the Drug Trafficking Act 1994 continues to have effect for the concealing or **3.07** transferring of the proceeds of drug trafficking prior to 24 February 2003 (but after 3 November 1994[4]). Section 93C of the Criminal Justice Act 1988 continues to have effect for concealing or transferring the proceeds of certain other criminal conduct including all indictable offences,[5] prior to that date (but after 15 February 1994[6]).

Section 327 example

In the case of *Loizou*,[7] £87,010 of cash, said to be the proceeds of cigarette smuggling, was **3.08** passed between the occupants of two motor vehicles parked in the car park of a Holiday Inn. Those who were party to the transaction were charged with section 327 by way of transferring criminal property. The case is important because the Court of Appeal ruled that, for a money laundering offence to be committed the property must be criminal before the transfer.

Sentencing

A person guilty of an offence under section 327 is liable: **3.09**

- on summary conviction to imprisonment for a term not exceeding six months or to a fine not exceeding the statutory maximum or to both, or
- on conviction on indictment, to imprisonment for a term not exceeding 14 years or to a fine or to both.[8]

See paragraph 3.105 below for sentencing authorities.

An offence under section 327 is a lifestyle offence for the purposes of section 75 of POCA,[9] **3.10** meaning that the extended benefit presumptions apply for the purposes of confiscation.

Indictment

The multiple ways of committing concealing etc

The section 327 offence may be committed in five ways. Where an offence created by an **3.11** enactment states the offence to be the doing of any one of a number of different acts in the alternative, those acts may be stated in the alternative in an indictment.[10] It is likely that section 327(1) will be construed in that way—as creating a single offence that can be

---

[2] Proceeds of Crime Act 2002 (Commencement No 4, Transitional Provisions and Savings) Order 2003 (SI 2003/120), Art 3 (as amended by SI 2003/333, Art 14).
[3] *R v Anwoir* [2008] EWCA Crim 1354, para 24.
[4] The commencement date of the Drug Trafficking Act 1994, s 69).
[5] As defined by Criminal Justice Act 1988, s 71(9)(c) and s 93A(7).
[6] The commencement date of that offence (SI 1994/71).
[7] *R v L, G, Q, and M (Loizou)* [2005] EWCA Crim 1579.
[8] s 334(1).
[9] POCA, Sch 2, para 2.
[10] Indictment Rules 1971, r 7.

committed in a number of ways: concealing, disguising, etc.[11] This would accord with the case law relating to handling stolen goods.[12] Therefore, a single count on the indictment may theoretically allege both the concealing and disguising of criminal property, or even all of the acts referred to in section 327(1). However, the prosecution is obliged to identify the possible methods of commission relevant to the case and should specify those methods and only those methods.[13]

Prosecution to give particulars

3.12 The prosecution should set out the factors upon which it relies and from which it is submitted the jury could draw proper inferences as to the criminal nature of the source of the property either by giving particulars, or at least in the course of the opening speech.[14] General assertions are not good enough. Precision is required from the outset of the case both in respect of the way that the offence is alleged to have been committed (i.e. whether concealed etc) and why the property is criminal. This is particularly important because the property must be criminal property at the time of the money laundering transaction by virtue of a previous criminal offence. This principle, however, causes uncertainty and differences of view where, for example, legitimately earned income is concealed for the purpose of avoiding tax. Whether such property is criminal property is discussed fully in paragraph 2.33.

Form

STATEMENT OF OFFENCE

CONCEALING Etc CRIMINAL PROPERTY, contrary to section 327 of the Proceeds of Crime Act 2002.

PARTICULARS OF OFFENCE

<Defendant> on <Date>, {concealed | disguised | converted | transferred | removed from {England and Wales / Scotland / Northern Ireland} } criminal property namely <property particulars> (by <conduct particulars>).

Example

STATEMENT OF OFFENCE

Transferring Criminal Property, contrary to section 327(1)(d) of the Proceeds of Crime Act 2002.

PARTICULARS OF OFFENCE

Lisa Loizou, John McCarthy, James Quilligan and Anastasios Gourzoilidis, together with Petros Arampatzis, on the 20th June 2004, transferred £87,010 in cash, which was criminal property, knowing or suspecting that the said cash constituted a person's benefit from criminal conduct.[15]

---

[11] Archbold 2007, para [33-11].
[12] Theft Act 1968, s 22(1).
[13] See *R v Nicklin* 64 Cr App R 205 by analogy with handling.
[14] See *R v Gabriel* [2006] EWCA Crim 229 para 26 commenting favourably on *Louizou* [2004] EWCA 1579 where the prosecution had done just that.
[15] See *R v Louizou* [2004] EWCA 1579.

Elements

Concealing etc

Concealing, disguising, converting, transferring, and removing are ordinary words and **3.13** need little by way of definition. However, the first two of these (concealing and disguising (section 327(1)(a) and (b))) are partially defined in the Act:

> 327 . . .
> (3) Concealing or disguising criminal property includes concealing or disguising its nature, source, location, disposition, movement or ownership or any rights with respect to it.

It is plain from that subsection and from the context as a whole that the terms are intended to be broad in their effect. Between them, they cover dealing with criminal property in a multitude of ways.

In the case of *R v Fazal*[16] D had allowed another person to lodge stolen monies into his bank **3.14** account. An issue arose as to whether in law he had 'converted' criminal property in these circumstances.

Victims purchased goods on the Internet which were never delivered although payment **3.15** was made. D permitted another to use his bank account. He submitted there was no case to answer as D had not converted the money, there being no act of conversion by him, only by others, even if he had acquired the relevant suspicion and knowledge. He contended that he might have been guilty of an offence under section 328 but none was charged. The Court of Appeal in dismissing the appeal held that D had 'converted' the stolen monies by allowing another to use his account. A person might lodge receive, retain, or withdraw money from his account each of which would amount to converting the money concerned, by asking or allowing another agent, innocent or not, to do so. That did not prevent the owner of the account who used or operated it, albeit with the help of an agent, innocent or not, from converting the money. The reference to 'converting' in POCA was not necessarily the civil tort of conversion but could be not far removed from its nature.

Conversion in civil law is a broad tort essentially concerned with wrongfully taking, receiv- **3.16** ing, or retaining another's property and although there is no *mens rea* requirement it involves dealing with another's property so far as to interfere with the owner's title to it. Where money was lodged and credited to D's bank account, and the retaining and withdrawing from it all occurred with the full approval, authority, and co-operation of D, those acts amounted to successive acts by D of converting criminal property.

There are, however, possible alternative views on the way that the operative words in section **3.17** 327 should be interpreted. Apart from the question of whether the words 'converts', 'transfers', and 'removes' should be construed as having any mental element or any purposive behaviour—which would bring the offence more into line with the FATF Recommendations and the Third Directive[17]—there is also the question of whether the words should be seen and interpreted simply as ordinary words used in ordinary language and not given the 'term of art' meaning that may be associated with civil proceedings.

The converting and transferring of criminal property in the pursuit of ordinary legal pro- **3.18** ceedings with a view to obtaining the court's adjudication upon the parties' rights and duties

---

[16] [2009] EWCA 1697.
[17] See Chapter 1.

is not to be regarded as a prohibited act under section 327[18] (see paragraphs 3.74–3.75 below).

Criminal property

3.19 To be *criminal property*, the property which is concealed etc:

- must constitute a person's benefit from criminal conduct or represent such a benefit (in whole or part, directly or indirectly); and
- the alleged offender must know or suspect that it constitutes or represents such a benefit.

The *mens rea* of the offence is defined by this latter element. It is not necessary for the Crown to prove that property derives from a specific kind of crime. If it derives from criminal conduct that is sufficient.[19] The offence does not require dishonesty or a specific criminal intent.

Limitations and defences

3.20 Each of the three principal money laundering offences is subject to the following limitations which have the effect, if appplicable, of no money laundering offence being committed (in each case worded as 'but a person does not commit an offence if. . .'):

- authorised disclosure/intention to make an authorised disclosure but had a reasonable excuse for not doing so;
- carrying out a function under the Act;
- belief in lawfulness of the conduct in a foreign jurisdiction;
- deposit-taking body taking a deposit under the threshold amount.

Additionally, the section 329 arrangements offence alone is subject to a further limitation:

- The adequate consideration limitation.

These limitations to the offences are also referred to as defences and exceptions.

3.21 As a matter of first principle, the burden of proving the elements of any offence is upon the prosecution. However, where the defendant relies upon a limitation to an offence, the question of where the burden of proof lies is less straightforward. POCA is silent as to who has the burden of proof for these limitations, so it is necessary for the courts to determine the question.

Limitation for the prosecution to prove beyond reasonable doubt

3.22 It is notable that the wording of the POCA provisions is distinct from that used in the previous money laundering regimes:

- In section 93B of the Criminal Justice Act 1988:
  (2) It is a defence to a charge of committing an offence under this section that the person charged acquired or used the property or had possession of it for adequate consideration.
- In the section 50 of the Drug Trafficking Act 1994:
  (4) In proceedings ... under this section, it is a defence to prove—
  . . .
     (c) that—
        (i) he intended to [make an authorised disclosure]

---

[18] See *Bowman v Fels* [2005] 1 WLR 3083, para 97.
[19] *R v Anwoir* [2008] EWCA Crim 1354.

Demonstrably, therefore, the previous regimes provided for a reverse burden. The POCA **3.23** regime is different. In *Hogan v The DPP*[20] the Administrative Court held, in relation to the adequate consideration limitation, that:

> Once the issue is raised, in my view the appellant is correct and it is for the Crown to show that there was not adequate consideration, and to do so in relation to both halves of that question, namely the fact of the consideration advanced and the adequacy of the consideration, if proved.

The court's reasons were: **3.24**

- The drafting change from the 1988 Act appeared deliberate.
- Once the issue of adequate consideration has been raised, the issue should be regarded as an element of the offence to be proved by the Crown.
- Where there is ambiguity in statutory wording in the context of a penal statute such as POCA, that ambiguity should be resolved so as to narrow rather than broaden criminal liability.

The reasoning of the court in *Hogan* applies equally to the other limitations and it seems **3.25** likely that in each case it would be for the prosecution to prove the facts beyond reasonable doubt, once the issue had been raised. Alternatively, it is possible that later courts will hold that an alternative reasoning should apply to some or all of the other limitations.

Alternative view

Where an offence is subject to a limitation and the defendant relies upon the exception in his **3.26** defence it may be for the defendant to prove the limitation on the balance of probabilities.

So in *R v Edwards*,[21] the defendant had been convicted in the Crown Court of selling intoxi- **3.27** cating liquor without a justices' licence contrary to section 160(1)(*a*) of the Licensing Act 1964. That section provides:

> Subject to the provisions of this Act, if any person — (*a*) sells or exposes for sale by retail any intoxicating liquor without holding a justices' licence or canteen licence authorising him to hold an excise licence for the sale of that liquor . . . he shall be guilty of an offence under this section.

The prosecution had called no evidence that the defendant did not have a licence and he appealed on the ground that the burden was on the prosecution to establish the lack of a licence. The Court of Appeal held that the burden was on the defendant to prove that he held a licence and that as he had not done so he was rightly convicted.

In *Nimmo v Alexander Cowan & Sons Ltd*[22] the House of Lords held that if the linguistic construc- **3.28** tion of the statute did not clearly indicate upon whom the burden should lie, the court should look to other considerations to determine the intention of Parliament, such as the mischief at which the Act was aimed and practical considerations affecting the burden of proof and, in par- ticular, the ease or difficulty that the respective parties would encounter in discharging the burden. In that case the House was considering section 29(1) of the Factories Act 1961 which provides:

> There shall, so far as is reasonably practicable, be provided and maintained safe means of access to every place at which any person has at any time to work, and every such place shall, so far as is reasonably practicable, be made and kept safe for any person working there.

---

[20] [2007] 1 WLR 2944.
[21] [1975] QB 27.
[22] [1968] AC 107.

They decided by a majority of three to two that it would be for the defendant to excuse himself by proving that it was not reasonably practicable to make it safe.

3.29   In *Hunt*[23] Lord Griffiths said:

> In *Reg. v. Edwards* [1975] Q.B. 27, 39-40 the Court of Appeal expressed their conclusion in the form of an exception to what they said was the fundamental rule of our criminal law that the prosecution must prove every element of the offence charged. They said that the exception
>
>> 'is limited to offences arising under enactments which prohibit the doing of an act save in specified circumstances or by persons of specified classes or with specified qualifications or with the licence or permission of specified authorities.'
>
> I have little doubt that the occasions upon which a statute will be construed as imposing a burden of proof upon a defendant which do not fall within this formulation are likely to be exceedingly rare. But I find it difficult to fit *Nimmo v. Alexander Cowan & Sons Ltd.* [1968] A.C. 107 into this formula, and I would prefer to adopt the formula as an excellent guide to construction rather than as an exception to a rule. In the final analysis each case must turn upon the construction of the particular legislation to determine whether the defence is an exception within the meaning of section 101 of the Act of 1980 which the Court of Appeal rightly decided reflects the rule for trials on indictment. With this one qualification I regard *Reg. v. Edwards* as rightly decided.

3.30   His Lordship stated that the key consideration was the ease or difficulty that the respective parties would encounter in discharging the burden if the burden was upon them:[24]

> I regard this . . . consideration as one of great importance for surely Parliament can never lightly be taken to have intended to impose an onerous duty on a defendant to prove his innocence in a criminal case, and a court should be very slow to draw any such inference from the language of a statute.

3.31   The critical considerations under POCA are likely to be the relative ease or difficulty of the defendant demonstrating that he made an authorised disclosure, was performing a duty under the act, believed in the lawfulness of the conduct abroad etc.

3.32   If any or all of the limitations is held to be an exception in the sense meant in *Edwards* and *Hunt*, then the issue is whether the imposition of such a burden on the defendant is compatible with their Convention rights.

3.33   So far as it is possible to do so, legislation must be read and given effect in a way which is compatible with the European Convention on Human Rights.[25] Article 6(2) of the Convention provides: 'Everyone charged with a criminal offence shall be presumed innocent until proven guilty.' Article 6(2) does not prohibit laws which transfer an evidential or persuasive burden to the accused so long as the overall burden of proving guilt stays with the prosecution.[26] Any rules which shift the evidential burden upon a defendant must be confined to reasonable limits.[27] This issue has been considered by the House of Lords in two leading cases, *R v DPP, ex p Kebilene*[28] and *R v Lambert*.[29]

---

[23]   *R v Hunt* [1986] 3 WLR 1115.
[24]   At 1128.
[25]   Human Rights Act 1998, s 3(1).
[26]   *Lingens and Leitgens v Austria* Series A No 103, (1981) 4 EHRR 373, para 4.
[27]   *Salabiaku v France* Series A No 141-A, (1988) 13 EHRR 379, para 28.
[28]   [2000] 2 AC 326.
[29]   [2001] UKHL 37, [2002] 2 AC 545. For cases applying the *Lambert* case see *R v Carass* [2002] WLR 1714 and *R v Daniel, The Times*, 8 April 2002.

In *Hogan* the court stated that though it had not heard full argument, if the limitations were **3.34** exceptions, they would nevertheless not have found the defendant to have the burden of proving the matter:

> Then it would seem to me that this represented too great an intrusion into the presumption of innocence, given the very low threshold by which someone may be exposed to criminal proceedings, based as I have said on the mere suspicion that the property concerned was criminal property.

Authorised disclosures

A person does not commit a section 327 offence if the authorised disclosure regime has been **3.35** complied with.[30]

Nor does a person commit a section 327 offence if he intended to make such a disclosure but **3.36** had a reasonable excuse for not doing so.[31] What would amount to a reasonable excuse for such a failure is not defined in the Act, and is yet to be considered by the courts.

This topic is discussed in full in Chapter 5. **3.37**

Carrying out a function under the Act

Prima facie, law enforcement personnel commit a money laundering offence when they seize **3.38** assets which they suspect to be the benefit of the offender's criminal conduct. The Act excludes that conduct from the ambit of the offence:

> (2) But a person does not commit such an offence if—
>
> . . .
>
>   (c) the act he does is done in carrying out a function he has relating to the enforcement of any provision of this Act or of any other enactment relating to criminal conduct or benefit from criminal conduct.

Lawful conduct outside the United Kingdom

A person does not commit a section 327 offence in certain circumstances if the conduct was **3.39** lawful in the place where it occurred.[32]

The foreign conduct exception is dealt with fully in Chapter 2. **3.40**

Deposit-taking below the threshold amount

Banks and other deposit-taking bodies are exempt from money laundering occurring in the **3.41** ordinary operation of accounts maintained by them by way of low value transactions below the *threshold amount,* currently £250. Section 327(2C) reads:

> 327. . .
>
> (2C) A deposit-taking body that does an act mentioned in paragraph (c) or (d) of subsection
>   (1) does not commit an offence under that subsection if—
>   (a) it does the act in operating an account maintained with it, and
>   (b) the value of the criminal property concerned is less than the threshold amount determined under section 339A for the act.

---

[30] s 327(2)(a).
[31] s 327(2)(b).
[32] s 327(2A).

Deposit-taking body is defined in section 340(14):

> 340...
> (14) 'Deposit-taking body' means—
>   (a) a business which engages in the activity of accepting deposits, or
>   (b) the National Savings Bank.

The defence only applies to the commission of the offence by means of converting or transferring. A deposit-taking body would still commit the section 327 offence for sums below the threshold amount, if it concealed, disguised, or removed the property from England and Wales etc.

3.42 The threshold amount may be varied by order or by way of a one-off arrangement:

> **339A Threshold amounts**
> (1) This section applies for the purposes of sections 327(2C), 328(5) and 329(2C).
> (2) The threshold amount for acts done by a deposit-taking body in operating an account is £250 unless a higher amount is specified under the following provisions of this section (in which event it is that higher amount).
> (3) An officer of Revenue and Customs, or a constable, may specify the threshold amount for acts done by a deposit-taking body in operating an account—
>   (a) when he gives consent, or gives notice refusing consent, to the deposit-taking body's doing of an act mentioned in section 327(1), 328(1) or 329(1) in opening, or operating, the account or a related account, or
>   (b) on a request from the deposit-taking body.
> (4) Where the threshold amount for acts done in operating an account is specified under subsection (3) or this subsection, an officer of Revenue and Customs, or a constable, may vary the amount (whether on a request from the deposit-taking body or otherwise) by specifying a different amount.
> (5) Different threshold amounts may be specified under subsections (3) and (4) for different acts done in operating the same account.
> (6) The amount specified under subsection (3) or (4) as the threshold amount for acts done in operating an account must, when specified, not be less than the amount specified in subsection (2).
> (7) The Secretary of State may by order vary the amount for the time being specified in subsection (2).
> (8) For the purposes of this section, an account is related to another if each is maintained with the same deposit-taking body and there is a person who, in relation to each account, is the person or one of the persons entitled to instruct the body as respects the operation of the account.

D. The Arrangements Offence (Section 328)

The offence

3.43 Section 328 of the Proceeds of Crime Act 2002 states:

> **328 Arrangements**
> (1) A person commits an offence if he enters into or becomes concerned in an arrangement which he knows or suspects facilitates (by whatever means) the acquisition, retention, use or control of criminal property by or on behalf of another person.

The section applies to conduct which commenced on or after 24 February 2003. It does not have effect where the conduct constituting the offence began before that date (and ended on or after that date).[33] Section 50 of the Drug Trafficking Act 1994 continues to have effect for assisting another person to retain the benefit of drug trafficking prior to that date (but after 3 November 1994[34]). Section 93A of the Criminal Justice Act 1988 continues to have effect for assisting another to retain the benefit of other criminal conduct including all indictable offences,[35] prior to that date (but after 15 February 1994[36]).

Section 328 example

In *I K*,[37] SK ran a money transfer business, and there was evidence that he was accepting large cash payments from MR to be sent to Pakistan. The cash given by MR was said to be the proceeds of a tax fraud perpetrated through MR's grocery business. It was said that in the circumstances in which the money came to SK, that is to say hidden in a box of fruit, he must have known or suspected that the money was the benefit of MR's criminal conduct. They were charged with the section 328 offence.[38]   **3.44**

Sentencing

A person guilty of an offence under section 328 is liable: **3.45**

- on summary conviction to imprisonment for a term not exceeding six months or to a fine not exceeding the statutory maximum or to both; or
- on conviction on indictment, to imprisonment for a term not exceeding 14 years or to a fine or to both.[39]

See paragraph 3.105 below for sentencing authorities.

An offence under section 328 is a lifestyle offence for the purposes of section 75 of POCA,[40]   **3.46**
meaning that the extended benefit presumptions apply for the purposes of confiscation.

Indictment

Multiple methods of commission

The section 328 offence may be committed in four ways: where the *acquisition*, *retention*, *use*,   **3.47**
or *control* of criminal property is *facilitated*. A single count on the indictment may allege one, several or even all of these (see para 3.11 above). However, where it is possible to identify which of these are applicable in a particular case, the indictment should specify them.

Form

STATEMENT OF OFFENCE

ARRANGING TO LAUNDER MONEY, contrary to section 328 of the Proceeds of Crime Act 2002.

---

[33] Proceeds of Crime Act 2002 (Commencement No 4, Transitional Provisions and Savings) Order 2003 (SI 2003/120), Art 3 (as amended by SI 2003/333, Art 14)

[34] The commencement date of the Drug Trafficking Act 1994 (s 69).

[35] As defined by Criminal Justice Act 1988, ss 71(9)(c) and 93A(7).

[36] The commencement date of that offence (SI 1994/71).

[37] *R v IK* [2007] 1 WLR 2262.

[38] See para 3.47 below.

[39] s 334(1).

[40] POCA, Sch 2, para 2.

PARTICULARS OF OFFENCE

<Defendant> on <Date>, {entered into | became concerned in} an arrangement knowing or suspecting that the arrangement would facilitate the {acquisition | retention | use | control} of criminal property namely <property particulars> {by | on behalf of} <name of person>).

Example

STATEMENT OF OFFENCE

ARRANGING TO LAUNDER MONEY, contrary to section 328 of the Proceeds of Crime Act 2002.

PARTICULARS OF OFFENCE

Between 1 October and 6 December 2003, SK and MR entered into or became concerned in an arrangement knowing or suspecting that the arrangement would facilitate the retention, use or control of MR's criminal property, namely banknotes.[41]

Elements

Enters into or becomes concerned in an arrangement

3.48 In *Bowman v Fels*[42] the Court of Appeal (Civil Division) considered the arrangements offence in the context of matrimonial proceedings. It said:[43]

> In s 328 the nature of the act is either entering into an arrangement or the vaguer concept of 'becom[ing] concerned in an arrangement'. To enter into an arrangement involves a single act at a single point in time; so too, on the face of it, does to 'become concerned' in an arrangement, even though the point at which someone may be said to have 'become' concerned may be open to argument.

3.49 Whilst 'becomes concerned in' may imply a lack of activity by the Defendant, it is clear that the alleged offender must in fact do an act to become concerned in an arrangement. It is notable in this regard that the conduct referred to in section 328(1) is referred to as the *prohibited act* elsewhere in the Act.[44]

3.50 The arrangement offence is wide in its scope, and in some ways might be considered a course of criminal conduct offence akin to a conspiracy but carried out by a single person. However, it is not identical in its effect to a conspiracy charge (see paragraphs 3.71–3.73 below).

3.51 It has been held that lawyers acting in the context of litigation, or the consensual resolution of such litigation, do not become concerned in an arrangement within in the meaning of the POCA[45] (see paragraphs 3.74–3.75 below) even though they suspect that the subject matter of the litigation is or may be criminal property.

Knows or suspects facilitates (by whatever means) the acquisition, retention, use or control. . .

3.52 Knowing or suspecting that the arrangement facilitates the acquisition, retention, use, or control of criminal property defines the *mens rea* of the offence. Although, in most cases,

---

[41] *IK* [2007] EWCA Crim 491, para 2.
[42] [2005] EWCA Civ 226
[43] Para 67.
[44] E.g. s 388(6).
[45] *Bowman v Fels* [2005] 1 WLR 3083.

it adds very little to the *mens rea* inherent in the definition of criminal property (that the person knows or suspects that the property is criminal property). Generally, it will be obvious that the arrangement facilitates the acquisition, retention, use, or control of property, the sole question is whether the person knows or suspects the property to be criminal.

Notably, the arrangements offence applies to cases where the defendant does not himself **3.53** handle criminal property. In other words D does not have to handle, possess or deal with the property for him to be guilty of this offence. D commits an offence if he enters into or becomes concerned in an arrangement whereby the retention or control of such property is facilitated.

Note that, by analogy with *R v Montila*[46] the arrangement must actually facilitate the acquisi- **3.54** tion, retention, use, or control of criminal property, as a matter of fact, as well as the person knowing or suspecting that it does.

. . . of criminal property

To be *criminal property*, the property which is the subject of the arrangement: **3.55**

- must constitute a person's benefit from criminal conduct or represent such a benefit (in whole or part, directly or indirectly); and
- the alleged offender must know or suspect that it constitutes or represents such a benefit.

The *mens rea* of the offence is this latter element together with knowing or suspecting that it facilitates the acquisition, retention, use, or control of criminal property. See the full discussion of *criminal property* in Chapter 2.

By or on behalf of another person

The acquisition, retention, use, or control of criminal property that is facilitated must be **3.56** acquisition, retention, use, or control of criminal property by or on behalf of another. A person cannot be guilty of the section 328 offence where the property is laundered by themselves, or on their own behalf.

However, D may be guilty of being concerned in an arrangement to facilitate, acquire, retain, **3.57** use, or control criminal property for himself if there are at least two defendants and each benefits: each has facilitated the relevant laundering by or on behalf of the other person. Count 12 in the case of *IK*[47] is an example of a case in which the defendant MR was convicted of being party to an arrangement which facilitated the acquisition, retention, use, or control of criminal property in these circumstances.

Criminal property at the time of the arrangement

Geary [2010] EWCA Crim 1925 is authority for the proposition that property must be **3.58** criminal at the time a money laundering arrangement is entered into within the meaning of section 328 of POCA.

---

[46] [2004] 1 WLR 3141 (HL).
[47] [2007] 1 WLR 2262.

3.59 D was charged with an offence contrary to section 328(1) of the Act. The particulars of offence were that he had:

> entered into or become concerned in an arrangement which [he] knew or suspected facilitated ... the acquisition, retention, use or control of criminal property, namely a credit balance of £123,600 belonging to Aviva plc/Norwich Union, by or on behalf of another person.

3.60 T, who worked in a bank, stole money from his employers and diverted it to H. H, in turn, passed £123,600 to D. D's case was that H had approached him and asked him to receive the money as he was going through a divorce and wanted to hide it from his wife. D agreed to help and retained £5000. The judge ruled that D was guilty of an offence contrary to section 328 on his own version of events. D pleaded guilty and was sentenced to 22 months imprisonment and then appealed.

3.61 On appeal, the Court of Appeal considered the issue of whether it was necessary before an offence was committed under section 328 for property which was the subject matter of the arrangement to be 'criminal at the time when the arrangement attaches to it' (see paragraph 18).

3.62 The court decided that (paragraph 19 per Moore-Bick LJ):

> In our view the natural and ordinary meaning of section 328(1) is that the arrangement to which it refers must be one which relates to property which is criminal property at the time when the arrangement begins to operate on it. To say that it extends to property which was originally legitimate but became criminal only as a result of carrying out the arrangement is to stretch the language of the section beyond its proper limits.

3.63 The court further decided in *Geary* that sections 327, 328, and 329 should be interpreted in accordance with their natural meaning in the interests of legal certainty (paragraph 37):

> Part 7 of the Act, as the heading indicates, is concerned with money laundering and sections 327, 328 and 329 are all directed to dealing with criminal property in one way or another. In each case the natural meaning of the statutory language is that in each case the property in question must have become criminal property as a result of some conduct which occurred prior to the act which is alleged to constitute the offence, whether that be concealing, disguising, converting, transferring or removing it contrary to section 327 or entering into or becoming concerned in an arrangement which facilitates its acquisition, retention, use or control by another contrary to section 328. We think that the same must be true of acquiring, using or having possession of criminal property contrary to section 329(1). Moreover, it follows from what we have said that the only authorities directly in point on the interpretation of sections 327 and 328 support that conclusion.

Limitations and defences

Authorised disclosures

3.64 A person does not commit a section 328 offence if the authorised disclosure regime has been complied with.[48]

3.65 Nor does a person commit a section 328 offence if he intended to make such a disclosure but had a reasonable excuse for not doing so.[49] What would amount to a reasonable excuse for such a failure is not defined in the Act, and is yet to be considered by the courts.

---

[48] s 328(2)(a)
[49] s 328(2)(b).

This topic is discussed in full in Chapter 5.   3.66

Carrying out a function under the Act

A person does not commit a section 328 offence if he was carrying out a function under the   3.67
Act[50] (see paragraph 3.38 above).

Certain lawful conduct outside the United Kingdom

A person does not commit a section 328 offence in certain circumstances if the conduct was   3.68
lawful in the place where it occurred.[51]

The foreign conduct exception is dealt with fully in Chapter 2.   3.69

Deposit taking below the threshold amount

A deposit-taking body does not commit offence a section 328, by operating an account   3.70
maintained with it, if the value of the property is below the threshold amount (see paragraphs 3.41–3.42 above).

Arrangements contrasted with conspiracy

The arrangements offence is an extremely wide one. After the case of *Saik* in which it was held   3.71
that the *mens rea* in conspiracy to launder money is that of knowledge, rather than knowledge or suspicion for the substantive offences, the prosecution have sought to charge substantive offences were possible—often the section 328 offence.

One example of a case which is unlikely to be covered by the arrangements offence, as   3.72
opposed to a conspiracy has been discussed in the Criminal Law Review.[52]

> The conduct of a number of defendants who have made repeated transfers, etc? If D1 transfers
> property for X, and D2 in a separate transaction converts different property for X, and D3
> does likewise, etc., is it possible to indict X, D1, D2, and D3 in one count under s.328? These
> facts would obviously allow for three substantive offences under that section. In each transac-
> tion, the relevant defendant and X enter into an arrangement which they know/suspect facili-
> tates the use of criminal property by another. But, when engaged in his transaction with X,
> can D1 be said to be 'entering or concerned in an arrangement' in which D2 and D3 are
> concerned? Can X be indicted in the same count given that X is 'another' under the terms of
> this section? Is the conduct properly described as an 'arrangement' or more accurately as a
> series of arrangements?

In the case of *R v Ramzan*[53] the court determined that offences contrary to sections 49(2) of   3.73
the Drug Trafficking Act 1994 and 93C(2) of the Criminal Justice Act 1988, that is to say
the forerunners of the current section 327 concealing etc offence, were not 'activity' offences,
so that a single count may be preferred, without duplicity, to cover the whole period of the
individual transactions relied upon. However, the court specifically excluded from its considerations offences under section 50 of the Drug Trafficking Act, section 93A of the Criminal
Justice Act, and section 328 of POCA.[54]

---

[50] s 328(2)(c).
[51] s 328(2A).
[52] *R v Ramzan* [2007] Crim LR 79 by Professor Ormerod.
[53] [2006] EWCA Crim 1974.
[54] Para 61.

Arrangements contrasted with legal proceedings

3.74   The central issue in *Bowman v Fels*[55] was whether section 328 applies to the ordinary conduct of legal proceedings or any aspect of such conduct—including, in particular, any step taken to pursue proceedings and the obtaining of a judgment. If a person enters into or becomes concerned in legal proceedings the subject of which they know or suspect to be criminal property are they guilty of the section 328 offence? The short answer given by Court of Appeal Civil Division in that case was 'no'.

3.75   The court considered Article 7 of the First Money Laundering Directive, as replaced by the Second Money Laundering Directive:

> Member States shall ensure that the institutions and persons subject to this Directive refrain from carrying out transactions which they know or suspect to be related to money laundering until they have apprised the authorities . . .

And recital 17 to that Directive:

> There must be exemptions from any obligation to report information obtained either before, during or after judicial proceedings, or in the course of ascertaining the legal position for a client. Thus, legal advice remains subject to the obligation of professional secrecy unless the legal counsellor is taking part in money laundering activities, the legal advice is provided for money laundering purposes, or the lawyer knows that the client is seeking legal advice for money laundering purposes.

The failure to disclosure offence in section 330 specifically protects legal professional privilege as defined in the Act whereas section 328 does not. The court in *Bowman* relied on recital 17 of the EC Directive to suggest that privilege should be respected, and in reaching their conclusion that section 328 is not intended to apply to legal professionals conducting judicial proceedings at all, said as follows:[56]

> Although s 328 applies to any person and is not limited like s 330 to the regulated sector, s 328 only applies if a person 'enters into or becomes concerned in an arrangement' which he knows or suspects facilitates the acquisition, retention, use or control of criminal property. To our mind, it is as improbable that Parliament, being the UK legislator, had the ordinary conduct of legal proceedings to judgment in mind under s 328 (or indeed under ss 327 and 329) as it is to suppose that the European legislator had them in mind in article 7.

Furthermore:[57]

> as a matter of ordinary language, our impression on reading s 328 was and remains that, whatever Parliament may have had in mind by the phrase 'entering into or becomes concerned in an arrangement which . . . facilitates . . .', it is most unlikely that it was thinking of legal proceedings.

Consensual settlement of legal proceedings

3.76   As 'the consensual resolution of issues is an integral part of the conduct of ordinary civil litigation', the settlement of proceedings does not amount to an arrangement either.[58]

---

[55]   [2005] EWCA Civ 22.
[56]   Para 63.
[57]   Para 64.
[58]   Paras 99–102.

Consensual arrangements independent of litigation

However, there is a distinction between consensual steps (including a settlement) taken **3.77** in an ordinary litigious context and consensual arrangements independent of litigation. The latter would fall within the definition of an arrangement.[59] Accordingly, a lawyer who is taking steps to execute a 'consensual settlement' outside the context of litigation would be at risk of prosecution under section 328 as being concerned in a money laundering arrangement.

E. Acquisition, Use, and Possession Offence (Section 329)

The offence

Section 329 of the Proceeds of Crime Act 2002 states: **3.78**

Acquisition, use and possession
(1) A person commits an offence if he—
  (a) acquires criminal property;
  (b) uses criminal property;
  (c) has possession of criminal property.

The section applies to conduct which commenced on or after 24 February 2003. It does not have effect where the conduct constituting the offence began before that date (and ended on or after that date).[60] Section 51 of the Drug Trafficking Act 1994 continues to have effect for the acquisition, possession, or use of the proceeds of drug trafficking, prior to that date (but after 3 November 1994[61]). Section 93B of the Criminal Justice Act 1988 continues to have effect for the acquisition, possession, or use of the proceeds of other criminal property, including all indictable offences,[62] prior to that date (but after 15 February 1994[63]).

Section 329 examples

In *Gabriel (Janis)*,[64] the police had searched the defendant's house and found £10,000, **3.79** hidden under the mattress of a water bed, and on another occasion, £6,070 inside an air pistol case. Within the house the officer observed a 42-inch plasma television screen, an ornate mahogany fireplace, a conservatory with a swimming pool and sauna, a large fridge, spa jets in the bathroom, a computer, good quality stereo equipment throughout the house, and Playstation games and DVDs. There was also a closed-circuit television set up outside the house which could be viewed from a monitor in the living room. Evidence was read from Department for Work and Pensions and Inland Revenue (now HM Revenue & Customs) officials to the effect that the household received social security benefits of about £500 a week. The prosecution alleged that, in the circumstances, it could be inferred that the monies

---

[59] Para 101.
[60] Proceeds of Crime Act 2002 (Commencement No 4, Transitional Provisions and Savings) Order 2003 (SI 2003/120), Art 3 (as amended by SI 2003/333, Art 14).
[61] The commencement date of the Drug Trafficking Act 1994 (s 69).
[62] As defined by Criminal Justice Act 1988, ss 71(9)(c) and 93A(7).
[63] The commencement date of that offence (SI 1994/71).
[64] *R v Gabriel (Janis)*[2006] EWCA Crim 229.

were the proceeds of crime, and that the defendant, as the householders, knew it. She was charged with possessing criminal property.

3.80 In *Griffiths and Pattison*,[65] the defendant Pattison was an estate agent who bought, at substantial undervalue, a house, from a known drug dealer who was awaiting the determination of confiscation proceedings against him. Pattison was charged with, amongst other charges, acquiring criminal property, namely the house.

Sentencing

3.81 A person guilty of an offence under section 329 is liable:

- on summary conviction to imprisonment for a term not exceeding six months or to a fine not exceeding the statutory maximum or to both; or
- on conviction on indictment, to imprisonment for a term not exceeding 14 years or to a fine or to both.[66]

See paragraph 3.105 below for sentencing authorities.

3.82 Unlike the other two principal money laundering offences (sections 327 and 328), an offence under section 329 is not a *lifestyle offence* for the purposes of confiscation.

Indictment

3.83 The section 329 offence may be committed in three ways: acquiring, using, or possessing criminal property. A single count on the indictment may allege one, two, or all of these. However, where it is possible to identify which branch or branches is applicable in a particular case, the indictment should specify only that branch or those branches.

Form

STATEMENT OF OFFENCE

{ACQUIRING | USING | POSSESSING} CRIMINAL PROPERTY, contrary to section 329 of the Proceeds of Crime Act 2002.

PARTICULARS OF OFFENCE

<Defendant> on <Date>, {acquired | used | possessed} criminal property namely <property particulars>.

Example

COUNT 1
STATEMENT OF OFFENCE

ACQUIRING CRIMINAL PROPERTY, contrary to section 329(1)(a) of the Proceeds of Crime Act 2002.

PARTICULARS OF OFFENCE

Between 21 March 2005 and 14 April 2005, at various locations in Lincolnshire, acquired criminal property, namely scaffolding components.

---

[65] [2006] EWCA Crim 2155.
[66] s 334(1).

COUNT 2

STATEMENT OF OFFENCE

POSSESSING CRIMINAL PROPERTY, contrary to section 329(1)(c) of the Proceeds of Crime Act 2002.

PARTICULARS OF OFFENCE

Between 21 March 2005 and 6 October 2005, in Lincolnshire, possessed criminal property, namely scaffolding.[67]

Elements

Acquisition, use and possession

Acquisition, use, and possession are ordinary words to be interpreted by the jury. However, **3.84** as is discussed in Chapter 2, property must be criminal before it is acquired.[68]

The acquisition, use and possession of criminal property in the pursuit of ordinary legal **3.85** proceedings with a view to obtaining the court's adjudication upon the parties' rights and duties may not be regarded as a prohibited act under section 329.[69] This must follow from the judgment of *Bowman* in which case the subject matter of the matrimonial litigation was suspected to be criminal property.

Criminal property

To be *criminal property*, the property which is concealed etc: **3.86**

- must constitute a person's benefit from criminal conduct or represent such a benefit (in whole or part, directly or indirectly); and
- the alleged offender must know or suspect that it constitutes or represents such a benefit.

The *mens rea* of the offence is defined by this latter element. See the full discussion of *criminal property* in Chapter 2.

Limitations and defences

Authorised disclosures

A person does not commit a section 329 offence if the authorised disclosure regime has been **3.87** complied with.[70]

Nor does a person commit a section 329 offence if he intended to make such a disclosure but **3.88** had a reasonable excuse for not doing so.[71] What would amount to a reasonable excuse for such a failure is not defined in the Act, and is yet to be considered by the courts.

This topic is discussed in full in Chapter 5. **3.89**

Carrying out a function under the Act

A person does not commit a section 328 offence if he was carrying out a function under the **3.90** Act[72] (see paragraph 3.38 above).

---

[67] *Hogan v DPP* [2007] 1 WLR 2944 —though that case was tried summarily.
[68] *R v Kausar* [2009] EWCA Crim 2242.
[69] See para 97 of *Bowman v Fels*.
[70] s 329(2)(a).
[71] s 329(2)(b).
[72] s 329(2)(c)

Certain lawful conduct outside the United Kingdom

3.91 A person does not commit a section 328 offence in certain circumstances if the conduct was lawful in the place where it occurred[73] (see paragraphs 3.39–3.40 above).

Deposit taking below the threshold amount

3.92 A deposit-taking body does not commit a section 328 offence, by operating an account maintained with it, if the value of the property is below the threshold amount (see paragraphs 3.41–3.42 above).

Adequate consideration exception

3.93 Section 329 of the Proceeds of Crime Act 2002 includes an exception which is not applicable to the other two prohibited acts:

> **329**
>
> (2) But a person does not commit such an offence if—
>
> . . .
>
>   (c) he acquired or used or had possession of the property for adequate consideration;
>
> . . .
>
> (3) For the purposes of this section—
>
>   (a) a person acquires property for inadequate consideration if the value of the consideration is significantly less than the value of the property;
>
>   (b) a person uses or has possession of property for inadequate consideration if the value of the consideration is significantly less than the value of the use or possession;
>
>   (c) the provision by a person of goods or services which he knows or suspects may help another to carry out criminal conduct is not consideration.

3.94 If a person provides goods or services to another in exchange for money which they know or suspect to be criminal property, they do not commit an offence, if the goods or services provided by them are adequate consideration. What matters is whether the service or goods are provided as part of a genuine agreement at arm's length rather than 'significantly less than the value of the property'. This section was inserted to protect those who deal with criminal property in the ordinary course of business. The amount of the consideration (i.e. the price) may be high but 'adequate' in the sense that it is genuine for the service provided.

3.95 In *Hogan v The Director of Public Prosecutions*[74] the court gave some guidance as to the meaning of adequate consideration:

> What is the meaning of 'adequate consideration'? This must be a question of fact in each cases. In deciding it, my view is that a court is entitled—indeed has an obligation—to look at all the relevant circumstances drawn from the evidence. But the question is an objective one. It is a discrete question from the question of knowledge, belief or suspicion by the defendant as to whether the property constitutes a benefit from criminal conduct . . . an unrecorded payment for goods, made in cash, in a sum representing 20 per cent of their market value, would be strong evidence against adequate consideration under section 329 and also might be strong evidence that a defendant knew or suspected that the goods represented the benefit of criminal conduct, under section 340.

---

[73] s 329(2A).
[74] [2007] 1 WLR 2944.

The court also decided that it was for the Crown to prove that the consideration was not **3.96** adequate once the issue was raised by the defence. The Court of Appeal returned to this issue in the case of *R v Kausar*.[75]

The CPS guidance for prosecutors[76] states: **3.97**

> . . . a person does not commit an offence under this section if he acquired, used or had possession of the property for 'adequate consideration.' The defence replicates that available under the offences in S.93 B of the Criminal Justice Act 1988. It is available to cover those cases where the funds or property have been acquired by a purchase for a proper market price or similar exchange and to cater for any injustice which might otherwise arise: for example, in the case of tradesmen who are paid for ordinary consumable goods and services in money that comes from crime.

> This defence will also apply where professional advisors (such as solicitors or accountants) receive money for or on account of costs (whether from the client or from another person on the client's behalf). This defence would not be available to a professional where the value of the work carried out or intended to be carried out on behalf of the client was significantly less than the money received for or on account of costs.

Acquisition of criminal property through private legal fees

Where a solicitor acquires monies from a client they may have suspicions as to the source of **3.98** the property. A solicitor accepting money from a private client for the conduct of his defence on charges of acquisitive crime, cannot fail to have his suspicions aroused. If the solicitor acquires the money knowing or suspecting it to be criminal in nature, then prima facie they would be guilty of the section 329 offence. However, provided the fees charged are reasonable for the services rendered, the solicitor would have a defence in that he acquired the property for adequate consideration, namely those services.

The Law Society Guidance on money laundering confirms this view[77] but highlights a fur- **3.99** ther problem where money is held on account:

> 2.31 There may be a problem if a balance remains after the final bill has been settled, as returning this balance to the client may amount to the commission of a money laundering offence if you know or suspect that the money is criminal property. In that case it may be necessary to make a pre-transaction authorised disclosure and obtain appropriate consent to deal with the money before any transfers take place.

Contrasted with handling

Section 22 of the Theft Act 1968 defines the offence of handling: **3.100**

> **22 Handling stolen goods**
> (1) A person handles stolen goods if (otherwise than in the course of the stealing) knowing or believing them to be stolen goods he dishonestly receives the goods, or dishonestly undertakes or assists in their retention, removal, disposal or realisation by or for the benefit of another person, or if he arranges to do so.

The offence carries 14 years on indictment.

---

[75] [2009] EWCA Crim 2242.
[76] <http://www.cps.gov.uk>.
[77] The current Law Society guidance is contained in the Anti-money laundering practice note—29 October 2009 available at <http://www.lawsociety.org.uk/productsandservices/practicenotes/aml.page>. The updated section in the current guidance can be found at 5.5.2 Adequate consideration defence.

3.101 It can be seen that the principal money laundering offences, and in particular possessing criminal property under section 329, are wider than and in effect subsume the offence of handling. The differences between handling and possessing criminal property are:

- In handling the prosecution must prove that the defendant knew or believed the goods to be stolen, as opposed to the product of other crime.
- As to the extent of the state of knowledge, in *Hall*[78] it was stated with respect to handling that:

'I suspect that these goods may be stolen, but it may be on the other hand that they are not.' That state of mind, of course, does not fall within the words 'knowing or believing'.

So suspicion is not enough for handling, but it is enough for the money laundering offence.

- Handling requires dishonesty, possessing criminal property does not.
- Handling may not be committed in the course of stealing, but there is no such restriction on possessing criminal property. In the case of *Rose*,[79] the Court of Appeal held that stolen goods in the hands of the thief or a receiver are criminal property for the purposes of section 329 since D obtains a right to possession of them in accordance with section 340(10) (a) and (d). However, there are certain circumstances when a criminal cannot 'acquire' property which he has stolen/acquired as there may be no predicate offence.[80]
- The making of an authorised disclosure and obtaining consent is a defence to the offence of possessing criminal property but not handling.

3.102 One practical effect of POCA is that all handling offences can now be charged under the money laundering provisions. By creating the offence of possessing criminal property, Parliament has, in practice, removed the need for the prosecution to prove dishonesty in handling, and lowered the *mens rea* for the offence.

3.103 For an analysis of the differences between handling and possessing criminal property, see *R (Wilkinson) v DPP*[81] and the commentary on the case in Archbold News[82] and the further discussion in Criminal Law Review.[83]

F. Conspiracy to Money Launder

3.104 Where a conspiracy to money launder is charged, the necessary *mens rea* is that the person knows that the property is a person's benefit from crime, or that the person intends that the property is a person's benefit from crime. This topic is dealt with in detail in Chapter 2.

---

[78] *R v Hall* (1985) 81 Cr App R 260 (Boreham J).
[79] *CPS (Nottinghamshire) v Rose, The Times*, 6 March 2008.
[80] *R v Kausar* [2009] EWCA Crim 2242.
[81] [2006] EWHC 3012 (Admin).
[82] [2007] 1 Archbold News 5.
[83] DC Ormerod, 2006 Crim LR 853.

G. Sentencing

In *Griffiths* [84] it was said that organizing the cover-up of or laundering the proceeds of crime   **3.105**
is always serious, especially if organized or set up as an operation. Custodial sentences are
inevitable in almost every case, if not every case. In that case:

- Leslie Pattison, an estate agent who also provided financial services, was convicted of
  offences of entering into a money laundering arrangement, contrary to section 328(1)
  of the POCA, and acquiring criminal property, contrary to section 329(1) of the Act.
  He purchased a property worth £150,000 from a convicted drug dealer who had
  pending confiscation proceedings. He bought the property for £43,000—grossly under
  value. He was convicted after a trial and was sentenced to three years' imprisonment
  concurrent on each count. He was 45 years old, of good character, and had lost his livelihood as a consequence of the conviction. The Court of Appeal held that the appropriate sentence for the one-off attempt to hide profit in this case was one of 27 months'
  imprisonment.
- Philip Griffiths was a solicitor responsible for the conveyance of the property which was
  the subject of Pattison's conviction. The jury acquitted him of being party to a money
  laundering arrangement, and of acquiring criminal property but convicted him of failing
  to make the required disclosure under section 330. The Court of Appeal noted that the
  jury's verdict meant that he could not have known or suspected that the property was the
  proceeds of criminal conduct (or they would have convicted him of the money laundering
  offences), only that he had reasonable grounds for suspicion. He was 45 years old, of good
  character, and had lost his livelihood as a consequence of the conviction. His sentence of
  15 months was reduced by the Court of Appeal to one of six months.

The court also stated that credit for pleading guilty in this type of case is always substantial,
not only because it allows the court to accept that the professional defendant has appreciated
the gravity of his misconduct, but also because it has the effect of saving substantial court
time and public funds.

In *Duff* [85] a solicitor had pleaded guilty to two counts of failing to disclose knowledge or   **3.106**
suspicion of money laundering in circumstances in which he had first been handed £60,000,
part of which was for an investment, albeit all later returned, with £10,000 subsequently
being placed by that client into a company set up to solicit business for the solicitor. The
court rejected the submission that the custody threshold was not passed and dismissed an
appeal from a six-month sentence.

In *Gonzales & Sarmiento*, [86] £700,000 in currency was brought to this country from South   **3.107**
America in a single trip with efforts being made to hide involvement and avoid detection.
Three years' imprisonment was the sentence ultimately imposed by the Court of Appeal.

In *Yoonus*, [87] four years' imprisonment was ultimately imposed for a course of conduct of   **3.108**
laundering drugs money by converting sterling into foreign currency.

---

[84] *R v Griffiths and Pattison* [2006] EWCA Crim 2155.
[85] *R v Duff* [2003] 1 Cr App R (S) 88.
[86] *R v Gonzales and Sarmiento* [2002] EWCA Crim 2685.
[87] *R v Yoonus* [2005] 1 Cr App R (S) 46.

4

THE TERRORIST MONEY LAUNDERING
AND TERRORIST FINANCING OFFENCES

A. Introduction

4.01 Those who commit acts of terrorism may use legally generated sources of income, as well as relying on the proceeds of criminal activity to finance terrorism. As a result a wider definition is employed in relation to laundering offences in the context of terrorism. As described below, this issue has been addressed in the Terrorism Act 2000 (TA 2000) as amended by the Terrorism Act 2006 and the Counter-Terrorism Act 2008. Unlike other money laundering criminal offences the property in question does not have to be 'criminal' in nature and/or from a criminal source for the terrorist money laundering offences to be engaged.

The concept of terrorist money laundering is perhaps best seen as a metaphor or an example **4.02** of political rhetoric. The UK offences referred to as terrorist money laundering do not necessarily deal with the proceeds of criminal activity. Insofar as they do, they would also be offences under POCA. To the extent that these offences differ from the POCA offences, they are concerned instead with the nature and identity of the owner—in effect, criminalizing the assets of proscribed organizations—or whether the property is 'likely to be used for the purposes of terrorism'.

This chapter deals with the UK terrorist financing and money laundering laws and sets out **4.03** the international legal framework from which these laws are derived. It does not include the failure to disclose offences in sections 19 and 21A of the Terrorism Act 2000 as these are discussed elsewhere in Chapter 6 dealing with disclosures. It also sets out the offences created by the Al-Qaida and Taliban (United Nations Measures) Order 2006/2952, the Terrorism (United Nations Measures) Order 2009/1747, and the Terrorism (United Nations Measures) Order 2006/2657.

The Terrorism Act 2000 as amended by the Anti Terrorism Crime and Security Act 2001 also **4.04** creates offences of failing to disclose information about which the relevant person has knowledge or suspicion that another person has committed a terrorist financing offence under sections 15 to 18 of the Act. These offences are discussed in detail elsewhere in this book.

B. International Legal Provisions

The UK terrorist financing laws derive from international instruments. Terrorism has been a **4.05** central part of the international agenda for decades. There are 13 international Conventions relating to UN activities in this area. The General Assembly of the UN has been increasing their efforts of co-ordination while the Security Council has been active through the passing of Resolutions and the establishment of subsidiary bodies such as the Counter-Terrorism Committee Executive Directorate (CTED) in 2004. These international efforts can be found in a number of sources including the International Convention for the Suppression of the Financing of Terrorism 1999,[1] UN Security Council Resolution 1373 (2001) which obliges all UN member states to introduce certain measures to combat terrorism including criminalizing the financing of terrorism,[2] the FATF 9 Special Recommendations on Terrorist Financing[3] and the EC's Third Directive which has been discussed elsewhere.[4]

Other Resolutions have been passed including 1535 (2004) creating the CTED, and **4.06** Resolutions 1540, 1566, and 1624 (2005) which prohibit states from assisting terrorists or from giving them safe haven.

---

[1] UN Doc A/Res/54/109; 39 ILM 270. This treaty entered into force on 10 April 2002.
[2] UN Doc S/Res/1373 (2001), adopted on 28 September 2001. For an overview of the UN and FATF standards, see R Barnes and D Newcomb, *Global Responses to Terrorist Financing,* (June 2002) World Money Laundering Review, vol. 1 no. 6.
[3] These can be found at <http://www.fatf-gafi.org>.
[4] See Chapters 1 and 9.

C. UK Terrorist Money Laundering Provisions under Part III of the Terrorism Act 2000

Summary of sections 14 to 22 of the Terrorism Act 2000

4.07 The antiterrorist money laundering and financing laws in the UK are contained in sections 14 to 22 of the Terrorism Act 2000 (TA 2000). The financing and laundering offences are set out in sections 15 to 18. Under these provisions a person commits an offence when he invites another to provide money or other property, receives money or other property, or possesses money or other property and intends that the money should be used or has reasonable grounds to suspect that it may be used for the purposes of terrorism. A person also commits an offence when he provides money or other property knowing or suspecting that it will or may be used for the purposes of terrorism, or enters into or is concerned with arrangements either to fund terrorism or to launder terrorist property.

Section 63 extraterritorial jurisdiction

4.08 Section 63 provides that if a person does anything outside the UK and his actions would have constituted the commission of an offence under any of the sections 15 to 18 had they been done in the UK, then he shall be guilty of an offence.

D. Key Concepts under the Terrorism Act 2000

'Terrorism' section 1

4.09 Action for the purposes of terrorism does not refer only to action taken for the benefit of proscribed organizations. It has a wider meaning and 'terrorism' is defined broadly in section 1 of TA 2000.

    (1) In this Act 'terrorism' means the use or threat of action where—
        (a) the action falls within subsection (2),
        (b) the use or threat is designed to influence the government [or an international government organization[5]) or to intimidate the public or a section of the public, and
        (c) the use or threat is made for the purposes of advancing a political, religious, [racial][6] or ideological cause.
    (2) Action falls within this subsection if it—
        (a) involves serious violence against a person,
        (b) involves serious damage to property,
        (c) endangers a person's life, other than that of the person committing the action,
        (d) creates a serious risk to the health or safety of the public or a section of the public,
        (e) is designed seriously to interfere with or disrupt an electronic system.

---

[5] Words in square brackets inserted by the Terrorism Act 2006.
[6] Word inserted by the Counter-Terrorism Act 2008 which came into force on 16 February 2009.

(3) The use or threat of action falling within subsection (2) which involves the use of firearms or explosives is terrorism whether or not subsection (1)(b) is satisfied.[7]

This definition of terrorism includes action outside the UK and any reference in the defini-   **4.10** tion to any person or property is a reference to any person or property wherever situated.[8] Similarly, a reference to the public includes the public of a country other than the UK and a reference to 'the government' includes the government of a country other than the UK.[9]

Such action or the threat of it is not limited to countries governed by democratic or represen-   **4.11** tative principles and includes countries governed by dictators and tyrants. In *R v F (Terrorism)*[10] the Court of Appeal ruled that the meaning of section 1(1)(b) of TA 2000 was unambiguous and included all governments of whatever political persuasion. The Court observed that given the random nature of terrorist acts the citizens of a country governed by a tyrant had as much right to be protected from such activities as those who lived in a democratic or representative countries.

In *R v (Islamic Human Rights Commission) v Civil Aviation Authority*[11] the High Court dis-   **4.12** missed an application by the IHRC for a declaration that the actions of the CAA in granting permissions, approvals and exemptions under the Air Navigation Order in respect of the transport of munitions of war through UK airspace to the State of Israel was unlawful. An emergency injunction seeking to prohibit the CAA from granting any further permissions, approvals, or exemptions for the carriage of munitions of war to Israel was similarly dismissed. When giving judgment the court observed that taken literally the definition of 'terrorism' in section 1 was wide enough to cover all lawful acts of war, but on their proper construction, they did not cover Israel's conduct in either place.

'For the purposes of terrorism'

Sections 15 to 17 of the Act create offences of raising funds, using, possessing, or funding   **4.13** arrangements 'for the purposes of terrorism'. For example, under section 15(1) a person commits an offence if he invites another to provide money or other property and intends that it should be used, or has reasonable cause to suspect that it may be used, for the purposes of terrorism.

Action taken for the purposes of terrorism includes action taken for the benefit of organiza-   **4.14** tions proscribed by the Secretary of State.[12] Pursuant to section 3 of the TA 2000, the Secretary of State has a discretionary power to add organizations to a schedule of proscribed organizations if he believes them to be concerned in terrorism, subject to approval by affirmative resolution of each House of Parliament.[13] Under section 3(5) of the Act, an organization is concerned in terrorism if it '(a) commits or participates in acts of terrorism, (b) prepares for terrorism, (c) promotes or encourages terrorism, or (d) is otherwise

---

[7] TA 2000, s 1.
[8] Ibid., s 1(4)(a), (b).
[9] Ibid., s 1(4)(c), (d).
[10] [2007] QB 960 CA.
[11] [2007] AC D 5 (Ouseley J).
[12] TA 2000, s 1(5).
[13] Sch 2 to the Act contains a list of proscribed organizations. The House of Lords considered the statutory construction of TA 2000, s 3 and the meaning of a 'proscribed organization' in *R v Z* [2005] UKHL 35 (19 May 2005).

concerned in terrorism'.[14] This means that, in the example above, fund-raising for a proscribed organization is an offence under section 15 of TA 2000.

4.15 Three claimants on behalf of organizations proscribed under TA 2000 have challenged the legality of the criminal regime established by sections 15 to 19 of the Act. These claimants made applications for judicial review by or on behalf of three proscribed organizations, namely the People's Mojahedin Organization of Iran (PMOI), the Kurdistan Workers' Party (PKK) and Lashkar e Tayyabah.[15] Richards J held that the claimants had made out an arguable claim that this regime of offences consequential upon even an unlawful proscription of an organization gives rise to a disproportionate interference with an individual's rights under the European Convention on Human Rights. Ultimately, however, he refused leave for judicial review on the basis that the lawfulness of this regime of penalties is better assessed by the Proscribed Organizations Appeal Commission (POAC) established under TA 2000 than by way of judicial review.[16]

4.16 On 30 November 2007 POAC in a detailed judgment (Appeal No PC/02/2006) and exercising its powers under section 5(4) and (5) of TA 2000 allowed the appeal by PMOI and ordered the Secretary of State to lay before Parliament a statutory instrument removing/de-proscribing the PMOI. Although allowing the appeal, POAC made the following point in paragraph 354 of its judgment: 'Although it is correct to say that the Appellant's rights under the Convention are limited by the provisions of the 2000 Act . . . it is clear to us that these provisions are legitimate and proportionate.' An appeal by the Home Secretary to the Court of Appeal against this decision was dismissed.[17]

4.17 The Secretary of State removed the PMOI from the list of organizations proscribed under the TA 2000. Notwithstanding this the Council of the European Union nonetheless maintained the PMOI on a list of those to be targeted to combat terrorism in terms of freezing assets. The Court of First Instance of the European Communities annulled the EU decision.[18]

'Terrorist'

4.18 The word 'terrorist' is defined in the Act. Section 40 states:

> (1) In this part 'terrorist' means a person who—
>   (a) has committed an offence under sections 11, 12, 15 to 18, 54 and 56 to 63, or
>   (b) is or has been concerned in the commission, preparation or instigation of acts of terrorism.
> (2) The reference in subsection (1)(b) to a person who has been concerned in the commission, preparation or instigation of acts of terrorism includes a reference to a person who has been, whether before or after the passing of this Act, concerned in the commission, preparation or instigation of acts of terrorism within the meaning given by section 1.

---

[14] TA 2000, s 3(5).

[15] *R v Secretary of State for the Home Department, ex parte the PKK, PMOI, and Nisar Ahmed* [2002] EWHC 644 (Admin) Richards J, 17 April 2002.

[16] Ibid. See paras 52–4 for a description of this claim and see paras 91–2 for Mr Justice Richards' conclusion. The POAC is established under TA 2000, s 5.

[17] [2008] EWCA Civ 443.

[18] *PMOI v Council of European Union* [2009] 1 CMLR 44.

Part V of TA 2000 gives the police certain powers in relation to suspected terrorists, such **4.19** as the power of arrest without a warrant (section 41) and the power to search a person and seize anything found upon him which the constable reasonably suspects may constitute evidence that the person is a terrorist (section 43). These powers can be exercised in relation to any person who has committed a terrorist financing or laundering offence under sections 15 to 18, as they are included in the definition of a 'terrorist' under section 40.[19]

'Terrorist property' section 14

Section 14(1) of the TA 2000 defines 'terrorist property' as: **4.20**

    (a) money or other property which is likely to be used for the purposes of terrorism (including any resources of a proscribed organisation),
    (b) proceeds of the commission of acts of terrorism, and
    (c) proceeds of acts carried out for the purposes of terrorism.

Section 14(2) reads as follows: **4.21**

In subsection (1)—
    (a) a reference to proceeds of an act includes a reference to any property which wholly or partly, and directly or indirectly, represents the proceeds of the act (including payments or other rewards in connection with its commission) and
    (b) the reference to an organisation's resources includes a reference to any money or other property which is applied or made available, or is to be applied or made available, for use by the organisation.

It is not entirely clear what the phrase 'proceeds of the commission of acts of terrorism' **4.22** means. Most such acts are unlikely to produce any direct proceeds—money or other property and so it seems that the phrase will apply almost always to indirect proceeds. The definition of 'terrorist property' is so widely drawn in section 14 that it covers clean and dirty funds. It arguably would include for example funds from the sale of a Jihadist film celebrating a particular terrorist attack.

E. Definition of 'Terrorist Financing' in Regulation 2 Money Laundering Regulations 2007

Regulation 2 of the Money Laundering Regulations 2007 (MLR 2007) defines 'terrorist **4.23** financing' as including offences under the following provisions:

- Sections 15, 16, 17, 18, and 63 of the Terrorism Act 2000;[20]
- Paragraphs 7(2) and 7(3) of Schedule 3 to the Anti-Terrorism, Crime and Security Act 2001;
- Articles 7, 8, or 10 of the Al-Qaida and Taliban (United Nations Measures) Order 2006;[21]

---

[19] TA 2000, s 41(1)(a).
[20] Discussed below at paras 4.24 *et seq.*
[21] Discussed below at paras 4.57 *et seq.*

- Articles 7, 8, or 10 of the Terrorism (United Nations Measures) Order 2006;[22] and
- Articles 10, 11, 12, 13, 14 and 16 of the Terrorism (United Nations Measures) Order 2009.[23]

F. Section 15— Raising Funds for the Purposes of Terrorism

4.24 Section 15 of TA 2000 creates three offences related to raising funds for terrorist purposes. These are triable either in the magistrates or the Crown Court. Upon summary conviction (i.e. in the magistrates court) the section carries a maximum sentence of 6 [12][24] months or a fine not exceeding the statutory maximum, or both.[25] In the Crown Court, there is a maximum sentence of 14 years' imprisonment or a fine, or both.[26]

4.25 Section 15:

> (1) A person commits an offence if he —
>   (a) invites another to provide money or other property, and
>   (b) intends that it should be used, or has reasonable cause to suspect that it may be used, for the purposes of terrorism.
> (2) A person commits an offence if he —
>   (a) receives money or other property, and
>   (b) intends that it should be used or has reasonable cause to suspect that it may be used, for the purposes of terrorism.
> (3) A person commits an offence if he—
>   (a) provides money or other property, and
>   (b) knows or has reasonable cause to suspect that it will or may be used for the purposes of terrorism.
> (4) In this section a reference to the provision of money or other property is a reference to its being given, lent or otherwise made available, whether or not for consideration.[27]

4.26 As described above, action taken for the purposes of terrorism includes action taken for the benefit of organizations proscribed under the Act as being concerned in terrorism.[28] A list of proscribed organizations is set out in Schedule 2 to the Act. Action taken for the purposes of terrorism is not however limited to action taken for the benefit of proscribed organizations and includes action taken in connection with the conduct described in section 1 of the Act, which provides a definition of terrorism (see above).

4.27 If the conduct described in this section—inviting another to provide, receiving or providing money or other property with the intent or knowledge or reasonable cause to suspect that it will or may be used for the purposes of terrorism—occurs outside the UK, an offence is still committed under section 15 provided the requisite mental element can be shown.[29]

---

[22] Discussed below at paras 4.57 *et seq.*
[23] Discussed below at paras 4.61 *et seq.*
[24] Amended to 12 months by CJA 2003, s 282 (not yet in force).
[25] TA 2000, s 22(a).
[26] Ibid., s 22(b).
[27] Ibid., s 15.
[28] Ibid., s 1(5).
[29] Ibid., s 63.

Mens rea for section 15

In all three of these fund-raising offences, the *mens rea* can be either subjective or objective. **4.28**
It is subjective where the offender either intends that the property that he either invites
another to provide (section 15(1)) or himself receives (section 15(2)) should be used for the
purposes of terrorism or where he provides money (section 15(3)) knowing that it will or
may be used for the purposes of terrorism. However, a person may also be guilty of an offence
under section 15 where he neither intends that the property in question should, nor knows
that it will or may, be used for the purposes of terrorism. To be guilty of an offence it is
sufficient that he has reasonable cause to suspect that the money may be used for the purposes of terrorism. In other words, there is an objective mental element to the offences under
section 15.

The phrase 'has reasonable cause to suspect' can be compared to the objective standard **4.29**
to which money laundering reporting officers (MLROs) and those working in the regulated sector are held under the MLR 2007, which also carry criminal sanction. However,
whereas the Regulations impose that standard only on limited classes of people, the offence
under section 18 applies that standard to all individuals no matter what their role or
responsibilities.

G. Section 16—Use and Possession of Money or other
Property for the Purposes of Terrorism

Section 16 of TA 2000 creates an offence of using money or other property for the purposes **4.30**
of terrorism triable either in the magistrates or the Crown Court. Upon summary conviction
(i.e. in the magistrates court) the section carries a maximum sentence of 6 [12][30] months or
a fine not exceeding the statutory minimum, or both.[31] In the Crown Court, there is a maximum sentence of 14 years' imprisonment or a fine, or both.[32]

Under section 16 of TA 2000: **4.31**

   (1) A person commits an offence if he uses money or other property for the purposes of
        terrorism.
   (2) A person commits an offence if he——
        (a) possesses money or other property, and
        (b) intends that it should be used, or has reasonable cause to suspect that it may be used,
             for the purposes of terrorism.

Like section 15, references to action 'for the purposes of terrorism' include—but are not **4.32**
limited to—action taken for the benefit of proscribed organizations.[33] Therefore, if a person
uses money or other property for the benefit of a proscribed organization with the requisite
state of mind, he commits an offence under section 16. The offence is not limited to action

---

[30] Amended to 12 months by CJA 2003, s 282 (not yet in force).
[31] TA 2000, s 22(a).
[32] Ibid., s 22(b).
[33] Ibid., s 1(5).

taken for the benefit of a proscribed organization. The offence would catch D who possessed money or other property with intent that it should be used in a single terrorist act.

4.33   If conduct amounting to the *actus reus* of this offence occurs abroad, a section 16 offence still occurs.[34] Similarly, money or property may be used for the purposes of terrorist acts directed against any public and any government (i.e. not only the public and government of the UK) and an offence is committed under section 16.[35]

4.34   It appears from the wording of this section that it would not only cover relevant acts supporting a terrorist organization, whether proscribed or not, but would cover actions by a third party who might, in some way, aid or support a lone terrorist. It would appear also, in fact, to create an offence that would catch someone who is a lone terrorist or an individual (unattached to any terrorist organization) intending to commit a terrorist act, since it would cover the possession of money or other property intended to be used by that person for the purposes of terrorism. It would, therefore, seem to apply to such persons as Theodore Kaczynski, the Unabomber, or David Copeland, the person who bombed the Admiral Duncan pub in Soho in 1999, or any other terrorist acting alone and out of some sense of grievance against the government or against a section of society.

4.35   In *O'Driscoll v Secretary of State for the Home Department and The Metropolitan Police Commissioner,*[36] the High Court rejected the claim that the offence created by section 16 is incompatible with basic freedoms enshrined in the ECHR, namely the freedom of expression under Article 10 and the freedom of association under Article 11, when applied in relation to the use of possessions or money or other property for the benefit of a proscribed organization. In this case, Kennedy LJ held first that the offence under section 16 is clearly defined in law and in this regard noted that in order to prove the offence it is necessary to show that the defendant had a specific intent or state of mind (section 16(2)(b)).[37] Secondly, where an organization has been properly proscribed there can be no question about its terrorist nature and, again 'bearing in mind the need for proof of a guilty mind', section 16 cannot be regarded as disproportionate. In this regard, Kennedy LJ stated that '[t]his section is not about freedom of expression. It is about knowingly providing money or other property to support a proscribed organization.'[38] For these reasons and others, the claimant's renewed application for permission to seek judicial review was dismissed.

Mens rea for section 16

4.36   Like section 15, the mental element of the offence under section 16 can be either subjective (that the defendant intends the money or other property he possesses to be used for the purposes of terrorism) or objective (that he has reasonable cause to suspect that the money or other property may be used for the purposes of terrorism).[39] In *O'Driscoll*, the court appears to have focused only on the subjective aspect of the mental element of this offence as Kennedy

---

[34] Ibid., s 63(1).

[35] Ibid., s 1(4).

[36] [2002] EWHC 2477 (QB).

[37] *O'Driscoll v Secretary of State for the Home Department and The Metropolitan Police Commissioner,* [2002] EWHC 2477, para. [25].

[38] Ibid., para [26].

[39] In relation to the objective element under POCA, see paras 6.07 *et seq.*

LJ did not specifically address the proportionality of imposing criminal liability upon a person who should have but did not suspect that the money or other property he possesses may be used for the purposes of terrorism including for the benefit of a proscribed organization.

H. Section 17—Funding Arrangements for the Purposes of Terrorism

Section 17 of the TA 2000 creates an offence of entering into or becoming concerned in **4.37** an arrangement which results in money or other property being available to another, knowing or having reasonable cause to suspect that it will or may be used for the purposes of terrorism, triable either in the magistrates or the Crown Court. Upon summary conviction (i.e. in the magistrates court) the section carries a maximum sentence of 6 [12][40] months or a fine not exceeding the statutory minimum, or both.[41] In the Crown Court, there is a maximum sentence of 14 years' imprisonment or a fine, or both.[42]

Under section 17: **4.38**

> A person commits an offence if—
> (a) he enters into or becomes concerned in an arrangement as a result of which money or other property is made available or is to be made available to another, and
> (b) he knows or has reasonable cause to suspect that it will or may be used for the purposes of terrorism.

Like sections 15 and 16 discussed above, references to action 'for the purposes of terrorism' **4.39** includes—but is not limited to—action taken for the benefit of proscribed organizations.[43] Therefore, if a person enters into funding arrangements in which money is or will be made available to another and he knows or has reasonable cause to suspect that it will or may be used for the benefit of a proscribed organization with the requisite state of mind, he commits an offence under section 16.

If conduct amounting to the *actus reus* of this offence occurs abroad, a section 17 offence still **4.40** occurs.[44] Similarly, the funding arrangements may be in relation to acts of terrorism directed against any public and any government (i.e. not only the public and government of the UK) and an offence is committed under section 17.[45]

As in the other financing sections of TA 2000, the mental element of the section 17 offence **4.41** can be either subjective (that the defendant intends the money or other property he possesses to be used for the purposes of terrorism) or objective (that he has reasonable cause to suspect that the money or other property may be used for the purposes of terrorism).[46]

---

[40] Amended to 12 months by CJA 2003, s 282 (not yet in force).
[41] TA 2000, s 22(a).
[42] Ibid., s 22(b).
[43] Ibid., s 1(5).
[44] Ibid., s 63(1).
[45] Ibid., s 1(4).
[46] In relation to the objective element under POCA, see paras 6.07 *et seq.*

4.42 At the time of writing, there had been one case in which a conviction under section 17 has been appealed: *R v Meziane and another.* [47] This application was dismissed by the Court of Appeal and unfortunately due to reporting restrictions under the Contempt of Court Act 1981 the reasons for this decision have not been published.

I. Section 18—Money Laundering by Concealing, Removing from a Jurisdiction, or Transferring Terrorist Property

4.43 Section 18 of TA 2000 creates a specific money laundering offence triable either in the magistrates or the Crown Court. Upon summary conviction (i.e. in the magistrates court) the section carries a maximum sentence of 6 [12][48] months or a fine not exceeding the statutory minimum, or both.[49] In the Crown Court, there is a maximum sentence of 14 years' imprisonment or a fine, or both.[50]

4.44 Under section 18:

> (1) A person commits an offence if he enters into or becomes concerned in an arrangement which facilitates the retention or control by or on behalf of another person of terrorist property—
> (a) by concealment,
> (b) by removal from the [a][51] jurisdiction,
> (c) by transfer to nominees, or
> (d) in any other way.
> (2) It is a defence for a person charged with an offence under subsection (1) to prove that he did not know and had no reasonable cause to suspect that the arrangement related to terrorist property.

4.45 As discussed above, since the financing of terrorism may derive from both lawful and illegal sources, this terrorist money laundering offence is not limited to criminal proceeds. 'Terrorist property' is defined under section 14 of the Act as including the proceeds of terrorism offences and money likely to be used for the purposes of terrorism. The former category is perhaps unlikely to have much practical application, as by their nature terrorist offences are not intended and are not likely to have a financial return. It would include for instance a payment by a terrorist organization to an individual in return for carrying out terrorist acts. The latter category is also irrevocably assumed to include all of the resources of proscribed organizations:

> 14.—(1) In this Act "terrorist property" means—
> (a) money or other property which is likely to be used for the purposes of terrorism (including any resources of a proscribed organization),
> (b) proceeds of the commission of acts of terrorism, and
> (c) proceeds of acts carried out for the purposes of terrorism.

---

[47] [2004] All ER (D) 293 (Jun).
[48] Amended to 12 months by CJA 2003, s 282 (not yet in force).
[49] TA 2000, s 22(a).
[50] Ibid., s 22(b).
[51] Under TA 2000, s 63, in relation to acts of laundering done outside the UK, s 18(1)(b) should read as 'a jurisdiction' rather than 'the jurisdiction'.

(2) In subsection (1) —
   (a) a reference to proceeds of an act includes a reference to any property which wholly or partly, and directly or indirectly, represents the proceeds of the act (including payments or other rewards in connection with its commission), and
   (b) the reference to an organization's resources includes a reference to any money or other property which is applied or made available, or is to be applied or made available, for use by the organization.[52]

Property is defined under the Act as including 'property wherever situated and whether real **4.46** or personal, heritable or moveable, and things in action and other intangible or incorporeal property'.[53]

Like the other financing offences under the TA 2000, section 18 applies to conduct that **4.47** occurs outside the UK. Thus, by operation of section 63(2), a person is guilty of an offence under this section if he facilitates the retention or control of terrorist property by or on behalf of another person by removing that property from any jurisdiction.

Defence to charge under section 18

It is a defence to a charge under section 18 that the person proves that he did not know **4.48** and had no reasonable cause to suspect that the arrangement in question related to terrorist property.[54] For the reasons discussed in Chapter 3 above in connection with the 'reverse burden' provisions of POCA, it is submitted that this defence must establish an evidentiary burden only. This position is supported by the House of Lords' decision in *Sheldrake v DPP; Attorney-General's Reference (No 4 of 2002)*.[55] This case concerned the reverse burden established under section 11(2) of the TA 2000 (offence of membership of a proscribed organization). Under this provision, it is a defence for a person to prove that the organization was not proscribed on the last (or only) occasion on which he became a member or began to profess to be a member of the proscribed organization and that he has not taken part in any activities of the organization at any time while it was proscribed. The House of Lords held that, in order ensure basic standards of fairness were met in criminal proceedings, this should be read and given effect as imposing only an evidentiary burden on the defendant.

The mental element laid out in this defence is both subjective and objective: that the defen- **4.49** dant neither knew nor had reasonable cause to suspect that the arrangement in question related to terrorist property. As discussed above in relation to POCA, this objective element requires that the facts known by the defendant would not cause a reasonable person to suspect that the arrangement related to terrorist property.[56]

---

[52] Ibid., s 14.
[53] Ibid., s 121.
[54] Ibid., 18(2).
[55] [2005] 1 AC 264.
[56] In relation to the reasonable grounds for suspicion under POCA, see paras 2.73 *et seq.*

J. Section 23—Forfeiture

4.50   Where a person is convicted of a money laundering offence under sections 15 to 18 of TA 2000 the court before which they are convicted may make a forfeiture order by virtue of sections 23, 23A and 23B.

4.51   Where a person is convicted of an offence contrary to sections 15(1) or (2) or 16 the court may order the forfeiture of any money or other property which, at the time of the offence, he had in his possession or under his control, and which, at that time, he intended should be used, or had reasonable cause to suspect might be used, for the purposes of terrorism.

4.52   Where a person is convicted of an offence under section 15(3) the court may order the forfeiture of any money or other property which, at the time of the offence, he had in his possession or under his control, and which, at that time, he knew or had reasonable cause to suspect would or might be used for the purposes of terrorism.

4.53   Where a person is convicted of an offence under section 17 the court may order the forfeiture of the money or other property to which the arrangement in question related, and which at the time he knew or had reasonable cause to suspect would or might be used for terrorism.

4.54   Where someone is convicted of an offence under section 18 the court may order the forfeiture of the money or other property to which the arrangement in question relates.

4.55   Section 23 is based on section 13(2) of the Prevention of Terrorism (Temporary Provisions) Act 1989 (PT(TP)A 1989) and has similar effect but it gives the court one important new power. Subsection (6) allows for forfeiture of the proceeds of a terrorist property offence. The Explanatory Note for this section says: 'This could arise in a case where an accountant prepared accounts on behalf of a proscribed organization—thus facilitating the retention or control of the organization's money—and was paid for doing so. The money he received in payment could not be forfeited under section 13(2) of PT(TP)A 1989 because it was not intended or suspected for use in terrorism. It could not be confiscated under the Criminal Justice Act 1988 (c 33) because that confiscation regime excludes terrorist property offences. Subsection (6) closes this loophole between the confiscation scheme in the 1988 Act and the counter-terrorist forfeiture scheme.'

K. Section 62—Counter-Terrorism Act 2008

4.56   Section 62 gives HM Treasury powers to act against terrorist financing, money laundering, and certain other activities. The provisions relating to this are contained Schedule 7 to the Act. In respect of UK institutions, the Schedule provides for 'directions' to be made, which may require enhanced customer due diligence and monitoring, systematic reporting, or even for the institution to cease business with particular individuals. The Schedule also enables directions to be made in respect of non-EEA countries, when certain criteria are fulfilled. Failure to comply with a direction is a criminal offence under paragraph 30 of Schedule 7, subject to a defence of having taken all reasonable steps and acted with due diligence. The Schedule also provides for civil liability, although the same conduct can only be punished via one of the two routes.

L. The Al-Qaida and Taliban (United Nations Measures) Order 2006/2952

4.57 The Al-Qaida and Taliban (United Nations Measures) Order 2006 creates offences in respect of assets of designated persons.[57]

4.58 Article 7 of the Order prohibits dealing with funds or economic resources owned or held by a designated person, someone in their control, or their agent. It is a defence for a person to show that they did not know and had no reasonable cause to suspect that the funds or resources belonged to such a person. Article 8 prohibits making funds or economic resources available to the same category of people, and it is similarly a defence to show that a person did not know or have reasonable cause to suspect that they were making funds or resources available to such a person. Article 10 makes it an offence to circumvent Articles 7 or 8, or to attempt to do so.

4.59 Offences created by Articles 7, 8, and 10 are triable on indictment or summarily, with maximum sentences of seven years or a fine or both on indictment, or 12 months or a fine not exceeding the statutory maximum or both where the offence is tried summarily.[58]

4.60 Article 9 creates an exception in respect of those who merely credit an account with interest due or amounts resulting from obligations or payments due that arose prior to the account holder becoming a designated person. Article 11 enables the Treasury to grant licences exempting specific acts from the provisions; breach of such a licence is an offence punishable by two years' imprisonment or a fine or both when tried on indictment, or 12 months or a fine when tried summarily.[59]

M. The Terrorism (United Nations Measures) Order 2009/1747

4.61 The Terrorism (United Nations Measures) Order 2009 creates similar offences in respect of 'restricted' persons, as defined in Article 2.[60]

4.62 Article 10 of the Order prohibits dealing with funds or resources owned, held, or controlled by a restricted person or someone in their control or their agent. It is a defence for a person to show that they reasonably lacked knowledge and did not suspect that they were dealing with the funds or resources belonging to such a person.

4.63 Articles 11 to 14 prohibit making funds, financial services, or economic resources available to or for the benefit of a restricted person. It is a defence for a person to show that they reasonably lacked knowledge and did not suspect that they were making the funds, financial services or economic resources available to such a person, or, in the case of economic resources, they did not know and had no reasonable cause to suspect that they would be used in exchange for funds, goods, or services.

---

[57] As defined in the Al-Qaida and Taliban (United Nations Measures Order), Arts 3–5.
[58] Ibid., Art 13.
[59] Ibid., Art 13.
[60] Defined in Art 2 as a designated person or one owned or controlled by or acting on behalf of a designated person. The term 'designated person' is defined in Arts 3–7.

4.64 Article 15 creates an exception in relation to a 'relevant institution[61] if it is merely crediting an account with interest due[62] or amounts resulting from obligations that arose before the account was frozen[63] or amounts transferred by a third party:[64] however, in respect of Articles 15(1)(b) and 15(2) there is an obligation to inform the Treasury of the situation as soon as is practicably possible. As in the Al-Qaida and Taliban Order discussed above, the Treasury may grant licences to exempt specific acts,[65] and it is similarly an offence to attempt or manage to circumvent the provisions.[66]

4.65 All of the offences created are triable on indictment or summarily. In respect of offences under Articles 10, 11, 12, 13, 14, and 16 the maximum penalties are seven years or a fine or both on indictment, or six months or a fine not exceeding the statutory maximum or both summarily. The offence created by Article 17 carries a maximum penalty of two years or a fine or both on indictment, or six months or a fine or both when tried summarily.[67]

N. The Terrorism (United Nations Measures) Order 2006/2657

4.66 The Terrorism (United Nations Measures) Order 2006 created similar offences to those set out above, with minor differences. It continued to apply, until 31 August 2010, to anyone in respect of whom there was a Treasury direction under Article 4 immediately prior to the date on which the 2009 Order came into force; the 2006 Order also preserved the 2001 Order in relation to anyone in respect of whom there was a direction under that Order, again until 31 August 2010.

4.67 Article 7 prohibited dealing with funds or economic resources owned, held, or controlled by a designated person, a person who is involved in terrorist attacks or attempts or anyone owned or controlled by them, save in accordance with a licence or where a person does not know or have reasonable cause to suspect that they are dealing with such funds.

4.68 Article 8 makes it an offence to made funds, economic resources, or financial services available to or for the benefit of a person as described in Article 7, save in accordance with a licence or where a person does not know or have reasonable cause to suspect that they are making such funds, resources, or services available.

Her Majesty's Treasury v Mohammed Jabar Ahmed and others[68]

4.69 The first cases to be heard in the Supreme Court were three conjoined appeals concerning the legality of the Terrorism (United Nations Measures) Order 2006 and the Al-Qaida and Taliban (United Nations Measures) Order 2006. It was argued that the Orders fell outside the scope of section 1(1) of the United Nations Act of 1946, and that they were incompatible with the Human Rights Act 1998. The Supreme Court concluded unanimously that the

---

[61] Defined in Art 2.
[62] The Terrorism (United Nations Measures) Order 2009, Art 15(1)(a).
[63] Ibid., Art 15(1)(b).
[64] Ibid., Art 15(2).
[65] Ibid., Art 17; breach of such a licence is an offence.
[66] Ibid., Art 16.
[67] The Terrorism (United Nations Measures) Order 2009, Art 21.
[68] [2010] UKSC 2.

Terrorism (United Nations Measures) Order 2006 was *ultra vires* because its terms went beyond those required by the Security Council Resolution. The majority also quashed Article 3(1)(b) of the Al-Qaida and Taliban Order on the basis that the absence of any means of effectively reviewing decisions of the Sanctions Committee to place individuals on the list of designated persons rendered the provision *ultra vires*.

4.70 The government responded almost immediately by enacting the Terrorist Asset-Freezing Act 2010 as a temporary measure to validate the Terrorism (United Nations Measures) Orders 2001, 2006, and 2009. The provisions of the Act applied until 31 December 2010, by which time a more permanent legislative scheme was presumably put in place. Article 3(1)(b) is not in fact needed in order for the provisions to have effect under UK law owing to EC Regulation 881/2002; however, affirmative procedure regulations under section 2(2) of the European Communities Act 1972 are at present being considered in order to ensure that enforcement provisions are in place to implement the Regulation fully.

O. Section 22—Penalties

4.71 A person found guilty of an offence of any of sections 15 to 18 of the TA 2000 shall be liable on conviction on indictment to imprisonment for a term not exceeding 14 years, to a fine, or to both and liable on summary conviction for a term not exceeding six months [12 months][69] or to a fine not exceeding the statutory maximum or to both.

4.72 A person found guilty of an offence of any of sections 19 or 21A of the TA 2000 shall be liable on conviction on indictment to imprisonment for a term not exceeding five years, to a fine, or to both and liable on summary conviction for a term not exceeding six [12 months] or to a fine or both.

4.73 The maximum penalty for an offence under paragraph 30 of Schedule 7 to the Counter-Terrorism Act 2008 is two years or a fine when tried on indictment, or a fine alone when tried summarily.

4.74 Offences created by Articles 7, 8, and 10 of the Al Qaida and Taliban UN Order 2006/2952 are triable on indictment or summarily, with maximum sentences of seven years or a fine or both on indictment, or 12 months or a fine not exceeding the statutory maximum or both where the offence is tried summarily. An offence under Article 11 is punishable by two years' imprisonment or a fine or both when tried on indictment, or 12 months or a fine or both when tried summarily.

4.75 All of the offences created by the Terrorism (UN Measures) Order 2009 are triable on indictment or summarily. Articles 10, 11, 12, 13, 14, and 16 carry maximum penalties of seven years or a fine or both on indictment, or six months or a fine not exceeding the statutory maximum or both summarily. An offence under Article 17 can incur a maximum penalty of two years or a fine or both on indictment, or six months or a fine or both when tried summarily.

---

[69] Twelve is substituted for six by CJA 2003, s 282(2) and (3) on a day to be appointed. The increase has no application to offences committed before the substitution takes effect.

5

DISCLOSURE AND THE SARS REGIME

A. Introduction

5.01 This Chapter and Chapters 6, 7, and 8 deal with the law on money laundering disclosure and how this law works in practice. It is a complex area of law. There are two distinct, but overlapping, disclosure regimes under Part 7 of the Proceeds of Crime Act 2002 (POCA); there are also, under the Terrorism Act 2000 (TA 2000), provisions for disclosure about terrorist money laundering and terrorist financing.

5.02 The purpose of money laundering disclosures[1] is not set out explicitly by the Financial Action Task Force (FATF) in its 40 Recommendations or in the Third Money Laundering Directive, but may broadly be summarized as follows:

- Disclosure to the national Financial Intelligence Unit (FIU) is the means by which a regulated sector institution provides the authorities with information

---

[1] In the FATF Recommendations this refers to the requirement for disclosures by persons working in financial and other institutions regulated for anti-money laundering purposes.

(criminal intelligence) about suspected money laundering and terrorist financing.
- The timely disclosure of suspicious transactions enables the authorities, where appropriate, to take action such as obtaining a restraint order over suspect funds.
- Disclosure contributes to the overall aim of combating the laundering of the proceeds of serious crime and combating the financing of terrorism.

The anti-money laundering measures, including disclosure, in the 40 Recommendations **5.03** have been adopted in most jurisdictions throughout the world and, since October 2001, their scope has been extended by 9 Special Recommendations to cover terrorist financing. The UK law on disclosure is intended to implement the disclosure provisions in the FATF Recommendations[2] and in the Third Money Laundering Directive,[3] but it also has important elements that are distinct from and additional to the provisions in these international instruments. Of these, perhaps the most distinctive are the provisions for 'authorised disclosure', combined with a request for consent to transact, as a means of avoiding criminal liability for committing the principal money laundering offences.

In the UK mutual evaluation report by FATF,[4] dated 29 June 2007, the UK was judged to be **5.04** compliant with the recommendations relating to disclosures by financial institutions and other regulated entities: Recommendation 13 (suspicious transaction reporting) and Recommendation 14 (protection and no tipping off).

B. Disclosures and 'SARs'

The terminology of disclosure

In international documents and in UK statutes and regulations, a number of different words **5.05** and terms are used for anti-money laundering and counter-terrorist financing disclosure. FATF uses the term 'suspicious transaction report' (STR); the EC Third Directive refers to 'disclosures of information'. In POCA and in TA 2000, the word 'disclosure' is used. The different words and phrases mean essentially the same thing: within Part 7 of POCA, however, the qualified terms for different types of disclosure, in particular 'required disclosures' and 'authorised disclosures', mean quite different things, and these differences are dealt with below.

In UK practice, 'suspicious activity report' or 'SAR' is the generic term for disclosures used **5.06** by the FIU at SOCA, and by law enforcement, regulators, and the regulated sector. SOCA also uses the term 'consent reports' for disclosures about criminal property combined with a request for consent.

---

[2] Recommendations 13 and 14.
[3] Directive 2005/60/EC of the European Parliament and of the Council of 26 October 2005 on the prevention of the use of the financial system for the purpose of money laundering and terrorist financing (referred to below as the 'Third Money Laundering Directive').
[4] Third Mutual Evaluation Report Anti-Money Laundering and Combating the Financing of Terrorism, the United Kingdom, <http://www.fatf-gafi.org/dataoecd/55/29/39064399.pdf>.

Disclosure and the recipients of disclosure

5.07   All roads lead to the FIU: in the statutory scheme for disclosures about money laundering and terrorist financing, the FIU at SOCA occupies a central position and role. All disclosures should end up in the hands of the FIU, whose function is to receive SARs and maintain a database of information derived from SARs and to analyse and disseminate this information to law enforcement agencies. This does not mean that all disclosures made to nominated officers must be passed to SOCA because nominated officers perform a valuable task in scrutinizing and filtering internal disclosures. It does, however, mean that all disclosures that should properly be made, either from need or obligation, should ultimately be received by the FIU, whether submitted directly by the originator of the report or indirectly.

5.08   Many disclosures are not, in fact, made to the FIU, and the class or classes of person to whom a disclosure may be made differs according to the type of disclosure. The recipients of disclosures under POCA are: a 'constable', a 'customs officer', the FIU at SOCA and a 'nominated officer'; and under TA 2000 are a 'constable', an 'authorised officer' and a 'nominated officer'.

- *Constable*: in Part 7 of POCA, references to a constable are to be interpreted as including references to a person authorized for the purposes of Part 7 by the Director General of SOCA (section 340(13)). Note that there are also disclosures made specifically to a person so authorized by the Director General of SOCA: required disclosures under sections 330, 331, and 332 (although under section 330 there is the option to disclose to a nominated officer).

  In Part III of TA 2000, and sections 38B and 39 in Part IV, the meaning of 'constable' varies from section to section. In sections 19, 20, 21A, and 21B, references to a constable include a reference to a member of staff of SOCA authorized ('for the purposes of this section') by the Director General of SOCA. However, in sections 21, 21C, and 21D, as well as in sections 38B and 39, constable means a police officer.

- *Customs officer*: this term now means an officer of HM Revenue & Customs.[5]

- *The FIU at SOCA*: in Part 7 of POCA, references to the FIU at SOCA as a recipient of disclosure are to '. . . a person authorised for the purposes of this Part by the Director General of SOCA'.

- *Nominated officer*: a nominated officer is a person nominated by a discloser's employer to receive disclosures under various sections of Part 7 of POCA and Part III of TA 2000.[6] Outside the confines of statute, nominated officers are usually called Money Laundering Reporting Officers (MLROs). In this work, the terms are used interchangeably. (The status and role of the nominated officer is considered in detail in Section G, at paragraphs 5.109 *et seq*.)

  In TA 2000, the situation is complicated by the fact that there are explicit references to disclosure to a 'nominated officer' only in the added sections 21A and 21B. Three original sections—19, 20, and 21—merely provide for disclosure in accordance with a procedure established by a person's employer. In practice, this must be taken to mean disclosure to a nominated officer.

---

[5] Commissioners of Revenue and Customs Act 2005, s 6.

[6] Note that for the purposes of a disclosure to a nominated officer, references to a person's employer include any body, association, or organization (including a voluntary organization) in connection with whose activities the person exercises a function (whether or not for gain or reward) (s 340(12)).

- *Authorised officer:* amendments to Part III of TA 2000 that came into force on 26 December 2007 brought with them a new term: 'authorised officer'. In sections 21ZA and 21ZB, authorised officer means a member of staff of SOCA 'authorised for the purposes of this section' by the Director General of SOCA.

Types of disclosure in POCA, Parts 7 and 8

The word 'disclosure' is used in a number of different ways in Part 7 of POCA,[7] together with Chapter 1 of Part 8, which includes offences of prejudicing an investigation under section 342. There are different types of lawful disclosure, normally made as internal disclosures to nominated officers or as disclosures to SOCA.[8] There are also unlawful disclosures and permitted disclosures to other persons—see paragraph 5.11 below. **5.09**

Lawful disclosures

Lawful disclosures about suspected money laundering may be disclosures made under a duty to disclose, from necessity or voluntarily. **5.10**

Named money laundering disclosures
- 'authorised disclosure', under section 338;
- 'required disclosure', under sections 330, 331, and 332;
- 'protected disclosure', under section 337. (See paragraphs 5.12 and 5.13 below on protection from liability for disclosers.)

Other money laundering disclosures
- a disclosure by a nominated officer about criminal property;[9]
- a disclosure to SOCA by a constable or customs officer under section 339ZA;
- also provided for in POCA, but not yet brought into force, is a disclosure made in pursuance of a request for further information under section 339(2).

For good measure, it should be noted that there is also, in section 330(9A), the disclosure that is not a disclosure—or is not to be treated as such. This is a disclosure by a professional legal adviser or relevant professional adviser to a nominated officer for the purpose of obtaining advice about making a money laundering disclosure under section 330 (see Chapter 6, paragraphs 6.39–6.46).

Unlawful and permitted disclosures

The money laundering disclosures above are all disclosures, directly or indirectly, to the UK FIU; the unlawful and permitted disclosures below are disclosures made to other persons. **5.11**

Unlawful disclosures
- A disclosure (tipping off about a money laundering disclosure) under section 333A(1);

---

[7] Note that, outside the SARs regime in Part 7 of POCA, there are also requirements in the Regulations for money laundering disclosures to be made by supervisory authorities (Reg 24(2)) and by specified public authorities (Reg 49(1)): see Chapter 10.

[8] Some lawful disclosures may also be made to police officers or customs officers, but in practice disclosures are now, almost invariably, made either to nominated officers or to SOCA.

[9] On the status of a disclosure about criminal property by a nominated officer, see Chapter 6 at paras 6.99–6.102.

- a disclosure (tipping off about a money laundering investigation) under section 333A(3);
- a disclosure (prejudicing an investigation) under section 342(2)(A).

Permitted disclosures

These are exceptions to the prohibition on disclosure in the tipping off provisions:

- a disclosure under section 333B—'Disclosures within an undertaking or group, etc';
- a disclosure under section 333C—'Other permitted disclosures between institutions, etc';
- a disclosure under section 333D—'Other permitted disclosures, etc'.

Protection from liability for disclosers

Protected disclosures

5.12   A protected disclosure is not really an additional type of disclosure but is a term that describes certain types of disclosure specified in section 337[10] and the protection given to disclosers who make any of those disclosures. In fact, other disclosures are also given the same protection, but this is contained within the relevant sections:

- required disclosures made under sections 330, 331 and 332—protected under section 337(1);
- certain voluntary disclosures—protected under section 337(1);
- authorised disclosures—protected under section 338(4).

In addition, if the form and manner of disclosures is at some future date prescribed by the Secretary of State under the power given in section 339(1), this protection will be extended, by section 339(4), to a supplementary disclosure, that is the provision of further information, on request, by a person who has made a disclosure.

5.13   All lawful disclosures under Part 7 of POCA are protected in the same way.[11] Whether protected under section 337 or otherwise, the disclosure 'is not to be taken to breach any restriction on the disclosure of information (however imposed)'.

Types of disclosure in TA 2000

5.14   In Part III of TA 2000, together with sections 38B and 39 in Part IV, the word 'disclosure' is used in a number of different ways. There are different types of lawful disclosure, which may be made as internal disclosures to nominated officers or as disclosures to SOCA or to a police officer. These are also unlawful disclosures and permitted disclosures to other persons.

Lawful money laundering and terrorist financing disclosures

5.15   There are three types of lawful disclosure about terrorist property:

- a required disclosure: although the term 'required disclosure' is not used in Parts III and IV of TA 2000, disclosures are required to be made under sections 19, 21A, and 21C, and under section 38B;

---

[10] Section 337 is considered in Chapter 6, paras 6.141–6.149.
[11] At least, it must have been intended that this is so. But it is not clear that disclosures about criminal property made by nominated officers to SOCA are protected: see Chapter 6, at para 6.148.

- a disclosure of involvement in a transaction or arrangement as a defence or to avoid criminal liability under sections 21, 21ZA, and 21ZB;
- a voluntary disclosure under section 20(1).

Protected disclosures

In TA 2000, there are 'protected disclosures' under section 21B. There are also the related provisions of section 20 'Disclosure of information: permission' (see Chapter 7, paragraphs 7.80–7.84) which contain provisions similar to the protection given under section 21B. **5.16**

Unlawful and permitted disclosures

The money laundering and terrorist financing disclosures above are all disclosures, directly or indirectly, to the UK FIU; the unlawful and permitted disclosures below are disclosures made to other persons. **5.17**

Unlawful disclosures
- a disclosure (tipping off about a money laundering or terrorist financing disclosure) under section 21D(1);
- a disclosure (tipping off about a terrorist property investigation) under section 21D(3);
- a disclosure (likely to prejudice a terrorist investigation) under section 39(2);
- a disclosure (about a money laundering or terrorist financing disclosure or a terrorist disclosure) under section 39(4)(a).

Permitted disclosures

As in Part 7 of POCA, these are exceptions to the prohibition on disclosures in the tipping off provisions:

- a disclosure under section 21E—'Disclosures within an undertaking or group, etc';
- a disclosure under section 21F—'Other permitted disclosures between institutions, etc';
- a disclosure under section 21G—'Other permitted disclosures, etc'.

Other related disclosures

The types of disclosures set out above relate to terrorist money laundering and terrorist financing. There are also disclosure provisions relating to acts of terrorism. These are outside the scope of this work except where the provisions relate to both acts of terrorism and terrorist property,[12] as they do in section 38B: **5.18**

- Disclosure of information about acts of terrorism (section 38B).

C. The Two Different Disclosure Regimes under POCA: Required and Authorised Disclosures

The provisions in Part 7 of POCA relating to the different kinds of lawful disclosure are complex and may best be understood as creating two different disclosure regimes. One regime implements international obligations and applies to the regulated sector a requirement to make disclosures about known or suspected money laundering—*required* **5.19**

---

[12] See Chapter 7, paras 7.43–7.52.

disclosures. The other regime, which applies to everyone subject to the criminal law, creates a need to make *authorised disclosures* about criminal property. It also creates a related need, in most cases where an authorised disclosure has to be made, to seek appropriate consent to deal in some way with the criminal property.

5.20   Most money laundering reports fall under either one or the other of these two regimes. In practice, the circumstances that give rise either to a requirement or to a need to make a disclosure will often overlap. The practical implications of this overlap are considered below.[13]

Characteristics of required disclosures

5.21   *A required disclosure* is a disclosure of the information or matter giving rise to knowledge or suspicion (or, under sections 330 and 331, reasonable grounds to know or suspect) that a person is engaged in money laundering. That is the essence of a required disclosure and the required information was not further specified in POCA as originally enacted. As amended by the Serious Organised Crime and Police Act 2005[14] (SOCPA), however, the information must include, if known, the identity of the suspected money launderer and the whereabouts of the laundered property.

5.22   Required disclosures fall to be made under three sections: 330, 331, and 332, and therefore in three different sets of circumstances, but the nature of the required disclosure is the same in each case. The key features of a required disclosure are:

- A required disclosure is primarily a disclosure about another person who is known or suspected to be engaged in money laundering.
- A required disclosure is made in response to an obligation and one that is backed by criminal sanctions.
- All disclosures that persons employed in the regulated sector and MLROs in the regulated sector are obliged to make are required disclosures, and most (but not all) required disclosures are made by those in the regulated sector.

5.23   The obligation to make a required disclosure extends beyond the regulated sector to include MLROs in institutions that do not conduct business that brings them within the regulated sector.

Characteristics of authorised disclosures

5.24   Authorised disclosures are made out of necessity, not in compliance with an obligation. They may be made by any person who is at risk of committing a principal money laundering offence and needs to take advantage of the defence or exception in subsection (2)(a) of each of the money laundering sections: sections 327, 328, and 329.

5.25   An authorised disclosure is a disclosure '. . . that property is criminal property' made by a person either before, during or after doing a prohibited act under section 327(1), 328(1), or 329(1). Generally, the disclosure will be made before doing the prohibited act and is coupled with a request for consent to do the prohibited act. For such a disclosure to qualify as authorized, it must comply with the terms of section 338(1): see paragraphs 6.106 and 6.108.

---

[13] See paras 5.62 and 5.63.
[14] Amendments inserted in POCA, ss 330, 331 and 332 by Serious Organised Crime and Police Act 2005, s 104.

The key features of an authorised disclosure are: **5.26**

- An authorised disclosure is a disclosure about criminal property and not, as such, about another person.
- There is no obligation placed on anyone to make an authorised disclosure.
- The reason for making an authorised disclosure is the need for a defence to one or more of the principal money laundering offences.
- Any person may need to make and may make an authorised disclosure; whether that person is employed in the regulated sector or not is irrelevant.

D. The SARs Regime: Structure and Purpose

The legal framework

The legal provisions for money laundering and terrorist financing disclosures impose obliga-   **5.27**
tions on those working in the regulated sector and, separately, create a need to make disclosures that applies to those inside and outside the regulated sector. Every one of these provisions
is backed by criminal offences carrying maximum sentences of imprisonment ranging
from 5 to 14 years.[15]

The primary legislation

There have been money laundering reporting provisions of some kind in UK law since   **5.28**
1986,[16] but Part 7 of POCA did much more than consolidate the disparate provisions in
earlier legislation for reporting the laundering of the proceeds of drug trafficking and of other
crime.[17] It greatly expanded both the requirement to disclose that was placed on those working in the regulated sector and the need to make disclosures as a defence to a money laundering offence. POCA and TA 2000, as amended, have extended the reach of anti-money
laundering law and have widened the range of circumstances in which money laundering
disclosures have to be made.

The secondary legislation

The Money Laundering Regulations 1993 created a regulated sector and gave structure to   **5.29**
the anti-money laundering measures, including disclosure, that were intended to prevent
and deter criminals from misusing the financial system to launder the proceeds of crime. The
regulated sector, originally confined to banks and financial services institutions (with the
notable exception of money service businesses[18]), was required to put in place and maintain
anti-money laundering systems, including customer due diligence measures and the reporting of suspicious transactions. The regulated sector was greatly expanded by the Money

---

[15] For tipping off and other *unlawful* disclosures, there are criminal offences with maximum sentences of imprisonment of two to five years.
[16] The Drug Trafficking Offences Act 1986, s 24(3).
[17] Criminal Justice Act 1988, as amended, and the Drug Trafficking Act 1994.
[18] Money service businesses were brought into the regulated sector for money laundering purposes by the Money Laundering Regulations 2001.

Laundering Regulations 2003[19] to include accountants, lawyers, estate agents, casino operators, and others.

Participants in the SARs regime

5.30 The three main participants are the reporting sector, the UK's Financial Intelligence Unit,
and the law enforcement agencies.

- *The reporting sector* consists of a large number of private sector organizations, mainly but
  not wholly regulated bodies, across a wide variety of businesses and professions. Within
  these organizations the nominated officer or MLRO has a critical role. (On the 'nominated officer', see Section G, paragraphs 5.109 *et seq.*)

  Note: The 'reporting sector' is wider than the 'regulated sector' because some required
  disclosures are made by MLROs in businesses outside the regulated sector and authorised
  disclosures may be made by anyone. In practice, most authorised disclosures (disclosures
  about criminal property) will be made by the regulated sector and almost all other authorised disclosures will be made by persons working in businesses outside the regulated sector.
  The reporting sector, therefore, consists mainly of companies and professional firms, large
  and small, as well as unincorporated businesses and sole traders.
- *The FIU* (now located within SOCA, but formerly part of the National Criminal
  Intelligence Service (NCIS)) is at the centre of the SARs regime and has the crucial role of
  receiving, analysing, and disseminating the information provided in SARs. It also has
  responsibility for giving appropriate consent following receipt of a disclosure about criminal property and request for consent to do a prohibited act.
- *The end-users* are those responsible for tackling money laundering and other financial and
  acquisitive crime: police forces, HM Revenue & Customs, and other law enforcement
  agencies.[20] They are also participants in the operation of the consent regime, and more
  than half of the decisions made on requests for consent are made by SOCA in conjunction
  with a law enforcement agency.

5.31 The law in Part 7 of POCA that relates to money laundering disclosures is primarily concerned with the making of reports, required and authorised disclosures, and with the process
and timetable for obtaining consent. It therefore deals largely with the role of the reporting
sector; to a lesser degree, it deals with the FIU in the context of the FIU's dealings with disclosers in connection with appropriate consent; but it does not deal at all with the role of the
end-users of SARs.[21]

---

[19] The regulated sector was further, but not greatly, expanded by the Money Laundering Regulation 2007.

[20] Annex F to the Suspicious Activity Reports Regime Annual Report 2010 (available on <http://www.soca
.gov.uk>) lists the 'Current End Users of SARs with "Direct" Access'. There are 55 police forces, six multi-
agency teams, nine law enforcement agencies, and six other bodies or organizations. The report notes that: 'The
SARs database is available to a small number of trained users within each organisation, not to an organisation
as a whole.'

[21] The policy and legislative emphasis was all on producing SARs: issues relating to the receipt, analysis, and
dissemination of SARs by the FIU and to the use of the resulting criminal intelligence by law enforcement agencies received less attention. For the practical result of this unbalanced approach, see the Review of the regime for
handling Suspicious Activity Reports, KMPG, July 2003.

Table 5.1 Suspicious activity reports and consent reports received by the FIU (at NCIS or SOCA) from 1999 to 2009

Year	Total SARs received by the FIU	'Consent reports' received by the FIU
1999	15,115	N/A
2000	18,447	N/A
2001	29,976	N/A
2002	56,023	N/A
2003	94,708	3,278
2004	143,638	15,110
2005	195,702	9,513
2006	213,561	9,674
2007	208,257	11,762
2008	221,466	13,677
2009	230,352	13,694

Suspicious activity reports: the statistics

From 1999 to 2009

Figures for the total number of SARs and for 'consent SARs' for the years 1999 to 2009   **5.32**
inclusive are set out above.[22] These figures relate partly to the period before Part 7 of POCA
was brought into force on 24 February 2003, but they also cover the whole period since then
up to the end of 2009, during which there have been numerous amendments to POCA and
TA 2000, as well as revised money laundering regulations.

Article33 of the Third Money Laundering Directive requires member states to maintain   **5.33**
comprehensive statistics on matters relevant to the effectiveness of their systems to combat
money laundering and terrorist financing. Since SOCA assumed responsibility for the FIU
early in 2006, the preparation and publication of detailed statistics on the SARs regime[23] has
improved greatly. Each year, SOCA publishes detailed SARs statistics in the Annual Report
of the SARs Regime Committee.

Total SARs received

All or almost all of the SARs for the years 1999 to 2002 would have come from the regulated   **5.34**
sector, which at that time, under the Money Laundering Regulations 1993, consisted of
banks and other financial services institutions. Since 24 February 2003, the total number of
SARs has included 'consent reports', not all of which are submitted by the regulated sector.
The total figures for SARs for 2004 and since reflect the fact that the Money Laundering

---

[22] The figures for the number of disclosures made to NCIS for the years 1999 to 2003 are taken from Hansard (written answer of 16 March 2004 on Suspicious Transaction Reports by Caroline Flint). Later figures, which relate in part to the period when NCIS was still responsible for the FIU, have been helpfully provided by SOCA.
[23] The SARs Annual Reports are published in November each year and contain statistics covering a 12-month period from October to September.

Regulations 2003, which came into force on 1 March 2004, greatly widened the regulated sector.

'Consent reports' received

5.35 Consent reports are disclosures about criminal property containing a request for consent to carry out a 'prohibited act'. They are not made in compliance with any requirement to report money laundering, but are made in response to a concern about potential liability for a serious criminal offence—one (or more) of the principal money laundering offences—and for the specific purpose of taking advantage of the defence or exception provided by the making of an authorised disclosure. Although anyone may need to make a consent report, it is probable that the great majority of consent reports are in fact made by people working in the regulated sector.

5.36 Since 24 February 2003, the total number of SARs has included 'consent reports' and they form a small but significant percentage of the total number of reports received by the FIU. By 2004 the number of consent reports had reached over 15,000 per year. The number of consent reports fell after the decision of the Court of Appeal in the case of *Bowman v Fels*,[24] which was given on 8 March 2005, but has since begun to rise again.

The FIU and law enforcement agencies: making use of SARs

5.37 In the period up to the end of 2005, the processing of all these reports was slow and inefficient, and little use was made by law enforcement agencies of this potentially valuable information in order to combat money laundering and acquisitive crime.[25] At that time, it could scarcely be said that there was any coherent system or a 'SARs regime' worthy of the name. This unsatisfactory and wasteful situation was recognized by the government with the appointment in 2005 of Sir Stephen Lander to conduct a review of the SARs regime.

The Lander review of the SARs regime

5.38 The key recommendation of the Lander report[26] was that SOCA, to which the FIU would be transferred from NCIS, should take overall responsibility for the working of the SARs regime. This was a brave and important recommendation because SOCA could only directly control the performance of the FIU and was taking on a responsibility for the performance of both the reporting sector and the end-users, whose performance it could seek to influence but could not directly control. The exercise of that overall responsibility demanded a new approach to the SARs regime and a reliance on co-operation between the participants in order to achieve common goals.

5.39 The implementation by SOCA of the Lander review has greatly improved the situation and made the SARs regime a reality: in particular, the nature and extent of the practical difficulties created by the consent regime have been markedly lessened by SOCA's implementation of the recommendations in the Lander report.

5.40 The performance of all participants in the SARs regime, as well as SOCA's discharge of its overall responsibility under Recommendation 1, is monitored by the SARs Regime

---

[24] [2005] EWCA Civ 226.

[25] Review of the regime for handling Suspicious Activity Reports, KPMG, July 2003.

[26] Commonly referred to as the Lander Report, the full title of the report is Review of the Suspicious Activity Reports Regime (The SARs Review), March 2006, <http://www.soca.gov.uk/downloads/SOCAtheSARsReview_FINAL_Web.pdf>.

Committee,[27] which exercises an independent oversight of the regime. The effective implementation by SOCA of the Lander recommendations has done much to unify and bring coherence to the SARs regime and to build the necessary co-operation between the participants.

The disclosure provisions: ends and means

The underlying purpose of SARs is to contribute criminal intelligence, that is, information **5.41** about suspected money launderers and criminal property, in order to help the law enforcement agencies to detect criminal activity, to recover the proceeds of crime and to combat money laundering and other acquisitive crime. POCA and the money laundering regulations provide the framework of anti-money laundering law that governs the operation of the SARs regime.

The money laundering disclosure provisions can only achieve their purpose and contribute **5.42** to tackling money laundering and serious crime if all participants in the SARs regime carry out their respective functions effectively. This requires that the necessary disclosures are made to SOCA; that they are entered into a database and analysed; that the information from SARs is disseminated as appropriate by SOCA and is made available to the law enforcement agency best able act on it; and that the police and other law enforcement agencies make effective use of the information from SARs.

Compliance by the private sector, which involves a massive commitment of resources, needs **5.43** to be matched by adequate resourcing in the public sector and, as importantly, a willingness on the part of the FIU and law enforcement agencies to accept new responsibilities and to develop a new working relationship with the sizeable part of the public that comprises the reporting sector.

The handling of SARs by the FIU and their analysis and dissemination to law enforcement **5.44** agencies has been much improved since 2006. The law enforcement agencies, which now have to report twice yearly on their use of SARs,[28] have taken steps to address the concern that inadequate use was being made of all the SARs information available to them. The Suspicious Activity Reports Regime Annual Report, 2008,[29] noted that: 'The assessment in last year's Annual Report was that use of SARs by law enforcement agencies was patchy with significant areas of weakness', but concluded '. . . that the use of SARs has increased to the extent that they are now an aspect of all law enforcement agencies' work'. Since then, that trend has continued and SARs are now routinely used in the prevention and detection of crime by police forces and other law enforcement agencies.

For the SARs regime to work well, each of the three main participants has not only to fulfil **5.45** its own function, but all three have to work co-operatively. The legal framework for the SARs regime in POCA seemed designed to impede rather than to foster co-operation, but with the implementation of the recommendations of the Lander review, the SARs regime is moving

---

[27] The SARs Regime Committee is a committee of the SOCA Board, whose membership is drawn from all three participants in the regime, as well as the Home Office, HM Treasury and the FSA. (See the Suspicious Activity Reports Regime Annual Reports for 2007 and 2008.)

[28] Lander Report, recommendation 16.

[29] Published by SOCA and available on the SOCA website at <http://www.soca.gov.uk/assessPublications/downloads/SAR-Annual-Report-08-pn.pdf>.

towards a more productive partnership approach to identifying, reporting, and tackling money laundering and acquisitive crime.

E. The SARs Regime in Practice

Internal reports

5.46   Almost all SARs, that is disclosures to the SOCA FIU, are made by MLROs after receiving and considering an internal disclosure, that is a disclosure by an individual working in the regulated sector or outside it but in an organization that has appointed an MLRO. The function of the MLRO is not to forward an internal disclosure but to consider it and to reach an independent decision, under section 331 or 332, on whether a disclosure to SOCA should be made. It is likely that many more internal disclosures, mainly required disclosures, are made than SARs,[30] particularly in the big retail banks.

5.47   The form and manner in which an internal disclosure is made is determined by the policy and practice of the business or other organization in which the internal discloser works; the content of the disclosure, however, must comply with the terms of the relevant section. Most internal disclosures will be 'required disclosures' and the content must comply with the requirements of section 330(5); 'authorised disclosures' must simply be disclosures '. . . that property is criminal property' in accordance with section 338(1)(a).

Suspicious activity reports

5.48   The term 'suspicious activity report' or 'SAR' is generally used for the reports made to SOCA and it applies to all types of money laundering disclosure under POCA, including 'consent reports',[31] and all types of money laundering and terrorist financing disclosure under the Terrorism Act 2000. Anyone may either need or want to make a SAR, but in practice the great majority of SARs will be made by MLROs in the regulated sector after they have received internal disclosures from persons employed in their organization.

5.49   There is no prescribed form for making SARs, but there is a standard form which can be downloaded from the SOCA website and completed online. The current modular SAR Online form is the report form for the whole regulated sector, but it still clearly shows (particularly in Module 3, which relates to banking transactions) its origins in the form originally devised for banks and the financial services industry under the 1993 Money Laundering Regulations.

5.50   Section 339 of POCA contains a power for the Secretary of State to prescribe the form in which a SAR is made to SOCA. A consultation paper on the proposals for a prescribed form was issued in 2007 by the Home Office, but it was decided after the consultation that, for the present, no prescribed form would be introduced. This was largely for the encouraging reason that SOCA's 'SAR Online' method of reporting was increasingly being used and the

---

[30] The total number of internal disclosures can only be roughly estimated, but it is likely to be much higher than the number of SARs, and may be more than 300,000 per year.

[31] See para 5.06 above on the use of this term.

percentage of reports made electronically had risen to over 90 per cent and was continuing to rise.[32]

SAR Online

SAR Online, which incorporates the SOCA preferred form, provides a convenient and prac-   **5.51**
tical way to report for anyone in the regulated sector and outside it. For the discloser, it also
has the advantage that submission of the SAR Online form automatically generates a receipt
by email which contains SOCA's allocated reference number for the report. Using SAR
Online avoids the inputting errors that are bound to occur when paper reports are processed
by the FIU and its increasing use has helped to improve the speed and efficiency of the SARs
system and to keep down SOCA's costs.

Improvements in the process of disclosure and the assistance given to disclosers by the FIU   **5.52**
have made disclosing easier even for those who only make reports occasionally. The procedure for using 'SAR Online' to make a report is now well signposted on the SOCA website[33]
and SOCA has a Financial Intelligence Helpdesk: telephone number 020 7238 8282. The
essential steps in the SAR Online process are set out below.

Registration

The necessary preliminary to making a report is for the reporter, usually a nominated officer,   **5.53**
to download the standard SAR form from the SOCA website and complete the source registration details in the first module of the form. This provides SOCA with identifying details
for the reporter and helps SOCA to communicate quickly and securely with the nominated
officer. The registration form needs only to be completed once unless it becomes necessary to
amend contact details.

Making required disclosures

Required disclosures are disclosures of knowledge or suspicion 'that another person is   **5.54**
engaged in money laundering'. As amended, the provisions relating to required disclosures[34]
now specifically require disclosure of information, if known, about the person laundering
money and the whereabouts of the laundered property.

When completing the SAR online report form, the key elements to be included, in as much   **5.55**
detail as is known, are the subject details (in Module 3 of the form), i.e. information about
the person suspected, and the reasons for suspicion (in Module 6). A third main element is
information about any transaction relating to suspected criminal property: this type of
information will normally feature in SARs from financial institutions, but will not always be
available. In the form, the reporter should, where possible, use the standard glossary terms
and search prefixes in the SARs Glossary of Terms[35] published by SOCA on its website.

Required disclosures to SOCA may be made under section 330 by any person in the regu-   **5.56**
lated sector, but in practice most required disclosures are made, under section 331, by

---

[32] See the Home Office document issued following the consultation on a prescribed form: 'The Proceeds of
Crime Act 2002: Tackling Money Laundering, Suspicious Activity Reports: Prescribed Form and Manner,
Summary of Responses to the Consultation Exercise and Next Steps'.
 [33] <http://www.soca.gov.uk/financialIntel/index.html>.
 [34] Disclosures made under ss 330, 331, and 332.
 [35] See the SAR Glossary of Terms (and search prefixes): <http://www.soca.gov.uk/about-soca/library/doc_
download/88-sars-glossary-of-terms.pdf>.

MLROs in the regulated sector. A smaller number of required disclosures may also be made, under section 332, by MLROs both within and outside the regulated sector.

5.57 There is no separate form for disclosures under TA 2000. Where a disclosure is made about a terrorist money laundering or terrorist property offence, this should be indicated in the 'Disclosure type' field on the form.

Making consent reports

5.58 An authorised disclosure under section 338 or a disclosure to SOCA by a MLRO resulting from an internal authorised disclosure is a disclosure about criminal property. Except in a few cases where a report is being made during or after doing the 'prohibited act', such a disclosure will need to include a request for consent to carry out a prohibited act.

5.59 Approximately 12,500 'consent reports', disclosures about criminal property with a request for appropriate consent, are made to SOCA each year, usually by nominated officers. The same SAR Online form is used as for required disclosures. As noted below, many consent reports about criminal property will also be required disclosures about a person suspected of money laundering.

5.60 In order to give the best chance of an early decision on consent from SOCA, the need for consent should be clearly flagged. The SAR form, on the first page of module two, contains a box marked 'Consent Required', that needs to be ticked. The consent report should clearly identify the money or other property that is said to be criminal property and the reason for suspecting that it is 'a person's benefit from criminal conduct'. It should also specify the proposed prohibited act(s) for which consent is sought.

5.61 Consent is often needed urgently and this is recognized by SOCA: 'All requests for appropriate consent are treated as a priority within SOCA.' So that the consent request is immediately identified, a reporter should mark the report form and use the 'Immediate Attention' search prefix for consent: XXS99XX, (which indicates 'Consent: SAR where the reporter is seeking appropriate consent under S335 of the Proceeds of Crime Act 2002.').

Dual purpose reports

5.62 Although in law, under Part 7 of POCA, there are two distinct reporting regimes with quite different characteristics (see paragraphs 5.19–5.26), the facts will in many cases create both a requirement to make a SAR under section 331 and the need to make a 'consent report' SAR. In practice, MLROs will not generally be concerned about the particular section or sections under which they make a disclosure, but will be concerned with the question of whether or not they need to request consent. The information giving rise to a suspicion that property is criminal property will, in all probability, also give rise to a suspicion that another person is engaged in money laundering, and include information about the identity of that person and the whereabouts of the criminal property. So a disclosure may well be both a required disclosure and an authorised disclosure about criminal property combined with a request for consent.

5.63 The circumstances of most required disclosures do not give rise to a need for consent, but the circumstances that make a consent report necessary will, almost always, also require a disclosure by the MLRO under section 331 or section 332. In practice, a single SAR is made that fulfils both the regulated sector disclosure obligation and the need for a consent report. Similarly, a MLRO who is a nominated officer outside the regulated sector may receive an internal disclosure which is both a voluntary protected disclosure and an authorised disclosure. Again, the MLRO would make a single SAR to the FIU at SOCA.

F. The Consent Regime

Where a person is intending to deal in some way with property, but suspects that the property or part of it is criminal property, that person needs to make an authorised disclosure before doing the 'prohibited act' and the disclosure needs to contain a request for appropriate consent.[36] An authorised disclosure will usually be made as an internal disclosure to a nominated officer. **5.64**

The legal framework, the process of requesting consent and the process by which actual or deemed consent is given or refused are often referred to together as the 'consent regime',[37] a subset of the SARs regime. (See Chapter 6 at paragraphs 6.122–6.140 for the statutory provisions relating to the consent regime in sections 335 and 336 of POCA.) **5.65**

The disclosure and request for consent
Who needs to make authorised disclosures?
The making of an authorised disclosure under section 338 can provide the means to take advantage of an exception or defence to the three principal money laundering offences. These offences may be committed by anyone (not just those working in the regulated sector), so the protection given by making an authorised disclosure and obtaining consent to transact may be needed by anyone. **5.66**

When is appropriate consent needed?
Whenever a person does a prohibited act in relation to criminal property, that person commits a money laundering offence unless he comes within one of the exceptions or defences in sub-section (2) of sections 327, 328, and 329. In most instances, the only available exception or defence will be disclosure plus consent, that is 'appropriate consent' obtained before the person carries out any transaction which would constitute a prohibited act. **5.67**

Consent to do what?
Consent is required to do a 'prohibited act': one of the acts set out in sub-section (1) of sections 327, 328, and 329. These acts cover just about every way of dealing with property and include acquisition, possession, and use, as well as concealing, disguising, and transferring property. In addition, there is the widely drafted offence of entering into or becoming concerned in a money laundering arrangement. **5.68**

How is consent obtained?
Most people who need—and recognize that they need—consent to do a prohibited act will do so in the course of working in a business or professional organization, probably one that is in the regulated sector. Most authorised disclosures, therefore, are made as internal disclosures to a nominated officer or MLRO and most consent reports to SOCA will be made by MLROs. **5.69**

---

[36] The relevant law is in subsection (2) of ss 327, 328, and 329, and in s 338: see Chapter 6, paras 6.103–6.108.
[37] See the Home Office consultation document on the consent regime: 'Obligations to Report Money Laundering: The Consent Regime'.

5.70 In practice, therefore, most consent reports to SOCA will be made by the regulated sector or by companies or firms outside the regulated sector that have nevertheless appointed a 'nominated officer'. It will be the MLRO who receives an internal authorised disclosure and decides whether it is necessary to make a disclosure about criminal property to SOCA and seek appropriate consent from SOCA. If the MLRO decides that a consent report should be made, the disclosure will normally be made using SAR Online. (See above at paragraphs 5.51 *et seq.*)

5.71 Subject to any later discussion with SOCA and consequent amendment, the nature of both the criminal property and the prohibited act for which consent may be given is set out in the SAR. Consent is more likely to be given where the property and the intended prohibited act are clearly identified and described, and where information about the circumstances and the purpose of a proposed transaction is set out in the SAR so that, for instance, SOCA may be able to decide quickly that no useful purpose would be served by refusing consent. (Note that as well as actual consent given by SOCA there are provisions for deemed consent: see below at paragraphs 6.124 *et seq.*)

From whom is consent obtained?

5.72 The internal discloser, the 'alleged offender'[38] who actually needs consent to carry out some transaction, will usually make a disclosure to and seek consent from a nominated officer. But the nominated officer cannot give consent unless and until he has made a consent report to SOCA and has obtained consent. In practice, it will almost always be the nominated officer who obtains consent from the FIU at SOCA. In most cases, the consent decision will be made by SOCA in conjunction with a law enforcement agency, usually a police force or HMRC.

5.73 If consent is given by SOCA, the MLRO can give consent to the person who really needs it. That person can then carry out the transaction which had been specified in the disclosure to SOCA. It is important to note exactly what the terms of the appropriate consent cover. They will be defined by the terms of the request contained in the disclosure unless, when giving consent, SOCA revises them. If any other action involving the suspected criminal property is contemplated, it would be necessary to consider whether that would involve a further prohibited act for which a new consent would be needed.

How long does it take to obtain a decision?

5.74 The day-to-day handling of consent requests has been much improved in recent years. In a number of cases, SOCA will be able to make the decision to grant consent itself and this can often be done very quickly. Where the report and request needs to be referred to a police force or other law enforcement agency, the decision whether to grant or refuse consent will take longer. The FIU has committed itself to responding to consent requests as soon as practicable and the SARs Regime Report [39] published in November 2010 summarizes the position on 'turnaround times' as follows: 'On average 30.7% of all consent requests (both those dealt with only by SOCA and those referred to other law enforcement agencies) were turned around on the day of receipt or the following day (day 0 or day 1). 54.3% were turned around on days 0, 1 or 2. The average turnaround time for responding to consent requests was 2.8 days.'

---

[38] An inappropriate choice of words (see para 6.107), but this is the term used in s 338 for a person who makes an authorised disclosure.

[39] See pp 14 and 15 of the report which gives information about and statistics on the consent provisions of POCA.

How is the decision to give or refuse consent notified?

Whether the decision is made by the FIU itself or in conjunction with one of the law **5.75** enforcement agencies, the FIU at SOCA is responsible for responding to the request for consent. They will inform the reporter of the consent decision by telephone, confirming it in writing. Where consent is given, the SOCA website makes it clear that reporters do not need to wait for written consent before they can do the 'prohibited act' for which consent was sought.

After the consent report is made

The consent procedure under sections 335 and 336 puts into the hands of SOCA and the law **5.76** enforcement agencies a power to intervene, refuse consent, and prevent any financial or property transaction involving suspected criminal property from going ahead for up to about six weeks. This is an extraordinary power to be exercised by police officers and other law enforcement officers, without judicial authority or even a requirement for decisions to be made by designated senior officers.

Although for property to be criminal property it must have been obtained through criminal **5.77** conduct, disclosures to SOCA about criminal property have to be made on the basis of nothing more than suspicion. It may turn out that the suspicion is unfounded and the property is not in fact criminal property, but as Hamblen J noted in *Shah and another v HSBC Private Bank (UK) Ltd*:[40] 'If a bank has a suspicion it must seek appropriate consent and the means of doing so is by making an authorised disclosure under section 338 . At the time of so doing the bank cannot know whether or not criminal property is involved, but that makes no difference to the disclosure/consent regime to be followed.'

Once a 'consent report' has been made to SOCA, the proposed transaction will be effectively **5.78** blocked for seven working days unless SOCA grants consent at some point before the expiry of the notice period. If appropriate consent is refused, the proposed transaction, and often other linked transactions or the operation of a bank account, will be, in effect, frozen without any order from a court. This continues for the length of the moratorium period—a further 31 calendar days, unless SOCA grants consent during that period.

The grant or refusal of consent

What are the possible outcomes?

There are three possible outcomes following a request for consent: **5.79**

- Actual consent may be given.
- Consent may be refused within seven working days, followed, perhaps, by law enforcement action such as an application for a restraint order.
- Deemed consent is obtained after lapse of time, that is:
  - — if consent is not refused, after expiry of the 'notice period' of seven working days; or
  - — if consent is refused, after expiry of the 'moratorium period' of 31 (calendar) days.

The position where consent is refused

The law in POCA and TA 2000 sets the timescales of the notice period and the moratorium **5.80** period, but makes no requirements on SOCA and law enforcement agencies about how they

---

[40] [2009] EWHC 79 (QB).

should exercise the power over financial and business transactions that they possess through refusal of consent. No criteria governing the exercise of the discretion to refuse consent were published until the Home Office Circular 29/2008 was issued (see below).

5.81 The absence of criteria governing the exercise of the discretion to refuse consent fuelled concerns in the reporting sector and in the judiciary about the potential for '. . . the arbitrary and capricious exercise of power . . . ',[41] whether by SOCA or by a law enforcement agency. This issue was considered by the Court of Appeal in *R (on the application of UMBS Online Ltd) v Serious Organised Crime Agency*.[42] Ward LJ noted that: 'As matters stood at the time of the first hearing before us there were no published criteria for checking whether or not SOCA were acting lawfully. Their inner workings were totally lacking transparency.'

Review of decisions to refuse consent

5.82 Many consent reports are made in circumstances where the transactions for which consent is sought are imminent and where any delay may seriously affect the interests of the relevant customer or client and, perhaps, of third parties. SOCA aims to make consent decisions as quickly as is practicable, but where consent is refused the practical problems and the urgency do not go away once the decision is made. The harmful consequences of the refusal of consent may begin to occur immediately and may be exacerbated by every day that passes. There is a real need for the decision to refuse consent to be kept under review and reassessed in the light of any relevant new information.

5.83 The need for review and the related question of what should prompt a review by SOCA came before the Court of Appeal in the *UMBS Online Ltd* case. In his judgment, Ward LJ said:

> Since it is accepted by SOCA that they must keep the matter under review, they must give the bank consent when there is no longer any good reason for withholding it. They can and must act independently of a request from anybody. Nothing in the Act requires the potential offender under section 328 to be responsible, and the only one responsible, for seeking a review of the refusal of consent. A request from the person directly affected by the freezing of the account must trigger the duty to look at the matter again.

5.84 Those whose interests may be seriously harmed by the continued refusal of consent to transact are the customers and third parties, not the banks or other organizations that make the consent reports:

> It is absurd for SOCA to suggest that they can only act on a request from the bank. The bank may no longer be interested in the matter. The bank has done its duty by reporting its suspicion and now it may simply sit on its hands and take care not to operate the account until the expiry of the moratorium. It is not directly affected but its customer is and the customers of the customer are. They are entitled to ask SOCA to review the matter and SOCA are obliged to do so. In my judgment the second reason given by SOCA for refusing to revisit the matter was erroneous in point of law.

For what reason(s) can consent be refused?

5.85 In law, the power to refuse consent is unfettered. It is subject to no qualification or restriction other than the statutory time limits. Although refusal of consent can too easily cause serious

---

[41] Judge Norris QC in *New Bridge Holdings & Enjien Ltd v Barclays Bank* [2006] EWHC 3773 (Ch), quoted by Longmore LJ in *K Ltd v National Westminster Bank Plc* [2006] EWCA Civ 1039.
[42] [2007] WL 1292620 (CA (Civ Div)), [2007] EWCA Civ 375.

harm to the rights and interests of companies and individuals, no provision was made in POCA or in subordinate legislation or in a Code of Practice to prevent the inappropriate and arbitrary refusal of consent. There was no requirement, for instance, that there should be reasonable grounds for refusal of consent or that the person refusing consent should consider in any way the consequences of refusal either to suspected persons or to third parties.

As Ward LJ observed in the *UMBS Online Ltd* case: **5.86**

> If the proper balance is to be struck between undue interference with personal liberties and the need constantly to fight crime, then the least that can be demanded of SOCA is that they do not withhold consent without good reason.

This situation was radically unsatisfactory, the more so because of the lack of judicial over-   **5.87**
sight of the way that the consent regime operated: see the comments of Sedley LJ in the *UMBS Online Ltd* case:

> In setting up the Serious Organised Crime Agency, the state has set out to create an Alsatia—a region of executive action free of judicial over-sight. Although the statutory powers can intrude heavily, and sometimes ruinously, into civil rights and obligations, the supervisory role which the court would otherwise have is limited by its primary obligation to give effect to Parliament's clearly expressed intentions.

SOCA recognized that this position was untenable and developed guidelines for the respon-   **5.88**
sible exercise by its own staff of the power to refuse consent. While it could commend those guidelines to the law enforcement agencies that make recommendations to SOCA and, effectively, make most consent decisions, it had no power to ensure that they were applied by them.

The Home Office circular

In late 2008, the Home Office issued a circular[43] which incorporates guidance on the criteria   **5.89**
to be applied when considering whether appropriate consent should be given or refused. These are contained in a 'Consent Policy', at Annex A to the circular. It is intended that the guidance in the Consent Policy should be followed by all law enforcement agencies, with the aim of achieving a consistent approach to dealing with requests for consent.

The key issue of the balancing of interests and of decision-makers giving due weight to pri-   **5.90**
vate rights is dealt with in the Consent Policy under the heading of Proportionality:

> Proportionality: However, decisions on whether to grant or refuse consent, including the formation of recommendations by LEAs, are also informed by the need to balance the public interest of the impact on crime with other interests. This includes the private rights of those involved in the activity which is subject to the consent request, and those of the reporter. All parties may have contractual and/or property rights which may be affected by a refusal of consent. Officers should also bear in mind the practical implications for these parties. If the case does not prove to involve money laundering a decision to refuse consent will cause a legitimate transaction to be frustrated. The results of this might include:
> - significant financial loss,
> - a legitimate business might cease trading; or
> - severe financial or personal consequences to an individual (for example if [it] concerns the purchase of residential property).

---

[43] Home Office circular 029/2008, 'The Proceeds of Crime Act 2002: obligations to report money launder-ing—the consent regime'. (Implementation date: 5 December 2008.)

> The result of such a balancing of interests is that, *in the majority of cases*, consent should only be refused when a criminal investigation with a view to bringing restraint proceedings is likely to follow or is already under way. However consent may be refused for other reasons (for example, to permit an application for a property freezing order) subject to the outcome of the same balancing exercise.

5.91 This is a welcome, if long overdue, statement. It is, however, a statement of policy couched in fairly general terms and does not attempt to provide detailed practical guidance. It will be the responsibility of each law enforcement agency to ensure that individual officers making recommendations[44] to SOCA apply this policy. It remains to be seen whether, in the absence of detailed guidance, the quality and consistency of decisions to grant or refuse consent improve and whether, in future, the decisions properly reflect the spirit as well as the letter of the Consent Policy.

Banks and their customers: a conflict of duties

5.92 Compliance by banks with the law on authorised disclosure and the operation of the consent regime can often cause conflict with the interests of the banks' customers and with instructions received from their customers. This conflict creates a situation of constant difficulty for banks; for some of their customers at least, it causes significant hardship (as, on occasions, it does for the customers' customers and other third parties).

5.93 Banks, particularly the major retail banks, process an enormous number of financial transactions every day. The banking sector provides about 78 per cent of all SARs and about 50 per cent of consent SARs[45] and research has shown that 52 per cent of all SARs are submitted by four banks (which hold 83 per cent of all current accounts in the UK).[46]

5.94 The customer's expectation for immediacy and speed—that its bank will, as soon as practicable, carry out its instructions, e.g. to transfer money to another bank—allows no time for the bank to resolve any queries before a decision is made (even where the bank is not inhibited from doing so by concerns about possible tipping off).

5.95 Where a bank suspects that funds in a customer's account are or include criminal property and the customer is requesting a transfer of money to another bank, there is a conflict between the contractual duty that the bank owes to its customer and the bank's need to comply with the effective requirements of the reporting and consent regime. Although sympathetic to the plight of customers affected, the courts have recognized that there can only be one way to resolve the conflict.

5.96 *In Squirrell Ltd v National Westminster Bank Plc*, HM Customs and Excise,[47] the company sought an order that its accounts be unfrozen so that the bank could honour its mandate and transfer money as instructed by Squirrell Ltd. The bank had a relevant suspicion of money laundering under section 328 and made an authorised disclosure. In effect, the action of the bank had frozen Squirrell Ltd's bank account. The court considered the

---

[44] For the decision-making process and the relationship between SOCA and other law enforcement agencies, see para 5 of the circular and para 3 of Annex A.

[45] The SARs statistics are taken from the SARs Regime Annual Report 2010.

[46] In the SARs Regime Annual Report 2010, the source of these latter figures is given as the British Bankers Association.

[47] *Squirrell Ltd v National Westminster Bank Plc, HM Customs and Excise*, [2005] EWHC 664.

application of the 'authorised disclosure' and 'appropriate consent' provisions and concluded that:

> The combined effect of these provisions is to force a party in Natwest's position to report its suspicions to the relevant authorities and not to move suspect funds or property either for 7 working days or, if a notice of refusal is sent by the relevant authority, for a maximum of 7 working plus 31 calendar days. Furthermore the anti–tip off provisions of s 338 of POCA prohibit the party from making any disclosure which is likely to prejudice any investigation which might be conducted following an authorised disclosure under s 338.[48]

In his judgment, Laddie J went on to say: **5.97**

> In my view the course adopted by Natwest was unimpeachable. It did precisely what this legislation intended it to do. In the circumstances there can be no question of me ordering it to operate the account in accordance with Squirrell's instructions. To do so would be to require it to commit a criminal offence. Even if I had power to do that, which I doubt, it could not be a proper exercise of my discretion. Sympathy for the position in which Squirrell finds itself do not override those considerations.[49]

The decision in *Squirrell Ltd* was followed in 2006 in the case of *K Ltd v National Westminster* **5.98**
Bank Plc.[50] In that case, Longmore LJ confirmed the way that banks must respond to this conflict:

> There can be no doubt that, if a banker knows or suspects that money in a customer's account is criminal property and, without making disclosure or without authorised consent (if disclosure is made), he processes a customer's cheque in such a way as to transfer that money into the account of another person, he facilitates the use or control of that criminal property and thus commits an offence under section 328 of the 2002 Act. It would be no defence to a charge under that section that the Bank was contractually obliged to obey its customer's instructions.
>
> If the law of the land makes it a criminal offence to honour the customer's mandate in these circumstances there can, in my judgment, be no breach of contract for the Bank to refuse to honour its mandate.[51]

On that central issue the law is settled, and settled in favour of the banks. It enables the banks **5.99**
and the nominated officers of banks to take advantage of the authorised disclosure exception and avoid criminal liability for an offence of money laundering. It does so, necessarily, at the expense of the interests of customers, whose instructions can, in these circumstances, be ignored or overridden with impunity. There are, however, related issues where the voice of the customer has, in recent cases, been heard and listened to. Neither the bank nor SOCA— the upper and the nether mill stones between which the customer is ground down—has entirely had its own way.

The bank's suspicion

Where a bank makes an 'authorised disclosure' in respect of a suspicion about criminal prop- **5.100**
erty, it will generally be a nominated officer who makes the relevant disclosure to the FIU at SOCA.[52] That suspicion is a subjective suspicion of the nominated officer. There is no requirement that it should be a 'reasonable' suspicion and this severely limits the grounds on

---

[48] *Squirrell Ltd* at para 18.
[49] Ibid., at para 21.
[50] *K Ltd v National Westminster Bank Plc* [2006] EWCA Civ 1039.
[51] *K Ltd* at paras 9 and 10.
[52] See Chapter 6, paras 6.99–6.102.

which a customer can attack the decision to make a disclosure. The question considered by the Court of Appeal in *Jayesh Shah, Shaleetha Mahabeer v HSBC Private Bank (UK) Limited*[53] was: where a bank claims that it acted properly in making a disclosure on the basis of a suspicion that the customer's funds were criminal property, is that claim or assertion 'justiciable' at all?

5.101 Yes, said the Court of Appeal (in the judgment of Longmore LJ) insofar as the customer can require the bank to prove its case that it had the relevant suspicion.

5.102 The court rejected a submission made on behalf of the bank that, in effect, the bank had only to put in evidence the fact that it had the relevant suspicion. Longmore LJ noted that: 'It must be remembered that it is for the bank to prove that it suspected Mr Shah to be involved in money-laundering', and later commented that: 'Accepting Mr Lissack's submission at this summary stage would, in effect, be giving carte blanche to every bank to decline to execute their customer's instructions without any court investigation.'[54]

5.103 A further submission on behalf of the bank was made that '. . . no court would (or should) order disclosure of any relevant documents particularly the documents reporting the bank's suspicions to SOCA (or whatever authority it was to which they did report)'. Longmore LJ went on to say: 'This amounts to saying that the dispute is completely unjusticiable and that, therefore, the bank must win.'[55]

5.104 The response of the Court of Appeal to this unattractive submission is given in the succeeding paragraph of Longmore LJ's judgment, which provides a balanced summary of the present state of this contentious aspect of anti-money laundering law:

> One appreciates, of course, that the 2002 Act has put banks in a most unenviable position. They are at risk of criminal prosecution if they entertain suspicions but do not report them or, if they report them, and then nevertheless carry out their customer's instructions without authorisation. If they act as instructed, their customers are likely to become incensed and some of those so incensed may begin litigation. But it cannot be right that proper litigation should be summarily dismissed without any appropriate inquiry of any kind. The normal procedures of the court are not to be side-stepped merely because Parliament has enacted stringent measures to inhibit the notorious evil of money-laundering, unless there is express statutory provision to that effect. In R (UBMS) v SOCA[56] Sedley LJ said (para 58) that, in setting SOCA up, the state had set out to create an Alsatia which he defined, in terms now adopted by no less an institution than Wikipedia, as:-
>
> > 'a region of executive action free of judicial oversight.'
>
> This appeal shows that there is at least, some judicial oversight in as much as there should, at least, not be summary judgment at this stage.[57]

The bank, its customer, and SOCA

5.105 The *UMBS Online*[58] case to which Longmore LJ refers in the passage quoted above is the leading case on the relationship of the SOCA FIU to both the bank and its customers and,

---

[53] *Jayesh Shah, Shaleetha Mahabeer v HSBC Private Bank (UK) Limited* [2010] EWCA Civ 31.
[54] Ibid. at paras 24 and 30.
[55] Ibid. at para 31.
[56] Sic: the correct name of the company is UMBS Online Ltd.
[57] *Shah* at para 32.
[58] See above at para 5.81 and note 43.

by extension, to all those who either make consent reports to SOCA or are the subject of such reports.

The starting point is that once an authorised disclosure has been made and consent has been **5.106** refused by SOCA: 'No one may deal with the suspect account and . . . the reality is that the account is frozen and there is precious little the customer, and his customers, can do about it.'[59] The courts will not interfere with SOCA's lawful decision to withhold 'appropriate consent', but the *UMBS* case establishes the important principle that SOCA should not withhold consent without good reason and the corollary that a refusal of consent must be kept under review so that if and when the reason for refusal is no longer valid consent must then be given.

In his judgment, Ward LJ said that: **5.107**

> SOCA is an immensely powerful statutory body whose decisions have the consequence of imperilling private and business banking activity based, initially at least, on no more than a reported suspicion of money laundering. If the proper balance is to be struck between undue interference with personal liberties and the need constantly to fight crime, then the least that can be demanded of SOCA is that they do not withhold consent without good reason.[60]

The court recognized that interference with the bank mandate by the action of SOCA in refus- **5.108** ing consent represents a serious interference with a customer's affairs that may cause significant harm and real injustice. Parliament had given to SOCA this power to intervene, but the power was time-limited and had to be exercised responsibly.[61]

G. The Role of the Nominated Officer

The legal basis

In the UK law on money laundering and terrorist financing, the MLRO has a central role. **5.109** This owes little to either FATF Recommendation 13,[62] which is directed at regulated institutions not at individuals, or to Article 22 of the EC Third Money Laundering Directive. In fact, there is nowhere in the primary legislation where the nominated officer's role is set out and the nature and scope of the nominated officer's reporting obligations are described.

Responsibilities of nominated officers in relation to disclosure

The responsibilities of nominated officers in dealing with disclosures appear, explicitly or **5.110** implicitly, in a number of offence-creating and other sections in the two pieces of primary legislation: POCA and TA 2000. These responsibilities differ according to whether they are inside or outside the regulated sector and are, therefore, set out in separate tables. Where an organization conducts both regulated and non-regulated business, the specific responsibilities that apply depend on whether the relevant internal disclosure is or is not based on information arising during the course of regulated sector business.

---

[59] *UMBS Online* at para 5.
[60] Ibid. at para 36.
[61] On the *UMBS Online case* and the requirement for SOCA to keep under review any refusal of consent, see paras 5.79–5.88 above.
[62] Recommendation 13. If a financial institution suspects or has reasonable grounds to suspect that funds are the proceeds of a criminal activity, or are related to terrorist financing, it should be required, directly by law or regulation, to report promptly its suspicions to the financial intelligence unit (FIU).

Nominated officers in the regulated sector

5.111 The disclosure responsibilities of nominated officers in the regulated sector under POCA and under TA 2000 are set out below:

Table 5.2 Disclosure responsibilities of nominated officers in the regulated sector

Proceeds of Crime Act 2002	
Section 331	Considering *required* disclosures under section 330
Section 330(9A)	Advising a professional legal adviser or relevant professional adviser about a potential disclosure in accordance with section 330(9A)
Section 332 Sections 335(9) and 336(11)	Considering *authorised* disclosures under section 338 and dealing with consent issues
Section 332	Considering protected disclosures under section 337
Terrorism Act 2000	
Section 20(4)(b)	Considering voluntary protected disclosures under section 20
Section 21(6)	Considering disclosures under section 21
Section 21A(7)	Considering obligatory disclosures under section 21A
Section 21B(5)	Considering protected disclosures under section 21

Nominated officers outside the regulated sector

5.112 The disclosure responsibilities of nominated officers outside the regulated sector under POCA and under TA 2000 are set out below:

Table 5.3 Disclosure responsibilities of nominated officers outside the regulated sector

Proceeds of Crime Act 2002	
Section 332 Sections 335 (9) and 336 (11)	Considering *authorised* disclosures under section 338 and dealing with consent issues
Section 332	Considering voluntary protected disclosures under section 337
Terrorism Act 2000	
Section 19(4)	Considering obligatory disclosures under section 19
Section 20(4)(b)	Considering voluntary protected disclosures under section 20
Section 21(6)	Considering disclosures under section 21
Section 21B (5)	Considering protected disclosures under Section 21

Appointment and functions of nominated officers under the Regulations

5.113 The job of the nominated officer is a difficult and demanding one, and both regulators and industry bodies emphasize the need for nominated officers to be sufficiently senior in the organizations in which they work for them to influence policies and for their decisions to be respected.[63] They need also to be well trained and to be unequivocally supported by senior management.

---

[63] See, for instance, within the FSA Handbook, Senior Management Arrangements, Systems and Controls, especially SYSC 6.1 Compliance and SYSC 6.3 Financial crime. See also the JMLSG Guidance for the

Regulation 20(1) requires regulated sector institutions to establish and maintain risk-sensitive anti-money laundering policies and procedures. The policies and procedures that relate to reporting are set out in Regulation 20(2)(d). They provide for an individual in the organization to be a nominated officer under Part 7 of the Proceeds of Crime Act 2002 and Part 3 of the Terrorism Act 2000 and for persons in the organization who suspect money laundering or terrorist financing to comply with the statutory disclosure requirements. **5.114**

The clearest statement of the purpose and function of the 'nominated officer' (in the regulated sector) is contained in Regulation 20 of the Money Laundering Regulations 2007, under the general heading of 'Policies and procedures'. Regulation 20(2)(d)(iii) provides that: '. . . where a disclosure is made to the nominated officer, he must consider it in the light of any relevant information which is available to the relevant person and determine whether it gives rise to knowledge or suspicion or reasonable grounds for knowledge or suspicion that a person is engaged in money laundering or terrorist financing'. **5.115**

This statement of the nominated officer's responsibility in relation to disclosures does not cover all of the types of report that a nominated officer may receive, nor does it apply to all nominated officers. From the way that it is worded, Regulation 20(2)(d) appears to relate to required disclosures, but not to authorised disclosures. Also, it does not apply, other than by analogy, to nominated officers outside the regulated sector, whose appointment is made voluntarily by their employers. **5.116**

Responsibilities of the nominated officer

In practice, MLROs usually have a number of other anti-money laundering and compliance responsibilities, but central to their role is the reporting responsibility as 'nominated officer': as such, they are subject to specific statutory obligations which are backed by criminal penalties for non-compliance. Note that a MLRO may well be a nominated officer under both sections 331 and 332, if he works for an institution that conducts both regulated and non-regulated business. **5.117**

Around 200,000 disclosures a year are made to SOCA and the great majority of those are made by nominated officers after receiving and considering internal disclosures. The internal disclosure to the nominated officer fulfils any obligation on the part of the person in the regulated sector who initially suspects that a person is engaged in money laundering and/or satisfies the need of a person to make an authorised disclosure to take advantage of a defence to one of the money laundering offences. **5.118**

Considering internal disclosures

Most SARs, particularly those made by the banks and financial services institutions, are required disclosures made in compliance with regulated sector obligations. The main function of an MLRO in the regulated sector is to consider and act on these internal required disclosures. However, the more complex and challenging responsibility for all nominated officers is that of dealing with authorised disclosures and the procedures relating to consent to do a prohibited act.[64] This responsibility carries with it greater risks for the MLRO of falling foul of the criminal law. **5.119**

UK Financial Sector, Part 1, (December 2007), Chapters 1 to 3, especially 'Standing of the MLRO' at paras 3.7–3.16.

[64] See Section F above, at paras 5.64 *et seq.*, on the 'consent regime'.

5.120   Unless there is a suspicion of terrorist financing, the concern of the nominated officer will be with one or both of two questions:

- Having considered the internal disclosure, do I know or suspect, or do I have reasonable grounds for knowing or suspecting, that another person is engaged in money laundering?
- In the case of an authorised disclosure, is the relevant property 'criminal property', i.e. is the property, with which the internal discloser is proposing to deal in some way, property that I know or suspect was obtained through criminal conduct?

5.121   If the answer to the first question is yes, the nominated officer is obliged to make a required disclosure to SOCA (unless he can neither identify the money launderer nor the location of the laundered property). If the answer to the second question is yes, the nominated officer needs to make a disclosure to SOCA that property is criminal property.

5.122   The factual circumstances may lead the nominated officer to answer yes to both questions. If so, a single disclosure will be made to SOCA. Assuming the disclosure is made before any prohibited act, the 'consent report' will be made in which the information given would identify the *property* suspected and what transaction is intended in respect of which consent is required and would also identify the *other person* suspected of being engaged in money laundering. Note that, despite the pejorative use of the term 'alleged offender' in the statute, the internal discloser is not an 'other person' under sections 330 or 331. (See paragraph 6.39 in Chapter 6.)

Authorised disclosures and appropriate consent

5.123   If the nominated officer considers an internal authorised disclosure and determines that disclosure is necessary, he should make a disclosure about the criminal property to SOCA. In most cases, the authorised disclosure will have been made to the nominated officer before the prohibited act is carried out and the discloser will require appropriate consent. The nominated officer will therefore need also to seek consent for the discloser (that is the person who made the internal disclosure) to do a prohibited act.

5.124   Thereafter, the nominated officer is responsible for giving appropriate consent to the discloser but only when actual consent has been given by SOCA or when one of the conditions in section 336(3) and 336(4) is fulfilled under which it is deemed that appropriate consent has been given. Dealing with authorised disclosures and requests for consent is a heavy responsibility for nominated officers and one that is made more difficult and stressful by the constraints, real and perceived,[65] of the tipping off offences.

Risk and responsibility: the decision to disclose to SOCA

5.125   The nominated officer is not an agent of the internal discloser nor is he simply the conduit through which a disclosure is passed on to SOCA.[66] In UK law, the responsibilities of the original discloser and the responsibilities of the nominated officer to whom an internal disclosure is made are separate and distinct.

---

[65] See Chapter 8 at paras 8.16–8.22.

[66] But note the position under ss 21ZA and 21ZB where no specific provision is made for disclosure to a nominated officer.

A defensive attitude to reporting is encouraged by the criminal penalties attached to failure **5.126** to make a required disclosure and by the fact that, in the course of conducting ordinary business such as a banking transaction, a person may commit a principal money laundering offence simply by failing to act on a suspicion and make an authorised disclosure. In the words of Hamblen J in the *Shah and another v HSBC Private Bank (UK) Ltd* case:[67] 'Under POCA the mere fact of suspicion is the trigger for an authorised disclosure to be made.'

A person who is employed in any organization that has a nominated officer and who is con- **5.127** sidering whether they need to make a disclosure might, therefore, make the disclosure to the nominated officer in order to remove any risk to themselves. Such an approach—'if in doubt, disclose'—may be understandable for internal disclosers,[68] but the nominated officer should make a considered decision on the information available and with an awareness of the potential consequences of a disclosure to SOCA.

The responsibility of the nominated officer to make a judgement to the best of his ability on **5.128** the known facts is particularly important in relation to disclosures about criminal property. To make a consent report is to create the potential for delay and interference with business and brings with it the very real possibility of serious harm to the rights and interests of suspected persons (who may be innocent of any criminality) and of third parties.

Nominated officers need also to bear in mind that the protection from liability afforded to **5.129** disclosers under POCA and under TA 2000 may not cover a disclosure made where there was no proper factual basis for disclosure or the law was wrongly applied.

Nominated officers: sanctions for non-compliance

The nominated officer and disclosures under POCA

As noted above (at paragraphs 5.110–5.112), the legal responsibilities of nominated officers **5.130** are derived from a number of provisions in POCA and TA 2000, as well as from the Money Laundering Regulations 2007 in the case of MLROs in the regulated sector.[69]

Once appointed, that is, nominated by his employer to receive all relevant disclosures under **5.131** POCA, a nominated officer is subject to criminal penalties for failure to carry out those responsibilities correctly. The sanctions for breach of the legal requirements by nominated officers, inside and outside the regulated sector, are summarized below.

- Failure to make a required disclosure: sections 331 and 332
  Under section 331(1), a nominated officer in the regulated sector who fails to make a required disclosure commits a criminal offence. Similarly, a nominated officer who fails to make a required disclosure under section 332(1) also commits an offence. The maximum penalty for this offence if five years' imprisonment.
- Giving consent to a prohibited act where the necessary conditions have not been satisfied: section 336

---

[67] [2009] EWHC 79 (QB).
[68] Section 330(9A) explicitly recognizes the advisory role of the nominated officer, albeit in the limited context of the privilege exception.
[69] For the sanctions for failure to comply with the requirements of the Money Laundering Regulations 2007, see Chapter 9.

Where a nominated officer has made a disclosure that property is criminal property and has asked for appropriate consent from SOCA, the nominated officer must not give consent to a prohibited act unless the necessary conditions in section 336 have been satisfied. A nominated officer who gives such consent where the necessary conditions have not been satisfied commits a criminal offence under section 336(5). The maximum penalty for this offence is five years' imprisonment.

The nominated officer and disclosures under TA 2000

5.132   The position under TA 2000 is quite different from that under POCA: the responsibilities of nominated officers are largely implied and there are no criminal offences that apply only to nominated officers. The contrast with the position under POCA can be seen in the provisions of sections 20 and 21, and most clearly in relation to the added section 21A of TA 2000.

5.133   A nominated officer may receive and make disclosures under section 20, which provides for the making of voluntary disclosures; there is, therefore, no sanction for failing to make a disclosure. Section 20, however, also refers back to the making of disclosures under section 19 which are in substance, if not in name, required disclosures: 'A person may make a disclosure to a constable in the circumstances mentioned in section 19(1) and (2).' Failure by a person to make a disclosure under section 19 is an offence, but one of the defences to it is the making of a disclosure in accordance with the internal disclosure procedure established by a person's employer. Where such an internal disclosure under section 19 is made to a nominated officer, there are no separate provisions, in either section 19 or section 20, requiring the nominated officer to make a disclosure to SOCA.

5.134   Under section 21, a nominated officer may receive a disclosure from a person who has made use of the procedure for making disclosures established by his employer. There is no legal obligation on the nominated officer to make a disclosure to SOCA, but the position is similar to that of the nominated officer who has received an authorised disclosure under POCA.

5.135   Section 21A essentially mirrors section 330 of POCA but with a number of differences determined by the different subject matter of the disclosure required. Each of these sections relates to a disclosure about 'another person' where it is known or suspected, or there are reasonable grounds for knowing or suspecting, that that person: '. . . is engaged in money laundering' (section 330 of POCA) or '. . . has committed an offence under any of sections 15 to 18' (that is, a terrorist property offence).

5.136   In POCA, the section following, section 331, is a parallel offence-creating section aimed at nominated officers. It relates specifically to information or other matter that comes to a nominated officer 'in consequence of a disclosure under section 330'. Where the necessary conditions are satisfied, the nominated officer commits an offence if he fails to make the required disclosure to SOCA. In TA 2000, there is no such offence-creating section aimed at nominated officers that runs parallel to section 21A.

H. Conclusion

5.137   The disclosure provisions in Part 7 greatly expanded the scope of the SARs regime and led to a marked increase in the number of SARs submitted to the UK FIU. SARs have become a source of criminal intelligence[70] that is valued by SOCA and increasingly used by law enforcement agencies. Although in some cases an individual SAR sparks off an investigation that leads to arrest and conviction for a serious crime and/or recovery of the proceeds of crime, it is the cumulative effect of SARs that seems to be proving increasingly useful—through cross-matching of data from a number of SARs on the same subject and from data-matching within the SARs database and with other databases.

Part 7 of POCA marked a significant step forward towards a coherent anti-money launder-   **5.138**
ing system, but the law that underlies the SARs regime is over-complicated and lacks focus and flexibility. Arguably, the current law has fundamental defects; it is certainly much in need of review and reform. Nevertheless, the SARs regime has come a long way since February 2003 and most of that distance has been travelled since March 2006. Despite the defects in the law, there can be little doubt that the SARs regime is in better health now than it was then.

The next two Chapters, 6 and 7, deal successively with the law on disclosure under POCA   **5.139**
and TA 2000. Chapter 8 deals with tipping off and other unlawful disclosures under both statutes.

---

[70] For SARs statistics and information about the operation of the SARs regime, see the Annual Reports of the SARs Regime Committee (from 2007).

6

DISCLOSURE AND THE DISCLOSURE OFFENCES UNDER THE PROCEEDS OF CRIME ACT 2002

A. Introduction

6.01 This chapter covers the law on disclosure under Part 7 and Chapter 1 of Part 8 of The Proceeds of Crime Act 2002 (POCA). It includes required disclosures and the failure to disclose offences which affect almost exclusively those in the regulated sector as well as the law relating to authorised disclosures and the consent regime. Tipping off and the other offences of unlawful disclosure, under both POCA and the Terrorism Act 2000 (TA 2000), are dealt with in Chapter 8.

6.02 The law on disclosure in POCA is set out below, and in Chapter 8, under headings reflecting the four main categories of disclosure:

- required disclosures;
- authorised disclosures and appropriate consent;
- protected disclosures;
- unlawful disclosures.

The different types of disclosure and the characteristics of the two separate disclosure regimes that exist under POCA are considered in Chapter 5 at paragraphs 5.09 *et seq.*

B. Disclosure and Offences of Failure to Disclose

Sections 330 and 331 together govern the process of disclosure by the regulated sector where **6.03** there is knowledge or suspicion of money laundering or reasonable grounds to suspect that a person is engaged in money laundering: section 330 deals with disclosure by a person employed in the regulated sector and section 331 deals with disclosure by the 'nominated officer' or MLRO.

Section 332 concerns disclosures by nominated officers, both inside and outside the regu- **6.04** lated sector, following receipt by them of voluntary protected disclosures under section 337 and authorised disclosures under section 338.

The reporting provisions in sections 330, 331, and 332 create *positive obligations* on those **6.05** employed in the regulated sector and on nominated officers. The obligations in these sections are not, however, set out as positive obligations followed by provisions aimed to ensure compliance and create sanctions for non-compliance. The three sections are drafted as offence-creating sections with the disclosure obligations first appearing, like photographic negatives, in the context of failure to make a disclosure as one of the necessary conditions for the commission of the relevant offence.

Section 330: failure to disclose: regulated sector

Section 330 imposes on persons carrying out regulated business an obligation, where speci- **6.06** fied circumstances exist, to make money laundering disclosures and it creates a criminal offence of failure to disclose. A person commits an offence if four conditions (set out in subsections (2) to (4)) are satisfied.

The first offence condition

This condition deals with the mental element of the offence: **6.07**

> The first condition is that he—
> (a) knows or suspects, or
> (b) has reasonable grounds for knowing or suspecting, that another person is engaged in money laundering.

Knowledge or suspicion is the essential mental element in money laundering and is part of the definition of criminal property.[1] The first condition extends that mental element to include the objective test of having 'reasonable grounds' for such knowledge or suspicion.

In the Explanatory Notes published with POCA, this is referred to as a 'negligence test' and **6.08** the rationale for its inclusion is expressed in the following comment on section 330: 'The section reflects the fact that persons who are carrying out activities in the regulated sector should be expected to exercise a higher level of diligence in handling transactions than those employed in other businesses.' In introducing the objective test, the government was looking to achieve a culture change in the regulated sector and the Home Office Minister, Mr Bob Ainsworth, said in the House of Commons: '. . .we consider that an objective test is necessary because we want the financial industry at large to be much more diligent in identifying and reporting instances of money laundering'.

---

[1] POCA, s 340(3)(b).

6.09 How far the addition of this objective element actually widens the offence in practice is a moot point. In a trial for an offence without this objective element, where the defendant claimed that he neither knew nor suspected, the prosecutor would call evidence to establish the grounds for knowledge or suspicion and that the defendant was aware of these and would invite the jury to infer that the defendant did in fact have the requisite knowledge or suspicion. It is probably a matter of degree. Where the objective element is absent, the prosecution would need to adduce circumstantial evidence that was more cogent than simply giving 'reasonable grounds' for such knowledge or suspicion.

6.10 Liability under section 330 for committing an offence of failing to disclose in the absence of subjective knowledge or suspicion is limited by section 330(7), which provides that a person does not commit the offence where that person has not been given appropriate anti-money laundering training.[2]

The second offence condition

6.11 This condition limits the application of the offence to regulated sector business:

> The second condition is that the information or other matter—
> (a) on which his knowledge or suspicion is based, or
> (b) which gives reasonable grounds for such knowledge or suspicion, came to him in the course of a business in the regulated sector.[3]

The wording of the second condition excludes information that comes to a person outside the course of a business or in the course of a business that is outside the regulated sector. Where an organization conducts both regulated sector business and other business, it would seem also to exclude information that comes to a person when conducting non-regulated sector business. The wording of Regulation 3 (Application of the Regulations) and 4 (Exclusions) supports this distinction.[4] Whether information has come to a person in the course of a business in the regulated sector should generally be clear where an organization, such as a bank, conducts exclusively or almost exclusively regulated sector business, but it may be less clear where an organization conducts, perhaps in roughly equal measure, regulated business and non-regulated business.

6.12 Many companies and professional firms which conduct both regulated and non-regulated business may decide, as a matter of good practice, to apply the CDD, record-keeping, and other regulated sector requirements across their entire business activities. A decision to do so would not, however, bring non-regulated business within the scope of the second condition.

The third offence condition

6.13 This condition concerns the identification of the suspected money launderer and/or the laundered property. It is intended to restrict required disclosures to those which can provide useful information for law enforcement purposes: that is, to circumstances where the identity of the money launderer or the whereabouts of the laundered property is known or

---

[2] See below, at paras 6.22 and 6.23.
[3] For the definition of business in the regulated sector, see POCA, s 330(12)(a) and POCA, Sch 9, as amended by the Proceeds of Crime Act 2002 (Business in the Regulated Sector and Supervisory Authorities) Order 2007) SI 2007/3287.
[4] The Money Laundering Regulations 2007.

can be identified, or where, broadly speaking, the information in the disclosure received should assist in identifying the money launderer or the whereabouts of the laundered property:

> The third condition is—
> (a) that he can identify the other person mentioned in subsection (2) or the whereabouts of any of the laundered property, or
> (b) that he believes, or it is reasonable to expect him to believe, that the information or other matter mentioned in subsection (3) will or may assist in identifying that other person or the whereabouts of any of the laundered property.

The third condition, inserted by section 104 of the Serious Organised Crime and Police Act 2005, is aimed at reducing the number of reports that, though quite properly made, provide no useable information about a known or suspected money launderer or about known or suspected laundered property.

6.14 Note that subsection (3A)(b) contains an objective element '. . .he believes, *or it is reasonable to expect him to believe*' (emphasis added) that the information or other matter giving rise to knowledge or suspicion will or may assist in identifying the money launderer or the whereabouts of the laundered property. This objective element, in the same terms, features in the equivalent provision not only for nominated officers in the regulated sector (section 331(3A)) but also for nominated officers outside the regulated sector (section 332(3A)).

The fourth offence condition

6.15 This condition contains the *actus reus* of the offence.

> The fourth condition is that he does not make the required disclosure to—
> (a) a nominated officer, or
> (b) a person authorised for the purposes of this Part by the Director General of the SOCA, as soon as is practicable after the information or other matter mentioned in subsection (3) comes to him.

The offence is committed not by a 'guilty act', as such, but by a guilty omission to act when under a legal obligation to do so. It is the fourth condition that creates the positive obligation to make a required disclosure whenever the first three conditions apply to a person in the regulated sector.

What must be disclosed

6.16 What must be disclosed in a required disclosure is set out in section 330(5):

> The required disclosure is a disclosure of—
> (a) the identity of the other person mentioned in subsection (2), if he knows it,
> (b) the whereabouts of the laundered property, so far as he knows it, and
> (c) the information or other matter mentioned in subsection (3).

The term 'laundered property' is defined in the added subsection (5A):

> (5A) The laundered property is the property forming the subject-matter of the money laundering that he knows or suspects, or has reasonable grounds for knowing or suspecting, that other person to be engaged in.

6.17 The required disclosure may be made directly to SOCA or to the nominated officer of the institution where the person is employed. In practice, internal procedures will usually require that the disclosure is made to the nominated officer. Once that internal disclosure is made, the employee is protected from liability under section 330 arising from their knowledge or suspicion of money laundering, or having reasonable grounds for knowing or suspecting.

Specimen indictment

6.18 The offence of failure to disclose is triable either in the magistrates' court or in the Crown Court.

STATEMENT OF OFFENCE

Failure to disclose contrary to section 330 of the P\roceeds of Crime Act 2002.

PARTICULARS OF OFFENCE

A B, on a date between the . . . day of . . . and the . . . day of . . ., knowing or suspecting or having reasonable grounds for knowing or suspecting, on the basis of information that came to him in the course of a business in the regulated sector, that C D was a person engaged in money laundering and being able to identify C D and the whereabouts of the laundered property, did not make the required disclosure to a nominated officer or to the Serious Organised Crime Agency as soon as practicable after the information came to him.

Sentence

6.19 A person guilty of the offence under section 330 is liable:[5]

- on summary conviction, to imprisonment for a term not exceeding six months or to a fine not exceeding the statutory maximum or to both; or
- on conviction on indictment, to imprisonment for a term not exceeding five years or to a fine or to both.

Section 330: defences

6.20 There are a number of defences or exceptions to the offence of failing to make a required disclosure, as set out in section 330(6), (7), (7A), and (7B). The provisions are complicated, but there are essentially four defences:

- reasonable excuse under section 330(6)(a);
- lack of training under section 330(6)(c) and (7);
- money laundering outside the UK under section 330(7A);
- privileged circumstances: firstly, professional legal advisers and relevant professional advisers under section 330(6)(b) and, secondly, persons providing assistance or support under section 330(6)(c) and (7B).

Reasonable excuse

6.21 Section 330(6)(a) provides that a person does not commit an offence under this section if: '(a) he has a reasonable excuse for not making the required disclosure, . . .'. There is no authority on what would constitute a reasonable excuse under section 330(6)(a) for failing to make a disclosure. What would be reasonable is likely to be construed narrowly by the courts since the duty to disclose is regarded as important and applies only to those working

---

[5] Section 334(2).

in the regulated sector who, as required by the Regulations, must have the benefit of anti-money laundering guidance and training.[6]

Lack of training

There is a defence of lack of training in section 330(6)(c) and (7). A person does not commit **6.22** an offence under this section if sub-section (7) applies to him:

> (7) This subsection applies to a person if—
>   (a) he does not know or suspect that another person is engaged in money laundering, and
>   (b) he has not been provided by his employer with such training as is specified by the Secretary of State by order for the purposes of this section.

This provision is consistent with the reasoning for applying the objective test to those working in the regulated sector: they should be more aware than others of money laundering and should recognize and respond to reasonable grounds for knowing or suspecting that another person is engaged in money laundering. That, however, is only reasonable where they have received training in accordance with the regulations.

The specified training for persons working in the regulated sector is training in accordance **6.23** with Regulation 21 of the Money Laundering Regulations 2007. This requires employers in the regulated sector to take appropriate measures so that all relevant employees are:

> (a) made aware of the law relating to money laundering and terrorist financing; and
> (b) regularly given training in how to recognize and deal with transactions and other activities which may be related to money laundering or terrorist financing.

Money laundering outside the UK

A further exception is contained in section 330(7A):   **6.24**

> (7A) Nor does a person commit an offence under this section if—
>   (a) he knows, or believes on reasonable grounds, that the money laundering is occurring in a particular country or territory outside the United Kingdom, and
>   (b) the money laundering—
>   (i) is not unlawful under the criminal law applying in that country or territory, and
>   (ii) is not of a description prescribed in an order made by the Secretary of State.[7]

This defence or exception[8] limits the scope of the offence of failure to disclose, but probably does so only to a limited degree since it is not easy for a person to be satisfied that the elements of the defence or exception are all in place.

Whether the exception to the requirement to disclose will apply in any particular case requires **6.25** a step-by-step consideration of the circumstances. The usual starting point will be that a person in the regulated sector suspects that another person is engaged in money laundering and the information giving rise to suspicion suggests that the activity of money laundering is taking place somewhere outside the UK. The exception will only apply if two conditions are fulfilled:

---

  [6] Money Laundering Regulations 2007, Reg 21.

  [7] The Secretary of State has not, as yet, made any order prescribing money laundering of a particular description under this section.

  [8] It is drafted in similar terms to sub-section 2(A) in ss 327, 328, and 329, though for a different purpose. The Secretary of State has made an order prescribing 'relevant criminal conduct' under these sections: The Proceeds of Crime Act 2002 (Money Laundering: Exceptions to Overseas Conduct Defence) Order 2006.

- Firstly, the person is unlikely to have exact knowledge about the suspected money laundering, but for the exception to apply he must believe *on reasonable grounds* that the money laundering is occurring *in a particular country or territory* outside the UK. For the purposes of the first condition, the 'money laundering' should be construed as money laundering as defined in POCA. An act of money laundering carried on outside the United Kingdom, that is an act which would constitute an offence of money laundering if done in the UK, would still be an offence of money laundering under POCA.[9]
- Secondly, having identified the particular country or territory, the person must be sure that the money laundering activity being carried out in that country or territory *is not unlawful under the criminal law applying in that country or territory*. The person needs certainty about the relevant foreign law. This places on a person wishing to take advantage of this exception a burden that may be difficult and/or expensive to discharge.

6.26 Even if the person is satisfied that these two conditions are fulfilled, there is a further provision which amounts to a potential exception to the exception or defence in section 330(7A). The effect of this provision is that the exception or defence will not apply where the money laundering in a foreign country or territory is money laundering of a description prescribed in an order made by the Secretary of State. At present, this further complication is only theoretical, since—as noted above—the Secretary of State has not yet made an order under section 330(7A)(b)(ii). The meaning of this provision, which is unclear, is considered in the following paragraph.

6.27 Section 330(7A)(b)(ii) refers to money laundering that 'is not of a description prescribed in an order made by the Secretary of State'. What money laundering of a particular description means in this context is uncertain, but it may refer to the laundering of the proceeds of a particular type of predicate criminal activity. The provision may be intended to apply to the situation where dealing with the proceeds of a particular activity would not constitute the criminal offence of money laundering in the relevant country but would be money laundering under UK law. An example would be dealing in some way with the proceeds of brothel-keeping in a place where it is not an offence to run a brothel.[10] In those circumstances, the defence or exception under sub-section (7A) would apply unless and until the Secretary of State makes an order prescribing, for the purposes of this section, money laundering of this description.

The 'privileged circumstances' exception

6.28 Section 330(6)(b) provides an exception to commission of the offence in the form of a statutory privilege exemption:

> (6) But he does not commit an offence under this section if—
>
> . . .
>
> > (b) he is a professional legal adviser or relevant professional adviser and—
> > > (i) if he knows either of the things mentioned in subsection (5)(a) and (b), he knows the thing because of information or other matter that came to him in privileged circumstances, or
> > > (ii) the information or other matter mentioned in subsection (3) came to him in privileged circumstances,

---

[9] POCA, s 340(11)(d).

[10] An offence under Sexual Offences Act 1956, s 33. This is a lifestyle offence under POCA, Sch 2, para 8(1). In the folklore of money laundering, the Nevada brothel-keeper ranks alongside the Spanish bullfighter.

The privilege exception in section 330(6) applies, therefore, in two situations: **6.29**

- where the professional legal adviser or relevant professional adviser knows the identity of the suspected money launderer or the whereabouts of the laundered property because of information that came to him in privileged circumstances; and
- where the information or other matter on which his knowledge or suspicion of money laundering is based, or which gives reasonable grounds for such knowledge or suspicion, came to him not only '. . . in the course of a business in the regulated sector', but also in privileged circumstances.

Under POCA as enacted, this exception applied only to a professional legal adviser but it   **6.30**
has since been expanded to include an 'other relevant professional adviser': that is, an accountant, auditor, or tax adviser who comes within the terms of the definition in section 330(14).

The practical effect of this statutory defence or exception is to exempt a lawyer or other rel-   **6.31**
evant professional adviser from the requirement to make a disclosure under section 330 in the specified circumstances. Although broadly similar to the circumstances in which legal professional privilege under common law applies, the scope of the statutory exception is not the same. 'The general aim of section 330(6)(b)', in the words of Lord Justice Brookes in *Bowman v Fels*, 'is clearly to protect legal professionals, by enabling them—in the interests of the public and clients generally—to render basic legal services, despite any suspicions such professionals may have and whatever may ultimately prove to be the true factual position.'[11]

'Privileged circumstances' are defined in section 330(10):   **6.32**

> (10) Information or other matter comes to a professional legal adviser or relevant professional adviser in privileged circumstances if it is communicated or given to him—
>   (a) by (or by a representative of) a client of his in connection with the giving by the adviser of legal advice to the client,
>   (b) by (or by a representative of) a person seeking legal advice from the adviser, or
>   (c) by a person in connection with legal proceedings or contemplated legal proceedings.

The crime/fraud provision

Just as legal professional privilege is subject to the 'crime/fraud' exception, so the statutory   **6.33**
privilege exception does not apply 'to information or other matter which is communicated or given with the intention of furthering a criminal purpose'.[12]

The privilege exception extended

The statutory privilege exception in sub-section (6), as originally enacted, applied only   **6.34**
to the advisers, that is to the lawyer or other relevant professional adviser who is actually advising the client. Common law legal professional privilege has always been understood to extend to other persons connected with the adviser such as a partner, assistant, or secretary as well as another lawyer or other person instructed as an expert to advise on the matter. Section 330(7B) now extends the statutory privilege exception to other

---

[11] *Bowman v Fels* (2005 EWCA Civ 226).
[12] s 330(11), and considered by the Court of Appeal in *Bowman v Fels* (2005 EWCA Civ 226) at paras 92 to 95 inclusive.

persons in partnership with the adviser or employed by the adviser to provide assistance or support:

> (7B) This sub-section applies to a person if:—
>> (a) he is employed by, or is in partnership with, a professional legal adviser or a relevant professional adviser to provide the adviser with assistance or support,
>> (b) the information or other matter mentioned in subsection (3) comes to the person in connection with the provision of such assistance or support, and
>> (c) the information or other matter came to the adviser in privileged circumstances.

Anti-money laundering guidance

6.35 Section 330(8) provides further protection to those who conduct business in the regulated sector. If a person is tried for an offence of failing to disclose, the court *must* consider whether he followed any relevant anti-money laundering guidance:

> (8) In deciding whether a person committed an offence under this section the court must consider whether he followed any relevant guidance which was at the time concerned—
>> (a) issued by a supervisory authority or any other appropriate body,
>> (b) approved by the Treasury, and
>> (c) published in a manner it approved as appropriate in its opinion to bring the guidance to the attention of persons likely to be affected by it.

6.36 Anti-money laundering guidance is, therefore, only relevant guidance for the purposes of subsection (8) if it complies with the three conditions. It must be:

- *Issued by a supervisory body or other appropriate body.* It must be issued by a 'supervisory authority', as defined in Schedule 9 of POCA,[13] or any other 'appropriate body',[14] that is any body which is regulated or is representative of any trade, profession, business, or employment carried on by the 'alleged offender'.[15]
- *Approved by the Treasury.*[16] Relevant guidance is submitted to the Treasury and is considered by Treasury officials and by members of the government's Money Laundering Advisory Committee. Subject to any agreed amendment of the guidance arising from this process, formal approval may then be given by the Treasury.
- *Published in a manner approved by the Treasury.* The third condition in subsection (8) requires that the guidance is brought to the attention of those likely to be affected by it. No particular formality is involved, but the Treasury needs to be satisfied that the guidance is readily accessible and that it is appropriately covered in the training referred to in section 333(7)(b).

6.37 Supervisory authorities and other appropriate bodies are not obliged to submit their anti-money laundering guidance for approval by the Treasury, and a court may well take such guidance into account even if it is not approved. Nevertheless, the protection of section 330(8) only applies to approved guidance. At present, some relevant guidance is approved, some is not: in the wake of the revision of guidance made necessary by the

---

[13] As amended by Proceeds of Crime Act 2002 (Business in the Regulated Sector and Supervisory Authorities) Order 2007, para 2.

[14] s 330(13).

[15] For the use of the term 'alleged offender' in Part 7 of POCA, see paras 6.39 and 6.110.

[16] That is, Treasury approval in accordance with POCA 2002, ss 330(8) and 331(7); TA 2000, s 21A(6); and Money Laundering Regulations 2007, Reg 45(2).

Money Laundering Regulations 2007 it appears that an increasing number of supervisory authorities and appropriate bodies have sought Treasury approval. The Treasury has formally approved guidance prepared by the Joint Money Laundering Steering Group, HMRC, and a number of other regulators, supervisors, and professional bodies. A full list of approved guidance is set out in Table 10.3 in Chapter 10 below.

The provisions of section 330(8) are generally regarded as giving a degree of protection to **6.38** persons in the regulated sector. They will do so to the extent that a person follows the relevant guidance. They may, however, be a sword in the hands of a prosecutor as well as a shield in the hands of the defendant; which they are in any particular case will depend on whether the evidence shows that a defendant to a charge under section 330 followed—and relied on—any relevant guidance or, without good reason, failed to follow such guidance.

Disclosure to a nominated officer

What does and does not constitute a disclosure to a nominated officer is dealt with in section **6.39** 330(9) and (9A):

> (9) A disclosure to a nominated officer is a disclosure which—
>> (a) is made to a person nominated by the alleged offender's employer to receive disclosures under this section, and
>> (b) is made in the course of the alleged offender's employment.

Together, subsection (5), which deals with the content of the disclosure, and subsection (9), which deals with the circumstances in which it is made, effectively define what is to count as a required disclosure under section 330, subject to subsection (9A) below. In doing so, they also define the scope of the duty of disclosure that applies to a person employed in the regulated sector. Such a person is referred to in section 330(9) as the 'alleged offender', a term that seems to be inappropriate and unnecessary.[17]

Disclosure for advice—a limited exception

Subsection (9A), which creates an exception to subsection (9) for a specific purpose, intro- **6.40** duces the anomalous concept of a disclosure that is not a disclosure or is to be treated for the purposes of section 330 as not counting as a disclosure:

> (9A) But a disclosure which satisfies paragraphs (a) and (b) of subsection (9) is not to be taken as a disclosure to a nominated officer if the person making the disclosure—
>> (a) is a professional legal adviser or relevant professional adviser,
>> (b) makes it for the purpose of obtaining advice about making a disclosure under this section, and
>> (c) does not intend it to be a disclosure under this section.

Section 330(9A) was added by section 106(2) of SOCPA 2005 and came into force on 1 July **6.41** 2005. This provision was introduced to deal with a specific situation that could arise for a nominated officer who has received a disclosure from a professional legal adviser or relevant professional adviser.

Where a professional legal adviser or relevant professional adviser comes into possession of **6.42** information within the terms of the 'privileged circumstances' exception in section 330(6)(b),

---

[17] A person in the regulated sector who makes a required disclosure to a nominated officer is exactly fulfilling his duty under section 330. To describe such a person as an 'alleged offender' (rather than 'person' or 'discloser' or some other neutral word or phrase) is both inaccurate and pejorative.

the adviser would not commit an offence if he makes no disclosure and should not make a disclosure. The adviser, however, may wish to have the advice of the nominated officer on whether the circumstances would potentially require a disclosure and whether the privileged circumstances exception does in fact apply to it.

6.43   If, in such a situation, the adviser makes an internal disclosure, the nominated officer may be faced with the problem which section 330(9A) is intended to resolve. This would arise where the information in the internal disclosure is such that:

- the nominated officer would be required under section 331 to make a disclosure to SOCA; and
- the privileged circumstances exception does apply to the adviser.

The problem is that the privileged circumstances exception would not apply to the nominated officer because the information giving rise to suspicion would not come *to the nominated officer* 'in privileged circumstances'.

6.44   Disclosure to the nominated officer would lead either to a disclosure being made to SOCA, which would negate the protection from disclosure which the statutory exception in section 330 is intended to provide, or, if no disclosure under section 331 is made to SOCA, to the nominated officer being exposed to the risk of prosecution for an offence of failure to disclose.

6.45   It may be that a nominated officer who, in that situation, decided not to report in order to safeguard the privileged circumstances protection would have a reasonable excuse under section 331(6), but the lack of specific provision to deal with the situation created uncertainty and was likely to inhibit informed discussion between an adviser and a nominated officer.

6.46   Subsection (9A) allows an adviser to inform the nominated officer about his knowledge or suspicion and about the information or other matters on which his knowledge or suspicion is based for the purpose of obtaining advice on whether or not he should be making an actual disclosure. Under these provisions, the nominated officer can receive from an adviser information about suspected money laundering that is 'not to be taken as a disclosure' and which, therefore, does not raise any duty on the part of the nominated officer to make a disclosure to SOCA. It enables the nominated officer to consider and to give advice to the professional legal adviser or relevant professional adviser on whether the circumstances do or do not require a disclosure.

Section 331: failure to disclose: nominated officers in the regulated sector

6.47   When an internal money laundering report or disclosure under section 330 is received by a nominated officer or MLRO the disclosure obligation, and with it the liability to criminal sanctions for failure to comply, pass to the nominated officer. As in section 330, so in sections 331 and 332, a positive obligation to report is implied by a condition of the offence being the failure to make a required disclosure.

Nominated officers

6.48   The nominated officer[18] in any organization will probably have been nominated to deal with money laundering and terrorist financing disclosure generally, including disclosures under section 330 which are the subject of section 331. Each institution in the regulated sector will have its own policies and procedures, but the nominated officer's duty on receipt of an

---

[18]   The role of the nominated officer is discussed in more detail in Section G in Chapter 5 at para 5.109 *et seq.*

internal disclosure is stated in general terms in Regulation 20(2)(d)(iii) of the Money Laundering Regulations 2007:

> (iii) where a disclosure is made to the nominated officer, he must consider it in the light of any relevant information which is available to the relevant person and determine whether it gives rise to knowledge or suspicion or reasonable grounds for knowledge or suspicion that a person is engaged in money laundering or terrorist financing.

Where, having considered the internal disclosure, the nominated officer determines that there is the necessary knowledge or suspicion, or reasonable grounds to know or suspect, that another person is engaged in money laundering, he must make the required disclosure if he has the necessary information about the identity of the other person and/or the whereabouts of the laundered property. The required disclosure in the case of the nominated officer would be a disclosure to SOCA. **6.49**

Section 331(1) places an obligation on nominated officers in the regulated sector to make required disclosures by creating a criminal offence of failing to disclose. A nominated officer commits that offence if the four conditions in subsections (2) to (4) are satisfied. **6.50**

The first offence condition

This condition deals with the mental element of the offence and is the same as for required disclosures under section 330, with the objective 'reasonable grounds' test added to the basic mental element of subjective knowledge or suspicion: **6.51**

> (2) The first condition is that he—
>   (a) knows or suspects, or
>   (b) has reasonable grounds for knowing or suspecting, that another person is engaged in money laundering.

The second offence condition

This condition concerns the source of the information giving rise to knowledge or suspicion of money laundering, which must come to the nominated officer from a required disclosure under section 330: **6.52**

> (3) The second condition is that the information or other matter—
>   (a) on which his knowledge or suspicion is based, or
>   (b) which gives reasonable grounds for such knowledge or suspicion, came to him in consequence of a disclosure made under section 330.

The third offence condition

This condition concerns the identification of the suspected money launderer and/or the laundered property. As in section 330, it is intended to restrict required disclosures to those which can provide useful information for law enforcement purposes: that is, to circumstances where the identity of the money launderer or the whereabouts of the laundered property is known or can be identified, or where, broadly speaking, the information in the disclosure received should assist in identifying the money launderer or the whereabouts of the laundered property: **6.53**

> (3A) The third condition is—
>   (a) that he knows the identity of the other person mentioned in subsection (2), or the whereabouts of any of the laundered property, in consequence of a disclosure made under section 330,

(b) that that other person, or the whereabouts of any of the laundered property, can be identified from the information or other matter mentioned in subsection (3), or

(c) that he believes, or it is reasonable to expect him to believe, that the information or other matter will or may assist in identifying that other person or the whereabouts of any of the laundered property.

The fourth offence condition

6.54 Where these three conditions are present, the nominated officer is required to make a disclosure to SOCA as soon as practicable. The fourth condition, set out in section 331(4), and the two definition subsections that follow it, mirror the provisions in section 330(4), (5), and (5A):

> (4) The fourth condition is that he does not make the required disclosure to a person authorised for the purposes of this Part by the Director General of SOCA as soon as is practicable after the information or other matter mentioned in subsection (3) comes to him.

6.55 Under section 331(5), what the nominated officer is required to disclose is essentially the same as in section 330(5), and in section 331(5A) the laundered property is defined in the same terms as in section 330(5A). The disclosure by the nominated officer to SOCA should, therefore, contain:

- if disclosed to him in the internal disclosure under section 330, the identity of the person suspected of money laundering;
- the whereabouts of the laundered property, so far as disclosed to him under section 330; and
- the information giving rise to knowledge or suspicion of money laundering.

Specimen indictment

6.56 The offence under section 331 is triable either in the magistrates' court or in the Crown Court.

STATEMENT OF OFFENCE

Failure to disclose contrary to section 331 of the Proceeds of Crime Act 2002.

PARTICULARS OF OFFENCE

A B, a nominated officer in the regulated sector, on a date between the . . . day of . . . and the . . . day of . . ., knowing or suspecting or having reasonable grounds for knowing or suspecting, on the basis of information that came to him in consequence of a disclosure made under section 330, that C D was a person engaged in money laundering and knowing, as a result of the said disclosure, the identity of C D and the whereabouts of the laundered property, did not make the required disclosure to the Serious Organised Crime Agency as soon as practicable after the said information came to him.

Sentence

6.57 Under section 334(2), a nominated officer guilty of an offence under section 331 is liable:

- on summary conviction, to imprisonment for a term not exceeding six months or to a fine not exceeding the statutory maximum or to both; or
- on conviction on indictment, to imprisonment for a term not exceeding five years or to a fine or to both.

Section 331: defences and exclusions

There are two defences under section 331: a defence of reasonable excuse and a defence that **6.58** applies where the money laundering is taking place outside the United Kingdom.

Reasonable excuse

There is a defence of reasonable excuse, in section 331(6), in the same terms as the defence in **6.59** section 330(6)(a):

> (6) But he does not commit an offence under this section if he has a reasonable excuse for not making the required disclosure.

Since the nominated officer should be a responsible person in a senior position with a knowledge and understanding of anti-money laundering matters, 'reasonable excuse' is likely to be construed as narrowly or more narrowly than under section 330(6)(a).

Money laundering outside the UK

A second defence relates to money laundering outside the UK: **6.60**

> (6A) Nor does a person commit an offence under this section if—
>   (a) he knows, or believes on reasonable grounds, that the money laundering is occurring in a particular country or territory outside the United Kingdom, and
>   (b) the money laundering—
>   (i) is not unlawful under the criminal law applying in that country or territory, and
>   (ii) is not of a description prescribed in an order made by the Secretary of State.

The nature and extent of this defence or exception, which is in the same terms as the defence under section 330(7A), is considered at paragraphs 6.24–6.27 above.

Relevant guidance

In section 331(7) there is the same evidential provision as in section 330(8) that in a trial for **6.61** the offence of failing to disclose the court must consider whether the defendant followed any 'relevant guidance'. (See paragraphs 6.35–6.38.)

Section 332: failure to disclose: other nominated officers

Although the detailed provisions of sections 330 and 331 are complex, their purpose and **6.62** the relationship between the two sections is straightforward. Section 330 creates the requirement for disclosure by those working in the regulated sector, normally disclosure to a nominated officer. Section 331 creates the corresponding requirement for the nominated officer to consider the disclosure under section 330 and, if the conditions are fulfilled, to make a disclosure to SOCA. In each case, there are criminal penalties for failure to disclose.

The scope and purpose of section 332 and its relationship to other sections (to sections 330 **6.63** and 331, as well as to sections 337 and 338) is less straightforward.

The scope of section 332

The heading of the section is misleading. After section 331 'Failure to disclose: nominated **6.64** officers in the regulated sector', the heading of section 332 'Failure to disclose: other nominated officers' suggests that the section concerns nominated officers *other than* those in the regulated sector.[19] The wording of section 332(1), however, does not limit the application of

---

[19] On the status of section headings and other headings within an Act, see Francis Bennion, *Statutory Interpretation* (Butterworths, 4th edition, 2002), Part XV, Section 255, at pp 635–6.

the offence of failure to disclose to nominated officers outside the regulated sector. On the plain wording of subsection (1), section 332 applies to all nominated officers.[20]

> (1) A person nominated to receive disclosures under section 337 or 338 commits an offence if the conditions in subsections (2) to (4) are satisfied.

The purpose of section 332

6.65 The purpose of the section is made clear in the Explanatory Notes to POCA:

> Section 332 creates an offence where a nominated officer who receives a report under section 337 or 338 (in other words, a disclosure in relation to one of the principal money laundering offences or a voluntary disclosure) which causes him to know or suspect that money laundering is taking place does not disclose that report as soon as practicable after the information comes to him . . . This [section] applies to nominated officers both in the regulated sector and outside the regulated sector.

6.66 The nominated officer who receives a voluntary protected disclosure under section 337 or an authorised disclosure under section 338 is under an obligation to make a disclosure, a 'required disclosure', to SOCA if the first three conditions (in section 332(2), (3) and (3A)) apply.

Nominated officers outside the regulated sector

6.67 There is no obligation on any business or professional firm that is outside the regulated sector to appoint a nominated officer and there is no legal obligation on the part of any person employed in a business outside the regulated sector to make a money laundering disclosure. If, however, an employer in a non-regulated business appoints a nominated officer to receive internal reports, both protected voluntary disclosures and authorised disclosures, the person appointed as nominated officer does have a legal duty, under section 332, to consider and deal with those disclosures in essentially the same way as a nominated officer in the regulated sector.

6.68 Nominated officers outside the regulated sector will not receive required disclosures under section 331 because those who are employed in their organization do not conduct 'relevant business' and are not subject to the reporting obligation in section 330.[21] In receiving and dealing with voluntary protected and authorised disclosures, however, the nominated officer is subject to the same obligation to make a required disclosure and liable to the same penalties for failure under section 332 as the nominated officer in the regulated sector.

The offence of failure to disclose

6.69 Section 332 creates an offence based on a set of conditions broadly similar to the offence conditions in section 331, but the subject matter of section 332 is more diverse. Section 331 concerns only required disclosures under section 330. Section 332 concerns two quite different types of disclosure: voluntary protected disclosures under section 337 and authorised disclosures under section 338.

6.70 The provisions of section 332 are intended to apply equally to voluntary protected disclosures and to authorised disclosures, on the basis that the wording of conditions that is

---

[20] And see, in para 6.65 below, the final sentence of the quotation from the Explanatory Notes to POCA.
[21] But note the position of the MLRO in an institution that conducts both regulated and non-regulated business: see Chapter 5 at paras 5.117 *et seq*.

appropriate to protected disclosures can be applied to and is equally appropriate to authorised disclosures. The nature and characteristics of authorised disclosures, however, differ greatly from those of voluntary protected disclosures, just as they do from those of required disclosures (see Section C of Chapter 5, at paragraphs 5.19 *et seq*.) Applying the offence conditions in section 332 to authorised disclosures under section 338 is problematical: for this reason, the way that the four offence conditions may be applied to disclosures under section 338 is dealt with separately below (at paragraphs 6.77–6.93).

Failure to disclose following receipt of a disclosure under section 337

Subsections (2) to (4) of section 332 set out the offence conditions in the same way as in section 331(2) to (4). The conditions are very similar except that the objective element—'reasonable grounds for knowing or suspecting'—is omitted from the first condition. **6.71**

The first offence condition

This condition deals with the mental element of the offence and, perhaps because the section applies to all nominated officers including those outside the regulated sector, this is purely subjective knowledge or suspicion. **6.72**

> (2) The first condition is that he knows or suspects that another person is engaged in money laundering.

The second offence condition

This condition concerns the source of the information giving rise to knowledge or suspicion of money laundering. It applies to information received by the nominated officer in either a voluntary protected disclosure or an authorised disclosure. **6.73**

> (3) The second condition is that the information or other matter on which his knowledge or suspicion is based came to him in consequence of a disclosure made under the applicable section.[22]

The second condition, as applied to a disclosure under section 337, is that the information or other matter on which his knowledge or suspicion is based came to the nominated officer from an internal voluntary disclosure which was itself based on information or other matter that came to the discloser 'in the course of his trade, profession, business or employment'.

The third offence condition

This condition concerns the identification of the suspected money launderer and/or the laundered property. The first two conditions are, in effect, qualified by the third condition, added by section 104 of SOCPA. It is intended to restrict required disclosures to those which can provide useful information for law enforcement purposes: that is, to circumstances where the identity of the money launderer or the whereabouts of the laundered property is known or can be identified, or where, broadly speaking, the information in the disclosure received should assist in identifying the money launderer or the whereabouts of the laundered property: **6.74**

> (3A) The third condition is
> (a) that he knows the identity of the other person mentioned in subsection (2), or the whereabouts of any of the laundered property, in consequence of a disclosure made under the applicable section,

---

[22] Section 332(5B): The phrase 'applicable section' in subsection (3) means 'section 337 or, as the case may be, section 338'.

(b) that that other person, or the whereabouts of any of the laundered property, can be identified from the information or other matter mentioned in subsection (3), or

(c) that he believes, or it is reasonable to expect him to believe, that the information or other matter will or may assist in identifying that other person or the whereabouts of any of the laundered property.

Note that in the third condition, there is an alternative objective mental element (in section 3A(c)), that 'it is reasonable to expect him to believe', which is made applicable to nominated officers outside the regulated sector as well as to those in the regulated sector.

The fourth offence condition

6.75 Where these three conditions are present, the nominated officer is required to make a disclosure to SOCA. The condition is expressed not as a positive requirement, but as the fourth—and last—offence condition. The nominated officer commits the offence of failure to disclose if he fails to make the required disclosure:

(4) The fourth condition is that he does not make the required disclosure to a person authorised for the purposes of this Part by the Director General of SOCA as soon as is practicable after the information or other matter mentioned in subsection (3) comes to him.

What must be disclosed

6.76 What must be disclosed in the required disclosure is set out in the new subsection (5), inserted by section 104(6) of SOCPA:

(5) The required disclosure is a disclosure of—
(a) the identity of the other person mentioned in subsection (2), if disclosed to him under the applicable section,
(b) the whereabouts of the laundered property, so far as disclosed to him under the applicable section, and
(c) the information or other matter mentioned in subsection (3).

The 'laundered property' is defined in subsection (5A) as 'the property forming the subject-matter of the money laundering that he knows or suspects that other person to be engaged in'.

Failure to disclose following receipt of a disclosure under section 338

6.77 For disclosures received by the nominated officer under section 338, that is authorised disclosures, the same four offence conditions in section 332 apply. These conditions are appropriate to the subject matter and the terms of a voluntary protected disclosure under section 337 (as they would be, with the addition of an objective mental element, to the circumstances of a required disclosure under section 330). They do not, however, readily fit the different subject matter and terms of a disclosure under section 338.

6.78 The problem in applying these conditions to disclosures under section 338 stems from the fact that the characteristics of authorised disclosures are quite different from those of protected disclosures (or of required disclosures under section 330).[23] The most significant difference is that an authorised disclosure is a disclosure about criminal property and not, other than incidentally, a disclosure of knowledge or suspicion that another person is engaged in money laundering. The following paragraphs consider how the offence conditions can be

---

[23] See Section C in Chapter 5, at paras 5.19–5.26.

applied to authorised disclosures under section 338 and where the application of these conditions is problematical.

Insofar as the conditions can be applied to the circumstances revealed by an authorised disclosure it is because, in practice, those circumstances will usually also give rise to information that fulfils the conditions of a required disclosure (as under section 330 or section 331) or a voluntary disclosure. **6.79**

The first offence condition

This condition is that he knows or suspects that another person is engaged in money laundering. **6.80**

An authorised disclosure is not about 'another person' who 'is engaged in money laundering': it is a disclosure 'that property is criminal property'. It is also a disclosure by 'the alleged offender'. Despite, however, the use in section 338 of the pejorative phrase 'alleged offender' about a person who needs to make and does make an authorised disclosure, an alleged offender is not a person who *is engaged in money laundering*. He is not a person who is committing the criminal offence of money laundering, and never will be so long as he fulfils the condition in subsection (2)(a) of sections 327, 328, and/or 329. **6.81**

Authorised disclosures will usually, but not necessarily, contain information about one or more persons who are suspected of being engaged in money laundering. This information would be incidental to the purpose of an authorised disclosure and to its essential content. **6.82**

Given the very wide definition of criminal property, especially the terms of section 340(4), there may be circumstances in which a person has to make an authorised disclosure (about criminal property), but where there is *no* person, whether identifiable or not, who 'is engaged in money laundering'. In that case, the first offence condition would not be present and there could be no requirement for the nominated officer to make a disclosure. **6.83**

The second offence condition

This condition is that the information or other matter on which his knowledge or suspicion is based came to him in consequence of a disclosure made under either section 337 or section 338. **6.84**

In a formal sense, this condition is fulfilled when the nominated officer receives an authorised disclosure containing information giving rise to the necessary 'knowledge or suspicion'. However, the knowledge or suspicion referred to in section 332(3) is that described in subsection (2): knowledge or suspicion 'that another person is engaged in money laundering'. In an authorised disclosure the knowledge or suspicion is not about a person but is knowledge or suspicion that the particular property which is the subject of the disclosure is criminal property, that is, it constitutes or represents a person's benefit from criminal conduct. **6.85**

As noted above, there may be criminal property in circumstances where there is no person who *is* engaged in money laundering. In practice, however, an authorised disclosure is very likely to include information about 'another person' that gives rise to knowledge or suspicion that that person is engaged in money laundering. In that case, the second offence condition would be fulfilled. **6.86**

The third offence condition

6.87 This condition concerns the identification of the suspected money launderer and/or the laundered property:

> The third condition is—
> (a) that he knows the identity of the other person mentioned in subsection (2), or the whereabouts of any of the laundered property, in consequence of a disclosure made under the applicable section,
> (b) that that other person, or the whereabouts of any of the laundered property, can be identified from the information or other matter mentioned in subsection (3), or
> (c) that he believes, or it is reasonable to expect him to believe, that the information or other matter will or may assist in identifying that other person or the whereabouts of any of the laundered property.

6.88 The three alternative formulations of the third condition are set out in descending order of exactness of knowledge or usefulness of information in identifying the other person or the whereabouts of the laundered property. The terms used do not fit a disclosure about criminal property, but where an authorised disclosure does include information about another person known or suspected to be engaged in money laundering, the third condition may well be fulfilled.

6.89 It should be noted, firstly, that the 'alleged offender' cannot be equated with 'another person engaged in money laundering' (see paragraph 6.85 above) and, secondly, that 'the laundered property' for the purposes of the required disclosure is not necessarily the same as the 'criminal property' in the authorised disclosure. The criminal property about which the internal discloser makes an authorised disclosure may, however, be the same as or form a part of the suspected 'laundered property' of a person known or suspected to be engaged in money laundering.

The position of the nominated officer

6.90 In practice, but for reasons that are incidental to both the essential content and the purpose of the authorised disclosure received, the nominated officer may well find that the first three conditions are fulfilled, so that he has to make a required disclosure about another person whom he knows or suspects is engaged in money laundering.

6.91 The nominated officer will also, quite independently of any required disclosure, have a responsibility to respond to the internal authorised disclosure and the discloser's likely need for consent. The disclosure made by the nominated officer will, therefore, usually be both a required disclosure to comply with section 332 and a disclosure 'that property is criminal property',[24] combined with a request for consent. (On this latter aspect of the disclosure, see paragraphs 6.99–6.102.)

The fourth offence condition

6.92 This condition is that he does not make the required disclosure to SOCA as soon as is practicable after the information or other matter giving rise to knowledge or suspicion of money laundering comes to him. Where information contained in the internal authorised disclosure effectively fulfils the first three offence conditions, the nominated officer must make the required disclosure.

---

[24] See the discussion of dual purpose reports at paras 5.62 and 5.63.

There could, however, be circumstances where a nominated officer who has received an **6.93** authorised disclosure is not required to make a disclosure to SOCA because there is no person suspected of being engaged in money laundering and because, although there is property identified as criminal property in the internal authorised disclosure, there is no 'laundered property' within the terms of section 332(5A).

Specimen indictment

The offence under section 332 is triable either in the magistrates' court or in the Crown **6.94** Court.

STATEMENT OF OFFENCE

Failure to disclose contrary to section 332 of the Proceeds of Crime Act 2002.

PARTICULARS OF OFFENCE

A B, a nominated officer, on a date between the . . . day of . . . and the . . . day of . . ., knowing or suspecting, on the basis of information that came to him in consequence of a disclosure under section 337, that C D was a person engaged in money laundering, and knowing, in consequence of the said disclosure, the identity of C D and the whereabouts of the laundered property, did not make the required disclosure to the Serious Organised Crime Agency as soon as practicable after the said information came to him.

Sentence

Under section 334(2), a person guilty of an offence under section 332 is liable: **6.95**

- on summary conviction, to imprisonment for a term not exceeding six months or to a fine not exceeding the statutory maximum or to both; or
- on conviction on indictment, to imprisonment for a term not exceeding five years or to a fine or to both.

Defences and exceptions

There are two defences under section 332, which are essentially the same as the defences in **6.96** section 331(6) and (6A): a defence of reasonable excuse and a defence that applies where money laundering is taking place outside the United Kingdom.

Reasonable excuse

There is no authority on what would count as a reasonable excuse under section 332(6). For **6.97** a nominated officer, whether inside or outside the regulated sector, it seems likely that 'reasonable excuse' would be construed narrowly.

> (6) But he does not commit an offence under this section if he has a reasonable excuse for not making the required disclosure.

Money laundering outside the UK

A second defence relates to money laundering carried on outside the UK: **6.98**

> (7) Nor does a person commit an offence under this section if—
>   (a) he knows, or believes on reasonable grounds, that the money laundering is occurring in a particular country or territory outside the United Kingdom, and
>   (b) the money laundering—
>   (i) is not unlawful under the criminal law applying in that country or territory, and
>   (ii) is not of a description prescribed in an order made by the Secretary of State.

This defence or exception is in the same terms as in sections 330(7A) and 331(6A). The nature and extent of it is considered above at paragraphs 6.24–6.27.

Disclosure by the nominated officer 'that property is criminal property'

6.99 The making of the required disclosure enables the nominated officer to comply with his obligation under section 332, but—in itself—does nothing to fulfil his responsibility to respond to the internal authorised disclosure and to assist the person who has made the internal disclosure, where necessary, with the obtaining of appropriate consent.

6.100 The authorised disclosure made by the 'alleged offender' to the nominated officer is, strictly speaking, a *voluntary* disclosure, albeit one impelled by necessity. The disclosure and request for consent are made so that the discloser, who would otherwise be at risk of committing a money laundering offence, can take advantage of a particular statutory defence or exception to the serious criminal offence of money laundering.[25] As Hamblen J recognized in the case of *Shah and another v HSBC Private Bank (UK) Ltd,*[26] such a person may be 'effectively com-pelled' to make an authorised disclosure under POCA: 'He is doing what the law forces him to do.'

6.101 On receiving an internal authorised disclosure, the nominated officer will need to consider carefully the information from the internal discloser in order to:

- to assess the information from the internal discloser giving rise to suspicion;
- to ascertain whether the relevant property has been correctly identified by the discloser as 'criminal property'; and
- to consider the nature of the transaction which the internal discloser wants to carry out and to check whether that transaction would be a 'prohibited act' (under one or more of sections 327, 328, and 329) for which the internal discloser would need 'appropriate consent'.

6.102 These three areas of concern for the nominated officer have a quite different focus to the four offence conditions in section 332: the purpose of a disclosure to SOCA that property is criminal property is to assist the internal discloser, the 'alleged offender', to obtain appropri-ate consent where that is needed as a defence to a potential money laundering offence. Such a disclosure by a nominated officer is not a 'required disclosure': it is, like an authorised dis-closure, a *voluntary* disclosure, but is, similarly, one made in response to a need rather than an obligation.

C. Authorised Disclosures and Appropriate Consent

6.103 A person intending to deal in some way with property who comes into possession of infor-mation that causes him to know or suspect that the property is a person's benefit from crimi-nal conduct is, without having any criminal intent, at risk of committing a criminal offence. This would not be an offence of failing to disclose, but one of the principal money laundering

---

[25] ss 327(2)(a), 328(2)(a), and 329(2)(a). In most, but not all, cases an authorised disclosure will need to be and will be accompanied by a request for appropriate consent.
[26] [2009] EWHC 79 (QB).

offences in sections 327, 328, or 329. In most cases the only defence available will be that of making an authorised disclosure and seeking appropriate consent.

Section 338: authorised disclosures

An authorised disclosure is a disclosure that property is criminal property made by a person, **6.104** the 'alleged offender', as a means of avoiding potential liability for one or more of the principal money laundering offences.

The circumstances or conditions under which a person 'does not commit such an offence' **6.105** although he is dealing with criminal property in a way that amounts to a prohibited act are set out in subsection (2) of sections 327, 328, and 329. The first two (alternative) conditions relate to authorised disclosures:

> (2) But a person does not commit such an offence if—
> > (a) he makes an authorised disclosure under section 338 and (if the disclosure is made before he does the act mentioned in subsection (1)) he has the appropriate consent;
> > (b) he intended to make such a disclosure but had a reasonable excuse for not doing so;

The definition of authorised disclosure

Authorised disclosure is defined in section 338(1): **6.106**

> (1) For the purposes of this Part a disclosure is authorised if—
> > (a) it is a disclosure to a constable, a customs officer or a nominated officer by the alleged offender that property is criminal property, and
> > . . .
> > (c) the first, second or third condition set out below is satisfied.

An authorised disclosure is a disclosure about criminal property made 'by the alleged **6.107** offender'. The term 'alleged offender' is an unfortunate term and its use in Part 7 of POCA is inconsistent.[27] In section 338(1)(a), 'alleged offender' must mean the person at risk of committing a principal money laundering offence.

An authorised disclosure may be made directly to a constable (that is, to a police officer or to **6.108** SOCA) or to a customs officer, but may also be made as an internal disclosure to a nominated officer. The need to make an authorised disclosure may arise outside the context of any trade, profession, business, or employment or may arise in a work context where there is no nominated officer. In practice, however, most authorised disclosures are made by people working in the regulated sector or in other businesses where a nominated officer has been appointed, so there is the option of making the disclosure to a nominated officer in accordance with the terms of section 338(5).

The conditions

For a disclosure to qualify as authorised, it must satisfy one of the three conditions laid down **6.109** in section 338(2), (2A) and (3). These relate to the timing of the disclosure: before, during or after the 'prohibited act'.[28]

---

[27] It is used in s 338(1) to (3) and (5), but not, for instance, in s 335(2). It is also used, with bizarre inappropriateness, in s 330(9) and (13). (See also para 6.39.)
[28] This term is defined in s 338(6): references to the prohibited act are to an act mentioned in ss 327(1), 328(1) or 329(1) (as the case may be).

The first condition

6.110 For a person in the uncomfortable position of an 'alleged offender', it is preferable to make the disclosure before doing the prohibited act and to obtain consent for doing it. Whether that is possible will depend on when the person comes to know or suspect that the property is a person's benefit from criminal conduct:

> (2) The first condition is that the disclosure is made before the alleged offender does the prohibited act.

The second condition

6.111 The second condition in subsection (2A), which was inserted by SOCPA,[29] deals with the situation in which the disclosure is made while the alleged offender is doing the prohibited act:

> (2A) The second condition is that—
> > (a) the disclosure is made while the alleged offender is doing the prohibited act,
> > (b) he began to do the act at a time when, because he did not then know or suspect that the property constituted or represented a person's benefit from criminal conduct, the act was not a prohibited act, and
> > (c) the disclosure is made on his own initiative and as soon as is practicable after he first knows or suspects that the property constitutes or represents a person's benefit from criminal conduct.

6.112 At first sight, this condition seems odd because an 'act' is typically something done at a particular point in time, but section 329 includes 'possession' and 'use' as prohibited acts. Possession is a continuing state; use may be continuous or intermittent, but to describe either possession or use as an 'act' strains the meaning of the word. Nevertheless, for the purposes of section 329, possession and use of criminal property are 'prohibited acts'.

6.113 In *Bowman v Fels*,[30] the Court of Appeal commented on this aspect of the money laundering offences:

> . . .each of ss 327–9 speaks of doing an act in precise terms suggestive of a focus on a particular point in time. This is so in the case of ss 327 and 329, even though use or possession of criminal property may be continuing, with the result that a charge may be brought and may succeed by reference to any point during a period. In s 328 the nature of the act is either entering into an arrangement or the vaguer concept of 'becom[ing] concerned in an arrangement'. To enter into an arrangement involves a single act at a single point in time; so too, on the face of it, does to 'become concerned' in an arrangement, even though the point at which someone may be said to have 'become' concerned may be open to argument.

6.114 The second condition is only satisfied where all three elements of subsection (2A) are in place as, for instance, where a person has come into possession of property, some time later comes to know or suspect that the property is the proceeds of crime, and then makes a disclosure as soon as practicable.

---

[29] SOCPA 2005, s 106(5).
[30] (2005) EWCA Civ 226.

The third condition

The third condition deals with the situation in which the disclosure is made after the alleged **6.115** offender does the prohibited act. This is the least favourable situation for the alleged offender:

> (3) The third condition is that
> (a) the disclosure is made after the alleged offender does the prohibited act,
> (b) there is a good reason for his failure to make the disclosure before he did the act, and
> (c) the disclosure is made on his own initiative and as soon as it is practicable for him to make it.

As with the second condition, the third is only satisfied where all three elements of the sub- **6.116** section are in place, and in section 338(3)(b) there is a provision that, in effect, requires the alleged offender to explain and justify his failure to disclose earlier—to show that 'there is a good reason for his failure to make the disclosure before he did the act'. There is as yet no authority on what would constitute a good reason under section 338(3)(b). In the context of the UK's prescriptive disclosure regime, the phrase 'good reason' is likely to be construed narrowly.

Authorised disclosures and the apparatus of consent are not derived from the FATF 40 **6.117** Recommendations or the Third Money Laundering Directive so these sources can provide no direct help on what might be a good reason. There could well be circumstances in which doing a prohibited act and reporting afterwards would best serve the anti-money laundering objective, but it would be a bold 'alleged offender' who took on himself the responsibility for acting in this way. The penal provisions that attach to a failure to make an authorised disclosure are not conducive to the exercise of discretion, however sensible and well-intentioned.

However, in the different context of the reporting obligations of the regulated sector under **6.118** the Third Money Laundering Directive, this scenario is specifically considered in Recital 30 and in Article 24:

> Recital 30
> By way of derogation from the general prohibition on executing suspicious transactions, the institutions and persons covered by this Directive may execute suspicious transactions before informing the competent authorities, where refraining from the execution thereof is impossible or likely to frustrate efforts to pursue the beneficiaries of a suspected money laundering or terrorist financing operation.

Recital 30 in the Preamble to the Third Money Laundering Directive is given effect in Article **6.119** 24, paragraph 2, below:

> Article 24
> 1. Member States shall require the institutions and persons covered by this Directive to refrain from carrying out transactions which they know or suspect to be related to money laundering or terrorist financing until they have completed the necessary action in accordance with Article 22(1)(a).[31] In conformity with the legislation of the Member States, instructions may be given not to carry out the transaction.
> 2. Where such a transaction is suspected of giving rise to money laundering or terrorist financing and where to refrain in such manner is impossible or is likely to frustrate efforts to

---

[31] The necessary action is, in summary, to promptly inform the FIU of suspected money laundering or terrorist financing.

pursue the beneficiaries of a suspected money laundering or terrorist financing operation, the institutions and persons concerned shall inform the FIU immediately afterwards.

Protection

6.120 Authorised disclosures are not protected disclosures under section 337, but the same protection provided by section 337(1) is given to authorised disclosures by section 338(4): 'An authorised disclosure is not to be taken to breach any restriction on the disclosure of information (however imposed).'

Nominated officers and authorised disclosures

6.121 Most disclosures to SOCA about criminal property, combined with a request for consent, are made by nominated officers, following an internal authorised disclosure by a person (the 'alleged offender') who may be about to deal in some way with criminal property. These disclosures by nominated officers to SOCA are themselves usually referred to as 'authorised disclosures', but they are not, strictly speaking, authorised disclosures. Their legal status is problematical: they are disclosures 'that property is criminal property', as referred to in section 336(2)(a), but they are neither authorised disclosures under section 338(1), nor required disclosures under section 332.[32] Such disclosures seem to lie outside the two disclosure regimes—for required and authorised disclosures. (See above, at paragraphs 6.99–6.102).

Section 335: appropriate consent

Actual consent

6.122 Appropriate consent, consent to do a prohibited act, may be either actual consent or deemed consent. Actual consent may be obtained from a constable (the term includes designated staff at SOCA) or from a customs officer where an authorised disclosure is made directly to a constable or customs officer by the alleged offender. Most authorised disclosures, however, are made to a nominated officer and if actual consent is obtained, it will be from the nominated officer:

(1) The appropriate consent is—
  (a) the consent of a nominated officer to do a prohibited act if an authorised disclosure is made to the nominated officer;
  (b) the consent of a constable to do a prohibited act if an authorised disclosure is made to a constable;
  (c) the consent of a customs officer to do a prohibited act if an authorised disclosure is made to a customs officer.

Although section 335(1) reads like a definition, it is incomplete. Because consent may be deemed as well as actual consent, its full definition extends over section 325(1) to (4) inclusive.

6.123 The prohibited acts in respect of which consent may be needed are contained in the criminal offences of money laundering, which are broadly drafted to cover any act involving property, including use and possession.[33] Anyone, therefore, may need to make an authorised

---

[32] See the discussion of required disclosures under s 332, following receipt by a nominated officer of an authorised disclosure under s 338, above, at paras 6.77 *et seq.*

[33] Section 335(8): references to a prohibited act are to an act mentioned in ss 327(1), 328(1), or 329(1) (as the case may be).

disclosure and seek consent. The provisions do not apply only to those who work in the regulated sector or only to situations arising in the course of a 'trade, profession, business or employment'. Since, however, the regulated sector embraces most of the business and professional activity thought to be particularly vulnerable to money laundering, most authorised disclosures and requests for consent are made by those working in regulated sector organizations or other organizations where a nominated officer has been appointed.

Deemed consent

The circumstances in which appropriate consent is deemed to have been received by the person seeking consent, following an authorised disclosure to a constable or customs officer, are set out in subsections (2) to (4) of section 335:   **6.124**

> (2) A person must be treated as having the appropriate consent if—
>   (a) he makes an authorised disclosure to a constable or a customs officer, and
>   (b) the condition in subsection (3) or the condition in subsection (4) is satisfied.
> (3) The condition is that before the end of the notice period he does not receive notice from a constable or customs officer that consent to the doing of the act is refused.
> (4) The condition is that–
>   (a) before the end of the notice period he receives notice from a constable or customs officer that consent to the doing of the act is refused, and
>   (b) the moratorium period has expired.

The 'person' referred to in neutral language in section 335 is the 'alleged offender' in section 338.

In effect, there are three ways in which consent may be obtained and different timescales for each: **6.125**

- Actual consent may be given—in practice, almost always by SOCA—at any time during the notice period (defined in subsection (5)—see below).
- Deemed consent is obtained if notice of refusal of consent is not received before the end of the notice period.
- If consent is refused, deemed consent will nevertheless be obtained when the moratorium period has expired.

Notice period

The notice period is defined in section 335(5):   **6.126**

> (5) The notice period is the period of seven working days starting with the first working day after the person makes the disclosure.
> . . .
> (7) A working day is a day other than a Saturday, a Sunday, Christmas Day, Good Friday or a day which is a bank holiday under the Banking and Financial Dealings Act 1971 (c. 80) in the part of the United Kingdom in which the person is when he makes the disclosure.

The notice period allows SOCA and law enforcement agencies to consider the information disclosed and decide whether consent should be given or refused.

Moratorium period

The moratorium period is defined in section 335(6) as the period of 31 calendar days starting with the day on which the person receives notice that consent to the doing of the act is refused. The moratorium period allows the relevant law enforcement agency to investigate   **6.127** the situation revealed by the disclosure and the criminal property that is the subject of the disclosure, and then to take any necessary action such as applying for a restraint order.

6.128 Consent 'to do a prohibited act' that is deemed to have been obtained at the expiry of the moratorium period may be illusory since the relevant property may have been restrained and the intended act may no longer be possible. In any event, in the light of changed circumstances, the person who, some five weeks earlier, sought consent to do a prohibited act may no longer wish to have anything to do with the suspected criminal property.

6.129 The timescales set out in section 335 apply where a person makes a disclosure directly to a constable or a customs officer, but this is not a typical situation. In practice, most authorised disclosures are made to nominated officers and it is the timescales set out in section 336 that apply.

Section 336: nominated officer: consent

6.130 Where a person has made an authorised disclosure to a nominated officer and needs consent to do a prohibited act, the nominated officer can only give consent when actual consent has first been obtained from SOCA or there is deemed consent. Section 336 sets out the framework of conditions and timescales within which a nominated officer has to act in responding to an authorised disclosure and request for consent. It is an offence-creating section: see paragraphs 6.136–6.139 below.

The conditions for giving consent

6.131 A nominated officer must not give appropriate consent to the doing of a prohibited act unless one of three conditions is satisfied.

The first condition

6.132 The first condition describes the situation where the nominated officer makes a disclosure 'that property is criminal property' to SOCA and receives actual consent from SOCA:

> (2) The condition is that–
> > (a) he makes a disclosure that property is criminal property to a person authorised for the purposes of this Part by the Director General of the Serious Organised Crime Agency, and
> > (b) such a person gives consent to the doing of the act.

The second condition

6.133 If actual consent is not obtained, deemed consent may be obtained in essentially the same two ways as under section 335. The second condition concerns deemed consent at the expiry of the notice period:

> (3) The condition is that–
> > (a) he makes a disclosure that property is criminal property to a person authorised for the purposes of this Part by the Director General of the Serious Organised Crime Agency, and
> > (b) before the end of the notice period he does not receive notice from such a person that consent to the doing of the act is refused.

The third condition

6.134 The third condition concerns deemed consent at the expiry of the moratorium period:

(4) The condition is that–
    (a) he makes a disclosure that property is criminal property to a person authorised for the purposes of this Part by the Director General of the Serious Organised Crime Agency,
    (b) before the end of the notice period he receives notice from such a person that consent to the doing of the act is refused, and
    (c) the moratorium period has expired.

The notice period and the moratorium period

The length of the notice period is the same as in section 335 and 'working day' is **6.135** defined in the same way. The length of the moratorium period is also the same, but note that the definition in section 336(8) differs slightly in the way that the starting date is determined:[34]

(7) The notice period is the period of seven working days starting with the first working day after the nominated officer makes the disclosure.
(8) The moratorium period is the period of 31 days starting with the day on which the nominated officer is given notice that consent to the doing of the act is refused.

Proving the offence under section 336

A nominated officer commits an offence if he gives consent where none of the three conditions applies. The offence of giving consent unlawfully is set out in section 336(5): **6.136**

(5) A person who is a nominated officer commits an offence if—
    (a) he gives consent to a prohibited act in circumstances where none of the conditions in subsections (2), (3) and (4) is satisfied, and
    (b) he knows or suspects that the act is a prohibited act.

Although succinctly defined,[35] 'prohibited act' is a complex term, containing elements **6.137** derived from sections 327(1), 328(1), or 329(1) and from the definition of criminal property in section 340(3). A prohibited act is an act of dealing with criminal property under sections 327, 328, or 329; 'criminal property' is property that constitutes or represents a person's benefit from criminal conduct *and* the alleged offender knows or suspects that it constitutes or represents such a benefit.

The elements of the offence that the prosecution have to prove, therefore, are that: **6.138**

- The defendant was a nominated officer at the relevant time.
- The defendant gave consent to an act (e.g. the transfer of money to another).
- The act was a 'prohibited act', an act of 'dealing with' criminal property (see above, paragraph 6.137).
- The defendant knew or suspected at the time that the act was a 'prohibited act'.
- The defendant was not authorised, by actual consent from SOCA or by deemed consent, to give consent to the act of transfer.

---

[34] Under s 335, it is '. . .the day on which the person receives notice that consent to the doing of the act is refused'. Under s 336, it is '. . .the day on which the nominated officer is given notice that consent to the doing of the act is refused'. In practice, consent will usually be given by telephone, so that there will be no room for any actual difference.
[35] In s 336(10): 'References to a prohibited act are to an act mentioned in section 327(1), 328(1) or 329(1) (as the case may be).'

Specimen indictment

6.139 The offence is triable either in the magistrates' court or in the Crown Court.

STATEMENT OF OFFENCE

Unlawfully giving consent to a prohibited act contrary to section 336 of the Proceeds of Crime Act 2002

PARTICULARS OF OFFENCE

A B, a nominated officer, on the . . . day of . . ., gave consent to a prohibited act by C D, namely the transfer of [a sum of money] to E F when he, A B, did not have consent to the doing of that act and he knew or suspected that the act was a prohibited act.

Sentence

6.140 A person guilty of an offence under section 336(5) is liable:

- on summary conviction, to imprisonment for a term not exceeding six months or to a fine not exceeding the statutory maximum or to both; or
- on conviction on indictment, to imprisonment for a term not exceeding five years or to a fine or to both.

D. Ancillary Provisions

Protection for disclosers

6.141 The nature of the protection that is given is stated in section 337(1):

> (1) A disclosure which satisfies the following three conditions is not to be taken to breach any restriction on the disclosure of information (however imposed).

This broadly worded protection in section 337 implements Article 26 of the Third Money Laundering Directive, which is concerned with institutions and persons in the regulated sector and with the disclosures they are obliged to make. It also applies to some disclosures outside the regulated sector:

> Article 26[36]
> The disclosure in good faith as foreseen in Articles 22(1) and 23 by an institution or person covered by this Directive or by an employee or director of such an institution or person of the information referred to in Articles 22 and 23 shall not constitute a breach of any restriction on disclosure of information imposed by contract or by any legislative, regulatory or administrative provision, and shall not involve the institution or person or its directors or employees in liability of any kind.

6.142 Subsections (2) to (4) of section 337 set out the three conditions that need to be satisfied for a disclosure to be a protected disclosure under this section.

---

[36] Article 26 itself seeks to give effect to Recommendation 14a) of the FATF 40 Recommendations:
Recommendation 14—Financial institutions, their directors, officers and employees should be:
a) Protected by legal provisions from criminal and civil liability for breach of any restriction on disclosure of information imposed by contract or by any legislative, regulatory or administrative provision, if they report their suspicions in good faith to the FIU, even if they did not know precisely what the underlying criminal activity was, and regardless of whether illegal activity actually occurred.

The first condition

This condition limits the protection to situations where the 'information or other matter' **6.143**
comes to the discloser in the course of business, but this may be business within or outside
the regulated sector:

> (2) The first condition is that the information or other matter disclosed came to the person
> making the disclosure (the discloser) in the course of his trade, profession, business or
> employment.

The second condition

The wording of the second condition, which concerns the mental element, closely reflects the **6.144**
relevant wording in the disclosure sections, section 330(2) and section 331(2), that give
rise to the need for protection. The wording of the first alternative—relating to subjective
knowledge or suspicion—also reflects that of section 332(2):

> (3) The second condition is that the information or other matter—
>   (a) causes the discloser to know or suspect, or
>   (b) gives him reasonable grounds for knowing or suspecting, that another person is
>   engaged in money laundering.

The third condition

This condition concerns the making of the disclosure and the person to whom the disclosure **6.145**
is made. It also limits the protection, in that it will only apply where the disclosure is made
as soon as practicable, and this restriction applies both to internal disclosures made by an
employee to a nominated officer and to disclosures made to a constable or a customs
officer:

> (4) The third condition is that the disclosure is made to a constable, a customs officer or a
>   nominated officer as soon as is practicable after the information or other matter comes
>   to the discloser.

Subsection (5) defines a 'disclosure to a nominated officer' in the context of section 337: **6.146**

> (5) A disclosure to a nominated officer is a disclosure which—
>   (a) is made to a person nominated by the discloser's employer to receive disclosures
>   under section 330[37] or this section,[38] and
>   (b) is made in the course of the discloser's employment.

What disclosures are protected?

These conditions, therefore, provide for the following disclosures to be protected under sec- **6.147**
tion 337:

- required disclosures by persons working in the regulated sector (under section 330);
- required disclosures by nominated officers in the regulated sector (under section 331);
- required disclosures by nominated officers (under section 332); and
- voluntary disclosures by persons working in a trade, profession, business, or employment
  outside the regulated sector.

---

[37] A person nominated to receive disclosures under s 330 is a nominated officer in the regulated sector: see
s 331(1).
[38] A person nominated to receive disclosures under s 337 is any nominated officer (that is, a nominated
officer either in or outside the regulated sector): see s 332(1).

6.148 There are other lawful disclosures under Part 7 of POCA that are or may be similarly protected under separate provisions in other sections:

- Authorised disclosures under section 338 (protected by the provision in section 338(4)[39]).
- Further disclosures made in response to a formal request by SOCA under section 339(2). (Note that the provision for such further disclosures is linked to the provision for a prescribed disclosure form under section 339, and no order has yet been made by the Secretary of State for a prescribed form.)
- Disclosures to SOCA made by a nominated officer 'that property is criminal property'. The status of these disclosures is uncertain;[40] equally uncertain is whether they are protected disclosures, although it must surely have been intended that they should be. They do not, however, seem to be effectively protected either by section 337 or by section 338(4). In practice, most such disclosures about criminal property will also be or include disclosure about a person engaged in money laundering, so that they will, in fact, be protected under section 337.

Protection for information disclosed

6.149 Subsection (4A) of section 337, inserted by section 104 of SOCPA, extends the protection to cover information given in accordance with the requirement[41] that the content of the required disclosure must include, where known, the identity of the suspected money launderer, the whereabouts of the laundered property and the information giving rise to the suspicion:

> (4A) Where a disclosure consists of a disclosure protected under subsection (1) and a disclosure of either or both of—
> (a) the identity of the other person mentioned in subsection (3), and
> (b) the whereabouts of property forming the subject-matter of the money laundering that the discloser knows or suspects, or has reasonable grounds for knowing or suspecting, that other person to be engaged in, the disclosure of the thing mentioned in paragraph (a) or (b) (as well as the disclosure protected under subsection (1)) is not to be taken to breach any restriction on the disclosure of information (however imposed).

Form and manner of disclosures

6.150 Section 339 empowers the Home Office to prescribe the form and manner of disclosures and, as amended, creates a summary offence of making a disclosure otherwise than in the form and manner prescribed:

> (1) The Secretary of State may by order prescribe the form and manner in which a disclosure under section 330, 331, 332 or 338 must be made.

6.151 In July 2007 the Home Office issued a consultation document on introducing a prescribed form and signalled its intention to invoke the power in section 339(1) for the Secretary of State, by order, to prescribe the form and manner in which disclosures can lawfully be made.

---

[39] See para 6.120 above.
[40] See the discussion about the status of these disclosures in the context of required disclosures under s 332, at paras 6.81–6.83 and 6.99–6.102, above.
[41] Contained in ss 330(5), 331(5), and 332(5).

The summary of responses to the consultation exercise was published in February 2008.[42] In **6.152** its conclusion the Home Office said that: 'Following the issues arising from the consultation process, the Government has accepted a recommendation from SOCA not to proceed at present with the introduction by Order of a prescribed form and manner of reporting suspicions of money laundering.'[43] For the present, therefore, the use of the power in section 339(1) remains on hold. SOCA has a modular report form, readily available through SAR Online, that it prefers disclosers to use, but there is no prescription.[44]

Disclosures by constables

It is important that all external disclosures reach the FIU at SOCA as soon as possible, and **6.153** section 339ZA makes provision for this where a disclosure is made not to SOCA, but to a police officer or customs officer:

> Where a disclosure is made under this Part to a constable or an officer of Revenue and Customs, the constable or officer of Revenue and Customs must disclose it in full to a person authorised for the purposes of this Part by the Director General of the Serious Organised Crime Agency as soon as practicable after it has been made.

E. Conclusion

Money laundering disclosures under POCA are the main part, but not the whole, of the **6.154** disclosure or 'SARs' regime. The other part, consisting of disclosures about terrorist money laundering and other terrorist property offences, forms the subject matter of the next chapter.

---

[42] 'The Proceeds of Crime Act 2002: Tackling Money Laundering. Suspicious Activity Reports: Prescribed Form and Manner, Summary of Responses to the Consultation Exercise and Next Steps'. This is available on the Home Office website at <http://www.homeoffice.gov.uk/documents>.

[43] One positive development which influenced the thinking of the Home Office and SOCA was that the statistics showed a steadily increasing use of the SOCA preferred form and, particularly, the making of SARs electronically through 'SAR Online' (<http://www.soca.gov.uk>). This has reduced the processing time required by SOCA for disclosures without the need for compulsion.

[44] See Chapter 5, at paras 5.51–5.52.

7

DISCLOSURE AND THE DISCLOSURE OFFENCES UNDER THE TERRORISM ACT 2000

A. Introduction

7.01   Part III of the Terrorism Act 2000 (TA 2000) contains, like Part 7 of the Proceeds of Crime Act 2002 (POCA), a number of provisions relating to disclosure and consent. These provisions, which concern disclosures about both money laundering and terrorist property, have been heavily amended and added to since the Terrorism Bill was first enacted. There are also disclosure provisions that relate to acts of terrorism. The resulting law is far from straightforward, but in practice disclosure about terrorist money laundering and terrorist property offences, and the related consent provisions, have been largely integrated into the SARs regime.

7.02   The terrorist property offences are set out in sections 15 to 17, which cover fund-raising, funding arrangements and the use and possession of terrorist property, and in section 18 which concerns terrorist money laundering. These criminal offences are considered in Chapter 4 above; the civil provisions relating to cash seizure and forfeiture are dealt with in Chapter 11.

Terrorist property

The definition of the politically tricky and legally difficult term 'terrorism'[1] is dealt with in   **7.03**
Chapter 4; the definition of terrorist property, in section 14 of the Act, is set out
below:

> (1) In this Act 'terrorist property' means–
>> (a) money or other property which is likely to be used for the purposes of terrorism
>> (including any resources of a proscribed organization),
>> (b) proceeds of the commission of acts of terrorism, and
>> (c) proceeds of acts carried out for the purposes of terrorism.
> (2) In subsection (1)–
>> (a) a reference to proceeds of an act includes a reference to any property which wholly
>> or partly, and directly or indirectly, represents the proceeds of the act (including pay-
>> ments or other rewards in connection with its commission), and
>> (b) the reference to an organization's resources includes a reference to any money or other
>> property which is applied or made available, or is to be applied or made available, for
>> use by the organization.

Other relevant terms are defined in the interpretation section, section 121.[2]

B. The Disclosure Provisions: Overview

As substantially added to and amended,[3] the sections that now make up the disclosure regime   **7.04**
under TA 2000 are complex and not easy to follow. In this and the next chapter, they are
considered not in the numerical order of the sections, but under headings which reflect the
main features of the disclosure regime.

Required disclosures and other lawful disclosures are dealt with in this chapter: **7.05**

- *Required disclosures about 'another person'* suspected of committing a terrorist property
offence under sections 15 to 18. [Sections 19, 21A and 21C.]
- *Required disclosures of information about acts of terrorism.* [Section 38B.][4]
- *Disclosures about 'terrorist property'* as a defence to offences under sections 15 to 18.
[Sections 21, 21ZA and 21ZB.]
- *Protected disclosures.* [Section 21B; also disclosures under the permissive provisions of
section 20.]

---

[1] See the helpful chapter by Iain Cameron on 'Terrorist Financing in International Law' in *International and European Financial Criminal Law* (Lexis Nexis Butterworths 2006, chapter 4 at pp 65–95). The definition of 'terrorism' was slightly amended by the Counter-Terrorism Act 2008 to include the word 'racial' in s 1(1)(c).
[2] There is also an index of defined expressions in s 122.
[3] Amendments, which came into force on 26 December 2007, were made by the Terrorism Act 2000 and Proceeds of Crime Act 2002 (Amendment) Regulations 2007/3398. New offences of tipping off, very similar to those in POCA, s 333A, and with similar specific defences, were added to the Act under enabling powers in the European Communities Act 1972. There were also amendments made to the disclosure and consent provisions under the Act.
[4] Disclosures under s 38B, largely outside the scope of this book, are included in order to deal with the degree of potential overlap with terrorist property disclosures.

7.06 Unlawful disclosures and permitted disclosures (exceptions to tipping off and other offences of unlawful disclosure) are dealt with in Chapter 8:

- *Unlawful disclosures* (tipping-off, etc). [Sections 21D and 39.[5]]
- *Permitted disclosures*. [Sections 21E, 21F and 21G[6].]

Comparison of disclosure provisions in POCA 2002 and TA 2000

7.07 A rough equivalence in the construction of a disclosure regime can be seen between Part 7 of POCA (with section 342) and Part III of TA 2000 (with sections 39 and 63), but there are many differences and not a few anomalies.

Table 7.1 Comparison of disclosure provisions in POCA 2002 and TA 2000

	TA 2000	POCA 2002
REQUIRED DISCLOSURE		
Required disclosure that another person has committed an offence under any of sections 15 to 18, from information in the course of a business *outside* the regulated sector	Section 19	[No equivalent in POCA, but note section 332—required disclosure by nominated officers *outside* the regulated sector]
Required disclosure that another person has committed an offence under any of sections 15 to 18, from information in the course of a business *inside* the regulated sector	Section 21A	Section 330—required disclosure
DISCLOSURE AND/OR CONSENT AS A DEFENCE		
Disclosure that property is terrorist property as a defence to an offence under sections 15 to 18	Section 21 and sections 21ZA and 21ZB	Section 338: (authorised disclosure as a defence to offences under sections 327–329)
Consent to involvement or continued involvement in a terrorist property transaction or arrangement	Section 21(1) and sections 21ZA and 21ZB	Section 335 and Section 336
PROTECTED DISCLOSURES		
Protected disclosures (regulated sector)	Section 21B	Section 337
Disclosure of information about terrorist property, with 'permission'	Section 20	No equivalent in POCA
UNLAWFUL DISCLOSURES		
Tipping-off offences (regulated sector)	Section 21D	Section 333A
Offences of tipping off and/or prejudicing an investigation	Section 39	Section 342

Note: Offence-creating sections are underlined.

---

[5] See Section D in Chapter 8, at paras 8.60 *et seq*.
[6] See Chapter 8 at paras 8.71 *et seq*.

C. Required Disclosures: Business Outside the Regulated Sector

Section 19: disclosure of information: duty

This section places a duty on a person working in a business outside the regulated sector to **7.08** disclose information where he believes or suspects that another person has committed a terrorist property or money laundering offence. The duty to disclose covers not only money laundering under section 18, but the other terrorist property offences: fund-raising for the purposes of terrorism under section 15, use and possession of property for the purposes of terrorism under section 16, and funding arrangements for the purposes of terrorism under section 17.

Other than in the section heading, section 19 does not express the requirement to disclose as **7.09** a positive duty. The circumstances in which the duty applies are set out in section 19(1) and (1A), but that duty is implied by the offence of failure to disclose created by section 19(2):

(1) This section applies where a person
   (a) believes or suspects that another person has committed an offence under any of sections 15 to 18, and
   (b) bases his belief or suspicion on information which comes to his attention in the course of a trade, profession, business or employment.

As originally enacted, section 19 applied whenever belief or suspicion of terrorist financing **7.10** or money laundering arose in the context of any kind of business or employment.[7] Section 21A, inserted by Schedule 2, Part 3, of the Anti-Terrorism, Crime and Security Act 2001, has created a separate offence of failure to disclose that applies to those conducting business in the regulated sector and the application of section 19 is, accordingly, now restricted by section 19(1A):

(1A) But this section does not apply if the information came to the person in the course of a business in the regulated sector.[8]

The offence of failure to disclose

Section 19(2) creates a criminal offence which consists of a guilty omission to make a **7.11** disclosure:

(2) The person commits an offence if he does not disclose to a constable as soon as is reasonably practicable—
   (a) his belief or suspicion, and
   (b) the information on which it is based.

Making the disclosure

Under section 19(2), the disclosure must be made to a constable, but in this context disclosure **7.12** to a 'constable' means disclosure either to a police officer or to SOCA. Note that in the sections dealing with disclosure in Part III of TA 2000 the word 'constable'[9] sometimes means 'police officer' and at other times has the extended meaning given in subsection (7B): 'The reference

---

[7] For the background to the provisions of TA 2000 as enacted and the changes made in the same year that it came into force, see the helpful summary in the Select Committee on Home Affairs First Report on the Anti-Terrorism, Crime and Security Bill (available at <http://www.parliament.uk>).

[8] s 19(7A) The reference to a business in the regulated sector must be construed in accordance with Sch 3A.

[9] For the use of the word 'constable' in both POCA and TA 2000, see Chapter 5 at para 5.08.

to a constable includes a reference to a member of the staff of the Serious Organised Crime Agency authorised for the purposes of this section by the Director General of that Agency.'

7.13 A disclosure under section 19 may be lawfully made either to a constable or, where practicable, to a nominated officer. Although, section 19(2) itself refers only to 'a constable', it needs to be read in conjunction with section 19(4), which provides for an internal disclosure to be a defence or exception to the offence of failure to disclose (see paragraphs 7.17 and 7.20 below).

7.14 Under POCA, a person who is working in a trade, profession, business, or employment that is not regulated for money laundering purposes is under no obligation to disclose knowledge or suspicion of money laundering, but may make a voluntary protected disclosure under section 337. Under TA 2000, however, such a person commits an offence if he does not disclose his belief or suspicion that another person has committed a terrorist property or money laundering offence. He must make the disclosure as soon as is reasonably practicable and disclose the information on which his belief or suspicion is based.

Specimen indictment

7.15 The offence under section 19(2) is triable either in the magistrates' court or in the Crown Court.

STATEMENT OF OFFENCE

Failure to disclose, contrary to section 19(2) Terrorism Act 2000.

PARTICULARS OF OFFENCE

A B, between the . . . day of . . . and the . . . day of . . ., believing or suspecting, on the basis of information which came to his attention in the course of his employment, that E F had committed a terrorist property offence did not disclose to a constable as soon as reasonably practicable his belief or suspicion and the information on which it was based.

Sentence

7.16 Under section 19(8), a person guilty of an offence under this section is liable:

- (a) on conviction on indictment, to imprisonment for a term not exceeding five years, to a fine or to both, or
- (b) on summary conviction, to imprisonment for a term not exceeding six months, or to a fine not exceeding the statutory maximum or to both.

Defences and exceptions

7.17 The offence under section 19 is subject to three defences or exceptions:

- a general defence of reasonable excuse;
- a defence of having made an internal disclosure—that is, a disclosure to a nominated officer;
- an exception to the duty of disclosure that applies to professional legal advisers in privileged circumstances.

Reasonable excuse

7.18 There is a general defence of reasonable excuse under section 19(3): 'It is a defence for a person charged with an offence under subsection (2) to prove that he had a reasonable excuse for not making the disclosure.'

There is at present no authority on what would amount to a reasonable excuse for failing **7.19** to make a required disclosure under this section, but what would be reasonable must be judged against the seriousness of the underlying subject matter—terrorism and terrorist financing—and the consequent importance with which the duty is likely to be viewed by the courts. The offence of failing to disclose consists of an omission to do something that would not normally be difficult to do unless a person is effectively prevented from making a disclosure by either physical or legal constraints.

Disclosure to a nominated officer

The alternative of disclosing to a nominated officer rather than directly to a constable appears **7.20** in section 19 (and in section 21) as a defence to the commission of a failure to disclose offence. Note that the burden of proof is placed on the defendant:

> (4) Where–
> > (a) a person is in employment,
> > (b) his employer has established a procedure for the making of disclosures of the matters specified in subsection (2), and
> > (c) he is charged with an offence under that subsection,
> > > it is a defence for him to prove that he disclosed the matters specified in that subsection in accordance with the procedure.

Section 19 makes no mention of the 'nominated officer', but the role of the nominated **7.21** officer in receiving disclosures is clearly implied by the reference to '. . . a procedure for the making of disclosures . . .' established by the person's employer. It is a defence for the person '. . .to prove that he disclosed the matters specified [in section 19(2)] in accordance with [this] procedure'. Since, however, section 19 concerns those employed outside the regulated sector where there is no obligation on employers to establish such a procedure, this alternative may not be available.

Privileged circumstances

In addition to these defences, there is, in section 19(5), an exclusion from the duty **7.22** to disclose information which applies in defined circumstances to professional legal advisers. A professional legal adviser is not required under section 19(2) to disclose information that he obtains in privileged circumstances or a belief or suspicion based on information that he obtains in privileged circumstances. The terms in which this exclusion is stated are essentially the same as in the 'professional legal adviser' exception in Part 7 of POCA:

> (6) For the purpose of subsection (5) information is obtained by an adviser in privileged circumstances if it comes to him, otherwise than with a view to furthering a criminal purpose—
> > (a) from a client or a client's representative, in connection with the provision of legal advice by the adviser to the client,
> > (b) from a person seeking legal advice from the adviser, or from the person's representative, or
> > (c) from any person, for the purpose of actual or contemplated legal proceedings

Information about foreign conduct

Specific provision is made in section 19(7) for the situation where it is believed or sus- **7.23** pected that another person 'has taken an action or been in possession of a thing' outside the UK and he would have committed an offence by doing so if he had been in the UK at the time:

> (7) For the purposes of subsection (1)(a) a person shall be treated as having committed an offence under one of sections 15 to 18 if—
> (a) he has taken an action or been in possession of a thing, and
> (b) he would have committed an offence under one of those sections if he had been in the United Kingdom at the time when he took the action or was in possession of the thing.

7.24 Subsection (7) appears to extend the scope of the duty to disclose under section 19(1)(a) to include disclosures of a belief of suspicion that a person 'has taken an action or been in possession of a thing' outside the United Kingdom. It is worded as a provision that, for the purpose of defining—and extending—the requirement to disclose, deems an offence to have been committed in circumstances where it is not in fact committed. It is not, however, clear that it is needed to extend the scope of the duty of disclosure, since sections 15 to 18 already have an extraterritorial reach under section 63.

7.25 Section 63 gives jurisdiction in respect of anything done outside the United Kingdom that would otherwise be an offence under sections 15 to 18:

> (1) If—
> (a) a person does anything outside the United Kingdom, and
> (b) his action would have constituted the commission of an offence under any of sections 15 to 18 if it had been done in the United Kingdom,
> he shall be guilty of the offence.

7.26 Section 63 also deals with the situation of an action abroad that would otherwise come under section 18(1)(b), i.e. removal from the jurisdiction, and would not be caught by the deeming provision in section 19(7):

> (2) For the purposes of subsection (1)(b), section 18(1)(b) shall be read as if for 'the jurisdiction' there were substituted 'a jurisdiction'.

7.27 The provisions of section 63 cover similar ground and appear to render section 19(7) unnecessary. The absence from section 63 of specific mention of being 'in possession of a thing', as in section 19(7)(a), probably does not lead to any difference in the scope of the provisions since possession and use are covered in section 16 and therefore come within section 63(1). It may be that the underlying purpose of section 19(7) is to ensure that potential disclosers pay as much attention to suspicious foreign conduct as to suspicious conduct in the UK.

D. Required Disclosures: the Regulated Sector

Section 21A

7.28 Section 21A, which broadly equates to section 330 of POCA, imposes on a person working in the regulated sector a positive obligation to disclose knowledge or suspicion that another person has committed or attempted to commit a terrorist property offence. As in section 330 of POCA, the duty to disclose is not set out explicitly but appears by implication from the conditions of the offence of failure to disclose:

> (1) A person commits an offence if each of the following three conditions is satisfied.

First offence condition

The mental element of the offence, which is the same as in section 330 of POCA, contains **7.29**
the objective alternative that the person in the regulated sector 'has reasonable grounds for
knowing or suspecting'. In relation to the stricter mental element applied to the regulated
sector, see paragraph 6.08 above:

> (2) The first condition is that he—
>   (a) knows or suspects, or
>   (b) has reasonable grounds for knowing or suspecting, that another person has com-
>   mitted an offence under any of sections 15 to 18.

The duty of disclosure covers not only knowledge or suspicion about money laundering
under section 18, that is the laundering of terrorist property, as widely defined,[10] but also
covers knowledge or suspicion about the other terrorist property offences, which concern
fund-raising, funding arrangements, and the use and possession of money for the purposes
of terrorism.

Second offence condition

The duty to disclose applies only where the relevant information came to the person in the **7.30**
course of a business in the regulated sector:

> (3) The second condition is that the information or other matter—
>   (a) on which his knowledge or suspicion is based, or
>   (b) which gives reasonable grounds for such knowledge or suspicion, came to him in
>   the course of a business in the regulated sector.

Third offence condition

The third condition contains the *actus reus* of the offence, a guilty omission rather than any **7.31**
positive act;[11] it also defines the duty of disclosure on those in the regulated sector:

> (4) The third condition is that he does not disclose the information or other matter to a
>   constable or a nominated officer as soon as is practicable after it comes to him.[12]

Conduct outside the United Kingdom

Specific provision is made for the situation where a person knows or suspects, or has reason- **7.32**
able grounds for suspecting, that another person 'has taken an action or been in possession
of a thing' outside the UK:

> (11) For the purposes of subsection (2) a person is to be taken to have committed an offence
>   there mentioned if:
>   (a) he has taken an action or been in possession of a thing and
>   (b) he would have committed the offence if he had been in the United Kingdom at the
>   time when he took the action or was in possession of the thing.

Section 21A(11) is in, essentially, the same terms as section 19(7): see above at paragraphs
7.23–7.27.

Specimen indictment

The offence under section 21A is triable either in the magistrates' court or in the Crown Court. **7.33**

---

[10] See above at para 7.03.
[11] Note that in TA 2000 'act' and 'action' include omission (s 121 Interpretation).
[12] A disclosure to a nominated officer is one that complies with s 21A(7).

STATEMENT OF OFFENCE

Failure to disclose, contrary to section 21A Terrorism Act 2000.

PARTICULARS OF OFFENCE

A B, on a date between the . . . day of . . . and the . . . day of . . ., knowing or suspecting, or having reasonable grounds for knowing or suspecting on the basis of information or other matter which came to him in the course of a business in the regulated sector, that C D had committed an offence of money laundering under section 18 did not disclose the information or other matter to a constable or a nominated officer as soon as practicable after it came to him.

Sentence

7.34 Under s 21A(12), a person guilty of an offence under this section is liable:

(a) on conviction on indictment, to imprisonment for a term not exceeding five years or to a fine or to both;

(b) on summary conviction, to imprisonment for a term not exceeding six months or to a fine not exceeding the statutory maximum or to both.

Defences and exceptions

7.35 There are three defences or exceptions to commission of the failure to disclose offence, which are expressed in very similar terms to defences or exceptions in sections 330(6) and (7B) of POCA. These are set out in section 21A(5)(a), (b), and (c), but they are really only two: a general defence of 'reasonable excuse' and an exception or exemption from the duty to disclose which applies, in defined circumstances, to a professional legal adviser or relevant professional adviser, and also applies to others in the adviser's organization who provide the adviser with assistance or support.

Reasonable excuse

7.36 There is no authority on the scope of the reasonable excuse defence, but it seems likely that the courts would construe the term narrowly both because of the importance and potential value of disclosures about terrorist property offences and because the duty to disclose under section 21A is restricted to those in the regulated sector:

(5) But a person does not commit an offence under this section if—
    (a) he has a reasonable excuse for not disclosing the information or other matter;

Privileged circumstances

7.37 The limited exception for professional legal advisers and relevant professional advisers provides the same exemption from the advisers' duty to disclose and the same protection for information or other matter received in privileged circumstances as in section 330 of POCA: see commentary in Chapter 6, at paragraphs 6.28–6.32. There is a small change of wording in the statutory crime/fraud exception between section 330(11) of POCA and section 21A(9) of TA 2000, but for no obvious reason and without apparent legal significance.[13]

7.38 Under section 21A(5), a person does not commit an offence if: '. . .he is a professional legal adviser or relevant professional adviser and the information or other matter came to him in privileged circumstances'.

---

[13] Perhaps the drafter thought that 'with a view to' is plainer English and has a more demotic feel to it than 'with the intention of'. (See the helpful material about drafting on the website of the Office of the Parliamentary Counsel: <http://www.cabinetoffice.gov.uk/parliamentarycounsel/drafting_techniques.aspx>.)

Privileged circumstances are defined for these purposes in subsection (8):

> Information or other matter comes to a professional legal adviser or relevant professional adviser in privileged circumstances if it is communicated or given to him—
> > (a) by (or by a representative of) a client of his in connection with the giving by the adviser of legal advice to the client,
> > (b) by (or by a representative of) a person seeking legal advice from the adviser, or
> > (c) by a person in connection with legal proceedings or contemplated legal proceedings.
> (9) But subsection (8) does not apply to information or other matter which is communicated or given with a view to furthering a criminal purpose.

The privileged circumstances exception extended

7.39 The exception has now been extended so that it covers persons who provide, in the circumstances specified in subsection (5A), assistance and support to professional legal advisers and relevant professional advisers. A person does not commit an offence under section 21A if subsection (5A) applies to him:

> (5A) This subsection applies to a person if—
> > (a) the person is employed by, or is in partnership with, a professional legal adviser or relevant professional adviser to provide the adviser with assistance or support,
> > (b) the information or other matter comes to the person in connection with the provision of such assistance or support, and
> > (c) the information or other matter came to the adviser in privileged circumstances.

Absence of a specified training provision

7.40 There is one exception or defence that is included in section 330(7) of POCA[14] which is unaccountably missing from section 21A of TA 2000. In POCA, this 'specified' training provision limits the application of the objective test—that a person 'has reasonable grounds for knowing or suspecting'—by protecting from criminal liability a person in the regulated sector who fails to make a disclosure where:

- that person has no subjective knowledge or suspicion; and
- that person has not received 'specified' training.

The omission of this provision from section 21A seems anomalous since the specified training required by Regulation 21 of the Money Laundering Regulations 2007 refers to training about both money laundering and terrorist finance.

Relevant guidance

7.41 The evidential provisions of subsection (6), which are in the same terms as section 330(8), may be a sword in the hands of a prosecutor or a shield in the hands of the defendant. Which it is depends on whether the evidence shows that a defendant to a charge under section 21A followed—and relied on—any relevant guidance or, without good reason, failed to follow such guidance:

> (6) In deciding whether a person committed an offence under this section the court must consider whether he followed any relevant guidance which was at the time concerned—
> > (a) issued by a supervisory authority or any other appropriate body,
> > (b) approved by the Treasury,[15] and

---

[14] See Chapter 6, at paras 6.22 and 6.23.
[15] For the meaning of 'approved by the Treasury', see Chapter 6 at paras 6.36 and 6.37.

(c) published in a manner it approved as appropriate in its opinion to bring the guidance to the attention of persons likely to be affected by it.

E. Other Required Disclosures

7.42 Offences involving acts of terrorism and the law relating to disclosure of information about acts of terrorism are outside the scope of this book, but there is a degree of overlap in the relevant provisions in Part III of the Terrorism Act 2000 ('Terrorist Property') and Part IV ('Terrorism Investigations'). For this reason, section 38B is considered below and offences of unlawful disclosure under section 39 are covered in Chapter 8 (at paragraph 8.86 *et seq.*).

Section 38B: information about acts of terrorism

7.43 This section was added by the Anti-Terrorism Crime and Security Act 2001[16] and came into force on 14 December 2001. It pre-dates and lies outside the framework of disclosure provisions (in POCA and in TA 2000, as amended) under which disclosures are made, directly or indirectly, to SOCA.

The requirement to disclose

7.44 The section creates a general obligation of disclosure: it applies to anyone who has relevant information as set out in section 38B(1):

(1) This section applies where a person has information which he knows or believes might be of material assistance—
   (a) in preventing the commission by another person of an act of terrorism, or
   (b) in securing the apprehension, prosecution or conviction of another person, in the United Kingdom, for an offence involving the commission, preparation or instigation of an act of terrorism.

The offence of failing to disclose

7.45 A person commits the offence under section 38B(2) if he does not disclose the information as soon as reasonably practicable to a constable.[17] In this section, 'constable' means a police officer[18] and does not have the extended meaning in section 19 and some other sections in Part III.[19]

Disclosures about acts of terrorism and disclosures about terrorist property

7.46 The circumstances that create a duty of disclosure under section 19 or section 21A may also bring a person within the terms of the duty of disclosure under section 38B. A person who knows or suspects that another person has committed or attempted to commit a terrorist property offence is likely also to be a person who 'has information which he knows or believes might be of material assistance' in the prevention or detection of terrorism (within the terms of section 38B(1)(a) and/or (b)). The kind of information that such a person might have and

---

[16] s 117(2).

[17] s 38B(3). In Northern Ireland, disclosure may be made either to a constable or a member of Her Majesty's forces.

[18] Apart from the extended meaning given to 'constable' in some sections of Part III of TA 2000, the term 'constable' itself is a common law term and is not statutorily defined (but see ss 29 and 30 of the Police Act 1996 on the attestation and jurisdiction of constables).

[19] See Chapter 5 at para 5.08.

might disclose in a SAR (e.g. details of a bank account or credit card details or personal information such as address or mobile telephone number) is also the kind of information that has proved useful in the investigation of terrorist offences.

There is, therefore, potential for overlap between the disclosure requirements relating to terrorist property and the broadly drafted requirement under section 38B for disclosure about acts of terrorism. Where this creates a double disclosure requirement, it is arguable that timely disclosure to SOCA of the information about a terrorist property offence should constitute a reasonable excuse under section 38B(4) if there is no additional information that the person could disclose under section 38B. **7.47**

Although there is a substantial degree of overlap between the disclosure requirements of section 38B and those of sections 19 and 21A, the duty of disclosure under section 38B is significantly wider. It applies to everyone and is not restricted to information that comes to a person in the course of regulated sector or other business. There will be many circumstances in which information about terrorist property would not create a duty to disclose under Part III but where a disclosure must be made under section 38B. For instance, where a person believes or suspects that certain money or other property is terrorist property on the basis of information that came to him outside the context of any business or employment: that person is under no obligation to make a report about terrorist property, although he may make a voluntary disclosure under section 20(1). If, however, the information about terrorist property might also be information of material assistance in preventing the commission of an act of terrorism, he would have a duty to make a disclosure under section 38B. **7.48**

Reasonable excuse

There is a defence of reasonable excuse under section 38B(4) in which the burden of proof is placed on the defendant: **7.49**

(4) It is a defence for a person charged with an offence under subsection (2) to prove that he had a reasonable excuse for not making the disclosure.

There is no authority at present on what would count as a reasonable excuse. Given the terrorist context, it seems likely that 'reasonable excuse' will be construed narrowly.

Jurisdiction

This provision applies where a person has the necessary state of mind, that is knowledge or belief that the information might be of material assistance in combating terrorism (in either of the ways set out in sub-sections (a) and (b) of section 38B). From the time that this is the case, the offence is a continuing offence and the jurisdiction provisions are, accordingly, widely drawn: **7.50**

(6) Proceedings for an offence under this section may be taken, and the offence may for the purposes of those proceedings be treated as having been committed, in any place where the person to be charged is or has at any time been since he first knew or believed that the information might be of material assistance as mentioned in subsection (1).

Specimen indictment

The offence under section 38B(2) is triable either in the magistrates' court or in the Crown Court. **7.51**

STATEMENT OF OFFENCE

Failure to disclose contrary to section 38B of the Terrorism Act 2000.

PARTICULARS OF OFFENCE

A B, between the . . . day of . . . and the . . . day of . . ., knowing or believing that he had information that might be of material assistance in preventing the commission by another person of an act of terrorism or in securing the apprehension, prosecution or conviction of another person, in the United Kingdom, for an offence involving the commission, preparation or instigation of an act of terrorism, failed to disclose that information to a constable.

Sentence

7.52 The offence carries the same penalty as offences of failure to disclose under sections 19 and 21A. Under section 38B(5), a person guilty of an offence under section 38B is liable:

(a) on conviction on indictment, to imprisonment for a term not exceeding five years, or to a fine or to both, or

(b) on summary conviction, to imprisonment for a term not exceeding six months, or to a fine not exceeding the statutory maximum or to both.

F. Disclosure by Constables

7.53 Section 21C,[20] which concerns only the relationship between constables (police officers) and SOCA as the UK's Financial Intelligence Unit, does not affect those in the reporting sector[21] who make or should make disclosures:

(1) Where a disclosure is made under a provision of this Part to a constable, the constable must disclose it in full as soon as practicable after it has been made to a member of staff of the Serious Organised Crime Agency authorised for the purposes of that provision by the Director General of that Agency.

(2) Where a disclosure is made under section 21 (cooperation with police) to a constable, the constable must disclose it in full as soon as practicable after it has been made to a member of staff of the Serious Organised Crime Agency authorised for the purposes of this subsection by the Director General of that Agency.

The role of the SOCA FIU is to receive, analyse, and disseminate SARs: the purpose of section 21C is to ensure that any disclosure made to a police officer is passed on to SOCA as soon as practicable.

G. Disclosure and/or Consent as a Defence

Section 21: co-operation with police

7.54 Section 21, which came into force on 19 February 2001, before POCA was enacted, contains consent provisions but without the structure and timescales of notice period and

---

[20] s 21C is unusual. POCA, as enacted, placed various duties on those who work in the regulated sector and on MLROs. Every one of those duties is backed by a criminal offence carrying a term of imprisonment. No duties, with or without criminal sanctions, were placed on anyone in the FIU or in law enforcement until the insertion in TA 2000 of this new section.

[21] The 'reporting sector' is wider than the regulated sector and includes others who need to make SARs. (See discussion of the term in Chapter 5 at para 5.30.)

moratorium period that POCA later introduced for appropriate consent in relation to authorised disclosures. This section contains two different provisions which set out the specific circumstances in which a person who would otherwise commit a terrorist property offence does not do so.

Express consent

Firstly, there is an 'express consent' provision that creates an exception to or gives a defence **7.55** to terrorist property offences:

> (1) A person does not commit an offence under any of sections 15 to 18 if he is acting with the express consent of a constable.

Note that in this section 'constable' means a police officer. This provision lies outside the structure, now common to POCA and TA 2000, of disclosure to and consent obtained from the SOCA FIU. The relationship envisaged is that between an individual police officer and a person who may be an informant. The relevant part of paragraph 32 of the Explanatory Notes to Terrorism Act 2000 reads: 'Subsection (1) of section 21 allows for the activities of informants who may have to be involved with terrorist property if they are not to be found out and protects others who may innocently become involved.'

Disclosure as an exception or defence

Secondly, there is, in section 21(2) to (4), provision for the making of a disclosure about **7.56** involvement in a terrorist property offence which can provide another exception to the commission of an offence under sections 15 to 18. It applies only where a disclosure is made *after* a person becomes concerned in a transaction, but if the necessary conditions are fulfilled, it can give a defence to a person already involved in a transaction or arrangement relating to terrorist property:

> (2) Subject to subsections (3) and (4), a person does not commit an offence under any of sections 15 to 18 by involvement in a transaction or arrangement[22] relating to money or other property if he discloses to a constable—
> (a) his suspicion or belief that the money or other property is terrorist property, and
> (b) the information on which his suspicion or belief is based.
> (3) Subsection (2) applies only where a person makes a disclosure—
> (a) after he becomes concerned in the transaction concerned,
> (b) on his own initiative, and
> (c) as soon as is reasonably practicable.

The disclosure to a police officer enables the officer either to take no immediate action and **7.57** allow the person's involvement to continue or to forbid continued involvement, according to the needs of the case or investigation. The making of the disclosure, if it fulfils the conditions in subsection (3), provides the defence unless the person is forbidden by a constable to continue his involvement in the transaction or arrangement to which the disclosure relates and he continues his involvement. The disclosure itself therefore provides a person with deemed consent until a constable forbids further involvement.

---

[22] Subsection (7) provides that reference in this section to a transaction or arrangement relating to money or other property includes a reference to use or possession.

A constable's veto

7.58   As noted above, in section 21 'constable' means a police officer.[23] For the purposes of disclosure under this section and of the exercise of the power under section 21(4) to forbid continued involvement, the term is not extended to include a designated officer of SOCA:

> Subsection (2) does not apply to a person if—
> > (a) a constable forbids him to continue his involvement in the transaction or arrangement to which the disclosure relates, and
> > (b) he continues his involvement.

Internal disclosure

7.59   As in sections 19 and 20, a person in employment may, where there exists a system for internal disclosures, make an internal disclosure. Where such a person wishes to make a disclosure, subsection (6) provides the alternative, in effect if not explicitly, of disclosure to a nominated officer:[24]

> (6) Where—
> > (a) a person is in employment, and
> > (b) his employer has established a procedure for the making of disclosures of the same kind as may be made to a constable under subsection (2), this section shall have effect in relation to that person as if any reference to disclosure to a constable included a reference to disclosure in accordance with the procedure.

Disclosure to SOCA

7.60   Although, from the wording of subsections (2) to (4), this provision for disclosure to a police officer appears also to lie outside the regime for making disclosures to the SOCA FIU, it is brought into it in one of two ways: either section 21(6) or 21C(2) applies. An internal disclosure under section 21(6) would normally lead to a disclosure to SOCA by the nominated officer; alternatively, section 21C(2) requires a police officer who receives a disclosure under section 21 to disclose to SOCA.

Reasonable excuse

7.61   There is a defence of 'reasonable excuse' for a person who intended to make a disclosure, but did not do so. The burden of proof is placed on the defendant:

> It is a defence for a person charged with an offence under any of sections 15(2) and (3) and 16 to 18 to prove that—
> > (a) he intended to make a disclosure of the kind mentioned in subsections (2) and (3), and
> > (b) there is reasonable excuse for his failure to do so.

The defence does not apply to section 15(1), which only concerns an invitation to provide money or other property: it is a terrorist financing offence, but not an offence involving actual terrorist property.

---

[23] See Chapter 5, at para 5.08, for discussion of the way that the term is used in POCA and TA 2000.
[24] See paras 7.20 and 7.21 above for disclosure to a nominated officer under s 19(4).

Section 21ZA: arrangements with prior consent

Disclosure and consent

Where section 21 provided for consent to continued involvement in a transaction or arrange- **7.62**
ment relating to terrorist property, section 21ZA provides for consent before becoming
involved.

This section provides an exception or defence to any of the offences under sections 15 to 18 **7.63**
of TA 2000:

(1) A person does not commit an offence under any of sections 15 to 18 by involvement in
a transaction or an arrangement relating to money or other property if, before becoming
involved, the person—
  (a) discloses to an authorised officer the person's suspicion or belief that the money or
  other property is terrorist property and the information on which the suspicion or
  belief is based, and
  (b) has the authorised officer's consent to becoming involved in the transaction or
  arrangement.
(6) The reference in this section to a transaction or arrangement relating to money or other
property includes a reference to use or possession.

The relevant disclosure is a disclosure 'that the money or other property is terrorist property'
and a disclosure of the information on which the suspicion or belief that it is terrorist property is based.

Authorised officer

The disclosure must be made to an 'authorised officer', as defined in section 21ZA(5): **7.64**
'In this section "authorised officer" means a member of the staff of the Serious Organised
Crime Agency authorised for the purposes of this section by the Director General of
that Agency.'

In other situations under the reporting provisions in POCA and TA 2000, there is provision **7.65**
for a person in employment to make a disclosure 'to a nominated officer' or in accordance
with a procedure for disclosure established by his employer (which, in practice must amount
to the same thing). Such an internal disclosure discharges any responsibility of the discloser
and/or protects the discloser from criminal liability. It seems unhelpful—and anomalous—
that no explicit provision is made for a person to make an internal disclosure to a nominated
officer under procedures established by his employer.

Because this exception or defence specifically requires disclosure to an authorised officer, it **7.66**
would not protect a person who made a disclosure to a nominated officer unless and until the
nominated officer made a disclosure in the terms of section 21ZA(1)(a) to an authorised
officer, that is to the SOCA FIU.

Where the facility for internal disclosure exists, there seems to be no reason why a per- **7.67**
son should not take advantage of the advice and assistance of a nominated officer: disclosure to an authorised officer via the nominated officer would still be disclosure to an
authorised officer under section 21ZA. In these circumstances, however, the responsibility to disclose, and the associated risk of criminal liability, would not pass to the nominated officer, but would remain with the original discloser until a disclosure to SOCA has
been made.

Deemed consent

7.68   If actual consent is not given by an authorised officer, deemed consent may be obtained under section 21ZA(2). This provides for deemed consent to become effective at the expiry of the notice period if the discloser is not informed by the authorised officer that consent is refused. The 'notice period', defined in subsection (3), is the same as the notice period for appropriate consent under section 335 of POCA, that is, the period of seven working days[25] starting with the first working day after the person makes the disclosure:

> (2)   A person is treated as having an authorised officer's consent if before the end of the notice period the person does not receive notice from an authorised officer that consent is refused.

7.69   There is, however, no equivalent to the 'moratorium period' under section 335. The refusal of consent to a person to become involved in a transaction or arrangement relating to money or other property suspected, rightly or wrongly, to be terrorist property may last indefinitely. The prohibition on involvement will only end if the authorised officer reconsiders the decision and gives actual consent under section 21ZA(1)(b).

Reasonable excuse

7.70   Although there is no 'reasonable excuse' provision in section 21ZA itself, the section needs to be read in conjunction with section 21ZC. If a disclosure under section 21ZA is not made, a person charged with an offence under sections 15 to 18 may have a reasonable excuse defence under section 21ZC:

> It is a defence for a person charged with an offence under any of sections 15 to 18 to prove that—
> (a)   the person intended to make a disclosure of the kind mentioned in section 21ZA or 21ZB, and
> (b)   there is a reasonable excuse for the person's failure to do so.

Section 21ZB: disclosure after entering into arrangements

7.71   Section 21ZA concerned disclosure and obtaining prior consent to involvement in a terrorist property arrangement; this section concerns disclosure after becoming involved in a terrorist property arrangement. These two sections, both introduced into Part III of TA 2000 on 26 December 2007,[26] can be seen to form the two halves of the whole provision for disclosure and consent as a defence to a terrorist property offence: one dealing with disclosures *before* and one dealing with disclosures *after* the event. Section 21ZB, however, also overlaps substantially with the original provisions in section 21. The way that the section works is in a number of respects closer to section 21 than to its other half, section 21ZA.

The disclosure

7.72   This section provides an exception or defence to any of the offences under sections 15 to 18 TA 2000:

---

[25]   A working day is a day other than a Saturday, a Sunday, Christmas Day, Good Friday, or a day that is a bank holiday under the Banking and Financial Dealings Act 1971 (c. 80) in the part of the United Kingdom in which the person is when making the disclosure.

[26]   Added to the Terrorism Act 2000 by the Terrorism Act 2000 and Proceeds of Crime Act 2002 (Amendment) Regulations 2007/3398.

(1) A person does not commit an offence under any of sections 15 to 18 by involvement in a transaction or an arrangement relating to money or other property[27] if, after becoming involved, the person discloses to an authorised officer—
  (a) the person's suspicion or belief that the money or other property is terrorist property, and
  (b) the information on which the suspicion or belief is based.

The disclosure provides an exception to commission of a terrorist property offence and what has to be disclosed is the same in section 21ZB as in section 21ZA. This section concerns disclosure after the event and the exception only applies where there is a reasonable excuse for failure to make prior disclosure and the disclosure fulfils the two conditions in section 21ZB(2)(b). **7.73**

The necessary conditions for the defence to apply are set out in section 21ZB(2). This section applies only where: **7.74**

  (a) there is a reasonable excuse for the person's failure to make the disclosure before becoming involved in the transaction or arrangement, and
  (b) the disclosure is made on the person's own initiative and as soon as it is reasonably practicable for the person to make it.

The power to forbid continued involvement

In section 21ZB there is no explicit consent provision: the disclosure itself provides a defence to a terrorist property offence, but—as in section 21—there is a provision for prohibiting continued involvement. Under section 21, the power to forbid continued involvement is exercised by a police officer; under section 21ZB, that power is exercised by an authorised officer, that is by SOCA: **7.75**

  (3) This section does not apply to a person if—
  (a) an authorised officer forbids the person to continue involvement in the transaction or arrangement to which the disclosure relates, and
  (b) the person continues that involvement.

Reasonable excuse for failure to disclose

Section 21ZB, like section 21ZA, needs to be read in conjunction with section 21ZC. If a disclosure under section 21ZB is not made, a person charged with an offence under sections 15 to 18 may have a reasonable excuse defence under section 21ZC: **7.76**

  It is a defence for a person charged with an offence under any of sections 15 to 18 to prove that—
  (a) the person intended to make a disclosure of the kind mentioned in section 21ZA or 21ZB, and
  (b) there is a reasonable excuse for the person's failure to do so.

Section 21(2) and section 21ZB

Sections 21(2) and section 21ZB both provide an exception to criminal liability under sections 15 to 18 for a person who makes a disclosure after becoming involved in a transaction or arrangement relating to suspected terrorist property. Despite significant differences, the overlap between these provisions is considerable. **7.77**

---

[27] The reference in this section to a transaction or arrangement relating to money or other property includes a reference to use or possession (s 21ZB(5)).

H. Protected Disclosures

Section 21B: protected disclosures

7.78 Section 21B provides protection for a person who makes a terrorist property disclosure in the same way as section 337 of POCA protects the discloser in respect of certain money laundering disclosures. Its scope is, however, narrower: it applies only to disclosures arising from business in the regulated sector:[28]

> (1) A disclosure which satisfies the following three conditions is not to be taken to breach any restriction on the disclosure of information (however imposed).
> (2) The first condition is that the information or other matter disclosed came to the person making the disclosure (the discloser) in the course of a business in the regulated sector.
> (3) The second condition is that the information or other matter—
> > (a) causes the discloser to know or suspect, or
> > (b) gives him reasonable grounds for knowing or suspecting, that another person has committed or attempted to commit an offence under any of sections 15 to 18.
> (4) The third condition is that the disclosure is made to a constable or a nominated officer as soon as is practicable after the information or other matter comes to the discloser.

7.79 The protection given by this section applies only to disclosures under section 21A and it is the only protection provision in Part III of TA 2000 (but see section 20(3) below).

Section 20: disclosure of information: permission

7.80 At first sight, this section is puzzling. It provides 'permission' to make a voluntary disclosure and to make a required disclosure. It seems odd, in the first case, that a person should need permission to act as a responsible citizen and make a voluntary disclosure about terrorist property; and, in the second case, equally odd that a person should need permission to do what he is obliged by law to do—that is, make a required disclosure:

> (1) A person may disclose to a constable—
> > (a) a suspicion or belief that any money or other property is terrorist property or is derived from terrorist property;
> > (b) any matter on which the suspicion or belief is based.
> (2) A person may make a disclosure to a constable in the circumstances mentioned in section 19(1) and (2).

7.81 The wording of section 20(3) is similar to, but not the same as, the wording of section 21B(1):

- Section 20 Disclosure of information: permission.

  'Section 20(3)—subsections (1) and (2) shall have effect notwithstanding any restriction on the disclosure of information imposed by statute or otherwise.'
- Section 21B Protected disclosures

  'Section 21B(1)—a disclosure which satisfies the following three conditions is not to be taken to breach any restriction on the disclosure of information (however imposed).'

---

[28] s 21B(6): 'The reference to a business in the regulated sector must be construed in accordance with schedule 3A.'

The wording of section 20(3) suggests that the purpose of the 'permission' provisions is **7.82** to make clear that they override any statutory or other restriction on the disclosure of information. The effect of the section is, therefore, in the case of voluntary disclosures that the discloser has permission to ignore any restriction that would otherwise prevent him or inhibit him from making the intended disclosure. In the case of a required disclosure, the provision permits a person who is required to make a disclosure to ignore any conflicting obligation. In the case of required disclosures, this *permission* is itself qualified by one exception, the professional legal adviser exception in section 19(5).

It is not clear whether 'permission' under section 20 provides the same protection as 'protec- **7.83** tion' under section 21B. Whereas the express purpose of section 21B is to protect disclosers, section 20, from its wording, seems to be aimed not so much at the interests of disclosers, but at the interests of law enforcement by making the disclosure provisions fully effective.

Under section 20(1), a person 'may disclose to a constable', which, in this section, means **7.84** disclosure to a police officer or to SOCA.[29] There is also a provision that allows a person in employment, where procedures for internal disclosure exist, to make the disclosure to the nominated officer.[30]

I. Conclusion

The remaining money laundering and terrorist financing disclosure provisions in TA 2000 **7.85** concern, firstly, tipping off and other unlawful disclosures and, secondly, permitted disclosures which are exceptions to the prohibition on tipping off. These disclosure provisions and the similar ones in POCA are considered together in the next chapter.

---

[29] s 20(5).
[30] s 20(4).

8

OFFENCES OF UNLAWFUL DISCLOSURE

A. Introduction

8.01 This chapter brings together the law relating to offences of unlawful disclosure under both the Proceeds of Crime Act 2002 (POCA) and the Terrorism Act 2000 (TA 2000): these are offences of tipping off and prejudicing an investigation. In both statutes, there are tipping off offences which apply to those who are working in a business in the regulated sector; there are also other offences of prejudicing an investigation which are of general application:

- tipping off offences (regulated sector) under section 333A(1) and (3) of POCA;
- the offence of making a disclosure likely to prejudice an investigation under section 342(2) of POCA;

- tipping off offences (regulated sector) under section 21D(1) and (3) of TA 2000;
- offences of disclosure likely to prejudice an investigation under section 39 of TA 2000.

This chapter also deals with permitted disclosures, which are exceptions to the prohibition on disclosure contained in the tipping off offences under both statutes: **8.02**

- permitted disclosures under sections 333B, 333C, and 333D of POCA;
- permitted disclosures under sections 21D, 21E, and 21F of TA 2000.

Tipping off and the other offences of unlawful disclosure respond to a concern that the investigation of money laundering and terrorist financing and the recovery of criminal property or terrorist property should not be impeded or prejudiced by suspects being alerted to the fact that they are under suspicion and/or under investigation by inappropriate disclosures, whether deliberate or inadvertent. **8.03**

B. Background

The UK law

There have been offences of tipping off in UK law since the Criminal Justice Act 1993 inserted new offences into the Drug Trafficking Offences Act 1986 (section 26C) and the Criminal Justice (Scotland) Act 1987 (section 43B).[1] The Drug Trafficking Offences Act 1986 already included, in section 31, an offence of prejudicing a drug trafficking investigation. The new anti-money laundering law introduced by POCA brought with it an offence of tipping off (section 333) and an offence of prejudicing an investigation (section 342). **8.04**

Important changes to the primary legislation were made by the Terrorism Act 2000 and Proceeds of Crime Act 2002 (Amendment) Regulations 2007, changes that came into force on 26 December 2007. The tipping off offence in section 333 of POCA was repealed and replaced by two new offences and, for the first time, tipping off offences were introduced into TA 2000. The new tipping off offences implement in UK law Recommendation 14 b) of the Financial Action Task Force 40 Recommendations on Money Laundering and the requirements of the EC Directives on money laundering. The two statutes now have almost identical tipping off offences, as well as other offences of unlawful disclosure which are broadly similar. **8.05**

Recommendations of the Financial Action Task Force

FATF Recommendation 14 b) applies to all regulated institutions, that is to financial and designated businesses and professions and those who work in them.[2] It states that the regulated institutions should be: 'prohibited by law from disclosing the fact that a suspicious transaction report (STR) or related information is being reported to the FIU.' **8.06**

---

[1] The tipping off offences were inserted by Criminal Justice Act 1993, ss 18 and 19.
[2] Designated non-financial businesses and professions as set out in Recommendation 12.

The First Money Laundering Directive

8.07   The First Money Laundering Directive,[3] in 1991, managed a similar brevity while widening the coverage of the prohibition. Article 8 reads:

> Credit and financial institutions and their directors and employees shall not disclose to the customer concerned nor to other third persons that information has been transmitted to the authorities in accordance with Articles 6 and 7[4] or that a money laundering investigation is being carried out.

The Third Money Laundering Directive

8.08   Article 28 of the Third Money Laundering Directive further widened the scope of the prohibition to include reference to terrorist financing.

Article 28, paragraph 1, reads:

> The institutions and persons covered by this Directive and their directors and employees shall not disclose to the customer concerned or to other third persons the fact that information has been transmitted in accordance with Articles 22 and 23[5] or that a money laundering or terrorist financing investigation is being or may be carried out.

8.09   The concern that underlies the prohibition on disclosure may be understandable, but whether the prohibition provides a necessary, effective and proportionate response to that concern is open to question. In practice, the tipping off provisions significantly interfere with the ordinary conduct of financial, business, and legal transactions, as well as harming relationships with clients and customers. In an apparent attempt to mitigate these consequences, the Third Money Laundering Directive introduced a number of detailed exceptions to the prohibition on disclosure. These exceptions, set out in paragraphs 2 to 6 inclusive, have greatly complicated the tipping off provisions in Article 28; how far they have improved them is debatable.

8.10   The prohibition on disclosure in Article 28 and the detailed exceptions to it have been incorporated in the substantially revised tipping off provisions now included in both POCA and TA 2000.

C. Unlawful Disclosures under the Proceeds of Crime Act 2002

8.11   In POCA as enacted in 2002, there were two sections that created offences of unlawful disclosure: section 333 Tipping Off and section 342 Offences of Prejudicing Investigation. These criminal offences, which applied not just to those in the regulated sector but to everyone subject to the criminal law, have now been substantially amended in response to the Third Money Laundering Directive of 2005.[6]

---

[3] Council Directive 91/308/EEC of 10 June 1991 on prevention of the use of the financial system for the purpose of money laundering. (For convenience, referred to as the 'First Money Laundering Directive'; similarly, references to the Second and Third Money Laundering Directives.) Art 8 in the First Money Laundering Directive became Art 8.1 following the amendments introduced by the Second Money Laundering Directive of 2001.

[4] Arts 6 and 7 deal with money laundering disclosures.

[5] Arts 22 and 23 deal with money laundering and terrorist financing disclosures.

[6] Primary legislation amended by statutory instrument—the Terrorism Act 2000 and Proceeds of Crime Act 2002 (Amendment) Regulations 2007/3398—under powers in the European Communities Act 1972.

Section 333 has been repealed and replaced by a new offence of tipping off, in section 333A, **8.12** that applies only to those in the regulated sector. The new section also includes a separate offence of prejudicing an investigation. Section 342 has been amended so that the offence of making a disclosure likely to prejudice an investigation under that section will no longer apply where the circumstances come within the new regulated sector offence of making a disclosure that is likely to prejudice an investigation.[7] These changes were brought into force on 26 December 2007.

Section 333A: tipping off: regulated sector

This section creates two criminal offences, the first of which is broadly similar to the former **8.13** tipping off offence except that it applies only to the regulated sector. The second of the offences created by section 333A is broadly similar to the offence of prejudicing an investigation in section 342(2)(a), but again it applies only to the regulated sector.

The first offence: tipping off under section 333A(1)

The essential elements of the offence are that the offender *unlawfully* discloses that he or **8.14** someone else has made a *lawful* disclosure of information that came to that person in the course of a business in the regulated sector and the *unlawful* disclosure is likely to prejudice any investigation that might be conducted following the *lawful* disclosure:

(1) A person commits an offence if—
    (a) the person discloses any matter within subsection (2);
    (b) the disclosure is likely to prejudice any investigation[8] that might be conducted following the disclosure referred to in that subsection; and
    (c) the information on which the disclosure is based came to the person in the course of a business in the regulated sector.
(2) The matters are that the person or another person has made a disclosure under this Part—
    (a) to a constable,
    (b) to an officer of Revenue and Customs,
    (c) to a nominated officer, or
    (d) to a member of staff of the Serious Organised Crime Agency authorised for the purposes of this Part by the Director General of that Agency,
of information that came to that person in the course of a business in the regulated sector.

Although an investigation conducted following disclosure is likely to be a criminal inves- **8.15** tigation, it might not be. It could be a confiscation investigation or a civil recovery investigation: the wording of section 333A(1)(b) would cover a civil as well as any criminal investigation.

The nature of the tipping off offence

The offence of tipping off consists in the unlawful disclosure itself: it is not a 'result crime'. **8.16** A disclosure, whether communicated by words or action, of any matter within subsection (2), will amount to an offence of tipping off if it is likely to prejudice an investigation, whether or not any such prejudice is actually caused by it. Equally, the fact that prejudice to an investigation is caused by something said or done by a person will not mean that the

---

[7] See paras 8.26 *et seq.*
[8] Reference to types of investigation in Part 8: 'any investigation' is not qualified—either by type of investigation or the investigating authority carrying it out.

person has committed an offence unless he has made a disclosure of some matter within subsection (2) and that disclosure was, at that time, likely to prejudice an investigation.

8.17 It may be that the fear of committing a criminal offence has led some people in the regulated sector to interpret the prohibition more widely than the wording of the section justifies. No offence is committed unless:

- prejudice to an investigation is likely; and
- the discloser knows or suspects that this is so.

Likelihood of prejudice

8.18 The disclosure must be likely to prejudice any investigation that might be conducted following the lawful disclosure, that is, either an internal disclosure or a Suspicious Activity Report (SAR). The likelihood of prejudice under section 333A(1)(b) must be judged objectively at the time of the disclosure that is alleged to amount to tipping off.

Awareness of the likelihood of prejudice

8.19 Those in the regulated sector considering whether they can properly disclose information to another person may be concerned that there are facts or circumstances of which they are unaware that do actually make it likely that prejudice will be caused. This possibility, however, would not mean that an offence is committed because for a person to be guilty of the offence, that person must be aware—must know or suspect—that the disclosure is likely to prejudice an actual or potential investigation. Note that this important provision about the mental state of the discloser is not in the offence-creating section (333A), but appears in section 333D—'Other permitted disclosures, etc':

> (3) A person does not commit an offence under section 333A(1) if the person does not know or suspect that the disclosure is likely to have the effect mentioned in section 333A(1)(b).

The tipping off offence in practice

8.20 The tipping off offence under section 333A(1) can create real difficulty in practice for the reporting sector, particularly where a person has made a consent report about a client or customer. While that person waits for consent and perhaps for a longer period thereafter if consent is refused, any intended financial or property transaction is effectively frozen. No satisfactory response can be given to the client who wants to know why the anticipated transaction has not been carried out.

8.21 Contrasting the position of the legitimate customer or client with that of a person intent on using the bank or other regulated sector business to launder money illustrates how unhelpful, even counter-productive, the tipping off law is in practice:

- The legitimate client, who may know little about money laundering and money laundering law, is likely to be baffled and frustrated when there has been a sudden and unexplained failure to carry out a money transfer or complete some property transaction.
- Faced with the same situation, however, a person deliberately engaged in money laundering and aware of the risks is likely to guess immediately that a money laundering disclosure has been made to the authorities. Such a person is, in effect, 'tipped off' by the legitimate actions of the person making an authorised disclosure and by the legal effects of such a disclosure.

8.22 Although, in this way, the law places many people, mainly in the regulated sector, in a very difficult position, a person does *not* commit a tipping off offence simply because the suspected money launderer or some other person becomes aware that a money laundering disclosure has been made. Whether that awareness results from the fact that a transaction has not gone ahead or from the fact that the person who has made a disclosure can give no satisfactory answer when asked why the transaction has not proceeded, no tipping off offence would be committed. Only where a person has made an unlawful *disclosure* within the terms of section 333A can there be an offence of tipping off.

Specimen indictment

The offence of tipping off under section 333A(1) is triable either in the magistrates' court or in the Crown Court. **8.23**

STATEMENT OF OFFENCE

Tipping off contrary to section 333A(1) Proceeds of Crime Act 2002.

PARTICULARS OF OFFENCE

A B, on the . . . day of . . ., disclosed to C D that E F had made a money laundering disclosure to the Serious Organised Crime Agency of information that came to E F in the course of a business in the regulated sector, and the disclosure by A B, based on information that came to him in the course of a business in the regulated sector, was likely to prejudice any investigation that might be conducted following the money laundering disclosure by E F.

Sentence

A person guilty of an offence under section 333A(1) is liable: **8.24**

(a) on summary conviction to imprisonment for a term not exceeding three months, or to a fine not exceeding level 5 on the standard scale, or to both;
(b) on conviction on indictment to imprisonment for a term not exceeding two years, or to a fine, or to both.

Defences and exceptions

There are a number of detailed defences and exceptions that apply to both tipping off offences under section 333A. These are referred to in section 333A(5) and set out fully in paragraphs 8.31 *et seq.*: **8.25**

(5) This section is subject to—
    (a) section 333B (disclosures within an undertaking or group etc),
    (b) section 333C (other permitted disclosures between institutions etc), and
    (c) section 333D (other permitted disclosures etc).

The second offence: tipping off under section 333A(3)

This offence is committed where the offender makes an unlawful disclosure about a money laundering investigation and the unlawful disclosure is likely to prejudice that investigation, but the offence is only committed where the information on which the unlawful disclosure is based came to the offender in the course of a business in the regulated sector: **8.26**

(3) A person commits an offence if—
    (a) the person discloses that an investigation into allegations that an offence under this Part has been committed is being contemplated or is being carried out;
    (b) the disclosure is likely to prejudice that investigation; and
    (c) the information on which the disclosure is based came to the person in the course of a business in the regulated sector.

8.27 Like the offence under section 333A(1), this offence is not a result crime, but consists in the act of disclosing. Note that this offence is drawn more narrowly than the equivalent offence in section 333A(1)(b) above. It only applies to a criminal money laundering investigation and only where that investigation 'is being contemplated or is being carried out'.

Awareness of the likelihood of prejudice

8.28 As with the tipping off offence under section 333A(1), there is a provision which, in effect, adds a mental element to the offence. This important provision about the mental state of the discloser is not in the offence-creating section (333A), but appears in section 333D—'Other permitted disclosures, etc':

> (4) A person does not commit an offence under section 333A(3) if the person does not know or suspect that the disclosure is likely to have the effect mentioned in section 333A(3)(b).

The offence is, therefore, only committed where a person knows or suspects that the disclosure is likely to prejudice an actual or potential investigation. The disclosure must be likely to prejudice an investigation *and* the person must be aware that it is likely to do so.

Specimen indictment

8.29 The offence under section 333A(3) is triable either in the magistrates' court or in the Crown Court.

STATEMENT OF OFFENCE

Tipping off contrary to section 333A(3) Proceeds of Crime Act 2002.

PARTICULARS OF OFFENCE

A B, on the . . . day of . . ., disclosed to C D that a money laundering investigation was being carried out by an officer of HM Revenue & Customs in relation to property belonging to C D and the disclosure by A B, based on information that came to him in the course of a business in the regulated sector, was likely to prejudice that investigation.

Sentence

8.30 A person guilty of an offence under section 333A(3) is liable:

> (a) on summary conviction to imprisonment for a term not exceeding three months, or to a fine not exceeding level 5 on the standard scale, or to both;
> (b) on conviction on indictment to imprisonment for a term not exceeding two years, or to a fine, or to both.

Defences and exceptions to the tipping off offences under section 333A

8.31 Section 333A is followed by four more new sections, 333B to 333E, which set out and define a number of detailed and complicated exceptions to the offences in section 333A. As noted above, these are largely derived from and faithfully implement the detailed provisions of paragraphs 2 to 6 inclusive of Article 28 of the Third Money Laundering Directive.

Section 333B: disclosures within an undertaking or group, etc

8.32 Section 333B(1) permits, without further qualification, disclosures within an undertaking in the regulated sector:

> (1) An employee, officer or partner of an undertaking does not commit an offence under section 333A if the disclosure is to an employee, officer or partner of the same undertaking.

Section 333B(2) and (4) permit disclosures within a group of credit or financial institutions **8.33** and between professional advisers within different undertakings that share common ownership, management, or control, but only in defined circumstances. There are separate provisions for credit and financial institutions on the one hand and professional advisers on the other, but with the qualification in each case that the disclosure is only permitted where it is to an institution or professional adviser subject to the same or equivalent money laundering requirements:

> (2) A person does not commit an offence under section 333A in respect of a disclosure by a credit institution or a financial institution if—
>
> (a) the disclosure is to a credit institution or a financial institution,
>
> (b) the institution to whom the disclosure is made is situated in an EEA State or in a country or territory imposing equivalent money laundering requirements, and
>
> (c) both the institution making the disclosure and the institution to whom it is made belong to the same group.
>
> (3) In subsection (2) 'group' has the same meaning as in Directive 2002/87/EC of the European Parliament and of the Council of 16th December 2002 on the supplementary supervision of credit institutions, insurance undertakings and investment firms in a financial conglomerate.

Definition of 'group'

In this section, 'group' '. . .shall mean a group of undertakings, which consists of a parent **8.34** undertaking, its subsidiaries and the entities in which the parent undertaking or its subsidiaries hold a participation, as well as undertakings linked to each other by a relationship within the meaning of Article 12(1) of Directive 83/349/EEC'.[9] For the purposes of a permitted disclosure under this section, the extension of the meaning of 'group' to linked undertakings within the terms of Article 12(1) of Directive 83/349/EEC is probably not of much practical relevance.

Professional legal advisers and relevant professional advisers

The provisions of section 333B(4) extend to professional legal advisers and relevant profes **8.35** sional advisers a *permission* to disclose that is similar to the exception that applies to credit institutions and financial institutions:

> (4) A professional legal adviser or a relevant professional adviser does not commit an offence under section 333A if—
>
> (a) the disclosure is to [a] professional legal adviser or a relevant professional adviser,
>
> (b) both the person making the disclosure and the person to whom it is made carry on business in an EEA State or in a country or territory imposing equivalent money laundering requirements, and
>
> (c) those persons perform their professional activities within different undertakings that share common ownership, management or control.

Section 333C: other permitted disclosures between institutions, etc

Section 333C(1) further widens the scope of permitted disclosures to allow certain dis **8.36** closures between credit or financial institutions of the same type and between professional advisers of the same kind, but only in defined circumstances and subject to restrictive conditions set out in section 333C(2). Notably, the exception only applies if

---

[9] Directive 2002/87/EC of the European Parliament and of the Council of 16 December 2002.

'the disclosure is *for the purpose only* of preventing an offence under this Part of this Act' (emphasis added):

> (1) This section applies to a disclosure—
>> (a) by a credit institution to another credit institution,
>> (b) by a financial institution to another financial institution,
>> (c) by a professional legal adviser to another professional legal adviser, or
>> (d) by a relevant professional adviser of a particular kind to another relevant professional adviser of the same kind.

The four conditions

8.37　The conditions for the exception to apply, set out in section 333C(2), restrict the application of the exception by reference to four features of the disclosure: the subject or subject matter of the disclosure, the purpose of the disclosure, equivalence of money laundering requirements and equivalence of duties of confidentiality and data protection:

> (2) A person does not commit an offence under section 333A in respect of a disclosure to which this section applies if—
>> (a) the disclosure relates to—
>>> (i) a client or former client of the institution or adviser making the disclosure and the institution or adviser to whom it is made,
>>> (ii) a transaction involving them both, or
>>> (iii) the provision of a service involving them both;
>> (b) the disclosure is for the purpose only of preventing an offence under this Part of this Act;
>> (c) the institution or adviser to whom the disclosure is made is situated in an EEA State or in a country or territory imposing equivalent money laundering requirements; and
>> (d) the institution or adviser making the disclosure and the institution or adviser to whom it is made are subject to equivalent duties of professional confidentiality and the protection of personal data (within the meaning of section 1 of the Data Protection Act 1998).

The purpose of the disclosure

8.38　Section 333C(2)(b) seems to require that the person making the disclosure must, when doing so, have the intention or purpose *only* of preventing a terrorist property offence. The single act of disclosure, however, may serve more than one purpose, and the three circumstances in which the exception would operate, set out in subsection (2)(a), are circumstances in which the person making the disclosure would be very likely to have other professional or commercial purposes that would be served by the disclosure.

8.39　Where such a disclosure does in fact serve another professional or commercial purpose, the good faith of the discloser might not be accepted by an investigator, making the discloser vulnerable to investigation and prosecution. The risk of this would be greater where, as is quite likely to be the case, the discloser will be aware of the other purpose that would be served by a disclosure and would or might, were it not for the prohibition on disclosure, make a disclosure for that other purpose. It seems likely that such considerations will inhibit any reliance on the provisions of section 333C.

Section 333D: other permitted disclosures etc

8.40　This section creates further exceptions to the commission of an offence under section 333A: an important general exception in section 333D(3) and (4) concerning the mental element of each of the offences under section 333A, and three specific exceptions in section 333D(1) and (2) which provide for further permitted disclosures:

- disclosures to supervisory authorities;
- disclosures for law enforcement purposes;
- disclosures to clients by professional advisers.

Disclosures to the supervisory authority

Section 333D(1)(a) creates the exception for disclosure to supervisory authorities.[10] These **8.41** authorities are themselves under a duty promptly to inform Serious Organised Crime Agency (SOCA) if in the course of carrying out any of their functions under the Money Laundering Regulations 2007 (MLR 2007), they know or suspect that a person is or has engaged in money laundering or terrorist financing:[11]

> (1) A person does not commit an offence under section 333A if the disclosure is—
>   (a) to the authority that is the supervisory authority for that person by virtue of the Money Laundering Regulations 2007;
>   . . .

Disclosure for law enforcement purposes

This second exception will exempt from liability for a tipping off offence any person carrying **8.42** out an investigatory function under the Act or a law enforcement function. The exception is expressed in terms of purpose rather than status so that, in appropriate circumstances, it could apply to a person who is not a constable or other law enforcement officer:

> (1) A person does not commit an offence under section 333A if the disclosure is—
>   . . .
>   (b) for the purpose of—
>   (i) the detection, investigation or prosecution of a criminal offence (whether in the United Kingdom or elsewhere),
>   (ii) an investigation under this Act, or
>   (iii) the enforcement of any order of a court under this Act.

Disclosures to clients by professional advisers

Section 333D(2) creates an exception which applies to professional legal advisers and rele- **8.43** vant professional advisers, but only in narrowly defined circumstances. Under section 333A there is no 'privileged circumstances' exception equivalent to that in the former section 333(2)(c); instead, there is this limited exception which is directly derived from Article 28(6) of the Third Money Laundering Directive.

The exception under section 333D(2) permits disclosures by professional advisers to their **8.44** clients, but only where the disclosure is made for the purpose of dissuading the client from committing a crime:

> (2) A professional legal adviser or a relevant professional adviser does not commit an offence under section 333A if the disclosure—
>   (a) is to the adviser's client, and
>   (b) is made for the purpose of dissuading the client from engaging in conduct amounting to an offence.

---

[10] For what is a supervisory authority, see POCA, Sch 9 and MLR 2007, Reg 23 and Sch 3.
[11] MLR 2007, Reg 24(2).

General defence—the mental element

8.45 Section 333D(3) and (4) create an important general exception applying to the two offences under section 333A. It provides that a person does not commit an offence under either section 333A(1) or section 333A(3) if the person does not know or suspect that the disclosure is likely to prejudice a potential or actual investigation. In effect, this inserts a mental element into both offences under section 333A. This provision is essentially the same as the exception to the former tipping off offence (in section 333(2)(a)):

> (3) A person does not commit an offence under section 333A(1) if the person does not know or suspect that the disclosure is likely to have the effect mentioned in section 333A(1)(b).
>
> (4) A person does not commit an offence under section 333A(3) if the person does not know or suspect that the disclosure is likely to have the effect mentioned in section 333A(3)(b).

Section 333E: interpretation of sections 333A to 333D

8.46 The complex provisions that make up the new tipping off offences and the various exceptions to them are supplemented, in section 333E, by an interpretation section:

> (1) For the purposes of sections 333A to 333D, Schedule 9 has effect for determining—
> (a) what is a business in the regulated sector, and
> (b) what is a supervisory authority.
> (2) In those sections—
> 'credit institution' has the same meaning as in Schedule 9;
> 'financial institution' means an undertaking that carries on a business in the regulated sector by virtue of any of paragraphs (b) to (i) of paragraph 1(1) of that Schedule.
> (3) References in those sections to a disclosure by or to a credit institution or a financial institution include disclosure by or to an employee, officer or partner of the institution acting on its behalf.
> (4) For the purposes of those sections a country or territory imposes 'equivalent money laundering requirements' if it imposes requirements equivalent to those laid down in Directive 2005/60/EC of the European Parliament and of the Council of 26th October 2005 on the prevention of the use of the financial system for the purpose of money laundering and terrorist financing.
> (5) In those sections 'relevant professional adviser' means an accountant, auditor or tax adviser who is a member of a professional body which is established for accountants, auditors or tax advisers (as the case may be) and which makes provision for—
> (a) testing the competence of those seeking admission to membership of such a body as a condition for such admission; and
> (b) imposing and maintaining professional and ethical standards for its members, as well as imposing sanctions for non-compliance with those standards.

Section 342: offences of prejudicing an investigation

8.47 This section creates two quite separate offences, only the first of which is an offence of unlawful disclosure:

> (1) This section applies if a person knows or suspects that an appropriate officer or (in Scotland) a proper person is acting (or proposing to act) in connection with a confiscation investigation, a civil recovery investigation or a money laundering investigation which is being or is about to be conducted.
> (2) The person commits an offence if—
> (a) he makes a disclosure which is likely to prejudice the investigation, or ...

The offence under section 342(2)(a)

As with tipping off, the offence consists in the unlawful disclosure itself: to make a disclosure **8.48** is to reveal information. The result of the disclosure is not relevant to the offence, or only relevant insofar as the actual outcome may be evidence that the disclosure was in fact likely to prejudice the investigation. An innocent action by a person, such as not proceeding with a transfer of property or other transaction, may alert a money launderer and have the effect of prejudicing an investigation, but no offence would be committed.

Conversely, where a person makes an unlawful disclosure within the terms of section 342(2) **8.49** (a), it would be no defence to show that no prejudice was in fact caused to the investigation. Again, however, the outcome may be relevant to the issue of whether the disclosure was likely to prejudice the investigation.

Specimen indictment

The offence under section 342(2) is triable either in the magistrates' court or in the Crown **8.50** Court.

STATEMENT OF OFFENCE

Making a disclosure likely to prejudice an investigation contrary to section 342(2) Proceeds of Crime Act 2002

PARTICULARS OF OFFENCE

A B on the . . . day of . . ., knowing or suspecting that C D, a constable, was proposing to act in connection with a money laundering investigation about to be conducted, made a disclosure to E F which was likely to prejudice the investigation.

Sentence

A person guilty of an offence under section 342(2) is liable: **8.51**

    (a) on summary conviction, to imprisonment for a term not exceeding six months or to a fine not exceeding the statutory maximum or to both, or

    (b) on conviction on indictment, to imprisonment for a term not exceeding five years or to a fine or to both.

Defences and exceptions

There is a general defence relating to the mental element of the offence and three particular **8.52** defences or exceptions to the offence under section 342(2):

- lack of awareness that the disclosure is likely to prejudice the investigation;
- disclosure in relation to a law enforcement function;
- disclosure which would come within the regulated sector offence under section 333A(3);
- disclosure made in accordance with provisions in the Coroners and Justice Act 2009;
- disclosure by a professional legal adviser in 'privileged circumstances'.

General defence relating to the mental element

In effect, this provision forms part of the mental element of the offence itself. As with the **8.53** tipping off offences created by section 333A, no offence is committed unless prejudice to an investigation is likely *and* the discloser knows or suspects that this is so:

    (3) A person does not commit an offence under subsection (2)(a) if—
        (a) he does not know or suspect that the disclosure is likely to prejudice the investigation,

Law enforcement exception

8.54 The exception in section 342(2)(b) would seem, in practice, to be largely confined to the functions of law enforcement officers:

> (3) A person does not commit an offence under subsection (2)(a) if—
>
> . . .
>
> > (b) the disclosure is made in the exercise of a function under this Act or any other enact-ment relating to criminal conduct or benefit from criminal conduct or in compliance with a requirement imposed under or by virtue of this Act, or

Exception in respect of regulated sector disclosures

8.55 Under POCA as originally enacted the offence under section 342 applied to everyone, whether they were in the regulated sector or outside it, subject to the exceptions in section 342(3)(a), (b) and (c). As from 26 December 2007, the application of section 342 is limited by subsection (3)(ba). This provision creates an exception where the unlawful disclosure is of a matter which would form the basis for a tipping off offence under either section 333A(1) or section 333A(3): specifically, where the disclosure is about a money laundering disclosure or an actual or contemplated criminal money laundering investigation, and where the infor-mation on which the unlawful disclosure is based came to a person through regulated sector business:

> (3) A person does not commit an offence under subsection (2)(a) if—
>
> . . .
>
> > (ba) the disclosure is of a matter within section 333A(2) or (3)(a) (money laundering: tip-ping off) and the information on which the disclosure is based came to the person in the course of a business in the regulated sector,

8.56 Although section 342(3)(ba) will, in practice, largely exclude those who work in the regu-lated sector from liability under the section, it should be noted that they may still commit the offence of unlawful disclosure under section 342 in certain circumstances. Firstly, where the information on which the unlawful disclosure is based came to the person otherwise than in the course of regulated sector business and, secondly, where the person makes a disclosure about an investigation other than a money laundering investigation, such as a confiscation or civil recovery investigation.

Exception in accordance with the Coroners and Justice Act 2009

8.57 A further exception, which has been added by the Coroners and Justice Act 2009 and is effective from 6 April 2010, has been added as section 342(3)(bb): 'the disclosure is made in the exercise of a function under Part 7 of the Coroners and Justice Act 2009 (crimi-nal memoirs etc) or in compliance with a requirement imposed under or by virtue of that Act'.

Privileged circumstances exception

8.58 The exception in section 342(3)(c) is the professional legal adviser exception, the scope of which is set out in subsections (4) and (5):

> (3) A person does not commit an offence under subsection (2)(a) if—
>
> . . .
>
> > (c) he is a professional legal adviser and the disclosure falls within subsection (4).
>
> (4) A disclosure falls within this subsection if it is a disclosure—
>
> > (a) to (or to a representative of) a client of the professional legal adviser in connection with the giving by the adviser of legal advice to the client, or

(b) to any person in connection with legal proceedings or contemplated legal proceedings.

(5) But a disclosure does not fall within subsection (4) if it is made with the intention of furthering a criminal purpose.

Section 342(4) enables a solicitor or other professional legal adviser to inform and advise **8.59** a client in circumstances where the adviser knows or suspects about an actual or impending investigation, except where the intention of the relevant adviser in making a disclosure to the client is to further a criminal purpose. Section 342(4)(a) allows the professional legal adviser to disclose information to the actual client or a representative of the client in any advice situation; section 342(4)(b) allows the professional legal adviser to disclose information to anyone in connection with actual or contemplated legal proceedings.

D. Unlawful Disclosures under the Terrorism Act 2000

Section 21D: tipping off: regulated sector

This section introduced into TA 2000 two new offences of unlawful disclosure which are **8.60** essentially the same as the two offences under section 333A of POCA. These offences came into force on 26 December 2007.

The first offence: tipping off under section 21D(1)

The first of the offences is the classic 'tipping off' offence: making an *unlawful* disclosure **8.61** about a *lawful* disclosure:

(1) A person commits an offence if—
    (a) the person discloses any matter within subsection (2);
    (b) the disclosure is likely to prejudice any investigation that might be conducted following the disclosure referred to in that subsection; and
    (c) the information on which the disclosure is based came to the person in the course of a business in the regulated sector.
(2) The matters are that the person or another person has made a disclosure under a provision of this Part—
    (a) to a constable,
    (b) in accordance with a procedure established by that person's employer for the making of disclosures under that provision,
    (c) to a nominated officer, or
    (d) to a member of staff of the Serious Organised Crime Agency authorised for the purposes of that provision by the Director General of that Agency,
of information that came to that person in the course of a business in the regulated sector.

In substance, this offence differs from the offence under section 333A(1) of POCA only **8.62** in respect of the description of the 'matters' unlawfully disclosed: disclosures either under Part 7 of POCA or Part III of TA 2000. Section 21D(2) lists the matters, that is the lawful disclosures, which may form the subject matter of tipping off. These are terrorist property or money laundering disclosures to a constable (in this section meaning a police officer) or to SOCA, as well as disclosures under subsection (2)(b) and (c) (internal disclosures). The procedural provision in subsection (2)(b) must, in effect, mean disclosure to a nominated officer, but seems to be separately included because of the wording used in section 19(4) which does not refer explicitly to a 'nominated officer'. Similar inexplicit wording is used in section 20(4) and section 21(6).

8.63 Although the offence elements are set out clearly, the section can be confusing because it involves both lawful and unlawful 'disclosures' and concerns 'persons' who are lawful disclosers and/or unlawful disclosers. The section is set out below with additions in square brackets to clarify its effect. Note that in subsection (2), the references to 'the lawful discloser' are references to the person who has made a lawful disclosure, but who may also be 'the unlawful discloser':

> (1) A person commits an offence if—
>> (a) the person [*unlawfully*] discloses any matter within subsection (2);
>> (b) the [*unlawful*] disclosure is likely to prejudice any investigation that might be conducted following the [*lawful*] disclosure referred to in that subsection; and
>> (c) the information on which the [*unlawful*] disclosure is based came to the person [*the unlawful discloser*] in the course of a business in the regulated sector.
> (2) The matters are that the person [*the unlawful discloser*] or another person has made a [*lawful*] disclosure under a provision of this Part—
>> (a) to a constable,
>> (b) in accordance with a procedure established by that person's [*the lawful discloser's*] employer for the making of [*lawful*] disclosures under that provision,
>> (c) to a nominated officer, or
>> (d) to a member of staff of the Serious Organised Crime Agency authorised for the purposes of that provision by the Director General of that Agency,
> of information that came to that person [*the lawful discloser*] in the course of a business in the regulated sector.

The nature of the tipping off offence

8.64 The offence of tipping off consists in the act of disclosing, that is communicating information to another person, in circumstances where that disclosure is *likely* to prejudice any investigation that *might* be conducted. The penal provisions of section 21D, like those in section 333A of POCA, are directed at those who work in the regulated sector and enforce a prohibition on the making of disclosures likely to be prejudicial. See above, at paragraphs 8.14–8.22 for a more detailed discussion of the nature of the tipping off offence.

Specimen indictment

8.65 The offence under section 21D(1) is triable either in the magistrates' court or in the Crown Court.

STATEMENT OF OFFENCE

Tipping off contrary to section 21D(1) Terrorism Act 2000.

PARTICULARS OF OFFENCE

A B on the . . . day of . . . disclosed to C D that E F had made a terrorist property disclosure to an authorised member of staff at the Serious Organised Crime Agency and the disclosure to C D, based on information that came to A B in the course of a business in the regulated sector, was likely to prejudice any investigation that might be conducted following the terrorist property disclosure.

Sentence

8.66 Under section 21D(4), a person who is guilty of an offence under section 21D(1) is liable:

> (a) on summary conviction to imprisonment for a term not exceeding three months, or to a fine not exceeding level 5 on the standard scale, or to both;

(b) on conviction on indictment to imprisonment for a term not exceeding two years, or to a fine, or to both.

Defences and exceptions

Section 21D is followed by four more sections, 21E to 21H, which set out a number of detailed defences and exceptions to the offences in section 21D(1) and (3). These are dealt with below at paragraphs 8.71 *et seq.* **8.67**

The second offence: tipping off under section 21D(3)

The second of the offences is contained in section 21D(3). This offence is the same as that created by section 333A(3) except that the investigation concerned is about an alleged offence under Part III of TA 2000 rather than an offence under Part 7 of POCA. For an offence to be committed, the unlawful disclosure must be likely to prejudice the investigation: **8.68**

(3) A person commits an offence if—
(a) the person discloses that an investigation into allegations that an offence under this Part has been committed is being contemplated or is being carried out;
(b) the disclosure is likely to prejudice that investigation; and
(c) the information on which the disclosure is based came to the person in the course of a business in the regulated sector.

Specimen indictment

The offence under section 21D(3) is triable either in the magistrates' court or in the Crown Court. **8.69**

STATEMENT OF OFFENCE

Tipping off contrary to section 21D(3) Terrorism Act 2000.

PARTICULARS OF OFFENCE

A B, on the . . . day of . . ., disclosed to C D that an investigation was being carried out into allegations that a terrorist property offence had been committed and the disclosure by A B, based on information that came to A B in the course of a business in the regulated sector, was likely to prejudice that investigation.

Sentence

Under section 21D(4), a person who is guilty of an offence under section 21D(3) is liable: **8.70**

(a) on summary conviction to imprisonment for a term not exceeding three months, or to a fine not exceeding level 5 on the standard scale, or to both;
(b) on conviction on indictment to imprisonment for a term not exceeding two years, or to a fine, or to both.

Defences and exceptions to the tipping off offences under section 21D

Section 21D is followed by four more sections, 21E to 21H, which set out and define a number of detailed and complicated exceptions to the offences in section 21D. These exceptions, which are essentially the same as those to the tipping off offences under POCA, are derived from and implement the provisions of paragraphs 2 to 6, inclusive, of Article 28 of the Third Money Laundering Directive. **8.71**

Section 21E: disclosure within an undertaking or group, etc

8.72 Section 21E(1) permits, without further qualification, disclosures within an undertaking in the regulated sector:

> (1) An employee, officer or partner of an undertaking does not commit an offence under section 21D if the disclosure is to an employee, officer or partner of the same undertaking.

8.73 Section 21E(2) and (4) permit disclosures within a group of credit or financial institutions and between professional advisers within different undertakings that share common ownership, management or control, but only in defined circumstances. There are separate provisions for credit and financial institutions on the one hand and professional advisers on the other, but with the qualification in each case that the disclosure is only permitted where it is to an institution or professional adviser subject to the same or equivalent money laundering requirements:

> (2) A person does not commit an offence under section 21D in respect of a disclosure by a credit institution or a financial institution if—
>   (a) the disclosure is to a credit institution or a financial institution,
>   (b) the institution to whom the disclosure is made is situated in an EEA State or in a country or territory imposing equivalent money laundering requirements, and
>   (c) both the institution making the disclosure and the institution to whom it is made belong to the same group.
> (3) In subsection (2) 'group' has the same meaning as in Directive 2002/87/EC of the European Parliament and of the Council of 16th December 2002 on the supplementary supervision of credit institutions, insurance undertakings and investment firms in a financial conglomerate.

Definition of 'group'

8.74 In this section, 'group' '. . .shall mean a group of undertakings, which consists of a parent undertaking, its subsidiaries and the entities in which the parent undertaking or its subsidiaries hold a participation, as well as undertakings linked to each other by a relationship within the meaning of Article 12(1) of Directive 83/349/EEC'.[12] For the purposes of a permitted disclosure under this section, the extension of the meaning of 'group' to linked undertakings within the terms of Article 12(1) of Directive 83/349/EEC is probably not of much practical relevance.

Professional legal advisers and relevant legal advisers

8.75 The provisions of section 21E(4) extend to professional legal advisers and relevant professional advisers a *permission* to disclose that is similar to the exception that applies to credit institutions and financial institutions:

> (4) A professional legal adviser or a relevant professional adviser does not commit an offence under section 21D if—
>   (a) the disclosure is to a professional legal adviser or a relevant professional adviser,
>   (b) both the person making the disclosure and the person to whom it is made carry on business in an EEA state or in a country or territory imposing equivalent money laundering requirements, and
>   (c) those persons perform their professional activities within different undertakings that share common ownership, management or control.

---

[12] Directive 2002/87/EC of the European Parliament and of the Council of 16 December 2002.

Section 21F: other permitted disclosures between institutions, etc

Section 21F(1) further widens the scope of permitted disclosures to allow certain disclosures **8.76** between credit or financial institutions of the same type and between professional advisers of the same kind, but only in defined circumstances and subject to restrictive conditions set out in section 21F(2). Notably, the exception only applies if 'the disclosure is *for the purpose only* of preventing an offence under this Part of the Act' (emphasis added):

    (1) This section applies to a disclosure—
        (a) by a credit institution to another credit institution,
        (b) by a financial institution to another financial institution,
        (c) by a professional legal adviser to another professional legal adviser, or
        (d) by a relevant professional adviser of a particular kind to another relevant professional adviser of the same kind.

The four conditions

The conditions for the exception to apply, set out in section 21F(2), restrict the application **8.77** of the exception by reference to four features of the disclosure: the subject or subject matter of the disclosure, the purpose of the disclosure, equivalence of money laundering requirements and equivalence of duties of confidentiality and data protection:

    (2) A person does not commit an offence under section 21D in respect of a disclosure to which this section applies if—
        (a) the disclosure relates to—
            (i) a client or former client of the institution or adviser making the disclosure and the institution or adviser to whom it is made,
            (ii) a transaction involving them both, or
            (iii) the provision of a service involving them both;
        (b) the disclosure is for the purpose only of preventing an offence under this Part of this Act;
        (c) the institution or adviser to whom the disclosure is made is situated in an EEA State or in a country or territory imposing equivalent money laundering requirements; and
        (d) the institution or adviser making the disclosure and the institution or adviser to whom it is made are subject to equivalent duties of professional confidentiality and the protection of personal data (within the meaning of section 1 of the Data Protection Act 1998).

The purpose of the disclosure

Section 21F(2)(b) seems to require that the person making the disclosure must, when doing **8.78** so, have the intention or purpose *only* of preventing a terrorist property offence. The single act of disclosure, however, may serve more than one purpose, and the three circumstances in which the exception would operate, set out in subsection (2)(a), are circumstances in which the person making the disclosure would be very likely to have other professional or commercial purposes that would be served by the disclosure.

Where such a disclosure does in fact serve another professional or commercial purpose, the **8.79** good faith of the discloser might not be accepted by an investigator, making the discloser vulnerable to investigation and prosecution. The risk of this would be greater where, as is quite likely to be the case, the discloser will be aware of the other purpose that would be served by a disclosure and would or might, were it not for the prohibition on disclosure, make a disclosure for that other purpose. It seems likely that such considerations will inhibit any reliance on the provisions of section 21F.

Section 21G: other permitted disclosure, etc

8.80 This section creates further exceptions to the commission of an offence under section 21D: an important general exception in section 21G(3) and (4) concerning the mental element of each of the offences under section 21D, and three specific exceptions in section 21G(1) and (2) which provide for further permitted disclosures:

- disclosures to supervisory authorities;
- disclosures for law enforcement purposes;
- disclosures to clients by professional legal advisers and relevant professional advisers.

Disclosures to the supervisory authority

8.81 Section 21G(1)(a) creates the exception for disclosure to supervisory authorities.[13] These authorities are themselves under a duty promptly to inform SOCA if in the course of carrying out any of their functions under the Money Laundering Regulations 2007, they know or suspect that a person is or has engaged in money laundering or terrorist financing:[14]

> (1) A person does not commit an offence under section 21D if the disclosure is—
>> (a) to the authority that is the supervisory authority for that person by virtue of the Money Laundering Regulations 2007 (SI 2007/2157);

Disclosure for law enforcement purposes

8.82 This second exception will exempt from liability for a tipping off offence any person carrying out an investigatory function under the Act or a law enforcement function. The exception is expressed in terms of purpose rather than status so that, in appropriate circumstances, it could apply to a person who is not a constable or other law enforcement officer:

> (1) A person does not commit an offence under section 21D if the disclosure is—
>> . . .
>> (b) for the purpose of—
>>> (i) the detection, investigation or prosecution of a criminal offence (whether in the United Kingdom or elsewhere),
>>> (ii) an investigation under the Proceeds of Crime Act 2002, or
>>> (iii) the enforcement of any order of a court under that Act.

Disclosures to clients by professional advisers

8.83 This exception applies to professional legal advisers and relevant professional advisers in narrowly defined circumstances. Under section 21D there is no 'privileged circumstances' exception equivalent to that in the former section 333 of POCA. Instead, there is this limited exception which is directly derived from Article 28(6) of the Third Money Laundering Directive. The exception under section 21G(2) permits disclosures by professional advisers to their clients, but only where the disclosure is made for the purpose of dissuading the client from committing a crime:

> (2) A professional legal adviser or a relevant professional adviser does not commit an offence under section 21D if the disclosure—
>> (a) is to the adviser's client, and

---

[13] For what is a supervisory authority, see Money Laundering Regulations 2007, Reg 23 and Sch 3.
[14] Money Laundering Regulations 2007, Reg 24(2).

(b) is made for the purpose of dissuading the client from engaging in conduct amounting to an offence.

General defence—the mental element

Section 21G(3) and (4) create an important general exception applying to the two offences **8.84** under section 21D. They provide that a person does not commit an offence under either section 21D(1) or section 21D(3) if the person does not know or suspect that the disclosure is likely to prejudice a potential or actual investigation. In effect, this inserts a mental element into both offences under section 21D. This provision is essentially the same as the exception to the former tipping off offence (in section 333(2)(a)):

(3) A person does not commit an offence under section 21D(1) if the person does not know or suspect that the disclosure is likely to have the effect mentioned in section 21D(1)(b).

(4) A person does not commit an offence under section 21D(3) if the person does not know or suspect that the disclosure is likely to have the effect mentioned in section 21D(3)(b).

Section 21H: interpretation of sections 21D to 21G

The complex provisions that make up the new tipping off offences and the various exceptions **8.85** to them are supplemented, in section 21H, by an interpretation section:

(1) The references in sections 21D to 21G—
  (a) to a business in the regulated sector, and
  (b) to a supervisory authority, are to be construed in accordance with Schedule 3A.

(2) In those sections—
  "credit institution" has the same meaning as in Schedule 3A;
  "financial institution" means an undertaking that carries on a business in the regulated sector by virtue of any of paragraphs (b) to (i) of paragraph 1(1) of that Schedule.

(3) References in those sections to a disclosure by or to a credit institution or a financial institution include disclosure by or to an employee, officer or partner of the institution acting on its behalf.

(4) For the purposes of those sections a country or territory imposes 'equivalent money laundering requirements' if it imposes requirements equivalent to those laid down in Directive 2005/60/EC of the European Parliament and of the Council of 26th October 2005 on the prevention of the use of the financial system for the purpose of money laundering and terrorist financing.

(5) In those sections 'relevant professional adviser' means an accountant, auditor or tax adviser who is a member of a professional body which is established for accountants, auditors or tax advisers (as the case may be) and which makes provision for—
  (a) testing the competence of those seeking admission to membership of such a body as a condition for such admission; and
  (b) imposing and maintaining professional and ethical standards for its members, as well as imposing sanctions for non-compliance with those standards.

Offences of unlawful disclosure under section 39 of TA 2000

Section 39 in Part IV of TA 2000 creates two offences of unlawful disclosure, which apply to **8.86** everyone subject to the criminal law. The first of these offences, under section 39(2)(a), is an offence of prejudicing a terrorist investigation. The second offence, under section 39(4)(a), is a classic tipping off offence: the making of an *unlawful* disclosure likely to prejudice an investigation by a person who knows or has reasonable cause to suspect that a *lawful* disclosure has been made.

The scope of the offences under section 39

8.87   Offences involving acts of terrorism[15] and the law relating to disclosure of information about acts of terrorism are outside the scope of this book, but the disclosure offences under section 39 concern the investigation of both acts of terrorism and terrorist property offences. Section 39 needs, therefore, to be read in conjunction with section 32 and section 38B. Section 32 is an interpretation section (see below, at paragraph 8.91); section 38B creates a general duty to disclose belief or suspicion about acts of terrorism and makes it a criminal offence to fail to disclose such information.[16]

8.88   The application of section 39 is limited in one respect, that is where there would be duplication of the offences of tipping off in the regulated sector under section 21D:

> (6A) Subsections (2) and (4) do not apply if—
>> (a) the disclosure is of a matter within section 21D(2) or (3)(a) (terrorist property: tipping off), and
>> (b) the information on which the disclosure is based came to the person in the course of a business in the regulated sector.

8.89   Although section 39 does not apply where the facts would also give rise to an offence under section 21D, it will apply to those in the regulated sector because the subject matter of the potential unlawful disclosures is wider under section 39 than under section 21D. In particular, the offence under section 39(2) relates to a terrorist investigation, as defined in section 32, and section 39(4) concerns tipping off about lawful disclosures made under section 38B as well as terrorist property disclosures under sections 19 to 21B.

The first offence: unlawful disclosure under section 39(2)

8.90   The first of the two offences of unlawful disclosure created by section 39 concerns a 'terrorist investigation', a term defined in section 32 (below):

> (1) Subsection (2) applies where a person knows or has reasonable cause to suspect that a constable is conducting or proposes to conduct a terrorist investigation.

The circumstances in which the offence may be committed are defined not by reference to an actual or contemplated investigation, as in other offences of unlawful disclosure, but according to whether a person knows or has—objectively—reasonable cause to suspect.

Definition of terrorist investigation

8.91   A terrorist investigation is defined in section 32:

> In this Act 'terrorist investigation' means an investigation of—
>> (a) the commission, preparation or instigation of acts of terrorism,
>> (b) an act which appears to have been done for the purposes of terrorism,
>> (c) the resources of a proscribed organisation,
>> (d) the possibility of making an order under section 3(3), or
>> (e) the commission, preparation or instigation of an offence under this Act or under Part 1 of the Terrorism Act 2006 other than an offence under section 1 or 2 of that Act.

---

[15] In TA 2000, 'act' includes omission (s 121) and 'terrorism' is defined in s 1, as amended by the Counter-Terrorism Act 2008.

[16] See Chapter 7 at paras 7.43–7.52.

A terrorist investigation is primarily an investigation about acts of terrorism, but the provision is broadly defined, so that subsections (b) and (c) in particular, as well as subsection (e), would bring investigations into terrorist property and terrorist finance within its scope.

The offence is set out in section 39(2):   **8.92**

(2) The person commits an offence if he—
    (a) discloses to another anything which is likely to prejudice the investigation, or
    (b) interferes with material which is likely to be relevant to the investigation.

The disclosure offence under section 39(2)(a) is widely drawn and applies to anyone coming within the broad terms of subsection (1), which includes an objective test of 'reasonable cause to suspect'.

Specimen indictment

The offence under section 39(2) is triable either in the magistrates' court or in the Crown   **8.93**
Court.

STATEMENT OF OFFENCE

Disclosure likely to prejudice an investigation contrary to section 39(2) Terrorism Act 2000.

PARTICULARS OF OFFENCE

A B, on the . . . day of . . ., knowing or having reasonable cause to suspect that a constable was conducting a terrorist investigation, disclosed to C D information which was likely to prejudice the investigation.

Sentence

A person who is guilty of an offence under section 39(2) is liable: **8.94**

    (a) on conviction on indictment, to imprisonment for a term not exceeding five years, to a fine or to both, or
    (b) on summary conviction, to imprisonment for a term not exceeding six months, to a fine not exceeding the statutory maximum or to both.

Defences and exceptions

There are two general defences under section 39(5), as well as a specific exception for   **8.95**
professional legal advisers, which apply to both of the offences created by section 39(2). These are considered below at paragraphs 8.99 *et seq*.

The second offence: unlawful disclosure under section 39(4)

The second of the disclosure offences, under section 39(4)(a), concerns an unlawful   **8.96**
disclosure that is likely to prejudice an investigation.

(3) Subsection (4) applies where a person knows or has reasonable cause to suspect that a disclosure has been or will be made under any of sections 19 to 21B or 38B.
(4) The person commits an offence if he—
    (a) discloses to another anything which is likely to prejudice an investigation resulting from the disclosure under that section,
    . . .

Specimen indictment

The offence under section 39(4) is triable either in the magistrates' court or in the Crown   **8.97**
Court.

STATEMENT OF OFFENCE

Disclosure likely to prejudice an investigation contrary to section 39(4) Terrorism Act 2000.

PARTICULARS OF OFFENCE

A B, on the . . . day of . . ., knowing or having reasonable cause to suspect that a disclosure under section 38B had been made, [or that a disclosure under any of sections 19 to 21B or 38B would be made,] disclosed to C D information which was likely to prejudice an investigation resulting from the disclosure under that section [or any such disclosure].

Sentence

8.98   Under section 39(7) a person guilty of an offence under section 39(4) is liable:

(a) on conviction on indictment, to imprisonment for a term not exceeding five years, to a fine or to both, or

(b) on summary conviction, to imprisonment for a term not exceeding six months, to a fine not exceeding the statutory maximum or to both.

Defences and exceptions

8.99   Apart from the regulated sector exclusion in section 39(6A),[17] there are two general defences under section 39(5) as well as a specific exception that applies to professional legal advisers.

General defence—the mental element

8.100   There is a general defence, in section 39(5)(a), which relates to the mental element of the offence:

(5) It is a defence for a person charged with an offence under subsection (2) or (4) to prove—

(a) that he did not know and had no reasonable cause to suspect that the disclosure or interference was likely to affect a terrorist investigation,

. . .

It is not clear why the word 'affect' has been used rather than 'prejudice' as in section 39(4)(a), but it seems likely that it should be read as meaning adversely affect or prejudice.

8.101   The burden of proof is placed on the defendant to establish the defence under section 39(5)(a). This evidential provision, which applies by virtue of section 118(5)(a), must be read subject to section 118(1) and (2):

(1) Subsection (2) applies where in accordance with a provision mentioned in subsection (5) it is a defence for a person charged with an offence to prove a particular matter.

(2) If the person adduces evidence which is sufficient to raise an issue with respect to the matter the court or jury shall assume that the defence is satisfied unless the prosecution proves beyond reasonable doubt that it is not.

General defence of reasonable excuse

8.102   There is a second general defence, which is that of reasonable excuse:

(5) It is a defence for a person charged with an offence under subsection (2) or (4) to prove—

. . .

(b) that he had a reasonable excuse for the disclosure or interference.

---

[17]   See para 8.88 above.

There is no authority on what would amount to a reasonable excuse but the burden of proof is placed on the defendant to establish the defence and in the context of terrorist investigations the test of reasonableness is likely to be stringent.

Privileged circumstances exclusion

This provision excludes from the ambit of the two offences under section 39 disclosures made **8.103** by professional legal advisers in privileged circumstances, as defined in subsection (6):

> (6) Subsections (2) and (4) do not apply to a disclosure which is made by a professional legal adviser—
>
>> (a) to his client or to his client's representative in connection with the provision of legal advice by the adviser to the client and not with a view to furthering a criminal purpose, or
>>
>> (b) to any person for the purpose of actual or contemplated legal proceedings and not with a view to furthering a criminal purpose.

E. Conclusion

Tipping off offences

The UK now has offences of tipping off in both POCA and TA 2000 which apply to those in **8.104** the regulated sector. These offences are intended to implement the provisions of Article 28[18] in the Third Money Laundering Directive and they include a number of detailed and complicated exceptions or defences. There are also offences of prejudicing an investigation which are of general application.

There is a clear rationale for having offences of prejudicing an investigation, but it is much **8.105** less clear that there is any need for or useful purpose served by the tipping off offences. When a SAR has been made, any responsible person would recognize that there is a need to avoid alerting the person suspected of money laundering or any other person likely to inform the suspected money launderer. It does not follow from this that a criminal offence of tipping off is either necessary or useful. While there is a risk that an unthinking disclosure of information may tip off a money launderer, that is a risk that might be better dealt with by guidance and training, supplemented by appropriate administrative or regulatory sanctions. Where, however, a person deliberately tips off a suspected money launderer or accomplice, it is—subject to the specific circumstances of the case—very likely that that person is committing other more serious criminal offences such as money laundering or attempting to pervert the course of justice.

It is unsurprising that there are very few prosecutions. The Home Office statistics record **8.106** three prosecutions—and three convictions—under the former section 333 tipping off offence between 2003 and 2007. (One person received a conditional discharge, one was given a community sentence and one was fined.)

If the tipping off offences are rarely used and it is questionable whether they have any positive **8.107** effect in combating money laundering or assisting law enforcement, they certainly have

---

[18] Art 28, which prohibits disclosure, needs to be read in conjunction with Art 39, paras 1 and 2, which deals with sanctions.

harmful and unnecessary side effects on the conduct of legitimate business. They are directed at those who work in the regulated sector and they promote a fear culture in the regulated sector which prevents the sensible exercise of discretion and is antithetical to the risk-based approach. The broader effect of the tipping off offences is to cause considerable interference with the conduct of business and with professional and business relationships that those in the regulated sector have with their customers and clients.

8.108 The most unhelpful aspect of the tipping off offences is that they are counter-productive. It is the combined effect of the operation of the consent regime and the tipping off offences that is itself most likely to alert money launderers to the fact that they are under suspicion and have been reported to the authorities.[19]

---

[19] See above at paras 8.20 and 8.21.

9

REGULATION:
THE REGULATED SECTOR AND ITS
OBLIGATIONS

A. Introduction

This and the next chapter are concerned with the regulatory measures intended to prevent **9.01** and detect money laundering and terrorist financing in those areas of business and professional activity that are thought to be particularly vulnerable to the misuse of their services. This chapter covers Parts 1 to 3 of the Money Laundering Regulations 2007 ('the Regulations') and deals with general matters such as Interpretation and the application of the Regulations in Part 1, with customer due diligence (CDD) in Part 2, and with Record Keeping, Procedures and Training in Part 3.

Background

9.02 The Regulations substantially implement the EU Third Money Laundering Directive in the UK. Both of these pieces of legislation reflect the Recommendations of the international Financial Action Task Force (FATF) which was set up to tackle money laundering on a worldwide basis.

9.03 The Regulations came in to force on 15 December 2007. The Regulations revoked in their entirety the 2003 Regulations and largely implemented the Third Money Laundering Directive, which was issued in October 2005 with a view to ensuring that the legislation of the European Union followed the revised Recommendations published by FATF, as well as with a view to improving anti-money laundering and counter-terrorist financing measures generally.

9.04 Apart from the criminalization of money laundering in Recommendations 1 to 3 inclusive, and the measures intended to enhance international co-operation, the FATF 40 Recommendations, now 20 years old, are primarily directed towards creating a regime of procedures and controls applied to a specific group of businesses and professions, collectively the regulated sector, that are considered to be particularly at risk of being used for the purpose of laundering money or processing terrorist funds.

9.05 The same emphasis is found in the three EU directives which closely follow the FATF Recommendations and incorporate them into the framework of EU legislation. The aim spelled out in the title of all three directives is the '. . . prevention of the use of the financial system for the purpose of money laundering' (with terrorist financing now added).

9.06 Implementing in the UK successive EU directives, the Money Laundering Regulations of 1993, 2001, 2003, and 2007 are even more focussed on the measures for prevention and detection to be applied by the regulated sector, because other elements in the Recommendations and the EU directives are put into effect in the UK through primary legislation, as in the three money laundering offence sections in Part 7 of POCA.

Overview of the Regulations

9.07 The Regulations place substantial responsibilities and obligations on relevant persons. In summary, the obligations under the Regulations are, broadly speaking, as follows:

- to apply customer due diligence measures;
- to conduct ongoing monitoring of a business relationship;
- to keep specified records;
- to make suspicious activity reports where money laundering or terrorist financing is suspected;
- to raise the awareness of employees about money laundering and terrorist financing and to train them;
- to establish and maintain policies and procedures in order to prevent activities related to money laundering and terrorist financing.

9.08 In the Regulations, the scope of the regulatory requirements and how they should be put into practice are most clearly set out in Regulation 20 which describes the '. . .appropriate and risk-sensitive policies and procedures. . .' that a 'relevant person' must establish and maintain in order to manage and monitor the money laundering and terrorist financing risk.[1] Other parts of the Regulations specify in detail the customer due diligence and ongoing monitoring measures as well as the requirement to keep records. The obligation on those in the regulated sector to make suspicious activity reports (SARs) is referred to in Regulation 20 in the context of reporting procedures and the role of the nominated officer (or MLRO), but the detailed provisions are contained in Part 7 of POCA.

The mandatory nature of the many detailed obligations in the Regulations is brought into **9.09** sharpest focus by considering the criminal offence, with a maximum penalty of two years' imprisonment, that may be committed by a failure to comply with any one of the numerous[2] specific requirements in the Regulations. The topics of supervision, monitoring, and sanctions for non-compliance are dealt with in Chapter 10.

B. The Regulated Sector—'Relevant Persons'

Who is subject to the Regulations?

In terms both of the scale and number of the institutions involved and the volume of **9.10** financial transactions undertaken, banks and other financial institutions continue to be the core of the regulated sector. The remaining 'relevant persons' form a disparate group whose common feature is that the businesses that they conduct or the professional services that they provide are considered to be vulnerable to money laundering or terrorist financing.

Throughout the Regulations, those businesses and individuals which are subject to the provi- **9.11** sions of the anti-money laundering regime, are referred to as 'relevant persons'. In Schedule 9 of POCA they are referred to as being part of the 'regulated sector'. Whilst the two schemes use different terminology, those included in the two categories are identical. In this chapter, the term 'relevant persons' is generally used.

The full list of relevant persons is set out in Regulation 3 read together with Schedule 1 and **9.12** is subject to certain exceptions given in Regulation 4. The detailed definitions of relevant persons in Regulation 3 are necessary because there are a number of different ways in which persons come within the definition of 'relevant person': for example, by function, by professional status, or through the conduct of particular business activities.

The list of relevant persons is summarized in Tables 1 and 2. The tables are intended **9.13** to show the reach of the Regulations, but should not be used as a definitive guide to whether a particular person is covered. Further reference should be made to the Regulations themselves, published guidance, the person's regulatory body, or the Financial Services Authority (FSA), who provide a 'Perimeter Enquiry line' for resolving issues as to scope.[3]

---

[1] The full provisions of Regulation 20 are dealt with below at paras 9.141–9.144.
[2] See Chapter 10 at paras 10.121–10.126.
[3] The FSA can be contacted on 020 7066 0082; or via the web link <http://www.fsa.gov.uk/pages/About/What/financial_crime/money_laundering/3mld/index.shtml>.

9.14 The categories of relevant person only apply when the person is acting in the course of business in the UK. Plainly, a person's business activities may fall partly within the definition and partly without—in which case only those activities within the definition are covered by the Regulations. Furthermore, a person may be in more than one category, e.g. solicitors may well be tax advisers, insolvency practitioners, or trust or company service providers, as well as independent legal professionals.

Table 9.1 Relevant persons—credit and financial institutions

Term	Meaning
Credit institutions	Undertakings receiving deposits or other repayable funds from the public or granting credits for their own account (or a branch which carries out directly all or some of the transactions inherent in the business of credit institutions), for example banks and building societies.[4]
Financial institutions[5]	(i) Undertakings (including Money Service Businesses) carrying out one or more of the activities listed in points 2 to 12 and 14 of Annex 1 to the Banking Consolidation Directive[6] (for example lending, financial leasing, money broking and issuing travellers' cheques and bankers' drafts), excluding undertakings covered under 'credit institutions' above, or whose only listed activity is trading for their own account in products listed in point 7 of that directive.
	(ii) Insurance companies authorized under, and carrying out activities covered by, the Life Assurance Consolidation Directive[7] (for example life assurance and annuities).
	(iii) Persons providing investment services or performing investment activities relating to various financial instruments, as listed in the Markets in Financial Instruments Directive.[8]
	(iv) Collective investment undertakings, when offering units or shares.
	(v) Insurance intermediaries (excluding tied insurance intermediaries) acting in respect of contracts of long-term insurance.[9]
	(vi) Branches located in an EEA state carrying out the activities mentioned in (i)–(v) above, irrespective of where their head offices are located.
	(vii) The National Savings Banks.
	(viii) The Director of Savings when money is raised under the National Loans Act 1968.

[4] The Regulations, Reg 3(1)(a) and 3(2), and the Banking Consolidation Directive 2006/48/EC, Art 4(1)(a).

[5] Reg 3(3).

[6] Directive 2006/48/EC of the European Parliament and of the Council of 14 June 2006. The relevant text is set out in Sch 1 to the Regulations.

[7] Directive 2002/83/EC of the European Parliament and of the Council of 5 November 2002.

[8] Directive 2004/39/EC of the European Parliament and of the Council of 12 April 2004 on markets in financial instruments. Annex I lists the investment services and activities in section 1 and the financial instruments in section C. The category excludes those exempted by Article 2 of the directive.

[9] 'Insurance intermediaries' are defined in Directive 2002/92/EC of the European Parliament and of the Council of 9 December 2002 on insurance mediation, Art 2(5); 'tied insurance intermediaries' in Art 2(7) of that directive. 'Contracts of long term insurance' is defined in the Financial Services and Markets Act 2000 (Regulated Activities) Order 2001, Art 3(1) and Pt II of Sch 1.

Table 9.2 Relevant persons—designated non-financial businesses and professions (DNFBPs)

Term	Meaning
Auditors	Any firm or individual who is a statutory auditor within the meaning of Part 42 of the Companies Act 2006 (statutory auditors), when carrying out statutory audit work within the meaning of section 1210 of the Act.[10]
Insolvency practitioners	Any person who acts as an insolvency practitioner within the meaning of section 388 of the Insolvency Act 1986 (meaning of 'act' as insolvency practitioner) or Article 3 of the Insolvency (Northern Ireland) Order 1989.[11]
External accountants	A firm or sole practitioner who by way of business provides accountancy services to other persons, when providing such services.[12]
Tax advisers	A firm or sole practitioner who by way of business provides advice about the tax affairs of other persons, when providing such services.[13]
Independent legal professionals	A firm or sole practitioner who by way of business provides legal or notarial services to other persons, when participating in financial or real property transactions concerning (a) the buying and selling of real property or business entities; (b) the managing of client money, securities or other assets; (c) the opening or management of bank, savings or securities accounts; (d) the organization of contributions necessary for the creation, operation or management of companies; or (e) the creation, operation or management of trusts, companies or similar structures; whether assisting in the planning or execution of the transaction or otherwise acting for or on behalf of a client in the transaction.[14]
Trust or company service providers	A firm or sole practitioner who by way of business provides any of the following services to other persons: (a) forming companies or other legal persons; (b) acting, or arranging for another person to act— (i) as a director or secretary of a company, (ii) as a partner of a partnership, or (iii) in a similar position in relation to other legal persons; (c) providing a registered office, business address, correspondence or administrative address or other related services for a company, partnership or any other legal person or arrangement; (d) actioning, or arranging for another person to act, as (i) a trustee of an express trust or similar legal arrangement, or (ii) a nominee shareholder for a person other than a company whose securities are listed on a regulated market, when providing such services.[15]
Estate agents	A firm or sole practitioner, who, or whose employees, carry out estate agency work (within the meaning given by section 1 of the Estate Agents Act 1979 (estate agency work)), when in the course of carrying out such work.[16]
High-value dealers	A firm or sole trader who by way of business trades in goods (including an auctioneer dealing in goods), when he receives, in respect of any transaction, a payment(s) in cash of at least 15,000 euros in total, whether the transaction is executed in a single operation or in several operations which appear to be linked.[17]
Casinos	A holder of a casino operating licence, 'casino operating licence' having the meaning given by section 65(2) of the Gambling Act 2005 (nature of licence).

---

[10] Reg 3(4).
[11] Reg 3(6).
[12] Reg 3(7).
[13] Reg 3(8).
[14] Reg 3(9).
[15] Reg 3(10).
[16] Reg 3(11).
[17] Reg 3(12).

9.15 Tables 9.1 and 9.2 list all the categories of relevant persons under the Regulations. There are also a number of other significant terms in the Regulations that are, in effect, subsets of the categories listed above. They are listed in Table 9.3.

Table 9.3. Notable sub-categories of relevant person

Term	Meaning
Money service businesses	Undertakings which by way of business operate a currency exchange office, transmit money (or any representations of monetary value) by any means or cash cheques which are made payable to customers. The Regulations refer to them in the context of defining financial institutions, and impose a registration regime on them. As they perform an activity listed in Schedule 1 of the Regulations[18] (point 7(b)), they are within the first subcategory of financial institutions in Regulation 3(3)(a) and are therefore relevant persons.
Telecommunications, digital and IT payment service providers	Undertakings that provide payment services falling within paragraph 1(g) of Schedule 1 to the Payment Services Regulations 2009.[19] The Regulations impose a registration regime on them. As they perform an activity listed in Schedule 1 of the Regulations[20] (point 4), they are within the first subcategory of financial institutions in Regulation 3(3)(a) and are therefore relevant persons.
Consumer credit financial institutions	Undertakings that fall within the first category of financial institutions in Regulation 3(3)(a) (see Table 1) and require a licence to carry on a consumer credit business,[21] with various exceptions.[22] The OFT is their supervisory authority and may maintain a register of them.

Exclusions

9.16 Regulation 4 provides for various exclusions in respect of persons who would otherwise be relevant persons. There is a significant exception of general application in Regulation 4(2), below, but the exclusions in Regulation 4(1) and (3) are specific.

9.17 The exclusions in Regulation 4(1) relate to specified persons or institutions or to specified persons when carrying out certain designated activities. These are summarized below:

- The Regulations do not apply to a society registered under the Industrial and Provident Societies Act 1956 or to a society registered under the Industrial and Provident Societies Act (Northern Ireland) 1969 when they conduct certain types of business specified in Regulation 4(1)(a) and (b).
- The Regulations do not apply, in the circumstances detailed in Regulation 4(1)(c) and (d), to a person when carrying out particular activities in respect of which that person is exempt

---

[18] Extracts from Annex 1 to the Banking Consolidation Directive.

[19] 'The execution of payment transactions where the consent of the payer to execute the payment transaction is given by means of any telecommunication, digital or IT device and the payment is made to the telecommunication, IT system or network operator acting only as an intermediary between the payment service user and the supplier of the goods or services.'

[20] Extracts from Annex 1 to the Banking Consolidation Directive.

[21] Under Consumer Credit Act 1974, s 21 (businesses needing a licence).

[22] The exceptions include Money Service Businesses, Authorized Persons, and Telecommunication, Digital and IT Payment Service Providers (Reg 22(1)).

in relation to the Financial Services and Markets Act 2000 (Exemption) Order 2001 or, in specified circumstances, to a person who was an exempted person for the purposes of section 45 of the Financial Services Act 1986.
- Under Regulation 4(1)(e), the Regulations do not apply to 'a person whose main activity is that of a high-value dealer, when he engages in financial activity on an occasional or very limited basis as set out in paragraph 1 of Schedule 2 to these Regulations'.
- Regulation 4(1)(f) concerns a person who prepares a home information pack.[23]

Occasional financial activity

In Regulation 4(2) there is an important general exclusion for any person who might otherwise **9.18** come within the definition of a relevant person: 'These Regulations do not apply to a person who falls within regulation 3 solely as a result of his engaging in financial activity on an occasional or very limited basis as set out in paragraph 1 of Schedule 2 to these Regulations.'[24]

Paragraph 1 of Schedule 2 to the Regulations provides that, for the purposes of Regulation **9.19** 4(1)(e) and (2), a person is to be considered as engaging in financial activity on an occasional or very limited basis if *all* the following conditions are fulfilled:

- (a) the person's total annual turnover in respect of the financial activity does not exceed £64,000;
- (b) the financial activity is limited in relation to any customer to no more than one transaction exceeding 1,000 euro, whether the transaction is carried out in a single operation, or a series of operations which appear to be linked;
- (c) the financial activity does not exceed 5 per cent of the person's total annual turnover;
- (d) the financial activity is ancillary and directly related to the person's main activity;
- (e) the financial activity is not the transmission or remittance of money (or any representation of monetary value) by any means;
- (f) the person's main activity is not that of a person falling within Regulation 3(1)(a) to (f) or (h);
- (g) the financial activity is provided only to customers of the person's main activity and is not offered to the public.

Under Regulation 4(3), Parts 2 to 5 of the Regulations, that is the operative parts,[25] do not **9.20** apply to the following specified persons:

- (a) the Auditor General for Scotland;
- (b) the Auditor General for Wales;
- (c) the Bank of England;
- (d) the Comptroller and Auditor General;
- (e) the Comptroller and Auditor General for Northern Ireland;
- (f) the Official Solicitor to the Supreme Court, when acting as trustee in his official capacity;
- (g) the Treasury Solicitor.

---

[23] Note that on 20 May 2010 the government announced that the requirement to have a home information pack was suspended. The government has stated its intention to repeal provisions in Part 5 of the Housing Act 2004 and thereby abolish HIPs.
[24] In Reg 4(1)(e), above, there is a specific instance of this general exclusion in respect of high-value dealers.
[25] Part 1 of the Regulations, headed 'General', concerns the interpretation and application of the Regulations; Part 6 deals with 'Miscellaneous' matters.

The Regulations: interpretation

9.21   The regulated sector now consists of a wide variety of institutions and individuals carrying on many different business and professional activities, so Regulation 2 necessarily contains a lengthy list of definitions (and Regulation 2 is itself supplemented by further definitions of 'relevant persons' in Regulation 3). The most important general definitions in Regulation 2 are set out below:

- 'business relationship' means a business, professional, or commercial relationship between a relevant person and a customer, which is expected by the relevant person, at the time when contact is established, to have an element of duration;
- 'occasional transaction' means a transaction (carried out other than as part of a business relationship) amounting to 15,000 euro or more, whether the transaction is carried out in a single operation or several operations which appear to be linked;
- 'firm' means any entity, whether or not a legal person, that is not an individual and includes a body corporate and a partnership or other unincorporated association;
- ' high value dealer' has the meaning given by Regulation 3(12):
- 'money laundering' means an act which falls within section 340(11) of the Proceeds of Crime Act 2002;
- 'terrorist financing' means an offence under—
    - (a) section 15 (fund-raising), 16 (use and possession), 17 (funding arrangements), 18 (money laundering) or 63 (terrorist finance: jurisdiction) of the Terrorism Act 2000;
    - (b) paragraph 7(2) or (3) of Schedule 3 to the Anti-Terrorism, Crime and Security Act 2001 (freezing orders);
    - (c) article 7, 8 or 10 of the Terrorism (United Nations Measures) Order 2006 ; [. . .]
    - (d) article 7, 8 or 10 of the Al-Qaida and Taliban (United Nations Measures) Order 2006; [or]
    - (e) article 10, 11, 12, 13, 14 or 16 of the Terrorism (United Nations Measures) Order 2009;
- 'cash' means notes, coins or travellers' cheques in any currency.[26]

'Authorised persons' and 'the Authority'

9.22   The term 'authorised persons' also appears in the Regulations, but has no separate meaning in them: it refers to persons authorised by the FSA for the purposes of the Financial Services and Markets Act 2000 (FSMA). Authorised persons are also relevant persons subject to supervision for anti-money laundering purposes by the FSA as a 'supervisory authority' under Regulation 23 and liable to enforcement action by the FSA as a 'designated authority' under Regulation 36. In the Regulations, the FSA is referred to as 'the Authority'.

The risk-based approach

Background

9.23   The risk-based approach was not really a significant feature of the measures to combat money laundering and terrorist financing, either at a national or international level, until about 2005, but is now well established. Such an approach is recognized in the FATF 40 Recommendations (as revised in 2003 and incorporating amendments to October 2004).

---

[26] The same definition of cash is contained also in POCA, Sch 9 and in TA 2000, Sch 3A. Note, however, the wider definition in POCA, s 289 for the purposes of cash seizure and forfeiture under Part 5 of POCA.

Recommendation 5, dealing with CDD and record-keeping, requires that regulated sector institutions should apply the specified CDD measures:

> . . .but may determine the extent of such measures on a risk sensitive basis depending on the type of customer, business relationship or transaction. The measures that are taken should be consistent with any guidelines issued by competent authorities. For higher risk categories, financial institutions should perform enhanced due diligence. In certain circumstances, where there are low risks, countries may decide that financial institutions can apply reduced or simplified measures.

Since 2005, FATF has taken further steps to develop and promote understanding of the risk-based approach. In March 2006, FATF set up an advisory group which comprised FATF members and observers, but also included representatives from the private sector. This group first considered the risk-based approach in principle and how it should apply to banks and financial services institutions. After international consultation on draft guidance with both public and private sectors, a guidance paper on the risk-based approach was adopted by FATF in June 2007. This was the first occasion that FATF had developed guidance using a public-private partnership approach. **9.24**

In a section of the guidance paper headed 'The purpose of the Risk-Based Approach', the rationale for the risk-based approach is explained in this way: **9.25**

> By adopting a risk-based approach, competent authorities and financial institutions are able to ensure that measures to prevent or mitigate money laundering and terrorist financing are commensurate to the risks identified. This will allow resources to be allocated in the most efficient ways. The principle is that resources should be directed in accordance with priorities so that the greatest risks receive the highest attention.

Over the following two years after June 2007, FATF developed a series of sectoral guidance papers to assist both public authorities and the private sector in applying a risk-based approach to combating money laundering and terrorist financing. Each of the guidance papers relates to a specific business or profession within the regulated sector and was developed in conjunction with representatives of the relevant business or profession.[27] **9.26**

The Third Money Laundering Directive

Similarly, Article 8 of the Third Directive, issued in 2005, contains CDD measures that are described in essentially the same terms as in FATF Recommendation 5 and require that the institutions and persons covered by the Directive shall apply each of the specified customer due diligence measures '. . . but may determine the extent of such measures on a risk-sensitive basis depending on the type of customer, business relationship, product or transaction'. **9.27**

The FSA and the risk-based approach

In the UK, the FSA has taken the lead in promoting the risk-based approach. In a letter to supervisors dated 31 August 2006,[28] Philip Robinson[29] announced the FSA's change to a more risk-based approach, and on the next day the FSA deleted its Money Laundering **9.28**

---

[27] <http://www.fatf-gafi.org/document/63/0,3343,en_32250379_32236920_44513535_1_1_1_1,00.html>.

[28] Published on the FSA website.

[29] Then Financial Crime Sector Leader at the FSA. Philip Robinson was also influential in the development of FATF's guidance on the risk-based approach as co-chair of the Electronic Advisory Group that produced the original FATF guidance paper on the risk-based approach.

Sourcebook and replaced it by high-level provisions that were '. . .intended to drive a more effective, risk-based approach'.[30]

9.29   In announcing its new anti-money laundering regime, under the heading 'What does the new regime mean for firms?', the FSA noted that: 'The risk-based approach is not necessarily the cheapest or easiest approach to money laundering, but it is the most cost-effective, proportionate and flexible.' It went on to say: 'The new regime places greater emphasis on senior management responsibility for managing money laundering risk and ensuring that systems and controls are used in a risk-based manner with an increased focus on higher risk customers and products.'

Applying the risk-based approach

9.30   The risk-based approach can only be applied where relevant persons have a significant area of discretion in the way that the obligation is performed. As FATF has recognized: 'There are circumstances in which the application of the risk-based approach will not apply, or may be limited . . . The limitations to the risk-based approach are usually the result of legal or regulatory requirements that mandate certain actions to be taken.' The risk-based approach is not, for instance, applicable to the provisions in UK law for required disclosures of suspected money laundering.

The risk-based approach in the Regulations

9.31   Regulation 20(1) sets out a broad requirement that a relevant person 'must establish and maintain appropriate and risk-sensitive policies and procedures' relating to all aspects of the regulatory requirements, including 'risk assessment and management'.[31] The main context, however, in which the risk-based approach is applied in the Regulations is in connection with the specific requirements for CDD.

9.32   The way in which the risk-based approach is to be applied to CDD is set out in Regulation 7(3):

> (3) A relevant person must—
>   (a) determine the extent of customer due diligence measures on a risk-sensitive basis depending on the type of customer, business relationship, product or transaction; and
>   (b) be able to demonstrate to his supervisory authority that the extent of the measures is appropriate in view of the risks of money laundering and terrorist financing.

Guidance on the application of the risk-based approach

9.33   The authoritative Joint Money Laundering Steering Group (JMLSG) guidance[32] places the risk-based approach to anti-money laundering in the broader context of risk management in the financial services industry and the responsibility of senior management to manage the affairs of its business with due regard to the risks inherent in it. The guidance, in paragraph 4.2, details the steps involved in a risk-based approach to 'assessing the most cost

---

[30] See the FSA Handbook (Senior Management Systems and Controls), SYSC 3.2.6A R–SYSC 3.2.6J G.

[31] How practicable the application of risk-sensitive policies and procedures is to particular anti-money laundering measures will necessarily vary (see the FATF statement above), but this is not explicitly recognized in Reg 20.

[32] Addressed primarily to relevant persons in the financial services sector, but containing much that is helpful to other relevant persons. (See Chapter 1 at paras 1.137 and 1.138).

effective and proportionate way to manage and mitigate the money laundering and terrorist financing risks faced by the firm'. These steps are to:

- identify the money laundering and terrorist financing risks that are relevant to the firm;
- assess the risks presented by the firm's particular
  - ○ customers;
  - ○ products;
  - ○ delivery channels;
  - ○ geographical areas of operation;
- design and implement controls to manage and mitigate these assessed risks;
- monitor and improve the effective operation of these controls; and
- record appropriately what has been done, and why.

9.34 In the view of the JMLSG, a risk-based approach will '. . .serve to balance the cost burden placed on individual firms and their customers with a realistic assessment of the threat in connection with money laundering or terrorist financing. It focuses the effort where it is needed and will have most impact'.

C. Customer Due Diligence: the Main Provisions

CDD—introduction

9.35 The CDD requirements are detailed and occupy the whole of Part 2: Regulations 5 to 18 inclusive. These apply to all relevant persons[33] and are intended primarily as preventative measures, to make it less easy for anyone to engage and use the services of the regulated sector for the purposes of money laundering or terrorist financing.

9.36 In this chapter, the CDD requirements are dealt with in three parts. The main provisions relating to CDD and ongoing monitoring, in Regulations 5 to 12, are covered in this part. Part D deals with the provisions relating to simplified CDD and with enhanced CDD and enhanced ongoing monitoring in Regulations 13 and 14; Part E deals with the provisions for 'reliance' and other ancillary matters in Regulations 15 to 18.

The new approach to CDD in the 2007 Regulations

9.37 The main change from the regime under the Money Laundering Regulations 2003 is the introduction of an approach to customer due diligence on a risk-sensitive basis. In effect, the Regulations apply a three-tiered approach to customer due diligence, which reflects the risk-based approach which should now underlie the way that many of the regulatory requirements are complied with, in particular the CDD obligations.

Terminology

9.38 The term CDD is used in the Regulations and elsewhere both to refer to CDD measures generally, including simplified and enhanced CDD, and to refer to what might be described as 'standard' CDD, that is CDD which is neither simplified nor enhanced. 'Simplified due diligence' and 'enhanced customer due diligence' are terms used in the Regulations, and

---

[33] Apart from Regulation 10 which applies specific CDD measures to casinos—see paras 9.70–9.74.

what they allow or require are set out in Regulations 13 and 14. Where appropriate, the term 'standard CDD' is also used below.

The three-tiered approach

9.39 *Standard CDD* applies to all situations unless simplified CDD is applicable or the circumstances may require the relevant person to apply enhanced CDD.

9.40 *Simplified CDD* applies to situations where the relevant person has 'reasonable grounds for believing that the customer, transaction or product related to such transaction' falls within one of a number of specified circumstances such that standard CDD is not required. These specified circumstances are as set out in Regulation 7(1), except for when the relevant person 'suspects money laundering or terrorist financing'.[34]

9.41 *Enhanced CDD* applies to certain situations on a risk-sensitive basis where there is a higher risk of money laundering or terrorist financing, including any situation in which the customer or intended customer is a politically exposed person (a 'PEP').[35]

Regulation 5—what is CDD?

9.42 Customer due diligence measures consist of identifying and verifying the identity of the customer and any beneficial owner of the customer, and obtaining information on the purpose and intended nature of the business relationship. Regulation 5 defines 'customer due diligence measures' and sets out the scope of the obligation placed on relevant persons:

    (a) identifying the customer and verifying the customer's identity on the basis of documents, data, or information obtained from a reliable and independent source;

    (b) identifying, where there is a beneficial owner who is not the customer, the beneficial owner and taking adequate measures, on a risk-sensitive basis, to verify his identity so that the relevant person is satisfied that he knows who the beneficial owner is, including, in the case of a legal person, trust or similar legal arrangement, measures to understand the ownership and control structure of the person, trust or arrangement; and

    (c) obtaining information on the purpose and intended nature of the business relationship.

Regulation 5(b)—beneficial owner

9.43 Generally speaking, it is impossible to ascertain the true nature of a financial transaction and evaluate the risk of it relating to money laundering unless one is aware of the identity of any underlying party. The immediate customer of a relevant person may be acting on behalf of another; the ultimate beneficiary of the transaction may be hidden.

9.44 The identification of beneficial owners is obviously necessary in order to prevent money launderers evading due diligence by the use of individual nominees or the use of a corporate entity or a trust to obscure ownership. In many cases where a customer or intending customer wishes, for instance, to open a bank account on behalf of another person the situation and the reason for it is clear, legitimate, and unproblematical. The requirement under Regulation 5(b) may be easily satisfied. However, the implementation in UK law of

---

[34] See para 9.52.
[35] Regulation 14: see paras 9.82 *et seq.*

the obligations in relation to beneficial owners, derived from Article 8.1(b) of the Third
Money Laundering Directive, were far from straightforward.

The provisions in the Directive could not, without significant adaptation,[36] be applied to   **9.45**
the distinctive nature of trusts under UK law. The Treasury originally proposed that any
practical difficulties should be resolved by the issue of guidance by supervisory or industry
bodies, but, following extensive discussions involving the Law Society and the STEP
(the Society of Trust and Estate Practitioners),[37] the government was persuaded that it was
necessary for the meaning of 'beneficial owner' in UK anti-money laundering law to be made
clear in the Regulations.[38] The meaning of beneficial owner is now extensively defined in
Regulation 6.

Regulation 6—identifying the beneficial owner

Under Regulation 5(b), the relevant person is required to verify the identity of the beneficial   **9.46**
owner and where that is a legal person, trust or 'similar arrangement' to take measures to
understand the ownership and control structure of that body.[39]

Regulation 6 separately defines beneficial owner in a number of different contexts, such as in   **9.47**
the case of a body corporate, partnership or trust. In any other case, Regulation 6(9) provides
that: '"beneficial owner" means the individual who ultimately owns or controls the customer
or on whose behalf a transaction is being conducted'. Where the person behind the transaction is not an individual but a legal person, there may be multiple beneficial owners
as defined by Regulation 6. The detailed definitions contained within that Regulation are
summarized in Table 9.4 below.

Table 9.4 Meaning of beneficial owner

Legal entity	Definition of beneficial owner
Body corporate	any individual who— (a) as respects any body other than a company whose securities are listed on a regulated market, ultimately owns or controls (whether through direct or indirect ownership or control, including through bearer share holdings) more than 25 per cent of the shares or voting rights in the body; or (b) as respects any body corporate, otherwise exercises control over the management of the body.[40]
Partnership (other than a limited liability partnership)	any individual who— (a) ultimately is entitled to or controls (whether the entitlement or control is direct or indirect) more than a 25 per cent share of the capital or profits of the partnership or more than 25 per cent of the voting rights in the partnership; or (b) otherwise exercises control over the management of the partnership.[41]

(Continued)

---

[36] The Law Society secured support from Brussels for its view that flexible implementation of the Directive
was required (see the letter dated 29 May 2007 from Charlie McCreevey, a member of the European Commission,
to the President of the Law Society, Fiona Woolf CBE, on the Law Society website).

[37] See <http://www.step.org/system_pages/small_navigation/about_step.aspx>.

[38] See the letter from the President of the Law Society to the Economic Secretary to the Treasury, Ed Balls
MP, dated 18 June 2007 on the Law Society website.

[39] See para 9.42 above.

[40] Reg 6(1).

[41] Reg 6(2).

Table 9.4 Meaning of beneficial owner (*Continued*)

Legal entity	Definition of beneficial owner
Trust	(a) any individual who is entitled to a specified interest [42] in at least 25 per cent of the capital of the trust property; (b) as respects any trust other than one which is set up or operates entirely for the benefit of individuals falling within sub-paragraph (a), the class of persons in whose main interest the trust is set up or operates; (c) any individual who has control[43] over the trust.[44]
Any other legal entity or arrangement	(a) where the individuals who benefit from the entity or arrangement have been determined, any individual who benefits from at least 25 per cent of the property of the entity or arrangement; (b) where the individuals who benefit from the entity or arrangement have yet to be determined, the class of persons in whose main interest the entity or arrangement is set up or operates; (c) any individual who exercises control over at least 25 per cent of the property of the entity or arrangement.[45] Note that where an individual is the beneficial owner of a body corporate which benefits from or exercises control over the property of the entity or arrangement, the individual is to be regarded as benefiting from or exercising control over the property of the entity or arrangement.[46]
Estate of a deceased person in the course of administration	(a) in England and Wales and Northern Ireland, the executor, representative, or administrator for the time being of original or by a deceased person; (b) in Scotland, the executor for the purposes of the Executors (Scotland) Act 1900.[47]
Any other case	The individual who ultimately owns or controls the customer on whose behalf a transaction is being conducted.[48]

9.48 Where a relevant person is required to apply CDD measures in the case of a trust, legal entity (other than a body corporate), or a legal arrangement (other than a trust), and the class of persons in whose main interest the trust, entity, or arrangement is set up or operates is identified as a beneficial owner, the relevant person is not required to identify all the members of the class.[49]

9.49 Trustees of debt issues (debentures, loan stock, bonds, any other instrument creating or acknowledging indebtedness) are not required to identify the beneficial owners of such instruments.[50]

---

[42] A vested interest which is in possession or in remainder or reversion (or, in Scotland, in fee): and defeasible or indefeasible (Reg 6(4)).

[43] Under Reg 6(4), 'control' means a power (whether exercisable alone, jointly with another person, or with the consent of another person) under the trust instrument or by law to dispose of, advance, lend, invest, pay, or apply trust property; vary the trust; add or remove a person as a beneficiary or to or from a class of beneficiaries; appoint or remove trustees; direct, withhold consent to or veto the exercise of such a power.

[44] Reg 6(3).

[45] Reg 6(6).

[46] Reg 6(7).

[47] Reg 6(8).

[48] Reg 6(9).

[49] Reg 7(4).

[50] Reg 12.

Customer due diligence and ongoing monitoring

The Regulations require a relevant person, whether an individual or a corporate entity, to **9.50** take particular due diligence measures when a new customer is taken on, to remain vigilant and review the position in certain defined circumstances, and to monitor the customer's business transactions throughout the business relationship. Subject to further provisions in Part 2, especially those requiring enhanced due diligence and ongoing monitoring, Regulations 7 and 8 set out how CDD and ongoing monitoring should be conducted.

Regulation 7: the application of CDD measures

In brief, CDD requires the relevant person to identify and verify the identity of the customer;[51] **9.51** to identify the beneficial owner[52] and to take adequate measures[53] to verify his identity; and to obtain information on the purpose and intended nature of the business relationship.[54]

Regulation 7 sets out the times and circumstances in which CDD measures are to be applied **9.52** by a relevant person to new and existing customers:[55]

> (1) Subject to regulations 9, 10, 12, 13, 14, 16(4) and 17, a relevant person must apply customer due diligence measures when he—
>   (a) establishes a business relationship;
>   (b) carries out an occasional transaction;
>   (c) suspects money laundering or terrorist financing;
>   (d) doubts the veracity or adequacy of documents, data or information previously obtained for the purposes of identification or verification.
> (2) Subject to regulation 16(4), a relevant person must also apply customer due diligence measures at other appropriate times to existing customers on a risk-sensitive basis.

Occasional transaction

'Occasional transaction' is a defined term[56] and means a transaction (carried out other than **9.53** as part of a business relationship) amounting to 15,000 euros or more, whether the transaction is carried out in a single operation or several operations which appear to be linked. Accordingly, a relevant person does not need to apply customer due diligence measures when he carries out a transaction (whether carried out in a single operation or several linked operations) that is not part of a business relationship if it involves less than 15,000 euros.

Otherwise than in the specified situations[57] under those regulations referred to at the start of **9.54** Regulation 7(1), a relevant person[58] must, therefore, apply customer due diligence measures:

- *when* he establishes a business relationship (although see below in relation to the timing of the verification of identity in certain circumstances);

---

[51] Note that where the customer is not physically present, the relevant person must apply *enhanced* customer due diligence measures.

[52] Where there is a beneficial owner who is not the customer.

[53] On a risk-sensitive basis.

[54] Where a relevant person is unable to apply CDD measures, there are requirements to cease transactions, etc: see Reg 11(1).

[55] For the application of CDD measures to existing customers, see para 9.57.

[56] Defined in Reg 2.

[57] Relating to timing (Reg 9), casinos (Reg 10), trustees of debt issues (Reg 12), simplified CDD (Reg 13), enhanced CDD and ongoing monitoring (Reg 14), anonymous accounts and passbooks (Reg 16(4)), and reliance on another (Reg 17).

[58] When he is 'acting in the course of business carried on by [him] in the United Kingdom' (Reg 3(1)).

- *when* he carries out an occasional transaction (although see below in relation to the timing of the verification of identity in certain circumstances);
- *when* he suspects money laundering or terrorist financing; and
- *when* he doubts the veracity or adequacy of documents, data or information previously obtained for the purposes of identification or verification.

9.55 The first two points above concern the application of CDD measures, in effect, at the start of business; the third and fourth points, however, require a relevant person to respond to situations that may arise at any time. While the requirement to apply CDD measures if doubts arise about the CDD originally carried out seems straightforward, the third point is less clear. It is suggested that it should be interpreted widely as meaning when the relevant person suspects money laundering or terrorist financing that is connected in any way to the customer's business. That should prompt, at the least, a review and re-application of CDD.

9.56 Where a relevant person actually suspects the customer of money laundering or terrorist financing, the required application of further CDD measures may, in reality, be overtaken by other actions and stronger measures: the relevant person would have to make a required disclosure to SOCA[59] and would certainly need to look carefully at the circumstances in order to decide whether to terminate the business relationship.

Existing customers

9.57 In addition, by virtue of Regulation 7(2), a relevant person must also apply CDD measures 'at other appropriate times' to existing customers on a risk-sensitive basis. In relation to shell banks and anonymous accounts, this is subject to the requirements and timing set out in Regulation 16.[60]

The risk-based approach

9.58 By virtue of Regulation 7(3), a relevant person must:

> (a) determine the extent of customer due diligence measures on a risk-sensitive basis depending on the type of customer, business relationship, product or transaction; and
>
> (b) be able to demonstrate to his supervisory authority that the extent of the measures is appropriate in view of the risks of money laundering and terrorist financing.[61]

Exceptions

9.59 Where a relevant person is required to apply CDD measures in the case of a trust, legal entity (other than a body corporate) or a legal arrangement (other than a trust), and the class of persons in whose main interest the trust, entity, or arrangement is set up or operates is identified as a beneficial owner, the relevant person is not required to identify all the members of the class.[62]

---

[59] Under POCA, s 330 or TA 2000, s 21A.

[60] See below at paras 9.112 and 9.113.

[61] The requirement to demonstrate appropriate risk-sensitive compliance to the supervisory authority does not apply to the National Savings Bank or the Director of Savings.

[62] Reg 7(4).

Trustees of debt issues (debentures, loan stock, bonds, any other instrument creating or **9.60** acknowledging indebtedness) are not required to identify the beneficial owners of such instruments.[63]

Regulation 8—ongoing monitoring

Separate, although related, to the requirement to apply customer due diligence measures is **9.61** the requirement to conduct 'ongoing monitoring'. Where Regulation 7 required CDD measures to be applied at the start and a vigilant alertness thereafter to changing circumstances, once a business relationship is established Regulation 8 imposes a positive, ongoing duty to scrutinize transactions and to keep relevant data up to date.

Regulation 8(1) requires that: 'A relevant person must conduct ongoing monitoring of a **9.62** business relationship.' What ongoing monitoring of a business relationship means is explained in Regulation 8(2):

> (a) scrutiny of transactions undertaken throughout the course of the relationship (including, where necessary, the source of funds) to ensure that the transactions are consistent with the relevant person's knowledge of the customer, his business and risk profile; and
> (b) keeping the documents, data or information obtained for the purpose of applying customer due diligence measures up to date.

As with the requirement to apply CDD measures, under Regulation 8(3), a relevant person **9.63** must determine the extent of ongoing monitoring on a risk-sensitive basis depending on the type of customer, business relationship, product, or transaction. He must also be able to demonstrate to his supervisory authority that the extent of the ongoing monitoring is appropriate in view of the risks of money laundering and terrorist financing.[64]

In the circumstances set out in Regulation 14, enhanced ongoing monitoring is required: see **9.64** paragraphs 9.82 *et seq.*

Regulation 9—timing of verification

Generally, both the identification of the customer (and any beneficial owner) and verifica- **9.65** tion of identity must take place before establishing a business relationship or carrying out an occasional transaction.[65] Regulation 9, however, allows some relaxation of the timing of *verification* of the identity of a customer or beneficial owner where a relevant person establishes a business relationship or carries out an occasional transaction.

Under Regulation 9(2), when a relevant person establishes a business relationship or carries **9.66** out an occasional transaction, he must verify the identity of the customer (and any beneficial owner) before the establishment of the business relationship or the carrying out of the occasional transaction, except as noted below.

Exceptions

In the establishment of a business relationship, the verification of identity (but not, for **9.67** obvious reasons, the identification) may be completed *during* the establishment of the

---

[63] Reg 12.
[64] Although it is not clearly expressed, it would also appear that the requirement to demonstrate to the supervisory authority does not apply to the National Savings Bank or the Director of Savings.
[65] Reg 9(1).

business relationship where, under Regulation 9(3), '. . .(a) this is necessary not to interrupt the normal conduct of business; and (b) there is little risk of money laundering or terrorist financing occurring, provided that the verification is completed as soon as practicable after contact is first established'.

9.68 The strict requirement under Regulation 9(2) for the timing of verification of identity is also moderated in relation to beneficiaries under a life insurance policy and to bank account holders:

- The verification of the identity of the beneficiary under a life insurance policy may take place *after* the business relationship has been established provided that it takes place *at or before* the time of payout or *at or before* the time the beneficiary exercises a right vested under the policy.[66]
- The verification of the identity of a bank account holder may take place *after* the bank account has been opened provided that there are adequate safeguards in place to ensure that the account is not closed and transactions are not carried out by or on behalf of the account holder (including any payment from the account to the account holder) before verification has been completed.[67]

9.69 A further, but different, exception applies to casinos where strict provisions are considered necessary: generally, casinos must verify the identity of customers prior to allowing them access to gaming facilities. See below on the provisions of Regulation 10.

Regulation 10—casinos

9.70 In addition to the customer due diligence measures that apply to all relevant persons, casinos are subject to specific requirements for the verification of the identity of their customers. Generally, casinos must verify the identity of customers prior to allowing them access to gaming facilities. However, where casinos have adequate monitoring procedures in place, they may do so only where betting reaches 2,000 euros in any 24-hour period.

9.71 Under Regulation 10(1), a casino[68] must 'establish and verify the identity'[69] of all customers to whom the casino makes facilities for gaming available *before* entry to any premises where such facilities are provided or, where the facilities are for remote gaming, *before* access is given to such facilities.

9.72 Alternatively, if the 'specified conditions' are met, a casino must establish and verify the identity of all customers who, in the course of any period of 24 hours, 'purchase from, or exchange with, the casino chips with a total value of 2,000 Euro or more'; 'pay the casino 2,000 Euro or more for the use of gaming machines'; or 'pay to, or stake with, the casino 2,000 Euro or more in connection with facilities for remote gaming'.

9.73 The specified conditions are set out in Regulation 10(2), as follows:

  (a) the casino verifies the identity of each customer before or immediately after such purchase, exchange, payment or stake takes place, and

---

[66] Reg 9(4).
[67] Reg 9(5).
[68] As defined in Reg 3(13).
[69] Note that the wording is different from the first limb of the definition of customer due diligence measures under Reg 5 ('identifying the customer and verifying the customer's identity').

   (b) the Gambling Commission is satisfied that the casino has appropriate procedures in place to monitor and record—
     (i) the total value of chips purchased from or exchanged with the casino;
     (ii) the total money paid for the use of gaming machines; or
     (iii) the total money paid or staked in connection with facilities for remote gaming,
       by each customer.

Regulation 10(3) sets out the meaning of the terms 'gaming', 'gaming machine', 'remote **9.74** operating licence', 'stake', 'premises', and 'remote gaming'.

Regulation 11—requirement to cease transactions

Where, in relation to any customer, a relevant person is unable to apply customer due **9.75** diligence measures in accordance with the provisions of Part 2, he:[70]

   (a) must not carry out a transaction with or for the customer through a bank account;
   (b) must not establish a business relationship or carry out an occasional transaction with the customer;
   (c) must terminate any existing business relationship with the customer;
   (d) must consider whether he is required to make a disclosure by Part 7 of the Proceeds of Crime Act 2002 or Part 3 of the Terrorism Act 2000.[71]

The requirement to cease transactions does not apply to lawyers or other professional **9.76** advisers[72] where they are:[73]
• ascertaining the legal position for their client; or
• defending or representing that client in, or concerning, legal proceedings, (including advice on the institution or avoidance of proceedings).

Regulation 12—Exception for trustees of debt issues

According to Regulation 12, a relevant person who is a trustee for debt issues is not required, **9.77** in respect of the holders of specified instruments or securities, to apply the customer due diligence measure referred to in paragraph (b) of Regulation 5, that is the requirement, where there is a beneficial owner who is not the customer, to identify and verify the identity of the beneficial owner:

  (1) A relevant person—
    (a) who is appointed by the issuer of instruments or securities specified in paragraph (2) as trustee of an issue of such instruments or securities; or
    (b) whose customer is a trustee of an issue of such instruments or securities, is not required to apply the customer due diligence measure referred to in regulation 5(b) in respect of the holders of such instruments or securities.
  (2) The specified instruments and securities are—
    (a) instruments which fall within [article 77 or 77A of the Financial Services and Markets Act 2000 (Regulated Activities) Order 2001]1 2; and
    (b) securities which fall within article 78 of that Order.

---

[70] Reg 11.
[71] In particular, under POCA, s 330 or TA 2000, s 21A. See Chapters 6 and 7 above.
[72] Auditor, accountant, or tax adviser who is a member of a professional body which is established for any such persons and which tests competence and imposes and maintains professional and ethical standards (Reg 11(3)).
[73] Reg 11(2).

D. Customer Due Diligence: Simplified Due Diligence, Enhanced Due Diligence, and Enhanced Ongoing Monitoring

Simplified due diligence

Regulation 13

9.78 An important aspect of the risk-based approach is that Regulation 13 provides for the circumstances in which a relevant person need not apply standard CDD measures:

> (1) A relevant person is not required to apply customer due diligence measures in the circumstances mentioned in regulation 7(1)(a), (b) or (d) where he has reasonable grounds for believing that the customer, transaction or product related to such transaction, falls within any of the following paragraphs.

9.79 The circumstances where simplified CDD is appropriate are where the relevant person has reasonable grounds for believing that the customer, transaction or product falls within one of eight specified categories, which relate either to *customers*, in paragraphs (2) to (6), or to *products*, in paragraphs (7) to (9). These are customers and products that must be considered to present a low risk of money laundering or terrorist financing.

9.80 In these circumstances a relevant person is not required to apply CDD measures when establishing a business relationship or carrying out an occasional transaction. Instead, the relevant person may apply simplified due diligence except: '. . . when suspecting money laundering or terrorist financing (in accordance with regulation 7(1)(c)) or at other appropriate times to existing customers on a risk-sensitive basis (in accordance with 7(2))'.

9.81 Those circumstances are when the relevant person has reasonable grounds for believing that:[74]

- The customer is one of the following:
  - itself a credit or financial institution which is subject to the requirements of the Money Laundering Directive;[75]
  - a company whose securities are listed on a regulated market subject to specified disclosure obligations;[76]
  - an independent legal professional operating a client account.[77]
- The customer is a public authority in the United Kingdom[78] or certain non-UK public authorities entrusted with public functions pursuant to the Treaty on the European Union, the Treaties on the European Communities or Community secondary legislation.[79]

---

[74] Reg 13.

[75] Reg 13(2)(a) or an equivalent regime in a non-EEA state (Reg 13(2)(b)).

[76] Reg 13(3).

[77] Reg 13(4). Provided that (a) where the pooled account is held in a non-EEA state that state imposes requirements to combat money laundering and terrorist financing which are consistent with international standards; and the independent legal professional is supervised in that state for compliance with those requirements; (b) information on the identity of the persons on whose behalf monies are held in the pooled account is available, on request, to the institution which acts as a depository institution for the account.

[78] Reg 13(5).

[79] Reg 13(6) and Sch 2.

- The product is one of the following:
  - certain low value or non-negotiable life insurance contracts and pension schemes;[80]
  - certain low value electronic money devices;[81]
  - certain other contractual products which accord with the conditions set out in paragraph 3 of Schedule 2 of the Regulations;[82]
  - a child trust fund.[83]

Enhanced due diligence

Regulation 14

Another important aspect of the risk-based approach is that in certain circumstances a relevant person must apply enhanced CDD and enhanced ongoing monitoring: **9.82**

(1) A relevant person must apply on a risk-sensitive basis enhanced customer due diligence measures and enhanced ongoing monitoring—
  (a) in accordance with paragraphs (2) to (4);
  (b) in any other situation which by its nature can present a higher risk of money laundering or terrorist financing.

Specific situations requiring enhanced CDD

Regulation 14(1)(a), in paragraphs (2), (3), and (4), requires a relevant person to apply **9.83**
'enhanced customer due diligence measures' and 'enhanced ongoing monitoring'[84] in the following circumstances:

- where the customer has not been physically present for identification purposes;
- where the relevant person is a credit institution[85] and has or proposes to have a correspondent banking relationship with a respondent institution from a non-EEA state; and
- where the relevant person proposes to have a business relationship or carry out an occasional transaction with a politically exposed person (PEP).

The general requirement for enhanced CDD

Regulation 14(1)(b) places an important duty on relevant persons to assess and manage the **9.84**
risk of money laundering and terrorist financing by requiring the relevant person to apply, on a risk-sensitive basis, enhanced CDD measures and enhanced ongoing monitoring '. . . in any other situation which by its nature can present a higher risk of money laundering or terrorist financing'.

Customer not physically present

Regulation 14(2) states that, where the customer has not been physically present for identi- **9.85**
fication purposes, 'a relevant person must take specific and adequate measures to compensate for the higher risk'. This puts an obligation on the relevant person to assess the extent of any higher risk of money laundering or terrorist financing and to identify and apply compensatory measures.

---

[80] Reg 13(7)(a)–(c).
[81] Reg 13(7)(d).
[82] Reg 13(8).
[83] Reg 13(9).
[84] Enhanced ongoing monitoring is dealt with below at paras 9.105 and 9.106.
[85] Credit institution is defined in Reg 3(2).

9.86   The Regulation gives three examples of measures to compensate for the higher risk:

- ensuring that the customer's identity is established by additional documents, data, or information;
- applying supplementary measures to verify or certify the documents supplied, or requiring confirmatory certification by a credit or financial institution which is subject to the Money Laundering Directive;
- ensuring that the first payment is carried out through an account opened in the customer's name with a credit institution.

Correspondent relationships

9.87   Where the relevant person is a credit institution[86] (the 'correspondent') and has or proposes to have a correspondent banking relationship with a respondent institution (the 'respondent') from a non-EEA state, Regulation 14(3) sets out the requirements of enhanced CDD. Whereas Regulation 14(2) above states a general requirement to take 'specific and adequate measures' and provides examples of such measures, Regulation 14(3) sets out, in specific and mandatory terms, a number of enhanced measures:

> A credit institution ('the correspondent') which has or proposes to have a correspondent banking relationship with a respondent institution ('the respondent') from a non-EEA state must—
>
> > (a) gather sufficient information about the respondent to understand fully the nature of its business;
> > (b) determine from publicly-available information the reputation of the respondent and the quality of its supervision;
> > (c) assess the respondent's anti-money laundering and anti-terrorist financing controls;
> > (d) obtain approval from senior management before establishing a new correspondent banking relationship;
> > (e) document the respective responsibilities of the respondent and correspondent; and
> > (f) be satisfied that, in respect of those of the respondent's customers who have direct access to accounts of the correspondent, the respondent—
> > > (i) has verified the identity of, and conducts ongoing monitoring in respect of, such customers; and
> > > (ii) is able to provide to the correspondent, upon request, the documents, data or information obtained when applying customer due diligence measures and ongoing monitoring.

Politically exposed persons

9.88   Article 13 of the Third Money Laundering Directive introduced into the anti-money laundering and counter-terrorist financing regime the category of 'politically exposed persons'. The rationale for this is explained in paragraphs 24 and 25 of the Preamble to the Directive:

> (24) ... Community legislation should recognise that certain situations present a greater risk of money laundering or terrorist financing. Although the identity and business profile of all customers should be established, there are cases where particularly rigorous customer identification and verification procedures are required.

---

[86] Credit institution is defined in Reg 3(2).

(25) This is particularly true of business relationships with individuals holding, or having held, important public positions, particularly those from countries where corruption is widespread. Such relationships may expose the financial sector in particular to significant reputational and/or legal risks. The international effort to combat corruption also justifies the need to pay special attention to such cases and to apply the complete normal customer due diligence measures in respect of domestic politically exposed persons or enhanced customer due diligence measures in respect of politically exposed persons residing in another Member State or in a third country.

9.89 The requirements in the Third Money Laundering Directive for enhanced due diligence in relation to PEPs have been implemented in UK law in the provisions of Regulation 14(4) to (6) and paragraph 4 of Schedule 2.

Applying enhanced CDD to PEPs

9.90 A relevant person must apply, on a risk-sensitive basis, enhanced CDD measures where they propose 'to have a business relationship or carry out an occasional transaction with a politically exposed person'.

9.91 Regulation 14(4) sets out the specific requirements of enhanced CDD in relation to PEPs. The relevant person must:

- have approval from senior management for establishing the business relationship with the PEP;
- take adequate measures to establish the source of wealth and source of funds which are involved in the proposed business relationship or occasional transaction; and
- where the business relationship is entered into, conduct enhanced ongoing monitoring of the relationship.[87]

What is a PEP?

9.92 Regulation 14(5) sets out a definition of 'politically exposed person', which is supplemented by detailed provisions in Schedule 2, paragraph 4 (1) (a):

(5) In paragraph (4), 'a politically exposed person' means a person who is—

    (a) an individual who is or has, at any time in the preceding year, been entrusted with a prominent public function by—
        (i) a state other than the United Kingdom;
        (ii) a Community institution;[88] or
        (iii) an international body,[89] including a person who falls in any of the categories listed in paragraph 4(1)(a) of Schedule 2;
    (b) an immediate family member of a person referred to in sub-paragraph (a), including a person who falls in any of the categories listed in paragraph 4(1)(c) of Schedule 2; or
    (c) a known close associate of a person referred to in sub-paragraph (a), including a person who falls in either of the categories listed in paragraph 4(1)(d) of Schedule 2.

---

[87] See below at paras 9.105 and 9.106.
[88] HM Revenue & Customs' guidance notes cite the European Parliament as an example.
[89] HM Revenue & Customs' guidance notes cite the United Nations as an example.

Information about PEPs

9.93   In many cases, identifying a PEP is not easy. Regulation 14(6) gives an indication of what may be reasonably required and puts some limits on the detective work involved. It provides that, for the purpose of deciding whether a person is a known close associate of a PEP, a relevant person need only have regard to information which is in his possession or is publicly known.

9.94   In broad terms, a PEP is a person entrusted with a 'prominent public function', or an 'immediate family member' of such a person, or a 'known close associate' of such a person. Effectively, and for ease of reference, there are three levels of PEPs:

- a person entrusted with a prominent public function (a 'primary PEP');
- a primary PEP's immediate family member (a 'secondary PEP');
- a primary PEP's known close associate (a 'tertiary PEP').

Primary PEPs

9.95   A primary PEP is an individual who is or has, at any time in the preceding year, been entrusted with a prominent public function by a state other than the United Kingdom, by a Community institution, or by an international body (including a person who falls in any of the categories listed in paragraph 4(1)(a) of Schedule 2).

9.96   Paragraph 4(1)(a) of Schedule 2 sets out a non-exhaustive list of categories of individuals (not including 'middle-ranking or more junior officials'[90]) 'who are or have been entrusted with prominent public functions', as follows:

  (i)   heads of state, heads of government, ministers and deputy or assistant ministers;
  (ii)   members of parliaments;
  (iii)   members of supreme courts, of constitutional courts or of other high-level judicial bodies whose decisions are not generally subject to further appeal, other than in exceptional circumstances;
  (iv)   members of courts of auditors or of the boards of central banks;
  (v)   ambassadors, chargés d'affaires and high-ranking officers in the armed forces; and
  (vi)   members of the administrative, management or supervisory bodies of state-owned enterprises.[91]

9.97   However, it is important to note that the above-mentioned list of categories is non-exhaustive,[92] such that other similar individuals could also be capable of falling within the definition of a PEP. The crucial deciding factor is whether they are or have, at any time in the preceding year, been entrusted with a prominent public function by a state other than the United Kingdom, by a Community institution, or by an international body.

9.98   The definition of a 'primary PEP' in paragraph 4(1)(a) is qualified by the statement in paragraph 4(1)(b) that: 'the categories set out in paragraphs (i) to (vi) of sub-paragraph (a) do not include middle-ranking or more junior officials'. This is helpful so far as it goes, but the phrase 'middle-ranking' is obviously open to wide interpretation, as is the word 'senior'.

---

[90]   See para 4(1)(b) of Sch 2.
[91]   There is no specific definition of a 'state-owned enterprise'. Generally, of course, it is right to say that the state can be a full or part owner of an enterprise (either a majority owner or a minority owner); it is unclear whether it is intended that a 'state-owned enterprise' extends to all levels of government ownership.
[92]   The Regulations use the word 'including'.

The word 'prominent', at least, in the phrase 'prominent public functions' seems to give a clearer indication of what is intended. It might, for instance, be argued that there are many senior public officials whose functions are public but not 'prominent'.

Secondary PEPs and tertiary PEPs

Since a primary PEP is an individual who is or has, at any time in the preceding year, been **9.99** entrusted with a prominent public function by a state other than the United Kingdom, by a Community institution, or by an international body, *including* a person who falls in any of the categories listed in paragraph 4(1)(a) of Schedule 2, an 'immediate family member' or a 'known close associate' also—in a somewhat circular manner—falls within the definition of a PEP.

Immediate family members

Paragraph 4(1)(c) of Schedule 2 states that immediate family members include: **9.100**

> (i)   a spouse;
> (ii) a partner;
> (iii) children and their spouses or partners; and
> (iv) parents.

However, again, it is important to note that the above-mentioned list of immediate fam- **9.101** ily members is non-exhaustive,[93] such that other similar individuals could also be capable of falling within the definition of a PEP. In particular, according to paragraph 4(2) of Schedule 2, 'partner' means a person who is considered by his national law as equivalent to a spouse.

Known close associates

Paragraph 4(1)(d) of Schedule 2 states that persons known to be close associates include: **9.102**

> (i)   any individual who is known to have joint beneficial ownership of a legal entity or legal arrangement, or any other close business relations, with a person referred to in regulation 14(5)(a);[94] and
> (ii) any individual who has sole beneficial ownership of a legal entity or legal arrangement which is known to have been set up for the benefit of a person referred to in regulation 14(5)(a).

Again, it should be noted that the above-mentioned list of known close associates is **9.103** non-exhaustive,[95] such that other similar individuals could also be capable of falling within the definition of a PEP. In practice, the obligation to identify known close associates of PEPs is, to some extent, kept within realistic bounds by Regulation 14(6), which states that: 'For the purpose of deciding whether a person is a known close associate . . ., a relevant person need only have regard to information which is in his possession or is publicly known.'

---

[93] The Regulations use the word 'include'.
[94] A person referred to in Reg 14(5)(a) (i.e. a primary PEP) is an individual who is or has, at any time in the preceding year, been entrusted with a prominent public function by a state other than the United Kingdom, by a Community institution, or by an international body (including a person who falls in any of the categories listed in para 4(1)(a) of Sch 2).
[95] The Regulations use the word 'include'.

How can a PEP be identified?

9.104   Together, Regulation 14 and Schedule 2 define a PEP, but in terms that create a difficult task for relevant persons. Identifying whether a customer or proposed customer is a PEP has proved to be a continuing practical problem for the regulated sector.[96]

Enhanced ongoing monitoring

9.105   The requirement to apply enhanced ongoing monitoring is set out in Regulation 14, alongside the requirement to apply enhanced customer due diligence. The situations in relation to which the requirement for enhanced ongoing monitoring apply are exactly the same as those relating to enhanced customer due diligence.

9.106   In broad terms, as with enhanced customer due diligence, a relevant person must apply enhanced customer due diligence measures in situations that present a higher risk of money laundering or terrorist financing. More specifically, according to Regulation 14, a relevant person must apply, on a risk-sensitive basis 'enhanced ongoing monitoring' in the following circumstances:

- where the customer has not been physically present for identification purposes;
- where the relevant person is a credit institution[97] and has or proposes to have a correspondent banking relationship with a respondent institution from a non-EEA state;
- where the relevant person proposes to have a business relationship or carry out an occasional transaction with a politically exposed person;
- in any other situation which by its nature can present a higher risk of money laundering or terrorist financing.

E. Customer Due Diligence: Ancillary Provisions

Regulation 15—branches and subsidiaries

9.107   To the extent that this is compatible with local law (see paragraph (2) below), Regulation 15 requires credit or financial institutions to ensure that their branches and subsidiaries apply CDD and other measures to at least the same standard as under the Regulations:

> (1) A credit or financial institution must require its branches and subsidiary undertakings[98] which are located in a non-EEA state to apply, to the extent permitted by the law of that state, measures at least equivalent to those set out in these Regulations with regard to customer due diligence measures, ongoing monitoring and record-keeping.

9.108   Where a credit or financial institution is unable to comply with the above requirement, there are alternative provisions in Regulation 15(2):

> (2) Where the law of a non-EEA state does not permit the application of such equivalent measures by the branch or subsidiary undertaking located in that state, the credit or financial institution must—

---

[96]   The Treasury may, from time to time, issue advice about high risk situations to the regulated sector. Such advice may include advice about dealing with customers in or receiving funds from countries that present a high risk of money laundering or terrorist financing. Such advice is published on the Treasury's website at <http://www.hm-treasury.gov.uk>.

[97]   Credit institution is defined in Reg 3(2).

[98]   The phrase 'subsidiary undertaking', for the purposes of this Regulation, is defined in Reg 15(3).

   (a) inform its supervisory authority accordingly; and

   (b) take additional measures to handle effectively the risk of money laundering and terrorist financing.

   . . .

Prohibitions on business

Regulations 16 and 18 both concern prohibitions on the conduct of business by banks, but in quite different circumstances. **9.109**

Under Regulation 16, credit institutions are prohibited from conducting business with a certain type of bank (a shell bank) and with a certain type of account (an anonymous account) that are considered to be particularly likely to facilitate and provide cover for money laundering. **9.110**

Regulation 18 gives the Treasury power to direct any relevant person not to conduct business with a person in a non-EEA state to which FATF has applied counter-measures.[99] **9.111**

Regulation 16—shell banks, etc

Shell banks

Regulation 16 requires credit institutions to ensure that they do not have a correspondent banking relationship with a 'shell bank' (as defined in paragraph 5 below). They must also avoid any such relationship with a bank known to permit its accounts to be used by a shell bank: **9.112**

   (1) A credit institution must not enter into, or continue, a correspondent banking relationship with a shell bank.

   (2) A credit institution must take appropriate measures to ensure that it does not enter into, or continue, a corresponding banking relationship with a bank which is known to permit its accounts to be used by a shell bank.

   . . .

   (5) A 'shell bank' means a credit institution, or an institution engaged in equivalent activities, incorporated in a jurisdiction in which it has no physical presence involving meaningful decision-making and management, and which is not part of a financial conglomerate or third-country financial conglomerate.[100]

Anonymous accounts

Regulation 16 also requires that credit and financial institutions do not set up new anonymous accounts and that they apply CDD measures to any existing anonymous accounts: **9.113**

   (3) A credit or financial institution carrying on business in the United Kingdom must not set up an anonymous account or an anonymous passbook for any new or existing customer.

---

[99] The HM Treasury website does not, at the time of writing, carry any general directions made specifically under Reg 18. Any such directions would presumably appear on its financial sanctions page, at <http://www.hm-treasury.gov.uk/fin_sanctions_index.htm>.

[100] Under Reg 16(6), 'In this regulation, "financial conglomerate" and "third-country financial conglomerate" have the meanings given by regulations 1(2) and 7(1) respectively of the Financial Conglomerates and Other Financial Groups Regulations 2004.'

(4) As soon as reasonably practicable on or after 15th December 2007 all credit and financial institutions carrying on business in the United Kingdom must apply customer due diligence measures to, and conduct ongoing monitoring of, all anonymous accounts and passbooks in existence on that date and in any event before such accounts or passbooks are used.

Regulation 18—directions where FATF counter-measures

9.114 In accordance with the aims of FATF in taking appropriate action with respect to non-co-operative countries and territories (NCCTs), the Treasury is given power to prevent business being conducted with a person in a country which is judged by FATF to be very high-risk in terms of money laundering or terrorist financing:

> 18. Directions where Financial Action Task Force applies counter-measures.
> The Treasury may direct any relevant person—
> (a) not to enter into a business relationship;
> (b) not to carry out an occasional transaction; or
> (c) not to proceed any further with a business relationship or occasional transaction, with a person who is situated or incorporated in a non-EEA state to which the Financial Action Task Force has decided to apply counter-measures.

Regulation 17—reliance

9.115 A financial transaction may involve numerous relevant persons conducting different aspects of it and, in order to comply strictly with the Regulations, CDD measures may have to be applied to the same customer successively by several regulated institutions. Even a simple house purchase may well involve lawyers, estate agents, and lenders on each side. Frequent repetition of CDD is wasteful of time and money (and unpopular with clients and customers). The 'reliance' provisions in Regulation 17 create an exception to the obligation under Regulation 7 to apply customer due diligence measures and allow a relevant person, in certain defined circumstances, to rely on CDD previously undertaken by another person.

9.116 Regulation 17 allows a relevant person to rely on another person who falls within any one of a number of specified categories,[101] or who the relevant person has reasonable grounds to believe is such a person, to apply 'any customer due diligence measures'. However, in order to be able to do so, the person relied upon must consent to being relied upon. In addition, 'notwithstanding the relevant person's reliance on the other person, the relevant person remains liable for any failure to apply such measures':

> (1) A relevant person may rely on a person who falls within paragraph (2) (or who the relevant person has reasonable grounds to believe falls within paragraph (2)) to apply any customer due diligence measures provided that—
> (a) the other person consents to being relied on; and
> (b) notwithstanding the relevant person's reliance on the other person, the relevant person remains liable for any failure to apply such measures.

9.117 The persons upon whom a relevant person may rely to apply 'any customer due diligence measures' are set out, in four alternative categories, in Regulation 17(2). The first two categories relate to persons in the UK and within the jurisdiction of the Regulations. The latter two categories relate to persons outside the UK.

---

[101] Set out in Reg 17(2)(a) to (d) inclusive.

Reliance on authorised persons and relevant persons

The categories of person in Regulation 17(2)(a) and (b) are persons in the UK whose **9.118** status is such that it is considered appropriate that they can be relied on for this purpose. Note that the provisions in subparagraph (a) are subject to an exclusion which is set out in Regulation 17(5):

> (2) The persons are—
> > (a) a credit or financial institution which is an authorised person;
> > (b) a relevant person who is—
> > > (i) an auditor, insolvency practitioner, external accountant, tax adviser or independent legal professional; and
> > > (ii) supervised for the purposes of these Regulations by one of the bodies listed in Part 1 of Schedule 3;

Reliance may not be placed on money service businesses or certain payment institutions.[102] **9.119**

Reliance on a person in another EEA state

Particular issues arise when dealing with transactions across national boundaries. The cus- **9.120** tomer or beneficial owner may be located abroad and the relevant person may not be best equipped to deal with the practicalities of customer due diligence in that jurisdiction. Regulation 17 provides separately for reliance on persons in other EEA states and persons in non-EEA states (for the latter, see paragraph 9.121 below):

> (c) a person who carries on business in another EEA state who is—
> > (i) a credit or financial institution,[103] auditor, insolvency practitioner,[104] external accountant, tax adviser or independent legal professional;
> > (ii) subject to mandatory professional registration recognised by law; and
> > (iii) supervised for compliance with the requirements laid down in the money laundering directive in accordance with section 2 of Chapter V of that directive;

Reliance on a person in a non-EEA state

This final provision is perhaps the least satisfactory in practice because of the use in it of the **9.121** notion of equivalence, which is considered below:

> (d) a person who carries on business in a non-EEA state who is—
> > (i) a credit or financial institution (or equivalent institution), auditor, insolvency practitioner, external accountant, tax adviser or independent legal professional;
> > (ii) subject to mandatory professional registration recognised by law;
> > (iii) subject to requirements equivalent to those laid down in the money laundering directive; and
> > (iv) supervised for compliance with those requirements in a manner equivalent to section 2 of Chapter V of the money laundering directive.

---

[102] Reg 17(5).

[103] In this regulation, 'financial institution' excludes any money service business, any authorised payment institution, an EEA authorised payment institution, or small payment institution (within the meaning of the Payment Services Regulations 2009) which provides payment services mainly falling within para 1(f) of Sch 1 to those Regulations.

[104] In para (2)(c)(i) and (d)(i), 'auditor' and 'insolvency practitioner' includes a person situated in another EEA state or a non-EEA state who provides services equivalent to the services provided by an auditor or insolvency practitioner.

Equivalence

9.122   It is uncertain how helpful the provisions in Regulation 17(2)(d) are in practice. They relate to reliance placed on 'a person who carries on business in a non-EEA state . . .', and in order to limit the reliance provisions to persons in whom the same degree of confidence can be placed as on persons carrying on business in another EEA state (as in Regulation 17(2)(c)), the provisions make use of the notion of equivalence. 'Equivalence' appears variously in the context of an equivalent institution, equivalent requirements and equivalent supervision.

9.123   The use of the notion of equivalence in these provisions means that a relevant person can only rely on another person under Regulation 17(2)(d) where they are satisfied, in effect, that the other person passes the equivalence tests in subparagraphs (i), (iii), and (iv). HM Treasury published a Statement on Equivalence on 12 May 2008, which remains on its website and has not been amended at the time of writing.[105] It says that member states participating in the EU Committee on the Prevention of Money Laundering and Terrorist Financing have agreed a list of equivalent third countries, for the purposes of relevant parts of the Third Directive. It says the list (which comprises 13 countries) 'is a voluntary, non-binding measure', which in the UK is relevant to assessing whether a jurisdiction is equivalent for the purposes of regulations 13 and 17. The House of Lords European Union Committee's 19th report, 'Money laundering and the financing of terrorism' (published on 14 July 2009) said: 'Our witnesses are unanimous in thinking that third country equivalence does not achieve its object of helping the private regulated sector. There is, as we have said, no definition of equivalence, and the Treasury "statement on equivalence" listing equivalent third countries was described by the Law Society as "voluntary, non binding and does not have the force of law . . . Regulated individuals or entities are required to make the assessment of equivalence themselves."'

Any customer due diligence measures

9.124   Regulation 17 does not specify what is meant by 'any customer due diligence measures'. It permits reliance beyond the essential CDD measures under Regulation 5: identifying and verifying the identity of the customer;[106] identifying the beneficial owner[107] and taking adequate measures[108] to verify his identity; and obtaining information on the purpose and intended nature of the business relationship. It seems that the phrase 'any customer due diligence measures' includes the associated requirements under Regulation 9 relating to the timing of the verification of the identity of the customer / beneficial owner.

9.125   The extent of customer due diligence by others on which reliance can be placed is indicated by the provisions in Regulation 19(4) relating to the keeping of records. These require that a relevant person who is relied on by another person must keep the specified records for five years '. . . for the purposes of Regulation 7, 10, 14 or 16(4) in relation to any business relationship or occasional transaction'. It therefore seems that the phrase 'any customer due diligence measures' includes the requirement under Regulation 10 in relation to casinos

---

[105] The Statement is at <http://webarchive.nationalarchives.gov.uk/+/http://www.hm-treasury.gov.uk/documents/financial_services/money/fin_crime_equivalence.cfm>.
[106] Note that where the customer is not physically present, the relevant person must apply enhanced customer due diligence measures.
[107] Where there is a beneficial owner who is not the customer.
[108] On a risk-sensitive basis.

establishing and verifying the identity of customers, as well as the requirement under Regulation 14 for enhanced due diligence and enhanced ongoing monitoring (but see below). Further, it seems that customer due diligence measures in relation to anonymous accounts and passbooks (Regulation 16(4)) are also included.

However, the position is less clear in relation to the requirement under Regulation 14 to apply enhanced customer due diligence measures. Unlike customer due diligence measures, enhanced customer due diligence measures are not prescribed[109] and include more than just identifying the customer/beneficial owner, verifying such identity, and obtaining information on the purpose and intended nature of the business relationship. It seems likely that it may be appropriate to rely on another for some enhanced CDD measures, but that in many cases it would not prove appropriate or practical to use the reliance provisions. **9.126**

Accordingly, it would appear that a relevant person cannot rely on another appropriate person to apply enhanced customer due diligence measures, save for in relation to identifying and verifying the identity of the customer. **9.127**

The fact that the relevant person will always remain liable for any failure by the person relied upon to apply customer due diligence measures means that in practice there is little incentive for a relevant person to rely upon another. Failure to apply customer due diligences measures exposes the relevant person to an unlimited civil penalty or criminal prosecution.[110] That is particularly the case when one considers that in reality one would only really be relying on another to identify and verify the identity of the customer/beneficial owner. **9.128**

Applying CDD measures by outsourcing

Outsourcing is quite different from 'reliance' and is no more than a particular method by which a relevant person carries out the CDD obligation, and the use of commercial third party credit reference and similar agencies to verify the identity of customers is widespread. **9.129**

To avoid confusion, Regulation 17(4) makes it clear that a relevant person can apply customer due diligence measures 'by means of an outsourcing service provider or agent'. If a relevant person does so, they remain liable for any failure to apply such measures: **9.130**

> (4) Nothing in this regulation prevents a relevant person applying customer due diligence measures by means of an outsourcing service provider or agent provided that the relevant person remains liable for any failure to apply such measures.

Failure to apply customer due diligences measures may expose the relevant person to an unlimited civil penalty and makes that person liable to criminal prosecution under Regulation 45.[111] **9.131**

---

[109] Save for in relation to a PEP.

[110] If found guilty, a relevant person is liable, on summary conviction, to a fine not exceeding the statutory maximum; or, on conviction on indictment, to imprisonment for a term not exceeding two years, to a fine, or to both.

[111] If found guilty, a relevant person is liable, on summary conviction, to a fine not exceeding the statutory maximum; or, on conviction on indictment, to imprisonment for a term not exceeding two years, to a fine, or to both.

F. The Requirements under Part 3 of the Regulations

Introduction

9.132 Part 3 of the Regulations concerns three aspects of the management of the risk of involvement by a relevant person in money laundering. Whereas the requirements in Part 2 are, in practice, directed primarily at individuals carrying front-line responsibilities, the provisions in Part 3 set out high-level responsibilities that need to be taken on by the senior management of regulated entities.

Record keeping

9.133 A relevant person is required to keep certain records for certain periods of time, whether in relation to their own occasional transactions or business relationships, or in relation to those of persons who rely on them pursuant to Regulation 17(1).

9.134 Regulation 19(1) requires a relevant person to keep the following records for at least the specified period:

- a copy of, or the references to, the evidence of the customer's identity obtained pursuant to Regulation 7,[112] 8,[113] 10,[114] 14,[115] or 16(4);[116]
- the supporting records (consisting of the original documents or copies) in respect of a business relationship or occasional transaction, which is the subject of customer due diligence measures or ongoing monitoring.

9.135 The specified period in relation to the first above-mentioned category of records is five years beginning on the date on which the occasional transaction is completed or the business relationship ends.

9.136 The specified period in relation to the second above-mentioned category of records is five years beginning either on the date on which the transaction is completed (where the records relate to a particular transaction) or on the date on which the business relationship ends (for all other records).

9.137 In addition to keeping records in relation to his own occasional transactions/business relationships, a relevant person, who is relied on[117] by another person, is required by Regulation 19(4) to keep the following records for five years beginning on the date on which he is relied on for the purposes of Regulation 7, 10, 14, or 16(4) in relation to any business relationship or occasional transaction:

---

[112] The requirement to apply customer due diligence measures.

[113] The requirement to conduct ongoing monitoring.

[114] The specific requirement on casinos to establish and verify identity.

[115] The requirement to apply enhanced customer due diligence measures and conduct enhanced ongoing monitoring.

[116] The requirement on credit institutions and financial institutions to apply customer due diligence measures and conduct ongoing monitoring in relation to anonymous accounts and passbooks.

[117] Where the reliance is pursuant to Reg 17(1) (Reg 19(8)).

- A copy of, or the references to, the evidence of the customer's identity obtained pursuant to Regulation 7,[118] 8,[119] 10,[120] 14,[121] or 16(4).[122]

Further, Regulation 19(5) requires that a person referred to in Regulation 17(2)(a) or **9.138** Regulation 17(2)(b) who is relied on[123] by a relevant person must, if requested by the person relying on him within the period of five years beginning on the date on which reliance began:

- as soon as reasonably practicable make available to the person who is relying on him any information about the customer (and any beneficial owner) which he obtained when applying customer due diligence measures; and
- as soon as reasonably practicable forward to the person who is relying on him copies of any identification and verification data and other relevant documents on the identity of the customer (and any beneficial owner) which he obtained when applying those measures.

A person referred to in Regulation 17(2)(a) or Regulation 17(2)(b) is 'a credit or financial **9.139** institution which is an authorised person' (i.e. authorised for the purposes of the Financial Services and Markets Act 2000) or 'a relevant person who is (i) an auditor, insolvency practitioner, external accountant, tax adviser or independent legal professional; and (ii) supervised for the purposes of these Regulations by one of the bodies listed in Part 1 of Schedule 3'. In reality, both categories of person are likely to fall within the definition of a relevant person. In effect, Regulation 19(4) and Regulation 19(5) require a relevant person who is relied upon by another relevant person to keep the specified records for five years from the date that they were relied on and to make them available or forward them to the relevant person relying on them. Any other interpretation is difficult to follow, as the Regulations only apply to relevant persons (as defined by Regulation 3) and Regulation 19(6) specifically deals with the position of third parties on whom reliance is placed.

Of course, Regulation 17(1) also permits a relevant person to rely on certain specified per- **9.140** sons who are not relevant persons, namely persons referred to in Regulation 17(2)(c) or Regulation 17(2)(d) (a 'third party'[124]). Because a third party does not fall within the definition of a relevant person (and, as such, the Regulations do not apply to them), they are not required by Regulation 19 to keep, make available, or forward records. However, Regulation 19(6) requires a relevant person who has relied on a third party[125] to take steps to ensure that the third party will, if requested by the relevant person within the period of five years beginning on the date on which reliance began:

- as soon as reasonably practicable make available to him any information about the customer (and any beneficial owner) which the third party obtained when applying customer due diligence measures; and

---

[118] The requirement to apply customer due diligence measures.

[119] The requirement to conduct ongoing monitoring.

[120] The specific requirement on casinos to establish and verify identity.

[121] The requirement to apply enhanced customer due diligence measures and conduct enhanced ongoing monitoring.

[122] The requirement on credit institutions and financial institutions to apply customer due diligence measures and conduct ongoing monitoring in relation to anonymous accounts and passbooks.

[123] Where the reliance is pursuant to Reg 17(1) (Reg 19(8)).

[124] They are referred to in Reg 17(6) as a 'third party'.

[125] Where, under Reg 19(8), the reliance is pursuant to Reg 17(1).

- as soon as reasonably practicable forward to him copies of any identification and verification data and other relevant documents on the identity of the customer (and any beneficial owner) which the third party obtained when applying those measures.

Regulation 20—policies and procedures

9.141 The Regulations require that relevant persons have in place policies and procedures to ensure that their organization is vigilant against being used for money laundering and has the necessary information upon which to make sound risk-based decisions, but generally they do not prescribe how this must be achieved. The onus is placed on the relevant person (and, in particular, on senior management) to consider the nature of the business and to identify appropriate policies. It is an offence not to establish such policies.[126]

9.142 Regulation 20 requires a relevant person to 'establish and maintain appropriate and risk-sensitive policies and procedures', in order to prevent activities related to money laundering and terrorist financing, relating to:

- customer due diligence measures;
- ongoing monitoring;
- reporting;
- record-keeping;
- internal control;
- risk assessment and management;
- the monitoring and management of compliance with, and the internal communication of, such policies and procedures.

9.143 Although the requirement is to establish and maintain appropriate and risk-sensitive policies and procedures in order to prevent activities related to money laundering and terrorist financing, Regulation 20(2) specifies that these policies and procedures include (but are not limited to):

    a. Policies and procedures that provide for the identification and scrutiny of:
        i. complex or unusually large transactions;
        ii. unusual patterns of transactions which have no apparent economic or visible lawful purpose; and
        iii. any other activity which the relevant person regards as particularly likely by its nature to be related to money laundering or terrorist financing.
    b. Policies and procedures that specify the taking of additional measures, where appropriate, to prevent the use for money laundering or terrorist financing of products and transactions which might favour anonymity.
    c. Policies and procedures to determine whether a customer is a politically exposed person.[127]
    d. Policies and procedures[128] under which:
        i. an individual in the relevant person's organization is a nominated officer[129] under Part 7 of the Proceeds of Crime Act 2002 and Part 3 of the Terrorism Act 2000;

---

[126] Reg 45(1).

[127] The meaning of 'politically exposed person' is the same as in Reg 14(4) (Reg 20(6)).

[128] The requirement to establish and maintain these policies and procedures does not apply to a relevant person who is an individual who neither employs nor acts in association with any other person.

[129] 'Nominated officer' means a person who is nominated to receive disclosures under of the Proceeds of Crime Act 2002, Pt 7 as amended (money laundering) or Terrorism Act 2000, Pt 3 as amended (terrorist property).

ii. anyone in the organization to whom information or other matter comes in the course of the business as a result of which he knows or suspects or has reasonable grounds for knowing or suspecting that a person is engaged in money laundering or terrorist financing is required to comply with Part 7 of the Proceeds of Crime Act 2002[130] or, as the case may be, Part 3 of the Terrorism Act 2000;[131] and

iii. where a disclosure is made to the nominated officer, he must consider it in the light of any relevant information which is available to the relevant person and determine whether it gives rise to knowledge or suspicion or reasonable grounds for knowledge or suspicion that a person is engaged in money laundering or terrorist financing.[132]

In addition, Regulation 20(4) and Regulation 20(5) place further specific requirements on **9.144** credit institutions and financial institutions. Each must establish and maintain systems which enable it to respond fully and rapidly to enquiries from identified persons[133] as to (a) whether it maintains, or has maintained during the previous five years, a business relationship with any person; and (b) the nature of that relationship. In addition, each must communicate where relevant the policies and procedures which it establishes and maintains in accordance with Regulation 20 to its branches and subsidiary undertakings[134] which are located outside the United Kingdom.

Training

Regulation 21 requires a relevant person to take 'appropriate measures' so that all relevant **9.145** employees of his are:

- made aware of the law relating to money laundering and terrorist financing; and
- regularly given training in how to recognize and deal with transactions and other activities which may be related to money laundering or terrorist financing.

Regulation 21 does not prescribe how or how often training is to be given. **9.146**

G. Conclusion

The duties placed on relevant persons by Parts 2 and 3 of the Regulations are onerous and **9.147** the cost of compliance is substantial. They are complemented in Parts 4 and 5 by provisions for supervision and registration, as well as extensive enforcement powers, both civil and criminal. These form the subject of the next chapter.

---

[130] See Chapter 6 above.
[131] See Chapter 7 above.
[132] POCA, ss 331 and 332. See Chapter 6 above at paras 6.47 *et seq.*
[133] Namely, financial investigators accredited under Proceeds of Crime Act 2002, s 3 (accreditation and training), persons acting on behalf of the Scottish Ministers in their capacity as an enforcement authority under the Proceeds of Crime Act 2002, officers of Revenue and Customs, or constables.
[134] The meaning of 'subsidiary undertaking' is the same as in Reg 15.

10

REGULATION: SUPERVISION, REGISTRATION, AND ENFORCEMENT

A. Introduction

10.01 This and the previous chapter are concerned with the regulatory measures intended to prevent and detect money laundering and terrorist financing in those areas of business and professional activity that are thought to be particularly vulnerable to the misuse of their services. This chapter covers Parts 4 to 6 of the Money Laundering Regulations 2007 ('the Regulations') and deals with the supervision of relevant persons, the registration of some otherwise unregulated businesses that are now within the regulated sector, and the provisions for enforcement by civil and criminal penalties.

10.02 The Regulations place on the legal and natural persons—institutions and individuals—that are subject to them substantial responsibilities to implement a range of detailed measures in order to prevent and detect money laundering and terrorist financing. Most, but not all, of those who are subject to the Regulations were already regulated for other purposes: the banks and financial services industry are subject to the regime of financial regulation under the Financial Services and Markets Act 2000 (FSMA) and accountants and lawyers are regulated by their professional bodies. For existing supervisors and regulators, the Regulations

234

have added a further area of responsibility in respect of which the regulatory body is required to monitor and supervise the persons that it regulates in order to ensure compliance with the anti-money laundering and counter-terrorist financing obligations set out in the Regulations.

Supervision and registration—an overview

Part 4 of the Regulations deals with the supervision of a relevant person and contains impor- **10.03**
tant provisions relating to supervisory authorities and their duties. Most of Part 4, however, is taken up with detailed provisions that do not concern the regulated sector as a whole. These relate to the registration of high-value dealers, money service businesses and certain other businesses that do not otherwise have a supervisory or regulatory authority. The registration provisions are contained in Regulations 25 to 35 inclusive.

Supervision for the purposes of the Regulations is, generally, the responsibility of existing **10.04**
regulators of the relevant business or profession. However, the 2003 Regulations brought into the regulated sector money service businesses and high-value dealers, neither of whom had an existing regulator that could take on the supervisory role with respect to money laundering. The Commissioners of Customs & Excise (as it then was) were given the responsibility under Part 3 of the 2003 Regulations to maintain registers of money service businesses and high-value dealers, the responsibility of supervision of these businesses, and powers of entry and search, as well as a power to impose penalties in order to ensure effective supervision.

B. Supervision

Background

The context from which the role of supervisory authorities is derived is paragraph 1 of **10.05**
Article 37 of the Third Money Laundering Directive, which places a duty on member states to '. . . require the competent authorities at least to effectively monitor and to take the necessary measures with a view to ensuring compliance with the requirements of this Directive by all the institutions and persons covered by this Directive'.

Competent authorities

The phrase 'competent authorities', extensively used in both the FATF Recommendations **10.06**
and in the Third Money Laundering Directive, is not defined in either document (other than in the Interpretative Notes to the FATF Recommendations and then only for the purposes of Recommendation 40 which concerns international co-operation).[1]

The meaning of the phrase appears to vary according to the context, but the breadth of **10.07**
meaning or possible meanings (at least in the FATF Recommendations) can be understood by considering the range of authorities referred to in Recommendations 26 to 32 under

---

[1] For the purposes of Recommendation 40, '"...Competent authority" refers to all administrative and law enforcement authorities concerned with combating money laundering and terrorist financing, including the FIU and supervisors'.

the subheading 'Competent authorities, their powers and resources': these include financial intelligence units (FIUs), law enforcement authorities, and supervisors.

10.08 The Third Money Laundering Directive requires that all relevant persons are supervised by a 'competent authority'—a 'supervisory authority' under the Regulations.

Supervisory authorities

10.09 The regulated sector now consists of a range of businesses and professions that cover a wide spectrum of business and professional activity. Most of these businesses and professions are already regulated for reasons of public interest that are separate from any concerns about money laundering and terrorist financing. Despite the addition to the regulated sector of the various businesses and professions brought into it by the 2003 Regulations—and to a lesser extent by the 2007 Regulations—it is still the banks and financial institutions that dominate the regulated sector and it is the Financial Services Authority (FSA) which is the lead regulator. There are, however, a large number of other bodies that have responsibilities as a supervisory authority under the Regulations.[2]

10.10 The Third Money Laundering Directive requires that all relevant persons are supervised by a 'competent authority'—a supervisory authority under the Regulations. The applicable supervisory authority depends upon the category of relevant person. Generally speaking, the supervisory authority will be a body which already regulates the relevant person for other purposes.

10.11 The supervisory landscape is complex and untidy, but necessarily so. The complexity reflects the number and diversity of the businesses and professions now considered to be particularly vulnerable to money laundering and which have, therefore, been brought into the regulated sector.

10.12 The regulatory authority that supervises the banks and financial services industry, the FSA, is an independent non-governmental body. The spectrum of other supervisory authorities ranges from government departments to independent professional regulators. In addition, the functions of some relevant persons may mean that they are brought within the Regulations under more than one category of relevant person: for instance, a solicitor or an accountant acting as a tax advisor.

- *The FSA* (referred to in the Regulations as 'the Authority'). The financial services industry was, in effect, the regulated sector from 1994 to 2004. Since 1997, the FSA has been the regulator for the banks and almost all financial institutions. The financial services industry continues to be the major part of the regulated sector and the FSA, which has tackling financial crime as one of its strategic objectives, plays a leading role among regulators and supervisors.[3]

- *Government departments and other public bodies.* Because the regulated sector now contains a number of otherwise unregulated businesses, the Regulations provide for various government departments and other public bodies to act as supervisory authorities. The most significant of these is HMRC (that is, the Commissioners of Revenue & Customs, referred to in the Regulations as 'the Commissioners'). Other supervisory authorities are

---

[2] See 2007 Regulations, Reg 23 and Sch 3.
[3] In particular, through the AML Supervisors' Forum, convened by HM Treasury.

the Office of Fair Trading (OFT), the Department of Enterprise, Trade and Investment (DETI) which has certain responsibilities in Northern Ireland, the Secretary of State (that is, the Secretary of State for Business, Innovation and Skills), and the Gambling Commission.[4]

- *Other independent regulators.* There are numerous professional regulatory bodies, such as the Law Society and the Institute of Chartered Accountants in England and Wales, which now have an additional responsibility for anti-money laundering supervision. These are listed in Schedule 3 to the Regulations (and below in Table 10.2).

The Supervisory Authorities, apart from those for professional bodies, are given in Table 10.1. **10.13**

Table 10.1 Supervisory authorities (other than for the professions)

Supervisory Authority	Relevant Persons
The Financial Services Authority (referred to in the Regulations as 'the Authority')	(i) credit and financial institutions which are authorised persons;[5] (ii) trust or company service providers which are authorised persons; (iii) Annex I financial institutions.[6]
The Office of Fair Trading (OFT)	(i) consumer credit financial institutions; (ii) estate agents
HM Revenue and Customs (referred to in the Regulations as 'the Commissioners')	(i) high-value dealers; (ii) money service businesses which are not supervised by the Authority; (iii) trust or company service providers which are not supervised by the Authority or one of the bodies listed in Schedule 3; (iv) auditors, external accountants and tax advisers who are not supervised by one of the bodies listed in Schedule 3; (v) bill payment service providers which are not supervised by the Authority; (vi) telecommunication, digital and IT payment service providers which are not supervised by the Authority.
The Gambling Commission The Department for Enterprise, Trade and Innovation (DETI)	(i) Casinos. (ii) credit unions in Northern Ireland; (iii) insolvency practitioners authorised by it under Article 351 of the Insolvency (Northern Ireland) Order 1989.
The Secretary of State for Business, Innovation and Skills (referred to in the Regulations as 'the Secretary of State')[7]	(i) insolvency practitioners authorised by him under section 393 of the Insolvency Act 1986 (grant, refusal and withdrawal of authorisation).

---

[4] The Gambling Commission, which is an independent non-departmental public body, was set up under the Gambling Act 2005 to regulate commercial gambling in Great Britain.

[5] The term 'authorised person' has the meaning given to it in the FSMA. See also Chapter 9 at para 9.22.

[6] As set out in Annex 1 to the Regulations.

[7] In Northern Ireland, the DETI, which is also responsible for Credit Unions in Northern Ireland.

Table 10.2 Supervisory authorities for the professions

Categories of professional body	Supervisory Authority
Professional bodies: accountancy, taxation and insolvency	**Accountancy and book-keeping** Association of Chartered Certified Accountants Institute of Chartered Accountants in England and Wales Institute of Chartered Accountants in Ireland Institute of Chartered Accountants of Scotland Chartered Institute of Management Accountants Chartered Institute of Public Finance and Accountancy Institute of Financial Accountants Association of Accounting Technicians Association of International Accountants Institute of Certified Bookkeepers International Association of Book-keepers **Taxation** Association of Taxation Technicians Chartered Institute of Taxation **Insolvency** Insolvency Practitioners Association
Professional bodies: lawyers	Faculty of Advocates General Council of the Bar General Council of the Bar of Northern Ireland Law Society Law Society of Scotland Law Society of Northern Ireland Council for Licensed Conveyancers
Professional bodies: other	Faculty Office of the Archbishop of Canterbury

10.14 Set out above, in Table 10.2, are the professional bodies that supervise their members for professional purposes and are also the supervisory authorities for money laundering purposes under Regulation 23. Members of such professional bodies will be relevant persons to whom the Regulations apply when they are '. . . acting in the course of business carried on by them in the United Kingdom . . .' as 'relevant persons' within the terms of Regulation 3.

10.15 Where there is more than one supervisory authority for a relevant person, the supervisory authorities may agree that one of them will act as the supervisory authority for that person.[8] Where such an agreement has been made, the authority which has agreed to act as the supervisory authority must notify the relevant person or publish the agreement in such manner as it considers appropriate.[9] Where no such agreement has been made, the supervisory authorities for a relevant person must co-operate in the performance of their functions under the Regulations.[10]

Duties of supervisory authorities

10.16 The role of the supervisory authority is effectively to monitor the relevant persons for whom it is the supervisory authority and take necessary measures for the purpose of securing

---

[8] Reg 23(2).
[9] Reg 23(3).
[10] Reg 23(4).

compliance by such persons with the requirements of the Regulations.[11] A *supervisory author-ity* is to be distinguished from a *designated authority* under Part 5 of the Regulations. The former's role is to monitor and secure compliance; the latter has specific enforcement powers given under that Part.[12]

Supervisory authorities: monitoring and compliance duties

The duties of supervisory authorities for the purposes of the Regulations are stated in wide **10.17** and general terms in Regulation 24(1). The regulatory requirements themselves, set out in Parts 2 and 3 of the Regulations, provide the detail and effectively define the scope of the supervisory role in relation to money laundering and terrorist financing:

> (1) A supervisory authority must effectively monitor the relevant persons for whom it is the supervisory authority and take necessary measures for the purpose of securing compliance by such persons with the requirements of these Regulations.[13]

Supervisory authorities: reporting requirement

In addition to the general requirement to monitor relevant persons, Regulation 24 places an **10.18** obligation on supervisory authorities to inform SOCA where they have knowledge or suspicion of money laundering or terrorist financing:

> (2) A supervisory authority which, in the course of carrying out any of its functions under these Regulations, knows or suspects that a person is or has engaged in money laundering or terrorist financing must promptly inform the Serious Organised Crime Agency.
> (3) A disclosure made under paragraph (2) is not to be taken to breach any restriction, however imposed, on the disclosure of information.

This duty placed on supervisory authorities to report to SOCA lies outside the disclosure **10.19** regime in Part 7 of POCA, but Regulation 24(3) provides that any such disclosure is a protected disclosure in essentially the same terms as protected disclosures under section 337 of POCA.[14] The duty to report is placed on the authority, not on any individual or individuals within the authority, and the scope of the duty to report differs from that in sections 330 and 331 of POCA in that it relates to knowledge or suspicion of past as well as present money laundering or terrorist financing.[15]

C. Registration

Background

There is no general requirement for relevant persons—the businesses and professions in the **10.20** regulated sector—to be registered with a regulator or supervisory authority. Certain businesses that are not otherwise regulated are, however, subject to a system of mandatory

---

[11] Reg 24.

[12] See para 10.63 below.

[13] See also: '(4) The functions of the Authority under these Regulations shall be treated for the purposes of Parts 1, 2 and 4 of Schedule 1 to the 2000 Act (the Financial Services Authority) as functions conferred on the Authority under that Act.'

[14] On protected disclosures, see Chapter 6 at paras 6.147 and 6.148.

[15] Note that there is also a reporting requirement placed on a number of public bodies and office holders under Reg 49.

registration set out in Regulations 25 to 30. Under Regulation 23, the Commissioners are made the supervisory authority for these businesses and Regulation 25 places on the Commissioners a duty to maintain registers.

10.21 These provisions substantially implement the requirements of Article 36 of the Third Directive:

> 1. Member States shall provide that currency exchange offices and trust and company service providers shall be licensed or registered and casinos be licensed in order to operate their business legally. Without prejudice to future Community legislation, Member States shall provide that money transmission or remittance offices shall be licensed or registered in order to operate their business legally.

10.22 Casinos, that are included in the requirements of Article 36, are absent from the provisions in Regulations 25 to 34; unlike the other relevant persons who are covered by these provisions, casinos were already subject to statutory regulation by the Gambling Commission.

10.23 The categories of persons to whom the Third Directive applies[16] are not closed. Article 4 requires member states to ensure that the provisions of the Directive are extended, in whole or in part, to other '. . . professions and to categories of undertakings . . . which engage in activities which are particularly likely to be used for money laundering or terrorist financing purposes'.

10.24 Regulations 25 to 34 inclusive make detailed provisions for the registration of relevant persons who are not otherwise subject to supervision by a regulatory authority.

Registration with the Commissioners of Revenue & Customs

10.25 Certain categories of relevant persons who were not previously required to register with a regulator, are now required to do so. The Commissioners for Her Majesty's Revenue and Customs[17] must maintain a register of those whom they supervise, and it is prohibited to carry on business in one of those areas without being registered. In effect, the Regulations establish a licensing system whereby the Commissioners will refuse to register those who they hold not to be 'fit and proper'.

10.26 Regulation 25(1) places a duty on HMRC as a supervisory authority to maintain registers:

> (1) The Commissioners must maintain registers of—
>   (a) high value dealers;
>   (b) money service businesses for which they are the supervisory authority;
>   (c) trust or company service providers for which they are the supervisory authority;
>   (d) bill payment service providers for which they are the supervisory authority; and
>   (e) telecommunication, digital and IT payment service providers for which they are the supervisory authority.
>
> . . .

---

[16] As set out in Art 2(1) of the directive.

[17] The obligation is placed on 'the Commissioners', which is the term used in the Regulations. In this chapter, 'HMRC' is also used for the Commissioners of Her Majesty's Revenue & Customs (and 'FSA' is also used instead of 'the Authority').

The Regulations provide that the Commissioners may keep the registers in any form that they **10.27** think fit and may publish or make available for public inspection all or part of a register.

Requirement to be registered

The duty on the Commissioners to maintain registers is matched by a requirement on those **10.28** intending to act in the specified businesses to be registered and a prohibition on acting as a high-value dealer or in any of the other specified businesses unless that person is included in the register:

> (1) A person in respect of whom the Commissioners are required to maintain a register under regulation 25 must not act as a—
>> (a) high value dealer;
>> (b) money service business;
>> (c) trust or company service provider;
>> (d) bill payment service provider; or
>> (e) telecommunication, digital and IT payment service provider,
>
> unless he is included in the register.[18]

Under the provisions of Part 5 of the Regulations, the prohibition in Regulation 26 on conducting any of the specified businesses unless the relevant person is registered, is enforceable either by a civil penalty on by a prosecution for a criminal offence.[19]

Transitional provisions

There are transitional provisions in Regulation 50 which allowed those already operating in **10.29** one of the specified businesses to determine the date by which they need to be registered. These transitional provisions continued to be relevant up to 1 March 2010 (and, in some cases subject to the detailed provisions in Regulation 50, remain relevant beyond that date) in relation to the latest businesses to be brought under the supervision of the Commissioners, that is bill-payment service providers and telecommunication, digital and IT payment service providers.

Applications for registration

In order to register, a person is required by Regulation 27 to make an application in such a **10.30** manner and provide such information to the Commissioners (in such a form and verified in such a manner) as they may specify. If, at any time after the applicant has provided the Commissioners with any information, there is a material change affecting any matter contained in that information or it becomes apparent to that person that the information contains a significant inaccuracy, he must provide the Commissioners with details of the change or, as the case may be, a correction of the inaccuracy within 30 days beginning with the date of the occurrence of the change (or the discovery of the inaccuracy) or within such later time as may be agreed with the Commissioners.[20] A person who fails to comply with the requirement to provide the Commissioners with details of a material change or, as the case may be, a correction is liable to a civil penalty or a prosecution in the criminal courts.[21]

---

[18] Note that para (1) and regulation 29 are subject to the transitional provisions set out in regulation 50.
[19] For the civil and criminal penalties, see below at paras 10.102 *et seq.*
[20] Reg 27.
[21] See below: for civil penalties, para 10.110 and for criminal penalties, paras 10.118 *et seq.*

Refusal to register and cancellation of registration

10.31 Regulations 28, 29, and 30 deal with the circumstances in which the Commissioners *must* refuse such an application by a money services business or a trust or company service provider (but not a high-value dealer) (the 'fit and proper test'); the circumstances in which the Commissioners *may* refuse such an application by a money services business, trust or company service provider, or a high-value dealer; the circumstances in which the Commissioners *must* cancel the registration of a money services business or a trust or company service provider (but not a high-value dealer); and the circumstances in which the Commissioners *may* cancel the registration of a money services business, a trust or company service provider, or a high-value dealer or a payment service provider.

The fit and proper test

10.32 The duty of HMRC as a supervisory authority to exercise a discretion, within the terms of the Regulations, to register only persons who pass the 'fit and proper' test under Regulation 28 is derived from paragraph 2 of Article 36[22] of the Third Money Laundering Directive: 'Member States shall require competent authorities to refuse licensing or registration of the entities referred to in paragraph 1 if they are not satisfied that the persons who effectively direct or will direct the business of such entities or the beneficial owners of such entities are fit and proper persons.'

10.33 Regulation 28 aims to ensure that money service businesses and trust or company service providers are not owned or controlled by anyone who is not a fit and proper person and that any such business does not have, as its nominated officer, a person who is not a fit and proper person.

10.34 Regulation 28 sets out the circumstances in which the Commissioners *must* refuse to register an applicant as either a money service business or a trust or company service provider:

    (1) The Commissioners must refuse to register an applicant as a money service business or trust or company service provider if they are satisfied that—
        (a) the applicant;
        (b) a person who effectively directs, or will effectively direct, the business or service provider;
        (c) a beneficial owner of the business or service provider; or
        (d) the nominated officer of the business or service provider,
    is not a fit and proper person.

10.35 The Commissioners *must* refuse the application if the applicant; a person who effectively directs, or will effectively direct, the business or service provider; a beneficial owner of the business or service provider; or the nominated officer of the business or service provider is 'not a fit and proper person'.

10.36 Who is 'not a fit and proper person' is defined in the detailed provisions of Regulation 28(2) and (3). In summary, a person is not a fit and proper person who:

- has been convicted of one of a number of specified serious offences (involving money laundering, terrorist financing or certain fraud and revenue offences);
- is an un-discharged bankrupt or is disqualified as a director;

---

[22] For the rationale for this provision, see para 39 of the Preamble to the Third Money Laundering Directive.

- is or has been subject to a confiscation order under POCA; or
- has, personally or through a business, consistently failed to comply with the requirements of money laundering regulations or regulations on information on the payer accompanying the transfer of funds.

Finally, under Regulation 28(2)(h), there is a discretionary category: a person who '. . . is **10.37** otherwise not a fit and proper person with regard to the risk of money laundering or terrorist financing'.

Determination of applications for registration

Regulation 29 sets out the only circumstances in which, subject to Regulation 28, the **10.38** Commissioners *may* refuse such an application by a business specified in Regulation 25(1), namely if:

    (a) any requirement of, or imposed under, regulation 27 has not been complied with;
    (b) it appears to the Commissioners that any information provided pursuant to regulation 27 is false or misleading in a material particular; or
    (c) the applicant has failed to pay a charge imposed by them under regulation 35(1).

It also sets out the time frame in which the Commissioners must give the applicant notice of **10.39** the decision whether or not to register the applicant and the contents of such a notice. The Commissioners must, as soon as practicable after deciding to register a person, include him in the relevant register.

Cancellation of registration

Regulation 30 sets out the circumstances in which the Commissioners *must* cancel the regis- **10.40** tration of a money services business or a trust or company service provider (but not a high-value dealer); and the circumstances in which the Commissioners *may* cancel the registration of a money services business, a trust or company service provider, or a high-value dealer. It also sets out the requirement on the Commissioners, where they decide to cancel a person's registration, to give him notice in a specified form.

Further provisions relating to registration and the costs of supervision

Requirement to inform the FSA

Regulation 31 places a specific requirement on certain authorised persons to inform the FSA: **10.41** '(1) An authorised person whose supervisory authority is the Authority must, before acting as a money service business or a trust or company service provider or within 28 days of so doing, inform the Authority that he intends, or has begun, to act as such.'

Regulation 31 requires an authorised person[23] whose supervisory authority is the Financial **10.42** Services Authority, before acting as a money service business or a trust or company service provider or within 28 days of so doing, to inform the Financial Services Authority (in such form or verified in such manner as it may specify) that he intends, or has begun, to act as such. In addition, it requires such an authorised person *where* he ceases to act as a money service business or a trust or company service provider to immediately inform the Financial Services Authority in such form or verified in such manner as it may specify.

---

[23] Reg 2(1) defines an 'authorised person' as a person who is authorised for the purposes of the Financial Services and Markets Act 2000.

10.43   Unlike other requirements in the Regulations,[24] the Regulations do not provide any sanction for failure to comply with the above-mentioned two requirements, but 'authorised persons' are, in any event, subject to the supervisory regime for the financial services industry under the FSMA, including the enforcement powers of the FSA as their regulator.[25]

Registration of other (relevant) persons

10.44   Relevant persons in other sectors will only be required to register if the relevant supervisory authority decides to maintain a register.

10.45   Regulation 32 gives a discretionary power to identified supervisory authorities (i.e. the FSA, the OFT, and the Commissioners), in order to fulfil their duties under Regulation 24, to maintain a register in relation to specified persons and, where such a register is maintained, requires the relevant supervisory authority to take reasonable steps to bring its decision to the attention of those relevant persons in respect of whom the register is to be established.

10.46   **The Financial Services Authority**   Under Regulation 32(2), the FSA may maintain a register of Annex I financial institutions.[26]

10.47   **The Office of Fair Trading**   Under Regulation 32(3), the OFT may maintain registers of consumer credit financial institutions[27] and estate agents.

10.48   **The Commissioners of Revenue and Customs**   The Commissioners may maintain registers of auditors, external accountants, and tax advisers, who are not supervised by the Secretary of State, DETI or any of the professional bodies listed in Schedule 3.

Requirement to be registered

10.49   Corresponding to the discretionary power to maintain registers given to the above supervisory authorities, there is—where that power is exercised—effectively a duty placed on relevant persons by Regulation 33 to ensure that they are registered:

> Where a supervisory authority decides to maintain a register under regulation 32 in respect of any description of relevant persons and establishes a register for that purpose, a relevant person of that description *may* not carry on the business or profession in question for a period of more than six months beginning on the date on which the supervisory authority establishes the register unless he is included in the register.

10.50   A person who fails to comply with the requirement is liable to a civil penalty or to prosecution in the criminal courts.[28]

Registers maintained by the Commissioners under Regulation 32

10.51   So far as registers maintained by the Commissioners pursuant to Regulation 32 are concerned, Regulation 34(1) confirms that Regulations 27, 29,[29] 30(2), 30(3), and 30(4) 'apply

---

[24]   Generally speaking, a person who fails to comply with a requirement under the Regulations is liable to a civil penalty or a prosecution in the criminal courts.

[25]   The term 'authorised person' has the meaning given to it in the FSMA. The General Prohibition imposed by the FSMA, s 19 states that no person may carry on a regulated activity in the UK, or purport to do so, unless he is: (a) an authorised person; or (b) an exempt person. Contravention of this general prohibition is a criminal offence punishable by up to two years imprisonment (FSMA, s 23).

[26]   As defined by Reg 22(1).

[27]   The term 'consumer credit financial institution' is defined in Reg 22(1).

[28]   See below: for civil penalties, para 10.110 and for criminal penalties, paras 10.118 *et seq.*

[29]   With the omission of the words 'Subject to regulation 28' in Reg 29(1).

to registration in a register maintained by the Commissioners under regulation 32 as they apply to registration in a register maintained under regulation 25'. It is important to note that Regulation 28, concerning the 'fit and proper' test, does not apply.[30]

Registers maintained by the Financial Services Authority or the OFT under Regulation 32

So far as registers maintained by the Financial Services Authority or the OFT pursuant to Regulation 32 are concerned, Regulation 34(2) confirms that Regulation 27 applies to registration in a register 'under regulation 32 as it applies to registration in a register maintained under regulation 25 and, for this purpose, references to the Commissioners are to be treated as references to the Authority or the OFT, as the case may be'. **10.52**

Regulation 34(3) sets out the only circumstances in which the Financial Services Authority or the OFT *may* refuse to register an applicant for registration in a register maintained under regulation 32,[31] namely if: **10.53**

- any requirement of, or imposed under, Regulation 27[32] has not been complied with;
- it appears to the Authority or the OFT, as the case may be, that any information provided pursuant to Regulation 27[33] is false or misleading in a material particular; or
- the applicant has failed to pay a charge imposed by the Authority or the OFT, as the case may be, under Regulation 35(1).

Regulation 34(4)–(6) set out detailed procedures that *must* be followed by the Financial Services Authority or the OFT in relation to notifying the applicant of the decision to register or the provisional decision not to register, making the final decision following a provisional decision, notifying the applicant of the final decision, and registering the applicant following a decision to register. **10.54**

Regulation 34(7) sets out the circumstances in which the Financial Services Authority or the OFT *may* cancel a person's registration, namely if, at any time after registration, it appears to them that they would have had grounds to refuse registration under Regulation 34(3). **10.55**

Regulation 34(8)–(10) set out detailed procedures that the Financial Services Authority or the OFT *must* follow in relation to notifying a registered person of the proposal to cancel their registration, making the final decision, and notifying the registered person of the final decision. **10.56**

Costs of supervision

The FSA, the OFT, and HMRC may impose charges on applicants for registration and on relevant persons supervised by them, which must not exceed such amount as they consider will enable them to meet any expenses reasonably incurred by them in carrying out their functions under the Regulations or for any incidental purpose. **10.57**

---

[30] Reg 28 sets out the circumstances in which the Commissioners *must* refuse to register an applicant as a money service business or trust or company service provider (but not if the application is by an applicant as a high-value dealer) because they are satisfied that a specified person is not a 'fit and proper person'.

[31] Reg 34(3), which is similar to Reg 29(1).

[32] Reg 34(11) states that 'references to regulation 27 are to be treated as references to that paragraph as applied by paragraph (2)' of Reg 34.

[33] Reg 34(11) states that 'references to regulation 27 are to be treated as references to that paragraph as applied by paragraph (2)' of Reg 34.

D. Enforcement: Introduction

Regulation and enforcement

10.58 Regulators and supervisors generally have wide powers to monitor, investigate, and discipline in order to fulfil their function of setting, maintaining and, where necessary, enforcing appropriate ethical and professional standards in the conduct of the businesses and professions that they regulate. In the context of anti-money laundering regulation, regulators and supervisors are in a position to play an important part, along with responsible industry and professional bodies, in heightening awareness and a sense of responsibility and in raising standards. A risk-based approach to money laundering and terrorist financing regulation makes greater demands on both the regulator and the regulated, but has the potential to achieve more than a rules-based and tick-box approach.

10.59 Where institutions and individuals in the regulated sector fail in their responsibilities under the regulations, regulators and supervisors are able to make use of a variety of enforcement powers, carrying with them significant sanctions, in order to mark and penalize inadequate performance and any failure to comply with the regulations. These include the civil and criminal sanctions under Part 5 of the Regulations.

10.60 The range of disciplinary, regulatory, and civil powers available to regulators and supervisors gives them flexibility in responding to inadequate performance by the application of appropriate sanctions. Many regulators also have the power to prosecute for criminal offences arising from a breach of regulations. The use of criminal sanctions in the context of money laundering regulation is something of a blunt instrument: prosecution for criminal offences provides an additional means of enforcement, but is, perhaps, best reserved for dealing with serious breaches of the regulations.

The enforcement structure and the scope of Part 5

10.61 The enforcement structure, (that is, collectively, the various supervisory authorities and their differing powers of investigation and available sanctions), is complicated because it reflects the disparate nature of the various businesses and professions that now comprise the regulated sector. Much of Part 5 of the Regulations is concerned with only part of the regulated sector and with certain powers of enforcement given to a limited number of supervisory authorities that are known as 'designated authorities'.

The scope of Part 5

10.62 Part 5 of the Regulations deals with three topics:

- the investigative powers of 'designated authorities' and of the officers of designated authorities;
- civil penalties imposed by designated authorities, together with provisions for the review of and appeal against civil penalties;
- criminal penalties: these provisions apply to all relevant persons and create a criminal offence of failure to comply with specific requirements of the Regulations, an offence which can be committed in more than 25 different ways.

Designated authorities

10.63 As noted above, not all supervisory authorities are designated authorities and the interpretation provisions in Regulation 36 are crucial to understanding both the scope of and the limitations on the investigative powers in the following sections. In Part 5, 'designated authority' means:

- the Authority (that is, the FSA);
- the Commissioners (that is, HMRC);
- the OFT; and
- (in relation to credit unions in Northern Ireland) the DETI.

The enforcement powers are given to officers of those agencies along with officers of the **10.64** local weights and measures authority (generally the local authority), albeit that officers of the local weights and measures authority may only act pursuant to an arrangement with the OFT.[34]

Officers and relevant officers

Under Regulation 36, the terms 'officer' and 'relevant officer' have specific and restricted **10.65** meanings:

'officer' , except in *regulations 40(3), 41* and *47* means—

(a) an officer of the Authority, including a member of the Authority's staff or an agent of the Authority;
(b) an officer of Revenue and Customs;
(c) an officer of the OFT;
(d) a relevant officer; or
(e) an officer of DETI acting for the purposes of its functions under these Regulations in relation to credit unions in Northern Ireland;

. . .

' relevant officer' means—

(a) in Great Britain, an officer of a local weights and measures authority;
(b) in Northern Ireland, an officer of DETI acting pursuant to arrangements made with the OFT for the purposes of these Regulations.

E. Enforcement: Investigative Powers

Introduction

Regulations 37 and 38 give investigative powers to 'officers' and 'relevant officers', as **10.66** defined in Regulation 36. These are officers of designated authorities or other specified authorities.

These are widely drawn powers, including a power of warrantless entry to premises, that are **10.67** stated to be applicable to 'relevant persons' and to 'connected persons' (see below). In practice, however, the powers are limited by provisions in Regulations 37 and 38 as to the purpose for which they can be used.

---

[34] The extension of powers of warrantless entry and inspection in Reg 38 to officers of local weights and measures authorities (now called 'trading standards'), who are referred to as 'relevant officers', might be considered surprising. At the time of writing, no arrangements with the OFT appear to have been made.

Power to require information from relevant and connected persons

10.68 Regulation 37(1) provides an officer with the power to require by notice a relevant person or a person connected with a relevant person[35] to provide information, produce recorded information, or attend before an officer and answer questions. However, pursuant to Regulation 37(3), an officer may exercise powers under Regulation 37 *only* if the information sought to be obtained as a result is reasonably required in connection with the exercise by the designated authority for whom he acts of its functions under the Regulations:

> (1) An officer may, by notice to a relevant person or to a person connected with a relevant person, require the relevant person or the connected person, as the case may be—
> (a) to provide such information as may be specified in the notice;
> (b) to produce such recorded information as may be so specified; or
> (c) to attend before an officer at a time and place specified in the notice and answer questions.
>
> ...
>
> (3) An officer may exercise powers under this regulation only if the information sought to be obtained as a result is reasonably required in connection with the exercise by the designated authority for whom he acts of its functions under these Regulations.

10.69 An officer, as defined in Regulation 36, has a power under section 37 to require a relevant person or a person connected with a relevant person to provide information, to produce recorded information or to attend and answer questions. This is a substantial investigative power akin to that given to the Serious Fraud Office under section 2 of the Criminal Justice Act 1987. In 1987 this was a major new investigative power granted to—and restricted to—the Serious Fraud Office that was set up by section 1 of the Act. The section 2 powers given to the Director of the SFO are exercisable '. . . only for the purposes of an investigation under section 1. . .', that is, the investigation of '. . . any suspected offence which appears to him on reasonable grounds to involve serious or complex fraud.'

10.70 In recent years, powers of this kind have been given to other criminal investigators, but Regulation 37 involves a significant extension of the use of such powers. Under this regulation, similar powers are given to officers of a variety of public bodies and may be exercised not only for the purposes of any investigation, but also for any purpose in connection with the regulatory function of the relevant designated authority, such as monitoring compliance.

Connected persons

10.71 Regulation 37(2) provides that: 'For the purposes of paragraph (1), a person is connected with a relevant person if he is, or has at any time been, in relation to the relevant person, a person listed in Schedule 4 to these Regulations.'

10.72 Connected persons include officers, managers, employees, and agents of the relevant person where the person is a body corporate and employees or agents of an individual relevant person.

---

[35] A person connected with a relevant person is defined in Reg 37(2) and Sch 4.

Where an officer requires information to be provided or produced, the notice to the relevant **10.73** person or connected person must set out the reasons why the officer requires the information to be provided or produced. The information must be provided or produced before the end of 'such reasonable period as may be specified in the notice', and at the place specified in the notice. Where information is recorded otherwise than in legible form, there is a power to require the production of a copy of it in legible form or in a form from which it can readily be produced in visible and legible form.

Legal professional privilege

Under section 37(7) a person may not be required to provide or produce information or to **10.74** answer questions which he would be entitled to refuse on grounds of legal professional privilege in proceedings in the High Court, except that a lawyer may be required to provide the name and address of his client:

> (7) A person may not be required under this regulation to provide or produce information or to answer questions which he would be entitled to refuse to provide, produce or answer on grounds of legal professional privilege in proceedings in the High Court, except that a lawyer may be required to provide the name and address of his client.

Use of a compelled statement in evidence

Subject to the exception in relation to criminal proceedings noted below, Regulation 37(8) **10.75** provides that a statement made by a person who has been required to attend and answer questions '. . . is admissible in evidence in any proceedings, so long as it also complies with any requirements governing the admissibility of evidence in the circumstances in question'.

In criminal proceedings in which a person is charged with an offence (other than an offence **10.76** of perjury or other offence involving a false statement), no evidence relating to the statement may be adduced and no question relating to it may be asked, by or on behalf of the Prosecution, unless evidence relating to it is adduced or a question relating to it is asked, in the proceedings, by or on behalf of that person.[36] This is essentially the same as the position that applies where a person has been questioned by the SFO under section 2 of the Criminal Justice Act 1987, and similar statutory regimes, so as to preserve the privilege against self-incrimination.[37]

Failure to comply with information requirement

Where it appears to the court[38] that a person (the 'information defaulter') has failed to do **10.77** something that he was required to do under Regulation 37(1), Regulation 40(1) gives the court the power to make an order that may require the information defaulter to do the thing that he failed to do within such period as may be specified in the order; or otherwise to take such steps to remedy the consequences of the failure as may be so specified. However, such an order can only be made on an application made by a designated authority or by a local weights and measures authority or DETI (pursuant to arrangements made with the OFT by or on behalf of the authority or by DETI). If the court makes an order and the person fails

---

[36] Reg 37(9) and (10).
[37] See *Saunders v* UK (1997) 23 EHRR 313.
[38] For the purposes of Reg 40(4), 'court' means (a) in England and Wales and Northern Ireland, the High Court or the county court; (b) in Scotland, the Court of Session or the sheriff court.

to comply with the requirements of that order, it may be a contempt of court, for which ultimately that person could be committed to prison.

10.78   If the information defaulter is a body corporate, a partnership or an unincorporated body of persons which is not a partnership, the order may require any officer[39] of the body corporate, partnership, or body, who is (wholly or partly) responsible for the failure to meet such costs of the application as are specified in the order.

Intrusive investigation powers

10.79   Regulations 38 and 39 make provision for an officer, as defined in Regulation 36, to *enter and inspect* premises without a warrant (under section 38) or to *enter and search* with the authority of a warrant (under Regulation 39). Regulation 38, therefore, provides a power of warrantless entry to premises without notice, but the exact scope of the power of 'inspection' is not clear. Regulation 39 provides for the issue of a warrant to search premises in two different situations, the second of which (under Regulation 39(5)) is widely drawn and its ambit is not wholly free from doubt.

Entry and inspection without a warrant

10.80   Regulation 38(1) provides an officer with powers of entry and inspection, as follows:

> (1) Where an officer has reasonable cause to believe that any premises are being used by a relevant person in connection with his business or professional activities, he may on producing evidence of his authority at any reasonable time—
> (a) enter the premises;
> (b) inspect the premises;
> (c) observe the carrying on of business or professional activities by the relevant person;
> (d) inspect any recorded information found on the premises;
> (e) require any person on the premises to provide an explanation of any recorded information or to state where it may be found;
> (f) in the case of a money service business or a high value dealer, inspect any cash found on the premises.

10.81   There are a number of features about the nature and extent of these intrusive powers that should be noted. The power to enter and inspect is given not to a law enforcement officer as such, but to 'an officer' as defined in Regulation 36—see above at paragraph 10.65. The power, therefore, may be exercised by trained law enforcement officers or by other officers of designated authorities (as well as officers of a local weights and measures authority), who lack such training and experience. This power is given not in respect of any suspicion or belief of criminal or other unlawful conduct, but simply on the much wider basis that the premises in question are being used by a relevant person for his business or professional activities.

Entry to 'any premises' used by 'a relevant person'

10.82   Regulation 38(1) allows the power to be exercised in respect of any premises being used by a relevant person.

---

[39]   Reg 40(3). Note that in these circumstances, 'officer' does *not* mean 'officer' as defined by Reg 36.

- 'any premises': in this Regulation, the natural meaning of the phrase is qualified[40] and means '. . . any premises other than premises used *only* as a dwelling' (emphasis added). In the contemporary world—with sophisticated communications and the widespread use of laptops and other portable devices—this provision may offer only scant protection for a person's home.
- 'a relevant person': subject to the provisions of Regulation 38(4), it seems that the power to enter and inspect can be used in respect of *any* relevant person and is not restricted to being exercised in relation to relevant persons in the businesses or profession supervised by the designated authority on behalf of which the officer is acting or, even, in a business or profession supervised by a designated authority.

Pursuant to Regulation 38(4), an officer may exercise powers under Regulations 38(1) and 38(2) *only* if the information sought to be obtained as a result is reasonably required in connection with the exercise by the designated authority for whom he acts of its functions under the Regulations. **10.83**

Under Regulation 38(1)(d), an officer may require any person on the premises to provide an explanation of or the location of any document or other recorded information. It is suggested that any such requirement by an officer should be restricted strictly to an explanation or to information reasonably sufficient to enable the inspection to be effective. It is clearly important that any questioning involved does not go beyond those bounds and become an informal interview conducted without appropriate safeguards. **10.84**

Regulation 38 includes a power for an officer to take copies of, or make extracts from, any recorded information found in the course of an inspection.[41] **10.85**

Legal professional privilege

There is in Regulation 38 a saving provision for legal professional privilege. **10.86**

> (3) Paragraphs (1)(d) and (e) and (2) do not apply to recorded information which the relevant person would be entitled to refuse to disclose on grounds of legal professional privilege in proceedings in the High Court, except that a lawyer may be required to provide the name and address of his client and, for this purpose, regulation 37(11) applies to this paragraph as it applies to regulation 37(7).
> (4) An officer may exercise powers under this regulation only if the information sought to be obtained as a result is reasonably required in connection with the exercise by the designated authority for whom he acts of its functions under these Regulations.
> (5) In this regulation, 'premises' means any premises other than premises used only as a dwelling.

Entry to premises under warrant

Regulation 39 provides that a justice may issue a warrant '. . . if satisfied on information on oath given by an officer that there are reasonable grounds for believing . . .' that one of three sets of conditions, in paragraphs (2), (3), and (4), is satisfied. **10.87**

---

[40] Reg 38(5).
[41] Reg 38(2).

The first set of conditions

10.88 Under Regulation 39(2) there are two conditions, both of which need to be satisfied. The first condition is that there is on the premises specified in the warrant 'recorded information' in relation to which a requirement could be imposed under Regulation 37(1)(b) to produce such specified recorded information. The second condition is that, if such a requirement for production were to be imposed, either it would not be complied with or the recorded information to which it relates would be removed, tampered with, or destroyed.

The second set of conditions

10.89 The second set of conditions also relates to the circumstances of an order to produce recorded information. There are two conditions, both of which need to be satisfied. The first condition is that a person who has been given notice to produce specified recorded information '. . . has failed (wholly or in part) to comply with it'. The second condition is that there is on the premises specified in the warrant recorded information which has been required to be produced.

The third set of conditions

10.90 These conditions can only apply where there has been an exercise or attempted exercise of the power to enter premises without a warrant under Regulation 38. There are two conditions, both of which need to be satisfied. The first condition is that an officer has been obstructed in the exercise of a power under Regulation 38 and the second condition is that there is on the premises specified in the warrant 'recorded information or cash which could be inspected under regulation 38(1)(d) or (f)'.

10.91 Regulation 38(1)(d) allows an officer lawfully exercising a right of entry under Regulation 38 to inspect any recorded information found on the premises; Regulation 38(1)(f) relates only to cases where the premises entered and inspected are those of a money service business or a high-value dealer. In either of these cases, an officer lawfully acting under Regulation 38 may also inspect any cash found on the premises.

The warrant to enter and search

10.92 In summary, a justice may issue such a warrant under Regulation 39 if satisfied on information on oath given by an officer that there are reasonable grounds for believing that:

- there is on the premises specified in the warrant recorded information in relation to which a requirement could be imposed under *Regulation 37(1)(b)* and, if such a requirement were to be imposed, it would not be complied with or the recorded information to which it relates would be removed, tampered with or destroyed; or
- a person on whom a requirement has been imposed under *Regulation 37(1)(b)* has failed (wholly or in part) to comply with it and there is on the premises specified in the warrant recorded information which has been required to be produced; or
- an officer has been obstructed in the exercise of a power under *Regulation 38* and there is on the premises specified in the warrant recorded information or cash which could be inspected under *Regulation 38(1)(d)* or *(f)*.

A warrant under Regulation 39(5)

10.93 In addition, a justice may issue a warrant if satisfied on information on oath given by an officer that there are reasonable grounds for suspecting that an offence under the Regulations has been, is being, or is about to be committed by a relevant person and there is on the premises specified in the warrant recorded information relevant to whether that offence has been, or is being, or is about to be committed.

It should be noted that the limitation on the exercise of powers by an 'officer', as defined in **10.94** Regulation 36, (that the officer may exercise powers under Regulations 37 and 38 only if the information sought to be obtained as a result is reasonably required in connection with the exercise by the designated authority for whom he acts of its functions under these regulations), is effectively imported into the three alternative conditions which permit a justice to issue a warrant under Regulation 39(1).

However, no such limitation applies in respect of a warrant that a justice may issue under **10.95** Regulation 39(5). A warrant under Regulation 39(5) may be issued by a justice to an officer as defined in Regulation 36, not only in respect of relevant persons engaged in the business for which their employer is the supervisory authority, but any relevant person under the Regulations:[42]

> (5) A justice may issue a warrant under this paragraph if satisfied on information on oath given by an officer that there are reasonable grounds for suspecting that—
> > (a) an offence under these Regulations has been, is being or is about to be committed by a relevant person; and
> > (b) there is on the premises specified in the warrant recorded information relevant to whether that offence has been, or is being or is about to be committed.

In this context, it should be noted that Regulation 39(5) provides for the granting of a war- **10.96** rant (in similar broad terms to that of the grant of a warrant to a constable under the Police and Criminal Evidence Act), to a wide variety of civil servants, public servants, and others who may come within the definition of 'officer'. These include not only officers of Revenue & Customs, but officers of a local weights and measures authority and members of staff of the FSA and agents of the FSA.

There is, however, a specific limitation relating to the execution of a warrant obtained by the **10.97** FSA. Regulation 39(7) provides that where a warrant is issued by a justice under paragraph 1 or 5 of Regulation 39 on the basis of information on oath given by an officer of the Authority, the execution of the warrant, that is the entry to and search of premises and so forth that is authorised by the warrant, must be undertaken by a constable.

Regulation 39(6) sets out what an officer is authorised to do under a warrant: **10.98**

> (6) A warrant issued under this regulation shall authorise an officer—
> > (a) to enter the premises specified in the warrant;
> > (b) to search the premises and take possession of any recorded information or anything appearing to be recorded information specified in the warrant or to take, in relation to any such recorded information, any other steps which may appear to be necessary for preserving it or preventing interference with it;
> > (c) to take copies of, or extracts from, any recorded information specified in the warrant;

---

[42] Whether it would be appropriate might be a different matter. It is suggested that it would only be appropriate for an 'officer' to apply for a warrant in respect of a suspected offence under the Regulations by a relevant person supervised by the designated authorities for which the officer acts.

(d) to require any person on the premises to provide an explanation of any recorded information appearing to be of the kind specified in the warrant or to state where it may be found;

(e) to use such force as may reasonably be necessary.

Legal professional privilege

10.99 It should be noted that there is no specific provision in Regulation 39 in relation to legal professional privilege as there is, for instance, in sections 8(1)(d) and (10) of the Police and Criminal Evidence Act 1984. It may be that the exceptions in respect of privileged material in Regulations 37 and 38 are effectively imported into Regulation 39(1) by the three sets of conditions in Regulation 39(2) to (4). However, if that is so in respect of Regulation 39(1), it would not also apply to Regulation 39(5). For the reasons noted below, however, it is submitted that Regulation 39 should be read as subject to common law LPP, that is that 'items subject to legal privilege' should be excluded from the scope of any warrant issued under Regulation 39.

10.100 An important issue in the case of *Bowman v Fels* concerned the absence from section 328 of POCA of any provision restricting the requirement[43] to make an authorised disclosure with regard to items subject to legal privilege. In his judgment, Brookes LJ expressed the firm opinion of the court that LPP could only be excluded from section 328 (so as to oblige a solicitor to make a disclosure) if the intention of Parliament to exclude it could be demonstrated by '. . . clear words or necessary implication'.[44] In that case the court found neither condition for exclusion applied in relation to section 328 of POCA. That argument would, it is suggested, be all the stronger in relation to provisions in a piece of secondary legislation introduced by statutory instrument.[45]

Powers of 'relevant officers'

10.101 Regulation 41 provides limitations on the exercise of powers by 'relevant officers', as defined in Regulation 36. It is perhaps surprising that it was considered appropriate to grant the extensive powers in Part 5 of the Regulations to officers of local weights and measures authorities. In any event, Regulation 41 stipulates that a relevant officer may only exercise the investigatory powers under Regulations 37 to 39 pursuant to arrangements made with the OFT:

(a) by or on behalf of the local weights and measures authority of which he is an officer ("his authority"); or

(b) by DETI.

---

[43] Effectively a requirement, but strictly there is never a legal requirement to make an authorised disclosure, only a need to do so in order to avoid the risk of prosecution and possible imprisonment. See Chapter 5 at paras 5.24–5.26.

[44] [2005] EWCA Civ 226. See, in particular, part 11 of the judgment and paras 87 to 90 in part 13 of the judgment.

[45] Compare also the position under POCA warrants under s 352 which are subject to the provisions protecting privileged material from seizure in s 354.

F. Enforcement: Civil Penalties

Introduction

Sanctions for breach of the Regulations

Regulations 42 to 47 inclusive set out the provisions for civil and criminal penalties that may **10.102** be imposed for failure to comply with specified requirements of the Regulations. The criminal penalties are generally applicable to all relevant persons, but the civil penalties are applicable only to those relevant person supervised by one of the designated authorities.[46]

Civil and criminal penalties: background

As has been noted above, the various requirements in the Regulations that relevant **10.103** persons must comply with are derived closely from the Third Money Laundering Directive. In Article 39 of the Third Directive there is a general statement of the approach that member states should take in relation to sanctions for breach of the requirements when translated into domestic law. It is worth noting that the emphasis in paragraph 2 of Article 39 is on 'administrative penalties' (which may be taken to refer to regulatory sanctions) rather than criminal penalties:

Article 39

1. Member States shall ensure that natural and legal persons covered by this Directive can be held liable for infringements of the national provisions adopted pursuant to this Directive. The penalties must be effective, proportionate and dissuasive.
2. Without prejudice to the right of Member States to impose criminal penalties, Member States shall ensure, in conformity with their national law, that the appropriate administrative measures can be taken or administrative sanctions can be imposed against credit and financial institutions for infringements of the national provisions adopted pursuant to this Directive. Member States shall ensure that these measures or sanctions are effective, proportionate and dissuasive.

Civil penalties: enforcement by 'designated authorities'

Regulations 42 to 44 inclusive deal with the regime of civil penalties and the related review **10.104** and appeal procedures. The powers of civil enforcement are given to *designated authorities* only.[47]

The power to impose civil penalties

The Regulations give to designated authorities a power to impose civil penalties.[48] Regulation **10.105** 42(1) provides that a designated authority may impose a penalty of such amount as it considers appropriate on a relevant person who fails to comply with any requirement in Regulation 7(1), (2) or (3), 8(1) or (3), 9(2), 10(1), 11(1), 14(1), 15(1) or (2), 16(1), (2), (3) or (4), 19(1), (4), (5) or (6), 20(1), (4) or (5), 21, 26, 27(4) or 33, or a direction made under Regulation 18 and, for this purpose, 'appropriate' means effective, proportionate, and dissuasive.

---

[46] On designated authorities and their powers, see paras 10.63–10.65 above.
[47] Note that not all supervisory authorities are designated authorities: see Reg 36 and para 10.63 above.
[48] Reg 42(1).

10.106 A designated authority may impose a penalty of such amount as it considers appropriate on a relevant person who fails to comply with any requirements in the Regulations or with a direction made under Regulation 18, as specified in Regulation 42(1).

10.107 A civil penalty under Regulation 42(1) may be imposed on 'a relevant person': the wording of the regulation does not restrict the exercise of the power to a relevant person who is supervised by one of the designated authorities. It is suggested that, in practice, the power should only be used in this way.[49]

The 'due diligence' limitation

10.108 Regulation 42(2) contains an important provision which operates as a bar to imposing a civil penalty and which reflects the broad aim of the Regulations to ensure that relevant persons are vigilant and conscientious in applying the measures intended to prevent and detect money laundering:

> (2) The designated authority must not impose a penalty on a person under paragraph (1) where there are reasonable grounds for it to be satisfied—an objective test—that the person took all reasonable steps and exercised all due diligence to ensure that the requirement would be complied with.

10.109 The designated authorities must comply with the terms of Regulation 42 in imposing a penalty, including giving the relevant person an opportunity to make representations.

Civil penalties for failure to comply

10.110 As set out above, the Regulations place a large number of mandatory requirements on a relevant person. Under Regulation 42(1), a relevant person who fails to comply with any one of a number of identified requirements, or a direction made under Regulation 18, may be made the subject of a civil penalty by a designated authority. The size of the penalty is unlimited, but must be of such amount as the designated authority considers appropriate (i.e. effective, proportionate, and dissuasive).

Guidance to relevant persons

10.111 Regulation 42(3) makes it clear that, in deciding whether a person has failed to comply with a requirement of the Regulations, 'the designated authority must consider whether he followed any relevant guidance', which was at the time issued by a supervisory authority or any other appropriate body;[50] approved by the Treasury; and published in a manner approved by the Treasury as suitable in their opinion to bring the guidance to the attention of persons likely to be affected by it:

> (3) In deciding whether a person has failed to comply with a requirement of these Regulations, the designated authority must consider whether he followed any relevant guidance which was at the time—
> (a) issued by a supervisory authority or any other appropriate body;
> (b) approved by the Treasury; and
> (c) published in a manner approved by the Treasury as suitable in their opinion to bring the guidance to the attention of persons likely to be affected by it.

---

[49] Any wider use of this power by a designated authority would cut across the responsibilities of the supervisory authority actually responsible for supervision of the relevant person in question.

[50] Reg 42(4) confirms that an 'appropriate body' means any body which regulates or is representative of any trade, profession, business, or employment carried on by the person.

Table 10.3 lists the Guidance that has been approved by the Treasury.[51]   **10.112**

Table 10.3 Anti-money laundering guidance approved by the Treasury

Body	Scope
Joint Money Laundering Steering Group (JMLSG)	'Prevention of money laundering/combating terrorist financing. Guidance for the UK Financial Sector':[52] prepared by JMLSG, is addressed to firms in the industry sectors represented by its member bodies (the British Bankers Association and 30 other bodies representing financial institutions), and to those firms regulated by the FSA. All such firms, including those which are members of JMLSG trade associations but not regulated by the FSA, and those regulated by the FSA which are not members of JMLSG trade associations—should have regard to the contents of the guidance. The Law Society of Scotland encourages its members to have regard to the JMLSG guidance. The Treasury is in the process of approving a revised version at the time of writing.
Consultative Committee of Accountancy Bodies (CCAB)	'Anti-Money Laundering Guidance for the Accountancy Sector':[53] for all entities providing audit, accountancy, tax advisory, insolvency, or related services, such as trust and company services, by way of business, issued on behalf of the Institute of Chartered Accountants in England and Wales, the Institute of Chartered Accountants of Scotland, the Institute of Chartered Accountants in Ireland, the Association of Chartered Certified Accountants, the Chartered Institute of Management Accountants, and the Chartered Institute of Public Finance and Accountancy.
Her Majesty's Revenue and Customs (HMRC)	Detailed sector-specific guidance addressed to proprietors, directors, managers, employees, and nominated officers of the following businesses that are the subject of the Money Laundering Regulations 2007 (MLR 2007) and for whom HMRC is the supervisory authority:[54] • money service businesses (MSBs); • high-value dealers (HVDs); • trust or company service providers (TCSPs).
Office of Fair Trading (OFT)	'Guidance for estate agents and consumer credit financial institutions.'[55]
Gambling Commission	'Prevention of money laundering and combating the financing of terrorism—guidance for remote and non-remote casinos.'[56]
Auditing Practices Board (part of the Financial Reporting Council)	Guidance for auditors is available on the Financial Reporting Council website.[57] The Treasury is in the process of approving a revised version at the time of writing.
Notaries Society/Society of Scrivener Notaries	Guidance for notaries is available via, for instance, the Scrivener Notaries website.[58]
The Law Society	The anti-money laundering practice note[59] is intended to help solicitors comply with POCA, TA 2000 and the Regulations and all amending legislation. It also details good practice. The Law Society of Northern Ireland has also adopted the note.

---

[51] On guidance approved by HM Treasury, see Chapter 6 above, at paras 6.35–6.38.
[52] See <http://www.jmlsg.org.uk/>.
[53] See <http://www.ccab.org.uk under Press and Publications>.
[54] The new sector-specific guidance is only available on the HMRC website. See, for MSBs: <http://www.hmrc.gov.uk/mlr/mlr_msb.pdf>; for HVDs: <http://www.hmrc.gov.uk/mlr/mlr_hvd.pdf>; and for TCSPs: <http://www.hmrc.gov.uk/mlr/mlr_tcsp.pdf>.
[55] <http://www.oft.gov.uk/shared_oft/business_leaflets/general/oft954.pdf>.
[56] See <http://www.gamblingcommission.gov.uk/>.
[57] <http://www.frc.org.uk/apb/publications/practice.cfm>.
[58] <http://www.scrivener-notaries.org.uk/links.php>.
[59] <http://www.lawsociety.org.uk/productsandservices/practicenotes/aml.page>.

10.113 The Regulations specify the policies which relevant person must implement; relevant guidance suggests ways in which those policies may be drawn up and what, in practice, they might stipulate. They also provide advice and assistance on how specific requirements of the Regulations should be satisfied, including dealing with difficult aspects of interpretation and implementation of the Regulations, such as 'reliance' and 'equivalence' or the identification of PEPs. It remains the responsibility of the relevant person, however, to determine the policies that they in fact implement.

10.114 A relevant person is not bound by the terms of relevant guidance but departures from the guidance, and the rationale for so doing, should be documented, and firms will have to stand prepared to justify departures to their supervisory authority or the court.

Review of civil penalties and appeals

Civil penalties procedure

10.115 The procedure for challenging penalties imposed under Regulation 42 is set out in Regulations 43 and 44. There are two different procedures: (1) relating to *decisions* made by the Commissioners for HMRC to impose a penalty; and (2) relating to *proposals* by the FSA, or the OFT, or the DETI in Northern Ireland to impose a penalty.

10.116 A decision made by the Commissioners can be (1) referred back to the Commissioners for review; and/or (2) appealed to a tribunal. When the relevant person is notified by the Commissioners of their decision to impose a penalty, and their reason for imposing a penalty, the person must also be given notice of his/her rights to review and/or to appeal the decision. There is a time limit of 30 days from the date of notice for accepting the review or making an appeal, although there are a number of exceptions to this time limit. The person cannot review and appeal a decision simultaneously but he/she can review a decision and, if that is unfavourable, subsequently appeal the decision to the tribunal, providing that various conditions are met. On review or appeal, the original decision by the Commissioners can be confirmed, varied or withdrawn. On appeal, the tribunal can vary or quash any decision and substitute their own decision for any decision it quashes.

10.117 If the designated authority is the FSA, the OFT, or the DETI, it must give the person notice of the *proposal* to impose the penalty and the proposed amount, the reasons for imposing the penalty, and the right to make representations within a specified period (which may not be less than 28 days). On the expiry of this period, and after consideration of any representations made, the designated authority must then decide within a reasonable period whether to impose a penalty under this regulation. If a penalty is not imposed, the designated authority must give the person notice of this decision. If a penalty is imposed, as well as giving notice of the penalty and the amount, the designated authority must also give the person notice of the reasons for its decision and of the right to appeal. An appeal of a decision by the FSA or the OFT is to a tribunal; an appeal of a decision by the DETI is to the High Court.

G. Enforcement: Criminal Penalties

The criminal offences

10.118 Regulation 45 sets out the offence of failing to comply with the requirements of the Regulations. It covers all the significant obligations placed on relevant persons, including those relating to customer due diligence measures, record-keeping, training, and the establishment and maintenance of adequate and appropriate systems, policies and procedures to prevent money laundering and terrorist financing:

45.— Offences[60]

(1) A person who fails to comply with any requirement in regulation 7(1), (2) or (3), 8(1) or (3), 9(2), 10(1), 11(1)(a), (b) or (c), 14(1), 15(1) or (2), 16(1), (2), (3) or (4), 19(1), (4), (5) or (6), 20(1), (4) or (5), 21, 26, 27(4) or 33, or a direction made under regulation 18, is guilty of an offence and liable—
  (a) on summary conviction, to a fine not exceeding the statutory maximum;
  (b) on conviction on indictment, to imprisonment for a term not exceeding two years, to a fine or to both.

. . .

(4) A person is not guilty of an offence under this regulation if he took all reasonable steps and exercised all due diligence to avoid committing the offence.
(5) Where a person is convicted of an offence under this regulation, he shall not also be liable to a penalty under regulation 42.

Conviction under the Regulations can incur up to two years' imprisonment and/or an unlimited fine. **10.119**

Guidance

As in Regulation 42 concerning civil penalties[61] there is a provision in Regulation 45(3) **10.120** requiring a court before whom a person is prosecuted, in deciding whether a person has committed an offence, to consider whether he followed any relevant guidance that was:

  (a) issued by a supervisory authority or any other appropriate body;[62]
  (b) approved by the Treasury; and
  (c) published in a manner approved by the Treasury as suitable in their opinion to bring the guidance to the attention of persons likely to be affected by it.

The criminal offences

The four tables, Tables 10.4 to 10.7 below, set out in summary form the substance of the 'offences' **10.121** under Regulation 45. Strictly, there is only a single offence which can be committed in numerous different ways. These all relate to a failure by a relevant person to comply with an obligation in one of the regulations, except for the provision in Regulation 18 (see Chapter 9 at paragraph 9.114). This does not create an obligation on relevant persons, but gives to the Treasury a power to issue directions and the offence consists of a failure to comply with any such direction.[63]

Table 10.4: failure to comply with Regulations 7 to 11 inclusive in Part 2.

Table 10.4 contains the mandatory requirements relating to CDD and ongoing monitoring **10.122** that are contained in Regulations 7 to 11 inclusive. A failure to comply with any of these requirements constitutes a criminal offence.

---

[60] The title/heading of the regulation refers to 'offences' in the plural, but Reg 45(1) would seem to create a single offence of non-compliance which can be committed in many different ways.
[61] In Reg 42(3): see para 10.111 above.
[62] Reg 45(3): in para (2), an 'appropriate body' means any body which regulates or is representative of any trade, profession, business, or employment carried on by the alleged offender.
[63] See Chapter 9 at para 9.114.

Table 10.4 Failure to comply with Regulations 7 to 11 inclusive in Part 2

Regulation 7	
7(1)	The requirement in Regulation 7(1) to apply customer measures *when* a relevant person establishes a business relationship, carries out an occasional transaction, suspects money laundering or terrorist financing, and doubts the veracity or adequacy of documents, data or information previously obtained for the purposes of identification or verification.
7(2)	The requirement in Regulation 7(2) to apply customer due diligence measures 'at other appropriate times' to existing customers on a risk-sensitive basis.
7(3)	The requirement in Regulation 7(3) to determine the extent of customer due diligence measures on a risk-sensitive basis depending on the type of customer, business relationship, product or transaction; and to be able to demonstrate to his supervisory authority that the extent of the measures is appropriate in view of the risks of money laundering and terrorist financing.
Regulation 8	
8(1)	The requirement in Regulation 8(1) to conduct ongoing monitoring of a business relationship.
8(3)	The requirement in Regulation 8(3) to determine the extent of ongoing monitoring on a risk-sensitive basis depending on the type of customer, business relationship, product, or transaction; and to be able to demonstrate to his supervisory authority that the extent of the ongoing monitoring is appropriate in view of the risks of money laundering and terrorist financing.
Regulation 9	
9(2)	The requirement in Regulation 9(2) to verify the identity of the customer (and any beneficial owner) *before* the establishment of the business relationship or the carrying out of the occasional transaction.
Regulation 10	
10(1)	The requirement on a casino in Regulation 10(1) to establish and verify the identity of all customers to whom the casino makes facilities for gaming available before entry to any premises where such facilities are provided or, where the facilities are for remote gaming, before access is given to such facilities. Alternatively, if the 'specified conditions' are met, a casino must establish and verify the identity of all customers who, in the course of any period of 24 hours 'purchase from, or exchange with, the casino chips with a total value of 2,000 Euro or more'; 'pay the casino 2,000 Euro or more for the use of gaming machines'; or 'pay to, or stake with, the casino 2,000 Euro or more in connection with facilities for remote gaming'.
Regulation 11	
11(1)(a)–(c)	The requirements in Regulation 11(1)(a)–(c) that where customer due diligence measures cannot be applied to a customer, a relevant person must not transact through a bank account, establish a business relationship, or carry out an occasional transaction and must terminate any existing business relationship.

10.123 Note that, with regard to Regulation 11, it is only a criminal offence to fail to comply with the requirements of 11(1)(a), (b), or (c). The civil penalty provisions apply, with respect to those relevant persons supervised by designated authorities, to all the same requirements as the criminal provisions, but also apply to a failure to comply with Regulation (11)(1)(d).

Table 10.5: failure to comply with Regulations 14 to 16 inclusive in Part 2

10.124 Table 10.5 contains the mandatory requirements relating to enhanced CDD and enhanced ongoing monitoring contained in Regulation 14 and further mandatory requirements in

Regulations 15 and 16. A failure to comply with any of these requirements constitutes a criminal offence.

Table 10.5 Failure to comply with Regulations 14 to 16 inclusive in Part 2

Regulation 14	
14(1)	The requirement in Regulation 14(1) to conduct on a risk-sensitive basis enhanced customer due diligence measures and enhanced ongoing monitoring where a customer has not been physically present for identification purposes, a credit institution has or proposes to have a correspondent banking relationship with a respondent institution, a relevant person proposes to have a business relationship or carry out an occasional transaction with a politically exposed person, or in any other situation which presents a higher risk of money laundering or terrorist financing.
Regulation 15	
15(1)	The requirement in Regulation 15(1) that a credit or financial institution demands equivalent measures in respect of customer due diligence, ongoing monitoring, and record-keeping in its branches and subsidiary undertakings located in non-EEA states, to the extent permitted by local law.
15(2)	The requirement in Regulation 15(2) that a credit or financial institution informs its supervisory authority and takes additional measures to handle the risk of money laundering and terrorist financing, where the law of a non-EEA state does not permit the application of equivalent standards of customer due diligence, ongoing monitoring, and record-keeping to branches and subsidiaries.
Regulation 16	
16(1)	The requirement in Regulation 16(1) that a credit institution must not enter or continue a corresponding banking relationship with a shell bank.
16(2)	The requirement in Regulation 16(2) that a credit institution applies measures to ensure that it does not enter or continue a corresponding banking relationship with a bank that permits accounts to be used by a shell bank.
16(3)	The requirement in Regulation 16(3) that a UK credit or financial institution does not set up an anonymous account/passbook for new or existing customers.
16(4)	The requirement in Regulation 16(4) that, as soon as is reasonably practicable from the 15 December 2007, UK credit and financial institutions apply customer due diligence and ongoing monitoring to anonymous accounts/passbooks existing on that date and before such accounts/passbooks are used.

Table 10.6: failure to comply with Regulations 19 to 21 inclusive in Part 3

Table 10.6 contains the mandatory requirements relating to record-keeping, policies and **10.125** procedures, and training in Part 3 of the Regulations. A failure to comply with any of these requirements constitutes a criminal offence. These requirements, particularly those relating to policies and procedures, are of a more general nature than the detailed requirements relating to CDD and the offence of failing to comply with these requirements is particularly relevant to the wider obligations of senior managers, directors, and partners (see the provisions of Regulation 47 below).

Table 10.6 Failure to comply with Regulations 19 to 21 inclusive in Part 3

Regulation 19	
19(1)	The requirement in Regulation 19(1) that a relevant person keeps the records evidencing a customer's identity and supporting documents in respect of the business or an occasional transaction, which is the focus of customer due diligence or ongoing monitoring, for five years.
19(4)	The requirement in Regulation 19(4) that where a relevant person is relied upon by another person, in respect of any business relationship or occasional transaction, he keeps the records evidencing a customer's identity for five years from the date upon which he is relied on.
19(5)	The requirement in Regulation 19(5) that the persons listed in Regulations 17(2)(a) and (b), for example a financial institution which is an authorised person or an auditor who is a relevant person, provide access to any customer information and any identification and verification data obtained through the application of customer due diligence measures, when a request is made by a relevant person relying upon them within the period of five years from the beginning of such reliance.
19(6)	The requirement in Regulation 19(6) that where a relevant person relies on a 'third party' listed in Regulations 17(2)(c) and (d) to conduct customer due diligence measures, he must act to ensure that such third party will, on request within the period of five years from the beginning of such reliance, provide access to the information described in the note to Regulation 19(5) above.
Regulation 20	
20(1)	The requirement in Regulation 20(1) that a relevant person establishes and maintains appropriate risk-sensitive policies and procedures in order to prevent activities related to money laundering and terrorist financing.
20(4)	The requirement in Regulation 20(4) that a credit or financial institution establishes and maintains systems that facilitate full and rapid responses to enquiries as to whether it maintains, or has maintained during the past five years, a business relationship with any person, and the nature of that relationship.
20(5)	The requirement in Regulation 20(5) that a credit or financial institution makes appropriate communications of risk-sensitive policies and procedures described in Regulation 20 to branches and subsidiary undertakings located outside the UK.
Regulation 21	
	The requirement in Regulation 21 that a relevant person takes appropriate measures to teach all relevant employees the law relating to money laundering and terrorist financing, and to train them to recognize activities which may be related to money laundering and terrorist financing.

Table 10.7: failure to comply with Regulations 26, 27, and 33 in Part 4

10.126 Table 10.7 contains the mandatory requirements relating to registration and the provision of information to a supervisory authority that are contained in Regulations 26, 27, and 33. A failure to comply with any of these requirements, which only apply to a limited number of relevant persons, constitutes a criminal offence.

Table 10.7 Failure to comply with Regulations 26, 27, and 33 in Part 4

Regulation 26	The requirement in Regulation 26 that, unless they are included in a register of the Commissioners, persons must not act as: high-value dealers; money service businesses; trust or company service providers; bill payment service providers; or telecommunication, digital, and IT payment service providers.
Regulation 27(4)[64]	The requirement in Regulation 27(4) that where there is a material change or inaccuracy in the information provided to the Commissioners in respect of an application to be included in a register, the applicant must provide details of the change or correction within 30 days from the date of the change or discovery of the inaccuracy, or within such later time as agreed with the Commissioners.
Regulation 33	The requirement that where a supervisory authority exercises its power to maintain a register of relevant persons, a relevant person of that description may not carry on the business or profession in question for a period of more than six months from the date of establishment of the register, unless he is included in the register.

Prosecution of offences

Regulation 46 lists the bodies that are given authority to prosecute offences under Regulation 45. It is something of a mixed bag: it includes independent prosecuting authorities[65] (the Director of Public Prosecutions and the Director of Public Prosecutions for Northern Ireland) as well as government departments and even local authorities. The offence under Regulation 45 is a serious criminal offence which is triable on indictment and carries a maximum penalty of two years imprisonment.   **10.127**

It must be questionable whether, 25 years after the setting up of an independent national prosecuting authority,[66] the power to prosecute such offences (and with it the discretion to review cases and make prosecution decisions) should still be exercised by bodies, whether government departments or local authorities, which have potentially conflicting executive responsibilities and cannot be said to be independent: **10.128**

46.— Prosecution of offences

(1) Proceedings for an offence under regulation 45 may be instituted by—
    (a) the Director of Revenue and Customs Prosecutions or by order of the Commissioners;
    (b) the OFT;
    (c) a local weights and measures authority;
    (d) DETI;
    (e) the Director of Public Prosecutions; or
    (f) the Director of Public Prosecutions for Northern Ireland.

---

[64] Note that, pursuant to the provisions of Reg 34(1) and (2), it would appear that this offence also applies in relation to an application under Reg 32.

[65] A further independent prosecuting authority, the Director of Revenue & Customs Prosecutions, is included in Reg 46(1)(a), but the Revenue & Customs Prosecution Office has since been abolished and its functions have been transferred to the Crown Prosecution Service (that is, in this context, to the Director of Public Prosecutions under Reg 46(1)(e)).

[66] The Crown Prosecution Service, established under the Prosecution of Offences Act 1985, s 1.

(2) Proceedings for an offence under regulation 45 may be instituted only against a relevant person or, where such a person is a body corporate, a partnership or an unincorporated association, against any person who is liable to be proceeded against under regulation 47.

Offences by bodies corporate etc

10.129 The criminal offence of non-compliance under Regulation 45 can be committed by any relevant person whether a natural or legal person. Regulation 47 makes specific provision, where an offence is committed by a body corporate, for criminal liability to be extended to certain categories of individual on the basis of consent, connivance, or neglect:

> 47.— Offences by bodies corporate etc.
> (1) If an offence under regulation 45 committed by a body corporate is shown—
>> (a) to have been committed with the consent or the connivance of an officer of the body corporate; or
>> (b) to be attributable to any neglect on his part,
>
> the officer as well as the body corporate is guilty of an offence and liable to be proceeded against and punished accordingly.

Partnerships

10.130 Essentially the same provision as in Regulation 47(1) is reproduced in Regulation 47(2) with respect to partners:

> (2) If an offence under regulation 45 committed by a partnership is shown—
>> (a) to have been committed with the consent or the connivance of a partner; or
>> (b) to be attributable to any neglect on his part,
>
> the partner as well as the partnership is guilty of an offence and liable to be proceeded against and punished accordingly.

Unincorporated associations

10.131 Similarly, in the case of an unincorporated association, where the provision relating to 'consent, connivance or neglect' applies to an officer of the association, the officer as well as the association is guilty of an offence under Regulation 45.

Interpretation

10.132 The word 'officer', which has a specific meaning within Part 5 of the Regulations, has a separate and specific meaning in relation to regulation 47:

> (9) In this regulation—
> "officer"—
>> (a) in relation to a body corporate, means a director, manager, secretary, chief executive, member of the committee of management, or a person purporting to act in such a capacity; and
>> (b) in relation to an unincorporated association, means any officer of the association or any member of its governing body, or a person purporting to act in such capacity; and
> "partner" includes a person purporting to act as a partner.

Penalties

10.133 A person who is convicted of an offence under Regulation 45 is liable on summary conviction to a fine not exceeding the statutory maximum and, on conviction on indictment, to imprisonment for a term not exceeding two years, to a fine or to both.

11

CASH DECLARATION, SEIZURE, AND FORFEITURE

A. Cash Declarations

From 15 June 2007, people who are either entering the UK from a non-EU country, or are travelling from the UK to a non-EU country, and are carrying 10,000 euros or more (or the equivalent in other currencies) are required to declare the cash to customs officers[1] at the place of their departure from, or arrival in, the UK. **11.01**

Travellers who fail to comply with the obligation to declare, or provide incorrect or incomplete information, could face a penalty of up to £5,000 under the Control of Cash (Penalties) Regulations 2007. **11.02**

HM Revenue & Customs has stated that officers will not seize properly declared cash if they have no reason to doubt its legitimacy. However, it is important to note that cash over £1,000 of any denomination may be seized under the Proceeds of Crime Act 2002 if an officer has reasonable grounds to suspect that it is, or represents, property obtained through unlawful conduct or that it is intended to be used in unlawful conduct. In addition, such cash may be forfeited subsequently upon application to a magistrates' court. **11.03**

---

[1] The function of a 'customs' officer' now vests in 'an officer of Revenue and Customs' (Commissioners for Revenue and Customs Act 2005, s 6). From 21 July 2009, the Secretary of State for the Home Department was given concurrent jurisdiction to exercise functions in relation to general customs matters (Borders, Citizenship and Immigration Act 2009, s 1). This led to the transfer in August 2009 of several thousand customs officers to the newly formed UK Border Agency.

11.04 It is also important to note the following:

- Cash includes not only notes and coins in any currency, but also bankers' drafts and cheques of any kind (including travellers' cheques), as well as other types of monetary instrument including those that are incomplete.
- The countries of the EU are Austria, Belgium, Bulgaria, Cyprus, the Czech Republic, Denmark, Estonia, Finland, France, Germany, Gibraltar, Greece, Hungary, Ireland, Italy, Latvia, Lithuania, Luxembourg, Malta, the Netherlands, Poland, Portugal, Romania, Slovakia, Slovenia, Spain, (including the Canary Islands), Sweden, and the United Kingdom (not including the Isle of Man and the Channel Islands).
- There is no declaration required for people travelling between the UK and other EU countries.

11.05 Cash should be declared on form C9011 which can be downloaded from HM Revenue & Customs' website or obtained at the port or airport. Customs officers may ask to see evidence of the declaration so it is important to retain a copy of the completed form.

B. Recovery of Cash in Summary Proceedings

Introduction

11.06 Chapter 3 of Part 5 of POCA (recovery of cash in summary proceedings) introduced specific powers for police and customs officers, to search for, seize, and apply in summary proceedings for the detention and forfeiture of cash which is connected to unlawful conduct. The commencement date for these provisions of POCA was 30 December 2002 and since that time they have been increasingly used by law enforcement. Home Office figures show that in the 2008–2009 financial year customs officers made 525 seizures amounting to £13.3 million and police officers made 5,398 seizures amounting to £82.9 million. In addition, a further £10.5m was seized by members of staff of the Serious Organised Crime Agency[2] and the Regional Asset Recovery Teams.[3]

11.07 The cash recovery powers under POCA are in addition to pre-existing powers to seize and detain cash. Customs officers retain their powers under the Customs and Excise Management Act 1979 and police officers routinely use their powers under the Police and Criminal Evidence Act 1984 and the Misuse of Drugs Act 1971 to seize and retain cash as part of an investigation into whether an individual has committed a criminal offence. The powers afforded by POCA, however, enable seized cash to be forfeited without the need for a criminal conviction.

11.08 There are analogous cash recovery powers under the Anti-terrorism, Crime and Security Act 2001 (ATCSA) which provide for the seizure, detention, and forfeiture of cash connected to terrorism.[4] Like the cash recovery powers under POCA, the ATCSA powers are exercised in

---

[2] Members of staff of the Serious Organised Crime Agency may be designated with the powers of constables or customs officers under the Serious Organised Crime and Police Act 2005, s 43.

[3] Regional Asset Recovery Teams are formed from officers and staff seconded from various police forces, HM Revenue & Customs, the CPS, and the Serious Organised Crime Agency. They have been established in five of the nine Association of Chief Police Officers regions: West Midlands; North West; North East; London; and Wales.

[4] ATCSA, s 1 and Sch 1.

civil proceedings before a magistrates' court[5] and are exercisable in relation to any cash whether or not any proceedings have been brought for an offence in connection with the cash.[6] Forfeiture of terrorist cash is addressed separately in section C below.

The POCA cash forfeiture proceedings are *in rem*, directed at the cash in question and not at **11.09** the criminality of any particular individual. This places customs officers and police officers in the position of an ordinary claimant in civil proceedings, albeit that the proceedings are heard in a magistrates' court.[7] There is no requirement for the officer to prove that there has been any criminal investigation, charge, or conviction. The standard of proof is the civil standard and all the court need be satisfied of is that the cash is derived from or was intended to be used for some kind of (unspecified[8]) criminal activity.

In the light of the 'particularly striking success'[9] of the cash recovery powers under POCA, **11.10** the government has been and is keen to exploit further this area. On 6 April 2008, the Serious Crime Act 2007 came into force; sections 75 to 77 and Schedule 10 extend the investigation powers under Part 8 of POCA to 'detained cash investigations'[10] whilst section 79 and Schedule 11 extend cash recovery powers to 'accredited financial investigators'.[11] Under section 24 of the UK Borders Act 2007, which came into force on 1 April 2010, the recovery of cash powers under POCA are further extended to immigration officers where the relevant unlawful conduct relates to an offence under the Immigrations Acts.[12] Finally, under section 63 of the Policing and Crime Act 2009, the search powers under Part 5 of POCA are extended, from a date to be appointed, to vehicles, whilst section 64 will, from a date to be appointed, enable law enforcement authorities to forfeit detained cash without a court order in uncontested cases.

Key concepts

Cash

POCA expanded the definition of 'cash' to include, in addition to banknotes and coins in **11.11** any currency,[13] most forms of financial instrument found at any place in the UK:

289. . .

. . .

    (6) Cash means—
        (a) notes and coins in any currency,
        (b) postal orders,

---

[5] Or, in Scotland, the sheriff.
[6] ATCSA, s 1(2).
[7] Or, in Scotland, the sheriff.
[8] See paras 11.14–11.19 below.
[9] Home Office Consultation paper: 'Asset Recovery Action Plan', May 2007, p. 19.
[10] See para 11.51 below.
[11] An accredited financial investigator is a civilian investigator who has been accredited by the National Policing Improvement Agency under POCA, s 3. In order to exercise specified powers under the Act the accredited financial investigator will also have to fall within a description specified in an order made for the purposes of that provision by the Secretary of State under s 453 of the Act (POCA, s 303A).
[12] Immigration officers are appointed under the Immigration Act 1971, Sch 2 para 1(1). They are appointed by the Secretary of State to exercise the functions conferred on them by that and other Acts. The Act also allows officers of Revenue and Customs to be deployed as immigration officers.
[13] As per the antecedent cash seizure provisions in the Drug Trafficking Act 1994.

    (c) cheques of any kind, including travellers' cheques,

    (d) bankers' drafts,

    (e) bearer bonds and bearer shares,

found at any place in the United Kingdom.

The list may be extended by the Secretary of State in consultation with Scottish ministers[14] to account for developments in the scope and use of new forms of financial instruments.

Recoverable property

11.12   'Recoverable property' is defined in section 304(1) of the Act:

304 Property obtained through unlawful conduct

(1) Property obtained through unlawful conduct is recoverable property.

(2) But if property obtained through unlawful conduct has been disposed of (since it was so obtained), it is recoverable property only if it is held by a person into whose hands it may be followed.

(3) Recoverable property obtained through unlawful conduct may be followed into the hands of a person obtaining it on a disposal by—

    (a) the person who through the conduct obtained the property, or

    (b) a person into whose hands it may (by virtue of this subsection) be followed.

If the original recoverable property is disposed of in place of other cash, for example a different form of financial instrument, the subsequent cash may represent the original property and may also be recoverable property.[15] Alternatively, cash obtained through unlawful conduct which is subsequently disposed of may remain recoverable property if it can be followed into the hands of a person who received the cash, either from the person who originally obtained it or as a subsequent recipient.[16] Conversely, property which is recoverable property may cease to be recoverable property if one of the exceptions or exemptions in sections 308 or 309 of POCA applies; they include persons who obtain the property in good faith, for value and without notice that it was recoverable property.[17]

Unlawful conduct

11.13   The general definition of unlawful conduct under POCA extends the scope of the cash forfeiture regime applicable under the old scheme, which was concerned only with cash seized at borders and reasonably suspected of being connected to drug trafficking.[18] Under the new regime, which is concerned with cash seized anywhere in the UK, 'unlawful conduct' is defined by section 241 of the Act:

241 'Unlawful conduct'

(1) Conduct occurring in any part of the United Kingdom is unlawful conduct if it is unlawful under the criminal law of that part.

(2) Conduct which—

    (a) occurs in a country or territory outside the United Kingdom and is unlawful under the criminal law applying in that country or territory, and

---

[14] POCA, s 289(7).

[15] Ibid., s 305.

[16] Ibid., s 305 (2) and (3).

[17] Ibid., s 308(1).

[18] DTA 1994, ss 42–8.

(b) if it occurred in a part of the United Kingdom, would be unlawful under the criminal law of that part,

is also unlawful conduct.

(3) The court or sheriff must decide on a balance of probabilities whether it is proved—
    (a) that any matters alleged to constitute unlawful conduct have occurred, or
    (b) that any person intended to use any cash in unlawful conduct.

This is the same definition as is applied to the civil recovery powers under Chapter 2 of Part 5 of the Act.

Property obtained through unlawful conduct

So 'recoverable property' is property obtained through unlawful conduct. 'Property obtained through unlawful conduct' is itself defined by the Act: **11.14**

242 'Property obtained through unlawful conduct'

(1) A person obtains property through unlawful conduct (whether his own conduct or another's) if he obtains property by or in return for the conduct.
(2) In deciding whether any property was obtained through unlawful conduct—
    (a) it is immaterial whether or not any money, goods or services were provided in order to put the person in question in a position to carry out the conduct,
    (b) it is not necessary to show that the conduct was of a particular kind if it is shown that the property was obtained through conduct of one of a number of kinds, each of which would have been unlawful conduct.

Whilst section 242(2)(b) of the Act would appear to require the officer applying for for- **11.15** feiture, at the very least, to set out the matters that are alleged to constitute the particular kind or kinds of unlawful conduct by or in return for which the cash was obtained, the courts have, in relation to the cash forfeiture scheme, not considered the identification of the particular kind or kinds of criminal conduct to be a necessary pre-condition to the making of a forfeiture order.

In *Muneka*[19] the court held that the prosecution need not identify the particular **11.16** criminal activity, the source of the money or the criminal offence for which it is intended to use the money. All that has to be shown is that, on balance, the source of the money was a (unspecified) criminal offence or that the money was intended for use in a (unspecified) criminal offence.

The decision in *Muneka* was approved by the court in *Green*[20] on the basis that, although **11.17** given an extended meaning for the purposes of Part 5 of POCA, the cash forfeiture regime was principally concerned with 'cash' in the narrow or popular sense of the word, i.e. banknotes. The court held that the decisions in cases such as *Muneka* were:

> . . . no more than a reflection of the fact that in today's 'cashless society', the ordinary law abiding citizen does not normally have any need to keep large numbers of banknotes in his possession . . . [The decision in Muneka does] no more than recognise that conduct consisting

---

[19] [2005] EWHC 495 (Admin).

[20] [2005] EWHC 3168 where it was held that, in respect of proceedings for civil recovery brought by the Director of the Assets Recovery Agency, the Director need not allege the commission of any specific criminal offence but must set out the matters that are alleged to constitute the particular kind or kinds of unlawful conduct by or in return for which the property was obtained. See also *Olupitan and another v Assets Recovery Agency* [2008] EWCA Civ 104.

in the mere fact of having a very large sum of cash in the form of banknotes in one's possession in certain circumstances (e.g. at an airport) may well provide reasonable grounds for suspicion and demand an answer'.

11.18 In establishing that cash is recoverable property, there appears, therefore, to be no requirement for the prosecution to adduce evidence showing that the cash was obtained as a result
of the involvement by the person from whom the cash was seized (or any other person) in a
particular kind or kinds of criminal conduct. The cash can be considered to be recoverable
property merely if it can be shown that it was obtained by some unspecified person by or in
return for some unspecified criminal conduct.

11.19 Note, however, that in June 2008, the Court of Appeal considered this issue again in the
context of money laundering offences under Part 7 of POCA. In *R v Anwoir*[21] the court
considered the main civil recovery authorities as well as the main money laundering authorities and held that there are two ways in which the Crown can prove that property derives
from crime, (a) by showing that it derives from conduct of a specific kind or kinds and that
conduct of that kind or those kinds is unlawful, or (b) by evidence of the circumstances in
which the property is handled which are such as to give rise to the irresistible inference that
it can only be derived from crime.[22] Although the court in *Anwoir* did not consider the position in relation to cash forfeiture proceedings, it is submitted that the second test enumer-
ated by Latham LJ is applicable to the question in cash forfeiture proceedings as to whether
the source of the money was a criminal offence or whether the money was intended for use
in a criminal offence.

Tracing, mixing etc

11.20 Where property obtained through unlawful conduct ('the original property') has been disposed of, any property which represents the original property is also recoverable property.[23]
Thus, where 'cash' which is recoverable property is exchanged or disposed of in return for
other property which is also 'cash', the subsequent 'cash' may also be subject to civil recovery
under POCA:[24]

> **305 Tracing property, etc**
> (1) Where property obtained through unlawful conduct ('the original property') is or has
>   been recoverable, property which represents the original property is also recoverable
>   property.
> (2) If a person enters into a transaction by which—
>   (a) he disposes of recoverable property, whether the original property or property which (by
>   virtue of this Chapter) represents the original property, and
>   (b) he obtains other property in place of it,
>   the other property represents the original property.
> (3) If a person disposes of recoverable property which represents the original property, the
>   property may be followed into the hands of the person who obtains it (and it continues
>   to represent the original property).

11.21 If a person grants an interest in his recoverable property, the question whether the interest is
also recoverable is to be determined in the same manner as it is on any other disposal of

---

[21] [2008] EWCA Crim 1354.
[22] Per Latham LJ, para 21.
[23] POCA, s 305(1).
[24] Ibid., s 305(2).

recoverable property.[25] Where cash which is recoverable property is mixed with other cash legitimately obtained, only the portion of the total value of the cash which is attributable to the original recoverable property represents the property obtained through unlawful conduct:[26]

306 Mixing property

(1) Subsection (2) applies if a person's recoverable property is mixed with other property (whether his property or another's).
(2) The portion of the mixed property which is attributable to the recoverable property represents the property obtained through unlawful conduct.
(3) Recoverable property is mixed with other property if (for example) it is used—
    (a) to increase funds held in a bank account,
    (b) in part payment for the acquisition of an asset,
    (c) for the restoration or improvement of land,
    (d) by a person holding a leasehold interest in the property to acquire the freehold.

Where a person who has recoverable property obtains further property by way of profits **11.22** accruing in respect of the recoverable property, the accruing profits are also to be treated as recoverable property:[27]

307 Recoverable property: accruing profits

(1) This section applies where a person who has recoverable property obtains further property consisting of profits accruing in respect of the recoverable property.
(2) The further property is to be treated as representing the property obtained through unlawful conduct.

The minimum amount

The 'minimum amount' is the amount set under section 303 of the Act by the Secretary of **11.23** State as being the minimum amount that may be searched for, seized, and detained:

303 'The minimum amount'

(1) In this Chapter, the minimum amount is the amount in sterling specified in an order made by the Secretary of State after consultation with the Scottish Ministers.
(2) For that purpose the amount of any cash held in a currency other than sterling must be taken to be its sterling equivalent, calculated in accordance with the prevailing rate of exchange.

Note, however, that the court may order forfeiture of a part of the cash which is less than the minimum amount.

The minimum amount was set originally at £10,000.[28] It was subsequently reduced to **11.24** £5,000 with effect from 16 March 2002[29] before being further altered to £1,000 with effect from 31 July 2006.[30]

---

[25] Ibid., s 310(1).
[26] Ibid., s 306.
[27] Ibid., s 307.
[28] Proceeds of Crime Act 2002 (Recovery of Cash in Summary Proceedings: Minimum Amount) Order 2002 (SI 2002/3016).
[29] Proceeds of Crime Act 2002 (Recovery of Cash in Summary Proceedings: Minimum Amount) Order 2004 (SI 2004/420).
[30] Proceeds of Crime Act 2002 (Recovery of Cash in Summary Proceedings: Minimum Amount) Order 2006 (SI 2006/1699).

11.25 It is possible to aggregate quantities of cash below the minimum amount found in separate places and seize the total sum if, in reality, the cash is derived from a common source or is intended for a common destination and collectively the amount exceeds the minimum amount.[31]

Powers of search of premises and of persons

Search of premises

11.26 Under section 289 of the Act customs officers, police officers, or an accredited financial investigator[32] may search for cash reasonably suspected of being connected to unlawful conduct:

289 Searches

(1) If a customs officer, a constable or an accredited financial investigator is lawfully on any premises and has reasonable grounds for suspecting that there is on the premises cash—
   (a) which is recoverable property or is intended by any person for use in unlawful conduct, and
   (b) the amount of which is not less than the minimum amount,

he may search for the cash there.

. . .

11.27 In relation to private premises, the power to search does not include the power to enter premises and may therefore only be exercised where the officer is 'lawfully' present on the premises. Where an officer is invited in by the occupier, having informed that occupier of the reason for entry,[33] or where an officer is present on the premises in the exercise of a power of entry conferred by other legislation,[34] he is lawfully present on the premises.

Search of persons

11.28 A customs officer, police officer, or an accredited financial investigator[35] may also search a person for cash:

289 . . .

. . .

(2) If a customs officer, a constable or an accredited financial investigator has reasonable grounds for suspecting that a person (the suspect) is carrying cash—
   (a) which is recoverable property or is intended by any person for use in unlawful conduct, and
   (b) the amount of which is not less than the minimum amount,

he may exercise the following powers.

(3) The officer, constable or accredited financial investigator may, so far as he thinks it necessary or expedient, require the suspect—
   (a) to permit a search of any article he has with him,
   (b) to permit a search of his person.

---

[31] *Customs and Excise Commissioners v Duffy* [2002] EWHC 425.

[32] An accredited financial investigator's powers to search for cash apply only in relation to premises in England, Wales or Northern Ireland (POCA, s 289(5)(c)).

[33] *Riley v DPP* 91 Cr App R 14.

[34] That is, the Police and Criminal Evidence Act 1984 in the case of police officers or the Customs and Excise Management Act 1979 or other enactment in the case of customs officers.

[35] An accredited financial investigator may only search a person for cash in England, Wales, or Northern Ireland (POCA, s 289(5)(c)).

Note that the power may only be exercised so far as the officer thinks it necessary or expedient[36] and there must be reasonable grounds for suspecting that the amount of 'cash' is not less than the 'minimum amount'.[37]

An officer exercising powers of search of a person or any article the person has with him may **11.29** detain the suspect for so long as is necessary for their exercise,[38] but he cannot require a person to answer questions or to undergo an intimate or strip search.[39] Accordingly, an officer cannot require any person to remove an article of clothing worn (wholly or partly) on the trunk and worn either next to the skin or next to an article of underwear.[40]

A customs officer may only exercise the search powers where the suspected unlawful activity **11.30** is an 'assigned matter' within the meaning of the Customs and Excise Management Act 1979,[41] that is, drug trafficking, money laundering, evasion of VAT, excise and other indirect taxes and duties, and evasion of various import and export prohibitions and restrictions.

Search of vehicles

Under section 63 of the Policing and Crime Act 2009 (not yet in force), subsection (1) of **11.31** section 289 of POCA is amended, from a date to be appointed, to provide for the search of a vehicle:

> **289** . . .
>
> . . .
>
> (1A) The powers specified in subsection (1D) are exercisable if—
>> (a) a customs officer, a constable or an accredited financial investigator has reasonable grounds for suspecting that there is cash falling within subsection (1E) in a vehicle, and
>> (b) it appears to the officer, constable or investigator that the vehicle is under the control of a person (the suspect) who is in or in the vicinity of the vehicle.
>
> (1B) The powers are exercisable only if the vehicle is—
>> (a) in any place to which, at the time of the proposed exercise of the powers, the public or any section of the public has access, on payment or otherwise, as of right or by virtue of express or implied permission, or
>> (b) in any other place to which at that time people have ready access but which is not a dwelling.
>
> (1C) But if the vehicle is in a garden or yard or other land occupied with and used for the purposes of a dwelling, the customs officer, constable or accredited financial investigator may exercise the powers under subsection (1D) only if the officer, constable or investigator has reasonable grounds for believing—
>> (a) that the suspect does not reside in the dwelling, and
>> (b) that the vehicle is not in the place in question with the express or implied permission of a person who resides in the dwelling.
>
> (1D) The customs officer, constable or accredited financial investigator may, so far as the officer, constable or investigator thinks it necessary or expedient, require the suspect to—
>> (a) permit entry to the vehicle,
>> (b) permit a search of the vehicle.
>
> . . .

---

[36] POCA, s 289(3).
[37] Ibid., s 289(2)(b).
[38] Ibid., s 289(4).
[39] Ibid., s 289(8).
[40] Code of Practice made under POCA, s 292.
[41] POCA, s 289(5).

11.32   In order to require the search, the officer must have reasonable grounds for suspecting that there is cash in the vehicle which is recoverable property or is intended for use in unlawful conduct, and the amount of it is not less than the minimum amount.[42] In exercising powers by virtue of subsection (1D), the officer may detain the vehicle for so long as is necessary for their exercise and may detain the person in control of the vehicle (the suspect) for so long as is necessary for their exercise.[43]

Searches with and without prior approval

11.33   The search powers may be exercised only with the prior approval of a judicial officer or (if that is not practicable in any case) the approval of a senior officer. Prior approval need not be obtained where, in the circumstances, it is not practicable to obtain that approval before exercising the power.[44] In the case of a police officer, a senior officer means an officer of the rank of police inspector or above, and for customs officers an officer of equivalent rank to a police inspector.[45] In the case of an accredited financial investigator, a senior officer means an accredited financial investigator who falls within a description specified by the Secretary of State under section 453 of the Act.[46]

11.34   In all cases where judicial approval is not obtained prior to a search and cash is not seized or cash is seized but is not detained for more than 48 hours, i.e. before the matter comes before a court, the police officer or customs officer concerned must prepare a written report and submit it to an independent person appointed by the Secretary of State.[47] The report will detail why the officer considered that he had the power to carry out the search and why it was not practicable to obtain judicial approval of the search.[48]

11.35   At the end of each financial year, the 'appointed person' is required to send a report to the Secretary of State on the exercise of the search powers in circumstances where prior judicial approval was not obtained. The report must then be made public and a copy must be laid before Parliament. In the report, the appointed person must give his opinion as to the circumstances and manner in which the powers of search are being exercised in cases where he has received a report and he may make any recommendations he considers appropriate.[49]

Exercise of power

11.36   Whilst searches conducted by constables and customs officers will often be conducted under existing legislation provided by the Police and Criminal Evidence Act 1984 and the Customs and Excise Management Act 1979, in recognition of the sensitivity of search powers, the Secretary of State is required to publish a Code of Practice in connection with the exercise of the cash search and seizure powers under POCA.[50] The code is admissible in evidence in criminal or civil proceedings and is to be taken into account by a court or tribunal in any case in which it appears to the court or tribunal to be relevant.[51] On 6 April 2008, a revised Code

---

[42] Ibid., s 289(1E).
[43] Ibid., s 289(4), as amended.
[44] Ibid., s 290(1) and (2).
[45] Ibid., s 290(4)(a) and (b).
[46] Ibid., s 290(4)(c).
[47] Ibid., s 290(6) and (7).
[48] Ibid., s 290(7).
[49] Ibid., s 291.
[50] Ibid., s 292 (in relation to England, Wales, and Northern Ireland) and s 293 (in relation to Scotland).
[51] Ibid., s 292(7).

of Practice was published.[52] The Code sets out the steps that should be taken by officers prior to a search of a person or premises, and stipulates the manner in which searches should be conducted and recorded, including the extent to which persons may be questioned and/or detained.

Note that paragraph 47 of the revised Code makes provision for a caution[53] to be given to a **11.37** person subject to a search if the officer discovers cash during the search and the questioning which may follow covers whether the person has committed an offence. In *Pisciotto,*[54] however, the court held that if the questioning is for the purpose of civil proceedings, namely, the recovery of the cash in summary proceedings, and the officer is not addressing his questions to the issue of the questioned person having committed an offence and possible criminal proceedings, a caution need not be administered.

The Code also gives general guidance. Paragraph 6 of the revised Code states: **11.38**

> The right to respect for private life and home—and the right to peaceful enjoyment of possessions—are both safeguarded by the Human Rights Act 1998. Powers of search may involve significant interference with the privacy of those whose premises and persons are searched and therefore need to be fully and clearly justified before they are used. In particular, officers should consider at every stage whether the necessary objectives can be achieved by less intrusive means. In all cases officers should exercise their powers courteously and with respect for the persons and property of those concerned. The possibility of using reasonable force to give effect to the power of detention of a person and search of a person or premises should only be considered where this is necessary and proportionate in all the circumstances.

In order to exercise a power of search under section 289, the officer must have reasonable **11.39** grounds for suspecting that cash meeting the conditions set out in section 289(1) will be found. The test of 'reasonable suspicion' is a very low hurdle for an officer to overcome. The test will be satisfied if the officer considers that there is a possibility, which is more than fanciful, that cash meeting the conditions will be found.[55]

The Code of Practice, however, urges some restraint and advises that there must be some **11.40** objective basis for the suspicion based on facts, information, and/or intelligence and that reasonable suspicion can never be supported on the basis of personal factors alone such as race or religion[56] without reliable supporting intelligence or information or some specific behaviour by the person concerned. The Code of Practice also makes it clear that an officer carrying out a search under section 289 of the Act will be a public authority for the purposes of the Race Relations Act 2000.[57]

Furthermore, following public consultation on the exercise of search powers, the Code of **11.41** Practice now requires an officer, before taking any action pursuant to the powers covered by the code (or in urgent cases, as soon as possible after), to consult the community liaison

---

[52] Proceeds of Crime Act 2002 (Cash Searches: Code of Practice) Order 2008/947.
[53] Under PACE, Code C: detention, treatment and questioning of persons by police officers.
[54] [2009] EWHC 1991 (Admin).
[55] *Da Silva* [2006] EWCA Crim 1654.
[56] Paras 18 and 19 of the Code of Practice.
[57] Para 12 of the Code of Practice.

officer and/or any other relevant persons if there is reason to believe that his action might have an adverse effect on relations between law enforcement and the community.[58]

Seizure of cash

11.42   Under s 294 of the Act:

294 Seizure of cash

(1)   A customs officer, a constable or an accredited financial investigator may seize any cash if he has reasonable grounds for suspecting that it is—
(a)   recoverable property, or
(b)   intended by any person for use in unlawful conduct.
(2)   A customs officer, a constable or an accredited financial investigator may also seize cash part of which he has reasonable grounds for suspecting to be—
(a)   recoverable property, or
(b)   intended by any person for use in unlawful conduct,
if it is not reasonably practicable to seize only that part.

(3)   This section does not authorise the seizure of an amount of cash if it or, as the case may be, the part to which his suspicion relates, is less than the minimum amount.
(4)   This section does not authorise the seizure by an accredited financial investigator of cash found in Scotland.

11.43   Note that under subsection (3), if only part of the value of the cash found is suspected to be connected to unlawful conduct, the total amount may nevertheless be seized on the basis that it would not be reasonably practicable to seize only a part.[59] This provision is designed to cater for financial instruments other than banknotes, such as a bearer bond, which are indivisible.

11.44   Inevitably, if cash is found following a search exercised by an officer under POCA, the officer will not need much, if any, further justification to seize the cash. Arguably, the requisite suspicion will already have been formulated to enable the search. In addition, officers may seek to justify their suspicion solely on the basis that the banking system has not been used.

11.45   Cash may be seized under POCA at any time. Accordingly, cash seized by the police for a different purpose under PACE may be subsequently notionally 're-seized' under POCA when the original purpose for seizure no longer applies. In such circumstances, the statutory minimum amount and the strict time limits for the detention of the cash apply only from the point when the cash is 're-seized'.[60]

Detention of seized cash

11.46   Seized cash can be initially detained for a maximum of 48 hours not including weekends, Christmas Day, Good Friday, and bank holidays.[61] Within that period, unless an application for forfeiture is made or the cash is released, the officer must apply to the magistrates' court or (in Scotland) the sheriff for an extension. The court may then order continued detention

---

[58]   Para 8 of the Code of Practice (save for circumstances where the officer considers that the consultation could jeopardize an ongoing (sensitive) wider operation or investigation).
[59]   POCA s 294(2).
[60]   *Chief Constable of Merseyside Police v Hickman* [2006] EWHC 451 (Admin).
[61]   POCA, s 295 (1), (1A) and (1B). Note that in Scotland the time limit also does not include court holidays prescribed under Criminal Procedure (Scotland) Act 1995, s 8(2).

of the cash for up to six months.[62] The period of detention can be extended by repeated applications up to an aggregate maximum of two years from the first day of the first order.[63] Paragraphs 4 and 5 of the Magistrates' Courts (Detention and Forfeiture of Cash) Rules 2002[64] set out the procedure for the application which must be made on the form prescribed in those rules.

Before granting an order for extension, the officer must satisfy the justices that either of the conditions set out in section 295 are met: **11.47**

295 Detention of seized cash

. . .

   (5) The first condition is that there are reasonable grounds for suspecting that the cash is recoverable property and that either—

      (a) its continued detention is justified while its derivation is further investigated or consideration is given to bringing (in the United Kingdom or elsewhere) proceedings against any person for an offence with which the cash is connected, or

      (b) proceedings against any person for an offence with which the cash is connected have been started and have not been concluded.

   (6) The second condition is that there are reasonable grounds for suspecting that the cash is intended to be used in unlawful conduct and that either—

      (a) its continued detention is justified while its intended use is further investigated or consideration is given to bringing (in the United Kingdom or elsewhere) proceedings against any person for an offence with which the cash is connected, or

      (b) proceedings against any person for an offence with which the cash is connected have been started and have not been concluded.[65]

If an application for further detention is refused by the court, the period of detention will come to an end at the expiry of the existing time limit unless the court directs the immediate release of the cash (upon an application for release[66]) or the officer submits an application for forfeiture, in which case the cash will be detained until the proceedings (including any appeal) are concluded.[67] **11.48**

Where cash has been seized on the basis that part of its value is suspected to be connected to unlawful conduct and it is not reasonably practicable to seize only that part,[68] an order granting extended detention of all the cash may be made if one of the above conditions is satisfied and it is not reasonably practicable to detain only that part.[69] **11.49**

If a detention order is made the cash must at the first opportunity be paid into an interest-bearing account and held there, with the accrued interest being added to it on its forfeiture or release.[70] In the case of cash seized under section 294(2), i.e. cash in respect of which **11.50**

---

   [62] Ibid., s 295(2)(a), as amended by Policing and Crime Act 2009, s 64. The time limit applies until midnight of the final day of the period of the order: *Chief Constable of Merseyside Police v Reynolds, The Times,* 27 November 2004.

   [63] POCA, s 295(2).

   [64] SI 2998.

   [65] POCA, s 295 (5) and (6).

   [66] Ibid., s 297.

   [67] Ibid., s 298(4) and *R (Chief Constable of Lancashire Constabulary) v Burnley Magistrates' Court* [2003] EWHC 3308 (Admin).

   [68] POCA, s 294(2).

   [69] Ibid., s 295(7).

   [70] Ibid., s 296(1).

the officer's suspicion relates to only part, on paying the cash into the account the officer must release that part to which the suspicion does not relate unless it is required as evidence.[71]

Detained cash investigations

11.51   Since 6 April 2008,[72] the investigation powers under Part 8 of POCA have been applicable to detained cash investigations. A detained cash investigation is defined in section 341(3A) of POCA:

> **341 Investigations**
>
> . . .
>
> (3A)   For the purposes of this Part a detained cash investigation is—
>> (a)   an investigation for the purposes of Chapter 3 of Part 5 into the derivation of cash detained under section 295 or a part of such cash, or
>> (b)   an investigation for the purposes of Chapter 3 of Part 5 into whether cash detained under section 295, or a part of such cash, is intended by any person to be used in unlawful conduct.

Accordingly, the power to obtain a production order under sections 345 and 380 of POCA and the power to obtain a search warrant under sections 352 and 387 of POCA are extended to detained cash investigations.[73]

Release

11.52   The cash may be released at any time by an officer, after notifying the court, if he is satisfied that detention is no longer justified. Alternatively, the court may order release of the cash upon an application by the person from whom it was seized if it is satisfied that the conditions in section 295 are no longer met.[74] Note that, where an application is made for the release of the cash, the burden is on the applicant to satisfy the court that the section 295 conditions are no longer met.

11.53   The Magistrates' Courts (Detention and Forfeiture of Cash) Rules 2002[75] require that the applicant for further detention or release of the cash give seven days notice of the application to any person known to be affected by the existing order. This requirement clearly envisages that applications are initiated and heard in good time. However, a failure to comply with the Rules will not necessarily render the proceedings irretrievably flawed as the requirement for seven days' notice is declaratory, not mandatory.[76]

Forfeiture of seized cash

11.54   While cash is detained under section 295, an application may be made to the court for the forfeiture of the whole or any part of it:[77]

---

[71]   Ibid., s 296(2) and(3).
[72]   Serious Crime Act 2007, ss 75 to 77 and Sch 10.
[73]   POCA, ss 345(2), 380(3), 352(2) and 387(3).
[74]   Ibid., s 297. Note that victims or other owners who claim ownership of the cash may also apply to the court for its release, Ibid, s 301.
[75]   SI 2998.
[76]   *Chief Constable of Merseyside Police v Reynolds, The Times*, 27 November 2004.
[77]   POCA, s 298(1).

298 Forfeiture

(1) While cash is detained under section 295, an application for the forfeiture of the whole or any part of it may be made—
   (a) to a magistrates' court by the Commissioners of Customs and Excise, [78] an accredited financial investigator or a constable,
   (b) (in Scotland) to the sheriff by the Scottish Ministers.
(2) The court or sheriff may order the forfeiture of the cash or any part of it if satisfied that the cash or part—
   (a) is recoverable property, or
   (b) is intended by any person for use in unlawful conduct.

The procedure is set out in the Magistrates' Courts (Detention and Forfeiture of Cash) Rules 2002.[79] Under Rule 4(1), the application for forfeiture may be made to any magistrates' court, wherever situated.

Once an application for forfeiture is made, the cash will continue to be detained until such **11.55** time as the proceedings (including any appeal) are concluded[80] and the officer need not, therefore, apply for any further periods of detention.

Forfeiture proceedings are civil proceedings[81] such that, unless otherwise provided for,[82] the **11.56** Civil Procedure Rules and the normal rules of evidence in civil proceedings are applicable. The Civil Procedure Rules Part 32.2 sets out how evidence is to be given and facts are to be proved. Part PD 32.17 sets out the form and content of a witness statement to be used. In *Pisciotto*[83] the court held that section 78 of PACE only relates to criminal proceedings and cannot therefore be used to exclude evidence in cash recovery proceedings: civil powers to exclude evidence would have to be used if it was considered that the interests of justice so required the exclusion.

The Act places the burden on the officer applying for forfeiture to prove that the cash is **11.57** recoverable property or is intended by any person for use in unlawful conduct. The courts have consistently held in relation to analogous cases that, since the blameworthiness or otherwise of the person from whom the property was seized is not of itself an element in what has to be proved, the proceedings do not amount to the bringing of criminal proceedings.[84] Accordingly, Article 6 of ECHR is not engaged and the proceedings do not infringe Article 1 of Protocol 1 to ECHR.[85]

The test properly applied is whether or not the court is satisfied that it is more probable than **11.58** not that the cash is recoverable property or is intended for use by any person in unlawful conduct.[86] In practice, however, it is often necessary for the person from whom the cash has

---

[78] To be read as, the Commissioner for Revenue and Customs (Commissioners for Revenue and Customs Act 2005, s 6).

[79] SI 2002/2998.

[80] POCA, s 298(4).

[81] Ibid., s 240.

[82] E.g., The Magistrates' Courts (Hearsay Evidence in Civil Proceedings) Rules 1999 govern the admission of hearsay evidence in cash recovery proceedings.

[83] [2009] EWHC 1991 (Admin).

[84] See e.g. *R (Mudie) v Dover Magistrates' Court* [2003] EWCA Civ 237 and *Butt v HMCE* [2001] EWHC Admin 1066.

[85] *Butler v UK* (41661/98).

[86] *Butt v HMCE* [2001] EWHC 1066 in which the court rejected a submission that the standard of proof should be akin to the criminal standard.

been seized to prove the legitimacy of his cash. Possession of large amounts of cash in certain circumstances (e.g. at an airport) may itself raise suspicions and require an explanation.[87] In *Muneka*[88] the court held that a requirement for the respondent to provide a truthful explanation for the source of the cash in the face of facts so startling that they called for an explanation did not amount to a shift in the burden of proof.

11.59 The burden on the officer to satisfy the court as to the derivation or intended use of the cash may be met by inference without any direct evidence relating to an individual's involvement in unlawful conduct. The court could infer, from all the circumstances of the case, that it is more likely than not that the cash seized was recoverable property or was intended by any person for use in unlawful conduct.[89]

11.60 In *Muneka*[90] a finding that the person from whom the cash was seized, in the context of questions put to him as to whether the cash had been obtained through unlawful conduct or was intended for such a purpose and there being no reasonable explanation for the source or intended use of the seized cash, had lied to the officers and the court was held to be sufficient to satisfy the burden.

11.61 Where the cash is held by joint tenants, one of whom is an 'excepted joint owner',[91] the order for forfeiture may not apply to so much of the cash as the court thinks is attributable to the excepted joint owner's share.[92] It remains to be seen how this provision will operate in practice where the particular cash concerned is indivisible and where there are no provisions similar to the role of the trustee for civil recovery in High Court proceedings. It is of note that POCA appears to provide the court with the discretion not to account for the excepted joint owner's share.[93]

11.62 The court also has an apparent discretion to order the forfeiture of all the cash detained even where it is satisfied that only part is recoverable property or is intended for use by any person in unlawful conduct.[94] It is submitted that this is an error in drafting and was not the intention of Parliament: the Chapter read as a whole clearly envisages the release of any legitimately obtained cash which has been mixed with recoverable cash.[95]

Victims, other owners, and compensation

11.63 Any 'victim' who claims that the cash detained belongs to him may apply to the court at any time for the cash or part of it to be released to him.[96] If the court is satisfied that the cash belongs to the applicant, that he was deprived of it by unlawful conduct and that it was not

---

[87] *Director of the Assets Recovery Agency v Green and others* [2005] EWHC 3168 (Admin).

[88] [2005] EWHC 495 (Admin).

[89] *Bassick v Customs and Excise Commissioners* (1997) 161 JPN 602 (QBD).

[90] [2005] EWHC 495 (Admin).

[91] Defined in s 270(4) as a person who obtained the property in circumstances in which it would not be recoverable against him.

[92] POCA, s 298(3).

[93] POCA, s 298(3) states that the court *may* account for the excepted joint owners share. Note, however, that the Government's Explanatory Notes to the Act state that: 'the court *must* not forfeit the cash that it thinks attributable to the "innocent" partner's share.' It is submitted that the Government's interpretation of this section should be favoured.

[94] Ibid., s 298(2).

[95] See e.g. s 296(2)(3) and s 297(2)(3)(4).

[96] POCA, s 301(1).

recoverable property immediately before he was deprived of it, it may order the applicant's cash to be released to him.[97]

Any other true owner of the cash who is not the person from whom the cash was seized may apply to the court for the release of the cash. The court may order the release of the cash to that person or to the person from whom the cash was seized if it is satisfied that the cash belongs to the applicant, that the conditions for detention of the cash are not met and if the person from whom the cash was seized does not object.[98] **11.64**

If no order for forfeiture is made the person from whom it was seized or the person to whom the cash belongs may apply to the court for compensation.[99] The court may order compensation for any interest lost during any period following the initial 48-hour period of detention that the cash was not deposited in an interest-bearing account.[100] The court may also order reasonable compensation in exceptional circumstances for other loss suffered as a result of the detention of the cash.[101] **11.65**

Appeals

An appeal against an order of forfeiture or a decision not to make such an order may be made by any party to the proceedings to the Crown Court.[102] The appeal must be made within 30 days from the order or decision[103] and will be a full re-hearing of the application. The Crown Court may make any order it thinks appropriate and may release the cash if it decides not to order forfeiture.[104] **11.66**

An appeal by case stated against a decision of either the magistrates' court or the Crown Court may be made to the Divisional Court on a point of law. Judicial review of a decision of the Crown Court is also available with leave of the Administrative Court. **11.67**

Funding and costs

Funding

The court has no jurisdiction to grant criminal legal aid to a defendant in cash forfeiture proceedings.[105] Neither is the defendant able to use the detained cash to fund the costs of responding to the proceedings.[106] Civil legal aid is, however, available for all stages of the proceedings, including appeals, subject to the CLS General Funding Code. **11.68**

---

[97] Ibid., s 301(3).
[98] Ibid., s 301(4).
[99] Ibid., s 302(1).
[100] Ibid., s 302(2)(3).
[101] Ibid., s 302(4)(5).
[102] Ibid., s 299(1).
[103] Ibid., s 299(2).
[104] Ibid., s 299(3)(4).
[105] See the analogous case of *R (Mudie and another) v Dover Magistrates' Court and another* [2003] EWCA Civ 237 which was concerned with condemnation proceedings under the Customs and Excise Management Act 1979.
[106] *Customs and Excise Commissioners v Harris, The Times,* 24 February 1999.

Costs

11.69 The Magistrates' Courts (Detention and Forfeiture of Cash) Rules 2002 make rules in respect of the procedure to be followed for the detention and forfeiture of seized cash and provide that the application shall proceed by way of complaint:

> **11 Procedure at hearings**
>
> . . .
>
> (2) Subject to the foregoing provisions of these Rules, proceedings on such an application shall be regulated in the same manner as proceedings on a complaint, and accordingly for the purposes of these Rules, the application *shall be deemed to be a complaint*, the applicant a complainant, the respondents to be defendants and any notice given by the [designated officer] under rules 5(3), 6(4), 7(4), 8(4) or 10(4) to be a summons: but nothing in this rule shall be construed as enabling a warrant of arrest to be issued for failure to appear in answer to any such notice.

11.70 The Magistrates Court Act 1980 states:

> Part II
> Civil Jurisdiction and Procedure
>
> . . .
>
> *Costs*
>
> **64 Power to award costs and enforcement of costs**
>
> (1) On the hearing of a complaint, a magistrates' court shall have power in its discretion to make such order as to costs—
>> (a) on making the order for which the complaint is made, to be paid by the defendant to the complainant;
>> (b) on dismissing the complaint, to be paid by the complainant to the defendant,
>
> as it thinks just and reasonable; but if the complaint is for an order for the periodical payment of money, or for the revocation, revival or variation of such an order, or for the enforcement of such an order, the court may, whatever adjudication it makes, order either party to pay the whole or any part of the other's costs.
>
> . . .

11.71 The section gives the court *discretion* to award costs to the successful party. Costs ordered to be paid under the section shall be enforceable as a civil debt. However, whilst the usual rule is that costs should follow the event, in *Perinpanathan*[107] the court held that in cash forfeiture cases, the power to award costs under section 64 of the Magistrates' Court Act 1980 does not provide any 'steer' or indication to the court that costs should follow the event. Rather, in circumstances where the claim for forfeiture was unsuccessful, the court should consider whether the claimant had acted reasonably in pursuing the claim. In such cases, there should be no presumption that costs should follow the event.

11.72 It is to be noted that each application for further detention, forfeiture, and release of cash is a separate proceeding. The costs power in section 64 applies only to the costs incurred in the course of the proceedings that the court is dealing with. For example, if cash is detained a number of times by the court, but eventually released upon the application of the owner, only the costs incurred in the course of the application for release are in issue at the conclusion of those proceedings, unless the issue of costs in the detention proceedings has been adjourned.

---

[107] [2010] EWCA Civ 40.

C. Forfeiture of Terrorist Cash

Introduction

Schedule 1 of the Anti-terrorism, Crime and Security Act 2001 (ATCSA) expands and   **11.73**
replaces the cash forfeiture powers under the Terrorism Act 2000.[108] The ATCSA provisions
provide for the seizure, detention, and forfeiture of terrorist cash in civil proceedings before
a magistrates' court or (in Scotland) the sheriff and are broadly analogous to the provisions
for the recovery of cash in summary proceedings under Chapter 3 of Part 5 of POCA.

The cash forfeiture provisions under ATCSA are only one part of UK law enforcement's   **11.74**
wide-ranging powers to seize and freeze terrorist assets with a view to disrupting terrorists'
ability to raise, move, and use funds. Whilst a detailed review of all the powers available to
UK law enforcement in this area is beyond the scope of this work, it is worth noting that the
two main statutory regimes governing executive action in relation to terrorist assets are
ATCSA and Part III of the Terrorism Act 2000.

In addition, in accordance with UN Security Council Resolutions, the government has made   **11.75**
provisions through Orders in Council for the freezing of assets of individuals who are involved
with terrorism. The two main Orders in Council are the Terrorism (United Nations Measures)
Order 2009[109] and the Al-Qaida and Taliban (Asset Freezing) Regulations 2010.[110]

Notwithstanding the extensive powers available to UK law enforcement, the value of terror-   **11.76**
ist assets seized and/or forfeited in recent years is relatively small. Between 2001 and July
2006, in relation to terrorist cases there were:

- £400,000 of cash seizures under ATCSA;
- £100,000 of forfeited funds;
- £475,000 of funds seized under POCA; and
- £477,000 subject to Treasury asset freezes.[111]

Key concepts

Terrorist cash

Terrorist cash is defined in Schedule 1, paragraph 1 of ATCSA as cash which is within section   **11.77**
1(1) of the Act, or is earmarked as terrorist property:[112]

1 Forfeiture of terrorist cash

(1) Schedule 1 (which makes provision for enabling cash which—
    (a) is intended to be used for the purposes of terrorism,
    (b) consists of resources of an organisation which is a proscribed organisation, or

---

[108] The cash forfeiture provisions contained in ATCSA are concerned with the seizure of terrorist cash throughout the whole of the UK whereas the Terrorism Act 2000 provided for the seizure and forfeiture of terrorist cash only at the borders.

[109] SI 2009/1747.

[110] SI 2010/1197.

[111] 'Countering International Terrorism: The United Kingdom's Strategy', July 2006, CM 6888. Note that these figures do not include the £78 million that was frozen until 2002 as part of the UK action against the Taliban.

[112] ATCSA, Sch 1, para 1(a) and (b).

(c) is, or represents, property obtained through terrorism,
    to be forfeited in civil proceedings before a magistrates' court or (in Scotland) the
    sheriff is to have effect.

(2) The powers conferred by Schedule 1 are exercisable in relation to any cash whether or not
    any proceedings have been brought for an offence in connection with the cash.

11.78 The definition of 'cash' is given the same meaning as in section 289 of POCA.[113] 'Terrorism'
and 'proscribed organisation' are defined in Schedule 1, paragraph 19 of ATCSA as having
the same meaning as in the Terrorism Act 2000.[114]

Property obtained through terrorism and property earmarked as terrorist property

11.79 Property obtained through terrorism and property earmarked as terrorist property are
defined in Schedule 1, paragraphs 11 and 12:

11 Property obtained through terrorism

(1) A person obtains property through terrorism if he obtains property by or in return for acts
    of terrorism, or acts carried out for the purposes of terrorism.
(2) In deciding whether any property was obtained through terrorism—
    (a) it is immaterial whether or not any money, goods or services were provided in order to put
        the person in question in a position to carry out the acts,
    (b) it is not necessary to show that the act was of a particular kind if it is shown that the
        property was obtained through acts of one of a number of kinds, each of which have been
        an act of terrorism, or an act carried out for the purposes of terrorism.

12 Property earmarked as terrorist property

(1) Property obtained through terrorism is property earmarked as terrorist property.
(2) But if property obtained through terrorism has been disposed of (since it was so obtained),
    it is earmarked as terrorist property only if it is held by a person into whose hands it may
    be followed.
(3) Earmarked property obtained through terrorism may be followed into the hands of a
    person obtaining it on a disposal by—
    (a) the person who obtained the property through terrorism, or
    (b) a person into whose hands it may (by virtue of this sub-paragraph) be followed.

11.80 The term 'property' is defined in paragraph 17 and includes money, all forms of property,
real or personal, heritable or moveable, things in action, and other intangible or
incorporeal property. A person's property also includes any interest which he holds in
the property.

Mixing and tracing property, accruing profits

11.81 Paragraphs 13 to 15 prescribe the circumstances in which property is treated as representing
property earmarked as terrorist property. Paragraph 13 (tracing property) deals with disposals of property obtained through terrorism:

13 Tracing property

(1) Where property obtained through terrorism ('the original property') is or has been
    earmarked as terrorist property, property which represents the original property is also
    earmarked.
(2) If a person enters into a transaction by which—

---

[113] See para 11.11 above.
[114] Terrorism Act 2000, ss 1 and 3.

(a) he disposes of earmarked property, whether the original property or property which (by virtue of this Part) represents the original property, and he obtains other property in place of it,

the other property represents the original property.

(3) If a person disposes of earmarked property which represents the original property, the property may be followed into the hands of the person who obtains it (and continues to represent the original property).

References to the disposal of property are defined in paragraph 18 to include disposals of a **11.82** part of the property or the granting of an interest in the property.[115] A disposal also includes the making of a payment to another and situations where property is passed on under a will or intestacy or by operation of law.[116]

Paragraph 14 (mixing property) deals with mixtures of property obtained through terrorism **11.83** with other property:

14 Mixing property
(1) Sub-paragraph (2) applies if a person's property which is earmarked as terrorist property is mixed with other property (whether his property or another's).
(2) the property which is attributable to the property earmarked as terrorist property represents the property obtained through terrorism.
(3) Property earmarked as terrorist property is mixed with other property if (for example) it is used—
    (a) to increase funds held in a bank account,
    (b) in part payment for the acquisition of an asset,
    (c) for the restoration or improvement of land,
    (d) by a person holding a leasehold interest in the property to acquire the freehold.

Paragraph 15 (accruing profits) deals with the profits accrued in respect of property obtained **11.84** through terrorism or representative property:

15 Accruing profits
(1) This paragraph applies where a person who has property earmarked as terrorist property obtains further property consisting of profits accruing in respect of the earmarked property.
(2) The further property is to be treated as representing the property obtained through terrorism.

General exceptions

Paragraph 16 lists the persons into whose hands property earmarked as terrorist property **11.85** may not be followed such that the property ceases to be earmarked; they include persons who obtain the property in good faith, for value and without notice that it was earmarked.[117] However, the consideration paid for the property by the person into whose hands the property may not be followed continues to be earmarked property.[118]

Note that the general exceptions do not apply to innocent donees, that is, persons who have **11.86** obtained the earmarked property in good faith, without notice but not for value (for example,

---

[115] ATCSA, Sch 1, para 18(1)(a) and (b).
[116] Ibid., para 18(3) and (4).
[117] Ibid., para 16(1).
[118] Ibid., para 16(7).

a charity). This seems to be at odds with the underlying purpose of the legislation which is to reduce the incidence of terrorism by preventing terrorists from using forfeited assets as a means of financing terrorist activity; it is difficult to see on what basis forfeiting cash from an innocent donee is consistent with this purpose.[119]

11.87 Sub-paragraphs (2) to (6) of paragraph 16 set out other circumstances in which terrorist property will cease to be earmarked; they include property obtained in pursuance of a judgment in civil proceedings where the claim is based on the defendant's criminal conduct; where a payment is made following a compensation or restitution order in criminal proceedings and the property received would otherwise be earmarked;[120] and where a restitution order is required to be made by the Financial Services Authority[121] paying an amount which would otherwise be earmarked.

Seizure of terrorist cash

11.88 The circumstances in which terrorist cash may be seized by authorised officers are prescribed under Schedule 1, paragraph 2 of ATCSA:

> **2 Seizure of cash**
>
> (1) An authorised officer may seize any cash if he has reasonable grounds for suspecting that it is terrorist cash.
> (2) An authorised officer may also seize cash part of which he has reasonable grounds for suspecting to be terrorist cash if it is not reasonably practicable to seize only that part.

11.89 An authorised officer is defined at paragraph 19 as a customs officer,[122] immigration officer, or constable. Note that, unlike the analogous cash seizure provisions under POCA, there is no minimum amount as regards the seizure of terrorist cash under ATCSA.

11.90 Where an authorised officer has seized cash only part of which he has reasonable grounds for suspecting to be terrorist cash, because, for example, the cash is in a non-divisible form, subparagraph (2) of paragraph 4 stipulates the release of any cash which is not attributable to terrorist cash, after paying it into an interest-bearing account.[123]

11.91 The provision that cash is to be held in an interest-bearing account during the course of proceedings is designed to compensate the individual where a terrorist link proves unfounded.[124] Some commentators have suggested that there should be an alternative means of compensation in cash seizure cases for those Muslims with religious objections to profiting from interest.[125] The government, however, is reluctant to change the legislation and considers

---

[119] See the discussion in 'Forfeiture of terrorist property and tracing: sub-group 4: impact of the initiatives on other areas of the law' by the Society for Advanced Legal Studies, JMLC 2003, 6(3), 261–8.

[120] Compensation or restitution orders under the Powers of Criminal Courts (Sentencing) Act 2000 or a restitution order made by the court under the Financial Services and Markets Act 2000.

[121] Under the Financial Services and Markets Act 2000.

[122] The function of 'customs' officer' now vests in an 'officer of Revenue and Customs' (Commissioners for Revenue and Customs Act 2005, s 6).

[123] Unless the cash is required as evidence of an offence or evidence in proceedings under ATCSA, Sch 1.

[124] See the provisions for compensation under para 10 of Sch 1 in circumstances where no forfeiture order is made.

[125] 'Anti-terrorism, Crime and Security Act 2001 Review: Report', Privy Counsellor Review Committee (The Newton Committee), December 2003, HC100.

that those who feel strongly against monies accrued in this way could donate the profit to charitable and humanitarian causes.[126]

Exercise of the power to seize terrorist cash

11.92 The exercise of the power to seize cash under ATCSA is subject to the Code of Practice issued by the Secretary of State.[127] The Code of Practice stipulates that any decision to seize cash under ATCSA must be authorised by a police officer of the rank of inspector or above; by a chief immigration officer; or by a customs officer pay band 7 or above. Authorization should be obtained prior to actual seizure of the cash itself and verbal authorization should be supported by written authorization as soon as is reasonably practicable.[128]

11.93 Note that the Code of Practice provides that the powers to seize and detain cash under ATCSA should only be exercised by an immigration officer or customs officer exceptionally. Where such an officer develops a suspicion that cash found is liable to be seized under ATCSA, he/she should alert a police officer at the earliest opportunity in order to continue the investigation.[129] Paragraphs 9 to 16 of the Code of Practice give further instruction on the exercise of the power to seize cash under ATCSA and the procedures that should be followed.

Detention of terrorist cash

11.94 Cash seized under Schedule 1 of ATCSA may not be detained for more than 48 hours except by order of a magistrates' court or (in Scotland) the sheriff.[130] Within that period, unless an application for forfeiture is made or the cash is released, the authorised officer must apply to the magistrates' court or (in Scotland) the sheriff for an extension. The court may then order continued detention of the cash for up to three months.[131] The period of detention can be extended by repeated applications up to an aggregate maximum of two years from the first day of the first order.[132] Paragraphs 4 and 5 of the Magistrates' Courts (Detention and Forfeiture of Terrorist Cash) (No 2) Rules 2001[133] set out the procedure for the application which must be made on the form prescribed in those rules.

11.95 Schedule 1, paragraph 3(1A) provides, like the analogous provision in section 295(1) of POCA, that weekends, Christmas day, Good Friday and bank holidays are to be disregarded when determining the initial period of 48 hours detention.

---

[126] 'Counter-terrorism powers: reconciliation, security and liberty in an open society', Home Office discussion paper, February 2004, CM6147.
[127] 'Code of Practice for authorised officers acting under Schedule 1 to The Anti-Terrorism, Crime and Security Act 2001' issued under Terrorism Act 2000, Sch 14, para 9(1) (and amended by the Anti-Terrorism, Crime and Security Act 2001 (Commencement) Order 2001).
[128] Code of Practice, para 5.
[129] Ibid., para 6.
[130] ATCSA, Sch 1, para 3(1). The cash must be released and returned to the person from whom it was seized unless a court order is obtained within 48 hours of the cash being seized.
[131] ATCSA, Sch 1, para 3(2)(a).
[132] Ibid., para 3(2)(b). Note that the Code of Practice on the exercise of powers by authorised officers under this Schedule provides that an application to renew an order to detain cash beyond six months and up to the maximum limit of two years should be authorised by a police officer of the rank of superintendent or above (para 21). This guidance clearly anticipates that, if cash needs to be detained beyond the initial three-months period provided under Sch 1, para 3(2)(a), a further application can be made under para 3(2)(b) to detain the cash for any period not going beyond the end of the period of two years beginning with the date of the first order.
[133] SI 4013·

Conditions for continued detention

11.96   There are three alternative conditions for continued detention of the seized cash, as set out in sub-paragraphs (6) to (8) of paragraph 3:

3 Detention of seized cash

. . .

(6) The first condition is that there are reasonable grounds for suspecting that the cash is intended to be used for the purposes of terrorism and that either—

(a) its continued detention is justified while its intended use is further investigated or consideration is given to bringing (in the United Kingdom or elsewhere) proceedings against any person for an offence with which the cash is connected, or

(b) proceedings against any person for an offence with which the cash is connected have been started and have not been concluded.

(7) The second condition is that there are reasonable grounds for suspecting that the cash consists of resources of an organisation which is a proscribed organisation and that either—

(a) its continued detention is justified while investigation is made into whether or not it consists of such resources or consideration is given to bringing (in the United Kingdom or elsewhere) proceedings against any person for an offence with which the cash is connected, or

(b) proceedings against any person for an offence with which the cash is connected have been started and have not been concluded.

(8) The third condition is that there are reasonable grounds for suspecting that the cash is property earmarked as terrorist property and that either—

(a) its continued detention is justified while its derivation is further investigated or consideration is given to bringing (in the United Kingdom or elsewhere) proceedings against any person for an offence with which the cash is connected, or

(b) proceedings against any person for an offence with which the cash is connected have been started and have not been concluded.

11.97   Instructions to authorised officers on the procedure to be adopted when making an application for the detention of cash seized under Schedule 1 are contained in the Code of Practice issued by the Secretary of State.[134] The Code of Practice stipulates, inter alia, that when an order to detain cash has been granted, the authorised officer should keep under review whether continued detention of the cash is justified, save where forfeiture proceedings or proceedings brought by a victim under paragraph 9 have been commenced and not concluded or where criminal proceedings have been commenced in connection with the cash and not concluded.[135] If for any reason the authorised officer considers he is no longer justified in detaining the cash he/she should release it and return it to the person from whom it was seized.

Victims

11.98   Paragraph 9 makes provision for any victim to intervene in the proceedings:

9 Victims

(1) A person who claims that any cash detained under this Schedule, or any part of it, belongs to him may apply to a magistrates' court or (in Scotland) the sheriff for the cash or part to be released to him.

---

[134] 'Code of Practice for authorised officers acting under Schedule 1 to The Anti-Terrorism, Crime and Security Act 2001' (n 127 above).
[135] Code of Practice, para 20.

(2) The application may be made in the course of proceedings under paragraph 3 or 6 [forfeiture proceedings] or at any other time.

(3) If it appears to the court or sheriff concerned that—

    (a) the applicant was deprived of the cash claimed, or of property which it represents, by criminal conduct,

    (b) the property he was deprived of was not, immediately before he was deprived of it, property obtained by or in return for criminal conduct and nor did it then represent such property, and

    (c) the cash claimed belongs to him,

the court or sheriff may order the cash to be released to the applicant.

Release of detained cash

Under Schedule 1, paragraph 5, there are two situations in which cash or any part of the cash **11.99** detained under paragraph 3 may be released to the person from whom it was seized:

5 Release of detained cash

(1) This paragraph applies while any cash is detained under this Schedule.

(2) A magistrates' court or (in Scotland) the sheriff may direct the release of the whole or any part of the cash if satisfied, on an application by the person from whom it was seized, that the conditions in paragraph 3 for the detention of cash are no longer met in relation to the cash to be released.

(3) An authorised officer or (in Scotland) a procurator fiscal may, after notifying the magistrates' court, sheriff or justice under whose order cash is being detained, release the whole or any part of it if satisfied that the detention of the cash to be released is no longer justified.

(4) But cash is not to be released—

    (a) if an application for its forfeiture under paragraph 6, or for its release under paragraph 9, is made, until any proceedings in pursuance of the application (including any proceedings on appeal) are concluded.

    (b) if (in the United Kingdom or elsewhere) proceedings are started against any person for an offence with which the cash is connected, until the proceedings are concluded.

Forfeiture of terrorist cash

Where cash has been detained under Schedule 1 an application may be made to the court for **11.100** the forfeiture of the whole or any part of it:

6 Forfeiture

(1) While cash is detained under this Schedule, an application for the forfeiture of the whole or any part of it may be made—

    (a) to a magistrates' court by the Commissioners of Customs and Excise[136] or an authorised officer, or

    (b) (in Scotland) to the sheriff by the Scottish Ministers.

(2) The court or sheriff may order the forfeiture of the cash or any part of it if satisfied that the cash or part is terrorist cash.

(3) In the case of property earmarked as terrorist property which belongs to joint tenants one of whom is an excepted joint owner, the order may not apply to so much of it as the court or sheriff thinks is attributable to the excepted joint owner's share.

(4) An excepted joint owner is a joint tenant who obtained the property in circumstances in which it would not (as against him) be earmarked; and references to his share of the

---

[136] To be read as, the Commissioner for Revenue and Customs (Commissioners for Revenue and Customs Act 2005, s 6).

earmarked property are to so much of the property as would have been his if the joint tenancy had been severed.

The procedure is set out in the Magistrates' Courts (Detention and Forfeiture of Terrorist Cash) (No 2) Rules 2001.[137] Instructions to authorised officers on the procedure to be adopted when making an application for the forfeiture of cash detained under Schedule 1 are also contained in the Code of Practice issued by the Secretary of State.[138] The Code of Practice provides that an application for forfeiture under Schedule 1 must be authorised by a police officer of the rank of superintendent or above who, prior to any application being made, should review the facts in order to be satisfied on the balance of probabilities that the cash is cash to which Schedule 1 applies.[139]

11.101 Paragraph 8 provides that any interest accrued on forfeited cash is to be paid into the Consolidated Fund (or the Scottish Consolidated Fund in Scotland) though only after the period of 30 days in paragraph 7 has elapsed or after an appeal has been determined or otherwise disposed of.

11.102 It has been suggested that open hearings in an ordinary magistrates' court are not the appropriate forum for handling cash seizures in terrorist cases. Such hearings are relatively infrequent and often depend on sensitive intelligence that the police may not be able to convert into open evidence within the 48 hours currently permitted between the seizure and confirmation in court.[140]

11.103 This point was made by various critics of the legislation during the bill's passage through Parliament but was, at that time, not accepted by the government. In its response to the recommendations of the Newton Committee of the Privy Council, however, the government conceded the point was worthy of further consideration, as the indications from law enforcement agencies were that they would welcome the introduction of special provisions such as those contained for warrant hearings in arrests under the Terrorism Act.[141]

Appeals

11.104 Under Schedule 1, paragraph 7 appeals against forfeiture may be lodged with the Crown Court[142] by any party to the proceedings within 30 days from when the forfeiture order was made.[143] The court hearing the appeal may make any order it thinks appropriate, including an order for the release of the cash.[144]

11.105 Note that, under paragraph 7(A), an organization which is deproscribed following a successful appeal under section 5 of the Terrorism Act 2000, may appeal against a forfeiture order within 30 days from the date in which deproscription came into force, provided that the forfeiture order was made in reliance (in whole or in part) on the fact that the organization

---

[137] SI 2001/4013.

[138] 'Code of Practice for authorised officers acting under Schedule 1 to The Anti-Terrorism, Crime and Security Act 2001' (n 127 above).

[139] Code of Practice, para 22.

[140] 'Anti-terrorism, Crime and Security Act 2001 Review: Report', Privy Counsellor Review Committee (The Newton Committee), December 2003, HC100.

[141] 'Counter-terrorism powers: reconciliation, security and liberty in an open society', Home Office discussion paper, February 2004, CM6147.

[142] Or, in Scotland, to the Court of Session or, in Northern Ireland, to a county court.

[143] ATCSA, Sch 1, paras 7(1)–(2).

[144] Ibid., paras 7(3)–(4).

was proscribed and the cash was seized on or after the date of the initial refusal to deproscribe against which the appeal was brought.

Compensation

Paragraph 10 provides for compensation to be made where no forfeiture order is made **11.106**
following the detention of cash under Schedule 1:

10 Compensation

(1) If no forfeiture order is made in respect of any cash detained under this Schedule, the person to whom the cash belongs or from whom it was seized may make an application to the magistrates' court or (in Scotland) the sheriff for compensation.

(2) If, for any period after the initial detention of the cash for 48 hours determined in accordance with paragraph 3(1A), the cash was not held in an interest-bearing account while detained, the court or sheriff may order an amount of compensation to be paid to the applicant.

(3) The amount of compensation to be paid under sub-paragraph (2) is the amount the court or sheriff thinks would have been earned in interest in the period in question if the cash had been held in an interest-bearing account.

(4) If the court or sheriff is satisfied that, taking account of any interest to be paid under this Schedule or any amount to be paid under sub-paragraph (2), the applicant has suffered loss as a result of the detention of the cash and that the circumstances are exceptions, the court or sheriff may order compensation (or additional compensation) to be paid to him.

(5) The amount of compensation to be paid under sub-paragraph (4) is the amount the court or sheriff thinks reasonable, having regard to the loss suffered and any other relevant circumstances.

Sub-paragraphs (6) to (9) prescribe the persons who must pay the compensation ordered by the court. Sub-paragraph (10) stipulates that paragraph 10 does not apply if the court or sheriff has made an order under paragraph 9 such that the cash has already been returned to the victim.

12

THE LAW IN PRACTICE

A. Introduction

12.01   The preceding chapters of this book examine in great detail the complex legislation and case law that relate to the investigation and prosecution of money laundering and the regulation of the anti-money laundering compliance regime. This chapter attempts to bring together those disparate areas and seeks to put them into a real-world context with practical guidance, identifying specific issues that commonly occur and illustrating how the civil, criminal, and regulatory fields of money laundering and anti-money laundering compliance intertwine.

12.02   Money laundering law is unusual in the way that it can affect ordinary law-abiding individuals and in the extent to which it can, on occasions, suddenly and dramatically impact on their lives and businesses—for instance, as the result of the effective freezing of bank accounts on a suspicion by a bank of money laundering or the seizure of cash at an airport. A number of features of the law contribute to this situation, such as the minimal mental element of 'suspicion' in money laundering and in relation to suspicious activity reporting, the consent regime, the lack of specific intent in the money laundering offences, the extended powers to seize cash on the basis of an officer's 'reasonable suspicion'[1] and the widening of investigative and related powers, including the circumstances in which restraint orders can be obtained.

12.03   This chapter develops a hypothetical scenario through the various stages of investigation and prosecution from civil cash seizure to criminal trial, and illustrates many of the aspects of money laundering law referred to above. It deals, in particular, with situations demanding an urgent response to law enforcement action that can have immediate and harmful effects on a person's life and livelihood. It is not intended that this chapter will cover the issues

---

[1] The threshold amount, originally £10,000, has been progressively reduced to £1,000.

exhaustively and the reader is encouraged always to refer back to the specific relevant earlier chapter(s).

B. A Practical Scenario

The scenario below is shown in four parts, followed by the relevant issues and commentary **12.04** for each.

Part one: scenario

A was stopped by customs officers employed by the UK Border Agency (UKBA) at Heathrow **12.05** Airport on her way to Bulgaria, at 8pm on Thursday 1 April 2010. She was found to be in possession of about £80,000 worth of currency (mainly in €200 notes[2]). UKBA detained, questioned, and then released A. They seized and detained the cash, then, on 6 April 2010,[3] they applied successfully to the magistrates' court for an order for its further detention.

In the case in which the cash was being carried, UKBA officers found a page torn from **12.06** a notebook with various figures on it, apparently money calculations, and a telephone number (B's mobile telephone number).

Part one: issues: cash seizure

Introduction

Although they also form part of the legal procedures for civil recovery of the proceeds of **12.07** crime,[4] cash forfeiture proceedings[5] are, essentially, part of the wider regime developed to deal with money laundering (i.e. the concealing, disguising, converting, transferring, removing from England and Wales, acquiring, using, or possessing criminal property[6]). For this reason, cash forfeiture cases often arise out of or result in criminal investigations in relation to money laundering. However, they may also, of course, operate independently of any criminal investigation, particularly where there is insufficient evidence to identify the particular kind or kinds of unlawful conduct to which the cash[7] relates and/or where it is not possible to establish the state of mind of the person from whom the cash was seized.[8]

---

[2] The €200 note is now the highest denomination dealt with by money service businesses in the UK. SOCA confirmed in May 2010 that the €500 note had been withdrawn from sale from April, after an eight-month analysis of movements of the note in the UK showed that 90 per cent of the notes sold in the UK were in the hands of organized criminals.

[3] Under s 295(1) and (1B), the cash may be detained for 48 hours before an order for extension of the period of detention is obtained from a magistrates' court or (in Scotland) the sheriff. However, in calculating the period of 48 hours, no account should be taken of weekends, Christmas Day, Good Friday, or bank holidays. In 2010, Good Friday fell on 2 April.

[4] Chapter 2 of Part 5 of POCA.

[5] Chapter 3 of Part 5 of POCA.

[6] POCA, ss 327–9, albeit that the cash forfeiture regime extends to cash which is not just criminal property, but also that which is intended for use in unlawful conduct.

[7] Cash is defined by POCA, s 89 very widely and includes, but is not limited to, notes and coins in any currency, postal orders, cheques of any kind (including traveller's cheques), banker's drafts, bearer bonds and bearer shares.

[8] Under POCA, s 340 for a money laundering offence to have been committed the alleged offender must know or suspect that the cash constitutes or represents a person's benefit from 'criminal conduct'.

What powers have been used here?

12.08   The officers here,[9] where they have reasonable grounds for suspecting that A is carrying cash that is £1,000 or more in value (and that is either the proceeds of crime or intended for use in crime),[10] have powers to require A to permit a search of any article she has with her.[11] They may also require her to permit a search of her person[12] (see below). In addition, the officers can detain A for as long as is necessary for the exercise of the powers.[13]

12.09   There may be a question here about what grounds the officers had to search A, although the finding of a large amount of cash arguably renders it academic. Despite claims that the powers would be used in intelligence-led investigations,[14] it is common to see a case start with a speculative search like this, often at an airport. A declaration under cash declaration regulations is not required because the travel is within the EU.

12.10   There is no specific power to question a person (or compel them to answer questions) in possession of seized cash or, indeed, before any possession of cash is suspected or known. However, in practice, a refusal to answer questions makes it more likely that the person will be detained and searched, and that any cash with a value of £1,000 or more will be seized and ultimately forfeited. The risk of not answering questions must be weighed against the prospect of a court disbelieving the account that is given—because it is later contradicted or discredited, because the court finds it inherently implausible or because the person fails to elaborate on it or produce the paperwork to back it up.

What is a search?

12.11   The term 'search' is not defined, although intimate searches and strip searches are specifically excluded.[15] Any individual faced with a request from a uniformed officer to turn out their pockets or empty the bags that they are carrying is, in practice, fairly likely to comply and so the question of what precisely constitutes a search and what an officer is entitled to do in pursuance of one is very unlikely to arise. The specific exclusion of intimate searches and strip searches might imply that reasonable force short of that is permissible, but the position is unclear. If A refused to turn out her pockets, would the officers be entitled to reach in to them? Section 289(3) of POCA states that the officer or constable may, so far as he thinks it necessary or expedient, require the suspect to permit a search of any article he has with him or to permit a search of his person. In addition, section 289(4) of POCA states that an officer or constable may detain the suspect for so long as is necessary for those powers of search to be exercised. In such circumstances, it would appear that the officer would be entitled to reach into A's pockets; he could also detain her to do so.

---

[9]   Because they are customs officers—not by virtue of their employment by UKBA. POCA, s 289(2).

[10]   POCA, s 289(2); in addition, the powers are only exercisable so far as reasonable for the purpose of finding cash and, so far as a customs officer is concerned, only if he has reasonable grounds for suspecting that the unlawful conduct in question relates to an assigned matter within the meaning of the Customs and Excise Management Act 1979.

[11]   POCA, s 289(3)(a).

[12]   Ibid., s289(3)(b).

[13]   Ibid., s 289(4).

[14]   Bob Ainsworth MP, then Parliamentary Under Secretary at the Home Office, said in the House of Commons on 8 January 2002 that the powers would be '...used in a targeting fashion to back up intelligence-led operations'.

[15]   POCA, s 289(8).

Was prior approval given for the exercise of these powers?

The search powers considered above may only be exercised with the approval of a magistrate **12.12** or, if that is not practicable, a senior officer (meaning a police inspector or the Customs equivalent), unless it is not practicable to obtain that approval in advance.[16] Applications to a magistrate can be made without notice and decided without a hearing or at a private hearing.[17] If the powers are exercised without such an approval in a case where no cash is seized (or where cash is seized but not detained for more than 48 hours), the officer who exercised the powers must make a written report to a person appointed by the Secretary of State.[18]

Have the powers been exercised in accordance with the relevant code of practice?

The Secretary of State must issue a code of practice on the exercise by customs officers and **12.13** others of these powers.[19] A revised code was introduced on 6 April 2008. Failure to comply with the code would not in itself make the officer liable to any civil or criminal proceedings.[20] Depending on the failure, it may instead have an impact on the admissibility of certain evidence in any proceedings for forfeiture.

Was the search intelligence-led?

Whilst section 289 of POCA provides customs and police officers (and other specified indi- **12.14** viduals) with the power to search persons and articles they have with them for cash, in prac- tice 'cash' which is ultimately seized under POCA is normally identified and seized as a result of searches conducted under alternative legislation.[21] As mentioned above, if the powers of search and detention are exercised without approval in a case where no cash is seized (or where cash is seized but not detained for more than 48 hours), the officer who exercised the powers must make a written report to the 'appointed person'. In the year 2008–2009, of the 5,398 cash seizures made by police officers, none resulted in a report to the 'appointed person' and of the 525 seizures made by customs officers, only 12 resulted in a report to the 'appointed person'. In his report, published in June 2009, the 'appointed person' concluded:

> The reasons for the relatively low numbers of reports from HM Revenue and Customs have been set out in previous reports as a greater concentration on activities at frontiers rather than inland (*using powers under the Customs and Excise Management Act 1979 rather than the Proceeds of Crime Act 2002*). The explanation from the police is that criminal investigations usually lead to an arrest for drug trafficking, theft or money laundering and police invariably *use their powers under the Police and Criminal Evidence Act 1984 and the Misuse of Drugs Act 1971* to obtain warrants and seize property including cash. [Emphasis added.]

Further, with the transfer in August 2009 of several thousand customs officers to the newly **12.15** formed UK Border Agency, which enforces both immigration and customs regulations, it is likely that there will be an increase in cash seized following questioning and/or searches conducted under the Immigration Act 1971.

---

[16] Ibid., s 290.
[17] Magistrates' Courts (Detention and Forfeiture of Cash) Rules 2002, r 3.
[18] POCA, s 290.
[19] Ibid., s 292.
[20] Ibid., s 292(6).
[21] E.g. pursuant to a search warrant or search following arrest under the Police and Criminal Evidence Act 1984.

12.16 The main practical implication of the lack of use of the POCA search powers is that it appears to render otiose the raft of safeguards in the Act designed to limit the use of the power. These safeguards, which include the obligation to follow the Code of Practice in connection with the exercise of search and seizure powers under POCA, were designed to ensure that the search powers were used in a targeted fashion to back up intelligence-led operations. Evidently, however, this 'intelligence-led' focus is not how the cash forfeiture regime is operating in practice. Rather, cash subject to seizure and, ultimately, forfeiture proceedings, is commonly identified initially as a result of questioning (and production by the person questioned, without a search) and/or searches conducted under alternative legislation with fewer safeguards.

12.17 In this regard, it is interesting to note that, of the 12 reports made by customs and police officers to the 'appointed person' in the year 2008–9, which followed, by definition, searches conducted under POCA, all related to seizures at airports, 11 followed 'dog identification', one followed 'voluntary disclosure' and none were made as a result of 'intelligence received'. Further, in the year 2007–8, of the 47 reports made (out of a total of 5,098 seizures), 42 were made at airports, 39 followed 'dog identification', five followed 'observation', and only three were 'intelligence-led'.

12.18 In practice, many cash seizures do not result from a search of any kind and are not intelligence-led. In addition, many searches resulting in a cash seizure are not exercised using the powers under POCA.

What were the grounds to seize the cash?

12.19 An officer may seize 'cash' *if he has* reasonable grounds for suspecting that it, or part of it, is 'recoverable property' (in effect, the proceeds of crime) or intended for use in 'unlawful conduct'.[22] This contrasts with the tests applied before the magistrates' courts for continued detention (*that there are* reasonable grounds for such a suspicion[23]) and eventual forfeiture (*that the court is satisfied* that the cash or part of it is 'recoverable property' or is intended for use in 'unlawful conduct'[24]).

12.20 Here, absent a compelling explanation, the fact of a large amount of cash being carried with the intention of flying with it on a plane is probably unusual enough to raise a general suspicion that the 'cash' is either 'recoverable property' or intended for use in 'unlawful conduct'. Clearly there is no basis for settling on a firmer view as to which of those categories applies and what offences have been committed or are contemplated. Nevertheless, the grounds for suspicion must be set out clearly in the application for detention, including any additional specific facts (the age or appearance of the banknotes, for example) that tend to support those grounds.

What forms must be served on A?

12.21 A should be provided with a 'Receipt for Seized Cash' and a copy of 'Form A', which is the application to be used before the magistrates' court for the detention of the 'cash'. The form must state the name and address of the person from whom the 'cash' was seized and anyone

---

[22] POCA, s 294; s 294 also requires the cash, or the part to which his requisite suspicion relates, to be of a value of £1,000 or more, but in this scenario that requirement is fulfilled.

[23] Ibid., s 295(5) and (6).

[24] Ibid., s 298(2).

else likely to be affected, the amount seized (or estimated amount, although this is not permissible for any further applications), the date, time, and place of seizure, and the grounds for suspicion. [25]

Was the application to the court made in time?

The officers can detain the cash for up to 48 hours, but must then release it unless they have **12.22** first successfully applied to a magistrates' court for an order that it continue to be detained. However, various days are excluded from this calculation including weekends and bank holidays.[26] As the cash that A was carrying was seized on the day before Good Friday, and taking into consideration Easter Monday, the officers have made their application in time.

Defending a cash forfeiture application

As many cash searches/seizures, particular at frontiers, are not in practice intelligence-led, **12.23** often the suspicions upon which the cash is seized and subsequently detained are not based on any direct evidence linking the cash (or the person from whom it was seized) to a particular kind or kinds of unlawful activity. Rather, common reasons given for formulating the relevant suspicion are no more than the individual concerned has 'eschewed the banking system', or the individual is carrying a large sum of cash whilst travelling, and/or the officer was not satisfied by the individual's explanation for carrying the cash.

This lack of substantive evidence will often mean that the enforcement authority will make **12.24** continuous applications for the detention of the seized cash (up to a maximum aggregate period of two years) whilst it carries out an investigation. Indeed, the fact that customs and police officers are commonly making repeated applications for detention is evident by the recent amendment to section 295(2)(a) of POCA, which increased the maximum time interval between individual applications for continued detention from three months to six months. Of course, during this period, the person from whom the cash was seized must do without the cash, unless he applies to the court for release of the detained cash, in which case the burden of satisfying the court that the conditions for detention are no longer met is reversed and placed on the person from whom the cash was seized.[27]

Further, it is now no longer necessary for the enforcement authority to adduce evidence of, **12.25** or even allege, the particular kind or kinds of unlawful conduct from which the cash was obtained or for which its use was intended in order to obtain forfeiture of the cash. In practice, the courts have held that conduct consisting of the mere fact of having a very large sum of cash in the form of banknotes in one's possession in certain circumstances (e.g. at an airport) may well demand an answer.[28] Thus, in many cases the burden of proof is, it is submitted (although, the courts have held otherwise), effectively reversed: the burden will be on the applicant for release of the cash to provide an answer which satisfies the court as to the derivation and intended use of the cash. In effect, persons carrying cash in the value of £1,000 or more are at risk of having the cash seized (and potentially subsequently forfeited) unless they are able to give a compelling explanation as to its origin and destination.

---

[25] Magistrates' Courts (Detention and Forfeiture of Cash) Rules 2002, Schedule: Form A.
[26] POCA, s 295(1B).
[27] Ibid., s 297: Note that victims or others who claim ownership of the cash may also apply to the court for its release.
[28] E.g. *Green* [2005] EWHC 495 (Admin).

12.26 This situation is exacerbated by the insertion of sections 297A to 297G of POCA.[29] These sections, although not in force at the time of writing, will introduce into POCA provisions to enable law enforcement authorities to forfeit detained cash without a court order in uncontested cases. In these circumstances, it will be sufficient for a senior officer (in the case of the police, an inspector) to come to the conclusion that the cash is 'recoverable property'[30] or is intended by any person for use in unlawful conduct and to issue a notice to which no objection is made within a defined period—the cash will then be forfeited. Accordingly, save for agreeing to the cash being detained (on the basis of a lower threshold than applies to an application for forfeiture[31]), there will be no judicial oversight safeguarding forfeiture by such administrative action.

Part two: scenario

12.27 An investigation was commenced by the Metropolitan Police Service into suspected money laundering by B, the proprietor of a small retail money service business offering Bureau de Change and money transmission services. During police observations, it was noted that frequent visits to B's money service business were made by C, a market trader with a number of outlets who had been engaged in that business for many years. C used B's money service business to convert large sums of cash into other currencies, usually euros, and arrange for the transmission of that money abroad.

The police successfully applied to the court for a search warrant for B's home and business premises and C's home. The warrant was executed; computers, documents and other items were seized. In response to what they found in the course of the searches, the police arrested B and C. They were both interviewed under caution and then bailed to return to the police station in the future to allow for further enquiries to be undertaken.

Cash was also seized from C's home address: a total of £1,430 was seized (£940 in a bundle of notes under a paper weight on a mantelpiece in his living room and £490 in a wallet found in his bedroom).

Part two: issues: search, arrest, and cash seizure

Was the search warrant lawfully granted?

12.28 The application for a search and seizure warrant would be made on the basis that B and C are subject to a money laundering investigation.[32] The court must also be satisfied, in effect, that a production order was not an appropriate alternative in the particular circumstances of the case.[33] In the event of a dispute, the authorities are in favour of disclosure of the information provided to the court. [34]

---

[29] By the Policing and Crime Act 2009, s 65.

[30] Recoverable property is defined in POCA, s 304 as property obtained through 'unlawful conduct'.

[31] Detention requires reasonable grounds for suspecting that the cash is 'recoverable property' or intended to be used in unlawful conduct, as opposed to forfeiture requiring satisfaction that the cash is 'recoverable property' or intended for use in unlawful conduct.

[32] POCA, s 352; alternatively, search and seizure warrants can be, and perhaps more often are, obtained under the Police and Criminal Evidence 1984 (as well as search and seizures being conducted following arrest).

[33] POCA, s 353.

[34] *R (Energy Financing Team Ltd) v Bow Street Magistrates' Court and others* [2006] 1 WLR 1316; *R (Cronin) v Sheffield Justices* [2003] 1 WLR 752; *R (Redknapp) v Commissioner of the City of London Police* [2009] 1 WLR 2091; *R (Mercury Tax Group) v HMRC* [2008] EWHC 2721.

What is the evidence of money laundering against B and C?

C, a market trader, is apparently using the services of a money service business to convert **12.29**
large amounts of cash (sterling) into euros and to transfer that cash, by courier, to a foreign
country. The cash from C is or may be, in whole or in part, cash receipts of his legitimate
business. In so far as it is, the police suspect that C may be moving the cash (undeclared
takings) in order to evade tax. However, a failure to declare income for tax purposes does not
turn the proceeds of otherwise legitimate trading into criminal property.[35]

The police also suspect that C is using his cash-generating business as a cover to launder other **12.30**
cash that is the proceeds of crime, probably drug trafficking. If there is sufficient evidence to
support that suspicion, the facts would constitute a money laundering offence.

In a trial of allegations of money laundering, if the prosecution was unable to produce suf- **12.31**
ficient evidence of the specific offence(s) from which the cash was derived, or even the kind
of offence(s), the jury may draw the inference that the cash was criminal property from the
surrounding circumstances.[36]

C's frequent visits to B's premises and the sending abroad of large sums of cash may be **12.32**
asserted by the police as good reason for B to have suspected that C was engaged in money
laundering and that C's cash was the proceeds of crime. On the basis of B's continued business relationship with C, the police may suspect that B has been engaged in money laundering by converting and transferring C's proceeds of crime, knowing or suspecting that it was
criminal property. In addition, the circumstances of the seizure of cash from A may be
adduced as evidence against B (and C, if seized paperwork or other evidence shows that the
cash was his). Further, as B is in the regulated sector, he may have committed the offence of
failing to make the required disclosure.[37]

Under what powers is the cash seized at C's home? Is it above the minimum amount?

The cash at C's home could be seized as 'material found there which is likely to be of substan- **12.33**
tial value (whether or not by itself) to the investigation',[38] or alternatively under cash seizure
powers.[39] Although neither the money on C's mantelpiece nor the money in his wallet meet
the minimum amount threshold of £1,000 by themselves, for the purposes of cash seizure,
it is permissible to aggregate them if the cash is derived from a common source or is intended
for a common destination and collectively the amount exceeds the minimum amount.[40]

Here, in connection with the £490 found in the wallet, there would appear to be no basis **12.34**
for inferring a common source or destination. As a market trader he is likely to deal in cash
and, so unless there are good grounds to think that all of his business is criminal, it appears
that aggregation would not be lawful. If cash is seized for one purpose, for example, as evidence of an offence, and then notionally re-seized under cash forfeiture powers, the statutory

[35] *R v Janis Gabriel* [2006] EWCA Crim 229.
[36] Where the circumstances are such 'as to give rise to the irresistible inference that it can only be derived
from crime' (per Thomas LJ in *R v Anwoir* [2008] EWCA Crim 1354).
[37] POCA, s 330.
[38] Ibid., s 352; compare with the position under a warrant granted under Police and Criminal Evidence Act
1984, s 8, which permits the seizure of material that is 'relevant evidence' and 'likely to be of substantial value
(whether by itself or together with other material) to the investigation . . .'.
[39] POCA, s 294.
[40] *Customs and Excise Commissioners v Duffy* [2002] EWHC 425.

minimum amount and the strict time limits for the detention of the cash apply only from the point when the cash is re-seized.[41]

Part three: scenario

12.35 The police investigation into the activities of B and C was extended to D, the accountant who prepares tax returns for C, and to E, the solicitor who has acted for C in several property transactions and whose firm has also acted for B.

D had a production order served on her.

E was arrested and interviewed under caution in relation to allegations of money laundering,[42] then bailed to return to the police station in the future.

The police made a without notice successful application for pre-charge restraint orders against B and C. Each restraint order includes a requirement for B and C each to provide a statement of truth setting out all of their assets.[43]

Part three: issues: arrest, production order and restraint orders

Have the requirements for a production order been met?

12.36 For the production order to have been lawfully made there must be reasonable grounds for suspecting that the person subject to the money laundering investigation (in this scenario, D's client, C) has committed a money laundering offence.[44] There must also be reasonable grounds for believing that D is in possession or control of the specified material, that it is likely to be of substantial value (whether or not by itself) to the investigation, and that it is in the public interest for it to be produced or access given to it (weighing up the benefit to the investigation against the circumstances in which D has or controls it[45]—here, the relationship between accountant and client). Depending on the strength of the surveillance evidence (and any information from HM Revenue & Customs about C's tax returns), D may have an argument that the production order is excessive and apply to the court to discharge or vary it.[46] The production order does not require D to produce or give access to legally privileged material.[47]

What is the evidence of money laundering against E?

12.37 Any person who carries out property or financial transactions—whether as a bank official, as a lawyer, or otherwise—must inevitably, but unwittingly, 'launder' dirty money on many occasions: dirty money does not come neatly labelled as such. The key question in considering the potential criminal liability of E is what he knew, or suspected, or should have known or suspected.

---

[41] *Chief Constable of Merseyside Police v Hickman* [2006] EWHC 451 (Admin).

[42] Under POCA, money laundering includes transferring criminal property (s 327), possessing criminal property (s 329) and entering into or becoming concerned in an arrangement knowing or suspecting that it facilitates the acquisition, retention, use or control or criminal property by or on behalf of another (s 328).

[43] Although there is no specific power for such a requirement in POCA, s 41(7) provides that the court may make such an order as it believes is appropriate for the purpose of ensuring that the restraint order is effective and, indeed, such a requirement has long been recognized by the court and even under the pre-existing regime.

[44] POCA, s 346(2)(c).

[45] Ibid., ss 346(3)–(5).

[46] Ibid., ss 346(3)–50.

[47] Ibid., s 348(1).

The police suspect C has been using these transactions as a means of laundering the proceeds **12.38** of crime. If the evidence suggests that E knew or suspected that C was money laundering, the position is straightforward and the police are likely to charge E either with a money laundering arrangement offence under section 328 or with conspiracy to money launder. If the evidence is insufficient to establish actual knowledge or suspicion, there is also the offence of failing to report to be considered.

E is a solicitor acting in property transactions and so is in the regulated sector for the pur- **12.39** poses of the Money Laundering Regulations 2007 and for the purposes of the requirement in section 330 of POCA to report knowledge or suspicion that another person is engaged in money laundering. This requirement extends beyond actual knowledge or suspicion, and includes an objective test: a person in the regulated sector is required to report where they have reasonable grounds to know or suspect that another person is engaged in money laundering. What facts and circumstances were known to E at the time of carrying out the relevant property transaction will determine whether such grounds exist.

The Law Society's guidance, contained in its Practice Note on money laundering, advises **12.40** solicitors dealing with property transactions to look out for large payments from private funds, especially if the client has a low income. If concerned, they should ask their clients to explain the source of the funds, and assess whether that explanation is valid (for instance, the money may be from an inheritance or from the sale of another property).[48]

The options for the police are, of course, not limited to arresting E and making him subject **12.41** to police bail following interview under caution. They may instead apply for and serve a production order on him. If there are insufficient grounds for charging a money laundering offence or a failing to report offence, the police might still have concerns as to whether the solicitor had acted with appropriate due diligence. In those circumstances, the police could refer the matter to the Solicitors Regulation Authority, who could require E to produce the files for C's various transactions and investigate whether he has breached the Regulations.[49] A failure to comply with a requirement of the Regulations, in particular any of the detailed requirements in relation to customer due diligence, would constitute a criminal offence under Regulation 45.

Have the conditions for a restraint order been met?

A restraint order can be made against a suspect in a criminal investigation who has not yet **12.42** been charged: all that is required is that a criminal investigation has been started in England and Wales and that there is reasonable cause to believe that the alleged offender has benefited from his criminal conduct.[50] This contrasts with the position under the preceding legislation, where if proceedings had not yet begun the court had to be satisfied that the person was 'to be charged'.[51] If any of the alleged offending precedes the commencement of the relevant part of POCA,[52] the old law applies.

Applications for restraint orders are often made without notice. It is, therefore, very impor- **12.43** tant that the judge is informed of the position in a fair and balanced manner; indeed the

---

[48] Law Society Anti Money Laundering Practice Note, para 11.4.2.
[49] See the Solicitors' Code of Conduct 2007, rule 20.08.
[50] POCA, s 40(2).
[51] Criminal Justice Act 1988, s 76.
[52] Before 24 March 2003.

applicant has a duty of full and frank disclosure.[53] In particular, the witness statement provided by the police in support of the application for the restraint order should set out fully and accurately all the relevant information, including information favourable to B and/or C. If there are matters that would have made a difference to the success of the application or the terms of the order, but have not been included in the prosecution's statement, B and C may bring them to the court's attention in an application to vary or discharge the order.

What about third party interests?

12.44 B is a money service provider and may hold funds for other people. If the funds are not his then they should not be covered by the restraint order, but this may not be clear. Third parties with an interest in the restrained property have a right to apply to the court to have the order varied accordingly.

What steps could have been taken to pre-empt the restraint order?

12.45 Persons subject to a criminal investigation in respect of allegations of money laundering will often also be subject to an application by the investigator/prosecutor for a restraint order restraining them from dealing[54] with their assets.[55] Such applications may be made at any time following the commencement of the investigation[56] (significantly, they may be made before any criminal offences have been formally charged) and may be made without notice[57] to the defendant.[58] The purpose of such a restraint order is to prevent the dissipation of assets in advance of any confiscation proceedings such that they are available at that time and should, therefore, only be granted where there is a real risk of dissipation, although in certain cases the risk of dissipation will speak for itself.[59] However, it is no exaggeration to say that the power to apply for a restraint order (both before and after charge) has been embraced by investigating and prosecuting authorities and applications for restraint orders may now be regarded as the norm in large and medium scale cases (particularly where significant assets are identifiable).

12.46 In practice, therefore, suspects in criminal investigations should be alive to the real prospect that they may within a very short timescale have a restraint order served on them prohibiting them from dealing[60] with any[61] of their assets save for, in most cases (and at least until the order can be varied), £250 per week for living expenses. Not only does such an order severely restrict the use of assets, it inevitably leads to financial institutions being made aware of its existence with the accompanying severe reputation damage. Further, it is inadvisable for

---

[53] See para 12.48 below; see also *AJ and DJ*, 9 December 1992, unreported and *In the matter of Stanford International Bank Ltd* [2010] EWCA Civ 137.

[54] Restraint orders are often drafted with the standard terms 'The defendant must not (1) remove from England and Wales any of his assets which are in England and Wales; or (2) in any way dispose of, deal with or diminish the value of any of his assets whether they are in or outside England and Wales.'

[55] POCA, s 41.

[56] Ibid., s 40(2).

[57] Criminal Procedure Rules, r 59.1.

[58] The reference to the defendant is in terms of him being a defendant to the proceedings relating to the application for the restraint order, as opposed to a defendant in criminal proceedings (which may have not yet been commenced).

[59] *Re AJ and DJ* (unreported, 9 December 1992).

[60] Ibid.

[61] Restraint orders invariably seek to identify specific assets, but they generally apply to all of the defendant's assets whether or not identified within the order or, indeed, transferred to the defendant after the order is made (POCA, s 41(2)). In short, restraint orders generally apply to any asset the defendant has the power directly or indirectly to dispose of or deal with as if it were his own.

a person to seek to pre-empt the order by dissipating their assets prior to a restraint order being obtained, such as by giving them away, or by seeking to 'hide' them in a foreign juris-diction. This simply provides the investigator/prosecutor with stronger grounds to obtain a restraint order; it is also unlikely to prevent such assets from being taken into account by the court when it comes to quantifying the size of any subsequent confiscation order.[62]

It may, however, be possible to pre-empt the application for a restraint order in other ways, **12.47** thereby avoiding it all together, or at least lessening its impact. An individual who anticipates an application for a restraint order being made against him may wish to notify the investiga-tor/prosecutor of the extent and whereabouts of his assets and offer an undertaking to 'ring-fence' a certain amount of his assets and/or not dissipate them beyond a certain amount. He may also ask that any application for a restraint order is made on notice on the basis that, in the light of the notification and undertaking, there would be no operational justification for preventing the attendance of his representatives at the application.

In addition, the investigator/prosecutor would be bound by the duty of full and frank disclo- **12.48** sure to bring to the attention of the court any such contact/ correspondence such that any application on a without notice basis should be adjourned for the defendant's representatives to attend to allow them to make appropriate submissions as to whether a restraint order should be made and, if so, its scope. This approach will give the individual a greater chance of avoiding an application being made, or at least avoiding it being made without notice,[63] as well as avoiding the imposition of a restraint order or limiting its scope.

Although legal aid is available, once a restraint order is obtained, the defendant is prohibited **12.49** from using his assets to meet legal expenses incurred in relation to the restraint proceedings (or, indeed, the substantive criminal proceedings).[64] Accordingly, if an application for a restraint order is made on notice it will enable the defendant to use his own assets to pay for legal representation to challenge the application, rather than having to resort to working within the constraints of legal aid. Alternatively, a person who anticipates a without notice application may seek to pay in advance for his legal representation up to a certain point in time, for example, any charging decision. This will enable him to argue that the fees were incurred prior to the making of the order and therefore that the funds paid over in settlement of the fees should not be subject to the restrictions or a restraint order.[65] This would allow the defendant to use his assets not only to challenge the imposition of a restraint order, but also to apply to vary or discharge any restraint order that was ultimately made.

What steps can be taken after the restraint order has been obtained?

A restraint order is a far reaching order: effectively it prevents the defendant from dealing[66] **12.50** with his assets in any way other than basic living, business, and legal[67] expenses until the criminal investigation, and any ensuing prosecution, is concluded. In practice, this can mean

---

[62] On the basis of a finding of 'hidden assets'; see *R v Wright* [2006] EWCA Crim 1257: where the court has found that there are hidden assets, it will make a confiscation order in the value of the 'recoverable amount' (i.e. defendant's benefit from the criminal conduct concerned).

[63] See *Re AJ and DJ,* (n 59 above): where there is little likelihood of assets being dissipated in the short period between notice of an application being given and the hearing taking place, the prosecutor should always con-sider whether it would be more appropriate for the application to be heard on notice.

[64] POCA, s 41(4) and *Customs and Excise Commissioners v S* [2005] 1 WLR 1338.

[65] See *Irwin Mitchell v Revenue and Customs Prosecutions Office* [2008] EWCA Crim 1741.

[66] Ibid.

[67] But not legal expenses related to the restraint proceedings or the substantive criminal proceedings.

that his assets are restrained for a number of years. Furthermore, even where a defendant is alleged to have committed only one offence, prosecutors will often seek to characterize the offence being investigated as falling within the definition of 'criminal lifestyle'.[68] The result is that, at least until the contrary is demonstrated, the court will assume that all property (whether or not related to the instant criminal allegation) obtained by the defendant within the previous six years was his benefit from criminal conduct, which may have a direct and significant effect on the value of assets subject to the restraint order.

12.51   It is often, therefore, of fundamental importance for recipients of restraint orders to obtain a variation limiting the value of the assets subject to the order. A variation may be obtained by agreement with the prosecutor or by an application to the court. However, this may require persuasive evidence to be provided by the defendant as to his income and expenditure (in order to rebut the 'criminal lifestyle' assumption[s]) together with a sound analysis of the maximum possible value attributable to the benefit obtained by the defendant from the alleged criminal conduct. If this can be done, it may be possible to obtain a variation of the order limiting the value of assets subject to the order and thereby leaving the defendant free to deal with the remainder of his assets. However, it is likely that, in return, the defendant will be required to provide the prosecutor with a monthly account of his income and expenditure.

Part four: scenario

12.52   The investigations by UKBA (in respect of the seized cash) and by the police (in respect of the suspected money laundering and other criminal offences) continued. In addition, HM Revenue & Customs (HMRC) began an investigation into the tax affairs of C. Further, B, C, and E answered their bail at the police station, where they were charged by the custody sergeant.

Part four: issues: continued investigation and charge

To what extent can data from the various investigations be shared?

12.53   There will be a continuing exchange of information by UKBA, HMRC, and the police, as well as the Serious Organised Crime Agency (in relation to any intelligence and/or any suspicious activity reports). Data matching will be an integral part of the investigations, but there are restrictions. Information provided under compulsion pursuant the requirements of a restraint order may not be used against that person in a prosecution.[69] Also, information provided to the Legal Services Commission in the context of an application for legal aid (which may include information about the person's income and capital) may not be revealed to investigators or prosecutors.[70]

What are the appropriate charges for B (the operator of a money service business)?

12.54   The following may be appropriate charges for B:

- acquiring and/or possessing criminal property (section 329 of POCA);
- concealing, disguising, converting, or transferring criminal property and/or removing criminal property from England and Wales (section 327 of POCA);

---

[68] Within the meaning of POCA, s 75.
[69] *Re C (Restraint Order: Disclosure)* 4 September 2000.
[70] Access to Justice Act 1999, s 20.

- entering into or becoming concerned in an arrangement with C which he knows or suspects facilitates C's retention, use or control of criminal property (section 328 of POCA).

In addition, it would be possible to charge B with conspiring with C to conceal, disguise, **12.55** convert, transfer, and/or remove from England and Wales criminal property. However, as the mental element that has to be proved in a money laundering conspiracy offence is higher (actual knowledge)[71] than in a substantive money laundering offence (where mere suspicion is enough), such a charge should only be included where there is sufficient evidence of this level of knowledge.[72]

Further, although the offence of failing to make the required disclosure knowing or suspect- **12.56** ing, or having reasonable grounds for the same, that C is engaged in money laundering (under section 330 of POCA) may effectively operate as an alternative to the above more serious offences of money laundering, in reality it is submitted that this offence should be restricted to circumstances where the evidence only supports reasonable grounds for knowing or suspecting rather than actual knowledge or suspicion.

What are the appropriate charges for C (the market trader)?
The following may be appropriate charges for C: **12.57**

- acquiring, using and/or possessing criminal property (section 329 of POCA);
- concealing, disguising, converting, transferring, and/or removing from England and Wales criminal property (section 327 of POCA).[73]

As with B above, it would also be possible to charge C with: **12.58**

- conspiring with B to conceal, disguise, convert, transfer, and/or remove from England and Wales criminal property;
- conspiring with E to conceal, disguise, convert, and/or transfer criminal property.

What are the appropriate charges for E (the property solicitor)?
The following may be appropriate charges for E: **12.59**

- acquiring and/or possessing criminal property (section 329 of POCA);
- concealing, disguising, converting, and/or transferring criminal property (section 327 of POCA);
- entering into or becoming concerned in an arrangement with C which he knows or suspects facilitates C's retention, use, or control of criminal property (section 328 of POCA).

Again, it would also be possible to charge E with: **12.60**

- conspiring with C to conceal, disguise, convert, and/or transfer criminal property;
- failing to make the required disclosure knowing or suspecting, or having reasonable grounds for the same, that C is engaged in money laundering (section 330 of POCA).

---

[71] *R v El-Kurd and others* [2007] EWCA Crim 1888 (26 July 2007).
[72] See Chapter 2 on conspiracy to launder money. Note also that if a substantive count and a related conspiracy count are joined in an indictment, the prosecution will have to justify their inclusion; the prosecution may be required to elect whether to proceed on a substantive charge or on conspiracy. *R v Colin Watts* [1995] WL 1084341.
[73] Unlike with B, the arrangement offence does not apply because it is C's criminal property.

What will happen to the cash seizure proceedings while the criminal proceedings are ongoing?

12.61   The court can authorize the further detention of the seized cash for six months at a time during the criminal proceedings, while the cash seizure/forfeiture investigations continue, to a maximum period of two years. An application for forfeiture can be made at any time within that period. Conversely, an application to release it can be made by the person from whom it was seized or by the owner, if that is different. Where the subject matter of cash seizure/forfeiture proceedings and criminal proceedings overlap, as they do in this scenario, the court may adjourn the cash seizure/forfeiture proceedings pending the outcome of the criminal proceedings, although in any event any application for forfeiture must be made before the expiry of the two-year limit.[74]

12.62   In this scenario, there may be a risk either to B or to C (if he is the owner of all or some of the cash seized from A) that they will incriminate themselves in relation to the criminal proceedings by giving evidence about the provenance or intended use of the cash. For that reason, they may wish to accept the continued detention of the cash, or even accept the adjournment of any forfeiture application, until the criminal proceedings have concluded.

What are the likely issues in the criminal proceedings?

12.63   It is for the prosecution to decide whether to apply for the joinder of the trials of B, C, and E. If they do, the common legal and factual nexus of the cases against these three make it inevitable that joinder will be permitted. However, one factor that may be relevant is the information provided by B and C as a result of their respective restraint orders. If, for instance, B said that he had received several very large cash payments from C in recent years, this could not be used in prosecuting B, but may be useful in prosecuting C—a problem for which the most appropriate solution may well be separate trials.

12.64   Pre-trial, all of the defendants may attempt in correspondence to push the prosecution to clarify the allegations, specifically whether it is alleged that the funds handled by B and E on behalf of C were indeed criminal property,[75] and which offence(s) (or category of offence(s)) is thought to have been its provenance. While the prosecution is not obliged to provide these details, it helps the defendants to know the basis upon which the case is alleged against them. It is arguable at least that a case based on inferences of general criminality is weaker than one with evidence of a specific offence(s).

12.65   The disclosure obligations on the prosecution should also be considered carefully. The allegations of money laundering under sections 327, 328, and 329 of POCA[76] against B or E (and against C) depend on evidence that C's money is in fact criminal property and the grounds upon which B or E knew or suspected that to be the case. The evidence obtained from HMRC, the accountant D, and UKBA's cash seizure case is all potentially relevant, as is the surveillance evidence of C's visits to B's premises and the customer due diligence data

---

[74] In *R v Payton* (see below), although it was not an issue decided in the case, the Court of Appeal accepted, in principle, submissions that it is 'highly undesirable that civil proceedings for forfeiture should take place before or concurrently with criminal proceedings' and in submissions it was asserted that generally the police would lodge an application for forfeiture (and so effect the detention of the cash and preservation of the status quo) but then seek an adjournment of the application until the criminal proceedings (including any appeal) are concluded.

[75] This is particularly important in relation to the alleged offences under POCA, s 330 and the Money Laundering Regulations 2007, as neither offence requires proof of actual criminal property.

[76] Conversely, the offence under POCA, s 330 does not require proof of criminal property.

provided by C to B and/or E (if there was any). In addition, if C sets out in his defence case statement for instance that he had recently started importing high-value goods from overseas, it may be argued that the prosecution is obliged to gather and disclose any information they have on C's customers and suppliers, without which any trial would be unfair.

Is there any priority between proceedings?

Civil proceedings can be and often are pursued at the same time as criminal proceedings.[77] **12.66** Victims, rather than await the somewhat notional prospect of being awarded compensation at the conclusion of a criminal trial, may seek redress in the form of an award of damages through the civil courts, which apply lower evidential safeguards and a lower burden of proof than the criminal courts. In addition, sector regulators may bring disciplinary or regulatory proceedings against the person concerned. Actions may also be taken by the Insolvency Service where an individual is declared bankrupt or a company is wound up. Further, there may also be associated cash forfeiture proceedings relating to cash seized during searches during the investigation stage (the cash also being part of the evidential basis of the criminal prosecution).[78]

In rare circumstances, however, the civil proceedings may be stayed when associated criminal **12.67** proceedings are contemplated, or are taking place, and the continuation of the civil case may lead to injustice. The test to be applied is whether there is 'a real risk of prejudice which might lead to injustice' in one or both of the proceedings.[79] The burden of proof in showing whether such prejudice exists is on the party applying for the stay.

However, a defendant in criminal proceedings is not entitled to a stay of the civil action **12.68** simply because to continue in the civil proceedings would require him to incriminate himself or to disclose all or part of his defence in the criminal proceedings.[80] The privilege against self-incrimination (such as it is) applies only in criminal proceedings. Further, the right to silence in criminal proceedings has been eroded significantly in recent years as a result of the inferences that may now be drawn from a defendant's silence and the obligation to serve a defence case statement. As such, the requirement to disclose a defence in civil proceedings (which, by definition, is likely to be exculpatory) is unlikely to result in real prejudice to the defendant in subsequent criminal proceedings and a consequent stay.

It seems that one of the few circumstances which might justify a stay of civil proceedings is **12.69** where the burden of defending those proceedings at the same time as defending the criminal proceedings is too great. This argument will, however, only succeed in exceptional circumstances and the primary consideration will be the sheer scale of the task faced by a defendant being required to respond simultaneously to two separate but large scale proceedings. The burden will of course be greater, and the application for a stay more likely to succeed, if the defendant is a litigant in person in the civil proceedings.[81]

---

[77] A recent example is the civil litigation arising out of the 'Buncefield' explosion—the largest peacetime explosion in Europe—where the civil proceedings concluded before the commencement of the criminal trial.

[78] The issue does not arise in relation to civil recovery proceedings because, by their very nature, in practice such proceedings (to recover property that is or represents property obtained through unlawful conduct) are generally only instituted by the enforcement authority in the event that there is no criminal prosecution or following one that has failed (at the time of writing, the possibility of civil recovering proceedings following a successful trial as part of a settlement is unclear).

[79] *Mote v Secretary of State for Work and Pensions* [2007] EWCA Civ 1324.

[80] *V v C* [2001] EWCA Civ 1509.

[81] *R (Application of Ranson) v Institute of Actuaries* [2004] EWHC 3087.

12.70 The position is perhaps different in relation to situations where there are concurrent cash forfeiture proceedings, no doubt due to the fact that the seized cash is also an integral part of the evidential basis of the criminal prosecution. In *R v Payton*,[82] although it was not an issue decided in the case, the Court of Appeal accepted in principal submissions that it is 'highly undesirable that civil proceedings for forfeiture should take place before or concurrently with criminal proceedings' and that 'There is a real potential unfairness for a defendant to be put in the position of giving evidence on oath about matters which could affect his criminal trial before his criminal trial takes place' and that '(i)f the defendant chooses not to give such evidence, it might well result in forfeiture of cash seized before his criminal trial has concluded, or even started'. The Court of Appeal went on to state that 'It is, however, important that care is taken to ensure that the fair trial of a defendant is not prejudiced by anything arising in civil proceedings in the magistrates' court and steps should be taken accordingly. Liaison between police acting under Part 5 of the 2002 Act and the prosecuting authority is essential.' It was submitted during argument that 'the overwhelming likelihood is that the police would lodge an application for forfeiture (and so effect the detention of the cash and preservation of the status quo) but then seek an adjournment of the application until criminal proceedings (including any appeal) are concluded . . .The advantages . . . include the preservation of the status quo and ensuring that the defendant is not embarrassed into having to rehearse what may be part of his defence to the criminal allegation'.

What are the evidential considerations when there are concurrent civil and criminal proceedings?

12.71 Where concurrent civil and criminal proceedings are taking place, there is a risk that documents that the defendant is compelled to produce in the civil proceedings will be used against him in the criminal trial (unless the particular statute conferring the power to compel disclosure expressly provides otherwise). For example, where a bankrupt is obliged under the Insolvency Act 1986 to produce all books, papers, and other documentation in relation to his estate, the material produced by the bankrupt will be prima facie admissible against him in any subsequent criminal trial. Whilst the criminal trial judge retains the power to exclude such documents under section 78 of the Police and Criminal Evidence Act 1984, it is unlikely that contemporaneous documents created in the course of a trade or business will be excluded simply because they were obtained under compulsion.[83]

12.72 In any event, where pleadings and documents are read out in open court they become documents of public record. Further, even where documents are not read out in open court, but are filed at court, an application can be made to the court for access to the material.[84] Such application may be made, for example, by the criminal investigator/prosecutor.

12.73 Note, however, that it is now trite law that any statements made by a defendant under compulsion (whether made pursuant to an order in civil proceedings or in criminal proceedings) cannot, save in certain limited circumstances, be used in evidence against him in a criminal trial.[85] That being said, it is of course possible that such statements may be used to the

---

[82] *R v Payton (Barrington)* [2006] EWCA Crim 1226; [2006] Crim LR 997.
[83] *R v Hertfordshire CC Ex p Green Environmental Industries Ltd* [2000] 2 AC 412.
[84] Civil Procedure Rule 5.4C (supply of documents to a non-party).
[85] Following the decision of the ECHR in *Saunders v UK* (1996) 23 EHRR 313; this is to be contrasted with the position in relation to the compulsory provision of documentation and information (*Ex p Green Environmental Industries Ltd*, n 83).

defendant's detriment in other ways. For example, statements made under compulsion may lead to the identification of further lines of enquiry in the criminal investigation. Further, consideration should be given to the fact that anything said by the defendant not under compulsion and any representations made on a defendant's behalf in civil proceedings may be prima facie admissible in the criminal proceedings.

It is also important to note that section 13 of the Fraud Act 2006 provides that a person is **12.74** not to be excused from answering any question put to him, or complying with any order, in civil proceedings relating to property on the ground that doing so may incriminate him (or his spouse or civil partner) of an offence under the Fraud Act or a related offence (where a related offence is widely defined to mean conspiracy to defraud and any other offence involving any form of fraudulent conduct or purpose and that any risk of prosecution under the Proceeds of Crime Act 2002 should be disregarded).[86]

Alternatives to a trial—settling proceedings

Contested criminal trials are extremely expensive and time consuming for both prosecutors **12.75** and defendants, and in different ways carry substantial risks. For a defendant, the range of possible outcomes stretches from a complete acquittal with the benefit of a defendant's costs order (if the court considers it appropriate, and subject to taxation) to a criminal conviction and imprisonment (for individuals) or a ruinous fine (for companies), not to mention severe reputational damage. For a prosecutor, the major risks are more prosaic: cost and the impact on the prosecuting authority's reputation of a high-profile acquittal or collapsed case. In all but the clearest cases, the prospects for reaching a settlement between the parties should be contemplated seriously.

Money laundering prosecutions are not unusual in this respect, but two complications make **12.76** it more likely that settlement will be seriously contemplated (by both sides) in such cases.

The first complication is that money laundering charges are often seen together on an indict- **12.77** ment with charges of other serious financial crimes, such as corruption, fraud, market abuse, price-fixing, and tax evasion. These 'white collar' crimes are notoriously difficult to prosecute and the resulting cases are easily the most expensive and time consuming. They are prose- cuted by a range of authorities—the CPS (which now includes the RCPO), the FSA, the OFT, and the SFO—perhaps none of which can truly be said to have a proven track record of bringing them to a just conclusion and all of which face severe budgetary constraints. The defendants include companies that have a strong interest in protecting both their business and their reputation, and which will often be highly risk averse, and individuals (almost inevitably of previous good character) whose main concern will be to avoid imprisonment if at all possible.

This substantial overlap between money laundering prosecutions and 'white collar' financial **12.78** crime raises two issues. First, these are cases that will often also involve a substantial civil claim by alleged victims and/or the prospect of civil penalties provided by statute such that there is far more for the defendant (whether individual or corporate) to consider than in the classic criminal case. Second, as the nature of these cases is very often that the evidence is in the form of documentation and the only potential witnesses are those with some involvement in the impugned conduct, co-operation between prosecutors and defendants (or suspects

---

[86] *Kensington International Ltd v Republic of Congo* [2007] EWCA Civ 1128.

who are not charged) is often a practical necessity. The Serious Organised Crime and Police Act 2005[87] formalizes the process by which such co-operation agreements are made and the benefit that a co-operating defendant can expect.

12.79 The second complication that makes money laundering cases serious contenders for settlement is the confiscation regime. Defendants accused of dealing with criminal property (either as a stand-alone allegation or as an additional charge) often have assets that stand to be restrained and subsequently confiscated; the draconian nature of the restraint and confiscation regime makes it all-important for a defendant to deal with the case quickly and without a trial if possible. Prosecutors (as well as the investigators), controversially, stand to benefit financially from any funds paid in satisfaction of a confiscation order,[88] and the political imperatives behind confiscation make it highly valuable for a prosecuting authority to be able to present a high-profile confiscation order in an impressively large amount.

12.80 Despite these considerations, there remains a large gap between the practice of negotiating and agreeing settlements in England and Wales and what is popularly known as 'plea bargaining' in the United States. The prosecuting authorities in England and Wales do not have the same resources as the US Department of Justice, nor do they have the same backing from the law in the form of disproportionately high prison sentences following conviction after a trial or the routine approval from the courts for the settlements that they reach.

12.81 This latter point has been driven home recently in the cases of *R v Innospec Ltd*[89] in the Crown Court and *R v Dougall*[90] in the Court of Appeal. In both cases, the SFO had presented the court with a settlement[91] that they considered fair, but the court responded with the firm message that such deals should not presume to reach agreements on the sentence to be imposed, or otherwise attempt to fetter the court's discretion (e.g. in relation to the level of a confiscation order and/or civil recovery proceedings taking precedence).

12.82 Another form of settlement in the US is that of so-called deferred or non-prosecution agreements. However, such agreements are not recognized by the law of England and Wales. In addition, it is to be noted that, in *R v Innospec Ltd*, a case in which the SFO sought to deal with the defendant company (that had self-reported and co-operated) by way of civil recovery proceedings, the SFO was heavily criticized by the court, which commented that it will 'rarely be appropriate for criminal conduct by a company to be dealt with by means of a civil recovery order ... It is of the greatest public interest that the serious criminality of any, including companies, who engage in the corruption of foreign governments, is made patent for all to see by the imposition of criminal and not civil sanctions.'

12.83 Therefore, in terms of settlement, all that really remains is for a defendant to agree with the prosecution to plead guilty on the basis of particular facts (a 'basis of plea') and/or to agree to plead guilty to particular charges; in cases of serious or complex fraud, defendants may enter

---

[87] ss 71–5.
[88] The Asset Recovery Incentivisation Scheme (ARIS): Agencies receive 50 per cent of what they recover, with incentive allocations based on the agency's contribution to the total value of remittances from cash forfeiture orders, confiscation orders, and civil recovery and taxation cases.
[89] *R v Innospec Ltd* [2010] Crim LR 665.
[90] *R v Dougall (Robert)* [2010] EWCA Crim 1048; [2010] Crim LR 661.
[91] Under the Serious Organised Crime and Police Act 2005.

into SOCPA plea agreements with the prosecution which include a joint submission as to sentence. However, a basis of plea is always subject to the approval of the court and it is open to the court to reject a basis of plea where it does not represent a proper plea on the basis of the facts set out in the papers. The same applies to agreements in cases of serious or complex fraud: the judge retains the absolute discretion to refuse to accept the plea agreement and to sentence otherwise than in accordance with the sentencing submissions.

In recent times, the SFO has explicitly sought to reach comprehensive settlements (including **12.84** civil recovery proceedings) with defendants, particularly in the context of corruption cases. At the time of writing it remains unclear whether the SFO's strategy now will be to reverse the recent trend and proceed more combatively against defendants, or continue reaching settlements with more emphasis on keeping them out of the criminal courts altogether. It could of course choose a third way of dealing with appropriate cases in one way, and the remainder in another.

What is increasingly clear is that the process of dealing with cases of this kind, which overlaps **12.85** substantially with money laundering prosecutions and confiscation cases, is extremely complex and requires, from the outset of a case, a great deal of thought and skill on both sides. Crucially, that process contrasts with the classical model of a criminal case in that it is not (or potentially is not) a zero-sum game: if both sides behave intelligently and pursue their interests in a creative manner, the result of the case can be both a 'win' for the prosecutor (in the sense of a publicly penal result for the offender's wrongdoing and also achieving that goal with the minimum necessary expense and investment of time) and at the same time a 'win' for the defendant (or at least substantial mitigation to the damage that the defendant would otherwise suffer).

This reality makes it all the more important to ensure that the process is adequately resourced **12.86** on both sides and (particularly, as *Innospec* and *Dougall* have shown, where the settlement is to go before the court) that it does not lose sight of the legal framework surrounding it. There is, it is submitted, no contradiction between settling a case that both sides accept involves criminal property, and the over-arching aim of bringing it to a just and equitable conclusion.

APPENDIX 1

Proceeds of Crime Act 2002 (Extracts)

The extracts of this Act appear as amended by subsequent legislation.

Part 5 Civil Recovery Of The Proceeds Etc. Of Unlawful Conduct

Chapter 1 Introductory

240 General purpose of this Part

(1) This Part has effect for the purposes of—
  (a) enabling the enforcement authority to recover, in civil proceedings before the High Court or Court of Session, property which is, or represents, property obtained through unlawful conduct,
  (b) enabling cash which is, or represents, property obtained through unlawful conduct, or which is intended to be used in unlawful conduct, to be forfeited in civil proceedings before a magistrates' court or (in Scotland) the sheriff.
(2) The powers conferred by this Part are exercisable in relation to any property (including cash) whether or not any proceedings have been brought for an offence in connection with the property.

241 "Unlawful conduct"

(1) Conduct occurring in any part of the United Kingdom is unlawful conduct if it is unlawful under the criminal law of that part.
(2) Conduct which—
  (a) occurs in a country [or territory] outside the United Kingdom and is unlawful under the criminal law [applying in that country or territory] , and
  (b) if it occurred in a part of the United Kingdom, would be unlawful under the criminal law of that part,
  is also unlawful conduct.
(3) The court or sheriff must decide on a balance of probabilities whether it is proved—
  (a) that any matters alleged to constitute unlawful conduct have occurred, or
  (b) that any person intended to use any cash in unlawful conduct.

242 "Property obtained through unlawful conduct"

(1) A person obtains property through unlawful conduct (whether his own conduct or another's) if he obtains property by or in return for the conduct.
(2) In deciding whether any property was obtained through unlawful conduct—
  (a) it is immaterial whether or not any money, goods or services were provided in order to put the person in question in a position to carry out the conduct,
  (b) it is not necessary to show that the conduct was of a particular kind if it is shown that the property was obtained through conduct of one of a number of kinds, each of which would have been unlawful conduct.

Chapter 3 Recovery Of Cash In Summary Proceedings

Searches

289 Searches

(1) If a customs officer [, a constable or an accredited financial investigator] is lawfully on any premises [and] has reasonable grounds for suspecting that there is on the premises cash—
 (a) which is recoverable property or is intended by any person for use in unlawful conduct, and
 (b) the amount of which is not less than the minimum amount,
 he may search for the cash there.

(2) If a customs officer [, a constable or an accredited financial investigator] has reasonable grounds for suspecting that a person (the suspect) is carrying cash—
 (a) which is recoverable property or is intended by any person for use in unlawful conduct, and
 (b) the amount of which is not less than the minimum amount,
 he may exercise the following powers.

(3) The officer [, constable or accredited financial investigator] may, so far as he thinks it necessary or expedient, require the suspect—
 (a) to permit a search of any article he has with him,
 (b) to permit a search of his person.

(4) An officer [, constable or accredited financial investigator] exercising powers by virtue of subsection (3)(b) may detain the suspect for so long as is necessary for their exercise.

(5) The powers conferred by this section—
 (a) are exercisable only so far as reasonably required for the purpose of finding cash,
 (b) are exercisable by a customs officer only if he has reasonable grounds for suspecting that the unlawful conduct in question relates to an assigned matter (within the meaning of the Customs and Excise Management Act 1979 (c. 2)) [,]
 [(c) are exercisable by an accredited financial investigator only in relation to premises or (as the case may be) suspects in England, Wales or Northern Ireland.]

(6) Cash means—
 (a) notes and coins in any currency,
 (b) postal orders,
 (c) cheques of any kind, including travellers' cheques,
 (d) bankers' drafts,
 (e) bearer bonds and bearer shares,
 found at any place in the United Kingdom.

(7) Cash also includes any kind of monetary instrument which is found at any place in the United Kingdom, if the instrument is specified by the Secretary of State by an order made after consultation with the Scottish Ministers.

(8) This section does not require a person to submit to an intimate search or strip search (within the meaning of section 164 of the Customs and Excise Management Act 1979 (c. 2)).

290 Prior approval

(1) The powers conferred by section 289 may be exercised only with the appropriate approval unless, in the circumstances, it is not practicable to obtain that approval before exercising the power.

(2) The appropriate approval means the approval of a judicial officer or (if that is not practicable in any case) the approval of a senior officer.

(3) A judicial officer means—
 (a) in relation to England and Wales and Northern Ireland, a justice of the peace,
 (b) in relation to Scotland, the sheriff.

(4) A senior officer means—
 (a) in relation to the exercise of the power by a customs officer, a customs officer of a rank designated by the Commissioners of Customs and Excise as equivalent to that of a senior police officer,
 (b) in relation to the exercise of the power by a constable, a senior police officer.
 [(c) in relation to the exercise of the power by an accredited financial investigator, an accredited financial investigator who falls within a description specified in an order made for this purpose by the Secretary of State under section 453.]

(5) A senior police officer means a police officer of at least the rank of inspector.
(6) If the powers are exercised without the approval of a judicial officer in a case where—
  (a) no cash is seized by virtue of section 294, or
  (b) any cash so seized is not detained for more than 48 hours [(calculated in accordance with section 295(1B))],
the customs officer [, constable or accredited financial investigator] who exercised the powers must give a written report to the appointed person. (7) The report must give particulars of the circumstances which led him to believe that—
  (a) the powers were exercisable, and
  (b) it was not practicable to obtain the approval of a judicial officer.
(8) In this section and section 291, the appointed person means—
  (a) in relation to England and Wales and Northern Ireland, a person appointed by the Secretary of State,
  (b) in relation to Scotland, a person appointed by the Scottish Ministers.
(9) The appointed person must not be a person employed under or for the purposes of a government department or of the Scottish Administration; and the terms and conditions of his appointment, including any remuneration or expenses to be paid to him, are to be determined by the person appointing him.

291 Report on exercise of powers

(1) As soon as possible after the end of each financial year, the appointed person must prepare a report for that year.
  "Financial year" means—
  (a) the period beginning with the day on which this section comes into force and ending with the next 31 March (which is the first financial year), and
  (b) each subsequent period of twelve months beginning with 1 April.
(2) The report must give his opinion as to the circumstances and manner in which the powers conferred by section 289 are being exercised in cases where the customs officer [, constable or accredited financial investigator] who exercised them is required to give a report under section 290(6).
(3) In the report, he may make any recommendations he considers appropriate.
(4) He must send a copy of his report to the Secretary of State or, as the case may be, the Scottish Ministers, who must arrange for it to be published.
(5) The Secretary of State must lay a copy of any report he receives under this section before Parliament; and the Scottish Ministers must lay a copy of any report they receive under this section before the Scottish Parliament.

292 Code of practice

(1) The Secretary of State must make a code of practice in connection with the exercise by customs officers and (in relation to England and Wales and Northern Ireland) constables [and accredited financial investigators] of the powers conferred by virtue of section 289.
(2) Where he proposes to issue a code of practice he must—
  (a) publish a draft,
  (b) consider any representations made to him about the draft by the Scottish Ministers or any other person,
  (c) if he thinks it appropriate, modify the draft in the light of any such representations.
(3) He must lay a draft of the code before Parliament.
(4) When he has laid a draft of the code before Parliament he may bring it into operation by order.
(5) He may revise the whole or any part of the code issued by him and issue the code as revised; and subsections (2) to (4) apply to such a revised code as they apply to the original code.
(6) A failure by a customs officer [, a constable or an accredited financial investigator] to comply with a provision of the code does not of itself make him liable to criminal or civil proceedings.
(7) The code is admissible in evidence in criminal or civil proceedings and is to be taken into account by a court or tribunal in any case in which it appears to the court or tribunal to be relevant.

293 Code of practice (Scotland)

(1) The Scottish Ministers must make a code of practice in connection with the exercise by constables in relation to Scotland of the powers conferred by virtue of section 289.

(2) Where they propose to issue a code of practice they must—
   (a) publish a draft,
   (b) consider any representations made to them about the draft,
   (c) if they think it appropriate, modify the draft in the light of any such representations.

(3) They must lay a draft of the code before the Scottish Parliament.

(4) When they have laid a draft of the code before the Scottish Parliament they may bring it into operation by order.

(5) They may revise the whole or any part of the code issued by them and issue the code as revised; and subsections (2) to (4) apply to such a revised code as they apply to the original code.

(6) A failure by a constable to comply with a provision of the code does not of itself make him liable to criminal or civil proceedings.

(7) The code is admissible in evidence in criminal or civil proceedings and is to be taken into account by a court or tribunal in any case in which it appears to the court or tribunal to be relevant.

Seizure and detention

294 Seizure of cash

(1) A customs officer [, a constable or an accredited financial investigator] may seize any cash if he has reasonable grounds for suspecting that it is—
   (a) recoverable property, or
   (b) intended by any person for use in unlawful conduct.

(2) A customs officer [, a constable or an accredited financial investigator] may also seize cash part of which he has reasonable grounds for suspecting to be—
   (a) recoverable property, or
   (b) intended by any person for use in unlawful conduct,
   if it is not reasonably practicable to seize only that part.

(3) This section does not authorise the seizure of an amount of cash if it or, as the case may be, the part to which his suspicion relates, is less than the minimum amount.

[(4) This section does not authorise the seizure by an accredited financial investigator of cash found in Scotland.]

295 Detention of seized cash

(1) While the customs officer [, constable or accredited financial investigator] continues to have reasonable grounds for his suspicion, cash seized under section 294 may be detained initially for a period of 48 hours.

[(1A) The period of 48 hours mentioned in subsection (1) is to be calculated in accordance with subsection (1B).

(1B) In calculating a period of 48 hours in accordance with this subsection, no account shall be taken of—
   (a) any Saturday or Sunday,
   (b) Christmas Day,
   (c) Good Friday,
   (d) any day that is a bank holiday under the Banking and Financial Dealings Act 1971 in the part of the United Kingdom within which the cash is seized, or
   (e) any day prescribed under section 8(2) of the Criminal Procedure (Scotland) Act 1995 as a court holiday in a sheriff court in the sheriff court district within which the cash is seized.]

(2) The period for which the cash or any part of it may be detained may be extended by an order made by a magistrates' court or (in Scotland) the sheriff; but the order may not authorise the detention of any of the cash—
   (a) beyond the end of the period of [six months] beginning with the date of the order,
   (b) in the case of any further order under this section, beyond the end of the period of two years beginning with the date of the first order.

(3) A justice of the peace may also exercise the power of a magistrates' court to make the first order under subsection (2) extending the period.

(4) An application for an order under subsection (2)—

    (a) in relation to England and Wales and Northern Ireland, may be made by the Commissioners of Customs and Excise [, a constable or an accredited financial investigator],

    (b) in relation to Scotland, may be made by the Scottish Ministers in connection with their functions under section 298 or by a procurator fiscal,

and the court, sheriff or justice may make the order if satisfied, in relation to any cash to be further detained, that either of the following conditions is met.

(5) The first condition is that there are reasonable grounds for suspecting that the cash is recoverable property and that either—

    (a) its continued detention is justified while its derivation is further investigated or consideration is given to bringing (in the United Kingdom or elsewhere) proceedings against any person for an offence with which the cash is connected, or

    (b) proceedings against any person for an offence with which the cash is connected have been started and have not been concluded.

(6) The second condition is that there are reasonable grounds for suspecting that the cash is intended to be used in unlawful conduct and that either—

    (a) its continued detention is justified while its intended use is further investigated or consideration is given to bringing (in the United Kingdom or elsewhere) proceedings against any person for an offence with which the cash is connected, or

    (b) proceedings against any person for an offence with which the cash is connected have been started and have not been concluded.

(7) An application for an order under subsection (2) may also be made in respect of any cash seized under section 294(2), and the court, sheriff or justice may make the order if satisfied that—

    (a) the condition in subsection (5) or (6) is met in respect of part of the cash, and

    (b) it is not reasonably practicable to detain only that part.

(8) An order under subsection (2) must provide for notice to be given to persons affected by it.

296 Interest

(1) If cash is detained under section 295 for more than 48 hours [(calculated in accordance with section 295(1B))], it is at the first opportunity to be paid into an interest-bearing account and held there; and the interest accruing on it is to be added to it on its forfeiture or release.

(2) In the case of cash detained under section 295 which was seized under section 294(2), the customs officer [, constable or accredited financial investigator] must, on paying it into the account, release the part of the cash to which the suspicion does not relate.

(3) Subsection (1) does not apply if the cash or, as the case may be, the part to which the suspicion relates is required as evidence of an offence or evidence in proceedings under this Chapter.

297 Release of detained cash

(1) This section applies while any cash is detained under section 295.

(2) A magistrates' court or (in Scotland) the sheriff may direct the release of the whole or any part of the cash if the following condition is met.

(3) The condition is that the court or sheriff is satisfied, on an application by the person from whom the cash was seized, that the conditions in section 295 for the detention of the cash are no longer met in relation to the cash to be released.

(4) A customs officer, constable [or accredited financial investigator] or (in Scotland) procurator fiscal may, after notifying the magistrates' court, sheriff or justice under whose order cash is being detained, release the whole or any part of it if satisfied that the detention of the cash to be released is no longer justified.

Forfeiture

298 Forfeiture

(1) While cash is detained under section 295, an application for the forfeiture of the whole or any part of it may be made—

    (a) to a magistrates' court by the Commissioners of Customs and Excise [, an accredited financial investigator] or a constable,

(b) (in Scotland) to the sheriff by the Scottish Ministers.

(2) The court or sheriff may order the forfeiture of the cash or any part of it if satisfied that the cash or part—

 (a) is recoverable property, or

 (b) is intended by any person for use in unlawful conduct.

(3) But in the case of recoverable property which belongs to joint tenants, one of whom is an excepted joint owner, the order may not apply to so much of it as the court thinks is attributable to the excepted joint owner's share.

(4) Where an application for the forfeiture of any cash is made under this section, the cash is to be detained (and may not be released under any power conferred by this Chapter) until any proceedings in pursuance of the application (including any proceedings on appeal) are concluded.

[299 Appeal against decision under section 298

(1) Any party to proceedings for an order for the forfeiture of cash under section 298 who is aggrieved by an order under that section or by the decision of the court not to make such an order may appeal—

 (a) in relation to England and Wales, to the Crown Court;

 (b) in relation to Scotland, to the Sheriff Principal;

 (c) in relation to Northern Ireland, to a county court.

(2) An appeal under subsection (1) must be made before the end of the period of 30 days starting with the day on which the court makes the order or decision.

(3) The court hearing the appeal may make any order it thinks appropriate.

(4) If the court upholds an appeal against an order forfeiting the cash, it may order the release of the cash.]

300 Application of forfeited cash

(1) Cash forfeited under this Chapter, and any accrued interest on it—

 (a) if forfeited by a magistrates' court in England and Wales or Northern Ireland, is to be paid into the Consolidated Fund,

 (b) if forfeited by the sheriff, is to be paid into the Scottish Consolidated Fund.

(2) But it is not to be paid in—

 (a) before the end of the period within which an appeal under section 299 may be made, or

 (b) if a person appeals under that section, before the appeal is determined or otherwise disposed of.

Supplementary

301 Victims and other owners

(1) A person who claims that any cash detained under this Chapter, or any part of it, belongs to him may apply to a magistrates' court or (in Scotland) the sheriff for the cash or part to be released to him.

(2) The application may be made in the course of proceedings under section 295 or 298 or at any other time.

(3) If it appears to the court or sheriff concerned that—

 (a) the applicant was deprived of the cash to which the application relates, or of property which it represents, by unlawful conduct,

 (b) the property he was deprived of was not, immediately before he was deprived of it, recoverable property, and

 (c) that cash belongs to him,

 the court or sheriff may order the cash to which the application relates to be released to the applicant.

(4) If—

 (a) the applicant is not the person from whom the cash to which the application relates was seized,

 (b) it appears to the court or sheriff that that cash belongs to the applicant,

    (c) the court or sheriff is satisfied that the conditions in section 295 for the detention of that cash are no longer met or, if an application has been made under section 298, the court or sheriff decides not to make an order under that section in relation to that cash, and

    (d) no objection to the making of an order under this subsection has been made by the person from whom that cash was seized,

the court or sheriff may order the cash to which the application relates to be released to the applicant or to the person from whom it was seized.

302 Compensation

(1) If no forfeiture order is made in respect of any cash detained under this Chapter, the person to whom the cash belongs or from whom it was seized may make an application to the magistrates' court or (in Scotland) the sheriff for compensation.

(2) If, for any period beginning with the first opportunity to place the cash in an interest-bearing account after the initial detention of the cash for 48 hours [(calculated in accordance with section 295(1B)], the cash was not held in an interest-bearing account while detained, the court or sheriff may order an amount of compensation to be paid to the applicant.

(3) The amount of compensation to be paid under subsection (2) is the amount the court or sheriff thinks would have been earned in interest in the period in question if the cash had been held in an interest-bearing account.

(4) If the court or sheriff is satisfied that, taking account of any interest to be paid under section 296 or any amount to be paid under subsection (2), the applicant has suffered loss as a result of the detention of the cash and that the circumstances are exceptional, the court or sheriff may order compensation (or additional compensation) to be paid to him.

(5) The amount of compensation to be paid under subsection (4) is the amount the court or sheriff thinks reasonable, having regard to the loss suffered and any other relevant circumstances.

(6) If the cash was seized by a customs officer, the compensation is to be paid by the Commissioners of Customs and Excise.

(7) If the cash was seized by a constable, the compensation is to be paid as follows—

    (a) in the case of a constable of a police force in England and Wales, it is to be paid out of the police fund from which the expenses of the police force are met,

    (b) in the case of a constable of a police force in Scotland, it is to be paid by the police authority or joint police board for the police area for which that force is maintained,

    (c) in the case of a police officer within the meaning of the Police (Northern Ireland) Act 2000 (c. 32), it is to be paid out of money provided by the Chief Constable.

[(7A) If the cash was seized by an accredited financial investigator who was not an officer of Revenue and Customs or a constable, the compensation is to be paid as follows–

    (a) in the case of an investigator–

        (i) who was employed by a police authority in England and Wales under section 15 of the Police Act 1996 (c. 16) and was under the direction and control of the chief officer of police of the police force maintained by the authority, or

        (ii) who was a member of staff of the City of London police force,

    it is to be paid out of the police fund from which the expenses of the police force are met,

    (b) in the case of an investigator who was a member of staff of the Police Service of Northern Ireland, it is to be paid out of money provided by the Chief Constable,

    (c) in the case of an investigator who was a member of staff of a department of the Government of the United Kingdom, it is to be paid by the Minister of the Crown in charge of the department or by the department,

    (d) in the case of an investigator who was a member of staff of a Northern Ireland department, it is to be paid by the department,

    (e) in any other case, it is to be paid by the employer of the investigator.

(7B) The Secretary of State may by order amend subsection (7A).]

(8) If a forfeiture order is made in respect only of a part of any cash detained under this Chapter, this section has effect in relation to the other part.

[302A Powers for prosecutors to appear in proceedings

(1) The Director of Public Prosecutions or the Director of Public Prosecutions for Northern Ireland may appear for a constable [or an accredited financial investigator] in proceedings under this Chapter if the Director–
    (a) is asked by, or on behalf of, a constable [or (as the case may be) an accredited financial investigator] to do so, and
    (b) considers it appropriate to do so.

(2) The Director of Revenue and Customs Prosecutions may appear for the Commissioners for Her Majesty's Revenue and Customs or an officer of Revenue and Customs in proceedings under this Chapter if the Director–
    (a) is asked by, or on behalf of, the Commissioners for Her Majesty's Revenue and Customs or (as the case may be) an officer of Revenue and Customs to do so, and
    (b) considers it appropriate to do so.

(3) The Directors may charge fees for the provision of services under this section.

[(4) The references in subsection (1) to an accredited financial investigator do not include an accredited financial investigator who is an officer of Revenue and Customs but the references in subsection (2) to an officer of Revenue and Customs do include an accredited financial investigator who is an officer of Revenue and Customs.]]

303 " The minimum amount"

(1) In this Chapter, the minimum amount is the amount in sterling specified in an order made by the Secretary of State after consultation with the Scottish Ministers.

(2) For that purpose the amount of any cash held in a currency other than sterling must be taken to be its sterling equivalent, calculated in accordance with the prevailing rate of exchange.

[303A Financial investigators

(1) In this Chapter (apart from this section) any reference in a provision to an accredited financial investigator is a reference to an accredited financial investigator who falls within a description specified in an order made for the purposes of that provision by the Secretary of State under section 453.

(2) Subsection (1) does not apply to the second reference to an accredited financial investigator in section 290(4)(c).

(3) Where an accredited financial investigator of a particular description–
    (a) applies for an order under section 295,
    (b) applies for forfeiture under section 298, or
    (c) brings an appeal under, or relating to, this Chapter,

any subsequent step in the application or appeal, or any further application or appeal relating to the same matter, may be taken, made or brought by a different accredited financial investigator of the same description.]

Recoverable property

304 Property obtained through unlawful conduct

(1) Property obtained through unlawful conduct is recoverable property.

(2) But if property obtained through unlawful conduct has been disposed of (since it was so obtained), it is recoverable property only if it is held by a person into whose hands it may be followed.

(3) Recoverable property obtained through unlawful conduct may be followed into the hands of a person obtaining it on a disposal by—
    (a) the person who through the conduct obtained the property, or
    (b) a person into whose hands it may (by virtue of this subsection) be followed.

305 Tracing property, etc.

(1) Where property obtained through unlawful conduct ("the original property") is or has been recoverable, property which represents the original property is also recoverable property.

(2) If a person enters into a transaction by which—
    (a) he disposes of recoverable property, whether the original property or property which (by virtue of this Chapter) represents the original property, and

   (b) he obtains other property in place of it,

the other property represents the original property.

(3) If a person disposes of recoverable property which represents the original property, the property may be followed into the hands of the person who obtains it (and it continues to represent the original property).

306 Mixing property

(1) Subsection (2) applies if a person's recoverable property is mixed with other property (whether his property or another's).

(2) The portion of the mixed property which is attributable to the recoverable property represents the property obtained through unlawful conduct.

(3) Recoverable property is mixed with other property if (for example) it is used—

   (a) to increase funds held in a bank account,

   (b) in part payment for the acquisition of an asset,

   (c) for the restoration or improvement of land,

   (d) by a person holding a leasehold interest in the property to acquire the freehold.

307 Recoverable property: accruing profits

(1) This section applies where a person who has recoverable property obtains further property consisting of profits accruing in respect of the recoverable property.

(2) The further property is to be treated as representing the property obtained through unlawful conduct.

308 General exceptions

(1) If—

   (a) a person disposes of recoverable property, and

   (b) the person who obtains it on the disposal does so in good faith, for value and without notice that it was recoverable property,

the property may not be followed into that person's hands and, accordingly, it ceases to be recoverable.

(2) If recoverable property is vested, forfeited or otherwise disposed of in pursuance of powers conferred by virtue of this Part, it ceases to be recoverable.

(3) If—

   (a) in pursuance of a judgment in civil proceedings (whether in the United Kingdom or elsewhere), the defendant makes a payment to the claimant or the claimant otherwise obtains property from the defendant,

   (b) the claimant's claim is based on the defendant's unlawful conduct, and

   (c) apart from this subsection, the sum received, or the property obtained, by the claimant would be recoverable property,

the property ceases to be recoverable.

In relation to Scotland, "claimant" and "defendant" are to be read as "pursuer" and "defender" .

(4) If—

   (a) a payment is made to a person in pursuance of a compensation order under Article 14 of the Criminal Justice (Northern Ireland) Order 1994 (S.I. 1994/2795 (N.I. 15)), section 249 of the Criminal Procedure (Scotland) Act 1995 (c. 46) or section 130 of the Powers of Criminal Courts (Sentencing) Act 2000 (c. 6) [or in pursuance of a service compensation order under the Armed Forces Act 2006], and

   (b) apart from this subsection, the sum received would be recoverable property,

the property ceases to be recoverable.

(5) If—

   (a) a payment is made to a person in pursuance of a restitution order under section 27 of the Theft Act (Northern Ireland) 1969 (c. 16 (N.I.)) or section 148(2) of the Powers of Criminal Courts (Sentencing) Act 2000 or a person otherwise obtains any property in pursuance of such an order, and

(b) apart from this subsection, the sum received, or the property obtained, would be recoverable property,

the property ceases to be recoverable.

(6) If—
    (a) in pursuance of an order made by the court under section 382(3) or 383(5) of the Financial Services and Markets Act 2000 (c. 8) (restitution orders), an amount is paid to or distributed among any persons in accordance with the court's directions, and
    (b) apart from this subsection, the sum received by them would be recoverable property,

the property ceases to be recoverable.

(7) If—
    (a) in pursuance of a requirement of the Financial Services Authority under section 384(5) of the Financial Services and Markets Act 2000 (power of authority to require restitution), an amount is paid to or distributed among any persons, and
    (b) apart from this subsection, the sum received by them would be recoverable property,

the property ceases to be recoverable.

(8) Property is not recoverable while a restraint order applies to it, that is—
    (a) an order under section 41, 120 or 190, or
    (b) an order under any corresponding provision of an enactment mentioned in section 8(7)(a) to (g).

(9) Property is not recoverable if it has been taken into account in deciding the amount of a person's benefit from criminal conduct for the purpose of making a confiscation order, that is—
    (a) an order under section 6, 92 or 156, or
    (b) an order under a corresponding provision of an enactment mentioned in section 8(7)(a) to (g),
and, in relation to an order mentioned in paragraph (b), the reference to the amount of a person's benefit from criminal conduct is to be read as a reference to the corresponding amount under the enactment in question.

(10) Where—
    (a) a person enters into a transaction to which section 305(2) applies, and (b) the disposal is one to which subsection (1) or (2) applies,
this section does not affect the recoverability (by virtue of section 305(2)) of any property obtained on the transaction in place of the property disposed of.

309 Other exemptions

(1) An order may provide that property is not recoverable or (as the case may be) associated property if—
    (a) it is prescribed property, or
    (b) it is disposed of in pursuance of a prescribed enactment or an enactment of a prescribed description.

(2) An order may provide that if property is disposed of in pursuance of a prescribed enactment or an enactment of a prescribed description, it is to be treated for the purposes of section 278 as if it had been disposed of in pursuance of a recovery order.

(3) An order under this section may be made so as to apply to property, or a disposal of property, only in prescribed circumstances; and the circumstances may relate to the property or disposal itself or to a person who holds or has held the property or to any other matter.

(4) In this section, an order means an order made by the Secretary of State after consultation with the Scottish Ministers, and prescribed means prescribed by the order.

310 Granting interests

(1) If a person grants an interest in his recoverable property, the question whether the interest is also recoverable is to be determined in the same manner as it is on any other disposal of recoverable property.

(2) Accordingly, on his granting an interest in the property ("the property in question")—
    (a) where the property in question is property obtained through unlawful conduct, the interest is also to be treated as obtained through that conduct,
    (b) where the property in question represents in his hands property obtained through unlawful conduct, the interest is also to be treated as representing in his hands the property so obtained.

Interpretation

314 Obtaining and disposing of property

(1) References to a person disposing of his property include a reference—
   (a) to his disposing of a part of it, or
   (b) to his granting an interest in it,
   (or to both); and references to the property disposed of are to any property obtained on the disposal.
(2) A person who makes a payment to another is to be treated as making a disposal of his property to the other, whatever form the payment takes.
(3) Where a person's property passes to another under a will or intestacy or by operation of law, it is to be treated as disposed of by him to the other.
(4) A person is only to be treated as having obtained his property for value in a case where he gave unexecuted consideration if the consideration has become executed consideration.

315 Northern Ireland courts

In relation to the practice and procedure of courts in Northern Ireland, expressions used in this Part are to be read in accordance with rules of court.

316 General interpretation

(1) In this Part—
   "associated property" has the meaning given by section 245,
   "cash" has the meaning given by section 289(6) or (7),
   "constable" , in relation to Northern Ireland, means a police officer within the meaning of the Police (Northern Ireland) Act 2000 (c. 32),
   "country" includes territory,
   "the court" (except in sections 253(2) and (3) and 262(2) and (3) and Chapter 3) means the High Court or (in relation to proceedings in Scotland) the Court of Session,
   "dealing" with property includes disposing of it, taking possession of it or removing it from the United Kingdom,
   "enforcement authority" —
   [(a) in relation to England and Wales, means SOCA, the Director of Public Prosecutions, the Director of Revenue and Customs Prosecutions or the Director of the Serious Fraud Office,]
   (b) in relation to Scotland, means the Scottish Ministers,
   [(c) in relation to Northern Ireland, means SOCA, the Director of the Serious Fraud Office or the Director of Public Prosecutions for Northern Ireland,]
   "excepted joint owner" has the meaning given by section 270(4),
   "interest" , in relation to land—
   (a) in the case of land in England and Wales or Northern Ireland, means any legal estate and any equitable interest or power,
   (b) in the case of land in Scotland, means any estate, interest, servitude or other heritable right in or over land, including a heritable security,
   "interest" , in relation to property other than land, includes any right (including a right to possession of the property),
   "interim administration order" has the meaning given by section 256(2), " interim receiving order" has the meaning given by section 246(2),
   "the minimum amount" (in Chapter 3) has the meaning given by section 303,
   "part" , in relation to property, includes a portion,
   "premises" has the same meaning as in the Police and Criminal Evidence Act 1984 (c. 60),
   [" prohibitory property order" has the meaning given by section 255A(2);
   " property freezing order" has the meaning given by section 245A(2);]
   "property obtained through unlawful conduct" has the meaning given by section 242,
   "recoverable property" is to be read in accordance with sections 304 to 310,
   "recovery order" means an order made under section 266,
   "respondent" means—

(a) where proceedings are brought by the enforcement authority by virtue of Chapter 2, the person against whom the proceedings are brought,

(b) where no such proceedings have been brought but the enforcement authority has applied for [a property freezing order, an interim receiving order, a prohibitory property order or an] interim administration order, the person against whom he intends to bring such proceedings,

"share" , in relation to an excepted joint owner, has the meaning given by section 270(4),

"unlawful conduct" has the meaning given by section 241,

"value" means market value.

(2) The following provisions apply for the purposes of this Part.

(3) For the purpose of deciding whether or not property was recoverable at any time (including times before commencement), it is to be assumed that this Part was in force at that and any other relevant time.

(4) Property is all property wherever situated and includes—

(a) money,

(b) all forms of property, real or personal, heritable or moveable,

(c) things in action and other intangible or incorporeal property.

(5) Any reference to a person's property (whether expressed as a reference to the property he holds or otherwise) is to be read as follows.

(6) In relation to land, it is a reference to any interest which he holds in the land.

(7) In relation to property other than land, it is a reference—

(a) to the property (if it belongs to him), or (b) to any other interest which he holds in the property.

(8) References to the satisfaction of the enforcement authority's right to recover property obtained through unlawful conduct are to be read in accordance with section 279.

[(8A) In relation to an order in England and Wales or Northern Ireland which is a recovery order, a property freezing order, an interim receiving order or an order under section 276, references to the enforcement authority are, unless the context otherwise requires, references to the enforcement authority which is seeking, or (as the case may be) has obtained, the order.]

(9) Proceedings against any person for an offence are concluded when—

(a) the person is convicted or acquitted,

(b) the prosecution is discontinued or, in Scotland, the trial diet is deserted simpliciter, or

(c) the jury is discharged without a finding [otherwise than in circumstances where the proceedings are continued without a jury].

Part 7 Money Laundering

Offences

327 Concealing etc

(1) A person commits an offence if he—

(a) conceals criminal property;

(b) disguises criminal property;

(c) converts criminal property;

(d) transfers criminal property;

(e) removes criminal property from England and Wales or from Scotland or from Northern Ireland.

(2) But a person does not commit such an offence if—

(a) he makes an authorised disclosure under section 338 and (if the disclosure is made before he does the act mentioned in subsection (1)) he has the appropriate consent;

(b) he intended to make such a disclosure but had a reasonable excuse for not doing so;

(c) the act he does is done in carrying out a function he has relating to the enforcement of any provision of this Act or of any other enactment relating to criminal conduct or benefit from criminal conduct.

[(2A) Nor does a person commit an offence under subsection (1) if—

(a) he knows, or believes on reasonable grounds, that the relevant criminal conduct occurred in a particular country or territory outside the United Kingdom, and

    (b) the relevant criminal conduct—

        (i) was not, at the time it occurred, unlawful under the criminal law then applying in that country or territory, and

        (ii) is not of a description prescribed by an order made by the Secretary of State.

(2B) In subsection (2A) " the relevant criminal conduct" is the criminal conduct by reference to which the property concerned is criminal property.]

[(2C) A deposit-taking body that does an act mentioned in paragraph (c) or (d) of subsection (1) does not commit an offence under that subsection if—

    (a) it does the act in operating an account maintained with it, and

    (b) the value of the criminal property concerned is less than the threshold amount determined under section 339A for the act.]

(3) Concealing or disguising criminal property includes concealing or disguising its nature, source, location, disposition, movement or ownership or any rights with respect to it.

328 Arrangements

(1) A person commits an offence if he enters into or becomes concerned in an arrangement which he knows or suspects facilitates (by whatever means) the acquisition, retention, use or control of criminal property by or on behalf of another person.

(2) But a person does not commit such an offence if—

    (a) he makes an authorised disclosure under section 338 and (if the disclosure is made before he does the act mentioned in subsection (1)) he has the appropriate consent;

    (b) he intended to make such a disclosure but had a reasonable excuse for not doing so;

    (c) the act he does is done in carrying out a function he has relating to the enforcement of any provision of this Act or of any other enactment relating to criminal conduct or benefit from criminal conduct.

[(3) Nor does a person commit an offence under subsection (1) if—

    (a) he knows, or believes on reasonable grounds, that the relevant criminal conduct occurred in a particular country or territory outside the United Kingdom, and

    (b) the relevant criminal conduct—

        (i) was not, at the time it occurred, unlawful under the criminal law then applying in that country or territory, and

        (ii) is not of a description prescribed by an order made by the Secretary of State.

(4) In subsection (3)" the relevant criminal conduct" is the criminal conduct by reference to which the property concerned is criminal property.]

[(5) A deposit-taking body that does an act mentioned in subsection (1) does not commit an offence under that subsection if—

    (a) it does the act in operating an account maintained with it, and

    (b) the arrangement facilitates the acquisition, retention, use or control of criminal property of a value that is less than the threshold amount determined under section 339A for the act.]

329 Acquisition, use and possession

(1) A person commits an offence if he—

    (a) acquires criminal property;

    (b) uses criminal property;

    (c) has possession of criminal property.

(2) But a person does not commit such an offence if—

    (a) he makes an authorised disclosure under section 338 and (if the disclosure is made before he does the act mentioned in subsection (1)) he has the appropriate consent;

    (b) he intended to make such a disclosure but had a reasonable excuse for not doing so;

    (c) he acquired or used or had possession of the property for adequate consideration;

    (d) the act he does is done in carrying out a function he has relating to the enforcement of any provision of this Act or of any other enactment relating to criminal conduct or benefit from criminal conduct.

[(2A) Nor does a person commit an offence under subsection (1) if—

    (a) he knows, or believes on reasonable grounds, that the relevant criminal conduct occurred in a particular country or territory outside the United Kingdom, and

    (b) the relevant criminal conduct—
        (i)   was not, at the time it occurred, unlawful under the criminal law then applying in that country or territory, and
        (ii) is not of a description prescribed by an order made by the Secretary of State.
(2B) In subsection (2A) "the relevant criminal conduct" is the criminal conduct by reference to which the property concerned is criminal property.][
(2C) A deposit-taking body that does an act mentioned in subsection (1) does not commit an offence under that subsection if—
    (a) it does the act in operating an account maintained with it, and
    (b) the value of the criminal property concerned is less than the threshold amount determined under section 339A for the act.]
(3) For the purposes of this section—
    (a) a person acquires property for inadequate consideration if the value of the consideration is significantly less than the value of the property;
    (b) a person uses or has possession of property for inadequate consideration if the value of the consideration is significantly less than the value of the use or possession;
    (c) the provision by a person of goods or services which he knows or suspects may help another to carry out criminal conduct is not consideration.

330 Failure to disclose: regulated sector

(1) A person commits an offence if [the conditions in subsections (2) to (4) are satisfied].
(2) The first condition is that he—
    (a) knows or suspects, or
    (b) has reasonable grounds for knowing or suspecting,
    that another person is engaged in money laundering.
(3) The second condition is that the information or other matter—
    (a) on which his knowledge or suspicion is based, or
    (b) which gives reasonable grounds for such knowledge or suspicion,
    came to him in the course of a business in the regulated sector.
[(3A) The third condition is—
    (a) that he can identify the other person mentioned in subsection (2) or the whereabouts of any of the laundered property, or
    (b) that he believes, or it is reasonable to expect him to believe, that the information or other matter mentioned in subsection (3) will or may assist in identifying that other person or the whereabouts of any of the laundered property.
(4) The fourth condition is that he does not make the required disclosure to—
    (a) a nominated officer, or
    (b) a person authorised for the purposes of this Part by the Director General of [SOCA],
    as soon as is practicable after the information or other matter mentioned in subsection (3) comes to him.
(5) The required disclosure is a disclosure of—
    (a) the identity of the other person mentioned in subsection (2), if he knows it,
    (b) the whereabouts of the laundered property, so far as he knows it, and
    (c) the information or other matter mentioned in subsection (3).
(5A) The laundered property is the property forming the subject-matter of the money laundering that he knows or suspects, or has reasonable grounds for knowing or suspecting, that other person to be engaged in.
(6) But he does not commit an offence under this section if—
    (a) he has a reasonable excuse for not making the required disclosure,
    (b) he is a professional legal adviser [or [. . .]relevant professional adviser] and—
        (i)   if he knows either of the things mentioned in subsection (5)(a) and (b), he knows the thing because of information or other matter that came to him in privileged circumstances, or
        (ii) the information or other matter mentioned in subsection (3) came to him in privileged circumstances, or
    (c) subsection (7) [or (7B)] applies to him.]

(7) This subsection applies to a person if—
    (a) he does not know or suspect that another person is engaged in money laundering, and
    (b) he has not been provided by his employer with such training as is specified by the Secretary of State by order for the purposes of this section.

[(7A) Nor does a person commit an offence under this section if—
    (a) he knows, or believes on reasonable grounds, that the money laundering is occurring in a particular country or territory outside the United Kingdom, and
    (b) the money laundering—
        (i) is not unlawful under the criminal law applying in that country or territory, and
        (ii) is not of a description prescribed in an order made by the Secretary of State.]

[(7B) This subsection applies to a person if—
    (a) he is employed by, or is in partnership with, a professional legal adviser or a relevant professional adviser to provide the adviser with assistance or support,
    (b) the information or other matter mentioned in subsection (3) comes to the person in connection with the provision of such assistance or support, and
    (c) the information or other matter came to the adviser in privileged circumstances.]

(8) In deciding whether a person committed an offence under this section the court must consider whether he followed any relevant guidance which was at the time concerned—
    (a) issued by a supervisory authority or any other appropriate body,
    (b) approved by the Treasury, and
    (c) published in a manner it approved as appropriate in its opinion to bring the guidance to the attention of persons likely to be affected by it.

(9) A disclosure to a nominated officer is a disclosure which—
    (a) is made to a person nominated by the alleged offender's employer to receive disclosures under this section, and
    (b) is made in the course of the alleged offender's employment [. . .].

[(9A) But a disclosure which satisfies paragraphs (a) and (b) of subsection (9) is not to be taken as a disclosure to a nominated officer if the person making the disclosure—
    (a) is a professional legal adviser [or [. . .] relevant professional adviser],
    (b) makes it for the purpose of obtaining advice about making a disclosure under this section, and
    (c) does not intend it to be a disclosure under this section.]

(10) Information or other matter comes to a professional legal adviser [or [. . .]relevant professional adviser] in privileged circumstances if it is communicated or given to him—
    (a) by (or by a representative of) a client of his in connection with the giving by the adviser of legal advice to the client,
    (b) by (or by a representative of) a person seeking legal advice from the adviser, or
    (c) by a person in connection with legal proceedings or contemplated legal proceedings.

(11) But subsection (10) does not apply to information or other matter which is communicated or given with the intention of furthering a criminal purpose.

(12) Schedule 9 has effect for the purpose of determining what is—
    (a) a business in the regulated sector; (b) a supervisory authority.

(13) An appropriate body is any body which regulates or is representative of any trade, profession, business or employment carried on by the alleged offender.

[(14) A relevant professional adviser is an accountant, auditor or tax adviser who is a member of a professional body which is established for accountants, auditors or tax advisers (as the case may be) and which makes provision for—
    (a) testing the competence of those seeking admission to membership of such a body as a condition for such admission; and
    (b) imposing and maintaining professional and ethical standards for its members, as well as imposing sanctions for non-compliance with those standards.]

331 Failure to disclose: nominated officers in the regulated sector

(1) A person nominated to receive disclosures under section 330 commits an offence if the conditions in subsections (2) to (4) are satisfied.

(2) The first condition is that he—
    (a) knows or suspects, or

(b) has reasonable grounds for knowing or suspecting,

that another person is engaged in money laundering.

(3) The second condition is that the information or other matter—

(a) on which his knowledge or suspicion is based, or

(b) which gives reasonable grounds for such knowledge or suspicion,

came to him in consequence of a disclosure made under section 330.

[(3A) The third condition is—

(a) that he knows the identity of the other person mentioned in subsection (2), or the whereabouts of any of the laundered property, in consequence of a disclosure made under section 330,

(b) that that other person, or the whereabouts of any of the laundered property, can be identified from the information or other matter mentioned in subsection (3), or

(c) that he believes, or it is reasonable to expect him to believe, that the information or other matter will or may assist in identifying that other person or the whereabouts of any of the laundered property.

(4) The fourth condition is that he does not make the required disclosure to a person authorised for the purposes of this Part by the Director General of [SOCA] as soon as is practicable after the information or other matter mentioned in subsection (3) comes to him.

(5) The required disclosure is a disclosure of—

(a) the identity of the other person mentioned in subsection (2), if disclosed to him under section 330,

(b) the whereabouts of the laundered property, so far as disclosed to him under section 330, and

(c) the information or other matter mentioned in subsection (3).

(5A) The laundered property is the property forming the subject-matter of the money laundering that he knows or suspects, or has reasonable grounds for knowing or suspecting, that other person to be engaged in.

(6) But he does not commit an offence under this section if he has a reasonable excuse for not making the required disclosure.]

[(6A) Nor does a person commit an offence under this section if—

(a) he knows, or believes on reasonable grounds, that the money laundering is occurring in a particular country or territory outside the United Kingdom, and

(b) the money laundering—

(i) is not unlawful under the criminal law applying in that country or territory, and

(ii) is not of a description prescribed in an order made by the Secretary of State.]

(7) In deciding whether a person committed an offence under this section the court must consider whether he followed any relevant guidance which was at the time concerned—

(a) issued by a supervisory authority or any other appropriate body,

(b) approved by the Treasury, and

(c) published in a manner it approved as appropriate in its opinion to bring the guidance to the attention of persons likely to be affected by it.

(8) Schedule 9 has effect for the purpose of determining what is a supervisory authority.

(9) An appropriate body is a body which regulates or is representative of a trade, profession, business or employment.

332 Failure to disclose: other nominated officers

(1) A person nominated to receive disclosures under section 337 or 338 commits an offence if the conditions in subsections (2) to (4) are satisfied.

(2) The first condition is that he knows or suspects that another person is engaged in money laundering.

(3) The second condition is that the information or other matter on which his knowledge or suspicion is based came to him in consequence of a disclosure made under [the applicable section].

[(3A) The third condition is—

(a) that he knows the identity of the other person mentioned in subsection (2), or the whereabouts of any of the laundered property, in consequence of a disclosure made under the applicable section,

(b) that that other person, or the whereabouts of any of the laundered property, can be identified from the information or other matter mentioned in subsection (3), or

(c) that he believes, or it is reasonable to expect him to believe, that the information or other matter will or may assist in identifying that other person or the whereabouts of any of the laundered property.

(4) The fourth condition is that he does not make the required disclosure to a person authorised for the purposes of this Part by the Director General of [SOCA] as soon as is practicable after the information or other matter mentioned in subsection (3) comes to him.

(5) The required disclosure is a disclosure of—
   (a) the identity of the other person mentioned in subsection (2), if disclosed to him under the applicable section,
   (b) the whereabouts of the laundered property, so far as disclosed to him under the applicable section, and
   (c) the information or other matter mentioned in subsection (3).

(5A) The laundered property is the property forming the subject-matter of the money laundering that he knows or suspects that other person to be engaged in. (5B) The applicable section is section 337 or, as the case may be, section 338.

(6) But he does not commit an offence under this section if he has a reasonable excuse for not making the required disclosure.]

[(7) Nor does a person commit an offence under this section if—
   (a) he knows, or believes on reasonable grounds, that the money laundering is occurring in a particular country or territory outside the United Kingdom, and
   (b) the money laundering—
      (i) is not unlawful under the criminal law applying in that country or territory, and
      (ii) is not of a description prescribed in an order made by the Secretary of State.]

[. . .]

[333A Tipping off: regulated sector

(1) A person commits an offence if—
   (a) the person discloses any matter within subsection (2);
   (b) the disclosure is likely to prejudice any investigation that might be conducted following the disclosure referred to in that subsection; and
   (c) the information on which the disclosure is based came to the person in the course of a business in the regulated sector.

(2) The matters are that the person or another person has made a disclosure under this Part—
   (a) to a constable,
   (b) to an officer of Revenue and Customs,
   (c) to a nominated officer, or
   (d) to a member of staff of the Serious Organised Crime Agency authorised for the purposes of this Part by the Director General of that Agency,
of information that came to that person in the course of a business in the regulated sector.

(3) A person commits an offence if—
   (a) the person discloses that an investigation into allegations that an offence under this Part has been committed is being contemplated or is being carried out;
   (b) the disclosure is likely to prejudice that investigation; and
   (c) the information on which the disclosure is based came to the person in the course of a business in the regulated sector.

(4) A person guilty of an offence under this section is liable—
   (a) on summary conviction to imprisonment for a term not exceeding three months, or to a fine not exceeding level 5 on the standard scale, or to both;
   (b) on conviction on indictment to imprisonment for a term not exceeding two years, or to a fine, or to both.

(5) This section is subject to—
   (a) section 333B (disclosures within an undertaking or group etc),
   (b) section 333C (other permitted disclosures between institutions etc), and
   (c) section 333D (other permitted disclosures etc).]

[333B Disclosures within an undertaking or group etc

(1) An employee, officer or partner of an undertaking does not commit an offence under section 333A if the disclosure is to an employee, officer or partner of the same undertaking.

(2) A person does not commit an offence under section 333A in respect of a disclosure by a credit institution or a financial institution if—

   (a) the disclosure is to a credit institution or a financial institution,

   (b) the institution to whom the disclosure is made is situated in an EEA State or in a country or territory imposing equivalent money laundering requirements, and

   (c) both the institution making the disclosure and the institution to whom it is made belong to the same group.

(3) In subsection (2) "group" has the same meaning as in Directive 2002/87/EC of the European Parliament and of the Council of 16th December 2002 on the supplementary supervision of credit institutions, insurance undertakings and investment firms in a financial conglomerate.

(4) A professional legal adviser or a relevant professional adviser does not commit an offence under section 333A if—

   (a) the disclosure is to professional legal adviser or a relevant professional adviser,

   (b) both the person making the disclosure and the person to whom it is made carry on business in an EEA State or in a country or territory imposing equivalent money laundering requirements, and

   (c) those persons perform their professional activities within different undertakings that share common ownership, management or control.]

333C Other permitted disclosures between institutions etc

(1) This section applies to a disclosure—

   (a) by a credit institution to another credit institution,

   (b) by a financial institution to another financial institution,

   (c) by a professional legal adviser to another professional legal adviser, or

   (d) by a relevant professional adviser of a particular kind to another relevant professional adviser of the same kind.

(2) A person does not commit an offence under section 333A in respect of a disclosure to which this section applies if—

   (a) the disclosure relates to—

      (i)   a client or former client of the institution or adviser making the disclosure and the institution or adviser to whom it is made,

      (ii) a transaction involving them both, or

      (iii) the provision of a service involving them both;

   (b) the disclosure is for the purpose only of preventing an offence under this Part of this Act;

   (c) the institution or adviser to whom the disclosure is made is situated in an EEA State or in a country or territory imposing equivalent money laundering requirements; and

   (d) the institution or adviser making the disclosure and the institution or adviser to whom it is made are subject to equivalent duties of professional confidentiality and the protection of personal data (within the meaning of section 1 of the Data Protection Act 1998).]

[333D Other permitted disclosures etc

(1) A person does not commit an offence under section 333A if the disclosure is—

   (a) to the authority that is the supervisory authority for that person by virtue of the Money Laundering Regulations 2007 (S.I. 2007/2157); or

   (b) for the purpose of—

      (i)   the detection, investigation or prosecution of a criminal offence (whether in the United Kingdom or elsewhere),

      (ii) an investigation under this Act, or

      (iii) the enforcement of any order of a court under this Act.

(2) A professional legal adviser or a relevant professional adviser does not commit an offence under section 333A if the disclosure—

   (a) is to the adviser's client, and

(b) is made for the purpose of dissuading the client from engaging in conduct amounting to an offence.

(3) A person does not commit an offence under section 333A(1) if the person does not know or suspect that the disclosure is likely to have the effect mentioned in section 333A(1)(b).

(4) A person does not commit an offence under section 333A(3) if the person does not know or suspect that the disclosure is likely to have the effect mentioned in section 333A(3)(b).]

[333E **Interpretation of sections 333A to 333D**

(1) For the purposes of sections 333A to 333D, Schedule 9 has effect for determining—
    (a) what is a business in the regulated sector, and
    (b) what is a supervisory authority.

(2) In those sections—
    "credit institution" has the same meaning as in Schedule 9;
    "financial institution" means an undertaking that carries on a business in the regulated sector by virtue of any of paragraphs (b) to (i) of paragraph 1(1) of that Schedule.

(3) References in those sections to a disclosure by or to a credit institution or a financial institution include disclosure by or to an employee, officer or partner of the institution acting on its behalf.

(4) For the purposes of those sections a country or territory imposes " equivalent money laundering requirements" if it imposes requirements equivalent to those laid down in Directive 2005/60/EC of the European Parliament and of the Council of 26th October 2005 on the prevention of the use of the financial system for the purpose of money laundering and terrorist financing.

(5) In those sections " relevant professional adviser" means an accountant, auditor or tax adviser who is a member of a professional body which is established for accountants, auditors or tax advisers (as the case may be) and which makes provision for—
    (a) testing the competence of those seeking admission to membership of such a body as a condition for such admission; and
    (b) imposing and maintaining professional and ethical standards for its members, as well as imposing sanctions for non-compliance with those standards.]

334 **Penalties**

(1) A person guilty of an offence under section 327, 328 or 329 is liable—
    (a) on summary conviction, to imprisonment for a term not exceeding six months or to a fine not exceeding the statutory maximum or to both, or
    (b) on conviction on indictment, to imprisonment for a term not exceeding 14 years or to a fine or to both.

(2) A person guilty of an offence under [section 330, 331 or 332] is liable—
    (a) on summary conviction, to imprisonment for a term not exceeding six months or to a fine not exceeding the statutory maximum or to both, or
    (b) on conviction on indictment, to imprisonment for a term not exceeding five years or to a fine or to both.

[(3) A person guilty of an offence under section 339(1A) is liable on summary conviction to a fine not exceeding level 5 on the standard scale.]

Consent

335 **Appropriate consent**

(1) The appropriate consent is—
    (a) the consent of a nominated officer to do a prohibited act if an authorised disclosure is made to the nominated officer;
    (b) the consent of a constable to do a prohibited act if an authorised disclosure is made to a constable;
    (c) the consent of a customs officer to do a prohibited act if an authorised disclosure is made to a customs officer.

(2) A person must be treated as having the appropriate consent if—
    (a) he makes an authorised disclosure to a constable or a customs officer, and
    (b) the condition in subsection (3) or the condition in subsection (4) is satisfied.

(3) The condition is that before the end of the notice period he does not receive notice from a constable or customs officer that consent to the doing of the act is refused.

(4) The condition is that—

(a) before the end of the notice period he receives notice from a constable or customs officer that consent to the doing of the act is refused, and

(b) the moratorium period has expired.

(5) The notice period is the period of seven working days starting with the first working day after the person makes the disclosure.

(6) The moratorium period is the period of 31 days starting with the day on which the person receives notice that consent to the doing of the act is refused.

(7) A working day is a day other than a Saturday, a Sunday, Christmas Day, Good Friday or a day which is a bank holiday under the Banking and Financial Dealings Act 1971 (c. 80) in the part of the United Kingdom in which the person is when he makes the disclosure.

(8) References to a prohibited act are to an act mentioned in section 327(1), 328(1) or 329(1) (as the case may be).

(9) A nominated officer is a person nominated to receive disclosures under section 338.

(10) Subsections (1) to (4) apply for the purposes of this Part.

336 Nominated officer: consent

(1) A nominated officer must not give the appropriate consent to the doing of a prohibited act unless the condition in subsection (2), the condition in subsection (3) or the condition in subsection (4) is satisfied.

(2) The condition is that—

(a) he makes a disclosure that property is criminal property to a person authorised for the purposes of this Part by [the Director General of [SOCA]] , and

(b) such a person gives consent to the doing of the act.

(3) The condition is that—

(a) he makes a disclosure that property is criminal property to a person authorised for the purposes of this Part by [the Director General of [SOCA]] , and

(b) before the end of the notice period he does not receive notice from such a person that consent to the doing of the act is refused.

(4) The condition is that—

(a) he makes a disclosure that property is criminal property to a person authorised for the purposes of this Part by [the Director General of [SOCA]],

(b) before the end of the notice period he receives notice from such a person that consent to the doing of the act is refused, and

(c) the moratorium period has expired.

(5) A person who is a nominated officer commits an offence if—

(a) he gives consent to a prohibited act in circumstances where none of the conditions in subsections (2), (3) and (4) is satisfied, and

(b) he knows or suspects that the act is a prohibited act.

(6) A person guilty of such an offence is liable—

(a) on summary conviction, to imprisonment for a term not exceeding six months or to a fine not exceeding the statutory maximum or to both, or

(b) on conviction on indictment, to imprisonment for a term not exceeding five years or to a fine or to both.

(7) The notice period is the period of seven working days starting with the first working day after the nominated officer makes the disclosure.

(8) The moratorium period is the period of 31 days starting with the day on which the nominated officer is given notice that consent to the doing of the act is refused.

(9) A working day is a day other than a Saturday, a Sunday, Christmas Day, Good Friday or a day which is a bank holiday under the Banking and Financial Dealings Act 1971 (c. 80) in the part of the United Kingdom in which the nominated officer is when he gives the appropriate consent.

(10) References to a prohibited act are to an act mentioned in section 327(1), 328(1) or 329(1) (as the case may be).

(11) A nominated officer is a person nominated to receive disclosures under section 338.

Disclosures

337 Protected disclosures

(1) A disclosure which satisfies the following three conditions is not to be taken to breach any restriction on the disclosure of information (however imposed).

(2) The first condition is that the information or other matter disclosed came to the person making the disclosure (the discloser) in the course of his trade, profession, business or employment.

(3) The second condition is that the information or other matter—
   (a) causes the discloser to know or suspect, or
   (b) gives him reasonable grounds for knowing or suspecting,
   that another person is engaged in money laundering.

(4) The third condition is that the disclosure is made to a constable, a customs officer or a nominated officer as soon as is practicable after the information or other matter comes to the discloser.

[(4A) Where a disclosure consists of a disclosure protected under subsection (1) and a disclosure of either or both of—
   (a) the identity of the other person mentioned in subsection (3), and
   (b) the whereabouts of property forming the subject-matter of the money laundering that the discloser knows or suspects, or has reasonable grounds for knowing or suspecting, that other person to be engaged in,
   the disclosure of the thing mentioned in paragraph (a) or (b) (as well as the disclosure protected under subsection (1)) is not to be taken to breach any restriction on the disclosure of information (however imposed).]

(5) A disclosure to a nominated officer is a disclosure which—
   (a) is made to a person nominated by the discloser's employer to receive disclosures under [section 330 or] this section, and
   (b) is made in the course of the discloser's employment [. . .].

338 Authorised disclosures

(1) For the purposes of this Part a disclosure is authorised if—
   (a) it is a disclosure to a constable, a customs officer or a nominated officer by the alleged offender that property is criminal property,[and]
   [. . .]
   (c) the first [, second or third] condition set out below is satisfied.

(2) The first condition is that the disclosure is made before the alleged offender does the prohibited act.

[(2A) The second condition is that—
   (a) the disclosure is made while the alleged offender is doing the prohibited act,
   (b) he began to do the act at a time when, because he did not then know or suspect that the property constituted or represented a person's benefit from criminal conduct, the act was not a prohibited act, and
   (c) the disclosure is made on his own initiative and as soon as is practicable after he first knows or suspects that the property constitutes or represents a person's benefit from criminal conduct.]

(3) The [third] condition is that—
   (a) the disclosure is made after the alleged offender does the prohibited act,
   (b) [he has a reasonable excuse] for his failure to make the disclosure before he did the act, and
   (c) the disclosure is made on his own initiative and as soon as it is practicable for him to make it.

(4) An authorised disclosure is not to be taken to breach any restriction on the disclosure of information (however imposed).

(5) A disclosure to a nominated officer is a disclosure which—
   (a) is made to a person nominated by the alleged offender's employer to receive authorised disclosures, and
   (b) is made in the course of the alleged offender's employment [. . .].

(6) References to the prohibited act are to an act mentioned in section 327(1), 328(1) or 329(1) (as the case may be).

339 Form and manner of disclosures

(1) The Secretary of State may by order prescribe the form and manner in which a disclosure under section 330, 331, 332 or 338 must be made.

[(1A) A person commits an offence if he makes a disclosure under section 330, 331, 332 or 338 otherwise than in the form prescribed under subsection (1) or otherwise than in the manner so prescribed.

(1B) But a person does not commit an offence under subsection (1A) if he has a reasonable excuse for making the disclosure otherwise than in the form prescribed under subsection (1) or (as the case may be) otherwise than in the manner so prescribed.

(2) The power under subsection (1) to prescribe the form in which a disclosure must be made includes power to provide for the form to include a request to a person making a disclosure that the person provide information specified or described in the form if he has not provided it in making the disclosure.

(3) Where under subsection (2) a request is included in a form prescribed under subsection (1), the form must—

(a) state that there is no obligation to comply with the request, and

(b) explain the protection conferred by subsection (4) on a person who complies with the request.]

(4) A disclosure made in pursuance of a request under subsection (2) is not to be taken to breach any restriction on the disclosure of information (however imposed).

[. . .]

(7) Subsection (2) does not apply to a disclosure made to a nominated officer.

[339ZA Disclosures to SOCA

Where a disclosure is made under this Part to a constable or an officer of Revenue and Customs, the constable or officer of Revenue and Customs must disclose it in full to a person authorised for the purposes of this Part by the Director General of the Serious Organised Crime Agency as soon as practicable after it has been made.]

Threshold amounts

[339A Threshold amounts

(1) This section applies for the purposes of sections 327(2C), 328(5) and 329(2C).

(2) The threshold amount for acts done by a deposit-taking body in operating an account is £250 unless a higher amount is specified under the following provisions of this section (in which event it is that higher amount).

(3) An officer of Revenue and Customs, or a constable, may specify the threshold amount for acts done by a deposit-taking body in operating an account—

(a) when he gives consent, or gives notice refusing consent, to the deposit-taking body's doing of an act mentioned in section 327(1), 328(1) or 329(1) in opening, or operating, the account or a related account, or

(b) on a request from the deposit-taking body.

(4) Where the threshold amount for acts done in operating an account is specified under subsection (3) or this subsection, an officer of Revenue and Customs, or a constable, may vary the amount (whether on a request from the deposit-taking body or otherwise) by specifying a different amount.

(5) Different threshold amounts may be specified under subsections (3) and (4) for different acts done in operating the same account.

(6) The amount specified under subsection (3) or (4) as the threshold amount for acts done in operating an account must, when specified, not be less than the amount specified in subsection (2).

(7) The Secretary of State may by order vary the amount for the time being specified in subsection (2).

(8) For the purposes of this section, an account is related to another if each is maintained with the same deposit-taking body and there is a person who, in relation to each account, is the person or one of the persons entitled to instruct the body as respects the operation of the account.]

Interpretation

340 Interpretation

(1) This section applies for the purposes of this Part.

(2) Criminal conduct is conduct which—

(a) constitutes an offence in any part of the United Kingdom, or

(b) would constitute an offence in any part of the United Kingdom if it occurred there.

(3) Property is criminal property if—

(a) it constitutes a person's benefit from criminal conduct or it represents such a benefit (in whole or part and whether directly or indirectly), and

(b) the alleged offender knows or suspects that it constitutes or represents such a benefit.

(4) It is immaterial—

(a) who carried out the conduct;

(b) who benefited from it;

(c) whether the conduct occurred before or after the passing of this Act.

(5) A person benefits from conduct if he obtains property as a result of or in connection with the conduct.

(6) If a person obtains a pecuniary advantage as a result of or in connection with conduct, he is to be taken to obtain as a result of or in connection with the conduct a sum of money equal to the value of the pecuniary advantage.

(7) References to property or a pecuniary advantage obtained in connection with conduct include references to property or a pecuniary advantage obtained in both that connection and some other.

(8) If a person benefits from conduct his benefit is the property obtained as a result of or in connection with the conduct.

(9) Property is all property wherever situated and includes—

(a) money;

(b) all forms of property, real or personal, heritable or moveable;

(c) things in action and other intangible or incorporeal property.

(10) The following rules apply in relation to property—

(a) property is obtained by a person if he obtains an interest in it;

(b) references to an interest, in relation to land in England and Wales or Northern Ireland, are to any legal estate or equitable interest or power;

(c) references to an interest, in relation to land in Scotland, are to any estate, interest, servitude or other heritable right in or over land, including a heritable security;

(d) references to an interest, in relation to property other than land, include references to a right (including a right to possession).

(11) Money laundering is an act which—

(a) constitutes an offence under section 327, 328 or 329,

(b) constitutes an attempt, conspiracy or incitement to commit an offence specified in paragraph (a),

(c) constitutes aiding, abetting, counselling or procuring the commission of an offence specified in paragraph (a), or

(d) would constitute an offence specified in paragraph (a), (b) or (c) if done in the United Kingdom.

(12) For the purposes of a disclosure to a nominated officer—

(a) references to a person's employer include any body, association or organisation (including a voluntary organisation) in connection with whose activities the person exercises a function (whether or not for gain or reward), and

(b) references to employment must be construed accordingly.

(13) References to a constable include references to a person authorised for the purposes of this Part by [the Director General of [SOCA]] .

[(14) "Deposit-taking body" means—

(a) a business which engages in the activity of accepting deposits, or

(b) the National Savings Bank.]

Part 8 Investigations

Chapter 1 Introduction

341 Investigations

(1) For the purposes of this Part a confiscation investigation is an investigation into—
    (a) whether a person has benefited from his criminal conduct, or
    (b) the extent or whereabouts of his benefit from his criminal conduct.

(2) For the purposes of this Part a civil recovery investigation is an investigation into—
    (a) whether property is recoverable property or associated property,
    (b) who holds the property, or
    (c) its extent or whereabouts.

(3) But an investigation is not a civil recovery investigation if—
    (a) proceedings for a recovery order have been started in respect of the property in question,
    (b) an interim receiving order applies to the property in question,
    (c) an interim administration order applies to the property in question, or
    (d) the property in question is detained under section 295.

[(3A) For the purposes of this Part a detained cash investigation is—
    (a) an investigation for the purposes of Chapter 3 of Part 5 into the derivation of cash detained under section 295 or a part of such cash, or
    (b) an investigation for the purposes of Chapter 3 of Part 5 into whether cash detained under section 295, or a part of such cash, is intended by any person to be used in unlawful conduct.]

(4) For the purposes of this Part a money laundering investigation is an investigation into whether a person has committed a money laundering offence.

[(5) For the purposes of this Part an exploitation proceeds investigation is an investigation for the purposes of Part 7 of the Coroners and Justice Act 2009 (criminal memoirs etc) into—
    (a) whether a person is a qualifying offender,
    (b) whether a person has obtained exploitation proceeds from a relevant offence,
    (c) the value of any benefits derived by a person from a relevant offence, or
    (d) the available amount in respect of a person.
Paragraphs (a) to (d) are to be construed in accordance with that Part of that Act.]

342 Offences of prejudicing investigation

(1) This section applies if a person knows or suspects that an appropriate officer or (in Scotland) a proper person is acting (or proposing to act) in connection with a confiscation investigation, a civil recovery investigation [, a detained cash investigation] [, an exploitation proceeds investigation] or a money laundering investigation which is being or is about to be conducted.

(2) The person commits an offence if—
    (a) he makes a disclosure which is likely to prejudice the investigation, or
    (b) he falsifies, conceals, destroys or otherwise disposes of, or causes or permits the falsification, concealment, destruction or disposal of, documents which are relevant to the investigation.

(3) A person does not commit an offence under subsection (2)(a) if—
    (a) he does not know or suspect that the disclosure is likely to prejudice the investigation,
    (b) the disclosure is made in the exercise of a function under this Act or any other enactment relating to criminal conduct or benefit from criminal conduct or in compliance with a requirement imposed under or by virtue of this Act, or
    [(ba) the disclosure is of a matter within section 333A(2) or (3)(a) (money laundering: tipping off) and the information on which the disclosure is based came to the person in the course of a business in the regulated sector,]
    [(bb) the disclosure is made in the exercise of a function under Part 7 of the Coroners and Justice Act 2009 (criminal memoirs etc) or in compliance with a requirement imposed under or by virtue of that Act,]
    (c) he is a professional legal adviser and the disclosure falls within subsection (4).

(4) A disclosure falls within this subsection if it is a disclosure—
    (a) to (or to a representative of) a client of the professional legal adviser in connection with the giving by the adviser of legal advice to the client, or
    (b) to any person in connection with legal proceedings or contemplated legal proceedings.

(5) But a disclosure does not fall within subsection (4) if it is made with the intention of furthering a criminal purpose.

(6) A person does not commit an offence under subsection (2)(b) if—

    (a) he does not know or suspect that the documents are relevant to the investigation, or

    (b) he does not intend to conceal any facts disclosed by the documents from any appropriate officer or (in Scotland) proper person carrying out the investigation.

(7) A person guilty of an offence under subsection (2) is liable—

    (a) on summary conviction, to imprisonment for a term not exceeding six months or to a fine not exceeding the statutory maximum or to both, or

    (b) on conviction on indictment, to imprisonment for a term not exceeding five years or to a fine or to both.

(8) For the purposes of this section—

    (a) "appropriate officer" must be construed in accordance with section 378;

    (b) "proper person" must be construed in accordance with section 412 [;]

    [(c) Schedule 9 has effect for determining what is a business in the regulated sector.]

Schedule 9 Regulated Sector And Supervisory Authorities

Part 1 Regulated Sector

Business in the regulated sector

[1.

(1) A business is in the regulated sector to the extent that it consists of—

    (a) the acceptance by a credit institution of deposits or other repayable funds from the public, or the granting by a credit institution of credits for its own account;

    (b) the carrying on of one or more of the activities listed in points 2 to 12 and 14 of Annex 1 to the Banking Consolidation Directive by an undertaking other than—

        (i) a credit institution; or

        (ii) an undertaking whose only listed activity is trading for own account in one or more of the products listed in point 7 of Annex 1 to the Banking Consolidation Directive and which does not act on behalf of a customer (that is, a third party which is not a member of the same group as the undertaking);

    (c) the carrying on of activities covered by the Life Assurance Consolidation Directive by an insurance company authorised in accordance with that Directive;

    (d) the provision of investment services or the performance of investment activities by a person (other than a person falling within Article 2 of the Markets in Financial Instruments Directive) whose regular occupation or business is the provision to other persons of an investment service or the performance of an investment activity on a professional basis;

    (e) the marketing or other offering of units or shares by a collective investment undertaking;

    (f) the activities of an insurance intermediary as defined in Article 2(5) of the Insurance Mediation Directive, other than a tied insurance intermediary as mentioned in Article 2(7) of that Directive, in respect of contracts of long-term insurance within the meaning given by article 3(1) of, and Part II of Schedule 1 to, the Financial Services and Markets Act 2000 (Regulated Activities) Order 2001;

    (g) the carrying on of any of the activities mentioned in paragraphs (b) to (f) by a branch located in an EEA State of a person referred to in those paragraphs (or of an equivalent person in any other State), wherever its head office is located;

    (h) the activities of the National Savings Bank; (i) any activity carried on for the purpose of raising money authorised to be raised under the National Loans Act 1968 under the auspices of the Director of Savings;

    (j) the carrying on of statutory audit work within the meaning of section 1210 of the Companies Act 2006 (meaning of " statutory auditor" etc) by any firm or individual who is a statutory auditor within the meaning of Part 42 of that Act (statutory auditors);

    (k) the activities of a person appointed to act as an insolvency practitioner within the meaning of section 388 of the Insolvency Act 1986 (meaning of " act as insolvency practitioner") or article 3 of the Insolvency (Northern Ireland) Order 1989;

(l) the provision to other persons of accountancy services by a firm or sole practitioner who by way of business provides such services to other persons;

(m) the provision of advice about the tax affairs of other persons by a firm or sole practitioner who by way of business provides advice about the tax affairs of other persons;

(n) the participation in financial or real property transactions concerning—

    (i) the buying and selling of real property (or, in Scotland, heritable property) or business entities;

    (ii) the managing of client money, securities or other assets;

    (iii) the opening or management of bank, savings or securities accounts;

    (iv) the organisation of contributions necessary for the creation, operation or management of companies; or

    (v) the creation, operation or management of trusts, companies or similar structures,

    by a firm or sole practitioner who by way of business provides legal or notarial services to other persons;

(o) the provision to other persons by way of business by a firm or sole practitioner of any of the services mentioned in sub-paragraph (4);

(p) the carrying on of estate agency work (within the meaning given by section 1 of the Estate Agents Act 1979 (estate agency work)) by a firm or a sole practitioner who carries on, or whose employees carry on, such work;

(q) the trading in goods (including dealing as an auctioneer) whenever a transaction involves the receipt of a payment or payments in cash of at least 15,000 euros in total, whether the transaction is executed in a single operation or in several operations which appear to be linked, by a firm or sole trader who by way of business trades in goods;

(r) operating a casino under a casino operating licence (within the meaning given by section 65(2) of the Gambling Act 2005 (nature of licence)).

(2) For the purposes of sub-paragraph (1)(a) and (b) " credit institution" means—

    (a) a credit institution as defined in Article 4(1)(a) of the Banking Consolidation Directive; or

    (b) a branch (within the meaning of Article 4(3) of that Directive) located in an EEA state of an institution falling within paragraph (a) (or of an equivalent institution in any other State) wherever its head office is located.

(3) For the purposes of sub-paragraph (1)(n) a person participates in a transaction by assisting in the planning or execution of the transaction or otherwise acting for or on behalf of a client in the transaction.

(4) The services referred to in sub-paragraph (1)(o) are—

    (a) forming companies or other legal persons;

    (b) acting, or arranging for another person to act—

        (i) as a director or secretary of a company;

        (ii) as a partner of a partnership; or

        (iii) in a similar position in relation to other legal persons;

    (c) providing a registered office, business address, correspondence or administrative address or other related services for a company, partnership or any other legal person or arrangement;

    (d) acting, or arranging for another person to act, as—

        (i) a trustee of an express trust or similar legal arrangement; or

        (ii) a nominee shareholder for a person other than a company whose securities are listed on a regulated market.

(5) For the purposes of sub-paragraph (4)(d) "regulated market" —

    (a) in relation to any EEA State, has the meaning given by point 14 of Article 4(1) of the Markets in Financial Instruments Directive; and

    (b) in relation to any other State, means a regulated financial market which subjects companies whose securities are admitted to trading to disclosure obligations which are contained in international standards and are equivalent to the specified disclosure obligations.

(6) For the purposes of sub-paragraph (5) " the specified disclosure obligations" means disclosure requirements consistent with—

    (a) Article 6(1) to (4) of Directive 2003/6/EC of the European Parliament and of the Council of 28th January 2003 on insider dealing and market manipulation;

    (b) Articles 3, 5, 7, 8, 10, 14 and 16 of Directive 2003/71/EC of the European Parliament and of the Council of 4th November 2003 on the prospectuses to be published when securities are offered to the public or admitted to trading;

    (c) Articles 4 to 6, 14, 16 to 19 and 30 of Directive 2004/109/EC of the European Parliament and of the Council of 15th December 2004 relating to the harmonisation of transparency requirements in relation to information about issuers whose securities are admitted to trading on a regulated market; or

    (d) Community legislation made under the provisions mentioned in paragraphs (a) to (c).

(7) For the purposes of sub-paragraph (1)(j) and (l) to (q) "firm" means any entity, whether or not a legal person, that is not an individual and includes a body corporate and a partnership or other unincorporated association.

(8) For the purposes of sub-paragraph (1)(q) " cash" means notes, coins or travellers' cheques in any currency.]

2

[

]

Excluded activities

[2

(1) A business is not in the regulated sector to the extent that it consists of—

    (a) the issuing of withdrawable share capital within the limit set by section 6 of the Industrial and Provident Societies Act 1965 (maximum shareholding in society), or the acceptance of deposits from the public within the limit set by section 7(3) of that Act (carrying on of banking by societies), by a society registered under that Act;

    (b) the issuing of withdrawable share capital within the limit set by section 6 of the Industrial and Provident Societies Act (Northern Ireland) 1969 (maximum shareholding in society), or the acceptance of deposits from the public within the limit set by section 7(3) of that Act (carrying on of banking by societies), by a society registered under that Act;

    (c) the carrying on of any activity in respect of which a person who is (or falls within a class of persons) specified in any of paragraphs 2 to 23, 25 to 38 or 40 to 49 of the Schedule to the Financial Services and Markets Act 2000 (Exemption) Order 2001 is exempt;

    (d) the exercise of the functions specified in section 45 of the Financial Services Act 1986 (miscellaneous exemptions) by a person who was an exempted person for the purposes of that section immediately before its repeal;

    (e) the engaging in financial activity which fulfils all of the conditions set out in paragraphs (a) to (g) of sub-paragraph (3) of this paragraph by a person whose main activity is that of a high value dealer; or

    (f) the preparation of a home information pack (within the meaning of Part 5 of the Housing Act 2004 (home information packs)) or a document or information for inclusion in a home information pack.

(2) For the purposes of sub-paragraph (1)(e) a "high value dealer" means a person mentioned in paragraph 1(1)(q) when carrying on the activities mentioned in that paragraph.

(3) A business is not in the regulated sector to the extent that it consists of financial activity if—

    (a) the person's total annual turnover in respect of the financial activity does not exceed £64,000;

    (b) the financial activity is limited in relation to any customer to no more than one transaction exceeding 1,000 euros, whether the transaction is carried out in a single operation, or a series of operations which appear to be linked;

    (c) the financial activity does not exceed 5% of the person's total annual turnover;

    (d) the financial activity is ancillary to the person's main activity and directly related to that activity;

    (e) the financial activity is not the transmission or remittance of money (or any representation of monetary value) by any means;

    (f) the main activity of the person carrying on the financial activity is not an activity mentioned in paragraph 1(1)(a) to (p) or (r); and

(g) the financial activity is provided only to customers of the person's main activity and is not offered to the public.

(4) A business is not in the regulated sector if it is carried on by—

    (a) the Auditor General for Scotland;

    (b) the Auditor General for Wales;

    (c) the Bank of England;

    (d) the Comptroller and Auditor General;

    (e) the Comptroller and Auditor General for Northern Ireland;

    (f) the Official Solicitor to the Supreme Court, when acting as trustee in his official capacity; or

    (g) the Treasury Solicitor.]

[

3

[

]

Interpretation

[3

(1) In this Part—

"the Banking Consolidation Directive" means directive 2006/48/EC of the European Parliament and of the Council of 14th June 2006 relating to the taking up and pursuit of the business of credit institutions;

"the Insurance Mediation Directive" means directive 2002/92/EC of the European Parliament and of the Council of 9th December 2002 on insurance mediation;

"the Life Assurance Consolidation Directive" means directive 2002/83/EC of the European Parliament and of the Council of 5th November 2002 concerning life assurance; and

"the Markets in Financial Instruments Directive" means directive 2004/39/EC of the European Parliament and of the Council of 12th April 2004 on markets in financial instruments.

(2) In this Part references to amounts in euros include references to equivalent amounts in another currency.

(3) Terms used in this Part and in the Banking Consolidation Directive or the Markets in Financial Instruments Directive have the same meaning in this Part as in those Directives.]

Part 2 Supervisory Authorities

[4

(1) The following bodies are supervisory authorities—

    (a) the Commissioners for Her Majesty's Revenue and Customs;

    (b) the Department of Enterprise, Trade and Investment in Northern Ireland;

    (c) the Financial Services Authority;

    (d) the Gambling Commission;

    (e) the Office of Fair Trading;

    (f) the Secretary of State; and

    (g) the professional bodies listed in sub-paragraph (2).

(2) The professional bodies referred to in sub-paragraph (1)(g) are—

    (a) the Association of Accounting Technicians;

    (b) the Association of Chartered Certified Accountants;

    (c) the Association of International Accountants;

    (d) the Association of Taxation Technicians;

    (e) the Chartered Institute of Management Accountants;

    (f) the Chartered Institute of Public Finance and Accountancy;

    (g) the Chartered Institute of Taxation;

    (h) the Council for Licensed Conveyancers;

    (i) the Faculty of Advocates;

    (j) the Faculty Office of the Archbishop of Canterbury; (k) the General Council of the Bar;

    (l) the General Council of the Bar of Northern Ireland;

(m) the Insolvency Practitioners Association;

(n) the Institute of Certified Bookkeepers;

(o) the Institute of Chartered Accountants in England and Wales;

(p) the Institute of Chartered Accountants in Ireland;

(q) the Institute of Chartered Accountants of Scotland;

(r) the Institute of Financial Accountants;

(s) the International Association of Book-keepers;

(t) the Law Society;

(u) the Law Society for Northern Ireland; and

(v) the Law Society of Scotland.]

Part 3 Power To Amend

5

The Treasury may by order amend Part 1 or 2 of this Schedule.

Terrorism Act 2000 (Extracts)

The extracts of this Act appear as updated by subsequent legislation.

Part I Introductory

1 Terrorism: interpretation.

(1) In this Act "terrorism" means the use or threat of action where—
   (a) the action falls within subsection (2),
   (b) the use or threat is designed to influence the government [or an international govermental organisation] or to intimidate the public or a section of the public, and
   (c) the use or threat is made for the purpose of advancing a political, religious [, racial] or ideological cause.

(2) Action falls within this subsection if it—
   (a) involves serious violence against a person,
   (b) involves serious damage to property,
   (c) endangers a person's life, other than that of the person committing the action,
   (d) creates a serious risk to the health or safety of the public or a section of the public, or
   (e) is designed seriously to interfere with or seriously to disrupt an electronic system.

(3) The use or threat of action falling within subsection (2) which involves the use of firearms or explosives is terrorism whether or not subsection (1)(b) is satisfied.

(4) In this section—
   (a) "action" includes action outside the United Kingdom,
   (b) a reference to any person or to property is a reference to any person, or to property, wherever situated,
   (c) a reference to the public includes a reference to the public of a country other than the United Kingdom, and
   (d) " the government" means the government of the United Kingdom, of a part of the United Kingdom or of a country other than the United Kingdom.

(5) In this Act a reference to action taken for the purposes of terrorism includes a reference to action taken for the benefit of a proscribed organisation.

Part III Terrorist Property

Interpretation

14 Terrorist property

(1) In this Act "terrorist property" means—
   (a) money or other property which is likely to be used for the purposes of terrorism (including any resources of a proscribed organisation),
   (b) proceeds of the commission of acts of terrorism, and
   (c) proceeds of acts carried out for the purposes of terrorism.

(2) In subsection (1)—
   (a) a reference to proceeds of an act includes a reference to any property which wholly or partly, and directly or indirectly, represents the proceeds of the act (including payments or other rewards in connection with its commission), and
   (b) the reference to an organisation's resources includes a reference to any money or other property which is applied or made available, or is to be applied or made available, for use by the organisation.

Offences

15 Fund-raising

(1) A person commits an offence if he—
    (a) invites another to provide money or other property, and
    (b) intends that it should be used, or has reasonable cause to suspect that it may be used, for the purposes of terrorism.
(2) A person commits an offence if he—
    (a) receives money or other property, and
    (b) intends that it should be used, or has reasonable cause to suspect that it may be used, for the purposes of terrorism.
(3) A person commits an offence if he—
    (a) provides money or other property, and
    (b) knows or has reasonable cause to suspect that it will or may be used for the purposes of terrorism.
(4) In this section a reference to the provision of money or other property is a reference to its being given, lent or otherwise made available, whether or not for consideration.

16 Use and possession

(1) A person commits an offence if he uses money or other property for the purposes of terrorism.
(2) A person commits an offence if he—
    (a) possesses money or other property, and
    (b) intends that it should be used, or has reasonable cause to suspect that it may be used, for the purposes of terrorism.

17 Funding arrangements

A person commits an offence if—

(a) he enters into or becomes concerned in an arrangement as a result of which money or other property is made available or is to be made available to another, and
(b) he knows or has reasonable cause to suspect that it will or may be used for the purposes of terrorism.

18 Money laundering

(1) A person commits an offence if he enters into or becomes concerned in an arrangement which facilitates the retention or control by or on behalf of another person of terrorist property—
    (a) by concealment,
    (b) by removal from the jurisdiction,
    (c) by transfer to nominees, or
    (d) in any other way.
(2) It is a defence for a person charged with an offence under subsection (1) to prove that he did not know and had no reasonable cause to suspect that the arrangement related to terrorist property.

19 Disclosure of information: duty

(1) This section applies where a person—
    (a) believes or suspects that another person has committed an offence under any of sections 15 to 18, and
    (b) [bases his belief or suspicion on information which comes to his attention—
        (i) in the course of a trade, profession or business, or
        (ii) in the course of his employment (whether or not in the course of a trade, profession or business).]
[(1A) But this section does not apply if the information came to the person in the course of a business in the regulated sector.]
(2) The person commits an offence if he does not disclose to a constable as soon as is reasonably practicable—
    (a) his belief or suspicion, and
    (b) the information on which it is based.

(3) It is a defence for a person charged with an offence under subsection (2) to prove that he had a reasonable excuse for not making the disclosure.

(4) Where—

    (a) a person is in employment,

    (b) his employer has established a procedure for the making of disclosures of the matters specified in subsection (2), and

    (c) he is charged with an offence under that subsection, it is a defence for him to prove that he disclosed the matters specified in that subsection in accordance with the procedure.

(5) Subsection (2) does not require disclosure by a professional legal adviser of—

    (a) information which he obtains in privileged circumstances, or

    (b) a belief or suspicion based on information which he obtains in privileged circumstances.

(6) For the purpose of subsection (5) information is obtained by an adviser in privileged circumstances if it comes to him, otherwise than with a view to furthering a criminal purpose—

    (a) from a client or a client's representative, in connection with the provision of legal advice by the adviser to the client,

    (b) from a person seeking legal advice from the adviser, or from the person's representative, or

    (c) from any person, for the purpose of actual or contemplated legal proceedings.

(7) For the purposes of subsection (1)(a) a person shall be treated as having committed an offence under one of sections 15 to 18 if—

    (a) he has taken an action or been in possession of a thing, and

    (b) he would have committed an offence under one of those sections if he had been in the United Kingdom at the time when he took the action or was in possession of the thing.

[(7A) The reference to a business in the regulated sector must be construed in accordance with Schedule 3A.

(7B) The reference to a constable includes a reference to a [member of the staff of the Serious Organised Crime Agency] authorised for the purposes of this section by the Director General of [that Agency].]

(8) A person guilty of an offence under this section shall be liable—

    (a) on conviction on indictment, to imprisonment for a term not exceeding five years, to a fine or to both, or

    (b) on summary conviction, to imprisonment for a term not exceeding six months, or to a fine not exceeding the statutory maximum or to both.

20 Disclosure of information: permission

(1) A person may disclose to a constable—

    (a) a suspicion or belief that any money or other property is terrorist property or is derived from terrorist property;

    (b) any matter on which the suspicion or belief is based.

(2) A person may make a disclosure to a constable in the circumstances mentioned in section 19(1) and (2).

(3) Subsections (1) and (2) shall have effect notwithstanding any restriction on the disclosure of information imposed by statute or otherwise.

(4) Where—

    (a) a person is in employment, and

    (b) his employer has established a procedure for the making of disclosures of the kinds mentioned in subsection (1) and section 19(2),

subsections (1) and (2) shall have effect in relation to that person as if any reference to disclosure to a constable included a reference to disclosure in accordance with the procedure.

[(5) References to a constable include references to a [member of the staff of the Serious Organised Crime Agency] authorised for the purposes of this section by the Director General of [that Agency].]

21 Cooperation with police

(1) A person does not commit an offence under any of sections 15 to 18 if he is acting with the express consent of a constable.

(2) Subject to subsections (3) and (4), a person does not commit an offence under any of sections 15 to 18 by involvement in a transaction or arrangement relating to money or other property if he discloses to a constable—

(a) his suspicion or belief that the money or other property is terrorist property, and

(b) the information on which his suspicion or belief is based.

(3) Subsection (2) applies only where a person makes a disclosure—

(a) after he becomes concerned in the transaction concerned,

(b) on his own initiative, and

(c) as soon as is reasonably practicable.

(4) Subsection (2) does not apply to a person if—

(a) a constable forbids him to continue his involvement in the transaction or arrangement to which the disclosure relates, and

(b) he continues his involvement.

(5) It is a defence for a person charged with an offence under any of sections 15(2) and (3) and 16 to 18 to prove that—

(a) he intended to make a disclosure of the kind mentioned in subsections (2) and (3), and

(b) there is reasonable excuse for his failure to do so.

(6) Where—

(a) a person is in employment, and

(b) his employer has established a procedure for the making of disclosures of the same kind as may be made to a constable under subsection (2), this section shall have effect in relation to that person as if any reference to disclosure to a constable included a reference to disclosure in accordance with the procedure.

(7) A reference in this section to a transaction or arrangement relating to money or other property includes a reference to use or possession.

[21ZA Arrangements with prior consent

(1) A person does not commit an offence under any of sections 15 to 18 by involvement in a transaction or an arrangement relating to money or other property if, before becoming involved, the person—

(a) discloses to an authorised officer the person's suspicion or belief that the money or other property is terrorist property and the information on which the suspicion or belief is based, and

(b) has the authorised officer's consent to becoming involved in the transaction or arrangement.

(2) A person is treated as having an authorised officer's consent if before the end of the notice period the person does not receive notice from an authorised officer that consent is refused.

(3) The notice period is the period of 7 working days starting with the first working day after the person makes the disclosure.

(4) A working day is a day other than a Saturday, a Sunday, Christmas Day, Good Friday or a day that is a bank holiday under the Banking and Financial Dealings Act 1971 (c.80) in the part of the United Kingdom in which the person is when making the disclosure.

(5) In this section "authorised officer" means a member of the staff of the Serious Organised Crime Agency authorised for the purposes of this section by the Director General of that Agency.

(6) The reference in this section to a transaction or arrangement relating to money or other property includes a reference to use or possession.]

[21ZB Disclosure after entering into arrangements

(1) A person does not commit an offence under any of sections 15 to 18 by involvement in a transaction or an arrangement relating to money or other property if, after becoming involved, the person discloses to an authorised officer—

(a) the person's suspicion or belief that the money or other property is terrorist property, and

(b) the information on which the suspicion or belief is based.

(2) This section applies only where—

(a) there is a reasonable excuse for the person's failure to make the disclosure before becoming involved in the transaction or arrangement, and

(b) the disclosure is made on the person's own initiative and as soon as it is reasonably practicable for the person to make it.

(3) This section does not apply to a person if—
  (a) an authorised officer forbids the person to continue involvement in the transaction or arrange-ment to which the disclosure relates, and
  (b) the person continues that involvement.
(4) In this section "authorised officer" means a member of the staff of the Serious Organised Crime Agency authorised for the purposes of this section by the Director General of that Agency.
(5) The reference in this section to a transaction or arrangement relating to money or other property includes a reference to use or possession.]

[21ZC Reasonable excuse for failure to disclose

It is a defence for a person charged with an offence under any of sections 15 to 18 to prove that—

(a) the person intended to make a disclosure of the kind mentioned in section 21ZA or 21ZB, and
(b) there is a reasonable excuse for the person's failure to do so.]

[21A Failure to disclose: regulated sector

(1) A person commits an offence if each of the following three conditions is satisfied.
(2) The first condition is that he—
  (a) knows or suspects, or
  (b) has reasonable grounds for knowing or suspecting,
  that another person has committed [or attempted to commit] an offence under any of sections 15 to 18.
(3) The second condition is that the information or other matter—
  (a) on which his knowledge or suspicion is based, or
  (b) which gives reasonable grounds for such knowledge or suspicion,
  came to him in the course of a business in the regulated sector.
(4) The third condition is that he does not disclose the information or other matter to a constable or a nominated officer as soon as is practicable after it comes to him.
(5) But a person does not commit an offence under this section if—
  (a) he has a reasonable excuse for not disclosing the information or other matter;
  (b) he is a professional legal adviser [or relevant professional adviser] and the information or other matter came to him in privileged circumstances [;]
  [(c) subsection (5A) applies to him.]
[(5A) This subsection applies to a person if—
  (a) the person is employed by, or is in partnership with, a professional legal adviser or relevant professional adviser to provide the adviser with assistance or support,
  (b) the information or other matter comes to the person in connection with the provision of such assistance or support, and
  (c) the information or other matter came to the adviser in privileged circumstances.]
(6) In deciding whether a person committed an offence under this section the court must consider whether he followed any relevant guidance which was at the time concerned—
  (a) issued by a supervisory authority or any other appropriate body,
  (b) approved by the Treasury, and
  (c) published in a manner it approved as appropriate in its opinion to bring the guidance to the attention of persons likely to be affected by it.
(7) A disclosure to a nominated officer is a disclosure which—
  (a) is made to a person nominated by the alleged offender's employer to receive disclosures under this section, and
  (b) is made in the course of the alleged offender's employment and in accordance with the procedure established by the employer for the purpose.
(8) Information or other matter comes to a professional legal adviser [or relevant professional adviser] in privileged circumstances if it is communicated or given to him—
  (a) by (or by a representative of) a client of his in connection with the giving by the adviser of legal advice to the client,
  (b) by (or by a representative of) a person seeking legal advice from the adviser, or
  (c) by a person in connection with legal proceedings or contemplated legal proceedings.

(9) But subsection (8) does not apply to information or other matter which is communicated or given with a view to furthering a criminal purpose.

(10) Schedule 3A has effect for the purpose of determining what is—

(a) a business in the regulated sector;

(b) a supervisory authority.

(11) For the purposes of subsection (2) a person is to be taken to have committed an offence there mentioned if—

(a) he has taken an action or been in possession of a thing and

(b) he would have committed the offence if he had been in the United Kingdom at the time when he took the action or was in possession of the thing.

(12) A person guilty of an offence under this section is liable—

(a) on conviction on indictment, to imprisonment for a term not exceeding five years or to a fine or to both;

(b) on summary conviction, to imprisonment for a term not exceeding six months or to a fine not exceeding the statutory maximum or to both.

(13) An appropriate body is any body which regulates or is representative of any trade, profession, business or employment carried on by the alleged offender.

(14) The reference to a constable includes a reference to a [member of the staff of the Serious Organised Crime Agency] authorised for the purposes of this section by the Director General of [that Agency].

[(15) In this section "relevant professional adviser" means an accountant, auditor or tax adviser who is a member of a professional body which is established for accountants, auditors or tax advisers (as the case may be) and which makes provision for—

(a) testing the competence of those seeking admission to membership of such a body as a condition for such admission; and

(b) imposing and maintaining professional and ethical standards for its members, as well as imposing sanctions for non-compliance with those standards.]]

[21B Protected disclosures

(1) A disclosure which satisfies the following three conditions is not to be taken to breach any restriction on the disclosure of information (however imposed).

(2) The first condition is that the information or other matter disclosed came to the person making the disclosure (the discloser) in the course of a business in the regulated sector.

(3) The second condition is that the information or other matter—

(a) causes the discloser to know or suspect, or

(b) gives him reasonable grounds for knowing or suspecting,

that another person has committed [or attempted to commit] an offence under any of sections 15 to 18.

(4) The third condition is that the disclosure is made to a constable or a nominated officer as soon as is practicable after the information or other matter comes to the discloser.

(5) A disclosure to a nominated officer is a disclosure which—

(a) is made to a person nominated by the discloser's employer to receive disclosures under this section, and

(b) is made in the course of the discloser's employment and in accordance with the procedure established by the employer for the purpose.

(6) The reference to a business in the regulated sector must be construed in accordance with Schedule 3A.

(7) The reference to a constable includes a reference to a [member of the staff of the Serious Organised Crime Agency] authorised for the purposes of this section by the Director General of [that Agency].]

[21C Disclosures to SOCA

(1) Where a disclosure is made under a provision of this Part to a constable, the constable must disclose it in full as soon as practicable after it has been made to a member of staff of the Serious Organised Crime Agency authorised for the purposes of that provision by the Director General of that Agency.

(2) Where a disclosure is made under section 21 (cooperation with police) to a constable, the constable must disclose it in full as soon as practicable after it has been made to a member of staff of the Serious Organised Crime Agency authorised for the purposes of this subsection by the Director General of that Agency.]

[21D Tipping off: regulated sector

(1) A person commits an offence if—
   (a) the person discloses any matter within subsection (2);
   (b) the disclosure is likely to prejudice any investigation that might be conducted following the disclosure referred to in that subsection; and
   (c) the information on which the disclosure is based came to the person in the course of a business in the regulated sector.
(2) The matters are that the person or another person has made a disclosure under a provision of this Part—
   (a) to a constable,
   (b) in accordance with a procedure established by that person's employer for the making of disclosures under that provision,
   (c) to a nominated officer, or
   (d) to a member of staff of the Serious Organised Crime Agency authorised for the purposes of that provision by the Director General of that Agency,
   of information that came to that person in the course of a business in the regulated sector.
(3) A person commits an offence if—
   (a) the person discloses that an investigation into allegations that an offence under this Part has been committed is being contemplated or is being carried out;
   (b) the disclosure is likely to prejudice that investigation; and
   (c) the information on which the disclosure is based came to the person in the course of a business in the regulated sector.
(4) A person guilty of an offence under this section is liable—
   (a) on summary conviction to imprisonment for a term not exceeding three months, or to a fine not exceeding level 5 on the standard scale, or to both; (b) on conviction on indictment to imprisonment for a term not exceeding two years, or to a fine, or to both.
(5) This section is subject to—
   (a) section 21E (disclosures within an undertaking or group etc),
   (b) section 21F (other permitted disclosures between institutions etc), and
   (c) section 21G (other permitted disclosures etc).]

[21E Disclosures within an undertaking or group etc

(1) An employee, officer or partner of an undertaking does not commit an offence under section 21D if the disclosure is to an employee, officer or partner of the same undertaking.
(2) A person does not commit an offence under section 21D in respect of a disclosure by a credit institution or a financial institution if—
   (a) the disclosure is to a credit institution or a financial institution,
   (b) the institution to whom the disclosure is made is situated in an EEA State or in a country or territory imposing equivalent money laundering requirements, and
   (c) both the institution making the disclosure and the institution to whom it is made belong to the same group.
(3) In subsection (2) "group" has the same meaning as in Directive 2002/87/EC of the European Parliament and of the Council of 16th December 2002 on the supplementary supervision of credit institutions, insurance undertakings and investment firms in a financial conglomerate.
(4) A professional legal adviser or a relevant professional adviser does not commit an offence under section 21D if—
   (a) the disclosure is to a professional legal adviser or a relevant professional adviser,
   (b) both the person making the disclosure and the person to whom it is made carry on business in an EEA state or in a country or territory imposing equivalent money laundering requirements, and
   (c) those persons perform their professional activities within different undertakings that share common ownership, management or control.]

[21F Other permitted disclosures between institutions etc

(1) This section applies to a disclosure—
    (a) by a credit institution to another credit institution,
    (b) by a financial institution to another financial institution,
    (c) by a professional legal adviser to another professional legal adviser, or
    (d) by a relevant professional adviser of a particular kind to another relevant professional adviser of the same kind.

(2) A person does not commit an offence under section 21D in respect of a disclosure to which this section applies if—
    (a) the disclosure relates to—
        (i) a client or former client of the institution or adviser making the disclosure and the institution or adviser to whom it is made,
        (ii) a transaction involving them both, or
        (iii) the provision of a service involving them both;
    (b) the disclosure is for the purpose only of preventing an offence under this Part of this Act;
    (c) the institution or adviser to whom the disclosure is made is situated in an EEA State or in a country or territory imposing equivalent money laundering requirements; and
    (d) the institution or adviser making the disclosure and the institution or adviser to whom it is made are subject to equivalent duties of professional confidentiality and the protection of personal data (within the meaning of section 1 of the Data Protection Act 1998).]

[21G Other permitted disclosures etc

(1) A person does not commit an offence under section 21D if the disclosure is—
    (a) to the authority that is the supervisory authority for that person by virtue of the Money Laundering Regulations 2007 (S.I. 2007/2157); or
    (b) for the purpose of—
        (i) the detection, investigation or prosecution of a criminal offence (whether in the United Kingdom or elsewhere),
        (ii) an investigation under the Proceeds of Crime Act 2002, or
        (iii) the enforcement of any order of a court under that Act.

(2) A professional legal adviser or a relevant professional adviser does not commit an offence under section 21D if the disclosure—
    (a) is to the adviser's client, and
    (b) is made for the purpose of dissuading the client from engaging in conduct amounting to an offence.

(3) A person does not commit an offence under section 21D(1) if the person does not know or suspect that the disclosure is likely to have the effect mentioned in section 21D(1)(b).

(4) A person does not commit an offence under section 21D(3) if the person does not know or suspect that the disclosure is likely to have the effect mentioned in section 21D(3)(b).]

[21 Interpretation of sections 21D to 21G

(1) The references in sections 21D to 21G—
    (a) to a business in the regulated sector, and
    (b) to a supervisory authority,
are to be construed in accordance with Schedule 3A.

(2) In those sections—
"credit institution" has the same meaning as in Schedule 3A;
"financial institution" means an undertaking that carries on a business in the regulated sector by virtue of any of paragraphs (b) to (i) of paragraph 1(1) of that Schedule.

(3) References in those sections to a disclosure by or to a credit institution or a financial institution include disclosure by or to an employee, officer or partner of the institution acting on its behalf.

(4) For the purposes of those sections a country or territory imposes " equivalent money laundering requirements" if it imposes requirements equivalent to those laid down in Directive 2005/60/EC of the European Parliament and of the Council of 26th October 2005 on the prevention of the use of the financial system for the purpose of money laundering and terrorist financing.

(5) In those sections " relevant professional adviser" means an accountant, auditor or tax adviser who is a member of a professional body which is established for accountants, auditors or tax advisers (as the case may be) and which makes provision for—

   (a) testing the competence of those seeking admission to membership of such a body as a condition for such admission; and
   (b) imposing and maintaining professional and ethical standards for its members, as well as imposing sanctions for non-compliance with those standards.]

22 Penalties

A person guilty of an offence under any of sections 15 to 18 shall be liable—

(a) on conviction on indictment, to imprisonment for a term not exceeding 14 years, to a fine or to both, or
(b) on summary conviction, to imprisonment for a term not exceeding six months, to a fine not exceeding the statutory maximum or to both.

[22A Meaning of "employment"

In sections 19 to 21B—

   (a) "employment" means any employment (whether paid or unpaid) and includes—
      (i) work under a contract for services or as an office-holder,
      (ii) work experience provided pursuant to a training course or programme or in the course of training for employment, and
      (iii) voluntary work;
   (b) "employer" has a corresponding meaning.]

23

[Existing s.23 is not repealed but has been substituted and moved under a new heading entitled "Forfeiture".]

Forfeiture

[23 Forfeiture: terrorist property offences

(1) The court by or before which a person is convicted of an offence under any of sections 15 to 18 may make a forfeiture order in accordance with the provisions of this section.
(2) Where a person is convicted of an offence under section 15(1) or (2) or 16, the court may order the forfeiture of any money or other property which, at the time of the offence, the person had in their possession or under their control and which—
   (a) had been used for the purposes of terrorism, or
   (b) they intended should be used, or had reasonable cause to suspect might be used, for those purposes.
(3) Where a person is convicted of an offence under section 15(3) the court may order the forfeiture of any money or other property which, at the time of the offence, the person had in their possession or under their control and which—
   (a) had been used for the purposes of terrorism, or
   (b) which, at that time, they knew or had reasonable cause to suspect would or might be used for those purposes.
(4) Where a person is convicted of an offence under section 17 or 18 the court may order the forfeiture of any money or other property which, at the time of the offence, the person had in their possession or under their control and which—
   (a) had been used for the purposes of terrorism, or
   (b) was, at that time, intended by them to be used for those purposes.
(5) Where a person is convicted of an offence under section 17 the court may order the forfeiture of the money or other property to which the arrangement in question related, and which—
   (a) had been used for the purposes of terrorism, or
   (b) at the time of the offence, the person knew or had reasonable cause to suspect would or might be used for those purposes.

(6) Where a person is convicted of an offence under section 18 the court may order the forfeiture of the money or other property to which the arrangement in question related.

(7) Where a person is convicted of an offence under any of sections 15 to 18, the court may order the forfeiture of any money or other property which wholly or partly, and directly or indirectly, is received by any person as a payment or other reward in connection with the commission of the offence.]

[23A Forfeiture: other terrorism offences and offences with a terrorist connection

(1) The court by or before which a person is convicted of an offence to which this section applies may order the forfeiture of any money or other property in relation to which the following conditions are met—
  (a) that it was, at the time of the offence, in the possession or control of the person convicted; and
  (b) that—
      (i) it had been used for the purposes of terrorism,
      (ii) it was intended by that person that it should be used for the purposes of terrorism, or
      (iii) the court believes that it will be used for the purposes of terrorism unless forfeited.
(2) This section applies to an offence under—
  (a) any of the following provisions of this Act—
      section 54 (weapons training);
      section 57, 58 or 58A (possessing things and collecting information for the purposes of terrorism);
      section 59, 60 or 61 (inciting terrorism outside the United Kingdom);
  (b) any of the following provisions of Part 1 of the Terrorism Act 2006 (c. 11)—
      section 2 (dissemination of terrorist publications);
      section 5 (preparation of terrorist acts);
      section 6 (training for terrorism);
      sections 9 to 11 (offences involving radioactive devices or materials).
(3) This section applies to any ancillary offence (as defined in section 94 of the Counter-Terrorism Act 2008) in relation to an offence listed in subsection (2). (4) This section also applies to an offence specified in Schedule 2 to the Counter-Terrorism Act 2008 (offences where terrorist connection to be considered) as to which—
  (a) in England and Wales, the court dealing with the offence has determined, in accordance with section 30 of that Act, that the offence has a terrorist connection;
  (b) in Scotland, it has been proved, in accordance with section 31 of that Act, that the offence has a terrorist connection.
(5) The Secretary of State may by order amend subsection (2).
(6) An order adding an offence to subsection (2) applies only in relation to offences committed after the order comes into force.]

[23B Forfeiture: supplementary provisions

(1) Before making an order under section 23 or 23A, a court must give an opportunity to be heard to any person, other than the convicted person, who claims to be the owner or otherwise interested in anything which can be forfeited under that section.
(2) In considering whether to make an order under section 23 or 23A in respect of any property, a court shall have regard to—
  (a) the value of the property, and
  (b) the likely financial and other effects on the convicted person of the making of the order (taken together with any other order that the court contemplates making).
(3) A court in Scotland must not make an order under section 23 or 23A except on the application of the prosecutor—
  (a) in proceedings on indictment, when the prosecutor moves for sentence, and
  (b) in summary proceedings, before the court sentences the accused;
  and for the purposes of any appeal or review, an order under either of those sections made by a court in Scotland is a sentence.
(4) Schedule 4 makes further provision in relation to forfeiture orders under section 23 or 23A.]

Seizure of terrorist cash

[*Law on seizure of terrorist cash is now contained in ATCSA 2001 (Appendix 3)*]

Part IV Terrorist Investigations

Interpretation

32 Terrorist investigation

In this Act "terrorist investigation" means an investigation of—

(a) the commission, preparation or instigation of acts of terrorism,
(b) an act which appears to have been done for the purposes of terrorism,
(c) the resources of a proscribed organisation,
(d) the possibility of making an order under section 3(3), or
(e) the commission, preparation or instigation of an offence under this Act [or under Part 1 of the Terrorism Act 2006 other than an offence under section 1 or 2 of that Act].

Information and evidence

37 Powers

Schedule 5 (power to obtain information, &c.) shall have effect.

38 Financial information

Schedule 6 (financial information) shall have effect.

[38A Account monitoring orders

Schedule 6A (account monitoring orders) shall have effect.]

[38B Information about acts of terrorism

(1) This section applies where a person has information which he knows or believes might be of material assistance—
  (a) in preventing the commission by another person of an act of terrorism, or
  (b) in securing the apprehension, prosecution or conviction of another person, in the United Kingdom, for an offence involving the commission, preparation or instigation of an act of terrorism.
(2) The person commits an offence if he does not disclose the information as soon as reasonably practicable in accordance with subsection (3).
(3) Disclosure is in accordance with this subsection if it is made—
  (a) in England and Wales, to a constable,
  (b) in Scotland, to a constable, or
  (c) in Northern Ireland, to a constable or a member of Her Majesty's forces.
(4) It is a defence for a person charged with an offence under subsection (2) to prove that he had a reasonable excuse for not making the disclosure.
(5) A person guilty of an offence under this section shall be liable—
  (a) on conviction on indictment, to imprisonment for a term not exceeding five years, or to a fine or to both, or
  (b) on summary conviction, to imprisonment for a term not exceeding six months, or to a fine not exceeding the statutory maximum or to both.
(6) Proceedings for an offence under this section may be taken, and the offence may for the purposes of those proceedings be treated as having been committed, in any place where the person to be charged is or has at any time been since he first knew or believed that the information might be of material assistance as mentioned in subsection (1).]

39 Disclosure of information, &c

(1) Subsection (2) applies where a person knows or has reasonable cause to suspect that a constable is conducting or proposes to conduct a terrorist investigation.

(2) The person commits an offence if he—
  (a) discloses to another anything which is likely to prejudice the investigation, or
  (b) interferes with material which is likely to be relevant to the investigation.
(3) Subsection (4) applies where a person knows or has reasonable cause to suspect that a disclosure has been or will be made under any of [sections 19 to 21B or 38B].
(4) The person commits an offence if he—
  (a) discloses to another anything which is likely to prejudice an investigation resulting from the disclosure under that section, or
  (b) interferes with material which is likely to be relevant to an investigation resulting from the disclosure under that section.
(5) It is a defence for a person charged with an offence under subsection (2) or (4) to prove—
  (a) that he did not know and had no reasonable cause to suspect that the disclosure or interference was likely to affect a terrorist investigation, or
  (b) that he had a reasonable excuse for the disclosure or interference.
(6) Subsections (2) and (4) do not apply to a disclosure which is made by a professional legal adviser—
  (a) to his client or to his client's representative in connection with the provision of legal advice by the adviser to the client and not with a view to furthering a criminal purpose, or
  (b) to any person for the purpose of actual or contemplated legal proceedings and not with a view to furthering a criminal purpose.
[(6A) Subsections (2) and (4) do not apply if—
  (a) the disclosure is of a matter within section 21D(2) or (3)(a) (terrorist property: tipping off), and
  (b) the information on which the disclosure is based came to the person in the course of a business in the regulated sector.]
(7) A person guilty of an offence under this section shall be liable—
  (a) on conviction on indictment, to imprisonment for a term not exceeding five years, to a fine or to both, or
  (b) on summary conviction, to imprisonment for a term not exceeding six months, to a fine not exceeding the statutory maximum or to both.
(8) For the purposes of this section—
  (a) a reference to conducting a terrorist investigation includes a reference to taking part in the conduct of, or assisting, a terrorist investigation, and
  (b) a person interferes with material if he falsifies it, conceals it, destroys it or disposes of it, or if he causes or permits another to do any of those things.
[(9) The reference in subsection (6A) to a business in the regulated sector is to be construed in accordance with Schedule 3A.]

Part VI Miscellaneous

Terrorist bombing and finance offences

63 Terrorist finance: jurisdiction

(1) If—
  (a) a person does anything outside the United Kingdom, and
  (b) his action would have constituted the commission of an offence under any of sections 15 to 18 if it had been done in the United Kingdom,
  he shall be guilty of the offence.
(2) For the purposes of subsection (1)(b), section 18(1)(b) shall be read as if for " " the jurisdiction" " there were substituted " " a jurisdiction" " .

Part VIII General

114 Police powers

(1) A power conferred by virtue of this Act on a constable—
  (a) is additional to powers which he has at common law or by virtue of any other enactment, and
  (b) shall not be taken to affect those powers.

(2) A constable may if necessary use reasonable force for the purpose of exercising a power conferred on him by virtue of this Act (apart from paragraphs 2 and 3 of Schedule 7).

(3) Where anything is seized by a constable under a power conferred by virtue of this Act, it may (unless the contrary intention appears) be retained for so long as is necessary in all the circumstances.

115 Officers' powers

Schedule 14 (which makes provision about the exercise of functions by authorised officers for the purposes of sections 25 to 31 and examining officers for the purposes of Schedule 7) shall have effect.

117 Consent to prosecution

(1) This section applies to an offence under any provision of this Act other than an offence under—
  (a) section 36,
  (b) section 51,
  (c) paragraph 18 of Schedule 7,
  (d) paragraph 12 of Schedule 12, or
  (e) Schedule 13.

(2) Proceedings for an offence to which this section applies—
  (a) shall not be instituted in England and Wales without the consent of the Director of Public Prosecutions, and
  (b) shall not be instituted in Northern Ireland without the consent of the Director of Public Prosecutions for Northern Ireland.

[(2A) But if it appears to the Director of Public Prosecutions or the Director of Public Prosecutions for Northern Ireland that an offence to which this section applies has been committed [outside the United Kingdom or] for a purpose wholly or partly connected with the affairs of a country other than the United Kingdom, his consent for the purposes of this section may be given only with the permission—
  (a) in the case of the Director of Public Prosecutions, of the Attorney General; and
  (b) in the case of the Director of Public Prosecutions for Northern Ireland, of the Advocate General for Northern Ireland.

(2B) In relation to any time before the coming into force of section 27(1) of the Justice (Northern Ireland) Act 2002, the reference in subsection (2A) to the Advocate General for Northern Ireland is to be read as a reference to the Attorney General for Northern Ireland.]

118 Defences

(1) Subsection (2) applies where in accordance with a provision mentioned in subsection (5) it is a defence for a person charged with an offence to prove a particular matter.

(2) If the person adduces evidence which is sufficient to raise an issue with respect to the matter the court or jury shall assume that the defence is satisfied unless the prosecution proves beyond reasonable doubt that it is not.

(3) Subsection (4) applies where in accordance with a provision mentioned in subsection (5) a court—
  (a) may make an assumption in relation to a person charged with an offence unless a particular matter is proved, or
  (b) may accept a fact as sufficient evidence unless a particular matter is proved.

(4) If evidence is adduced which is sufficient to raise an issue with respect to the matter mentioned in subsection (3)(a) or (b) the court shall treat it as proved unless the prosecution disproves it beyond reasonable doubt.

(5) The provisions in respect of which subsections (2) and (4) apply are—
  (a) [sections 12(4), 39(5)(a), 54, 57, 58, 58A, 77 and 103] of this Act, and
  (b) sections 13, 32 and 33 of the Northern Ireland (Emergency Provisions) Act 1996 (possession and information offences) as they have effect by virtue of Schedule 1 to this Act.

119 Crown servants, regulators, &c

(1) The Secretary of State may make regulations providing for any of [sections 15 to 23A and 39] to apply to persons in the public service of the Crown.

(2) The Secretary of State may make regulations providing for section 19 not to apply to persons who are in his opinion performing or connected with the performance of regulatory, supervisory, investigative or registration functions of a public nature.

(3) Regulations—

    (a) may make different provision for different purposes,

    (b) may make provision which is to apply only in specified circumstances, and

    (c) may make provision which applies only to particular persons or to persons of a particular description.

120 Evidence

(1) A document which purports to be—

    (a) a notice or direction given or order made by the Secretary of State for the purposes of a provision of this Act, and

    (b) signed by him or on his behalf,

shall be received in evidence and shall, until the contrary is proved, be deemed to have been given or made by the Secretary of State.

(2) A document bearing a certificate which—

    (a) purports to be signed by or on behalf of the Secretary of State, and

    (b) states that the document is a true copy of a notice or direction given or order made by the Secretary of State for the purposes of a provision of this Act,

shall be evidence (or, in Scotland, sufficient evidence) of the document in legal proceedings.

(3) In subsections (1) and (2) a reference to an order does not include a reference to an order made by statutory instrument.

(4) The Documentary Evidence Act 1868 shall apply to an authorisation given in writing by the Secretary of State for the purposes of this Act as it applies to an order made by him.

[120A Supplementary powers of forfeiture

(1) A court by or before which a person is convicted of an offence under a provision mentioned in column 1 of the following table may order the forfeiture of any item mentioned in column 2 in relation to that offence.

Offence	Items liable to forfeiture
Section 54 (weapons training)	Anything that the court considers to have been in the possession of the person for purposes connected with the offence.
Section 57 (possession for terrorist purposes)	Any article that is the subject matter of the offence.
Section 58 (collection of information)	Any document or record containing information of the kind mentioned in subsection (1)(a) of that section.
Section 58A (eliciting, publishing or communicating information about members of armed forces etc)	Any document or record containing information of the kind mentioned in subsection (1)(a) of that section.

(2) Before making an order under this section, a court must give an opportunity to be heard to any person, other than the convicted person, who claims to be the owner or otherwise interested in anything which can be forfeited under this section.

(3) An order under this section does not come into force until there is no further possibility of it being varied, or set aside, on appeal (disregarding any power of a court to grant leave to appeal out of time).

(4) Where a court makes an order under this section, it may also make such other provision as appears to it to be necessary for giving effect to the forfeiture, including, in particular, provision relating to the retention, handling, disposal or destruction of what is forfeited.

(5) Provision made by virtue of subsection (4) may be varied at any time by the court that made it.

(6) The power of forfeiture under this section is in addition to any power of forfeiture under section 23A.]

121 Interpretation

In this Act—

"act" and " action" include omission

"article" includes substance and any other thing,

[. . .]

["customs officer" means an officer of Revenue and Customs,]

"dwelling" means a building or part of a building used as a dwelling, and a vehicle which is habitually stationary and which is used as a dwelling,

"explosive" means—

(a) an article or substance manufactured for the purpose of producing a practical effect by explosion,

(b) materials for making an article or substance within paragraph (a),

(c) anything used or intended to be used for causing or assisting in causing an explosion, and

(d) a part of anything within paragraph (a) or (c),

"firearm" includes an air gun or air pistol,

"immigration officer" means a person appointed as an immigration officer under paragraph 1 of Schedule 2 to the Immigration Act 1971,

"the Islands" means the Channel Islands and the Isle of Man,

"organisation" includes any association or combination of persons,

[. . .]

"premises" [, except in section 63D,] includes any place and in particular includes—

(a) a vehicle,

(b) an offshore installation within the meaning given in section 44 of the Petroleum Act 1998, and

(c) a tent or moveable structure,

"property" includes property wherever situated and whether real or personal, heritable or moveable, and things in action and other intangible or incorporeal property, " public place" means a place to which members of the public have or are permitted to have access, whether or not for payment,

"road" has the same meaning as in the Road Traffic Act 1988 (in relation to England and Wales), the Roads (Scotland) Act 1984 (in relation to Scotland) and the Road Traffic Regulation (Northern Ireland) Order 1997 (in relation to Northern Ireland), and includes part of a road, and

"vehicle" , except in sections 48 to 52 and Schedule 7, includes an aircraft, hovercraft, train or vessel.

122 Index of defined expressions

In this Act the expressions listed below are defined by the provisions specified.

Expression	Interpretation provision
Act	Section 121
Action	Section 121
Action taken for the purposes of terrorism	Section 1(5)
Article	Section 121
[. . .]	
[British Transport Police Force	Section 121]
[. . .]	
Cordoned area	Section 33
Customs officer	Section 121
Dwelling	Section 121
Examining officer	Schedule 7, paragraph 1

Expression	Interpretation provision
Explosive	Section 121
Firearm	Section 121
Immigration officer	Section 121
The Islands	Section 121
Organisation	Section 121
[Policed premises	Section 121]
Premises	Section 121
Property	Section 121
Proscribed organisation	Section 3(1)
Public place	Section 121
Road	Section 121
Scheduled offence (in Part VII)	Section 65
Terrorism	Section 1
Terrorist (in Part V)	Section 40
Terrorist investigation	Section 32
Terrorist property	Section 14
Vehicle	Section 121
Vehicle (in sections 48 to 51)	Section 52

Anti-Terrorism, Crime and Security Act 2001 (Extracts)

The extracts from this Act appear as amended by subsequent legislation.

Part 1 Terrorist Property

1 Forfeiture of terrorist cash

(1) Schedule 1 (which makes provision for enabling cash which—
    (a) is intended to be used for the purposes of terrorism,
    (b) consists of resources of an organisation which is a proscribed organisation, or
    (c) is, or represents, property obtained through terrorism,
to be forfeited in civil proceedings before a magistrates' court or (in Scotland) the sheriff) is to have effect.

(2) The powers conferred by Schedule 1 are exercisable in relation to any cash whether or not any proceedings have been brought for an offence in connection with the cash.

(3) Expressions used in this section have the same meaning as in Schedule 1.

(4) Sections 24 to 31 of the Terrorism Act 2000 (c. 11) (seizure of terrorist cash) are to cease to have effect.

(5) An order under section 127 bringing Schedule 1 into force may make any modifications of any code of practice then in operation under Schedule 14 to the Terrorism Act 2000 (exercise of officers' powers) which the Secretary of State thinks necessary or expedient.

Schedule 1 Forfeiture of Terrorist Cash

Part 1 Introductory

1 Terrorist cash

(1) This Schedule applies to cash ("terrorist cash") which—
    (a) is within subsection (1)(a) or (b) of section 1, or
    (b) is property earmarked as terrorist property.

(2) "Cash" means—
    (a) coins and notes in any currency,
    (b) postal orders,
    (c) cheques of any kind, including travellers' cheques,
    (d) bankers' drafts,
    (e) bearer bonds and bearer shares,
found at any place in the United Kingdom.

(3) Cash also includes any kind of monetary instrument which is found at any place in the United Kingdom, if the instrument is specified by the Secretary of State by order.

(4) The power to make an order under sub-paragraph (3) is exercisable by statutory instrument, which is subject to annulment in pursuance of a resolution of either House of Parliament.

Part 2 Seizure and Detention

2 Seizure of cash

(1) An authorised officer may seize any cash if he has reasonable grounds for suspecting that it is terrorist cash.

(2) An authorised officer may also seize cash part of which he has reasonable grounds for suspecting to be terrorist cash if it is not reasonably practicable to seize only that part.

3 Detention of seized cash

(1) While the authorised officer continues to have reasonable grounds for his suspicion, cash seized under this Schedule may be detained initially for a period of 48 hours.

[(1A) In determining the period of 48 hours specified in sub-paragraph (1) there shall be disregarded—

(a) any Saturday or Sunday;

(b) Christmas Day;

(c) Good Friday;

(d) any day that is a bank holiday under the Banking and Financial Dealings Act 1971 in the part of the United Kingdom in which the cash is seized;

(e) any day prescribed under section 8(2) of the Criminal Procedure (Scotland) Act 1995 as a court holiday in the sheriff court district in which the cash is seized.]

(2) The period for which the cash or any part of it may be detained may be extended by an order made by a magistrates' court or (in Scotland) the sheriff; but the order may not authorise the detention of any of the cash—

(a) beyond the end of the period of three months beginning with the date of the order, and

(b) in the case of any further order under this paragraph, beyond the end of the period of two years beginning with the date of the first order.

(3) A justice of the peace may also exercise the power of a magistrates' court to make the first order under sub-paragraph (2) extending the period.

[(3A) An application to a justice of the peace or the sheriff for an order under sub-paragraph (2) making the first extension of the period—

(a) may be made and heard without notice of the application or hearing having been given to any of the persons affected by the application or to the legal representative of such a person, and

(b) may be heard and determined in private in the absence of persons so affected and of their legal representatives.]

(4) An order under sub-paragraph (2) must provide for notice to be given to persons affected by it.

(5) An application for an order under sub-paragraph (2)—

(a) in relation to England and Wales and Northern Ireland, may be made by the Commissioners of Customs and Excise or an authorised officer,

(b) in relation to Scotland, may be made by a procurator fiscal,

and the court, sheriff or justice may make the order if satisfied, in relation to any cash to be further detained, that one of the following conditions is met.

(6) The first condition is that there are reasonable grounds for suspecting that the cash is intended to be used for the purposes of terrorism and that either—

(a) its continued detention is justified while its intended use is further investigated or consideration is given to bringing (in the United Kingdom or elsewhere) proceedings against any person for an offence with which the cash is connected, or

(b) proceedings against any person for an offence with which the cash is connected have been started and have not been concluded.

(7) The second condition is that there are reasonable grounds for suspecting that the cash consists of resources of an organisation which is a proscribed organisation and that either—

(a) its continued detention is justified while investigation is made into whether or not it consists of such resources or consideration is given to bringing (in the United Kingdom or elsewhere) proceedings against any person for an offence with which the cash is connected, or

(b) proceedings against any person for an offence with which the cash is connected have been started and have not been concluded.

(8) The third condition is that there are reasonable grounds for suspecting that the cash is property earmarked as terrorist property and that either—

(a) its continued detention is justified while its derivation is further investigated or consideration is given to bringing (in the United Kingdom or elsewhere) proceedings against any person for an offence with which the cash is connected, or

(b) proceedings against any person for an offence with which the cash is connected have been started and have not been concluded.

4 Payment of detained cash into an account

(1) If cash is detained under this Schedule for more than 48 hours [(determined in accordance with paragraph 3(1A))], it is to be held in an interest-bearing account and the interest accruing on it is to be added to it on its forfeiture or release.

(2) In the case of cash seized under paragraph 2(2), the authorised officer must, on paying it into the account, release so much of the cash then held in the account as is not attributable to terrorist cash.

(3) Sub-paragraph (1) does not apply if the cash is required as evidence of an offence or evidence in proceedings under this Schedule.

5 Release of detained cash

(1) This paragraph applies while any cash is detained under this Schedule.

(2) A magistrates' court or (in Scotland) the sheriff may direct the release of the whole or any part of the cash if satisfied, on an application by the person from whom it was seized, that the conditions in paragraph 3 for the detention of cash are no longer met in relation to the cash to be released.

(3) A authorised officer or (in Scotland) a procurator fiscal may, after notifying the magistrates' court, sheriff or justice under whose order cash is being detained, release the whole or any part of it if satisfied that the detention of the cash to be released is no longer justified.

(4) But cash is not to be released—

   (a) if an application for its forfeiture under paragraph 6, or for its release under paragraph 9, is made, until any proceedings in pursuance of the application (including any proceedings on appeal) are concluded,

   (b) if (in the United Kingdom or elsewhere) proceedings are started against any person for an offence with which the cash is connected, until the proceedings are concluded.

Part 3 Forfeiture

6 Forfeiture

(1) While cash is detained under this Schedule, an application for the forfeiture of the whole or any part of it may be made—

   (a) to a magistrates' court by the Commissioners of Customs and Excise or an authorised officer,

   (b) (in Scotland) to the sheriff by the Scottish Ministers.

(2) The court or sheriff may order the forfeiture of the cash or any part of it if satisfied that the cash or part is terrorist cash.

(3) In the case of property earmarked as terrorist property which belongs to joint tenants one of whom is an excepted joint owner, the order may not apply to so much of it as the court or sheriff thinks is attributable to the excepted joint owner's share.

(4) An excepted joint owner is a joint tenant who obtained the property in circumstances in which it would not (as against him) be earmarked; and references to his share of the earmarked property are to so much of the property as would have been his if the joint tenancy had been severed.

[7 Appeal against decision in forfeiture proceedings]

(1) A party to proceedings for an order under paragraph 6 ("a forfeiture order") who is aggrieved by a forfeiture order made in the proceedings or by the decision of the court or sheriff not to make a forfeiture order may appeal—

   (a) in England and Wales, to the Crown Court;

   (b) in Scotland, to the sheriff principal;

   (c) in Northern Ireland, to a county court.

(2) The appeal must be brought before the end of the period of 30 days beginning with the date on which the order is made or, as the case may be, the decision is given.

This is subject to paragraph 7A (extended time for appealing in certain cases of deproscription).

(3) The court or sheriff principal hearing the appeal may make any order that appears to the court or sheriff principal to be appropriate.

(4) If an appeal against a forfeiture order is upheld, the court or sheriff principal may order the release of the cash.]

[7A Extended time for appealing in certain cases where deproscription order made

(1) This paragraph applies where—

   (a) a successful application for a forfeiture order relies (wholly or partly) on the fact that an organisation is proscribed,

   (b) an application under section 4 of the Terrorism Act 2000 for a deproscription order in respect of the organisation is refused by the Secretary of State,

   (c) the forfeited cash is seized under this Schedule on or after the date of the refusal of that application,

   (d) an appeal against that refusal is allowed under section 5 of that Act,

   (e) a deproscription order is made accordingly, and

   (f) if the order is made in reliance on section 123(5) of that Act, a resolution is passed by each House of Parliament under section 123(5)(b).

(2) Where this paragraph applies, an appeal under paragraph 7 above against the forfeiture order may be brought at any time before the end of the period of 30 days beginning with the date on which the deproscription order comes into force.

(3) In this paragraph a "deproscription order" means an order under section 3(3)(b) or (8) of the Terrorism Act 2000.]

8 Application of forfeited cash

(1) Cash forfeited under this Schedule, and any accrued interest on it—

   (a) if forfeited by a magistrates' court in England and Wales or Northern Ireland, is to be paid into the Consolidated Fund,

   (b) if forfeited by the sheriff, is to be paid into the Scottish Consolidated Fund.

(2) But it is not to be paid in—

   (a) before the end of the period within which an appeal under paragraph 7 may be made, or

   (b) if a person appeals under that paragraph, before the appeal is determined or otherwise disposed of.

Part 4 Miscellaneous

9 Victims

(1) A person who claims that any cash detained under this Schedule, or any part of it, belongs to him may apply to a magistrates' court or (in Scotland) the sheriff for the cash or part to be released to him.

(2) The application may be made in the course of proceedings under paragraph 3 or 6 or at any other time.

(3) If it appears to the court or sheriff concerned that—

   (a) the applicant was deprived of the cash claimed, or of property which it represents, by criminal conduct,

   (b) the property he was deprived of was not, immediately before he was deprived of it, property obtained by or in return for criminal conduct and nor did it then represent such property, and

   (c) the cash claimed belongs to him,

   the court or sheriff may order the cash to be released to the applicant.

10 Compensation

(1) If no forfeiture order is made in respect of any cash detained under this Schedule, the person to whom the cash belongs or from whom it was seized may make an application to the magistrates' court or (in Scotland) the sheriff for compensation.

(2) If, for any period after the initial detention of the cash for 48 hours [(determined in accordance with paragraph 3(1A))], the cash was not held in an interest-bearing account while detained, the court or sheriff may order an amount of compensation to be paid to the applicant.

(3) The amount of compensation to be paid under sub-paragraph (2) is the amount the court or sheriff thinks would have been earned in interest in the period in question if the cash had been held in an interest-bearing account.

(4) If the court or sheriff is satisfied that, taking account of any interest to be paid under this Schedule or any amount to be paid under sub-paragraph (2), the applicant has suffered loss as a result of the

detention of the cash and that the circumstances are exceptional, the court or sheriff may order compensation (or additional compensation) to be paid to him.

(5) The amount of compensation to be paid under sub-paragraph (4) is the amount the court or sheriff thinks reasonable, having regard to the loss suffered and any other relevant circumstances.

(6) If the cash was seized by a customs officer, the compensation is to be paid by the Commissioners of Customs and Excise.

(7) If the cash was seized by a constable, the compensation is to be paid as follows—

(a) in the case of a constable of a police force in England and Wales, it is to be paid out of the police fund from which the expenses of the police force are met,

(b) in the case of a constable of a police force in Scotland, it is to be paid by the police authority or joint police board for the police area for which that force is maintained,

(c) in the case of a police officer within the meaning of the Police (Northern Ireland) Act 2000 (c. 32), it is to be paid out of money provided by the Chief Constable.

(8) If the cash was seized by an immigration officer, the compensation is to be paid by the Secretary of State.

(9) If a forfeiture order is made in respect only of a part of any cash detained under this Schedule, this paragraph has effect in relation to the other part. (10) This paragraph does not apply if the court or sheriff makes an order under paragraph 9.

11 Property obtained through terrorism

(1) A person obtains property through terrorism if he obtains property by or in return for acts of terrorism, or acts carried out for the purposes of terrorism.

(2) In deciding whether any property was obtained through terrorism—

(a) it is immaterial whether or not any money, goods or services were provided in order to put the person in question in a position to carry out the acts,

(b) it is not necessary to show that the act was of a particular kind if it is shown that the property was obtained through acts of one of a number of kinds, each of which would have been an act of terrorism, or an act carried out for the purposes of terrorism.

Part 5 Property Earmarked as Terrorist Property

12 Property earmarked as terrorist property

(1) Property obtained through terrorism is earmarked as terrorist property.

(2) But if property obtained through terrorism has been disposed of (since it was so obtained), it is earmarked as terrorist property only if it is held by a person into whose hands it may be followed.

(3) Earmarked property obtained through terrorism may be followed into the hands of a person obtaining it on a disposal by—

(a) the person who obtained the property through terrorism, or

(b) a person into whose hands it may (by virtue of this sub-paragraph) be followed.

13 Tracing property

(1) Where property obtained through terrorism ("the original property") is or has been earmarked as terrorist property, property which represents the original property is also earmarked.

(2) If a person enters into a transaction by which—

(a) he disposes of earmarked property, whether the original property or property which (by virtue of this Part) represents the original property, and

(b) he obtains other property in place of it,

the other property represents the original property.

(3) If a person disposes of earmarked property which represents the original property, the property may be followed into the hands of the person who obtains it (and it continues to represent the original property).

14 Mixing property

(1) Sub-paragraph (2) applies if a person's property which is earmarked as terrorist property is mixed with other property (whether his property or another's).

(2) The portion of the mixed property which is attributable to the property earmarked as terrorist property represents the property obtained through terrorism.

(3) Property earmarked as terrorist property is mixed with other property if (for example) it is used—

(a) to increase funds held in a bank account,

(b) in part payment for the acquisition of an asset,

(c) for the restoration or improvement of land,

(d) by a person holding a leasehold interest in the property to acquire the freehold.

15 Accruing profits

(1) This paragraph applies where a person who has property earmarked as terrorist property obtains further property consisting of profits accruing in respect of the earmarked property.

(2) The further property is to be treated as representing the property obtained through terrorism.

16 General exceptions

(1) If—

(a) a person disposes of property earmarked as terrorist property, and

(b) the person who obtains it on the disposal does so in good faith, for value and without notice that it was earmarked,

the property may not be followed into that person's hands and, accordingly, it ceases to be earmarked.

(2) If—

(a) in pursuance of a judgment in civil proceedings (whether in the United Kingdom or elsewhere), the defendant makes a payment to the claimant or the claimant otherwise obtains property from the defendant,

(b) the claimant's claim is based on the defendant's criminal conduct, and

(c) apart from this sub-paragraph, the sum received, or the property obtained, by the claimant would be earmarked as terrorist property,

the property ceases to be earmarked.

In relation to Scotland, "claimant" and "defendant" are to be read as "pursuer" and "defender"; and, in relation to Northern Ireland, "claimant" is to be read as "plaintiff".

(3) If—

(a) a payment is made to a person in pursuance of a compensation order under Article 14 of the Criminal Justice (Northern Ireland) Order 1994 (S.I. 1994/2795 (N.I. 15)), section 249 of the Criminal Procedure (Scotland) Act 1995 (c. 46) or section 130 of the Powers of Criminal Courts (Sentencing) Act 2000 (c. 6), [or in pursuance of a service compensation order under the Armed Forces Act 2006,] and

(b) apart from this sub-paragraph, the sum received would be earmarked as terrorist property,

the property ceases to be earmarked.

(4) If—

(a) a payment is made to a person in pursuance of a restitution order under section 27 of the Theft Act (Northern Ireland) 1969 (c.16 (NI)) or section 148(2) of the Powers of Criminal Courts (Sentencing) Act 2000 or a person otherwise obtains any property in pursuance of such an order, and

(b) apart from this sub-paragraph, the sum received, or the property obtained, would be earmarked as terrorist property,

the property ceases to be earmarked.

(5) If—

(a) in pursuance of an order made by the court under section 382(3) or 383(5) of the Financial Services and Markets Act 2000 (c. 8) (restitution orders), an amount is paid to or distributed among any persons in accordance with the court's directions, and

(b) apart from this sub-paragraph, the sum received by them would be earmarked as terrorist property,

the property ceases to be earmarked.

(6) If—

    (a) in pursuance of a requirement of the Financial Services Authority under section 384(5) of the Financial Services and Markets Act 2000 (c. 8) (power of authority to require restitution), an amount is paid to or distributed among any persons, and

    (b) apart from this sub-paragraph, the sum received by them would be earmarked as terrorist property,

the property ceases to be earmarked.

(7) Where—

    (a) a person enters into a transaction to which paragraph 13(2) applies, and

    (b) the disposal is one to which sub-paragraph (1) applies,

this paragraph does not affect the question whether (by virtue of paragraph 13(2)) any property obtained on the transaction in place of the property disposed of is earmarked.

Part 6 Interpretation

17 Property

(1) Property is all property wherever situated and includes—

    (a) money,

    (b) all forms of property, real or personal, heritable or moveable,

    (c) things in action and other intangible or incorporeal property.

(2) Any reference to a person's property (whether expressed as a reference to the property he holds or otherwise) is to be read as follows.

(3) In relation to land, it is a reference to any interest which he holds in the land.

(4) In relation to property other than land, it is a reference—

    (a) to the property (if it belongs to him), or

    (b) to any other interest which he holds in the property.

18 Obtaining and disposing of property

(1) References to a person disposing of his property include a reference—

    (a) to his disposing of a part of it, or

    (b) to his granting an interest in it,

(or to both); and references to the property disposed of are to any property obtained on the disposal.

(2) If a person grants an interest in property of his which is earmarked as terrorist property, the question whether the interest is also earmarked is to be determined in the same manner as it is on any other disposal of earmarked property.

(3) A person who makes a payment to another is to be treated as making a disposal of his property to the other, whatever form the payment takes.

(4) Where a person's property passes to another under a will or intestacy or by operation of law, it is to be treated as disposed of by him to the other.

(5) A person is only to be treated as having obtained his property for value in a case where he gave unexecuted consideration if the consideration has become executed consideration.

19 General interpretation

(1) In this Schedule—

"authorised officer" means a constable, a customs officer or an immigration officer,

"cash" has the meaning given by paragraph 1,

"constable", in relation to Northern Ireland, means a police officer within the meaning of the Police (Northern Ireland) Act 2000 (c. 32),

"criminal conduct" means conduct which constitutes an offence in any part of the United Kingdom, or would constitute an offence in any part of the United Kingdom if it occurred there,

"customs officer" means an officer commissioned by the Commissioners of Customs and Excise under section 6(3) of the Customs and Excise Management Act 1979 (c. 2),

"forfeiture order" has the meaning given by paragraph 7,

"immigration officer" means a person appointed as an immigration officer under paragraph 1 of Schedule 2 to the Immigration Act 1971 (c. 77), "interest" , in relation to land—

(a) in the case of land in England and Wales or Northern Ireland, means any legal estate and any equitable interest or power,

(b) in the case of land in Scotland, means any estate, interest, servitude or other heritable right in or over land, including a heritable security,

"interest" , in relation to property other than land, includes any right (including a right to possession of the property),

"part", in relation to property, includes a portion,

"property obtained through terrorism" has the meaning given by paragraph 11,

"property earmarked as terrorist property" is to be read in accordance with Part 5,

"proscribed organisation" has the same meaning as in the Terrorism Act 2000 (c. 11),

"terrorism" has the same meaning as in the Terrorism Act 2000,

"terrorist cash" has the meaning given by paragraph 1,

"value" means market value.

(2) Paragraphs 17 and 18 and the following provisions apply for the purposes of this Schedule. (3) For the purpose of deciding whether or not property was earmarked as terrorist property at any time (including times before commencement), it is to be assumed that this Schedule was in force at that and any other relevant time.

(4) References to anything done or intended to be done for the purposes of terrorism include anything done or intended to be done for the benefit of a proscribed organisation.

(5) An organisation's resources include any cash which is applied or made available, or is to be applied or made available, for use by the organisation.

(6) Proceedings against any person for an offence are concluded when—

(a) the person is convicted or acquitted,

(b) the prosecution is discontinued or, in Scotland, the trial diet is deserted simpliciter, or

(c) the jury is discharged without a finding [otherwise than in circumstances where the proceedings are continued without a jury].[. . .]

Money Laundering Regulations 2007
SI 2007/2157

**This Statutory Instrument appears as amended by
subsequent legislation.**

The Treasury are a government department designated for the purposes of section 2(2) of
the European Communities Act 1972 in relation to measures relating to preventing the use
of the financial system for the purpose of money laundering;

The Treasury, in exercise of the powers conferred on them by section 2(2) of the European
Communities Act 1972 and by sections 168(4)(b), 402(1)(b), 417(1) and 428(3) of the
Financial Services and Markets Act 2000, make the following Regulations:

Part 1 General

1 Citation, commencement etc.

(1) These Regulations may be cited as the Money Laundering Regulations 2007 and come into force
on 15th December 2007.
(2) These Regulations are prescribed for the purposes of sections 168(4)(b) (appointment of persons to
carry out investigations in particular cases) and 402(1)(b) (power of the Authority to institute
proceedings for certain other offences) of the 2000 Act.
(3) The Money Laundering Regulations 2003 are revoked.

2 Interpretation

(1) In these Regulations—
"the 2000 Act" means the Financial Services and Markets Act 2000;
"Annex I financial institution" has the meaning given by regulation 22(1);
"auditor" , except in regulation 17(2)(c) and (d), has the meaning given by regulation 3(4) and (5);
"authorised person" means a person who is authorised for the purposes of the 2000 Act;
"the Authority" means the Financial Services Authority;
"the banking consolidation directive" means Directive 2006/48/EC of the European Parliament
and of the Council of 14th June 2006 relating to the taking up and pursuit of the business of credit
institutions;
"beneficial owner" has the meaning given by regulation 6;
["bill payment service provider" means an undertaking which provides a payment service enabling
the payment of utility and other household bills;]
"business relationship" means a business, professional or commercial relationship between a relevant person and a customer, which is expected by the relevant person, at the time when contact is
established, to have an element of duration;
"cash" means notes, coins or travellers' cheques in any currency;
"casino" has the meaning given by regulation 3(13);
"the Commissioners" means the Commissioners for Her Majesty's Revenue and Customs;
"consumer credit financial institution" has the meaning given by regulation 22(1);
"credit institution" has the meaning given by regulation 3(2);
"customer due diligence measures" has the meaning given by regulation 5;

"DETI" means the Department of Enterprise, Trade and Investment in Northern Ireland;

"the electronic money directive" means Directive 2000/46/EC of the European Parliament and of the Council of 18th September 2000 on the taking up, pursuit and prudential supervision of the business of electronic money institutions;

"estate agent" has the meaning given by regulation 3(11);

"external accountant" has the meaning given by regulation 3(7);

"financial institution" has the meaning given by regulation 3(3);

"firm" means any entity, whether or not a legal person, that is not an individual and includes a body corporate and a partnership or other unincorporated association; " high value dealer" has the meaning given by regulation 3(12);

"the implementing measures directive" means Commission Directive 2006/70/EC of 1st August 2006 laying down implementing measures for the money laundering directive;

"independent legal professional" has the meaning given by regulation 3(9);

"insolvency practitioner" , except in regulation 17(2)(c) and (d), has the meaning given by regulation 3(6);

"the life assurance consolidation directive" means Directive 2002/83/EC of the European Parliament and of the Council of 5th November 2002 concerning life assurance;

"local weights and measures authority" has the meaning given by section 69 of the Weights and Measures Act 1985 (local weights and measures authorities);

"the markets in financial instruments directive" means Directive 2004/39/EC of the European Parliament and of the Council of 12th April 2004 on markets in financial instruments;

"money laundering" means an act which falls within section 340(11) of the Proceeds of Crime Act 2002;

"the money laundering directive" means Directive 2005/60/EC of the European Parliament and of the Council of 26th October 2005 on the prevention of the use of the financial system for the purpose of money laundering and terrorist financing;

"money service business" means an undertaking which by way of business operates a currency exchange office, transmits money (or any representations of monetary value) by any means or cashes cheques which are made payable to customers;

"nominated officer" means a person who is nominated to receive disclosures under Part 7 of the Proceeds of Crime Act 2002 (money laundering) or Part 3 of the Terrorism Act 2000 (terrorist property);

"non-EEA state" means a state that is not an EEA state;

"notice" means a notice in writing;

"occasional transaction" means a transaction (carried out other than as part of a business relationship) amounting to 15,000 euro or more, whether the transaction is carried out in a single operation or several operations which appear to be linked;

"the OFT" means the Office of Fair Trading;

"ongoing monitoring" has the meaning given by regulation 8(2);

["payment services" has the meaning given by regulation 2(1) of the Payment Services Regulations 2009;]

"regulated market" —

(a) within the EEA, has the meaning given by point 14 of Article 4(1) of the markets in financial instruments directive; and

(b) outside the EEA, means a regulated financial market which subjects companies whose securities are admitted to trading to disclosure obligations which are contained in international standards and are equivalent to the specified disclosure obligations;

"relevant person" means a person to whom, in accordance with regulations 3 and 4, these Regulations apply;

"the specified disclosure obligations" means disclosure requirements consistent with—

(a) Article 6(1) to (4) of Directive 2003/6/EC of the European Parliament and of the Council of 28th January 2003 on insider dealing and market manipulation;

(b) Articles 3, 5, 7, 8, 10, 14 and 16 of Directive 2003/71/EC of the European Parliament and of the Council of 4th November 2003 on the prospectuses to be published when securities are offered to the public or admitted to trading;

(c) Articles 4 to 6, 14, 16 to 19 and 30 of Directive 2004/109/EC of the European Parliament and of the Council of 15th December 2004 relating to the harmonisation of transparency requirements in relation to information about issuers whose securities are admitted to trading on a regulated market; or

(d) Community legislation made under the provisions mentioned in sub-paragraphs (a) to (c); "supervisory authority" in relation to any relevant person means the supervisory authority specified for such a person by regulation 23;

"tax adviser" (except in regulation 11(3)) has the meaning given by regulation 3(8);

["telecommunication, digital and IT payment service provider" means an undertaking which provides payment services falling within paragraph 1(g) of Schedule 1 to the Payment Services Regulations 2009;]

" terrorist financing" means an offence under—

(a) section 15 (fund-raising), 16 (use and possession), 17 (funding arrangements), 18 (money laundering) or 63 (terrorist finance: jurisdiction) of the Terrorism Act 2000;

(b) paragraph 7(2) or (3) of Schedule 3 to the Anti-Terrorism, Crime and Security Act 2001 (freezing orders);

(c) article 7, 8 or 10 of the Terrorism (United Nations Measures) Order 2006 ; [. . .]

(d) article 7, 8 or 10 of the Al-Qaida and Taliban (United Nations Measures) Order 2006;[or]

[(e) article 10, 11, 12, 13, 14 or 16 of the Terrorism (United Nations Measures) Order 2009;]

"trust or company service provider" has the meaning given by regulation 3(10).

(2) In these Regulations, references to amounts in euro include references to equivalent amounts in another currency.

(3) Unless otherwise defined, expressions used in these Regulations and the money laundering directive have the same meaning as in the money laundering directive and expressions used in these Regulations and in the implementing measures directive have the same meaning as in the implementing measures directive.

3 Application of the Regulations

(1) Subject to regulation 4, these Regulations apply to the following persons acting in the course of business carried on by them in the United Kingdom ("relevant persons")—

(a) credit institutions;

(b) financial institutions;

(c) auditors, insolvency practitioners, external accountants and tax advisers;

(d) independent legal professionals;

(e) trust or company service providers;

(f) estate agents;

(g) high value dealers;

(h) casinos.

(2) "Credit institution" means—

(a) a credit institution as defined in Article 4(1)(a) of the banking consolidation directive; or

(b) a branch (within the meaning of Article 4(3) of that directive) located in an EEA state of an institution falling within sub-paragraph (a) (or an equivalent institution whose head office is located in a non-EEA state) wherever its head office is located,

when it accepts deposits or other repayable funds from the public or grants credits for its own account (within the meaning of the banking consolidation directive).

(3) "Financial institution" means—

(a) an undertaking, including a money service business, when it carries out one or more of the activities listed in points 2 to 12 and 14 of Annex 1 to the banking consolidation directive (the relevant text of which is set out in Schedule 1 to these Regulations), other than—

(i) a credit institution;

(ii) an undertaking whose only listed activity is trading for own account in one or more of the products listed in point 7 of Annex 1 to the banking consolidation directive where the undertaking does not have a customer, and, for this purpose, "customer" means a third party which is not a member of the same group as the undertaking;

(b) an insurance company duly authorised in accordance with the life assurance consolidation directive, when it carries out activities covered by that directive;

(c) a person whose regular occupation or business is the provision to other persons of an investment service or the performance of an investment activity on a professional basis, when providing or performing investment services or activities (within the meaning of the markets in financial instruments directive), other than a person falling within Article 2 of that directive;

(d) a collective investment undertaking, when marketing or otherwise offering its units or shares;

(e) an insurance intermediary as defined in Article 2(5) of Directive 2002/92/EC of the European Parliament and of the Council of 9th December 2002 on insurance mediation, with the exception of a tied insurance intermediary as mentioned in Article 2(7) of that Directive, when it acts in respect of contracts of long-term insurance within the meaning given by article 3(1) of, and Part II of Schedule 1 to, the Financial Services and Markets Act 2000 (Regulated Activities) Order 2001;

(f) a branch located in an EEA state of a person referred to in sub-paragraphs (a) to (e) (or an equivalent person whose head office is located in a non-EEA state), wherever its head office is located, when carrying out any activity mentioned in sub-paragraphs (a) to (e);

(g) the National Savings Bank;

(h) the Director of Savings, when money is raised under the auspices of the Director under the National Loans Act 1968.

(4) "Auditor" means any firm or individual who is a statutory auditor within the meaning of Part 42 of the Companies Act 2006 (statutory auditors), when carrying out statutory audit work within the meaning of section 1210 of that Act.

(5) Before the entry into force of Part 42 of the Companies Act 2006 the reference in paragraph (4) to—

(a) a person who is a statutory auditor shall be treated as a reference to a person who is eligible for appointment as a company auditor under section 25 of the Companies Act 1989 (eligibility for appointment) or article 28 of the Companies (Northern Ireland) Order 1990; and

(b) the carrying out of statutory audit work shall be treated as a reference to the provision of audit services.

(6) "Insolvency practitioner" means any person who acts as an insolvency practitioner within the meaning of section 388 of the Insolvency Act 1986 (meaning of "act as insolvency practitioner") or article 3 of the Insolvency (Northern Ireland) Order 1989.

(7) "External accountant" means a firm or sole practitioner who by way of business provides accountancy services to other persons, when providing such services.

(8) "Tax adviser" means a firm or sole practitioner who by way of business provides advice about the tax affairs of other persons, when providing such services.

(9) "Independent legal professional" means a firm or sole practitioner who by way of business provides legal or notarial services to other persons, when participating in financial or real property transactions concerning—

(a) the buying and selling of real property or business entities;

(b) the managing of client money, securities or other assets;

(c) the opening or management of bank, savings or securities accounts;

(d) the organisation of contributions necessary for the creation, operation or management of companies; or

(e) the creation, operation or management of trusts, companies or similar structures,

and, for this purpose, a person participates in a transaction by assisting in the planning or execution of the transaction or otherwise acting for or on behalf of a client in the transaction.

(10) "Trust or company service provider" means a firm or sole practitioner who by way of business provides any of the following services to other persons—

(a) forming companies or other legal persons;

(b) acting, or arranging for another person to act—

(i) as a director or secretary of a company;

(ii) as a partner of a partnership; or

(iii) in a similar position in relation to other legal persons;

(c) providing a registered office, business address, correspondence or administrative address or other related services for a company, partnership or any other legal person or arrangement;

(d) acting, or arranging for another person to act, as—

(i) a trustee of an express trust or similar legal arrangement; or

(ii) a nominee shareholder for a person other than a company whose securities are listed on a regulated market,

when providing such services.

(11) "Estate agent" means—

(a) a firm; or

(b) sole practitioner,

who, or whose employees, carry out estate agency work (within the meaning given by section 1 of the Estate Agents Act 1979 (estate agency work)), when in the course of carrying out such work.

(12) "High value dealer" means a firm or sole trader who by way of business trades in goods (including an auctioneer dealing in goods), when he receives, in respect of any transaction, a payment or payments in cash of at least 15,000 euros in total, whether the transaction is executed in a single operation or in several operations which appear to be linked.

(13) "Casino" means the holder of a casino operating licence and, for this purpose, a " casino operating licence" has the meaning given by section 65(2) of the Gambling Act 2005 (nature of licence).

(14) In the application of this regulation to Scotland, for " "real property" " in paragraph (9) substitute " "heritable property" " .

4 Exclusions

(1) These Regulations do not apply to the following persons when carrying out any of the following activities—

(a) a society registered under the Industrial and Provident Societies Act 1965, when it—

(i) issues withdrawable share capital within the limit set by section 6 of that Act (maximum shareholding in society); or

(ii) accepts deposits from the public within the limit set by section 7(3) of that Act (carrying on of banking by societies);

(b) a society registered under the Industrial and Provident Societies Act (Northern Ireland) 1969, when it—

(i) issues withdrawable share capital within the limit set by section 6 of that Act (maximum shareholding in society); or

(ii) accepts deposits from the public within the limit set by section 7(3) of that Act (carrying on of banking by societies);

(c) a person who is (or falls within a class of persons) specified in any of paragraphs 2 to 23, 25 to 38 or 40 to 49 of the Schedule to the Financial Services and Markets Act 2000 (Exemption) Order 2001, when carrying out any activity in respect of which he is exempt;

(d) a person who was an exempted person for the purposes of section 45 of the Financial Services Act 1986 (miscellaneous exemptions) immediately before its repeal, when exercising the functions specified in that section;

(e) a person whose main activity is that of a high value dealer, when he engages in financial activity on an occasional or very limited basis as set out in paragraph 1 of Schedule 2 to these Regulations; or

(f) a person, when he prepares a home information pack or a document or information for inclusion in a home information pack.

(2) These Regulations do not apply to a person who falls within regulation 3 solely as a result of his engaging in financial activity on an occasional or very limited basis as set out in paragraph 1 of Schedule 2 to these Regulations.

(3) Parts 2 to 5 of these Regulations do not apply to—

(a) the Auditor General for Scotland;

(b) the Auditor General for Wales;

(c) the Bank of England;

(d) the Comptroller and Auditor General;

(e) the Comptroller and Auditor General for Northern Ireland;

(f) the Official Solicitor to the Supreme Court, when acting as trustee in his official capacity;

(g) the Treasury Solicitor.

(4) In paragraph (1)(f), "home information pack" has the same meaning as in Part 5 of the Housing Act 2004 (home information packs).

Part 2 Customer Due Diligence

5 Meaning of customer due diligence measures

"Customer due diligence measures" means—

(a) identifying the customer and verifying the customer's identity on the basis of documents, data or information obtained from a reliable and independent source;

(b) identifying, where there is a beneficial owner who is not the customer, the beneficial owner and taking adequate measures, on a risk-sensitive basis, to verify his identity so that the relevant person is satisfied that he knows who the beneficial owner is, including, in the case of a legal person, trust or similar legal arrangement, measures to understand the ownership and control structure of the person, trust or arrangement; and

(c) obtaining information on the purpose and intended nature of the business relationship.

6 Meaning of beneficial owner

(1) In the case of a body corporate, "beneficial owner" means any individual who—

(a) as respects any body other than a company whose securities are listed on a regulated market, ultimately owns or controls (whether through direct or indirect ownership or control, including through bearer share holdings) more than 25% of the shares or voting rights in the body; or

(b) as respects any body corporate, otherwise exercises control over the management of the body.

(2) In the case of a partnership (other than a limited liability partnership), "beneficial owner" means any individual who—

(a) ultimately is entitled to or controls (whether the entitlement or control is direct or indirect) more than a 25% share of the capital or profits of the partnership or more than 25% of the voting rights in the partnership; or

(b) otherwise exercises control over the management of the partnership.

(3) In the case of a trust, "beneficial owner" means—

(a) any individual who is entitled to a specified interest in at least 25% of the capital of the trust property;

(b) as respects any trust other than one which is set up or operates entirely for the benefit of individuals falling within sub-paragraph (a), the class of persons in whose main interest the trust is set up or operates;

(c) any individual who has control over the trust.

(4) In paragraph (3)—

"specified interest" means a vested interest which is—

(a) in possession or in remainder or reversion (or, in Scotland, in fee); and

(b) defeasible or indefeasible;

"control" means a power (whether exercisable alone, jointly with another person or with the consent of another person) under the trust instrument or by law to—

(a) dispose of, advance, lend, invest, pay or apply trust property;

(b) vary the trust;

(c) add or remove a person as a beneficiary or to or from a class of beneficiaries;

(d) appoint or remove trustees;

(e) direct, withhold consent to or veto the exercise of a power such as is mentioned in sub-paragraph (a), (b), (c) or (d).

(5) For the purposes of paragraph (3)—

(a) where an individual is the beneficial owner of a body corporate which is entitled to a specified interest in the capital of the trust property or which has control over the trust, the individual is to be regarded as entitled to the interest or having control over the trust; and

(b) an individual does not have control solely as a result of—

(i) his consent being required in accordance with section 32(1)(c) of the Trustee Act 1925 (power of advancement);

(ii) any discretion delegated to him under section 34 of the Pensions Act 1995 (power of investment and delegation);

(iii) the power to give a direction conferred on him by section 19(2) of the Trusts of Land and Appointment of Trustees Act 1996 (appointment and retirement of trustee at instance of beneficiaries); or

    (iv) the power exercisable collectively at common law to vary or extinguish a trust where the beneficiaries under the trust are of full age and capacity and (taken together) absolutely entitled to the property subject to the trust (or, in Scotland, have a full and unqualified right to the fee).

(6) In the case of a legal entity or legal arrangement which does not fall within paragraph (1), (2) or (3), "beneficial owner" means—

    (a) where the individuals who benefit from the entity or arrangement have been determined, any individual who benefits from at least 25% of the property of the entity or arrangement;

    (b) where the individuals who benefit from the entity or arrangement have yet to be determined, the class of persons in whose main interest the entity or arrangement is set up or operates;

    (c) any individual who exercises control over at least 25% of the property of the entity or arrangement.

(7) For the purposes of paragraph (6), where an individual is the beneficial owner of a body corporate which benefits from or exercises control over the property of the entity or arrangement, the individual is to be regarded as benefiting from or exercising control over the property of the entity or arrangement.

(8) In the case of an estate of a deceased person in the course of administration, "beneficial owner" means—

    (a) in England and Wales and Northern Ireland, the executor, original or by representation, or administrator for the time being of a deceased person;

    (b) in Scotland, the executor for the purposes of the Executors (Scotland) Act 1900.

(9) In any other case, "beneficial owner" means the individual who ultimately owns or controls the customer or on whose behalf a transaction is being conducted.

(10) In this regulation—

"arrangement" , "entity" and "trust" means an arrangement, entity or trust which administers and distributes funds;

"limited liability partnership" has the meaning given by the Limited Liability Partnerships Act 2000.

7 Application of customer due diligence measures

(1) Subject to regulations 9, 10, 12, 13, 14, 16(4) and 17, a relevant person must apply customer due diligence measures when he—

    (a) establishes a business relationship;

    (b) carries out an occasional transaction;

    (c) suspects money laundering or terrorist financing;

    (d) doubts the veracity or adequacy of documents, data or information previously obtained for the purposes of identification or verification.

(2) Subject to regulation 16(4), a relevant person must also apply customer due diligence measures at other appropriate times to existing customers on a risk-sensitive basis.

(3) A relevant person must—

    (a) determine the extent of customer due diligence measures on a risk-sensitive basis depending on the type of customer, business relationship, product or transaction; and

    (b) be able to demonstrate to his supervisory authority that the extent of the measures is appropriate in view of the risks of money laundering and terrorist financing.

(4) Where—

    (a) a relevant person is required to apply customer due diligence measures in the case of a trust, legal entity (other than a body corporate) or a legal arrangement (other than a trust); and

    (b) the class of persons in whose main interest the trust, entity or arrangement is set up or operates is identified as a beneficial owner,

the relevant person is not required to identify all the members of the class.

(5) Paragraph (3)(b) does not apply to the National Savings Bank or the Director of Savings.

8 Ongoing monitoring

(1) A relevant person must conduct ongoing monitoring of a business relationship.

(2) "Ongoing monitoring" of a business relationship means—

    (a) scrutiny of transactions undertaken throughout the course of the relationship (including, where necessary, the source of funds) to ensure that the transactions are consistent with the relevant person's knowledge of the customer, his business and risk profile; and

    (b) keeping the documents, data or information obtained for the purpose of applying customer due diligence measures up-to-date.

(3) Regulation 7(3) applies to the duty to conduct ongoing monitoring under paragraph (1) as it applies to customer due diligence measures.

9 Timing of verification

(1) This regulation applies in respect of the duty under regulation 7(1)(a) and (b) to apply the customer due diligence measures referred to in regulation 5(a) and (b).

(2) Subject to paragraphs (3) to (5) and regulation 10, a relevant person must verify the identity of the customer (and any beneficial owner) before the establishment of a business relationship or the carrying out of an occasional transaction.

(3) Such verification may be completed during the establishment of a business relationship if—

    (a) this is necessary not to interrupt the normal conduct of business; and

    (b) there is little risk of money laundering or terrorist financing occurring,

provided that the verification is completed as soon as practicable after contact is first established.

(4) The verification of the identity of the beneficiary under a life insurance policy may take place after the business relationship has been established provided that it takes place at or before the time of payout or at or before the time the beneficiary exercises a right vested under the policy.

(5) The verification of the identity of a bank account holder may take place after the bank account has been opened provided that there are adequate safeguards in place to ensure that—

    (a) the account is not closed; and

    (b) transactions are not carried out by or on behalf of the account holder (including any payment from the account to the account holder),

before verification has been completed.

10 Casinos

(1) A casino must establish and verify the identity of—

    (a) all customers to whom the casino makes facilities for gaming available—

        (i) before entry to any premises where such facilities are provided; or

        (ii) where the facilities are for remote gaming, before access is given to such facilities; or

    (b) if the specified conditions are met, all customers who, in the course of any period of 24 hours—

        (i) purchase from, or exchange with, the casino chips with a total value of 2,000 euro or more;

        (ii) pay the casino 2,000 [euro] or more for the use of gaming machines; or

        (iii) pay to, or stake with, the casino 2,000 euro or more in connection with facilities for remote gaming.

(2) The specified conditions are—

    (a) the casino verifies the identity of each customer before or immediately after such purchase, exchange, payment or stake takes place, and

    (b) the Gambling Commission is satisfied that the casino has appropriate procedures in place to monitor and record—

        (i) the total value of chips purchased from or exchanged with the casino;

        (ii) the total money paid for the use of gaming machines; or

        (iii) the total money paid or staked in connection with facilities for remote gaming,

by each customer.

(3) In this regulation—

"gaming", "gaming machine", "remote operating licence" and "stake" have the meanings given by, respectively, sections 6(1) (gaming & game of chance), 235 (gaming machine), 67 (remote gambling) and 353(1) (interpretation) of the Gambling Act 2005;

"premises" means premises subject to—

    (a) a casino premises licence within the meaning of section 150(1)(a) of the Gambling Act 2005 (nature of licence); or

    (b) a converted casino premises licence within the meaning of paragraph 65 of Part 7 of Schedule 4 to the Gambling Act 2005 (Commencement No. 6 and Transitional Provisions) Order 2006;

"remote gaming" means gaming provided pursuant to a remote operating licence.

11 Requirement to cease transactions etc

(1) Where, in relation to any customer, a relevant person is unable to apply customer due diligence measures in accordance with the provisions of this Part, he—

(a) must not carry out a transaction with or for the customer through a bank account;

(b) must not establish a business relationship or carry out an occasional transaction with the customer;

(c) must terminate any existing business relationship with the customer;

(d) must consider whether he is required to make a disclosure by Part 7 of the Proceeds of Crime Act 2002 or Part 3 of the Terrorism Act 2000.

(2) Paragraph (1) does not apply where a lawyer or other professional adviser is in the course of ascertaining the legal position for his client or performing his task of defending or representing that client in, or concerning, legal proceedings, including advice on the institution or avoidance of proceedings.

(3) In paragraph (2), "other professional adviser" means an auditor, accountant or tax adviser who is a member of a professional body which is established for any such persons and which makes provision for—

(a) testing the competence of those seeking admission to membership of such a body as a condition for such admission; and

(b) imposing and maintaining professional and ethical standards for its members, as well as imposing sanctions for non-compliance with those standards.

12 Exception for trustees of debt issues

(1) A relevant person—

(a) who is appointed by the issuer of instruments or securities specified in paragraph (2) as trustee of an issue of such instruments or securities; or

(b) whose customer is a trustee of an issue of such instruments or securities,

is not required to apply the customer due diligence measure referred to in regulation 5(b) in respect of the holders of such instruments or securities.

(2) The specified instruments and securities are—

(a) instruments which fall within [article 77 or 77A of the Financial Services and Markets Act 2000 (Regulated Activities) Order 2001]; and

(b) securities which fall within article 78 of that Order.

13 Simplified due diligence

(1) A relevant person is not required to apply customer due diligence measures in the circumstances mentioned in regulation 7(1)(a), (b) or (d) where he has reasonable grounds for believing that the customer, transaction or product related to such transaction, falls within any of the following paragraphs.

(2) The customer is—

(a) a credit or financial institution which is subject to the requirements of the money laundering directive; or

(b) a credit or financial institution (or equivalent institution) which—

(i) is situated in a non-EEA state which imposes requirements equivalent to those laid down in the money laundering directive; and

(ii) is supervised for compliance with those requirements.

(3) The customer is a company whose securities are listed on a regulated market subject to specified disclosure obligations.

(4) The customer is an independent legal professional and the product is an account into which monies are pooled, provided that—

(a) where the pooled account is held in a non-EEA state—

(i) that state imposes requirements to combat money laundering and terrorist financing which are consistent with international standards; and

(ii) the independent legal professional is supervised in that state for compliance with those requirements; and

(b) information on the identity of the persons on whose behalf monies are held in the pooled account is available, on request, to the institution which acts as a depository institution for the account.

(5) The customer is a public authority in the United Kingdom.

(6) The customer is a public authority which fulfils all the conditions set out in paragraph 2 of Schedule 2 to these Regulations.

(7) The product is—

    (a) a life insurance contract where the annual premium is no more than 1,000 euro or where a single premium of no more than 2,500 euro is paid;

    (b) an insurance contract for the purposes of a pension scheme where the contract contains no surrender clause and cannot be used as collateral;

    (c) a pension, superannuation or similar scheme which provides retirement benefits to employees, where contributions are made by an employer or by way of deduction from an employee's wages and the scheme rules do not permit the assignment of a member's interest under the scheme (other than an assignment permitted by section 44 of the Welfare Reform and Pensions Act 1999 (disapplication of restrictions on alienation) or section 91(5)(a) of the Pensions Act 1995 (inalienability of occupational pension)); or

    (d) electronic money, within the meaning of Article 1(3)(b) of the electronic money directive, where—

        (i) if the device cannot be recharged, the maximum amount stored in the device is no more than 150 euro; or

        (ii) if the device can be recharged, a limit of 2,500 euro is imposed on the total amount transacted in a calendar year, except when an amount of 1,000 euro or more is redeemed in the same calendar year by the bearer (within the meaning of Article 3 of the electronic money directive).

(8) The product and any transaction related to such product fulfils all the conditions set out in paragraph 3 of Schedule 2 to these Regulations.

(9) The product is a child trust fund within the meaning given by section 1(2) of the Child Trust Funds Act 2004.

14 Enhanced customer due diligence and ongoing monitoring

(1) A relevant person must apply on a risk-sensitive basis enhanced customer due diligence measures and enhanced ongoing monitoring—

    (a) in accordance with paragraphs (2) to (4);

    (b) in any other situation which by its nature can present a higher risk of money laundering or terrorist financing.

(2) Where the customer has not been physically present for identification purposes, a relevant person must take specific and adequate measures to compensate for the higher risk, for example, by applying one or more of the following measures—

    (a) ensuring that the customer's identity is established by additional documents, data or information;

    (b) supplementary measures to verify or certify the documents supplied, or requiring confirmatory certification by a credit or financial institution which is subject to the money laundering directive;

    (c) ensuring that the first payment is carried out through an account opened in the customer's name with a credit institution.

(3) A credit institution ("the correspondent") which has or proposes to have a correspondent banking relationship with a respondent institution ("the respondent") from a non-EEA state must—

    (a) gather sufficient information about the respondent to understand fully the nature of its business;

    (b) determine from publicly-available information the reputation of the respondent and the quality of its supervision;

    (c) assess the respondent's anti-money laundering and anti-terrorist financing controls;

    (d) obtain approval from senior management before establishing a new correspondent banking relationship;

    (e) document the respective responsibilities of the respondent and correspondent; and

    (f) be satisfied that, in respect of those of the respondent's customers who have direct access to accounts of the correspondent, the respondent—

        (i) has verified the identity of, and conducts ongoing monitoring in respect of, such customers; and

    (ii) is able to provide to the correspondent, upon request, the documents, data or information obtained when applying customer due diligence measures and ongoing monitoring.

(4) A relevant person who proposes to have a business relationship or carry out an occasional transaction with a politically exposed person must—

    (a) have approval from senior management for establishing the business relationship with that person;

    (b) take adequate measures to establish the source of wealth and source of funds which are involved in the proposed business relationship or occasional transaction; and

    (c) where the business relationship is entered into, conduct enhanced ongoing monitoring of the relationship.

(5) In paragraph (4), "a politically exposed person" means a person who is—

    (a) an individual who is or has, at any time in the preceding year, been entrusted with a prominent public function by—

        (i)   a state other than the United Kingdom;

        (ii) a Community institution; or

        (iii) an international body,

    including a person who falls in any of the categories listed in paragraph 4(1)(a) of Schedule 2;

    (b) an immediate family member of a person referred to in sub-paragraph (a), including a person who falls in any of the categories listed in paragraph 4(1)(c) of Schedule 2; or

    (c) a known close associate of a person referred to in sub-paragraph (a), including a person who falls in either of the categories listed in paragraph 4(1)(d) of Schedule 2.

(6) For the purpose of deciding whether a person is a known close associate of a person referred to in paragraph (5)(a), a relevant person need only have regard to information which is in his possession or is publicly known.

15 Branches and subsidiaries

(1) A credit or financial institution must require its branches and subsidiary undertakings which are located in a non-EEA state to apply, to the extent permitted by the law of that state, measures at least equivalent to those set out in these Regulations with regard to customer due diligence measures, ongoing monitoring and record-keeping.

(2) Where the law of a non-EEA state does not permit the application of such equivalent measures by the branch or subsidiary undertaking located in that state, the credit or financial institution must—

    (a) inform its supervisory authority accordingly; and

    (b) take additional measures to handle effectively the risk of money laundering and terrorist financing.

(3) In this regulation "subsidiary undertaking" —

    (a) except in relation to an incorporated friendly society, has the meaning given by section 1162 of the Companies Act 2006 (parent and subsidiary undertakings) and, in relation to a body corporate in or formed under the law of an EEA state other than the United Kingdom, includes an undertaking which is a subsidiary undertaking within the meaning of any rule of law in force in that state for purposes connected with implementation of the European Council Seventh Company Law Directive 83/349/EEC of 13th June 1983 on consolidated accounts;

    (b) in relation to an incorporated friendly society, means a body corporate of which the society has control within the meaning of section 13(9)(a) or (aa) of the Friendly Societies Act 1992 (control of subsidiaries and other bodies corporate).

(4) Before the entry into force of section 1162 of the Companies Act 2006 the reference to that section in paragraph (3)(a) shall be treated as a reference to section 258 of the Companies Act 1985 (parent and subsidiary undertakings).

16 Shell banks, anonymous accounts etc.

(1) A credit institution must not enter into, or continue, a correspondent banking relationship with a shell bank.

(2) A credit institution must take appropriate measures to ensure that it does not enter into, or continue, a corresponding banking relationship with a bank which is known to permit its accounts to be used by a shell bank.

(3) A credit or financial institution carrying on business in the United Kingdom must not set up an anonymous account or an anonymous passbook for any new or existing customer.

(4) As soon as reasonably practicable on or after 15th December 2007 all credit and financial institutions carrying on business in the United Kingdom must apply customer due diligence measures to, and conduct ongoing monitoring of, all anonymous accounts and passbooks in existence on that date and in any event before such accounts or passbooks are used.

(5) A "shell bank" means a credit institution, or an institution engaged in equivalent activities, incorporated in a jurisdiction in which it has no physical presence involving meaningful decision-making and management, and which is not part of a financial conglomerate or third-country financial conglomerate.

(6) In this regulation, "financial conglomerate" and "third-country financial conglomerate" have the meanings given by regulations 1(2) and 7(1) respectively of the Financial Conglomerates and Other Financial Groups Regulations 2004.

17 Reliance

(1) A relevant person may rely on a person who falls within paragraph (2) (or who the relevant person has reasonable grounds to believe falls within paragraph (2)) to apply any customer due diligence measures provided that—

   (a) the other person consents to being relied on; and

   (b) notwithstanding the relevant person's reliance on the other person, the relevant person remains liable for any failure to apply such measures.

(2) The persons are—

   (a) a credit or financial institution which is an authorised person;

   (b) a relevant person who is—

      (i) an auditor, insolvency practitioner, external accountant, tax adviser or independent legal professional; and

      (ii) supervised for the purposes of these Regulations by one of the bodies listed in Part 1 of Schedule 3;

   (c) a person who carries on business in another EEA state who is—

      (i) a credit or financial institution, auditor, insolvency practitioner, external accountant, tax adviser or independent legal professional;

      (ii) subject to mandatory professional registration recognised by law; and

      (iii) supervised for compliance with the requirements laid down in the money laundering directive in accordance with section 2 of Chapter V of that directive; or

   (d) a person who carries on business in a non-EEA state who is—

      (i) a credit or financial institution (or equivalent institution), auditor, insolvency practitioner, external accountant, tax adviser or independent legal professional;

      (ii) subject to mandatory professional registration recognised by law;

      (iii) subject to requirements equivalent to those laid down in the money laundering directive; and

      (iv) supervised for compliance with those requirements in a manner equivalent to section 2 of Chapter V of the money laundering directive.

(3) In paragraph (2)(c)(i) and (d)(i), "auditor" and "insolvency practitioner" includes a person situated in another EEA state or a non-EEA state who provides services equivalent to the services provided by an auditor or insolvency practitioner.

(4) Nothing in this regulation prevents a relevant person applying customer due diligence measures by means of an outsourcing service provider or agent provided that the relevant person remains liable for any failure to apply such measures.

[(5) In this regulation, "financial institution" excludes—

   (a) any money service business;

   (b) any authorised payment institution, EEA authorised payment institution or small payment institution (within the meaning of the Payment Services Regulations 2009) which provides payment services mainly falling within paragraph 1(f) of Schedule 1 to those Regulations.]

18 Directions where Financial Action Task Force applies counter-measures

The Treasury may direct any relevant person—

   (a) not to enter into a business relationship;

   (b) not to carry out an occasional transaction; or

(c) not to proceed any further with a business relationship or occasional transaction,

with a person who is situated or incorporated in a non-EEA state to which the Financial Action Task Force has decided to apply counter-measures.

Part 3 Record-Keeping, Procedures and Training

19 Record-keeping

(1) Subject to paragraph (4), a relevant person must keep the records specified in paragraph (2) for at least the period specified in paragraph (3).

(2) The records are—

(a) a copy of, or the references to, the evidence of the customer's identity obtained pursuant to regulation 7, 8, 10, 14 or 16(4);

(b) the supporting records (consisting of the original documents or copies) in respect of a business relationship or occasional transaction which is the subject of customer due diligence measures or ongoing monitoring.

(3) The period is five years beginning on—

(a) in the case of the records specified in paragraph (2)(a), the date on which—

    (i) the occasional transaction is completed; or

    (ii) the business relationship ends; or

(b) in the case of the records specified in paragraph (2)(b)—

    (i) where the records relate to a particular transaction, the date on which the transaction is completed;

    (ii) for all other records, the date on which the business relationship ends.

(4) A relevant person who is relied on by another person must keep the records specified in paragraph (2)(a) for five years beginning on the date on which he is relied on for the purposes of regulation 7, 10, 14 or 16(4) in relation to any business relationship or occasional transaction.

(5) A person referred to in regulation 17(2)(a) or (b) who is relied on by a relevant person must, if requested by the person relying on him within the period referred to in paragraph (4)—

(a) as soon as reasonably practicable make available to the person who is relying on him any information about the customer (and any beneficial owner) which he obtained when applying customer due diligence measures; and

(b) as soon as reasonably practicable forward to the person who is relying on him copies of any identification and verification data and other relevant documents on the identity of the customer (and any beneficial owner) which he obtained when applying those measures.

(6) A relevant person who relies on a person referred to in regulation 17(2)(c) or (d) (a "third party") to apply customer due diligence measures must take steps to ensure that the third party will, if requested by the relevant person within the period referred to in paragraph (4)—

(a) as soon as reasonably practicable make available to him any information about the customer (and any beneficial owner) which the third party obtained when applying customer due diligence measures; and

(b) as soon as reasonably practicable forward to him copies of any identification and verification data and other relevant documents on the identity of the customer (and any beneficial owner) which the third party obtained when applying those measures.

(7) Paragraphs (5) and (6) do not apply where a relevant person applies customer due diligence measures by means of an outsourcing service provider or agent.

(8) For the purposes of this regulation, a person relies on another person where he does so in accordance with regulation 17(1).

20 Policies and procedures

(1) A relevant person must establish and maintain appropriate and risk-sensitive policies and procedures relating to—

(a) customer due diligence measures and ongoing monitoring;

(b) reporting;

(c) record-keeping;

(d) internal control;

    (e) risk assessment and management;

    (f) the monitoring and management of compliance with, and the internal communication of, such policies and procedures,

in order to prevent activities related to money laundering and terrorist financing.

(2) The policies and procedures referred to in paragraph (1) include policies and procedures—

    (a) which provide for the identification and scrutiny of—

        (i) complex or unusually large transactions;

        (ii) unusual patterns of transactions which have no apparent economic or visible lawful purpose; and

        (iii) any other activity which the relevant person regards as particularly likely by its nature to be related to money laundering or terrorist financing;

    (b) which specify the taking of additional measures, where appropriate, to prevent the use for money laundering or terrorist financing of products and transactions which might favour anonymity;

    (c) to determine whether a customer is a politically exposed person;

    (d) under which—

        (i) an individual in the relevant person's organisation is a nominated officer under Part 7 of the Proceeds of Crime Act 2002 and Part 3 of the Terrorism Act 2000;

        (ii) anyone in the organisation to whom information or other matter comes in the course of the business as a result of which he knows or suspects or has reasonable grounds for knowing or suspecting that a person is engaged in money laundering or terrorist financing is required to comply with Part 7 of the Proceeds of Crime Act 2002 or, as the case may be, Part 3 of the Terrorism Act 2000; and

        (iii) where a disclosure is made to the nominated officer, he must consider it in the light of any relevant information which is available to the relevant person and determine whether it gives rise to knowledge or suspicion or reasonable grounds for knowledge or suspicion that a person is engaged in money laundering or terrorist financing.

(3) Paragraph (2)(d) does not apply where the relevant person is an individual who neither employs nor acts in association with any other person.

(4) A credit or financial institution must establish and maintain systems which enable it to respond fully and rapidly to enquiries from financial investigators accredited under section 3 of the Proceeds of Crime Act 2002 (accreditation and training), persons acting on behalf of the Scottish Ministers in their capacity as an enforcement authority under that Act, officers of Revenue and Customs or constables as to—

    (a) whether it maintains, or has maintained during the previous five years, a business relationship with any person; and

    (b) the nature of that relationship.

(5) A credit or financial institution must communicate where relevant the policies and procedures which it establishes and maintains in accordance with this regulation to its branches and subsidiary undertakings which are located outside the United Kingdom.

(6) In this regulation—

"politically exposed person" has the same meaning as in regulation 14(4);

"subsidiary undertaking" has the same meaning as in regulation 15.

21 Training

A relevant person must take appropriate measures so that all relevant employees of his are—

    (a) made aware of the law relating to money laundering and terrorist financing; and

    (b) regularly given training in how to recognise and deal with transactions and other activities which may be related to money laundering or terrorist financing.

Part 4 Supervision and Registration

Interpretation

22 Interpretation

(1) In this Part—

"Annex I financial institution" means any undertaking which falls within regulation 3(3)(a) other than—

    (a) a consumer credit financial institution;

    (b) a money service business; [...]

    (c) an authorised person;

    [(d) a bill payment service provider; or

    (e) a telecommunication, digital and IT payment service provider;]

"consumer credit financial institution" means any undertaking which falls within regulation 3(3)(a) and which requires, under section 21 of the Consumer Credit Act 1974 (businesses needing a licence), a licence to carry on a consumer credit business, other than—

    (a) a person covered by a group licence issued by the OFT under section 22 of that Act (standard and group licences);

    (b) a money service business; [...]

    (c) an authorised person [;]

    [(d) a bill payment service provider; or

    (e) a telecommunication, digital and IT payment service provider.]

(2) In paragraph (1), "consumer credit business" has the meaning given by section 189(1) of the Consumer Credit Act 1974 (definitions) and, on the entry into force of section 23(a) of the Consumer Credit Act 2006 (definitions of " consumer credit business" and " consumer hire business"), has the meaning given by section 189(1) of the Consumer Credit Act 1974 as amended by section 23(a) of the Consumer Credit Act 2006.

Supervision

23 Supervisory authorities

(1) Subject to paragraph (2), the following bodies are supervisory authorities—

    (a) the Authority is the supervisory authority for—

        (i)   credit and financial institutions which are authorised persons;

        (ii) trust or company service providers which are authorised persons;

        (iii) Annex I financial institutions;

    (b) the OFT is the supervisory authority for—

        (i)   consumer credit financial institutions;

        (ii) estate agents;

    (c) each of the professional bodies listed in Schedule 3 is the supervisory authority for relevant persons who are regulated by it;

    (d) the Commissioners are the supervisory authority for—

        (i)   high value dealers;

        (ii) money service businesses which are not supervised by the Authority;

        (iii) trust or company service providers which are not supervised by the Authority or one of the bodies listed in Schedule 3;

        (iv) auditors, external accountants and tax advisers who are not supervised by one of the bodies listed in Schedule 3 [;]

        [(v) bill payment service providers which are not supervised by the Authority;

        (vi) telecommunication, digital and IT payment service providers which are not supervised by the Authority.]

    (e) the Gambling Commission is the supervisory authority for casinos; (f) DETI is the supervisory authority for—

        (i)   credit unions in Northern Ireland;

        (ii) insolvency practitioners authorised by it under article 351 of the Insolvency (Northern Ireland) Order 1989;

    (g) the Secretary of State is the supervisory authority for insolvency practitioners authorised by him under section 393 of the Insolvency Act 1986 (grant, refusal and withdrawal of authorisation).

(2) Where under paragraph (1) there is more than one supervisory authority for a relevant person, the supervisory authorities may agree that one of them will act as the supervisory authority for that person.

(3) Where an agreement has been made under paragraph (2), the authority which has agreed to act as the supervisory authority must notify the relevant person or publish the agreement in such manner as it considers appropriate.

(4) Where no agreement has been made under paragraph (2), the supervisory authorities for a relevant person must cooperate in the performance of their functions under these Regulations.

24 Duties of supervisory authorities

(1) A supervisory authority must effectively monitor the relevant persons for whom it is the supervisory authority and take necessary measures for the purpose of securing compliance by such persons with the requirements of these Regulations.

(2) A supervisory authority which, in the course of carrying out any of its functions under these Regulations, knows or suspects that a person is or has engaged in money laundering or terrorist financing must promptly inform the Serious Organised Crime Agency.

(3) A disclosure made under paragraph (2) is not to be taken to breach any restriction, however imposed, on the disclosure of information.

(4) The functions of the Authority under these Regulations shall be treated for the purposes of Parts 1, 2 and 4 of Schedule 1 to the 2000 Act (the Financial Services Authority) as functions conferred on the Authority under that Act.

Registration of high value dealers, money service businesses and trust or company service providers

25 Duty to maintain registers

(1) The Commissioners must maintain registers of—
   (a) high value dealers;
   (b) money service businesses for which they are the supervisory authority; [...]
   (c) trust or company service providers for which they are the supervisory authority [;]
   [(d) bill payment service providers for which they are the supervisory authority; and
   (e) telecommunication, digital and IT payment service providers for which they are the supervisory authority.]

(2) The Commissioners may keep the registers in any form they think fit.

(3) The Commissioners may publish or make available for public inspection all or part of a register maintained under this regulation.

26 Requirement to be registered

(1) A person in respect of whom the Commissioners are required to maintain a register under regulation 25 must not act as a—
   (a) high value dealer;
   (b) money service business; [...]
   (c) trust or company service provider,
   [(d) bill payment service provider; or
   (e) telecommunication, digital and IT payment service provider,]
   unless he is included in the register.

(2) Paragraph (1) and regulation 29 are subject to the transitional provisions set out in regulation 50.

27 Applications for registration in a register maintained under regulation 25

(1) An applicant for registration in a register maintained under regulation 25 must make an application in such manner and provide such information as the Commissioners may specify.

(2) The information which the Commissioners may specify includes—
   (a) the applicant's name and (if different) the name of the business;
   (b) the nature of the business;
   (c) the name of the nominated officer (if any);
   (d) in relation to a money service business or trust or company service provider—
      (i) the name of any person who effectively directs or will direct the business and any beneficial owner of the business; and
      (ii) information needed by the Commissioners to decide whether they must refuse the application pursuant to regulation 28.

(3) At any time after receiving an application and before determining it, the Commissioners may require the applicant to provide, within 21 days beginning with the date of being requested to do so, such further information as they reasonably consider necessary to enable them to determine the application.

(4) If at any time after the applicant has provided the Commissioners with any information under paragraph (1) or (3)—
  (a) there is a material change affecting any matter contained in that information; or
  (b) it becomes apparent to that person that the information contains a significant inaccuracy,
  he must provide the Commissioners with details of the change or, as the case may be, a correction of the inaccuracy within 30 days beginning with the date of the occurrence of the change (or the discovery of the inaccuracy) or within such later time as may be agreed with the Commissioners.
(5) The obligation in paragraph (4) applies also to material changes or significant inaccuracies affecting any matter contained in any supplementary information provided pursuant to that paragraph.
(6) Any information to be provided to the Commissioners under this regulation must be in such form or verified in such manner as they may specify.

28 Fit and proper test

(1) The Commissioners must refuse to register an applicant as a money service business or trust or company service provider if they are satisfied that—
  (a) the applicant;
  (b) a person who effectively directs, or will effectively direct, the business or service provider;
  (c) a beneficial owner of the business or service provider; or
  (d) the nominated officer of the business or service provider,
  is not a fit and proper person.
(2) For the purposes of paragraph (1), a person is not a fit and proper person if he—
  (a) has been convicted of—
    (i) an offence under the Terrorism Act 2000;
    (ii) an offence under paragraph 7(2) or (3) of Schedule 3 to the Anti-Terrorism, Crime and Security Act 2001 (offences);
    (iii) an offence under the Terrorism Act 2006;
    (iv) an offence under Part 7 (money laundering) of, or listed in Schedule 2 (lifestyle offences: England and Wales), 4 (lifestyle offences: Scotland) or 5 (lifestyle offences: Northern Ireland) to, the Proceeds of Crime Act 2002;
    (v) an offence under the Fraud Act 2006 or, in Scotland, the common law offence of fraud;
    (vi) an offence under section 72(1), (3) or (8) of the Value Added Tax Act 1994 (offences); or
    (vii) the common law offence of cheating the public revenue;
  (b) has been adjudged bankrupt or sequestration of his estate has been awarded and (in either case) he has not been discharged; (c) is subject to a disqualification order under the Company Directors Disqualification Act 1986;
  (d) is or has been subject to a confiscation order under the Proceeds of Crime Act 2002;
  (e) has consistently failed to comply with the requirements of these Regulations, the Money Laundering Regulations 2003 or the Money Laundering Regulations 2001;
  (f) has consistently failed to comply with the requirements of regulation 2006/1781/EC of the European Parliament and of the Council of 15th November 2006 on information on the payer accompanying the transfer of funds;
  (g) has effectively directed a business which falls within sub-paragraph (e) or (f);
  (h) is otherwise not a fit and proper person with regard to the risk of money laundering or terrorist financing.
(3) For the purposes of this regulation, a conviction for an offence listed in paragraph (2)(a) is to be disregarded if it is spent for the purposes of the Rehabilitation of Offenders Act 1974.

29 Determination of applications under regulation 27

(1) Subject to regulation 28, the Commissioners may refuse to register an applicant for registration in a register maintained under regulation 25 only if—
  (a) any requirement of, or imposed under, regulation 27 has not been complied with;
  (b) it appears to the Commissioners that any information provided pursuant to regulation 27 is false or misleading in a material particular; or
  (c) the applicant has failed to pay a charge imposed by them under regulation 35(1).

(2) The Commissioners must within 45 days beginning either with the date on which they receive the application or, where applicable, with the date on which they receive any further information required under regulation 27(3), give the applicant notice of—
   (a) their decision to register the applicant; or
   (b) the following matters—
      (i) their decision not to register the applicant;
      (ii) the reasons for their decision;
      [(iii) the right to a review under regulation 43A; and]
      (iv) the right to appeal under [regulation 43].
(3) The Commissioners must, as soon as practicable after deciding to register a person, include him in the relevant register.

30 Cancellation of registration in a register maintained under regulation 25

(1) The Commissioners must cancel the registration of a money service business or trust or company service provider in a register maintained under regulation 25(1) if, at any time after registration, they are satisfied that he or any person mentioned in regulation 28(1)(b), (c) or (d) is not a fit and proper person within the meaning of regulation 28(2).
(2) The Commissioners may cancel a person's registration in a register maintained by them under regulation 25 if, at any time after registration, it appears to them that they would have had grounds to refuse registration under regulation 29(1).
(3) Where the Commissioners decide to cancel a person's registration they must give him notice of—
   (a) their decision and, subject to paragraph (4), the date from which the cancellation takes effect;
   (b) the reasons for their decision;
   [(c) the right to a review under regulation 43A; and]
   (d) the right to appeal under [regulation 43].
(4) If the Commissioners—
   (a) consider that the interests of the public require the cancellation of a person's registration to have immediate effect; and
   (b) include a statement to that effect and the reasons for it in the notice given under paragraph (3),
   the cancellation takes effect when the notice is given to the person.

Requirement to inform the Authority

31 Requirement on authorised person to inform the Authority

(1) An authorised person whose supervisory authority is the Authority must, before acting as a money service business or a trust or company service provider or within 28 days of so doing, inform the Authority that he intends, or has begun, to act as such.
(2) Paragraph (1) does not apply to an authorised person who—
   (a) immediately before 15th December 2007 was acting as a money service business or a trust or company service provider and continues to act as such after that date; and
   (b) before 15th January 2008 informs the Authority that he is or was acting as such.
(3) Where an authorised person whose supervisory authority is the Authority ceases to act as a money service business or a trust or company service provider, he must immediately inform the Authority.
(4) Any requirement imposed by this regulation is to be treated as if it were a requirement imposed by or under the 2000 Act.
(5) Any information to be provided to the Authority under this regulation must be in such form or verified in such manner as it may specify.

Registration of Annex I financial institutions, estate agents etc.

32 Power to maintain registers

(1) The supervisory authorities mentioned in paragraph (2), (3) or (4) may, in order to fulfil their duties under regulation 24, maintain a register under this regulation.
(2) The Authority may maintain a register of Annex I financial institutions.
(3) The OFT may maintain registers of—
   (a) consumer credit financial institutions; and
   (b) estate agents.

(4) The Commissioners may maintain registers of—
(a) auditors;
(b) external accountants; and
(c) tax advisers,

who are not supervised by the Secretary of State, DETI or any of the professional bodies listed in Schedule 3.

(5) Where a supervisory authority decides to maintain a register under this regulation, it must take reasonable steps to bring its decision to the attention of those relevant persons in respect of whom the register is to be established.

(6) A supervisory authority may keep a register under this regulation in any form it thinks fit.

(7) A supervisory authority may publish or make available to public inspection all or part of a register maintained by it under this regulation.

33 Requirement to be registered

Where a supervisory authority decides to maintain a register under regulation 32 in respect of any description of relevant persons and establishes a register for that purpose, a relevant person of that description may not carry on the business or profession in question for a period of more than six months beginning on the date on which the supervisory authority establishes the register unless he is included in the register.

34 Applications for and cancellation of registration in a register maintained under regulation 32

(1) Regulations 27, 29 (with the omission of the words " "Subject to regulation 28" " in regulation 29(1)) and 30(2), (3) and (4) apply to registration in a register maintained by the Commissioners under regulation 32 as they apply to registration in a register maintained under regulation 25.

(2) Regulation 27 applies to registration in a register maintained by the Authority or the OFT under regulation 32 as it applies to registration in a register maintained under regulation 25 and, for this purpose, references to the Commissioners are to be treated as references to the Authority or the OFT, as the case may be.

(3) The Authority and the OFT may refuse to register an applicant for registration in a register maintained under regulation 32 only if—
(a) any requirement of, or imposed under, regulation 27 has not been complied with;
(b) it appears to the Authority or the OFT, as the case may be, that any information provided pursuant to regulation 27 is false or misleading in a material particular; or
(c) the applicant has failed to pay a charge imposed by the Authority or the OFT, as the case may be, under regulation 35(1).

(4) The Authority or the OFT, as the case may be, must, within 45 days beginning either with the date on which it receives an application or, where applicable, with the date on which it receives any further information required under regulation 27(3), give the applicant notice of—
(a) its decision to register the applicant; or
(b) the following matters—
(i) that it is minded not to register the applicant;
(ii) the reasons for being minded not to register him; and
(iii) the right to make representations to it within a specified period (which may not be less than 28 days).

(5) The Authority or the OFT, as the case may be, must then decide, within a reasonable period, whether to register the applicant and it must give the applicant notice of—
(a) its decision to register the applicant; or
(b) the following matters—
(i) its decision not to register the applicant;
(ii) the reasons for its decision; and
(iii) the right to appeal under regulation 44(1)(b).

(6) The Authority or the OFT, as the case may be, must, as soon as reasonably practicable after deciding to register a person, include him in the relevant register.

(7) The Authority or the OFT may cancel a person's registration in a register maintained by them under regulation 32 if, at any time after registration, it appears to them that they would have had grounds to refuse registration under paragraph (3).

(8) Where the Authority or the OFT proposes to cancel a person's registration, it must give him notice of—

   (a) its proposal to cancel his registration;

   (b) the reasons for the proposed cancellation; and

   (c) the right to make representations to it within a specified period (which may not be less than 28 days).

(9) The Authority or the OFT, as the case may be, must then decide, within a reasonable period, whether to cancel the person's registration and it must give him notice of—

   (a) its decision not to cancel his registration; or

   (b) the following matters—

      (i) its decision to cancel his registration and, subject to paragraph (10), the date from which cancellation takes effect;

      (ii) the reasons for its decision; and

      (iii) the right to appeal under regulation 44(1)(b).

(10) If the Authority or the OFT, as the case may be—

   (a) considers that the interests of the public require the cancellation of a person's registration to have immediate effect; and

   (b) includes a statement to that effect and the reasons for it in the notice given under paragraph (9)(b), the cancellation takes effect when the notice is given to the person.

(11) In paragraphs (3) and (4), references to regulation 27 are to be treated as references to that paragraph as applied by paragraph (2) of this regulation.

Financial provisions

35 Costs of supervision

(1) The Authority, the OFT and the Commissioners may impose charges—

   (a) on applicants for registration;

   (b) on relevant persons supervised by them.

(2) Charges levied under paragraph (1) must not exceed such amount as the Authority, the OFT or the Commissioners (as the case may be) consider will enable them to meet any expenses reasonably incurred by them in carrying out their functions under these Regulations or for any incidental purpose.

(3) Without prejudice to the generality of paragraph (2), a charge may be levied in respect of each of the premises at which a person carries on (or proposes to carry on) business.

(4) The Authority must apply amounts paid to it by way of penalties imposed under regulation 42 towards expenses incurred in carrying out its functions under these Regulations or for any incidental purpose.

(5) In paragraph (2), "expenses" in relation to the OFT includes expenses incurred by a local weights and measures authority or DETI pursuant to arrangements made for the purposes of these Regulations with the OFT—

   (a) by or on behalf of the authority; or

   (b) by DETI.

Part 5 Enforcement

Powers of designated authorities

36 Interpretation

In this Part—

   "designated authority" means—

   (a) the Authority;

   (b) the Commissioners;

   (c) the OFT; and

   (d) in relation to credit unions in Northern Ireland, DETI;

   "officer" , except in regulations 40(3), 41 and 47 means—

   (a) an officer of the Authority, including a member of the Authority's staff or an agent of the Authority;

(b) an officer of Revenue and Customs;

(c) an officer of the OFT;

(d) a relevant officer; or

(e) an officer of DETI acting for the purposes of its functions under these Regulations in relation to credit unions in Northern Ireland;

"recorded information" includes information recorded in any form and any document of any nature;

" relevant officer" means—

(a) in Great Britain, an officer of a local weights and measures authority;

(b) in Northern Ireland, an officer of DETI acting pursuant to arrangements made with the OFT for the purposes of these Regulations.

37 Power to require information from, and attendance of, relevant and connected persons

(1) An officer may, by notice to a relevant person or to a person connected with a relevant person, require the relevant person or the connected person, as the case may be—

(a) to provide such information as may be specified in the notice;

(b) to produce such recorded information as may be so specified; or

(c) to attend before an officer at a time and place specified in the notice and answer questions.

(2) For the purposes of paragraph (1), a person is connected with a relevant person if he is, or has at any time been, in relation to the relevant person, a person listed in Schedule 4 to these Regulations.

(3) An officer may exercise powers under this regulation only if the information sought to be obtained as a result is reasonably required in connection with the exercise by the designated authority for whom he acts of its functions under these Regulations.

(4) Where an officer requires information to be provided or produced pursuant to paragraph (1)(a) or (b)—

(a) the notice must set out the reasons why the officer requires the information to be provided or produced; and

(b) such information must be provided or produced—

(i) before the end of such reasonable period as may be specified in the notice; and

(ii) at such place as may be so specified.

(5) In relation to information recorded otherwise than in legible form, the power to require production of it includes a power to require the production of a copy of it in legible form or in a form from which it can readily be produced in visible and legible form.

(6) The production of a document does not affect any lien which a person has on the document.

(7) A person may not be required under this regulation to provide or produce information or to answer questions which he would be entitled to refuse to provide, produce or answer on grounds of legal professional privilege in proceedings in the High Court, except that a lawyer may be required to provide the name and address of his client.

(8) Subject to paragraphs (9) and (10), a statement made by a person in compliance with a requirement imposed on him under paragraph (1)(c) is admissible in evidence in any proceedings, so long as it also complies with any requirements governing the admissibility of evidence in the circumstances in question.

(9) In criminal proceedings in which a person is charged with an offence to which this paragraph applies—

(a) no evidence relating to the statement may be adduced; and

(b) no question relating to it may be asked,

by or on behalf of the prosecution unless evidence relating to it is adduced, or a question relating to it is asked, in the proceedings by or on behalf of that person.

(10) Paragraph (9) applies to any offence other than one under—

(a) section 5 of the Perjury Act 1911 (false statements without oath);

(b) section 44(2) of the Criminal Law (Consolidation)(Scotland) Act 1995 (false statements and declarations); or

(c) Article 10 of the Perjury (Northern Ireland) Order 1979 (false unsworn statements).

(11) In the application of this regulation to Scotland, the reference in paragraph (7) to—

(a) proceedings in the High Court is to be read as a reference to legal proceedings generally; and

(b) an entitlement on grounds of legal professional privilege is to be read as a reference to an entitlement on the grounds of confidentiality of communications [—]

[(i) between a professional legal adviser and his client; or

(ii) made in connection with or in contemplation of legal proceedings and for the purposes of those proceedings.]

38 Entry, inspection without a warrant etc.

(1) Where an officer has reasonable cause to believe that any premises are being used by a relevant person in connection with his business or professional activities, he may on producing evidence of his authority at any reasonable time—

(a) enter the premises;

(b) inspect the premises;

(c) observe the carrying on of business or professional activities by the relevant person;

(d) inspect any recorded information found on the premises;

(e) require any person on the premises to provide an explanation of any recorded information or to state where it may be found;

(f) in the case of a money service business or a high value dealer, inspect any cash found on the premises.

(2) An officer may take copies of, or make extracts from, any recorded information found under paragraph (1).

(3) Paragraphs (1)(d) and (e) and (2) do not apply to recorded information which the relevant person would be entitled to refuse to disclose on grounds of legal professional privilege in proceedings in the High Court, except that a lawyer may be required to provide the name and address of his client and, for this purpose, regulation 37(11) applies to this paragraph as it applies to regulation 37(7).

(4) An officer may exercise powers under this regulation only if the information sought to be obtained as a result is reasonably required in connection with the exercise by the designated authority for whom he acts of its functions under these Regulations.

(5) In this regulation, "premises" means any premises other than premises used only as a dwelling.

39 Entry to premises under warrant

(1) A justice may issue a warrant under this paragraph if satisfied on information on oath given by an officer that there are reasonable grounds for believing that the first, second or third set of conditions is satisfied.

(2) The first set of conditions is—

(a) that there is on the premises specified in the warrant recorded information in relation to which a requirement could be imposed under regulation 37(1)(b); and

(b) that if such a requirement were to be imposed—

(i) it would not be complied with; or

(ii) the recorded information to which it relates would be removed, tampered with or destroyed.

(3) The second set of conditions is—

(a) that a person on whom a requirement has been imposed under regulation 37(1)(b) has failed (wholly or in part) to comply with it; and

(b) that there is on the premises specified in the warrant recorded information which has been required to be produced.

(4) The third set of conditions is—

(a) that an officer has been obstructed in the exercise of a power under regulation 38; and

(b) that there is on the premises specified in the warrant recorded information or cash which could be inspected under regulation 38(1)(d) or (f).

(5) A justice may issue a warrant under this paragraph if satisfied on information on oath given by an officer that there are reasonable grounds for suspecting that—

(a) an offence under these Regulations has been, is being or is about to be committed by a relevant person; and

(b) there is on the premises specified in the warrant recorded information relevant to whether that offence has been, or is being or is about to be committed.

(6) A warrant issued under this regulation shall authorise an officer—

(a) to enter the premises specified in the warrant;

(b) to search the premises and take possession of any recorded information or anything appearing to be recorded information specified in the warrant or to take, in relation to any such recorded information, any other steps which may appear to be necessary for preserving it or preventing interference with it;

   (c) to take copies of, or extracts from, any recorded information specified in the warrant;

   (d) to require any person on the premises to provide an explanation of any recorded information appearing to be of the kind specified in the warrant or to state where it may be found;

   (e) to use such force as may reasonably be necessary.

(7) Where a warrant is issued by a justice under paragraph (1) or (5) on the basis of information [on oath] given by an officer of the Authority, for " "an officer" " in paragraph (6) substitute " "a constable" " .

(8) In paragraphs (1), (5) and (7), "justice" means—

   (a) in relation to England and Wales, a justice of the peace;

   (b) in relation to Scotland, a justice within the meaning of section 307 of the Criminal Procedure (Scotland) Act 1995 (interpretation);

   (c) in relation to Northern Ireland, a lay magistrate.

(9) In the application of this regulation to Scotland, the references in paragraphs [(1), (5) and (7)] to information on oath are to be read as references to evidence on oath.

40 Failure to comply with information requirement

(1) If, on an application made by—

   (a) a designated authority; or

   (b) a local weights and measures authority or DETI pursuant to arrangements made with the OFT—

      (i) by or on behalf of the authority; or

      (ii) by DETI,

it appears to the court that a person (the "information defaulter") has failed to do something that he was required to do under regulation 37(1), the court may make an order under this regulation.

(2) An order under this regulation may require the information defaulter—

   (a) to do the thing that he failed to do within such period as may be specified in the order;

   (b) otherwise to take such steps to remedy the consequences of the failure as may be so specified.

(3) If the information defaulter is a body corporate, a partnership or an unincorporated body of persons which is not a partnership, the order may require any officer of the body corporate, partnership or body, who is (wholly or partly) responsible for the failure to meet such costs of the application as are specified in the order.

(4) In this regulation, "court" means—

   (a) in England and Wales and Northern Ireland, the High Court or the county court;

   (b) in Scotland, the Court of Session or the sheriff [court].

41 Powers of relevant officers

(1) A relevant officer may only exercise powers under regulations 37 to 39 pursuant to arrangements made with the OFT—

   (a) by or on behalf of the local weights and measures authority of which he is an officer ("his authority"); or

   (b) by DETI.

(2) Anything done or omitted to be done by, or in relation to, a relevant officer in the exercise or purported exercise of a power in this Part shall be treated for all purposes as having been done or omitted to be done by, or in relation to, an officer of the OFT.

(3) Paragraph (2) does not apply for the purposes of any criminal proceedings brought against the relevant officer, his authority, DETI or the OFT, in respect of anything done or omitted to be done by the officer.

(4) A relevant officer shall not disclose to any person other than the OFT and his authority or, as the case may be, DETI information obtained by him in the exercise of such powers unless—

   (a) he has the approval of the OFT to do so; or

   (b) he is under a duty to make the disclosure.

Civil penalties, review and appeals

42 Power to impose civil penalties

(1) A designated authority may impose a penalty of such amount as it considers appropriate on a relevant person who fails to comply with any requirement in regulation 7(1), (2) or (3), 8(1) or (3), 9(2), 10(1), 11(1), 14(1), 15(1) or (2), 16(1), (2), (3) or (4), 19(1), (4), (5) or (6), 20(1), (4) or (5), 21, 26, 27(4) or 33 or a direction made under regulation 18 and, for this purpose, " appropriate" means effective, proportionate and dissuasive.

(2) The designated authority must not impose a penalty on a person under paragraph (1) where there are reasonable grounds for it to be satisfied that the person took all reasonable steps and exercised all due diligence to ensure that the requirement would be complied with.

(3) In deciding whether a person has failed to comply with a requirement of these Regulations, the designated authority must consider whether he followed any relevant guidance which was at the time—
   (a) issued by a supervisory authority or any other appropriate body;
   (b) approved by the Treasury; and
   (c) published in a manner approved by the Treasury as suitable in their opinion to bring the guidance to the attention of persons likely to be affected by it.

(4) In paragraph (3), an "appropriate body" means any body which regulates or is representative of any trade, profession, business or employment carried on by the [person].

(5) Where the Commissioners decide to impose a penalty under this regulation, they must give the person notice of—
   (a) their decision to impose the penalty and its amount;
   (b) the reasons for imposing the penalty;
   (c) the right to a review under [regulation 43A]; and
   (d) the right to appeal under [regulation 43].

(6) Where the Authority, the OFT or DETI proposes to impose a penalty under this regulation, it must give the person notice of—
   (a) its proposal to impose the penalty and the proposed amount;
   (b) the reasons for imposing the penalty; and
   (c) the right to make representations to it within a specified period (which may not be less than 28 days).

(7) The Authority, the OFT or DETI, as the case may be, must then decide, within a reasonable period, whether to impose a penalty under this regulation and it must give the person notice of—
   (a) its decision not to impose a penalty; or
   (b) the following matters—
      (i)   its decision to impose a penalty and the amount;
      (ii) the reasons for its decision; and
      (iii) the right to appeal under regulation 44(1)(b).

(8) A penalty imposed under this regulation is payable to the designated authority which imposes it.

43 [Appeals against decisions of the Commissioners]

(1) This regulation applies to decisions of the Commissioners made under—
   (a) regulation 29, to refuse to register an applicant;
   (b) regulation 30, to cancel the registration of a registered person; and
   (c) regulation 42, to impose a penalty.

(2) Any person who is the subject of a decision to which this regulation applies may [appeal to the tribunal in accordance with regulation 43F].

[(3) The provisions of Part 5 of the Value Added Tax Act 1994 (appeals), subject to the modifications set out in paragraph 1 of Schedule 5 to these Regulations, apply in respect of appeals to a tribunal made under this regulation as they apply in respect of appeals made to the tribunal under section 83 (appeals) of that Act.

(4) A tribunal hearing an appeal under paragraph (2) has the power to—
   (a) quash or vary any decision of the supervisory authority, including the power to reduce any penalty to such amount (including nil) as it thinks proper, and
   (b) substitute its own decision for any decision quashed on appeal.

(5) The modifications in Schedule 5 have effect for the purposes of appeals made under this regulation.

(6) For the purposes of appeals under this regulation, the meaning of "tribunal" is as defined in section 82 of the Value Added Tax Act 1994.]

[43A Offer of review

(1) The Commissioners must offer a person (P) a review of a decision that has been notified to P if an appeal lies under regulation 43 in respect of the decision.

(2) The offer of the review must be made by notice given to P at the same time as the decision is notified to P.

(3) This regulation does not apply to the notification of the conclusions of a review.]

[43B Review by the Commissioners

(1) The Commissioners must review a decision if—
  (a) they have offered a review of the decision under regulation 43A, and
  (b) P notifies the Commissioners accepting the offer within 30 days from the date of the document containing the notification of the offer.

(2) But P may not notify acceptance of the offer if P has already appealed to the tribunal under regulation 43F.

(3) The Commissioners shall not review a decision if P has appealed to the tribunal under regulation 43F in respect of the decision.]

[43C Extensions of time

(1) If under regulation 43A, the Commissioners have offered P a review of a decision, the Commissioners may within the relevant period notify P that the relevant period is extended.

(2) If notice is given the relevant period is extended to the end of 30 days from—
  (a) the date of the notice, or
  (b) any other date set out in the notice or a further notice.

(3) In this regulation "relevant period" means—
  (a) the period of 30 days referred to in regulation 43B(1)(b), or
  (b) if notice has been given under paragraph (1) that period as extended (or as most recently extended) in accordance with paragraph (2).]

[43D Review out of time

(1) This regulation applies if—
  (a) the Commissioners have offered a review of a decision under regulation 43A, and
  (b) P does not accept the offer within the time allowed under regulation 43B(1)(b) or 43C(2).

(2) The Commissioners must review the decision under regulation 43B if—
  (a) after the time allowed, P notifies the Commissioners in writing requesting a review out of time,
  (b) the Commissioners are satisfied that P had a reasonable excuse for not accepting the offer or requiring review within the time allowed, and
  (c) the Commissioners are satisfied that P made the request without unreasonable delay after the excuse had ceased to apply.

(3) The Commissioners shall not review a decision if P has appealed to the tribunal under regulation 43F in respect of the decision.]

[43E Nature of review etc

(1) This regulation applies if the Commissioners are required to undertake a review under regulation 43B or 43D.

(2) The nature and extent of the review are to be such as appear appropriate to the Commissioners in the circumstances.

(3) For the purpose of paragraph (2), the Commissioners must, in particular, have regard to steps taken before the beginning of the review—
  (a) by the Commissioners in reaching the decision, and
  (b) by any person in seeking to resolve disagreement about the decision.

(4) The review must take account of any representations made by P at a stage which gives the Commissioners a reasonable opportunity to consider them.

(5) The review may conclude that the decision is to be—
    (a) upheld,
    (b) varied, or
    (c) cancelled.

(6) The Commissioners must give P notice of the conclusions of the review and their reasoning within—
    (a) a period of 45 days beginning with the relevant date, or
    (b) such other period as the Commissioners and P may agree.

(7) In paragraph (6) "relevant date" means—
    (a) the date the Commissioners received P's notification accepting the offer of a review (in a case falling within regulation 43A), or
    (b) the date on which the Commissioners decided to undertake the review (in a case falling within regulation 43D).

(8) Where the Commissioners are required to undertake a review but do not give notice of the conclusions within the time period specified in paragraph (6), the review is to be treated as having concluded that the decision is upheld.

(9) If paragraph (8) applies, the Commissioners must notify P of the conclusion which the review is treated as having reached.]

[43F Bringing of appeals against decisions of the Commissioners

(1) An appeal under regulation 43 is to be made to the tribunal before—
    (a) the end of the period of 30 days beginning with the date of the document notifying the decision to which the appeal relates, or
    (b) if later, the end of the relevant period (within the meaning of regulation 43C).

(2) But that is subject to paragraphs (3) to (5).

(3) In a case where the Commissioners are required to undertake a review under regulation 43B—
    (a) an appeal may not be made until the conclusion date, and
    (b) any appeal is to be made within the period of 30 days beginning with the conclusion date.

(4) In a case where the Commissioners are requested to undertake a review in accordance with regulation 43D—
    (a) an appeal may not be made—
        (i) unless the Commissioners have decided whether or not to undertake a review, and
        (ii) if the Commissioners decide to undertake a review, until the conclusion date; and
    (b) any appeal is to be made within the period of 30 days beginning with—
        (i) the conclusion date (if the Commissioners decide to undertake a review), or
        (ii) the date on which the Commissioners decide not to undertake a review.

(5) In a case where regulation 43E(8) applies, an appeal may be made at any time from the end of the period specified in regulation 43E(6) to the date 30 days after the conclusion date.

(6) An appeal may be made after the end of the period specified in paragraph (1), (3)(b), (4)(b) or (5) if the tribunal gives permission to do so.

(7) In this regulation " conclusion date" means the date of the document notifying the conclusions of the review.]

44 Appeals

(1) A person may appeal from a decision by—
    [...]
    (b) the Authority, the OFT or DETI under regulation 34 or 42.

(2) An appeal from a decision by—
    [...]
    (b) the Authority is to the [Upper Tribunal];
    (c) the OFT is to the [First-tier Tribunal]; and
    (d) DETI is to the High Court.
    [...]

(4) The provisions of Part 9 of the 2000 Act (hearings and appeals), subject to the modifications set out in paragraph 2 of Schedule 5 , apply in respect of appeals to the [Upper Tribunal] made under this regulation as they apply in respect of references made to that Tribunal under that Act.

[...]
[...]
(7) Notwithstanding paragraph (2)(c), until the coming into force of section 55 of the Consumer Credit Act 2006 (the Consumer Credit Appeals Tribunal), an appeal from a decision by the OFT is to the Financial Services and Markets Tribunal and, for these purposes, the coming into force of that section shall not affect—
  (a) the hearing and determination by the Financial Service and Markets Tribunal of an appeal commenced before the coming into force of that section ("the original appeal"); or
  (b) any appeal against the decision of the Financial Services and Markets Tribunal with respect to the original appeal.
(8) The modifications in Schedule 5 have effect for the purposes of appeals made under this regulation.

Criminal offences

45 Offences

(1) A person who fails to comply with any requirement in regulation 7(1), (2) or (3), 8(1) or (3), 9(2), 10(1), 11(1)(a), (b) or (c), 14(1), 15(1) or (2), 16(1), (2), (3) or (4), 19(1), (4), (5) or (6), 20(1), (4) or (5), 21, 26, 27(4) or 33, or a direction made under regulation 18, is guilty of an offence and liable—
  (a) on summary conviction, to a fine not exceeding the statutory maximum;
  (b) on conviction on indictment, to imprisonment for a term not exceeding two years, to a fine or to both.
(2) In deciding whether a person has committed an offence under paragraph (1), the court must consider whether he followed any relevant guidance which was at the time—
  (a) issued by a supervisory authority or any other appropriate body;
  (b) approved by the Treasury; and
  (c) published in a manner approved by the Treasury as suitable in their opinion to bring the guidance to the attention of persons likely to be affected by it.
(3) In paragraph (2), an "appropriate body" means any body which regulates or is representative of any trade, profession, business or employment carried on by the alleged offender.
(4) A person is not guilty of an offence under this regulation if he took all reasonable steps and exercised all due diligence to avoid committing the offence.
(5) Where a person is convicted of an offence under this regulation, he shall not also be liable to a penalty under regulation 42.

46 Prosecution of offences

(1) Proceedings for an offence under regulation 45 may be instituted by—
  (a) the Director of Revenue and Customs Prosecutions or by order of the Commissioners;
  (b) the OFT;
  (c) a local weights and measures authority;
  (d) DETI;
  (e) the Director of Public Prosecutions; or
  (f) the Director of Public Prosecutions for Northern Ireland.
(2) Proceedings for an offence under regulation 45 may be instituted only against a relevant person or, where such a person is a body corporate, a partnership or an unincorporated association, against any person who is liable to be proceeded against under regulation 47.
(3) Where proceedings under paragraph (1) are instituted by order of the Commissioners, the proceedings must be brought in the name of an officer of Revenue and Customs.
(4) Where a local weights and measures authority in England or Wales proposes to institute proceedings for an offence under regulation 45 it must give the OFT notice of the intended proceedings, together with a summary of the facts on which the charges are to be founded.
(5) A local weights and measures authority must also notify the OFT of the outcome of the proceedings after they are finally determined.
(6) A local weights and measures authority must, whenever the OFT requires, report in such form and with such particulars as the OFT requires on the exercise of its functions under these Regulations.
(7) Where the Commissioners investigate, or propose to investigate, any matter with a view to determining—
  (a) whether there are grounds for believing that an offence under regulation 45 has been committed by any person; or

    (b) whether such a person should be prosecuted for such an offence, that matter is to be treated as an assigned matter within the meaning of section 1(1) of the Customs and Excise Management Act 1979.

(8) Paragraphs (1) and (3) to (6) do not extend to Scotland.

[(9) In its application to the Commissioners acting in Scotland, paragraph (7)(b) shall be read as referring to the Commissioners determining whether to refer the matter to the Crown Office and Procurator Fiscal Service with a view to the Procurator Fiscal determining whether a person should be prosecuted for such an offence.]

47 Offences by bodies corporate etc.

(1) If an offence under regulation 45 committed by a body corporate is shown—
    (a) to have been committed with the consent or the connivance of an officer of the body corporate; or
    (b) to be attributable to any neglect on his part,
the officer as well as the body corporate is guilty of an offence and liable to be proceeded against and punished accordingly.

(2) If an offence under regulation 45 committed by a partnership is shown—
    (a) to have been committed with the consent or the connivance of a partner; or
    (b) to be attributable to any neglect on his part,
the partner as well as the partnership is guilty of an offence and liable to be proceeded against and punished accordingly.

(3) If an offence under regulation 45 committed by an unincorporated association (other than a partnership) is shown—
    (a) to have been committed with the consent or the connivance of an officer of the association; or
    (b) to be attributable to any neglect on his part,
that officer as well as the association is guilty of an offence and liable to be proceeded against and punished accordingly.

(4) If the affairs of a body corporate are managed by its members, paragraph (1) applies in relation to the acts and defaults of a member in connection with his functions of management as if he were a director of the body.

(5) Proceedings for an offence alleged to have been committed by a partnership or an unincorporated association must be brought in the name of the partnership or association (and not in that of its members).

(6) A fine imposed on the partnership or association on its conviction of an offence is to be paid out of the funds of the partnership or association.

(7) Rules of court relating to the service of documents are to have effect as if the partnership or association were a body corporate.

(8) In proceedings for an offence brought against the partnership or association—
    (a) section 33 of the Criminal Justice Act 1925 (procedure on charge of offence against corporation) and Schedule 3 to the Magistrates' Courts Act 1980 (corporations) apply as they do in relation to a body corporate;
    (b) section 70 (proceedings against bodies corporate) of the Criminal Procedure (Scotland) Act 1995 applies as it does in relation to a body corporate;
    (c) section 18 of the Criminal Justice (Northern Ireland) Act 1945 (procedure on charge) and Schedule 4 to the Magistrates' Courts (Northern Ireland) Order 1981 (corporations) apply as they do in relation to a body corporate.

(9) In this regulation—
"officer" —
    (a) in relation to a body corporate, means a director, manager, secretary, chief executive, member of the committee of management, or a person purporting to act in such a capacity; and
    (b) in relation to an unincorporated association, means any officer of the association or any member of its governing body, or a person purporting to act in such capacity; and
"partner" includes a person purporting to act as a partner.

Part 6 Miscellaneous

48 Recovery of charges and penalties through the court

Any charge or penalty imposed on a person by a supervisory authority under regulation 35(1) or 42(1) is a debt due from that person to the authority, and is recoverable accordingly.

49 Obligations on public authorities

(1) The following bodies and persons must, if they know or suspect or have reasonable grounds for knowing or suspecting that a person is or has engaged in money laundering or terrorist financing, as soon as reasonably practicable inform the Serious Organised Crime Agency—
 (a) the Auditor General for Scotland;
 (b) the Auditor General for Wales;
 (c) the Authority;
 (d) the Bank of England;
 (e) the Comptroller and Auditor General;
 (f) the Comptroller and Auditor General for Northern Ireland;
 (g) the Gambling Commission;
 (h) the OFT;
 (i) the Official Solicitor to the Supreme Court;
 (j) the Pensions Regulator;
 (k) the Public Trustee;
 (l) the Secretary of State, in the exercise of his functions under enactments relating to companies and insolvency;
 (m) the Treasury, in the exercise of their functions under the 2000 Act;
 (n) the Treasury Solicitor;
 (o) a designated professional body for the purposes of Part 20 of the 2000 Act (provision of financial services by members of the professions);
 (p) a person or inspector appointed under section 65 (investigations on behalf of Authority) or 66 (inspections and special meetings) of the Friendly Societies Act 1992;
 (q) an inspector appointed under section 49 of the Industrial and Provident Societies Act 1965 (appointment of inspectors) or section 18 of the Credit Unions Act 1979 (power to appoint inspector);
 (r) an inspector appointed under section 431 (investigation of a company on its own application), 432 (other company investigations), 442 (power to investigate company ownership) or 446 (investigation of share dealing) of the Companies Act 1985 or under Article 424, 425, 435 or 439 of the Companies (Northern Ireland) Order 1986;
 (s) a person or inspector appointed under section 55 (investigations on behalf of Authority) or 56 (inspections and special meetings) of the Building Societies Act 1986;
 (t) a person appointed under section 167 (appointment of persons to carry out investigations), 168(3) or (5) (appointment of persons to carry out investigations in particular cases), 169(1)(b) (investigations to support overseas regulator) or 284 (power to investigate affairs of a scheme) of the 2000 Act, or under regulations made under section 262(2)(k) (open-ended investment companies) of that Act, to conduct an investigation; and
 (u) a person authorised to require the production of documents under section 447 of the Companies Act 1985 (Secretary of State's power to require production of documents), Article 440 of the Companies (Northern Ireland) Order 1986 or section 84 of the Companies Act 1989 (exercise of powers by officer).
(2) A disclosure made under paragraph (1) is not to be taken to breach any restriction on the disclosure of information however imposed.

[49A Disclosure by the Commissioners

(1) The Commissioners may disclose to the Authority information held in connection with their functions under these Regulations if the disclosure is made for the purpose of enabling or assisting the Authority to discharge any of its functions under the Payment Services Regulations 2009.

(2) Information disclosed to the Authority under subsection (1) may not be disclosed by the Authority or any person who receives the information directly or indirectly from the Authority except—

(a) to, or in accordance with authority given by, the Commissioners;

(b) with a view to the institution of, or otherwise for the purposes of, any criminal proceedings;

(c) with a view to the institution of any other proceedings by the Authority, for the purposes of any such proceedings instituted by the Authority, or for the purposes of any reference to the Tribunal under the Payment Services Regulations 2009; or

(d) in the form of a summary or collection of information so framed as not to enable information relating to any particular person to be ascertained from it.

(3) Any person who discloses information in contravention of subsection (2) is guilty of an offence and liable—

(a) on summary conviction, to imprisonment for a term not exceeding three months, to a fine not exceeding the statutory maximum, or to both;

(b) on conviction on indictment, to imprisonment for a term not exceeding two years to a fine, or to both.

(4) It is a defence for a person charged with an offence under this regulation of disclosing information to prove that they reasonably believed

(a) that the disclosure was lawful; or

(b) that the information had already and lawfully been made available to the public.]

50 Transitional provisions: requirement to be registered

(1) Regulation 26 does not apply to an existing money service business, an existing trust or company service provider [, an existing high value dealer, an existing bill payment service provider or an existing telecommunication, digital and IT payment service provider] until—

(a) where it has applied in accordance with regulation 27 before the specified date for registration in a register maintained under regulation 25(1) (a "new register")—

(i) the date it is included in a new register following the determination of its application by the Commissioners; or

(ii) where the Commissioners give it notice under regulation 29(2)(b) of their decision not to register it, the date on which the Commissioners state that the decision takes effect or, where a statement is included in accordance with paragraph (3)(b), the time at which the Commissioners give it such notice;

(b) in any other case, the specified date.

(2) The specified date is—

(a) in the case of an existing money service business, 1st February 2008;

(b) in the case of an existing trust or company service provider, 1st April 2008;

(c) in the case of an existing high value dealer, the first anniversary which falls on or after 1st January 2008 of the date of its registration in a register maintained under regulation 10 of the Money Laundering Regulations 2003 [;]

[(d) in the case of an existing bill payment service provider or an existing telecommunication, digital and IT payment service provider, 1st March 2010.]

(3) In the case of an application for registration in a new register made before the specified date by an existing money service business, an existing trust or company service provider [, an existing high value dealer, an existing bill payment service provider or an existing telecommunication, digital and IT payment service provider], the Commissioners must include in a notice given to it under regulation 29(2)(b)—

(a) the date on which their decision is to take effect; or

(b) if the Commissioners consider that the interests of the public require their decision to have immediate effect, a statement to that effect and the reasons for it.

(4) In the case of an application for registration in a new register made before the specified date by an existing money services business or an existing trust or company service provider, the Commissioners must give it a notice under regulation 29(2) by—

(a) in the case of an existing money service business, 1st June 2008;

(b) in the case of an existing trust or company service provider, 1st July 2008; or

    (c) where applicable, 45 days beginning with the date on which they receive any further information required under regulation 27(3).

(5) In this regulation—

["existing bill payment service provider" and "existing telecommunication, digital and IT payment service provider" mean a bill payment service provider or a telecommunication, digital and IT payment service provider carrying on business in the United Kingdom immediately before 1st November 2009;]

"existing money service business" and an "existing high value dealer" mean a money service business or a high value dealer which, immediately before 15th December 2007, was included in a register maintained under regulation 10 of the Money Laundering Regulations 2003;

"existing trust or company service provider" means a trust or company service provider carrying on business in the United Kingdom immediately before 15th December 2007.

51 Minor and consequential amendments

Schedule 6, which contains minor and consequential amendments to primary and secondary legislation, has effect.

Signatory text

Alan Campbell; Frank Roy

Two Lords Commissioners of Her Majesty's Treasury

24th July 2007

Schedule 1 Activities Listed in Points 2 to 12 and 14 of Annex I to the Banking Consolidation Directive

  2. Lending including, inter alia: consumer credit, mortgage credit, factoring, with or without recourse, financing of commercial transactions (including forfeiting).

  3. Financial leasing.

[4. Payment services as defined in Article 4(3) of Directive 2007/64/EC of the European Parliament and of the Council of 13 November 2007 on payment services in the internal market.

  5. Issuing and administering other means of payment (including travellers' cheques and bankers' drafts) insofar as this activity is not covered by point 4.]

  6. Guarantees and commitments.

  7. Trading for own account or for account of customers in:

    (a) money market instruments (cheques, bills, certificates of deposit, etc.);
    (b) foreign exchange;
    (c) financial futures and options;
    (d) exchange and interest-rate instruments; or
    (e) transferable securities.

  8. Participation in securities issues and the provision of services related to such issues.

  9. Advice to undertakings on capital structure, industrial strategy and related questions and advice as well as services relating to mergers and the purchase of undertakings.

10. Money broking.

11. Portfolio management and advice.

12. Safekeeping and administration of securities.

14. Safe custody services

Schedule 2 Financial Activity, Simplified Due Diligence and Politically Exposed Persons

Financial activity on an occasional or very limited basis

1

For the purposes of regulation 4(1)(e) and (2), a person is to be considered as engaging in financial activity on an occasional or very limited basis if all the following conditions are fulfilled—

(a) the person's total annual turnover in respect of the financial activity does not exceed £64,000;

(b) the financial activity is limited in relation to any customer to no more than one transaction exceeding 1,000 euro, whether the transaction is carried out in a single operation, or a series of operations which appear to be linked;

(c) the financial activity does not exceed 5% of the person's total annual turnover;

(d) the financial activity is ancillary and directly related to the person's main activity;

(e) the financial activity is not the transmission or remittance of money (or any representation of monetary value) by any means;

(f) the person's main activity is not that of a person falling within regulation 3(1)(a) to (f) or (h);

(g) the financial activity is provided only to customers of the person's main activity and is not offered to the public.

Simplified due diligence

2

For the purposes of regulation 13(6), the conditions are—

(a) the authority has been entrusted with public functions pursuant to the Treaty on the European Union, the Treaties on the European Communities or Community secondary legislation;

(b) the authority's identity is publicly available, transparent and certain;

(c) the activities of the authority and its accounting practices are transparent;

(d) either the authority is accountable to a Community institution or to the authorities of an EEA state, or otherwise appropriate check and balance procedures exist ensuring control of the authority's activity.

3

For the purposes of regulation 13(8), the conditions are—

(a) the product has a written contractual base;

(b) any related transaction is carried out through an account of the customer with a credit institution which is subject to the money laundering directive or with a credit institution situated in a non-EEA state which imposes requirements equivalent to those laid down in that directive;

(c) the product or related transaction is not anonymous and its nature is such that it allows for the timely application of customer due diligence measures where there is a suspicion of money laundering or terrorist financing;

(d) the product is within the following maximum threshold—

(i) in the case of insurance policies or savings products of a similar nature, the annual premium is no more than 1,000 euro or there is a single premium of no more than 2,500 euro;

(ii) in the case of products which are related to the financing of physical assets where the legal and beneficial title of the assets is not transferred to the customer until the termination of the contractual relationship (whether the transaction is carried out in a single operation or in several operations which appear to be linked), the annual payments do not exceed 15,000 euro;

(iii) in all other cases, the maximum threshold is 15,000 euro;

(e) the benefits of the product or related transaction cannot be realised for the benefit of third parties, except in the case of death, disablement, survival to a predetermined advanced age, or similar events;

(f) in the case of products or related transactions allowing for the investment of funds in financial assets or claims, including insurance or other kinds of contingent claims—
  (i) the benefits of the product or related transaction are only realisable in the long term;
  (ii) the product or related transaction cannot be used as collateral; and
  (iii) during the contractual relationship, no accelerated payments are made, surrender clauses used or early termination takes place

Politically exposed persons

4

(1) For the purposes of regulation 14(5)—
  (a) individuals who are or have been entrusted with prominent public functions include the following—
    (i) heads of state, heads of government, ministers and deputy or assistant ministers;
    (ii) members of parliaments;
    (iii) members of supreme courts, of constitutional courts or of other high-level judicial bodies whose decisions are not generally subject to further appeal, other than in exceptional circumstances;
    (iv) members of courts of auditors or of the boards of central banks;
    (v) ambassadors, chargés d'affaires and high-ranking officers in the armed forces; and
    (vi) members of the administrative, management or supervisory bodies of state-owned enterprises;
  (b) the categories set out in paragraphs (i) to (vi) of sub-paragraph (a) do not include middle-ranking or more junior officials;
  (c) immediate family members include the following—
    (i) a spouse;
    (ii) a partner;
    (iii) children and their spouses or partners; and
    (iv) parents;
  (d) persons known to be close associates include the following—
    (i) any individual who is known to have joint beneficial ownership of a legal entity or legal arrangement, or any other close business relations, with a person referred to in regulation 14(5)(a); and
    (ii) any individual who has sole beneficial ownership of a legal entity or legal arrangement which is known to have been set up for the benefit of a person referred to in regulation 14(5)(a).
(2) In paragraph (1)(c), "partner" means a person who is considered by his national law as equivalent to a spouse.

Schedule 4 Connected Persons

Corporate bodies

1

If the relevant person is a body corporate ("BC"), a person who is or has been—
  (a) an officer or manager of BC or of a parent undertaking of BC;
  (b) an employee of BC;
  (c) an agent of BC or of a parent undertaking of BC.

Partnerships

2

If the relevant person is a partnership, a person who is or has been a member, manager, employee or agent of the partnership.

Unincorporated associations

3

If the relevant person is an unincorporated association of persons which is not a partnership, a person who is or has been an officer, manager, employee or agent of the association.

Individuals

4

If the relevant person is an individual, a person who is or has been an employee or agent of that individual.

Explanatory Note

These Regulations replace the Money Laundering Regulations 2003 (S.I. 2003/3075) with updated provisions which implement in part Directive 2005/60/EC (OJ No L 309, 25.11.2005, p.15) of the European Parliament and of the Council on the prevention of the use of the financial system for the purpose of money laundering and terrorist financing. A Transposition Note setting out how the main elements of this directive will be transposed into UK law is available from the Financial Services Team, HM Treasury, 1 Horse Guards Road, London SW1A 2HQ. An impact assessment has also been prepared. Copies of both documents have been placed in the library of each House of Parliament and are available on HM Treasury's website (www.hm-treasury.gov.uk).

The Regulations provide for various steps to be taken by the financial services sector and other persons to detect and prevent money laundering and terrorist financing. Obligations are imposed on "relevant persons" (defined in regulation 3 and subject to the exclusions in regulation 4), who are credit and financial institutions, auditors, accountants, tax advisers and insolvency practitioners, independent legal professionals, trust or company service providers, estate agents, high value dealers and casinos.

Relevant persons are required, when undertaking certain activities in the course of business, to apply customer due diligence measures where they establish a business relationship, carry out an occasional transaction, suspect money laundering or terrorist finance or doubt the accuracy of customer identification information (regulation 7). Customer due diligence measures (defined in regulation 5) consist of identifying and verifying the identity of the customer and any beneficial owner (defined in regulation 6) of the customer, and obtaining information on the purpose and intended nature of the business relationship. Relevant persons also have to undertake ongoing monitoring of their business relationships (regulation 8).

Regulation 9 sets out the general rule on the timing of the verification of the customer's identity and certain exceptions. Regulation 10 sets out when casinos must identify and verify their customers. Failure to apply such measures means that a person cannot establish or continue a business relationship with the customer concerned or undertake an occasional transaction (regulation 11). Regulation 12 provides an exception from the requirement to identify the beneficial owner for debt issues held in trust.

Relevant persons may apply simplified customer due diligence measures for the products, customers or transactions listed in regulation 13 and must apply enhanced measures in the four situations set out in regulation 14. Regulation 15 sets out the obligations on relevant persons in respect of their overseas branches and subsidiaries. Regulation 16 imposes obligations in respect of shell banks and anonymous accounts. Regulation 17 lists the persons on whom relevant persons can rely to perform customer due diligence measures. Regulation 18 provides for the Treasury to make directions where the Financial Action Task Force applies counter-measures to a non-EEA state.

Part 3 imposes obligations in respect of record-keeping (regulation 19), policies and procedures (regulation 20) and staff training (regulation 21).

Part 4 deals with supervision and registration. Regulation 23 allocates supervisory authorities for different relevant persons. Regulation 24 sets out the duties of supervisors. Money service businesses, high value dealers and trust or company service providers which are not otherwise registered are subject to a system of mandatory registration set out in regulations 25 to 30. Money service businesses and trust or company service providers must not be registered unless the business, its owners, its nominated officer and senior managers are fit and proper persons: regulation 28. Other sectors will only be required to register if the supervisor decides to maintain a register (regulations 33 and 34). Regulation 35 enables supervisors to impose charges on persons they supervise.

Part 5 provides enforcement powers for certain supervisors, including powers to obtain information and enter and inspect premises (regulations 37 to 41). Civil penalties may be imposed by these supervisors under regulation 42 on persons who fail to comply with the requirements of Parts 2, 3 and 4. Provision is made for reviews of and appeals against such penalties (regulations 43 and 44). Relevant persons who fail to comply with the requirements of Parts 2, 3 and 4 will also be guilty of a criminal offence: regulations 45 to 47. Persons convicted of a criminal offence may not also be liable to a civil penalty.

Part 6 contains provision for the recovery of penalties and charges through the court (regulation 48), imposes an obligation on certain public authorities to report suspicions of money laundering or terrorist financing (regulation 49) and makes transitional provision (regulation 50). Regulation 51 makes minor and consequential amendments to primary and secondary legislation.

Directive 2005/60/EC of the European Parliament and of the Council

of 26 October 2005
on the prevention of the use of the financial system for
the purpose of money laundering and terrorist financing.
(Text with EEA relevance)

THE EUROPEAN PARLIAMENT AND THE COUNCIL OF THE EUROPEAN UNION,

Having regard to the Treaty establishing the European Community, and in particular Article 47(2), first and third sentences, and Article 95 thereof,

Having regard to the proposal from the Commission,

Having regard to the opinion of the European Economic and Social Committee,[1]

Having regard to the opinion of the European Central Bank,[2]

Acting in accordance with the procedure laid down in Article 251 of the Treaty,[3]

Whereas:

(1) Massive flows of dirty money can damage the stability and reputation of the financial sector and threaten the single market, and terrorism shakes the very foundations of our society. In addition to the criminal law approach, a preventive effort via the financial system can produce results.

(2) The soundness, integrity and stability of credit and financial institutions and confidence in the financial system as a whole could be seriously jeopardised by the efforts of criminals and their associates either to disguise the origin of criminal proceeds or to channel lawful or unlawful money for terrorist purposes. In order to avoid Member States' adopting measures to protect their financial systems which could be inconsistent with the functioning of the internal market and with the prescriptions of the rule of law and Community public policy, Community action in this area is necessary.

(3) In order to facilitate their criminal activities, money launderers and terrorist financers could try to take advantage of the freedom of capital movements and the freedom to supply financial services which the integrated financial area entails, if certain coordinating measures are not adopted at Community level.

(4) In order to respond to these concerns in the field of money laundering, Council Directive 91/308/EEC of 10 June 1991 on prevention of the use of the financial system for the purpose of money laundering[4] was adopted. It required Member States to prohibit money laundering and to oblige the financial sector, comprising credit institutions and a wide range of other financial institutions, to identify their customers, keep appropriate records, establish internal procedures to train staff and guard against money laundering and to report any indications of money laundering to the competent authorities.

---

[1] Opinion delivered on 11 May 2005 (not yet published in the Official Journal).

[2] OJ C 40, 17.2.2005, p. 9.

[3] Opinion of the European Parliament of 26 May 2005 (not yet published in the Official Journal) and Council Decision of 19 September 2005.

[4] OJ L 166, 28.6.1991, p. 77. Directive as amended by Directive 2001/97/EC of the European Parliament and of the Council (OJ L 344, 28.12.2001, p. 76).

(5) Money laundering and terrorist financing are frequently carried out in an international context. Measures adopted solely at national or even Community level, without taking account of international coordination and cooperation, would have very limited effects. The measures adopted by the Community in this field should therefore be consistent with other action undertaken in other international fora. The Community action should continue to take particular account of the Recommendations of the Financial Action Task Force (hereinafter referred to as the FATF), which constitutes the foremost international body active in the fight against money laundering and terrorist financing. Since the FATF Recommendations were substantially revised and expanded in 2003, this Directive should be in line with that new international standard.

(6) The General Agreement on Trade in Services (GATS) allows Members to adopt measures necessary to protect public morals and prevent fraud and adopt measures for prudential reasons, including for ensuring the stability and integrity of the financial system.

(7) Although initially limited to drugs offences, there has been a trend in recent years towards a much wider definition of money laundering based on a broader range of predicate offences. A wider range of predicate offences facilitates the reporting of suspicious transactions and international cooperation in this area. Therefore, the definition of serious crime should be brought into line with the definition of serious crime in Council Framework Decision 2001/500/JHA of 26 June 2001 on money laundering, the identification, tracing, freezing, seizing and confiscation of instrumentalities and the proceeds of crime.[5]

(8) Furthermore, the misuse of the financial system to channel criminal or even clean money to terrorist purposes poses a clear risk to the integrity, proper functioning, reputation and stability of the financial system. Accordingly, the preventive measures of this Directive should cover not only the manipulation of money derived from crime but also the collection of money or property for terrorist purposes.

(9) Directive 91/308/EEC, though imposing a customer identification obligation, contained relatively little detail on the relevant procedures. In view of the crucial importance of this aspect of the prevention of money laundering and terrorist financing, it is appropriate, in accordance with the new international standards, to introduce more specific and detailed provisions relating to the identification of the customer and of any beneficial owner and the verification of their identity. To that end a precise definition of 'beneficial owner' is essential. Where the individual beneficiaries of a legal entity or arrangement such as a foundation or trust are yet to be determined, and it is therefore impossible to identify an individual as the beneficial owner, it would suffice to identify the class of persons intended to be the beneficiaries of the foundation or trust. This requirement should not include the identification of the individuals within that class of persons.

(10) The institutions and persons covered by this Directive should, in conformity with this Directive, identify and verify the identity of the beneficial owner. To fulfil this requirement, it should be left to those institutions and persons whether they make use of public records of beneficial owners, ask their clients for relevant data or obtain the information otherwise, taking into account the fact that the extent of such customer due diligence measures relates to the risk of money laundering and terrorist financing, which depends on the type of customer, business relationship, product or transaction.

(11) Credit agreements in which the credit account serves exclusively to settle the loan and the repayment of the loan is effected from an account which was opened in the name of the customer with a credit institution covered by this Directive pursuant to Article 8(1)(a) to (c) should generally be considered as an example of types of less risky transactions.

(12) To the extent that the providers of the property of a legal entity or arrangement have significant control over the use of the property they should be identified as a beneficial owner.

(13) Trust relationships are widely used in commercial products as an internationally recognised feature of the comprehensively supervised wholesale financial markets. An obligation to identify the beneficial owner does not arise from the fact alone that there is a trust relationship in this particular case.

---

[5] OJ L 182, 5.7.2001, p. 1.

(14) This Directive should also apply to those activities of the institutions and persons covered hereunder which are performed on the Internet.

(15) As the tightening of controls in the financial sector has prompted money launderers and terrorist financers to seek alternative methods for concealing the origin of the proceeds of crime and as such channels can be used for terrorist financing, the anti-money laundering and antiterrorist financing obligations should cover life insurance intermediaries and trust and company service providers.

(16) Entities already falling under the legal responsibility of an insurance undertaking, and therefore falling within the scope of this Directive, should not be included within the category of insurance intermediary.

(17) Acting as a company director or secretary does not of itself make someone a trust and company service provider. For that reason, the definition covers only those persons that act as a company director or secretary for a third party and by way of business.

(18) The use of large cash payments has repeatedly proven to be very vulnerable to money laundering and terrorist financing. Therefore, in those Member States that allow cash payments above the established threshold, all natural or legal persons trading in goods by way of business should be covered by this Directive when accepting such cash payments. Dealers in high-value goods, such as precious stones or metals, or works of art, and auctioneers are in any event covered by this Directive to the extent that payments to them are made in cash in an amount of EUR 15 000 or more. To ensure effective monitoring of compliance with this Directive by that potentially wide group of institutions and persons, Member States may focus their monitoring activities in particular on those natural and legal persons trading in goods that are exposed to a relatively high risk of money laundering or terrorist financing, in accordance with the principle of risk-based supervision. In view of the different situations in the various Member States, Member States may decide to adopt stricter provisions, in order to properly address the risk involved with large cash payments.

(19) Directive 91/308/EEC brought notaries and other independent legal professionals within the scope of the Community anti-money laundering regime; this coverage should be maintained unchanged in this Directive; these legal professionals, as defined by the Member States, are subject to the provisions of this Directive when participating in financial or corporate transactions, including providing tax advice, where there is the greatest risk of the services of those legal professionals being misused for the purpose of laundering the proceeds of criminal activity or for the purpose of terrorist financing.

(20) Where independent members of professions providing legal advice which are legally recognised and controlled, such as lawyers, are ascertaining the legal position of a client or representing a client in legal proceedings, it would not be appropriate under this Directive to put those legal professionals in respect of these activities under an obligation to report suspicions of money laundering or terrorist financing. There must be exemptions from any obligation to report information obtained either before, during or after judicial proceedings, or in the course of ascertaining the legal position for a client. Thus, legal advice shall remain subject to the obligation of professional secrecy unless the legal counsellor is taking part in money laundering or terrorist financing, the legal advice is provided for money laundering or terrorist financing purposes or the lawyer knows that the client is seeking legal advice for money laundering or terrorist financing purposes.

(21) Directly comparable services need to be treated in the same manner when provided by any of the professionals covered by this Directive. In order to ensure the respect of the rights laid down in the European Convention for the Protection of Human Rights and Fundamental Freedoms and the Treaty on European Union, in the case of auditors, external accountants and tax advisors, who, in some Member States, may defend or represent a client in the context of judicial proceedings or ascertain a client's legal position, the information they obtain in the performance of those tasks should not be subject to the reporting obligations in accordance with this Directive.

(22) It should be recognised that the risk of money laundering and terrorist financing is not the same in every case. In line with a risk-based approach, the principle should be introduced into Community legislation that simplified customer due diligence is allowed in appropriate cases.

(23) The derogation concerning the identification of beneficial owners of pooled accounts held by notaries or other independent legal professionals should be without prejudice to the obligations that those notaries or other independent legal professionals have pursuant to this Directive.

Those obligations include the need for such notaries or other independent legal professionals themselves to identify the beneficial owners of the pooled accounts held by them.

(24) Equally, Community legislation should recognise that certain situations present a greater risk of money laundering or terrorist financing. Although the identity and business profile of all customers should be established, there are cases where particularly rigorous customer identification and verification procedures are required.

(25) This is particularly true of business relationships with individuals holding, or having held, important public positions, particularly those from countries where corruption is widespread. Such relationships may expose the financial sector in particular to significant reputational and/or legal risks. The international effort to combat corruption also justifies the need to pay special attention to such cases and to apply the complete normal customer due diligence measures in respect of domestic politically exposed persons or enhanced customer due diligence measures in respect of politically exposed persons residing in another Member State or in a third country.

(26) Obtaining approval from senior management for establishing business relationships should not imply obtaining approval from the board of directors but from the immediate higher level of the hierarchy of the person seeking such approval.

(27) In order to avoid repeated customer identification procedures, leading to delays and inefficiency in business, it is appropriate, subject to suitable safeguards, to allow customers to be introduced whose identification has been carried out elsewhere. Where an institution or person covered by this Directive relies on a third party, the ultimate responsibility for the customer due diligence procedure remains with the institution or person to whom the customer is introduced. The third party, or introducer, also retains his own responsibility for all the requirements in this Directive, including the requirement to report suspicious transactions and maintain records, to the extent that he has a relationship with the customer that is covered by this Directive.

(28) In the case of agency or outsourcing relationships on a contractual basis between institutions or persons covered by this Directive and external natural or legal persons not covered hereby, any anti-money laundering and anti-terrorist financing obligations for those agents or outsourcing service providers as part of the institutions or persons covered by this Directive, may only arise from contract and not from this Directive. The responsibility for complying with this Directive should remain with the institution or person covered hereby.

(29) Suspicious transactions should be reported to the financial intelligence unit (FIU), which serves as a national centre for receiving, analysing and disseminating to the competent authorities suspicious transaction reports and other information regarding potential money laundering or terrorist financing. This should not compel Member States to change their existing reporting systems where the reporting is done through a public prosecutor or other law enforcement authorities, as long as the information is forwarded promptly and unfiltered to FIUs, allowing them to conduct their business properly, including international cooperation with other FIUs.

(30) By way of derogation from the general prohibition on executing suspicious transactions, the institutions and persons covered by this Directive may execute suspicious transactions before informing the competent authorities, where refraining from the execution thereof is impossible or likely to frustrate efforts to pursue the beneficiaries of a suspected money laundering or terrorist financing operation. This, however, should be without prejudice to the international obligations accepted by the Member States to freeze without delay funds or other assets of terrorists, terrorist organisations or those who finance terrorism, in accordance with the relevant United Nations Security Council resolutions.

(31) Where a Member State decides to make use of the exemptions provided for in Article 23(2), it may allow or require the self-regulatory body representing the persons referred to therein not to transmit to the FIU any information obtained from those persons in the circumstances referred to in that Article.

(32) There has been a number of cases of employees who report their suspicions of money laundering being subjected to threats or hostile action. Although this Directive cannot interfere with Member States' judicial procedures, this is a crucial issue for the effectiveness of the anti-money laundering and anti-terrorist financing system. Member States should be aware of this problem and should do whatever they can to protect employees from such threats or hostile action.

(33) Disclosure of information as referred to in Article 28 should be in accordance with the rules on transfer of personal data to third countries as laid down in Directive 95/46/EC of the European Parliament and of the Council of 24 October 1995 on the protection of individuals with regard to the processing of personal data and on the free movement of such data.[6] Moreover, Article 28 cannot interfere with national data protection and professional secrecy legislation.

(34) Persons who merely convert paper documents into electronic data and are acting under a contract with a credit institution or a financial institution do not fall within the scope of this Directive, nor does any natural or legal person that provides credit or financial institutions solely with a message or other support systems for transmitting funds or with clearing and settlement systems.

(35) Money laundering and terrorist financing are international problems and the effort to combat them should be global. Where Community credit and financial institutions have branches and subsidiaries located in third countries where the legislation in this area is deficient, they should, in order to avoid the application of very different standards within an institution or group of institutions, apply the Community standard or notify the competent authorities of the home Member State if this application is impossible.

(36) It is important that credit and financial institutions should be able to respond rapidly to requests for information on whether they maintain business relationships with named persons. For the purpose of identifying such business relationships in order to be able to provide that information quickly, credit and financial institutions should have effective systems in place which are commensurate with the size and nature of their business. In particular it would be appropriate for credit institutions and larger financial institutions to have electronic systems at their disposal. This provision is of particular importance in the context of procedures leading to measures such as the freezing or seizing of assets (including terrorist assets), pursuant to applicable national or Community legislation with a view to combating terrorism.

(37) This Directive establishes detailed rules for customer due diligence, including enhanced customer due diligence for high-risk customers or business relationships, such as appropriate procedures to determine whether a person is a politically exposed person, and certain additional, more detailed requirements, such as the existence of compliance management procedures and policies. All these requirements are to be met by each of the institutions and persons covered by this Directive, while Member States are expected to tailor the detailed implementation of those provisions to the particularities of the various professions and to the differences in scale and size of the institutions and persons covered by this Directive.

(38) In order to ensure that the institutions and others subject to Community legislation in this field remain committed, feedback should, where practicable, be made available to them on the usefulness and follow-up of the reports they present. To make this possible, and to be able to review the effectiveness of their systems to combat money laundering and terrorist financing Member States should keep and improve the relevant statistics.

(39) When registering or licensing a currency exchange office, a trust and company service provider or a casino nationally, competent authorities should ensure that the persons who effectively direct or will direct the business of such entities and the beneficial owners of such entities are fit and proper persons. The criteria for determining whether or not a person is fit and proper should be established in conformity with national law. As a minimum, such criteria should reflect the need to protect such entities from being misused by their managers or beneficial owners for criminal purposes.

(40) Taking into account the international character of money laundering and terrorist financing, coordination and cooperation between FIUs as referred to in Council Decision 2000/642/JHA of 17 October 2000 concerning arrangements for cooperation between financial intelligence units of the Member States in respect of exchanging information,[7] including the establishment of an EU FIU-net, should be encouraged to the greatest possible extent. To that end, the Commission should lend such assistance as may be needed to facilitate such coordination, including financial assistance.

---

[6] OJ L 281, 23.11.1995, p. 31. Directive as amended by Regulation (EC) No 1882/2003 (OJ L 284, 31.10.2003, p. 1).
[7] OJ L 271, 24.10.2000, p. 4.

(41) The importance of combating money laundering and terrorist financing should lead Member States to lay down effective, proportionate and dissuasive penalties in national law for failure to respect the national provisions adopted pursuant to this Directive. Provision should be made for penalties in respect of natural and legal persons. Since legal persons are often involved in complex money laundering or terrorist financing operations, sanctions should also be adjusted in line with the activity carried on by legal persons.

(42) Natural persons exercising any of the activities referred to in Article 2(1)(3)(a) and (b) within the structure of a legal person, but on an independent basis, should be independently responsible for compliance with the provisions of this Directive, with the exception of Article 35.

(43) Clarification of the technical aspects of the rules laid down in this Directive may be necessary to ensure an effective and sufficiently consistent implementation of this Directive, taking into account the different financial instruments, professions and risks in the different Member States and the technical developments in the fight against money laundering and terrorist financing. The Commission should accordingly be empowered to adopt implementing measures, such as certain criteria for identifying low and high risk situations in which simplified due diligence could suffice or enhanced due diligence would be appropriate, provided that they do not modify the essential elements of this Directive and provided that the Commission acts in accordance with the principles set out herein, after consulting the Committee on the Prevention of Money Laundering and Terrorist Financing.

(44) The measures necessary for the implementation of this Directive should be adopted in accordance with Council Decision 1999/468/EC of 28 June 1999 laying down the procedures for the exercise of implementing powers conferred on the Commission.[8] To that end a new Committee on the Prevention of Money Laundering and Terrorist Financing, replacing the Money Laundering Contact Committee set up by Directive 91/308/EEC, should be established.

(45) In view of the very substantial amendments that would need to be made to Directive 91/308/EEC, it should be repealed for reasons of clarity.

(46) Since the objective of this Directive, namely the prevention of the use of the financial system for the purpose of money laundering and terrorist financing, cannot be sufficiently achieved by the Member States and can therefore, by reason of the scale and effects of the action, be better achieved at Community level, the Community may adopt measures, in accordance with the principle of subsidiarity as set out in Article 5 of the Treaty. In accordance with the principle of proportionality, as set out in that Article, this Directive does not go beyond what is necessary in order to achieve that objective.

(47) In exercising its implementing powers in accordance with this Directive, the Commission should respect the following principles: the need for high levels of transparency and consultation with institutions and persons covered by this Directive and with the European Parliament and the Council; the need to ensure that competent authorities will be able to ensure compliance with the rules consistently; the balance of costs and benefits to institutions and persons covered by this Directive on a long-term basis in any implementing measures; the need to respect the necessary flexibility in the application of the implementing measures in accordance with a risk-sensitive approach; the need to ensure coherence with other Community legislation in this area; the need to protect the Community, its Member States and their citizens from the consequences of money laundering and terrorist financing.

(48) This Directive respects the fundamental rights and observes the principles recognised in particular by the Charter of Fundamental Rights of the European Union. Nothing in this Directive should be interpreted or implemented in a manner that is inconsistent with the European Convention on Human Rights,

---

[8] OJ L 184, 17.7.1999, p. 23.

HAVE ADOPTED THIS DIRECTIVE:

Chapter I

Subject Matter, Scope and Definitions

ARTICLE 1

1. Member States shall ensure that money laundering and terrorist financing are prohibited.
2. For the purposes of this Directive, the following conduct, when committed intentionally, shall be regarded as money laundering:
   (a) the conversion or transfer of property, knowing that such property is derived from criminal activity or from an act of participation in such activity, for the purpose of concealing or disguising the illicit origin of the property or of assisting any person who is involved in the commission of such activity to evade the legal consequences of his action;
   (b) the concealment or disguise of the true nature, source, location, disposition, movement, rights with respect to, or ownership of property, knowing that such property is derived from criminal activity or from an act of participation in such activity;
   (c) the acquisition, possession or use of property, knowing, at the time of receipt, that such property was derived from criminal activity or from an act of participation in such activity;
   (d) participation in, association to commit, attempts to commit and aiding, abetting, facilitating and counselling the commission of any of the actions mentioned in the foregoing points.
3. Money laundering shall be regarded as such even where the activities which generated the property to be laundered were carried out in the territory of another Member State or in that of a third country.
4. For the purposes of this Directive, 'terrorist financing' means the provision or collection of funds, by any means, directly or indirectly, with the intention that they should be used or in the knowledge that they are to be used, in full or in part, in order to carry out any of the offences within the meaning of Articles 1 to 4 of Council Framework Decision 2002/475/JHA of 13 June 2002 on combating terrorism.[9]
5. Knowledge, intent or purpose required as an element of the activities mentioned in paragraphs 2 and 4 may be inferred from objective factual circumstances.

ARTICLE 2

1. This Directive shall apply to:

   (1) credit institutions;
   (2) financial institutions;
   (3) the following legal or natural persons acting in the exercise of their professional activities:
      (a) auditors, external accountants and tax advisors;
      (b) notaries and other independent legal professionals, when they participate, whether by acting on behalf of and for their client in any financial or real estate transaction, or by assisting in the planning or execution of transactions for their client concerning the:
         (i) buying and selling of real property or business entities;
         (ii) managing of client money, securities or other assets;
         (iii) opening or management of bank, savings or securities accounts;
         (iv) organisation of contributions necessary for the creation, operation or management of companies;
         (v) creation, operation or management of trusts, companies or similar structures;
      (c) trust or company service providers not already covered under points (a) or (b);
      (d) real estate agents;
      (e) other natural or legal persons trading in goods, only to the extent that payments are made in cash in an amount of EUR 15 000 or more, whether the transaction is executed in a single operation or in several operations which appear to be linked;
      (f) casinos.

---

[9] OJ L 164, 22.6.2002, p. 3.

2. Member States may decide that legal and natural persons who engage in a financial activity on an occasional or very limited basis and where there is little risk of money laundering or terrorist financing occurring do not fall within the scope of Article 3(1) or (2).

ARTICLE 3

For the purposes of this Directive the following definitions shall apply:

(1) 'credit institution' means a credit institution, as defined in the first subparagraph of Article 1(1) of Directive 2000/12/EC of the European Parliament and of the Council of 20 March 2000 relating to the taking up and pursuit of the business of credit institutions,[10] including branches within the meaning of Article 1(3) of that Directive located in the Community of credit institutions having their head offices inside or outside the Community;

(2) 'financial institution' means:

(a) an undertaking other than a credit institution which carries out one or more of the operations included in points 2 to 12 and 14 of Annex I to Directive 2000/12/EC, including the activities of currency exchange offices (bureaux de change) and of money transmission or remittance offices;

(b) an insurance company duly authorised in accordance with Directive 2002/83/EC of the European Parliament and of the Council of 5 November 2002 concerning life assurance,[11] insofar as it carries out activities covered by that Directive;

(c) an investment firm as defined in point 1 of Article 4(1) of Directive 2004/39/EC of the European Parliament and of the Council of 21 April 2004 on markets in financial instruments;[12]

(d) a collective investment undertaking marketing its units or shares;

(e) an insurance intermediary as defined in Article 2(5) of Directive 2002/92/EC of the European Parliament and of the Council of 9 December 2002 on insurance mediation,[13] with the exception of intermediaries as mentioned in Article 2(7) of that Directive, when they act in respect of life insurance and other investment related services;

(f) branches, when located in the Community, of financial institutions as referred to in points (a) to (e), whose head offices are inside or outside the Community;

(3) 'property' means assets of every kind, whether corporeal or incorporeal, movable or immovable, tangible or intangible, and legal documents or instruments in any form including electronic or digital, evidencing title to or an interest in such assets;

(4) 'criminal activity' means any kind of criminal involvement in the commission of a serious crime;

(5) 'serious crimes' means, at least:

(a) acts as defined in Articles 1 to 4 of Framework Decision 2002/475/JHA;

(b) any of the offences defined in Article 3(1)(a) of the 1988 United Nations Convention against Illicit Traffic in Narcotic Drugs and Psychotropic Substances;

(c) the activities of criminal organisations as defined in Article 1 of Council Joint Action 98/733/ JHA of 21 December 1998 on making it a criminal offence to participate in a criminal organisation in the Member States of the European Union;[14]

(d) fraud, at least serious, as defined in Article 1(1) and Article 2 of the Convention on the Protection of the European Communities' Financial Interests;[15]

(e) corruption;

(f) all offences which are punishable by deprivation of liberty or a detention order for a maximum of more than one year or, as regards those States which have a minimum threshold for offences in their legal system, all offences punishable by deprivation of liberty or a detention order for a minimum of more than six months;

---

[10] OJ L 126, 26.5.2000, p. 1. Directive as last amended by Directive 2005/1/EC (OJ L 79, 24.3.2005, p. 9).
[11] OJ L 345, 19.12.2002, p. 1. Directive as last amended by Directive 2005/1/EC.
[12] OJ L 145, 30.4.2004, p. 1.
[13] OJ L 9, 15.1.2003, p. 3.
[14] OJ L 351, 29.12.1998, p. 1.
[15] OJ C 316, 27.11.1995, p. 49.

(6) 'beneficial owner' means the natural person(s) who ultimately owns or controls the customer and/ or the natural person on whose behalf a transaction or activity is being conducted. The beneficial owner shall at least include:
  (a) in the case of corporate entities:
    (i) the natural person(s) who ultimately owns or controls a legal entity through direct or indirect ownership or control over a sufficient percentage of the shares or voting rights in that legal entity, including through bearer share holdings, other than a company listed on a regulated market that is subject to disclosure requirements consistent with Community legislation or subject to equivalent international standards; a percentage of 25 % plus one share shall be deemed sufficient to meet this criterion;
    (ii) the natural person(s) who otherwise exercises control over the management of a legal entity:
  (b) in the case of legal entities, such as foundations, and legal arrangements, such as trusts, which administer and distribute funds:
    (i) where the future beneficiaries have already been determined, the natural person(s) who is the beneficiary of 25 % or more of the property of a legal arrangement or entity;
    (ii) where the individuals that benefit from the legal arrangement or entity have yet to be determined, the class of persons in whose main interest the legal arrangement or entity is set up or operates;
    (iii) the natural person(s) who exercises control over 25 % or more of the property of a legal arrangement or entity;
(7) 'trust and company service providers' means any natural or legal person which by way of business provides any of the following services to third parties:
  (a) forming companies or other legal persons;
  (b) acting as or arranging for another person to act as a director or secretary of a company, a partner of a partnership, or a similar position in relation to other legal persons;
  (c) providing a registered office, business address, correspondence or administrative address and other related services for a company, a partnership or any other legal person or arrangement;
  (d) acting as or arranging for another person to act as a trustee of an express trust or a similar legal arrangement;
  (e) acting as or arranging for another person to act as a nominee shareholder for another person other than a company listed on a regulated market that is subject to disclosure requirements in conformity with Community legislation or subject to equivalent international standards;
(8) 'politically exposed persons' means natural persons who are or have been entrusted with prominent public functions and immediate family members, or persons known to be close associates, of such persons;
(9) 'business relationship' means a business, professional or commercial relationship which is connected with the professional activities of the institutions and persons covered by this Directive and which is expected, at the time when the contact is established, to have an element of duration;
(10) 'shell bank' means a credit institution, or an institution engaged in equivalent activities, incorporated in a jurisdiction in which it has no physical presence, involving meaningful mind and management, and which is unaffiliated with a regulated financial group.

Article 4

1. Member States shall ensure that the provisions of this Directive are extended in whole or in part to professions and to categories of undertakings, other than the institutions and persons referred to in Article 2(1), which engage in activities which are particularly likely to be used for money laundering or terrorist financing purposes.

2. Where a Member State decides to extend the provisions of this Directive to professions and to categories of undertakings other than those referred to in Article 2(1), it shall inform the Commission thereof.

Article 5

The Member States may adopt or retain in force stricter provisions in the field covered by this Directive to prevent money laundering and terrorist financing.

Chapter II

Customer Due Diligence

Section 1

General provisions

ARTICLE 6

Member States shall prohibit their credit and financial institutions from keeping anonymous accounts or anonymous passbooks. By way of derogation from Article 9(6), Member States shall in all cases require that the owners and beneficiaries of existing anonymous accounts or anonymous passbooks be made the subject of customer due diligence measures as soon as possible and in any event before such accounts or passbooks are used in any way.

ARTICLE 7

The institutions and persons covered by this Directive shall apply customer due diligence measures in the following cases:

(a) when establishing a business relationship;

(b) when carrying out occasional transactions amounting to EUR 15 000 or more, whether the transaction is carried out in a single operation or in several operations which appear to be linked;

(c) when there is a suspicion of money laundering or terrorist financing, regardless of any derogation, exemption or threshold;

(d) when there are doubts about the veracity or adequacy of previously obtained customer identification data.

ARTICLE 8

1. Customer due diligence measures shall comprise:

(a) identifying the customer and verifying the customer's identity on the basis of documents, data or information obtained from a reliable and independent source;

(b) identifying, where applicable, the beneficial owner and taking risk-based and adequate measures to verify his identity so that the institution or person covered by this Directive is satisfied that it knows who the beneficial owner is, including, as regards legal persons, trusts and similar legal arrangements, taking risk-based and adequate measures to understand the ownership and control structure of the customer;

(c) obtaining information on the purpose and intended nature of the business relationship;

(d) conducting ongoing monitoring of the business relationship including scrutiny of transactions undertaken throughout the course of that relationship to ensure that the transactions being conducted are consistent with the institution's or person's knowledge of the customer, the business and risk profile, including, where necessary, the source of funds and ensuring that the documents, data or information held are kept up-to-date.

2. The institutions and persons covered by this Directive shall apply each of the customer due diligence requirements set out in paragraph 1, but may determine the extent of such measures on a risk-sensitive basis depending on the type of customer, business relationship, product or transaction. The institutions and persons covered by this Directive shall be able to demonstrate to the competent authorities mentioned in Article 37, including self-regulatory bodies, that the extent of the measures is appropriate in view of the risks of money laundering and terrorist financing.

ARTICLE 9

1. Member States shall require that the verification of the identity of the customer and the beneficial owner takes place before the establishment of a business relationship or the carrying-out of the transaction.

2. By way of derogation from paragraph 1, Member States may allow the verification of the identity of the customer and the beneficial owner to be completed during the establishment of a business relationship if this is necessary not to interrupt the normal conduct of business and where there is little risk of money laundering or terrorist financing occurring. In such situations these procedures shall be completed as soon as practicable after the initial contact.

3. By way of derogation from paragraphs 1 and 2, Member States may, in relation to life insurance business, allow the verification of the identity of the beneficiary under the policy to take place after the business relationship has been established. In that case, verification shall take place at or before the time of payout or at or before the time the beneficiary intends to exercise rights vested under the policy.

4. By way of derogation from paragraphs 1 and 2, Member States may allow the opening of a bank account provided that there are adequate safeguards in place to ensure that transactions are not carried out by the customer or on its behalf until full compliance with the aforementioned provisions is obtained.

5. Member States shall require that, where the institution or person concerned is unable to comply with points (a), (b) and (c) of Article 8(1), it may not carry out a transaction through a bank account, establish a business relationship or carry out the transaction, or shall terminate the business relationship, and shall consider making a report to the financial intelligence unit (FIU) in accordance with Article 22 in relation to the customer. Member States shall not be obliged to apply the previous subparagraph in situations when notaries, independent legal professionals, auditors, external accountants and tax advisors are in the course of ascertaining the legal position for their client or performing their task of defending or representing that client in, or concerning judicial proceedings, including advice on instituting or avoiding proceedings.

6. Member States shall require that institutions and persons covered by this Directive apply the customer due diligence procedures not only to all new customers but also at appropriate times to existing customers on a risk-sensitive basis.

ARTICLE 10

1. Member States shall require that all casino customers be identified and their identity verified if they purchase or exchange gambling chips with a value of EUR 2 000 or more.

2. Casinos subject to State supervision shall be deemed in any event to have satisfied the customer due diligence requirements if they register, identify and verify the identity of their customers immediately on or before entry, regardless of the amount of gambling chips purchased.

Section 2
Simplified customer due diligence

ARTICLE 11

1. By way of derogation from Articles 7(a), (b) and (d), 8 and 9(1), the institutions and persons covered by this Directive shall not be subject to the requirements provided for in those Articles where the customer is a credit or financial institution covered by this Directive, or a credit or financial institution situated in a third country which imposes requirements equivalent to those laid down in this Directive and supervised for compliance with those requirements.

2. By way of derogation from Articles 7(a), (b) and (d), 8 and 9(1) Member States may allow the institutions and persons covered by this Directive not to apply customer due diligence in respect of:

(a) listed companies whose securities are admitted to trading on a regulated market within the meaning of Directive 2004/39/EC in one or more Member States and listed companies from third countries which are subject to disclosure requirements consistent with Community legislation;

(b) beneficial owners of pooled accounts held by notaries and other independent legal professionals from the Member States, or from third countries provided that they are subject to requirements to combat money laundering or terrorist financing consistent with international standards and are supervised for compliance with those requirements and provided that the information on the identity of the beneficial owner is available, on request, to the institutions that act as depository institutions for the pooled accounts;

(c) domestic public authorities,

or in respect of any other customer representing a low risk of money laundering or terrorist financing which meets the technical criteria established in accordance with Article 40(1)(b).

3. In the cases mentioned in paragraphs 1 and 2, institutions and persons covered by this Directive shall in any case gather sufficient information to establish if the customer qualifies for an exemption as mentioned in these paragraphs.

4. The Member States shall inform each other and the Commission of cases where they consider that a third country meets the conditions laid down in paragraphs 1 or 2 or in other situations which meet the technical criteria established in accordance with Article 40(1)(b).

5. By way of derogation from Articles 7(a), (b) and (d), 8 and 9(1), Member States may allow the institutions and persons covered by this Directive not to apply customer due diligence in respect of:

    (a) life insurance policies where the annual premium is no more than EUR 1 000 or the single premium is no more than EUR 2 500;

    (b) insurance policies for pension schemes if there is no surrender clause and the policy cannot be used as collateral;

    (c) a pension, superannuation or similar scheme that provides retirement benefits to employees, where contributions are made by way of deduction from wages and the scheme rules do not permit the assignment of a member's interest under the scheme;

    (d) electronic money, as defined in Article 1(3)(b) of Directive 2000/46/EC of the European Parliament and of the Council of 18 September 2000 on the taking up, pursuit of and prudential supervision of the business of electronic money institutions,[16] where, if the device cannot be recharged, the maximum amount stored in the device is no more than EUR 150, or where, if the device can be recharged, a limit of EUR 2 500 is imposed on the total amount transacted in a calendar year, except when an amount of EUR 1 000 or more is redeemed in that same calendar year by the bearer as referred to in Article 3 of Directive 2000/46/EC, or in respect of any other product or transaction representing a low risk of money laundering or terrorist financing which meets the technical criteria established in accordance with Article 40(1)(b).

ARTICLE 12

Where the Commission adopts a decision pursuant to Article 40(4), the Member States shall prohibit the institutions and persons covered by this Directive from applying simplified due diligence to credit and financial institutions or listed companies from the third country concerned or other entities following from situations which meet the technical criteria established in accordance with Article 40(1)(b).

Section 3

Enhanced customer due diligence

ARTICLE 13

1. Member States shall require the institutions and persons covered by this Directive to apply, on a risk-sensitive basis, enhanced customer due diligence measures, in addition to the measures referred to in Articles 7, 8 and 9(6), in situations which by their nature can present a higher risk of money laundering or terrorist financing, and at least in the situations set out in paragraphs 2, 3, 4 and in other situations representing a high risk of money laundering or terrorist financing which meet the technical criteria established in accordance with Article 40(1)(c).

2. Where the customer has not been physically present for identification purposes, Member States shall require those institutions and persons to take specific and adequate measures to compensate for the higher risk, for example by applying one or more of the following measures:

    (a) ensuring that the customer's identity is established by additional documents, data or information;

    (b) supplementary measures to verify or certify the documents supplied, or requiring confirmatory certification by a credit or financial institution covered by this Directive;

---

[16] OJ L 275, 27.10.2000, p. 39.

(c) ensuring that the first payment of the operations is carried out through an account opened in the customer's name with a credit institution.

3. In respect of cross-frontier correspondent banking relationships with respondent institutions from third countries, Member States shall require their credit institutions to:

(a) gather sufficient information about a respondent institution to understand fully the nature of the respondent's business and to determine from publicly available information the reputation of the institution and the quality of supervision;

(b) assess the respondent institution's anti-money laundering and anti-terrorist financing controls;

(c) obtain approval from senior management before establishing new correspondent banking relationships;

(d) document the respective responsibilities of each institution;

(e) with respect to payable-through accounts, be satisfied that the respondent credit institution has verified the identity of and performed ongoing due diligence on the customers having direct access to accounts of the correspondent and that it is able to provide relevant customer due diligence data to the correspondent institution, upon request.

4. In respect of transactions or business relationships with politically exposed persons residing in another Member State or in a third country, Member States shall require those institutions and persons covered by this Directive to:

(a) have appropriate risk-based procedures to determine whether the customer is a politically exposed person;

(b) have senior management approval for establishing business relationships with such customers;

(c) take adequate measures to establish the source of wealth and source of funds that are involved in the business relationship or transaction;

(d) conduct enhanced ongoing monitoring of the business relationship.

5. Member States shall prohibit credit institutions from entering into or continuing a correspondent banking relationship with a shell bank and shall require that credit institutions take appropriate measures to ensure that they do not engage in or continue correspondent banking relationships with a bank that is known to permit its accounts to be used by a shell bank.

6. Member States shall ensure that the institutions and persons covered by this Directive pay special attention to any money laundering or terrorist financing threat that may arise from products or transactions that might favour anonymity, and take measures, if needed, to prevent their use for money laundering or terrorist financing purposes.

Section 4

Performance by third parties

ARTICLE 14

Member States may permit the institutions and persons covered by this Directive to rely on third parties to meet the requirements laid down in Article 8(1)(a) to (c). However, the ultimate responsibility for meeting those requirements shall remain with the institution or person covered by this Directive which relies on the third party.

ARTICLE 15

1. Where a Member State permits credit and financial institutions referred to in Article 2(1)(1) or (2) situated in its territory to be relied on as a third party domestically, that Member State shall in any case permit institutions and persons referred to in Article 2(1) situated in its territory to recognise and accept, in accordance with the provisions laid down in Article 14, the outcome of the customer due diligence requirements laid down in Article 8(1)(a) to (c), carried out in accordance with this Directive by an institution referred to in Article 2(1)(1) or (2) in another Member State, with the exception of currency exchange offices and money transmission or remittance offices, and meeting the requirements laid down in Articles 16 and 18, even if the documents or data on which these requirements have been based are different to those required in the Member State to which the customer is being referred.

2. Where a Member State permits currency exchange offices and money transmission or remittance offices referred to in Article 3(2)(a) situated in its territory to be relied on as a third party domestically, that Member State shall in any case permit them to recognise and accept, in accordance with Article 14, the outcome of the customer due diligence requirements laid down in Article 8(1)(a) to (c), carried out in accordance with this Directive by the same category of institution in another Member State and meeting the requirements laid down in Articles 16 and 18, even if the documents or data on which these requirements have been based are different to those required in the Member State to which the customer is being referred.

3. Where a Member State permits persons referred to in Article 2(1)(3)(a) to (c) situated in its territory to be relied on as a third party domestically, that Member State shall in any case permit them to recognise and accept, in accordance with Article 14, the outcome of the customer due diligence requirements laid down in Article 8(1)(a) to (c), carried out in accordance with this Directive by a person referred to in Article 2(1)(3)(a) to (c) in another Member State and meeting the requirements laid down in Articles 16 and 18, even if the documents or data on which these requirements have been based are different to those required in the Member State to which the customer is being referred.

ARTICLE 16

1. For the purposes of this Section, 'third parties' shall mean institutions and persons who are listed in Article 2, or equivalent institutions and persons situated in a third country, who meet the following requirements:

(a) they are subject to mandatory professional registration, recognised by law;
(b) they apply customer due diligence requirements and record keeping requirements as laid down or equivalent to those laid down in this Directive and their compliance with the requirements of this Directive is supervised in accordance with Section 2 of Chapter V, or they are situated in a third country which imposes equivalent requirements to those laid down in this Directive.

2. Member States shall inform each other and the Commission of cases where they consider that a third country meets the conditions laid down in paragraph 1(b).

ARTICLE 17

Where the Commission adopts a decision pursuant to Article 40(4), Member States shall prohibit the institutions and persons covered by this Directive from relying on third parties from the third country concerned to meet the requirements laid down in Article 8(1)(a) to (c).

ARTICLE 18

1. Third parties shall make information requested in accordance with the requirements laid down in Article 8(1)(a) to (c) immediately available to the institution or person covered by this Directive to which the customer is being referred.

2. Relevant copies of identification and verification data and other relevant documentation on the identity of the customer or the beneficial owner shall immediately be forwarded, on request, by the third party to the institution or person covered by this Directive to which the customer is being referred.

ARTICLE 19

This Section shall not apply to outsourcing or agency relationships where, on the basis of a contractual arrangement, the outsourcing service provider or agent is to be regarded as part of the institution or person covered by this Directive.

Chapter III

Reporting Obligations

Section 1

General provisions

ARTICLE 20

Member States shall require that the institutions and persons covered by this Directive pay special attention to any activity which they regard as particularly likely, by its nature, to be related to money laundering or terrorist financing and in particular complex or unusually large transactions and all unusual patterns of transactions which have no apparent economic or visible lawful purpose.

ARTICLE 21

1. Each Member State shall establish a FIU in order effectively to combat money laundering and terrorist financing.

2. That FIU shall be established as a central national unit. It shall be responsible for receiving (and to the extent permitted, requesting), analysing and disseminating to the competent authorities, disclosures of information which concern potential money laundering, potential terrorist financing or are required by national legislation or regulation. It shall be provided with adequate resources in order to fulfil its tasks.

3. Member States shall ensure that the FIU has access, directly or indirectly, on a timely basis, to the financial, administrative and law enforcement information that it requires to properly fulfil its tasks.

ARTICLE 22

1. Member States shall require the institutions and persons covered by this Directive, and where applicable their directors and employees, to cooperate fully:

    (a) by promptly informing the FIU, on their own initiative, where the institution or person covered by this Directive knows, suspects or has reasonable grounds to suspect that money laundering or terrorist financing is being or has been committed or attempted;

    (b) by promptly furnishing the FIU, at its request, with all necessary information, in accordance with the procedures established by the applicable legislation.

2. The information referred to in paragraph 1 shall be forwarded to the FIU of the Member State in whose territory the institution or person forwarding the information is situated. The person or persons designated in accordance with the procedures provided for in Article 34 shall normally forward the information.

ARTICLE 23

1. By way of derogation from Article 22(1), Member States may, in the case of the persons referred to in Article 2(1)(3)(a) and (b), designate an appropriate self-regulatory body of the profession concerned as the authority to be informed in the first instance in place of the FIU. Without prejudice to paragraph 2, the designated self-regulatory body shall in such cases forward the information to the FIU promptly and unfiltered.

2. Member States shall not be obliged to apply the obligations laid down in Article 22(1) to notaries, independent legal professionals, auditors, external accountants and tax advisors with regard to information they receive from or obtain on one of their clients, in the course of ascertaining the legal position for their client or performing their task of defending or representing that client in, or concerning judicial proceedings, including advice on instituting or avoiding proceedings, whether such information is received or obtained before, during or after such proceedings.

ARTICLE 24

1. Member States shall require the institutions and persons covered by this Directive to refrain from carrying out transactions which they know or suspect to be related to money laundering or terrorist financing until they have completed the necessary action in accordance with Article 22(1)(a). In conformity with the legislation of the Member States, instructions may be given not to carry out the transaction.

2. Where such a transaction is suspected of giving rise to money laundering or terrorist financing and where to refrain in such manner is impossible or is likely to frustrate efforts to pursue the beneficiaries of a suspected money laundering or terrorist financing operation, the institutions and persons concerned shall inform the FIU immediately afterwards.

ARTICLE 25

1. Member States shall ensure that if, in the course of inspections carried out in the institutions and persons covered by this Directive by the competent authorities referred to in Article 37, or in any other way, those authorities discover facts that could be related to money laundering or terrorist financing, they shall promptly inform the FIU.

2. Member States shall ensure that supervisory bodies empowered by law or regulation to oversee the stock, foreign exchange and financial derivatives markets inform the FIU if they discover facts that could be related to money laundering or terrorist financing.

ARTICLE 26

The disclosure in good faith as foreseen in Articles 22(1) and 23 by an institution or person covered by this Directive or by an employee or director of such an institution or person of the information referred to in Articles 22 and 23 shall not constitute a breach of any restriction on disclosure of information imposed by contract or by any legislative, regulatory or administrative provision, and shall not involve the institution or person or its directors or employees in liability of any kind.

ARTICLE 27

Member States shall take all appropriate measures in order to protect employees of the institutions or persons covered by this Directive who report suspicions of money laundering or terrorist financing either internally or to the FIU from being exposed to threats or hostile action.

Section 2

Prohibition of disclosure

ARTICLE 28

1. The institutions and persons covered by this Directive and their directors and employees shall not disclose to the customer concerned or to other third persons the fact that information has been transmitted in accordance with Articles 22 and 23 or that a money laundering or terrorist financing investigation is being or may be carried out.

2. The prohibition laid down in paragraph 1 shall not include disclosure to the competent authorities referred to in Article 37, including the self-regulatory bodies, or disclosure for law enforcement purposes.

3. The prohibition laid down in paragraph 1 shall not prevent disclosure between institutions from Member States, or from third countries provided that they meet the conditions laid down in Article 11(1), belonging to the same group as defined by Article 2(12) of Directive 2002/87/EC of the European Parliament and of the Council of 16 December 2002 on the supplementary supervision of credit institutions, insurance undertakings and investment firms in a financial conglomerate.[17]

---

[17] OJ L 35, 11.2.2003, p. 1.

4. The prohibition laid down in paragraph 1 shall not prevent disclosure between persons referred to in Article 2(1)(3)(a) and (b) from Member States, or from third countries which impose requirements equivalent to those laid down in this Directive, who perform their professional activities, whether as employees or not, within the same legal person or a network. For the purposes of this Article, a 'network' means the larger structure to which the person belongs and which shares common ownership, management or compliance control.

5. For institutions or persons referred to in Article 2(1)(1), (2) and (3)(a) and (b) in cases related to the same customer and the same transaction involving two or more institutions or persons, the prohibition laid down in paragraph 1 shall not prevent disclosure between the relevant institutions or persons provided that they are situated in a Member State, or in a third country which imposes requirements equivalent to those laid down in this Directive, and that they are from the same professional category and are subject to equivalent obligations as regards professional secrecy and personal data protection. The information exchanged shall be used exclusively for the purposes of the prevention of money laundering and terrorist financing.

6. Where the persons referred to in Article 2(1)(3)(a) and (b) seek to dissuade a client from engaging in illegal activity, this shall not constitute a disclosure within the meaning of the paragraph 1.

7. The Member States shall inform each other and the Commission of cases where they consider that a third country meets the conditions laid down in paragraphs 3, 4 or 5.

ARTICLE 29

Where the Commission adopts a decision pursuant to Article 40(4), the Member States shall prohibit the disclosure between institutions and persons covered by this Directive and institutions and persons from the third country concerned.

Chapter IV

Record Keeping and Statistical Data

ARTICLE 30

Member States shall require the institutions and persons covered by this Directive to keep the following documents and information for use in any investigation into, or analysis of, possible money laundering or terrorist financing by the FIU or by other competent authorities in accordance with national law:

(a) in the case of the customer due diligence, a copy or the references of the evidence required, for a period of at least five years after the business relationship with their customer has ended;

(b) in the case of business relationships and transactions, the supporting evidence and records, consisting of the original documents or copies admissible in court proceedings under the applicable national legislation for a period of at least five years following the carrying-out of the transactions or the end of the business relationship.

ARTICLE 31

1. Member States shall require the credit and financial institutions covered by this Directive to apply, where applicable, in their branches and majority-owned subsidiaries located in third countries measures at least equivalent to those laid down in this Directive with regard to customer due diligence and record keeping. Where the legislation of the third country does not permit application of such equivalent measures, the Member States shall require the credit and financial institutions concerned to inform the competent authorities of the relevant home Member State accordingly.

2. Member States and the Commission shall inform each other of cases where the legislation of the third country does not permit application of the measures required under the first subparagraph of paragraph 1 and coordinated action could be taken to pursue a solution.

3. Member States shall require that, where the legislation of the third country does not permit application of the measures required under the first subparagraph of paragraph 1, credit or financial institutions take additional measures to effectively handle the risk of money laundering or terrorist financing.

ARTICLE 32

Member States shall require that their credit and financial institutions have systems in place that enable them to respond fully and rapidly to enquiries from the FIU, or from other authorities, in accordance with their national law, as to whether they maintain or have maintained during the previous five years a business relationship with specified natural or legal persons and on the nature of that relationship.

ARTICLE 33

1. Member States shall ensure that they are able to review the effectiveness of their systems to combat money laundering or terrorist financing by maintaining comprehensive statistics on matters relevant to the effectiveness of such systems.

2. Such statistics shall as a minimum cover the number of suspicious transaction reports made to the FIU, the follow-up given to these reports and indicate on an annual basis the number of cases investigated, the number of persons prosecuted, the number of persons convicted for money laundering or terrorist financing offences and how much property has been frozen, seized or confiscated.

3. Member States shall ensure that a consolidated review of these statistical reports is published.

Chapter V

Enforcement Measures

Section 1

Internal procedures, training and feedback

ARTICLE 34

1. Member States shall require that the institutions and persons covered by this Directive establish adequate and appropriate policies and procedures of customer due diligence, reporting, record keeping, internal control, risk assessment, risk management, compliance management and communication in order to forestall and prevent operations related to money laundering or terrorist financing.

2. Member States shall require that credit and financial institutions covered by this Directive communicate relevant policies and procedures where applicable to branches and majority owned subsidiaries in third countries.

ARTICLE 35

1. Member States shall require that the institutions and persons covered by this Directive take appropriate measures so that their relevant employees are aware of the provisions in force on the basis of this Directive. These measures shall include participation of their relevant employees in special ongoing training programmes to help them recognise operations which may be related to money laundering or terrorist financing and to instruct them as to how to proceed in such cases. Where a natural person falling within any of the categories listed in Article 2(1)(3) performs his professional activities as an employee of a legal person, the obligations in this Section shall apply to that legal person rather than to the natural person.

2. Member States shall ensure that the institutions and persons covered by this Directive have access to up-to-date information on the practices of money launderers and terrorist financers and on indications leading to the recognition of suspicious transactions.

3. Member States shall ensure that, wherever practicable, timely feedback on the effectiveness of and follow-up to reports of suspected money laundering or terrorist financing is provided.

Section 2

Supervision

ARTICLE 36

1. Member States shall provide that currency exchange offices and trust and company service providers shall be licensed or registered and casinos be licensed in order to operate their business legally.

Without prejudice to future Community legislation, Member States shall provide that money transmission or remittance offices shall be licensed or registered in order to operate their business legally.

2. Member States shall require competent authorities to refuse licensing or registration of the entities referred to in paragraph 1 if they are not satisfied that the persons who effectively direct or will direct the business of such entities or the beneficial owners of such entities are fit and proper persons.

ARTICLE 37

1. Member States shall require the competent authorities at least to effectively monitor and to take the necessary measures with a view to ensuring compliance with the requirements of this Directive by all the institutions and persons covered by this Directive.

2. Member States shall ensure that the competent authorities have adequate powers, including the power to compel the production of any information that is relevant to monitoring compliance and perform checks, and have adequate resources to perform their functions.

3. In the case of credit and financial institutions and casinos, competent authorities shall have enhanced supervisory powers, notably the possibility to conduct on-site inspections.

4. In the case of the natural and legal persons referred to in Article 2(1)(3)(a) to (e), Member States may allow the functions referred to in paragraph 1 to be performed on a risk-sensitive basis.

5. In the case of the persons referred to in Article 2(1)(3)(a) and (b), Member States may allow the functions referred to in paragraph 1 to be performed by self-regulatory bodies, provided that they comply with paragraph 2.

Section 3

Cooperation

ARTICLE 38

The Commission shall lend such assistance as may be needed to facilitate coordination, including the exchange of information between FIUs within the Community.

Section 4

Penalties

ARTICLE 39

1. Member States shall ensure that natural and legal persons covered by this Directive can be held liable for infringements of the national provisions adopted pursuant to this Directive. The penalties must be effective, proportionate and dissuasive.

2. Without prejudice to the right of Member States to impose criminal penalties, Member States shall ensure, in conformity with their national law, that the appropriate administrative measures can be taken or administrative sanctions can be imposed against credit and financial institutions for infringements of the national provisions adopted pursuant to this Directive. Member States shall ensure that these measures or sanctions are effective, proportionate and dissuasive.

3. In the case of legal persons, Member States shall ensure that at least they can be held liable for infringements referred to in paragraph 1 which are committed for their benefit by any person, acting either individually or as part of an organ of the legal person, who has a leading position within the legal person, based on:

(a) a power of representation of the legal person;
(b) an authority to take decisions on behalf of the legal person, or
(c) an authority to exercise control within the legal person.

4. In addition to the cases already provided for in paragraph 3, Member States shall ensure that legal persons can be held liable where the lack of supervision or control by a person referred to in paragraph 3 has made possible the commission of the infringements referred to in paragraph 1 for the benefit of a legal person by a person under its authority.

Chapter VI

Implementing Measures

ARTICLE 40

1. In order to take account of technical developments in the fight against money laundering or terrorist financing and to ensure uniform implementation of this Directive, the Commission may, in accordance with the procedure referred to in Article 41(2), adopt the following implementing measures:

    (a) clarification of the technical aspects of the definitions in Article 3(2)(a) and (d), (6), (7), (8), (9) and (10);

    (b) establishment of technical criteria for assessing whether situations represent a low risk of money laundering or terrorist financing as referred to in Article 11(2) and (5);

    (c) establishment of technical criteria for assessing whether situations represent a high risk of money laundering or terrorist financing as referred to in Article 13;

    (d) establishment of technical criteria for assessing whether, in accordance with Article 2(2), it is justified not to apply this Directive to certain legal or natural persons carrying out a financial activity on an occasional or very limited basis.

2. In any event, the Commission shall adopt the first implementing measures to give effect to paragraphs 1(b) and 1(d) by 15 June 2006.

3. The Commission shall, in accordance with the procedure referred to in Article 41(2), adapt the amounts referred to in Articles 2(1)(3)(e), 7(b), 10(1) and 11(5)(a) and (d) taking into account Community legislation, economic developments and changes in international standards.

4. Where the Commission finds that a third country does not meet the conditions laid down in Article 11(1) or (2), Article 28(3), (4) or (5), or in the measures established in accordance with paragraph 1(b) of this Article or in Article 16(1)(b), or that the legislation of that third country does not permit application of the measures required under the first subparagraph of Article 31(1), it shall adopt a decision so stating in accordance with the procedure referred to in Article 41(2).

ARTICLE 41

1. The Commission shall be assisted by a Committee on the Prevention of Money Laundering and Terrorist Financing, hereinafter 'the Committee'.

2. Where reference is made to this paragraph, Articles 5 and 7 of Decision 1999/468/EC shall apply, having regard to the provisions of Article 8 thereof and provided that the implementing measures adopted in accordance with this procedure do not modify the essential provisions of this Directive. The period laid down in Article 5(6) of Decision 1999/468/EC shall be set at three months.

3. The Committee shall adopt its Rules of Procedure.

4. Without prejudice to the implementing measures already adopted, the implementation of the provisions of this Directive concerning the adoption of technical rules and decisions in accordance with the procedure referred to in paragraph 2 shall be suspended four years after the entry into force of this Directive. On a proposal from the Commission, the European Parliament and the Council may renew the provisions concerned in accordance with the procedure laid down in Article 251 of the Treaty and, to that end, shall review them prior to the expiry of the four-year period.

Chapter VII

Final Provisions

ARTICLE 42

By 15 December 2009, and at least at three-yearly intervals thereafter, the Commission shall draw up a report on the implementation of this Directive and submit it to the European Parliament and the Council. For the first such report, the Commission shall include a specific examination of the treatment of lawyers and other independent legal professionals.

ARTICLE 43

By 15 December 2010, the Commission shall present a report to the European Parliament and to the Council on the threshold percentages in Article 3(6), paying particular attention to the possible expediency and consequences of a reduction of the percentage in points (a)(i), (b)(i) and (b)(iii) of Article 3(6) from 25 % to 20 %. On the basis of the report the Commission may submit a proposal for amendments to this Directive.

ARTICLE 44

Directive 91/308/EEC is hereby repealed.

References made to the repealed Directive shall be construed as being made to this Directive and should be read in accordance with the correlation table set out in the Annex.

ARTICLE 45

1. Member States shall bring into force the laws, regulations and administrative provisions necessary to comply with this Directive by 15 December 2007. They shall forthwith communicate to the Commission the text of those provisions together with a table showing how the provisions of this Directive correspond to the national provisions adopted. When Member States adopt those measures, they shall contain a reference to this Directive or be accompanied by such a reference on the occasion of their official publication. The methods of making such reference shall be laid down by Member States.

2. Member States shall communicate to the Commission the text of the main provisions of national law which they adopt in the field covered by this Directive.

ARTICLE 46

This Directive shall enter into force on the 20th day after its publication in the *Official Journal of the European Union*.

ARTICLE 47

This Directive is addressed to the Member States.

Done at Strasbourg, 26 October 2005.

For the European Parliament   *For the Council*

The President   *The President*

J. BORRELL FONTELLES   D. ALEXANDER

FATF 40 Recommendations

October 2003
(incorporating all subsequent amendments until October 2004)

Introduction

Money laundering methods and techniques change in response to developing counter-measures. In recent years, the Financial Action Task Force (FATF)[1] has noted increasingly sophisticated combinations of techniques, such as the increased use of legal persons to disguise the true ownership and control of illegal proceeds, and an increased use of professionals to provide advice and assistance in laundering criminal funds. These factors, combined with the experience gained through the FATF's Non-Cooperative Countries and Territories process, and a number of national and international initiatives, led the FATF to review and revise the Forty Recommendations into a new comprehensive framework for combating money laundering and terrorist financing. The FATF now calls upon all countries to take the necessary steps to bring their national systems for combating money laundering and terrorist financing into compliance with the new FATF Recommendations, and to effectively implement these measures.

The review process for revising the Forty Recommendations was an extensive one, open to FATF members, non-members, observers, financial and other affected sectors and interested parties. This consultation process provided a wide range of input, all of which was considered in the review process.

The revised Forty Recommendations now apply not only to money laundering but also to terrorist financing, and when combined with the Eight Special Recommendations on Terrorist Financing provide an enhanced, comprehensive and consistent framework of measures for combating money laundering and terrorist financing. The FATF recognises that countries have diverse legal and financial systems and so all cannot take identical measures to achieve the common objective, especially over matters of detail. The Recommendations therefore set minimum standards for action for countries to implement the detail according to their particular circumstances and constitutional frameworks. The Recommendations cover all the measures that national systems should have in place within their criminal justice and regulatory systems; the preventive measures to be taken by financial institutions and certain other businesses and professions; and international co-operation.

The original FATF Forty Recommendations were drawn up in 1990 as an initiative to combat the misuse of financial systems by persons laundering drug money. In 1996 the Recommendations were revised for the first time to reflect evolving money laundering typologies. The 1996 Forty Recommendations have been endorsed by more than 130 countries and are the international anti-money laundering standard.

In October 2001 the FATF expanded its mandate to deal with the issue of the financing of terrorism, and took the important step of creating the Eight Special Recommendations on Terrorist Financing.

---

[1] The FATF is an inter-governmental body which sets standards, and develops and promotes policies to combat money laundering and terrorist financing. It currently has 36 members: 34 countries and governments and two international organisations; and more than 20 observers: five FATF-style regional bodies and more than 15 other international organisations or bodies. A list of all members and observers can be found on the FATF website at www.fatf-gafi.org.

These Recommendations contain a set of measures aimed at combating the funding of terrorist acts and terrorist organisations, and are complementary to the Forty Recommendations.[2]

A key element in the fight against money laundering and the financing of terrorism is the need for countries systems to be monitored and evaluated, with respect to these international standards. The mutual evaluations conducted by the FATF and FATF-style regional bodies, as well as the assessments conducted by the IMF and World Bank, are a vital mechanism for ensuring that the FATF Recommendations are effectively implemented by all countries.

The Forty Recommendations

A. Legal Systems

Scope of the criminal offence of money laundering

1. Countries should criminalise money laundering on the basis of the United Nations Convention against Illicit Traffic in Narcotic Drugs and Psychotropic Substances, 1988 (the Vienna Convention) and the United Nations Convention against Transnational Organized Crime, 2000 (the Palermo Convention).

Countries should apply the crime of money laundering to all serious offences, with a view to including the widest range of predicate offences. Predicate offences may be described by reference to all offences, or to a threshold linked either to a category of serious offences or to the penalty of imprisonment applicable to the predicate offence (threshold approach), or to a list of predicate offences, or a combination of these approaches.

Where countries apply a threshold approach, predicate offences should at a minimum comprise all offences that fall within the category of serious offences under their national law or should include offences which are punishable by a maximum penalty of more than one year's imprisonment or for those countries that have a minimum threshold for offences in their legal system, predicate offences should comprise all offences, which are punished by a minimum penalty of more than six months imprisonment.

Whichever approach is adopted, each country should at a minimum include a range of offences within each of the designated categories of offences.[3]

Predicate offences for money laundering should extend to conduct that occurred in another country, which constitutes an offence in that country, and which would have constituted a predicate offence had it occurred domestically. Countries may provide that the only prerequisite is that the conduct would have constituted a predicate offence had it occurred domestically.

Countries may provide that the offence of money laundering does not apply to persons who committed the predicate offence, where this is required by fundamental principles of their domestic law.

2. Countries should ensure that:

a) The intent and knowledge required to prove the offence of money laundering is consistent with the standards set forth in the Vienna and Palermo Conventions, including the concept that such mental state may be inferred from objective factual circumstances.

b) Criminal liability, and, where that is not possible, civil or administrative liability, should apply to legal persons. This should not preclude parallel criminal, civil or administrative proceedings with respect to legal persons in countries in which such forms of liability are available. Legal persons should be subject to effective, proportionate and dissuasive sanctions. Such measures should be without prejudice to the criminal liability of individuals.

Provisional measures and confiscation

3. Countries should adopt measures similar to those set forth in the Vienna and Palermo Conventions, including legislative measures, to enable their competent authorities to confiscate property laundered, proceeds from money laundering or predicate offences, instrumentalities used in or intended for use in

---

[2] The FATF Forty and Eight Special Recommendations have been recognised by the International Monetary Fund and the World Bank as the international standards for combating money laundering and the financing of terrorism.

[3] See the definition of "designated categories of offences" in the Glossary.

* Recommendations marked with an asterisk should be read in conjunction with their Interpretative Note.

the commission of these offences, or property of corresponding value, without prejudicing the rights of bona fide third parties.

Such measures should include the authority to: (a) identify, trace and evaluate property which is subject to confiscation; (b) carry out provisional measures, such as freezing and seizing, to prevent any dealing, transfer or disposal of such property; (c) take steps that will prevent or void actions that prejudice the State's ability to recover property that is subject to confiscation; and (d) take any appropriate investigative measures.

Countries may consider adopting measures that allow such proceeds or instrumentalities to be confiscated without requiring a criminal conviction, or which require an offender to demonstrate the lawful origin of the property alleged to be liable to confiscation, to the extent that such a requirement is consistent with the principles of their domestic law.

B. Measures to be Taken by Financial Institutions and Non-Financial Businesses and Professions to Prevent Money Laundering and Terrorist Financing

4. Countries should ensure that financial institution secrecy laws do not inhibit implementation of the FATF Recommendations.

Customer due diligence and record-keeping

5.* Financial institutions should not keep anonymous accounts or accounts in obviously fictitious names.

Financial institutions should undertake customer due diligence measures, including identifying and verifying the identity of their customers, when:

- establishing business relations;
- carrying out occasional transactions: (i) above the applicable designated threshold; or (ii) that are wire transfers in the circumstances covered by the Interpretative Note to Special Recommendation VII;
- there is a suspicion of money laundering or terrorist financing; or
- the financial institution has doubts about the veracity or adequacy of previously obtained customer identification data.

The customer due diligence (CDD) measures to be taken are as follows:

a) Identifying the customer and verifying that customer's identity using reliable, independent source documents, data or information.[4]
b) Identifying the beneficial owner, and taking reasonable measures to verify the identity of the beneficial owner such that the financial institution is satisfied that it knows who the beneficial owner is. For legal persons and arrangements this should include financial institutions taking reasonable measures to understand the ownership and control structure of the customer.
c) Obtaining information on the purpose and intended nature of the business relationship.
d) Conducting ongoing due diligence on the business relationship and scrutiny of transactions undertaken throughout the course of that relationship to ensure that the transactions being conducted are consistent with the institution's knowledge of the customer, their business and risk profile, including, where necessary, the source of funds.

Financial institutions should apply each of the CDD measures under (a) to (d) above, but may determine the extent of such measures on a risk sensitive basis depending on the type of customer, business relationship or transaction. The measures that are taken should be consistent with any guidelines issued by competent authorities. For higher risk categories, financial institutions should perform enhanced due diligence. In certain circumstances, where there are low risks, countries may decide that financial institutions can apply reduced or simplified measures.

Financial institutions should verify the identity of the customer and beneficial owner before or during the course of establishing a business relationship or conducting transactions for occasional customers. Countries may permit financial institutions to complete the verification as soon as reasonably practicable

---

[4] Reliable, independent source documents, data or information will hereafter be referred to as "identification data".

following the establishment of the relationship, where the money laundering risks are effectively managed and where this is essential not to interrupt the normal conduct of business.

Where the financial institution is unable to comply with paragraphs (a) to (c) above, it should not open the account, commence business relations or perform the transaction; or should terminate the business relationship; and should consider making a suspicious transactions report in relation to the customer.

These requirements should apply to all new customers, though financial institutions should also apply this Recommendation to existing customers on the basis of materiality and risk, and should conduct due diligence on such existing relationships at appropriate times.

6.* Financial institutions should, in relation to politically exposed persons, in addition to performing normal due diligence measures:

a) Have appropriate risk management systems to determine whether the customer is a politically exposed person.
b) Obtain senior management approval for establishing business relationships with such customers.
c) Take reasonable measures to establish the source of wealth and source of funds.
d) Conduct enhanced ongoing monitoring of the business relationship.

7. Financial institutions should, in relation to cross-border correspondent banking and other similar relationships, in addition to performing normal due diligence measures:

a) Gather sufficient information about a respondent institution to understand fully the nature of the respondent's business and to determine from publicly available information the reputation of the institution and the quality of supervision, including whether it has been subject to a money launder-ing or terrorist financing investigation or regulatory action.
b) Assess the respondent institution's anti-money laundering and terrorist financing controls.
c) Obtain approval from senior management before establishing new correspondent relationships.
d) Document the respective responsibilities of each institution.
e) With respect to "payable-through accounts", be satisfied that the respondent bank has verified the identity of and performed on-going due diligence on the customers having direct access to accounts of the correspondent and that it is able to provide relevant customer identification data upon request to the correspondent bank.

8. Financial institutions should pay special attention to any money laundering threats that may arise from new or developing technologies that might favour anonymity, and take measures, if needed, to prevent their use in money laundering schemes. In particular, financial institutions should have policies and procedures in place to address any specific risks associated with non-face to face business relationships or transactions.

9.* Countries may permit financial institutions to rely on intermediaries or other third parties to perform elements (a) – (c) of the CDD process or to introduce business, provided that the criteria set out below are met. Where such reliance is permitted, the ultimate responsibility for customer identification and verification remains with the financial institution relying on the third party.

The criteria that should be met are as follows:

a) A financial institution relying upon a third party should immediately obtain the necessary information concerning elements (a) – (c) of the CDD process. Financial institutions should take adequate steps to satisfy themselves that copies of identification data and other relevant documenta-tion relating to the CDD requirements will be made available from the third party upon request without delay.
b) The financial institution should satisfy itself that the third party is regulated and supervised for, and has measures in place to comply with CDD requirements in line with Recommendations 5 and 10.

It is left to each country to determine in which countries the third party that meets the conditions can be based, having regard to information available on countries that do not or do not adequately apply the FATF Recommendations.

10.* Financial institutions should maintain, for at least five years, all necessary records on transactions, both domestic or international, to enable them to comply swiftly with information requests from the competent authorities. Such records must be sufficient to permit reconstruction of individual transactions (including the amounts and types of currency involved if any) so as to provide, if necessary, evidence for prosecution of criminal activity.

Financial institutions should keep records on the identification data obtained through the customer due diligence process (e.g. copies or records of official identification documents like passports, identity cards, driving licenses or similar documents), account files and business correspondence for at least five years after the business relationship is ended.

The identification data and transaction records should be available to domestic competent authorities upon appropriate authority.

11.* Financial institutions should pay special attention to all complex, unusual large transactions, and all unusual patterns of transactions, which have no apparent economic or visible lawful purpose. The background and purpose of such transactions should, as far as possible, be examined, the findings established in writing, and be available to help competent authorities and auditors.

12.* The customer due diligence and record-keeping requirements set out in Recommendations 5, 6, and 8 to 11 apply to designated non-financial businesses and professions in the following situations:

a) Casinos – when customers engage in financial transactions equal to or above the applicable designated threshold.
b) Real estate agents – when they are involved in transactions for their client concerning the buying and selling of real estate.
c) Dealers in precious metals and dealers in precious stones - when they engage in any cash transaction with a customer equal to or above the applicable designated threshold.
d) Lawyers, notaries, other independent legal professionals and accountants when they prepare for or carry out transactions for their client concerning the following activities:
   • buying and selling of real estate;
   • managing of client money, securities or other assets;
   • management of bank, savings or securities accounts;
   • organisation of contributions for the creation, operation or management of companies;
   • creation, operation or management of legal persons or arrangements, and buying and selling of business entities.
e) Trust and company service providers when they prepare for or carry out transactions for a client concerning the activities listed in the definition in the Glossary.

Reporting of suspicious transactions and compliance

13.* If a financial institution suspects or has reasonable grounds to suspect that funds are the proceeds of a criminal activity, or are related to terrorist financing, it should be required, directly by law or regulation, to report promptly its suspicions to the financial intelligence unit (FIU).

14.* Financial institutions, their directors, officers and employees should be:

a) Protected by legal provisions from criminal and civil liability for breach of any restriction on disclosure of information imposed by contract or by any legislative, regulatory or administrative provision, if they report their suspicions in good faith to the FIU, even if they did not know precisely what the underlying criminal activity was, and regardless of whether illegal activity actually occurred.
b) Prohibited by law from disclosing the fact that a suspicious transaction report (STR) or related information is being reported to the FIU.

15.* Financial institutions should develop programmes against money laundering and terrorist financing. These programmes should include:

a) The development of internal policies, procedures and controls, including appropriate compliance management arrangements, and adequate screening procedures to ensure high standards when hiring employees.
b) An ongoing employee training programme.
c) An audit function to test the system.

16.* The requirements set out in Recommendations 13 to 15, and 21 apply to all designated non-financial businesses and professions, subject to the following qualifications:

a) Lawyers, notaries, other independent legal professionals and accountants should be required to report suspicious transactions when, on behalf of or for a client, they engage in a financial transaction in relation to the activities described in Recommendation 12(d). Countries are strongly encouraged to extend the reporting requirement to the rest of the professional activities of accountants, including auditing.

b) Dealers in precious metals and dealers in precious stones should be required to report suspicious transactions when they engage in any cash transaction with a customer equal to or above the applicable designated threshold.

c) Trust and company service providers should be required to report suspicious transactions for a client when, on behalf of or for a client, they engage in a transaction in relation to the activities referred to Recommendation 12(e).

Lawyers, notaries, other independent legal professionals, and accountants acting as independent legal professionals, are not required to report their suspicions if the relevant information was obtained in circumstances where they are subject to professional secrecy or legal professional privilege.

Other measures to deter money laundering and terrorist financing

17. Countries should ensure that effective, proportionate and dissuasive sanctions, whether criminal, civil or administrative, are available to deal with natural or legal persons covered by these Recommendations that fail to comply with anti-money laundering or terrorist financing requirements.

18. Countries should not approve the establishment or accept the continued operation of shell banks. Financial institutions should refuse to enter into, or continue, a correspondent banking relationship with shell banks. Financial institutions should also guard against establishing relations with respondent foreign financial institutions that permit their accounts to be used by shell banks.

19. Countries should consider the feasibility and utility of a system where banks and other financial institutions and intermediaries would report all domestic and international currency transactions above a fixed amount, to a national central agency with a computerised data base, available to competent authorities for use in money laundering or terrorist financing cases, subject to strict safeguards to ensure proper use of the information.

20. Countries should consider applying the FATF Recommendations to businesses and professions, other than designated non-financial businesses and professions, that pose a money laundering or terrorist financing risk.

Countries should further encourage the development of modern and secure techniques of money management that are less vulnerable to money laundering.

Measures to be taken with respect to countries that do not or insufficiently comply with
the FATF Recommendations

21. Financial institutions should give special attention to business relationships and transactions with persons, including companies and financial institutions, from countries which do not or insufficiently apply the FATF Recommendations. Whenever these transactions have no apparent economic or visible lawful purpose, their background and purpose should, as far as possible, be examined, the findings established in writing, and be available to help competent authorities. Where such a country continues not to apply or insufficiently applies the FATF Recommendations, countries should be able to apply appropriate countermeasures.

22. Financial institutions should ensure that the principles applicable to financial institutions, which are mentioned above are also applied to branches and majority owned subsidiaries located abroad, especially in countries which do not or insufficiently apply the FATF Recommendations, to the extent that local applicable laws and regulations permit. When local applicable laws and regulations prohibit this implementation, competent authorities in the country of the parent institution should be informed by the financial institutions that they cannot apply the FATF Recommendations.

Regulation and supervision

23.* Countries should ensure that financial institutions are subject to adequate regulation and supervision and are effectively implementing the FATF Recommendations. Competent authorities should take the necessary legal or regulatory measures to prevent criminals or their associates from holding or being the beneficial owner of a significant or controlling interest or holding a management function in a financial institution.

For financial institutions subject to the Core Principles, the regulatory and supervisory measures that apply for prudential purposes and which are also relevant to money laundering, should apply in a similar manner for anti-money laundering and terrorist financing purposes.

Other financial institutions should be licensed or registered and appropriately regulated, and subject to supervision or oversight for anti-money laundering purposes, having regard to the risk of money laundering or terrorist financing in that sector. At a minimum, businesses providing a service of money or value transfer, or of money or currency changing should be licensed or registered, and subject to effective systems for monitoring and ensuring compliance with national requirements to combat money laundering and terrorist financing.

24. Designated non-financial businesses and professions should be subject to regulatory and supervisory measures as set out below.

a) Casinos should be subject to a comprehensive regulatory and supervisory regime that ensures that they have effectively implemented the necessary anti-money laundering and terrorist-financing measures. At a minimum:
- casinos should be licensed;
- competent authorities should take the necessary legal or regulatory measures to prevent criminals or their associates from holding or being the beneficial owner of a significant or controlling interest, holding a management function in, or being an operator of a casino
- competent authorities should ensure that casinos are effectively supervised for compliance with requirements to combat money laundering and terrorist financing.

b) Countries should ensure that the other categories of designated non-financial businesses and professions are subject to effective systems for monitoring and ensuring their compliance with requirements to combat money laundering and terrorist financing. This should be performed on a risk-sensitive basis. This may be performed by a government authority or by an appropriate self-regulatory organisation, provided that such an organisation can ensure that its members comply with their obligations to combat money laundering and terrorist financing.

25.* The competent authorities should establish guidelines, and provide feedback which will assist financial institutions and designated non-financial businesses and professions in applying national measures to combat money laundering and terrorist financing, and in particular, in detecting and reporting suspicious transactions.

C. Institutional and Other Measures Necessary in Systems for Combating Money Laundering and Terrorist Financing

Competent authorities, their powers and resources

26.* Countries should establish a FIU that serves as a national centre for the receiving (and, as permitted, requesting), analysis and dissemination of STR and other information regarding potential money laundering or terrorist financing. The FIU should have access, directly or indirectly, on a timely basis to the financial, administrative and law enforcement information that it requires to properly undertake its functions, including the analysis of STR.

27.* Countries should ensure that designated law enforcement authorities have responsibility for money laundering and terrorist financing investigations. Countries are encouraged to support and develop, as far as possible, special investigative techniques suitable for the investigation of money laundering, such as controlled delivery, undercover operations and other relevant techniques. Countries are also encouraged to use other effective mechanisms such as the use of permanent or temporary groups specialised in asset investigation, and co-operative investigations with appropriate competent authorities in other countries.

28. When conducting investigations of money laundering and underlying predicate offences, competent authorities should be able to obtain documents and information for use in those investigations, and in prosecutions and related actions. This should include powers to use compulsory measures for the production of records held by financial institutions and other persons, for the search of persons and premises, and for the seizure and obtaining of evidence.

29. Supervisors should have adequate powers to monitor and ensure compliance by financial institutions with requirements to combat money laundering and terrorist financing, including the authority to conduct inspections. They should be authorised to compel production of any information from financial institutions that is relevant to monitoring such compliance, and to impose adequate administrative sanctions for failure to comply with such requirements.

30. Countries should provide their competent authorities involved in combating money laundering and terrorist financing with adequate financial, human and technical resources. Countries should have in place processes to ensure that the staff of those authorities are of high integrity.

31. Countries should ensure that policy makers, the FIU, law enforcement and supervisors have effective mechanisms in place which enable them to co-operate, and where appropriate co-ordinate domestically with each other concerning the development and implementation of policies and activities to combat money laundering and terrorist financing.

32. Countries should ensure that their competent authorities can review the effectiveness of their systems to combat money laundering and terrorist financing systems by maintaining comprehensive statistics on matters relevant to the effectiveness and efficiency of such systems. This should include statistics on the STR received and disseminated; on money laundering and terrorist financing investigations, prosecutions and convictions; on property frozen, seized and confiscated; and on mutual legal assistance or other international requests for co-operation.

Transparency of legal persons and arrangements

33. Countries should take measures to prevent the unlawful use of legal persons by money launderers. Countries should ensure that there is adequate, accurate and timely information on the beneficial ownership and control of legal persons that can be obtained or accessed in a timely fashion by competent authorities. In particular, countries that have legal persons that are able to issue bearer shares should take appropriate measures to ensure that they are not misused for money laundering and be able to demonstrate the adequacy of those measures. Countries could consider measures to facilitate access to beneficial ownership and control information to financial institutions undertaking the requirements set out in Recommendation 5.

34. Countries should take measures to prevent the unlawful use of legal arrangements by money launderers. In particular, countries should ensure that there is adequate, accurate and timely information on express trusts, including information on the settlor, trustee and beneficiaries, that can be obtained or accessed in a timely fashion by competent authorities. Countries could consider measures to facilitate access to beneficial ownership and control information to financial institutions undertaking the requirements set out in Recommendation 5.

D. International Co-operation

35. Countries should take immediate steps to become party to and implement fully the Vienna Convention, the Palermo Convention, and the 1999 United Nations International Convention for the Suppression of the Financing of Terrorism. Countries are also encouraged to ratify and implement other relevant international conventions, such as the 1990 Council of Europe Convention on Laundering, Search, Seizure and Confiscation of the Proceeds from Crime and the 2002 Inter-American Convention against Terrorism.

Mutual legal assistance and extradition

36. Countries should rapidly, constructively and effectively provide the widest possible range of mutual legal assistance in relation to money laundering and terrorist financing investigations, prosecutions, and related proceedings. In particular, countries should:

a) Not prohibit or place unreasonable or unduly restrictive conditions on the provision of mutual legal assistance.
b) Ensure that they have clear and efficient processes for the execution of mutual legal assistance requests.
c) Not refuse to execute a request for mutual legal assistance on the sole ground that the offence is also considered to involve fiscal matters.
d) Not refuse to execute a request for mutual legal assistance on the grounds that laws require financial institutions to maintain secrecy or confidentiality.

Countries should ensure that the powers of their competent authorities required under Recommendation 28 are also available for use in response to requests for mutual legal assistance, and if consistent with their domestic framework, in response to direct requests from foreign judicial or law enforcement authorities to domestic counterparts.

To avoid conflicts of jurisdiction, consideration should be given to devising and applying mechanisms for determining the best venue for prosecution of defendants in the interests of justice in cases that are subject to prosecution in more than one country.

37. Countries should, to the greatest extent possible, render mutual legal assistance notwithstanding the absence of dual criminality.

Where dual criminality is required for mutual legal assistance or extradition, that requirement should be deemed to be satisfied regardless of whether both countries place the offence within the same category of offence or denominate the offence by the same terminology, provided that both countries criminalise the conduct underlying the offence.

38.* There should be authority to take expeditious action in response to requests by foreign countries to identify, freeze, seize and confiscate property laundered, proceeds from money laundering or predicate offences, instrumentalities used in or intended for use in the commission of these offences, or property of corresponding value. There should also be arrangements for co-ordinating seizure and confiscation proceedings, which may include the sharing of confiscated assets.

39. Countries should recognise money laundering as an extraditable offence. Each country should either extradite its own nationals, or where a country does not do so solely on the grounds of nationality, that country should, at the request of the country seeking extradition, submit the case without undue delay to its competent authorities for the purpose of prosecution of the offences set forth in the request. Those authorities should take their decision and conduct their proceedings in the same manner as in the case of any other offence of a serious nature under the domestic law of that country. The countries concerned should cooperate with each other, in particular on procedural and evidentiary aspects, to ensure the efficiency of such prosecutions.

Subject to their legal frameworks, countries may consider simplifying extradition by allowing direct transmission of extradition requests between appropriate ministries, extraditing persons based only on warrants of arrests or judgements, and/or introducing a simplified extradition of consenting persons who waive formal extradition proceedings.

Other forms of co-operation

40.* Countries should ensure that their competent authorities provide the widest possible range of international co-operation to their foreign counterparts. There should be clear and effective gateways to facilitate the prompt and constructive exchange directly between counterparts, either spontaneously or upon request, of information relating to both money laundering and the underlying predicate offences. Exchanges should be permitted without unduly restrictive conditions. In particular:

a) Competent authorities should not refuse a request for assistance on the sole ground that the request is also considered to involve fiscal matters.
b) Countries should not invoke laws that require financial institutions to maintain secrecy or confidentiality as a ground for refusing to provide co-operation.
c) Competent authorities should be able to conduct inquiries; and where possible, investigations; on behalf of foreign counterparts.

Where the ability to obtain information sought by a foreign competent authority is not within the mandate of its counterpart, countries are also encouraged to permit a prompt and constructive exchange of information with non-counterparts. Co-operation with foreign authorities other than counterparts could occur directly or indirectly. When uncertain about the appropriate avenue to follow, competent authorities should first contact their foreign counterparts for assistance.

Countries should establish controls and safeguards to ensure that information exchanged by competent authorities is used only in an authorised manner, consistent with their obligations concerning privacy and data protection.

Glossary

In these Recommendations the following abbreviations and references are used:

"**Beneficial owner**" refers to the natural person(s) who ultimately owns or controls a customer and/or the person on whose behalf a transaction is being conducted. It also incorporates those persons who exercise ultimate effective control over a legal person or arrangement.

"**Core Principles**" refers to the Core Principles for Effective Banking Supervision issued by the Basel Committee on Banking Supervision, the Objectives and Principles for Securities Regulation issued by the International Organization of Securities Commissions, and the Insurance Supervisory Principles issued by the International Association of Insurance Supervisors.

"**Designated categories of offences**" means:

- participation in an organised criminal group and racketeering;
- terrorism, including terrorist financing;
- trafficking in human beings and migrant smuggling;
- sexual exploitation, including sexual exploitation of children;
- illicit trafficking in narcotic drugs and psychotropic substances;
- illicit arms trafficking;
- illicit trafficking in stolen and other goods;
- corruption and bribery;
- fraud;
- counterfeiting currency;
- counterfeiting and piracy of products;
- environmental crime;
- murder, grievous bodily injury;
- kidnapping, illegal restraint and hostage-taking;
- robbery or theft;
- smuggling;
- extortion;
- forgery;
- piracy; and
- insider trading and market manipulation.

When deciding on the range of offences to be covered as predicate offences under each of the categories listed above, each country may decide, in accordance with its domestic law, how it will define those offences and the nature of any particular elements of those offences that make them serious offences.

"**Designated non-financial businesses and professions**" means:

a) Casinos (which also includes internet casinos).

b) Real estate agents.

c) Dealers in precious metals.

d) Dealers in precious stones.

e) Lawyers, notaries, other independent legal professionals and accountants – this refers to sole practitioners, partners or employed professionals within professional firms. It is not meant to refer to "internal" professionals that are employees of other types of businesses, nor to professionals working for government agencies, who may already be subject to measures that would combat money laundering.

f) Trust and Company Service Providers refers to all persons or businesses that are not covered elsewhere under these Recommendations, and which as a business, provide any of the following services to third parties:

- acting as a formation agent of legal persons;
- acting as (or arranging for another person to act as) a director or secretary of a company, a partner of a partnership, or a similar position in relation to other legal persons;
- providing a registered office; business address or accommodation, correspondence or administrative address for a company, a partnership or any other legal person or arrangement;

- acting as (or arranging for another person to act as) a trustee of an express trust;
- acting as (or arranging for another person to act as) a nominee shareholder for another person.

"**Designated threshold**" refers to the amount set out in the Interpretative Notes.

"**Financial institutions**" means any person or entity who conducts as a business one or more of the following activities or operations for or on behalf of a customer:

1. Acceptance of deposits and other repayable funds from the public.[5]
2. Lending.[6]
3. Financial leasing.[7]
4. The transfer of money or value.[8]
5. Issuing and managing means of payment (e.g. credit and debit cards, cheques, traveller's cheques, money orders and bankers' drafts, electronic money).
6. Financial guarantees and commitments.
7. Trading in:
   (a) money market instruments (cheques, bills, CDs, derivatives etc.);
   (b) foreign exchange;
   (c) exchange, interest rate and index instruments;
   (d) transferable securities;
   (e) commodity futures trading.
8. Participation in securities issues and the provision of financial services related to such issues.
9. Individual and collective portfolio management.
10. Safekeeping and administration of cash or liquid securities on behalf of other persons.
11. Otherwise investing, administering or managing funds or money on behalf of other persons.
12. Underwriting and placement of life insurance and other investment related insurance.[9]
13. Money and currency changing.

When a financial activity is carried out by a person or entity on an occasional or very limited basis (having regard to quantitative and absolute criteria) such that there is little risk of money laundering activity occurring, a country may decide that the application of anti-money laundering measures is not necessary, either fully or partially.

In strictly limited and justified circumstances, and based on a proven low risk of money laundering, a country may decide not to apply some or all of the Forty Recommendations to some of the financial activities stated above.

"**FIU**" means financial intelligence unit.

"**Legal arrangements**" refers to express trusts or other similar legal arrangements.

"**Legal persons**" refers to bodies corporate, foundations, anstalt, partnerships, or associations, or any similar bodies that can establish a permanent customer relationship with a financial institution or otherwise own property.

"**Payable-through accounts**" refers to correspondent accounts that are used directly by third parties to transact business on their own behalf.

"**Politically Exposed Persons**" (PEPs) are individuals who are or have been entrusted with prominent public functions in a foreign country, for example Heads of State or of government, senior politicians, senior government, judicial or military officials, senior executives of state owned corporations, important political party officials. Business relationships with family members or close associates of PEPs involve

---

[5] This also captures private banking.

[6] This includes inter alia: consumer credit; mortgage credit; factoring, with or without recourse; and finance of commercial transactions (including forfaiting).

[7] This does not extend to financial leasing arrangements in relation to consumer products.

[8] This applies to financial activity in both the formal or informal sector *e.g.* alternative remittance activity. See the Interpretative Note to Special Recommendation VI. It does not apply to any natural or legal person that provides financial institutions solely with message or other support systems for transmitting funds. See the Interpretative Note to Special Recommendation VII.

[9] This applies both to insurance undertakings and to insurance intermediaries (agents and brokers).

reputational risks similar to those with PEPs themselves. The definition is not intended to cover middle ranking or more junior individuals in the foregoing categories.

"**Shell bank**" means a bank incorporated in a jurisdiction in which it has no physical presence and which is unaffiliated with a regulated financial group.

"**STR**" refers to suspicious transaction reports.

"**Supervisors**" refers to the designated competent authorities responsible for ensuring compliance by financial institutions with requirements to combat money laundering and terrorist financing.

"**the FATF Recommendations**" refers to these Recommendations and to the FATF Special Recommendations on Terrorist Financing.

Interpretative Notes

General

1. Reference in this document to "countries" should be taken to apply equally to "territories" or "jurisdictions".

2. Recommendations 5–16 and 21–22 state that financial institutions or designated non-financial businesses and professions should take certain actions. These references require countries to take measures that will oblige financial institutions or designated non-financial businesses and professions to comply with each Recommendation. The basic obligations under Recommendations 5, 10 and 13 should be set out in law or regulation, while more detailed elements in those Recommendations, as well as obligations under other Recommendations, could be required either by law or regulation or by other enforceable means issued by a competent authority.

3. Where reference is made to a financial institution being satisfied as to a matter, that institution must be able to justify its assessment to competent authorities.

4. To comply with Recommendations 12 and 16, countries do not need to issue laws or regulations that relate exclusively to lawyers, notaries, accountants and the other designated non-financial businesses and professions so long as these businesses or professions are included in laws or regulations covering the underlying activities.

5. The Interpretative Notes that apply to financial institutions are also relevant to designated non-financial businesses and professions, where applicable.

Recommendations 5, 12 and 16

The designated thresholds for transactions (under Recommendations 5 and 12) are as follows:

- Financial institutions (for occasional customers under Recommendation 5) - USD/EUR 15 000.
- Casinos, including internet casinos (under Recommendation 12) - USD/EUR 3 000
- For dealers in precious metals and dealers in precious stones when engaged in any cash transaction (under Recommendations 12 and 16) - USD/EUR 15 000.

Financial transactions above a designated threshold include situations where the transaction is carried out in a single operation or in several operations that appear to be linked.

Recommendation 5

Customer due diligence and tipping off

1. If, during the establishment or course of the customer relationship, or when conducting occasional transactions, a financial institution suspects that transactions relate to money laundering or terrorist financing, then the institution should:

   a) Normally seek to identify and verify the identity of the customer and the beneficial owner, whether permanent or occasional, and irrespective of any exemption or any designated threshold that might otherwise apply.
   b) Make a STR to the FIU in accordance with Recommendation 13.

2. Recommendation 14 prohibits financial institutions, their directors, officers and employees from disclosing the fact that an STR or related information is being reported to the FIU. A risk exists that customers could be unintentionally tipped off when the financial institution is seeking to perform its

customer due diligence (CDD) obligations in these circumstances. The customer's awareness of a possible STR or investigation could compromise future efforts to investigate the suspected money laundering or terrorist financing operation.

3. Therefore, if financial institutions form a suspicion that transactions relate to money laundering or terrorist financing, they should take into account the risk of tipping off when performing the customer due diligence process. If the institution reasonably believes that performing the CDD process will tip-off the customer or potential customer, it may choose not to pursue that process, and should file an STR. Institutions should ensure that their employees are aware of and sensitive to these issues when conducting CDD.

CDD for legal persons and arrangements

4. When performing elements (a) and (b) of the CDD process in relation to legal persons or arrangements, financial institutions should:

   a) Verify that any person purporting to act on behalf of the customer is so authorised, and identify that person.
   b) Identify the customer and verify its identity - the types of measures that would be normally needed to satisfactorily perform this function would require obtaining proof of incorporation or similar evidence of the legal status of the legal person or arrangement, as well as information concerning the customer's name, the names of trustees, legal form, address, directors, and provisions regulating the power to bind the legal person or arrangement.
   c) Identify the beneficial owners, including forming an understanding of the ownership and control structure, and take reasonable measures to verify the identity of such persons. The types of measures that would be normally needed to satisfactorily perform this function would require identifying the natural persons with a controlling interest and identifying the natural persons who comprise the mind and management of the legal person or arrangement. Where the customer or the owner of the controlling interest is a public company that is subject to regulatory disclosure requirements, it is not necessary to seek to identify and verify the identity of any shareholder of that company.

FATF 40 Recommendations 20 - © 2010 FATF/OECD

The relevant information or data may be obtained from a public register, from the customer or from other reliable sources.

Reliance on identification and verification already performed

5. The CDD measures set out in Recommendation 5 do not imply that financial institutions have to repeatedly identify and verify the identity of each customer every time that a customer conducts a transaction. An institution is entitled to rely on the identification and verification steps that it has already undertaken unless it has doubts about the veracity of that information. Examples of situations that might lead an institution to have such doubts could be where there is a suspicion of money laundering in relation to that customer, or where there is a material change in the way that the customer's account is operated which is not consistent with the customer's business profile.

Timing of verification

6. Examples of the types of circumstances where it would be permissible for verification to be completed after the establishment of the business relationship, because it would be essential not to interrupt the normal conduct of business include:

• Non face-to-face business.
• Securities transactions. In the securities industry, companies and intermediaries may be required to perform transactions very rapidly, according to the market conditions at the time the customer is contacting them, and the performance of the transaction may be required before verification of identity is completed.
• Life insurance business. In relation to life insurance business, countries may permit the identification and verification of the beneficiary under the policy to take place after having established the business relationship with the policyholder. However, in all such cases, identification and verification should occur at or before the time of payout or the time where the beneficiary intends to exercise vested rights under the policy.

7. Financial institutions will also need to adopt risk management procedures with respect to the conditions under which a customer may utilise the business relationship prior to verification. These procedures

should include a set of measures such as a limitation of the number, types and/or amount of transactions that can be performed and the monitoring of large or complex transactions being carried out outside of expected norms for that type of relationship. Financial institutions should refer to the Basel CDD paper[10] (section 2.2.6.) for specific guidance on examples of risk management measures for non-face to face business.

Requirement to identify existing customers

8. The principles set out in the Basel CDD paper concerning the identification of existing customers should serve as guidance when applying customer due diligence processes to institutions engaged in banking activity, and could apply to other financial institutions where relevant.

Simplified or reduced CDD measures

9. The general rule is that customers must be subject to the full range of CDD measures, including the requirement to identify the beneficial owner. Nevertheless there are circumstances where the risk of money laundering or terrorist financing is lower, where information on the identity of the customer and the beneficial owner of a customer is publicly available, or where adequate checks and controls exist elsewhere in national systems. In such circumstances it could be reasonable for a country to allow its financial institutions to apply simplified or reduced CDD measures when identifying and verifying the identity of the customer and the beneficial owner.

10. Examples of customers where simplified or reduced CDD measures could apply are:

- Financial institutions – where they are subject to requirements to combat money laundering and terrorist financing consistent with the FATF Recommendations and are supervised for compliance with those controls.
- Public companies that are subject to regulatory disclosure requirements.
- Government administrations or enterprises.

11. Simplified or reduced CDD measures could also apply to the beneficial owners of pooled accounts held by designated non financial businesses or professions provided that those businesses or professions are subject to requirements to combat money laundering and terrorist financing consistent with the FATF Recommendations and are subject to effective systems for monitoring and ensuring their compliance with those requirements. Banks should also refer to the Basel CDD paper (section 2.2.4.), which provides specific guidance concerning situations where an account holding institution may rely on a customer that is a professional financial intermediary to perform the customer due diligence on his or its own customers (*i.e.* the beneficial owners of the bank account). Where relevant, the CDD Paper could also provide guidance in relation to similar accounts held by other types of financial institutions.

12. Simplified CDD or reduced measures could also be acceptable for various types of products or transactions such as (examples only):

- Life insurance policies where the annual premium is no more than USD/EUR 1 000 or a single premium of no more than USD/EUR 2 500.
- Insurance policies for pension schemes if there is no surrender clause and the policy cannot be used as collateral.
- A pension, superannuation or similar scheme that provides retirement benefits to employees, where contributions are made by way of deduction from wages and the scheme rules do not permit the assignment of a member's interest under the scheme.

13. Countries could also decide whether financial institutions could apply these simplified measures only to customers in its own jurisdiction or allow them to do for customers from any other jurisdiction that the original country is satisfied is in compliance with and has effectively implemented the FATF Recommendations.

Simplified CDD measures are not acceptable whenever there is suspicion of money laundering or terrorist financing or specific higher risk scenarios apply.

---

[10] "Basel CDD paper" refers to the guidance paper on Customer Due Diligence for Banks issued by the Basel Committee on Banking Supervision in October 2001.

Recommendation 6

Countries are encouraged to extend the requirements of Recommendation 6 to individuals who hold prominent public functions in their own country.

Recommendation 9

This Recommendation does not apply to outsourcing or agency relationships.

This Recommendation also does not apply to relationships, accounts or transactions between financial institutions for their clients. Those relationships are addressed by Recommendations 5 and 7.

Recommendations 10 and 11

In relation to insurance business, the word "transactions" should be understood to refer to the insurance product itself, the premium payment and the benefits.

Recommendation 13

1. The reference to criminal activity in Recommendation 13 refers to:

a) all criminal acts that would constitute a predicate offence for money laundering in the jurisdiction; or

b) at a minimum to those offences that would constitute a predicate offence as required by Recommendation 1.

Countries are strongly encouraged to adopt alternative (a). All suspicious transactions, including attempted transactions, should be reported regardless of the amount of the transaction.

2. In implementing Recommendation 13, suspicious transactions should be reported by financial institutions regardless of whether they are also thought to involve tax matters. Countries should take into account that, in order to deter financial institutions from reporting a suspicious transaction, money launderers may seek to state *inter alia* that their transactions relate to tax matters.

Recommendation 14 (tipping off)

Where lawyers, notaries, other independent legal professionals and accountants acting as independent legal professionals seek to dissuade a client from engaging in illegal activity, this does not amount to tipping off.

Recommendation 15

The type and extent of measures to be taken for each of the requirements set out in the Recommendation should be appropriate having regard to the risk of money laundering and terrorist financing and the size of the business.

For financial institutions, compliance management arrangements should include the appointment of a compliance officer at the management level.

Recommendation 16

1. It is for each jurisdiction to determine the matters that would fall under legal professional privilege or professional secrecy. This would normally cover information lawyers, notaries or other independent legal professionals receive from or obtain through one of their clients: (a) in the course of ascertaining the legal position of their client, or (b) in performing their task of defending or representing that client in, or concerning judicial, administrative, arbitration or mediation proceedings. Where accountants are subject to the same obligations of secrecy or privilege, then they are also not required to report suspicious transactions.

2. Countries may allow lawyers, notaries, other independent legal professionals and accountants to send their STR to their appropriate self-regulatory organisations, provided that there are appropriate forms of co-operation between these organisations and the FIU.

Recommendation 23

Recommendation 23 should not be read as to require the introduction of a system of regular review of licensing of controlling interests in financial institutions merely for anti-money laundering purposes, but as to stress the desirability of suitability review for controlling shareholders in financial institutions (banks and non-banks in particular) from a FATF point of view. Hence, where shareholder suitability (or "fit and proper") tests exist, the attention of supervisors should be drawn to their relevance for anti-money laundering purposes.

Recommendation 25

When considering the feedback that should be provided, countries should have regard to the FATF Best Practice Guidelines on Providing Feedback to Reporting Financial Institutions and Other Persons.

Recommendation 26

Where a country has created an FIU, it should consider applying for membership in the Egmont Group. Countries should have regard to the Egmont Group Statement of Purpose, and its Principles for Information Exchange Between Financial Intelligence Units for Money Laundering Cases. These documents set out important guidance concerning the role and functions of FIUs, and the mechanisms for exchanging information between FIU.

Recommendation 27

Countries should consider taking measures, including legislative ones, at the national level, to allow their competent authorities investigating money laundering cases to postpone or waive the arrest of suspected persons and/or the seizure of the money for the purpose of identifying persons involved in such activities or for evidence gathering. Without such measures the use of procedures such as controlled deliveries and undercover operations are precluded.

Recommendation 38

Countries should consider:

a)   Establishing an asset forfeiture fund in its respective country into which all or a portion of confiscated property will be deposited for law enforcement, health, education, or other appropriate purposes.

b)   Taking such measures as may be necessary to enable it to share among or between other countries confiscated property, in particular, when confiscation is directly or indirectly a result of co-ordinated law enforcement actions. </APAL>

Recommendation 40

1. For the purposes of this Recommendation:

• "Counterparts" refers to authorities that exercise similar responsibilities and functions.

• "Competent authority" refers to all administrative and law enforcement authorities concerned with combating money laundering and terrorist financing, including the FIU and supervisors.

2. Depending on the type of competent authority involved and the nature and purpose of the co-operation, different channels can be appropriate for the exchange of information. Examples of mechanisms or channels that are used to exchange information include: bilateral or multilateral agreements or arrangements, memoranda of understanding, exchanges on the basis of reciprocity, or through appropriate international or regional organisations. However, this Recommendation is not intended to cover co-operation in relation to mutual legal assistance or extradition.

3. The reference to indirect exchange of information with foreign authorities other than counterparts covers the situation where the requested information passes from the foreign authority through one or more domestic or foreign authorities before being received by the requesting authority. The competent authority that requests the information should always make it clear for what purpose and on whose behalf the request is made.

4. FIUs should be able to make inquiries on behalf of foreign counterparts where this could be relevant to an analysis of financial transactions. At a minimum, inquiries should include:

- Searching its own databases, which would include information related to suspicious transaction reports.
- Searching other databases to which it may have direct or indirect access, including law enforcement databases, public databases, administrative databases and commercially available databases.

Where permitted to do so, FIUs should also contact other competent authorities and financial institutions in order to obtain relevant information.

FATF IX SPECIAL RECOMMENDATIONS

October 2011
(incorporating all subsequent amendments until February 2008)

FATF Special Recommendations on Terrorist Financing

Recognising the vital importance of taking action to combat the financing of terrorism, the FATF has agreed these Recommendations, which, when combined with the FATF Forty Recommendations on money laundering, set out the basic framework to detect, prevent and suppress the financing of terrorism and terrorist acts.

I. Ratification and implementation of UN instruments

Each country should take immediate steps to ratify and to implement fully the 1999 United Nations International Convention for the Suppression of the Financing of Terrorism.

Countries should also immediately implement the United Nations resolutions relating to the prevention and suppression of the financing of terrorist acts, particularly United Nations Security Council Resolution 1373.

II. Criminalising the financing of terrorism and associated money laundering

Each country should criminalise the financing of terrorism, terrorist acts and terrorist organisations. Countries should ensure that such offences are designated as money laundering predicate offences.

III. Freezing and confiscating terrorist assets

Each country should implement measures to freeze without delay funds or other assets of terrorists, those who finance terrorism and terrorist organisations in accordance with the United Nations resolutions relating to the prevention and suppression of the financing of terrorist acts.

Each country should also adopt and implement measures, including legislative ones, which would enable the competent authorities to seize and confiscate property that is the proceeds of, or used in, or intended or allocated for use in, the financing of terrorism, terrorist acts or terrorist organisations.

IV. Reporting suspicious transactions related to terrorism

If financial institutions, or other businesses or entities subject to anti-money laundering obligations, suspect or have reasonable grounds to suspect that funds are linked or related to, or are to be used for terrorism, terrorist acts or by terrorist organisations, they should be required to report promptly their suspicions to the competent authorities.

V. International Co-operation

Each country should afford another country, on the basis of a treaty, arrangement or other mechanism for mutual legal assistance or information exchange, the greatest possible measure of assistance in connection with criminal, civil enforcement, and administrative investigations, inquiries and proceedings relating to the financing of terrorism, terrorist acts and terrorist organisations.

Countries should also take all possible measures to ensure that they do not provide safe havens for individuals charged with the financing of terrorism, terrorist acts or terrorist organisations, and should have procedures in place to extradite, where possible, such individuals.

VI. Alternative Remittance

Each country should take measures to ensure that persons or legal entities, including agents, that provide a service for the transmission of money or value, including transmission through an informal money or value transfer system or network, should be licensed or registered and subject to all the FATF Recommendations that apply to banks and non-bank financial institutions. Each country should ensure that persons or legal entities that carry out this service illegally are subject to administrative, civil or criminal sanctions.

VII. Wire transfers

Countries should take measures to require financial institutions, including money remitters, to include accurate and meaningful originator information (name, address and account number) on funds transfers and related messages that are sent, and the information should remain with the transfer or related message through the payment chain.

Countries should take measures to ensure that financial institutions, including money remitters, conduct enhanced scrutiny of and monitor for suspicious activity funds transfers which do not contain complete originator information (name, address and account number).

VIII. Non-profit organisations

Countries should review the adequacy of laws and regulations that relate to entities that can be abused for the financing of terrorism. Non-profit organisations are particularly vulnerable, and countries should ensure that they cannot be misused:

(i)   by terrorist organisations posing as legitimate entities;
(ii) to exploit legitimate entities as conduits for terrorist financing, including for the purpose of escaping asset freezing measures; and
(iii) to conceal or obscure the clandestine diversion of funds intended for legitimate purposes to terrorist organisations.

IX. Cash Couriers

Countries should have measures in place to detect the physical cross-border transportation of currency and bearer negotiable instruments, including a declaration system or other disclosure obligation.

Countries should ensure that their competent authorities have the legal authority to stop or restrain currency or bearer negotiable instruments that are suspected to be related to terrorist financing or money laundering, or that are falsely declared or disclosed.

Countries should ensure that effective, proportionate and dissuasive sanctions are available to deal with persons who make false declaration(s) or disclosure(s). In cases where the currency or bearer negotiable instruments are related to terrorist financing or money laundering, countries should also adopt measures, including legislative ones consistent with Recommendation 3 and Special Recommendation III, which would enable the confiscation of such currency or instruments.

Interpretative Notes

Interpretative Note to Special Recommendation II: Criminalising the financing of terrorism and associated money laundering

Objective

1. Special Recommendation II (SR II) was developed with the objective of ensuring that countries have the legal capacity to prosecute and apply criminal sanctions to persons that finance terrorism. Given the close connection between international terrorism and inter alia money laundering, another objective of SR II is to emphasise this link by obligating countries to include terrorist financing offences as predicate offences for money laundering. The basis for criminalising terrorist financing should be the United Nations International Convention for the Suppression of the Financing of Terrorism, 1999.[1]

---

[1] Although the UN Convention had not yet come into force at the time that SR II was originally issued in October 2001 – and thus is not cited in the SR itself – the intent of the FATF has been from the issuance of SR II to reiterate

Definitions

2. For the purposes of SR II and this Interpretative Note, the following definitions apply:

a) The term funds refers to assets of every kind, whether tangible or intangible, movable or immovable, however acquired, and legal documents or instruments in any form, including electronic or digital, evidencing title to, or interest in, such assets, including, but not limited to, bank credits, travellers cheques, bank cheques, money orders, shares, securities, bonds, drafts, letters of credit.

b) The term terrorist refers to any natural person who: (i) commits, or attempts to commit, terrorist acts by any means, directly or indirectly, unlawfully and wilfully; (ii) participates as an accomplice in terrorist acts; (iii) organises or directs others to commit terrorist acts; or (iv) contributes to the commission of terrorist acts by a group of persons acting with a common purpose where the contribution is made intentionally and with the aim of furthering the terrorist act or with the knowledge of the intention of the group to commit a terrorist act.

c) The term terrorist act includes:

   i)   An act which constitutes an offence within the scope of, and as defined in one of the following treaties: Convention for the Suppression of Unlawful Seizure of Aircraft (1970), Convention for the Suppression of Unlawful Acts against the Safety of Civil Aviation (1971), Convention on the Prevention and Punishment of Crimes against Internationally Protected Persons, including Diplomatic Agents (1973), International Convention against the Taking of Hostages (1979), Convention on the Physical Protection of Nuclear Material (1980), Protocol for the Suppression of Unlawful Acts of Violence at Airports Serving International Civil Aviation, supplementary to the Convention for the Suppression of Unlawful Acts against the Safety of Civil Aviation (1988), Convention for the Suppression of Unlawful Acts against the Safety of Maritime Navigation (1988), Protocol for the Suppression of Unlawful Acts against the Safety of Fixed Platforms located on the Continental Shelf (1988), and the International Convention for the Suppression of Terrorist Bombings (1997); and

   ii) Any other act intended to cause death or serious bodily injury to a civilian, or to any other person not taking an active part in the hostilities in a situation of armed conflict, when the purpose of such act, by its nature or context, is to intimidate a population, or to compel a Government or an international organisation to do or to abstain from doing any act.

d) The term terrorist financing includes the financing of terrorist acts, and of terrorists and terrorist organisations.

e) The term terrorist organisation refers to any group of terrorists that: (i) commits, or attempts to commit, terrorist acts by any means, directly or indirectly, unlawfully and wilfully; (ii) participates as an accomplice in terrorist acts; (iii) organises or directs others to commit terrorist acts; or (iv) contributes to the commission of terrorist acts by a group of persons acting with a common purpose where the contribution is made intentionally and with the aim of furthering the terrorist act or with the knowledge of the intention of the group to commit a terrorist act.

Characteristics of the Terrorist Financing Offence

3. Terrorist financing offences should extend to any person who wilfully provides or collects funds by any means, directly or indirectly, with the unlawful intention that they should be used or in the knowledge that they are to be used, in full or in part: (a) to carry out a terrorist act(s); (b) by a terrorist organisation; or (c) by an individual terrorist.

4. Criminalising terrorist financing solely on the basis of aiding and abetting, attempt, or conspiracy does not comply with this Recommendation.

5. Terrorist financing offences should extend to any funds whether from a legitimate or illegitimate source.

6. Terrorist financing offences should not require that the funds: (a) were actually used to carry out or attempt a terrorist act(s); or (b) be linked to a specific terrorist act(s).

7. It should also be an offence to attempt to commit the offence of terrorist financing.

---

and reinforce the criminalisation standard as set forth in the Convention (in particular, Article 2). The Convention came into force in April 2003.

8. It should also be an offence to engage in any of the following types of conduct:

a) Participating as an accomplice in an offence as set forth in paragraphs 3 or 7 of this Interpretative Note;

b) Organising or directing others to commit an offence as set forth in paragraphs 3 or 7 of this Interpretative Note;

c) Contributing to the commission of one or more offence(s) as set forth in paragraphs 3 or 7 of this Interpretative Note by a group of persons acting with a common purpose. Such contribution shall be intentional and shall either: (i) be made with the aim of furthering the criminal activity or criminal purpose of the group, where such activity or purpose involves the commission of a terrorist financing offence; or (ii) be made in the knowledge of the intention of the group to commit a terrorist financing offence.

9. Terrorist financing offences should be predicate offences for money laundering.

10. Terrorist financing offences should apply, regardless of whether the person alleged to have committed the offence(s) is in the same country or a different country from the one in which the terrorist(s)/terrorist organisation(s) is located or the terrorist act(s) occurred/will occur.

11. The law should permit the intentional element of the terrorist financing offence to be inferred from objective factual circumstances.

12. Criminal liability for terrorist financing should extend to legal persons. Where that is not possible (i.e. due to fundamental principles of domestic law), civil or administrative liability should apply.

13. Making legal persons subject to criminal liability for terrorist financing should not preclude the possibility of parallel criminal, civil or administrative proceedings in countries in which more than one form of liability is available.

14. Natural and legal persons should be subject to effective, proportionate and dissuasive criminal, civil or administrative sanctions for terrorist financing.

Interpretative Note to Special Recommendation III: Freezing and Confiscating Terrorist Assets

Objectives

1. FATF Special Recommendation III consists of two obligations. The first requires jurisdictions to implement measures that will freeze or, if appropriate, seize terrorist-related funds or other assets without delay in accordance with relevant United Nations resolutions. The second obligation of Special Recommendation III is to have measures in place that permit a jurisdiction to seize or confiscate terrorist funds or other assets on the basis of an order or mechanism issued by a competent authority or a court.

2. The objective of the first requirement is to freeze terrorist-related funds or other assets based on reasonable grounds, or a reasonable basis, to suspect or believe that such funds or other assets could be used to finance terrorist activity. The objective of the second requirement is to deprive terrorists of these funds or other assets if and when links have been adequately established between the funds or other assets and terrorists or terrorist activity. The intent of the first objective is preventative, while the intent of the second objective is mainly preventative and punitive. Both requirements are necessary to deprive terrorists and terrorist networks of the means to conduct future terrorist activity and maintain their infrastructure and operations.

Scope

3. Special Recommendation III is intended, with regard to its first requirement, to complement the obligations in the context of the United Nations Security Council (UNSC) resolutions relating to the prevention and suppression of the financing of terrorist acts—S/RES/1267(1999) and its successor resolutions,[2] S/RES/1373(2001) and any prospective resolutions related to the freezing, or if appropriate

---

[2] When issued, S/RES/1267(1999) had a time limit of one year. A series of resolutions have been issued by the United Nations Security Council (UNSC) to extend and further refine provisions of S/RES/1267(1999). By successor resolutions are meant those resolutions that extend and are directly related to the original resolution S/RES/1267(1999). At the time of issue of this Interpretative Note, these resolutions included S/RES/1333(2000), S/RES/1363(2001), S/RES/1390(2002) and S/RES/1455(2003). In this Interpretative Note, the term S/RES/1267(1999) refers to S/RES/1267(1999) and its successor resolutions.

seizure, of terrorist assets. It should be stressed that none of the obligations in Special Recommendation III is intended to replace other measures or obligations that may already be in place for dealing with funds or other assets in the context of a criminal, civil or administrative investigation or proceeding[3] The focus of Special Recommendation III instead is on the preventative measures that are necessary and unique in the context of stopping the flow or use of funds or other assets to terrorist groups.

4. S/RES/1267(1999) and S/RES/1373(2001) differ in the persons and entities whose funds or other assets are to be frozen, the authorities responsible for making these designations, and the effect of these designations.

5. S/RES/1267(1999) and its successor resolutions obligate jurisdictions to freeze without delay the funds or other assets owned or controlled by Al-Qaida, the Taliban, Usama bin Laden, or persons and entities associated with them as designated by the United Nations Al-Qaida and Taliban Sanctions Committee established pursuant to United Nations Security Council Resolution 1267 (the Al-Qaida and Taliban Sanctions Committee), including funds derived from funds or other assets owned or controlled, directly or indirectly, by them or by persons acting on their behalf or at their direction, and ensure that neither these nor any other funds or other assets are made available, directly or indirectly, for such persons' benefit, by their nationals or by any person within their territory. The Al-Qaida and Taliban Sanctions Committee is the authority responsible for designating the persons and entities that should have their funds or other assets frozen under S/RES/1267(1999). All jurisdictions that are members of the United Nations are obligated by S/RES/1267(1999) to freeze the assets of persons and entities so designated by the Al-Qaida and Taliban Sanctions Committee.[4]

6. S/RES/1373(2001) obligates jurisdictions[5] to freeze without delay the funds or other assets of persons who commit, or attempt to commit, terrorist acts or participate in or facilitate the commission of terrorist acts; of entities owned or controlled directly or indirectly by such persons; and of persons and entities acting on behalf of, or at the direction of such persons and entities, including funds or other assets derived or generated from property owned or controlled, directly or indirectly, by such persons and associated persons and entities. Each individual jurisdiction has the authority to designate the persons and entities that should have their funds or other assets frozen. Additionally, to ensure that effective co-operation is developed among jurisdictions, jurisdictions should examine and give effect to, if appropriate, the actions initiated under the freezing mechanisms of other jurisdictions. When (i) a specific notification or communication is sent and (ii) the jurisdiction receiving the request is satisfied, according to applicable legal principles, that a requested designation is supported by reasonable grounds, or a reasonable basis, to suspect or believe that the proposed designee is a terrorist, one who finances terrorism or a terrorist organisation, the jurisdiction receiving the request must ensure that the funds or other assets of the designated person are frozen without delay.

Definitions

7. For the purposes of Special Recommendation III and this Interpretive Note, the following definitions apply:

a)   The term freeze means to prohibit the transfer, conversion, disposition or movement of funds or other assets on the basis of, and for the duration of the validity of, an action initiated by a competent authority or a court under a freezing mechanism. The frozen funds or other assets remain the property of the person(s) or entity(ies) that held an interest in the specified funds or other assets at the time of the freezing and may continue to be administered by the financial institution or other arrangements designated by such person(s) or entity(ies) prior to the initiation of an action under a freezing mechanism.

---

[3] For instance, both the UN Convention against Illicit Traffic in Narcotic Drugs and Psychotropic Substances (1988) and UN Convention against Transnational Organised Crime (2000) contain obligations regarding freezing, seizure and confiscation in the context of combating transnational crime. Those obligations exist separately and apart from obligations that are set forth in S/RES/1267(1999), S/RES/1373(2001) and Special Recommendation III.

[4] When the UNSC acts under Chapter VII of the UN Charter, the resolutions it issues are mandatory for all UN members.

[5] The UNSC was acting under Chapter VII of the UN Charter in issuing S/RES/1373(2001) (see previous footnote).

b) The term seize means to prohibit the transfer, conversion, disposition or movement of funds or other assets on the basis of an action initiated by a competent authority or a court under a freezing mechanism. However, unlike a freezing action, a seizure is effected by a mechanism that allows the competent authority or court to take control of specified funds or other assets. The seized funds or other assets remain the property of the person(s) or entity(ies) that held an interest in the specified funds or other assets at the time of the seizure, although the competent authority or court will often take over possession, administration or management of the seized funds or other assets.

c) The term confiscate, which includes forfeiture where applicable, means the permanent deprivation of funds or other assets by order of a competent authority or a court. Confiscation or forfeiture takes place through a judicial or administrative procedure that transfers the ownership of specified funds or other assets to be transferred to the State. In this case, the person(s) or entity(ies) that held an interest in the specified funds or other assets at the time of the confiscation or forfeiture loses all rights, in principle, to the confiscated or forfeited funds or other assets.[6]

d) The term funds or other assets means financial assets, property of every kind, whether tangible or intangible, movable or immovable, however acquired, and legal documents or instruments in any form, including electronic or digital, evidencing title to, or interest in, such funds or other assets, including, but not limited to, bank credits, travellers cheques, bank cheques, money orders, shares, securities, bonds, drafts, or letters of credit, and any interest, dividends or other income on or value accruing from or generated by such funds or other assets.

e) The term terrorist refers to any natural person who: (i) commits, or attempts to commit, terrorist acts[7] by any means, directly or indirectly, unlawfully and wilfully; (ii) participates as an accomplice in terrorist acts or terrorist financing; (iii) organises or directs others to commit terrorist acts or terrorist financing; or (iv) contributes to the commission of terrorist acts or terrorist financing by a group of persons acting with a common purpose where the contribution is made intentionally and with the aim of furthering the terrorist act or terrorist financing or with the knowledge of the intention of the group to commit a terrorist act or terrorist financing.

f) The phrase those who finance terrorism refers to any person, group, undertaking or other entity that provides or collects, by any means, directly or indirectly, funds or other assets that may be used, in full or in part, to facilitate the commission of terrorist acts, or to any persons or entities acting on behalf of, or at the direction of such persons, groups, undertakings or other entities. This includes those who provide or collect funds or other assets with the intention that they should be used or in the knowledge that they are to be used, in full or in part, in order to carry out terrorist acts.

g) The term terrorist organisation refers to any legal person, group, undertaking or other entity owned or controlled directly or indirectly by a terrorist(s).

h) The term designated persons refers to those persons or entities designated by the Al-Qaida and Taliban Sanctions Committee pursuant to S/RES/1267(1999) or those persons or entities designated and accepted, as appropriate, by jurisdictions pursuant to S/RES/1373(2001).

i) The phrase without delay, for the purposes of S/RES/1267(1999), means, ideally, within a matter of hours of a designation by the Al-Qaida and Taliban Sanctions Committee. For the purposes of S/RES/1373(2001), the phrase without delay means upon having reasonable grounds, or a reasonable basis, to suspect or believe that a person or entity is a terrorist, one who finances terrorism or a terrorist organisation. The phrase without delay should be interpreted in the context of the need to

---

[6] Confiscation or forfeiture orders are usually linked to a criminal conviction or a court decision whereby the confiscated or forfeited property is determined to have been derived from or intended for use in a violation of the law.

[7] A terrorist act includes an act which constitutes an offence within the scope of, and as defined in one of the following treaties: Convention for the Suppression of Unlawful Seizure of Aircraft, Convention for the Suppression of Unlawful Acts against the Safety of Civil Aviation, Convention on the Prevention and Punishment of Crimes against Internationally Protected Persons, including Diplomatic Agents, International Convention against the Taking of Hostages, Convention on the Physical Protection of Nuclear Material, Protocol for the Suppression of Unlawful Acts of Violence at Airports Serving International Civil Aviation, supplementary to the Convention for the Suppression of Unlawful Acts against the Safety of Civil Aviation, Convention for the Suppression of Unlawful Acts against the Safety of Maritime Navigation, Protocol for the Suppression of Unlawful Acts against the Safety of Fixed Platforms located on the Continental Shelf, International Convention for the Suppression of Terrorist Bombings, and the International Convention for the Suppression of the Financing of Terrorism (1999).

prevent the flight or dissipation of terrorist-linked funds or other assets, and the need for global, concerted action to interdict and disrupt their flow swiftly.

Freezing without delay terrorist-related funds or other assets

8. In order to fulfil the preventive intent of Special Recommendation III, jurisdictions should establish the necessary authority and adopt the following standards and procedures to freeze the funds or other assets of terrorists, those who finance terrorism and terrorist organisations in accordance with both S/RES/1267(1999) and S/RES/1373(2001):

a) **Authority to freeze, unfreeze and prohibit dealing in funds or other assets of designated persons.** Jurisdictions should prohibit by enforceable means the transfer, conversion, disposition or movement of funds or other assets. Options for providing the authority to freeze and unfreeze terrorist funds or other assets include:

 i) empowering or designating a competent authority or a court to issue, administer and enforce freezing and unfreezing actions under relevant mechanisms, or

 ii) enacting legislation that places responsibility for freezing the funds or other assets of designated persons publicly identified by a competent authority or a court on the person or entity holding the funds or other assets and subjecting them to sanctions for non-compliance.

 The authority to freeze and unfreeze funds or other assets should also extend to funds or other assets derived or generated from funds or other assets owned or controlled directly or indirectly by such terrorists, those who finance terrorism, or terrorist organisations.

 Whatever option is chosen there should be clearly identifiable competent authorities responsible for enforcing the measures.

 The competent authorities shall ensure that their nationals or any persons and entities within their territories are prohibited from making any funds or other assets, economic resources or financial or other related services available, directly or indirectly, wholly or jointly, for the benefit of: designated persons, terrorists; those who finance terrorism; terrorist organisations; entities owned or controlled, directly or indirectly, by such persons or entities; and persons and entities acting on behalf of or at the direction of such persons or entities.

b) **Freezing procedures.** Jurisdictions should develop and implement procedures to freeze the funds or other assets specified in paragraph (c) below without delay and without giving prior notice to the persons or entities concerned. Persons or entities holding such funds or other assets should be required by law to freeze them and should furthermore be subject to sanctions for non-compliance with this requirement. Any delay between the official receipt of information provided in support of a designation and the actual freezing of the funds or other assets of designated persons undermines the effectiveness of designation by affording designated persons time to remove funds or other assets from identifiable accounts and places. Consequently, these procedures must ensure (i) the prompt determination whether reasonable grounds or a reasonable basis exists to initiate an action under a freezing mechanism and (ii) the subsequent freezing of funds or other assets without delay upon determination that such grounds or basis for freezing exist. Jurisdictions should develop efficient and effective systems for communicating actions taken under their freezing mechanisms to the financial sector immediately upon taking such action. As well, they should provide clear guidance, particularly financial institutions and other persons or entities that may be holding targeted funds or other assets on obligations in taking action under freezing mechanisms.

c) **Funds or other assets to be frozen or, if appropriate, seized.** Under Special Recommendation III, funds or other assets to be frozen include those subject to freezing under S/RES/1267(1999) and S/RES/1373(2001). Such funds or other assets would also include those wholly or jointly owned or controlled, directly or indirectly, by designated persons. In accordance with their obligations under the United Nations International Convention for the Suppression of the Financing of Terrorism (1999) (the Terrorist Financing Convention (1999)), jurisdictions should be able to freeze or, if appropriate, seize any funds or other assets that they identify, detect, and verify, in accordance with applicable legal principles, as being used by, allocated for, or being made available to terrorists, those who finance terrorists or terrorist organisations. Freezing or seizing under the Terrorist Financing Convention (1999) may be conducted by freezing or seizing in the context of a criminal investigation or proceeding. Freezing action taken under Special Recommendation III shall be without prejudice to the rights of third parties acting in good faith.

d) **De-listing and unfreezing procedures.** Jurisdictions should develop and implement publicly known procedures to consider de-listing requests upon satisfaction of certain criteria consistent with international obligations and applicable legal principles, and to unfreeze the funds or other assets of de-listed persons or entities in a timely manner. For persons and entities designated under S/RES/1267(1999), such procedures and criteria should be in accordance with procedures adopted by the Al-Qaida and Taliban Sanctions Committee under S/RES/1267(1999).

e) **Unfreezing upon verification of identity.** For persons or entities with the same or similar name as designated persons, who are inadvertently affected by a freezing mechanism, jurisdictions should develop and implement publicly known procedures to unfreeze the funds or other assets of such persons or entities in a timely manner upon verification that the person or entity involved is not a designated person.

f) **Providing access to frozen funds or other assets in certain circumstances.** Where jurisdictions have determined that funds or other assets, which are otherwise subject to freezing pursuant to the obligations under S/RES/1267(1999), are necessary for basic expenses; for the payment of certain types of fees, expenses and service charges, or for extraordinary expenses,[8] jurisdictions should authorise access to such funds or other assets in accordance with the procedures set out in S/RES/1452(2002) and subject to approval of the Al-Qaida and Taliban Sanctions Committee. On the same grounds, jurisdictions may authorise access to funds or other assets, if freezing measures are applied pursuant to S/RES/1373(2001).

g) **Remedies.** Jurisdictions should provide for a mechanism through which a person or an entity that is the target of a freezing mechanism in the context of terrorist financing can challenge that measure with a view to having it reviewed by a competent authority or a court.

h) **Sanctions.** Jurisdictions should adopt appropriate measures to monitor effectively the compliance with relevant legislation, rules or regulations governing freezing mechanisms by financial institutions and other persons or entities that may be holding funds or other assets as indicated in paragraph 8(c) above. Failure to comply with such legislation, rules or regulations should be subject to civil, administrative or criminal sanctions.

Seizure and Confiscation

9. Consistent with FATF Recommendation 3, jurisdictions should adopt measures similar to those set forth in Article V of the United Nations Convention against Illicit Traffic in Narcotic Drugs and Psychotropic Substances (1988), Articles 12 to 14 of the United Nations Convention on Transnational Organised Crime (2000), and Article 8 of the Terrorist Financing Convention (1999), including legislative measures, to enable their courts or competent authorities to seize and confiscate terrorist funds or other assets.

Interpretative Note to Special Recommendation VI: Alternative Remittance

General

1. Money or value transfer systems have shown themselves vulnerable to misuse for money laundering and terrorist financing purposes. The objective of Special Recommendation VI is to increase the transparency of payment flows by ensuring that jurisdictions impose consistent anti-money laundering and counter-terrorist financing measures on all forms of money/value transfer systems, particularly those traditionally operating outside the conventional financial sector and not currently subject to the FATF Recommendations. This Recommendation and Interpretative Note underscore the need to bring all money or value transfer services, whether formal or informal, within the ambit of certain minimum legal and regulatory requirements in accordance with the relevant FATF Recommendations.

2. Special Recommendation VI consists of three core elements:

a) Jurisdictions should require licensing or registration of persons (natural or legal) that provide money/value transfer services, including through informal systems;

b) Jurisdictions should ensure that money/value transmission services, including informal systems (as described in paragraph 5 below), are subject to applicable FATF Forty Recommendations (2003)

---

[8] See Article 1, S/RES/1452(2002) for the specific types of expenses that are covered.

(in particular, Recommendations 4-16 and 21-25)[9] and the Eight Special Recommendations (in particular SR VII); and

c) Jurisdictions should be able to impose sanctions on money/value transfer services, including informal systems, that operate without a license or registration and that fail to comply with relevant FATF Recommendations.

Scope and Application

3. For the purposes of this Recommendation, the following definitions are used.

4. *Money or value transfer service* refers to a financial service that accepts cash, cheques, other monetary instruments or other stores of value in one location and pays a corresponding sum in cash or other form to a beneficiary in another location by means of a communication, message, transfer or through a clearing network to which the money/value transfer service belongs. Transactions performed by such services can involve one or more intermediaries and a third party final payment.

5. A money or value transfer service may be provided by persons (natural or legal) formally through the regulated financial system or informally through non-bank financial institutions or other business entities or any other mechanism either through the regulated financial system (for example, use of bank accounts) or through a network or mechanism that operates outside the regulated system. In some jurisdictions, informal systems are frequently referred to as alternative remittance services or underground (or parallel) banking systems. Often these systems have ties to particular geographic regions and are therefore described using a variety of specific terms. Some examples of these terms include hawala, hundi, fei-chien, and the black market peso exchange.[10]

6. Licensing means a requirement to obtain permission from a designated competent authority in order to operate a money/value transfer service legally.

7. Registration in this Recommendation means a requirement to register with or declare to a designated competent authority the existence of a money/value transfer service in order for the business to operate legally.

8. The obligation of licensing or registration applies to agents. At a minimum, the principal business must maintain a current list of agents which must be made available to the designated competent authority. An agent is any person who provides money or value transfer service under the direction of or by contract with a legally registered or licensed remitter (for example, licensees, franchisees, concessionaires).

Applicability of Special Recommendation VI

9. Special Recommendation VI should apply to all persons (natural or legal), which conduct for or on behalf of another person (natural or legal) the types of activity described in paragraphs 4 and 5 above as a primary or substantial part of their business or when such activity is undertaken on a regular or recurring basis, including as an ancillary part of a separate business enterprise.

10. Jurisdictions need not impose a separate licensing / registration system or designate another competent authority in respect to persons (natural or legal) already licensed or registered as financial institutions (as defined by the FATF Forty Recommendations (2003)) within a particular jurisdiction, which under such license or registration are permitted to perform activities indicated in paragraphs 4 and 5 above and which are already subject to the full range of applicable obligations under the FATF Forty Recommendations (2003) (in particular, Recommendations 4-16 and 21-25) and the Eight Special Recommendations (in particular SR VII).

Licensing or Registration and Compliance

11. Jurisdictions should designate an authority to grant licences and/or carry out registration and ensure that the requirement is observed. There should be an authority responsible for ensuring compliance by money/value transfer services with the FATF Recommendations (including the Eight Special Recommendations). There should also be effective systems in place for monitoring and ensuring

---

[9] When this Interpretative Note was originally issued, these references were to the 1996 FATF Forty Recommendations. Subsequent to the publication of the revised FATF Forty Recommendations in June 2003, this text was updated accordingly. All references are now to the 2003 FATF Forty Recommendations.

[10] The inclusion of these examples does not suggest that such systems are legal in any particular jurisdiction.

such compliance. This interpretation of Special Recommendation VI (i.e., the need for designation of competent authorities) is consistent with FATF Recommendation 23.

Sanctions

12. Persons providing money/value transfer services without a license or registration should be subject to appropriate administrative, civil or criminal sanctions.[11] Licensed or registered money/value transfer services which fail to comply fully with the relevant measures called for in the FATF Forty Recommendations (2003) or the Eight Special Recommendations should also be subject to appropriate sanctions.

Revised[12] Interpretative Note to Special Recommendation VII: Wire Transfers[13]

Objective

1. Special Recommendation VII (SR VII) was developed with the objective of preventing terrorists and other criminals from having unfettered access to wire transfers for moving their funds and for detecting such misuse when it occurs. Specifically, it aims to ensure that basic information on the originator of wire transfers is immediately available (1) to appropriate law enforcement and/or prosecutorial authorities to assist them in detecting, investigating, prosecuting terrorists or other criminals and tracing the assets of terrorists or other criminals, (2) to financial intelligence units for analysing suspicious or unusual activity and disseminating it as necessary, and (3) to beneficiary financial institutions to facilitate the identification and reporting of suspicious transactions. Due to the potential terrorist financing threat posed by small wire transfers, countries should aim for the ability to trace all wire transfers and should minimise thresholds taking into account the risk of driving transactions underground. It is not the intention of the FATF to impose rigid standards or to mandate a single operating process that would negatively affect the payment system. The FATF will continue to monitor the impact of Special Recommendation VII and conduct an assessment of its operation within three years of full implementation.

Definitions

2. For the purposes of this interpretative note, the following definitions apply.

a) The terms wire transfer and funds transfer refer to any transaction carried out on behalf of an originator person (both natural and legal) through a financial institution by electronic means with a view to making an amount of money available to a beneficiary person at another financial institution. The originator and the beneficiary may be the same person.

b) Cross-border transfer means any wire transfer where the originator and beneficiary institutions are located in different countries. This term also refers to any chain of wire transfers that has at least one cross-border element.

c) Domestic transfer means any wire transfer where the originator and beneficiary institutions are located in the same country. This term therefore refers to any chain of wire transfers that takes place entirely within the borders of a single country, even though the system used to effect the wire transfer may be located in another country. The term also refers to any chain of wire transfers that takes place entirely within the borders of the European Union.[14]

---

[11] Jurisdictions may authorise temporary or provisional operation of money / value transfer services that are already in existence at the time of implementing this Special Recommendation to permit such services to obtain a license or to register.

[12] This revision of the Interpretative Note to Special Recommendation VII was issued on 29 February 2008.

[13] It is recognised that countries will need time to make relevant legislative or regulatory changes and to allow financial institutions to make necessary adaptations to their systems and procedures. This period should not extend beyond December 2006.

[14] Having regard to the fact that:

The European Union constitutes an autonomous entity with its own sovereign rights and a legal order independent of the Member States, to which both the Member States themselves and their nationals are subject, within the European Union's areas of competence;

The European Union has enacted legislation binding upon its Member States, subject to control by a court of justice, which provides for the integration of payment services within an internal market in accordance with the principles of the free movement of capital and free provision of services; and

This legislation notably provides for the implementation of Special Recommendation VII as a single jurisdiction and requires that full information on the payer is made readily available, where appropriate upon request, to the

d) The term financial institution is as defined by the FATF Forty Recommendations (2003).[15] The term does not apply to any persons or entities that provide financial institutions solely with message or other support systems for transmitting funds.[16]

e) The originator is the account holder, or where there is no account, the person (natural or legal) that places the order with the financial institution to perform the wire transfer.

Scope

3. SR VII applies, under the conditions set out below, to cross-border and domestic transfers between financial institutions.

Cross-border wire transfers

4. Cross-border wire transfers should be accompanied by accurate and meaningful originator information. However, countries may adopt a de minimus threshold (no higher than USD or EUR 1 000). For cross-border transfers below this threshold:

a) Countries are not obligated to require ordering financial institutions to identify, verify record, or transmit originator information.

b) Countries may nevertheless require that incoming cross-border wire transfers contain full and accurate originator information.

5. Information accompanying qualifying cross-border wire transfers[17] must always contain the name of the originator and where an account exists, the number of that account. In the absence of an account, a unique reference number must be included.

6. Information accompanying qualifying wire transfers should also contain the address of the originator. However, countries may permit financial institutions to substitute the address with a national identity number, customer identification number, or date and place of birth.

7. Where several individual transfers from a single originator are bundled in a batch file for transmission to beneficiaries in another country, they shall be exempted from including full originator information, provided they include the originator's account number or unique reference number (as described in paragraph 8), and the batch file contains full originator information that is fully traceable within the recipient country.

Domestic wire transfers

8. Information accompanying domestic wire transfers must also include originator information as indicated for cross-border wire transfers, unless full originator information can be made available to the beneficiary financial institution and appropriate authorities by other means. In this latter case, financial institutions need only include the account number or a unique identifier provided that this number or identifier will permit the transaction to be traced back to the originator.

9. The information must be made available by the ordering financial institution within three business days of receiving the request either from the beneficiary financial institution or from appropriate authorities. Law enforcement authorities should be able to compel immediate production of such information.

---

beneficiary financial institution and relevant competent authorities. It is further noted that the European internal market and corresponding legal framework is extended to the members of the European Economic Area.

[15] When this Interpretative Note was originally issued, these references were to the 1996 FATF Forty Recommendations. Subsequent to the publication of the revised FATF Forty Recommendations in June 2003, this text was updated accordingly. All references are now to the 2003 FATF Forty Recommendations.

[16] However, these systems do have a role in providing the necessary means for the financial institutions to fulfil their obligations under SR VII and, in particular, in preserving the integrity of the information transmitted with a wire transfer.

[17] Throughout this Interpretative Note, the phrase 'qualifying cross-border wire transfers' means those cross-border wire transfers above any applicable threshold as described in paragraph 4.

Exemptions from SR VII

10. SR VII is not intended to cover the following types of payments:

a) Any transfer that flows from a transaction carried out using a credit or debit card so long as the credit or debit card number accompanies all transfers flowing from the transaction. However, when credit or debit cards are used as a payment system to effect a money transfer, they are covered by SR VII, and the necessary information should be included in the message.

b) Financial institution-to-financial institution transfers and settlements where both the originator person and the beneficiary person are financial institutions acting on their own behalf.

Role of ordering, intermediary and beneficiary financial institutions

Ordering financial institution

11. The ordering financial institution must ensure that qualifying wire transfers contain complete originator information. The ordering financial institution must also verify this information for accuracy and maintain this information in accordance with the standards set out in the FATF Forty Recommendations (2003).[18]

Intermediary financial institution

12. For both cross-border and domestic wire transfers, financial institutions processing an intermediary element of such chains of wire transfers must ensure that all originator information that accompanies a wire transfer is retained with the transfer.

13. Where technical limitations prevent the full originator information accompanying a cross-border wire transfer from remaining with a related domestic wire transfer (during the necessary time to adapt payment systems), a record must be kept for five years by the receiving intermediary financial institution of all the information received from the ordering financial institution.

Beneficiary financial institution

14. Beneficiary financial institutions should have effective risk-based procedures in place to identify wire transfers lacking complete originator information. The lack of complete originator information may be considered as a factor in assessing whether a wire transfer or related transactions are suspicious and, as appropriate, whether they are thus required to be reported to the financial intelligence unit or other competent authorities. In some cases, the beneficiary financial institution should consider restricting or even terminating its business relationship with financial institutions that fail to meet SRVII standards.

Enforcement mechanisms for financial institutions that do not comply with wire transfer rules and regulations

15. Countries should adopt appropriate measures to monitor effectively the compliance of financial institutions with rules and regulations governing wire transfers. Financial institutions that fail to comply with such rules and regulations should be subject to civil, administrative or criminal sanctions.

Interpretative Note to Special Recommendation VIII: Non-Profit Organisations

Introduction

1. Non-profit organisations (NPOs) play a vital role in the world economy and in many national economies and social systems. Their efforts complement the activity of the governmental and business sectors in providing essential services, comfort and hope to those in need around the world. The ongoing international campaign against terrorist financing has unfortunately demonstrated however that terrorists and terrorist organisations exploit the NPO sector to raise and move funds, provide logistical support, encourage terrorist recruitment or otherwise support terrorist organisations and operations. This misuse not only facilitates terrorist activity but also undermines donor confidence and jeopardises the very integrity of NPOs. Therefore, protecting the NPO sector from terrorist abuse is both a critical component of the global fight against terrorism and a necessary step to preserve the integrity of NPOs.

2. NPOs may be vulnerable to abuse by terrorists for a variety of reasons. NPOs enjoy the public trust, have access to considerable sources of funds, and are often cash-intensive. Furthermore, some NPOs have a global presence that provides a framework for national and international operations and financial

---

[18] See note 4.

transactions, often within or near those areas that are most exposed to terrorist activity. Depending on the legal form of the NPO and the country, NPOs may often be subject to little or no governmental oversight (for example, registration, record keeping, reporting and monitoring), or few formalities may be required for their creation (for example, there may be no skills or starting capital required, no background checks necessary for employees). Terrorist organisations have taken advantage of these characteristics of NPOs to infiltrate the sector and misuse NPO funds and operations to cover for or support terrorist activity.

Objectives and General Principles

3. The objective of Special Recommendation VIII (SR VIII) is to ensure that NPOs are not misused by terrorist organisations: (i) to pose as legitimate entities; (ii) to exploit legitimate entities as conduits for terrorist financing, including for the purpose of escaping asset freezing measures; or (iii) to conceal or obscure the clandestine diversion of funds intended for legitimate purposes but diverted for terrorist purposes. In this Interpretative Note, the approach taken to achieve this objective is based on the following general principles:

a) Past and ongoing abuse of the NPO sector by terrorists and terrorist organisations requires countries to adopt measures both: (i) to protect the sector against such abuse, and (ii) to identify and take effective action against those NPOs that either are exploited by or actively support terrorists or terrorist organizations.

b) Measures adopted by countries to protect the NPO sector from terrorist abuse should not disrupt or discourage legitimate charitable activities. Rather, such measures should promote transparency and engender greater confidence in the sector, across the donor community and with the general public that charitable funds and services reach intended legitimate beneficiaries. Systems that promote achieving a high degree of transparency, integrity and public confidence in the management and functioning of all NPOs are integral to ensuring the sector cannot be misused for terrorist financing.

c) Measures adopted by countries to identify and take effective action against NPOs that either are exploited by or actively support terrorists or terrorist organisations should aim to prevent and prosecute as appropriate terrorist financing and other forms of terrorist support. Where NPOs suspected of or implicated in terrorist financing or other forms of terrorist support are identified, the first priority of countries must be to investigate and halt such terrorist financing or support. Actions taken for this purpose should to the extent reasonably possible avoid any negative impact on innocent and legitimate beneficiaries of charitable activity. However, this interest cannot excuse the need to undertake immediate and effective actions to advance the immediate interest of halting terrorist financing or other forms of terrorist support provided by NPOs.

d) Developing co-operative relationships among the public, private and NPO sector is critical to raising awareness and fostering capabilities to combat terrorist abuse within the sector. Countries should encourage the development of academic research on and information sharing in the NPO sector to address terrorist financing related issues.

e) A targeted approach in dealing with the terrorist threat to the NPO sector is essential given the diversity within individual national sectors, the differing degrees to which parts of each sector may be vulnerable to misuse by terrorists, the need to ensure that legitimate charitable activity continues to flourish and the limited resources and authorities available to combat terrorist financing in each jurisdiction.

f) Flexibility in developing a national response to terrorist financing in the NPO sector is also essential in order to allow it to evolve over time as it faces the changing nature of the terrorist financing threat.

Definitions

4. For the purposes of SR VIII and this interpretative note, the following definitions apply:

a) The term non-profit organisation or NPO refers to a legal entity or organisation that primarily engages in raising or disbursing funds for purposes such as charitable, religious, cultural, educational, social or fraternal purposes, or for the carrying out of other types of 'good works'.

b) The terms FIU, legal arrangement and legal person are as defined by the FATF Forty Recommendations (2003) (the FATF Recommendations).

c) The term funds is as defined by the Interpretative Note to FATF Special Recommendation II.

d) The terms freezing, terrorist and terrorist organisation are as defined by the Interpretative Note to FATF Special Recommendation III.

e) The term appropriate authorities refers to competent authorities, self-regulatory bodies, accrediting institutions and other administrative authorities.

f) The term beneficiaries refers to those natural persons, or groups of natural persons who receive charitable, humanitarian or other types of assistance through the services of the NPO.

Measures

5. Countries should undertake domestic reviews of their NPO sector or have the capacity to obtain timely information on its activities, size and other relevant features. In undertaking these assessments, countries should use all available sources of information in order to identify features and types of NPOs, which by virtue of their activities or characteristics, are at risk of being misused for terrorist financing.[19] Countries should also periodically reassess the sector by reviewing new information on the sector's potential vulnerabilities to terrorist activities.

6. There is a diverse range of approaches in identifying, preventing and combating terrorist misuse of NPOs. An effective approach, however, is one that involves all four of the following elements: (a) Outreach to the sector, (b) Supervision or monitoring, (c) Effective investigation and information gathering and (d) Effective mechanisms for international co-operation. The following measures represent specific actions that countries should take with respect to each of these elements in order to protect their NPO sector from terrorist financing abuse.

a. Outreach to the NPO sector concerning terrorist financing issues

(i) Countries should have clear policies to promote transparency, integrity and public confidence in the administration and management of all NPOs.

(ii) Countries should encourage or undertake outreach programmes to raise awareness in the NPO sector about the vulnerabilities of NPOs to terrorist abuse and terrorist financing risks, and the measures that NPOs can take to protect themselves against such abuse.

(iii) Countries should work with the NPO sector to develop and refine best practices to address terrorist financing risks and vulnerabilities and thus protect the sector from terrorist abuse.[20]

(iv) Countries should encourage NPOs to conduct transactions via regulated financial channels, wherever feasible, keeping in mind the varying capacities of financial sectors in different countries and in different areas of urgent charitable and humanitarian concerns.

b. Supervision or monitoring of the NPO sector   Countries should take steps to promote effective supervision or monitoring of their NPO sector. In practice, countries should be able to demonstrate that the following standards apply to NPOs which account for (1) a significant portion of the financial resources under control of the sector; and (2) a substantial share of the sector's international activities.

(i) NPOs should maintain information on: (1) the purpose and objectives of their stated activities; and (2) the identity of the person(s) who own, control or direct their activities, including senior officers, board members and trustees. This information should be publicly available either directly from the NPO or through appropriate authorities.

(ii) NPOs should issue annual financial statements that provide detailed breakdowns of incomes and expenditures.

(iii) NPOs should be licensed or registered. This information should be available to competent authorities.[21]

(iv) NPOs should have appropriate controls in place to ensure that all funds are fully accounted for and are spent in a manner that is consistent with the purpose and objectives of the NPO's stated activities.

(v) NPOs should follow a "know your beneficiaries and associate NPOs"[22] rule, which means that the NPO should make best efforts to confirm the identity, credentials and good standing of their

---

[19] For example, such information could be provided by regulators, tax authorities, FIUs, donor organisations or law enforcement and intelligence authorities.

[20] The FATF's Combating the Abuse of Non-Profit Organisations: International Best Practices provides a useful reference document for such exercises.

[21] Specific licensing or registration requirements for counter terrorist financing purposes are not necessary. For example, in some countries, NPOs are already registered with tax authorities and monitored in the context of qualifying for favourable tax treatment (such as tax credits or tax exemptions).

[22] The term associate NPOs includes foreign branches of international NPOs.

beneficiaries and associate NPOs. NPOs should also undertake best efforts to document the identity of their significant donors and to respect donor confidentiality.

(vi) NPOs should maintain, for a period of at least five years, and make available to appropriate authorities, records of domestic and international transactions that are sufficiently detailed to verify that funds have been spent in a manner consistent with the purpose and objectives of the organisation. This also applies to information mentioned in paragraphs (i) and (ii) above.

(vii) Appropriate authorities should monitor the compliance of NPOs with applicable rules and regulations.[23] Appropriate authorities should be able to properly

sanction relevant violations by NPOs or persons acting on behalf of these NPOs.[24]

c. Effective information gathering and investigation

(i) Countries should ensure effective co-operation, co-ordination and information sharing to the extent possible among all levels of appropriate authorities or organisations that hold relevant information on NPOs.

(ii) Countries should have investigative expertise and capability to examine those NPOs suspected of either being exploited by or actively supporting terrorist activity or terrorist organisations.

(iii) Countries should ensure that full access to information on the administration and management of a particular NPO (including financial and programmatic information) may be obtained during the course of an investigation.

(iv) Countries should establish appropriate mechanisms to ensure that when there is suspicion or reasonable grounds to suspect that a particular NPO: (1) is a front for fundraising by a terrorist organisation; (2) is being exploited as a conduit for terrorist financing, including for the purpose of escaping asset freezing measures; or (3) is concealing or obscuring the clandestine diversion of funds intended for legitimate purposes, but redirected for the benefit of terrorists or terrorist organisations, this information is promptly shared with all relevant competent authorities in order to take preventative or investigative action.

d. Effective capacity to respond to international requests for information about an NPO of concern
Consistent with Special Recommendation V, countries should identify appropriate points of contact and procedures to respond to international requests for information regarding particular NPOs suspected of terrorist financing or other forms of terrorist support.

Interpretative Note to Special Recommendation IX: Cash Couriers

Objectives

1. FATF Special Recommendation IX was developed with the objective of ensuring that terrorists and other criminals cannot finance their activities or launder the proceeds of their crimes through the physical cross-border transportation of currency and bearer negotiable instruments. Specifically, it aims to ensure that countries have measures 1) to detect the physical cross-border transportation of currency and bearer negotiable instruments, 2) to stop or restrain currency and bearer negotiable instruments that are suspected to be related to terrorist financing or money laundering, 3) to stop or restrain currency or bearer negotiable instruments that are falsely declared or disclosed, 4) to apply appropriate sanctions for making a false declaration or disclosure, and 5) to enable confiscation of currency or bearer negotiable instruments that are related to terrorist financing or money laundering. Countries should implement Special Recommendation IX subject to strict safeguards to ensure proper use of information and without restricting either: (i) trade payments between countries for goods and services; or (ii) the freedom of capital movements in any way.

---

[23] In this context, rules and regulations may include rules and standards applied by self regulatory bodies and accrediting institutions.

[24] The range of such sanctions might include freezing of accounts, removal of trustees, fines, de-certification, de-licensing and de-registration. This should not preclude parallel civil, administrative or criminal proceedings with respect to NPOs or persons acting on their behalf where appropriate.

Definitions

2. For the purposes of Special Recommendation IX and this Interpretative Note, the following definitions apply.

3. The *term bearer negotiable instruments* includes monetary instruments in bearer form such as: travellers cheques; negotiable instruments (including cheques, promissory notes and money orders) that are either in bearer form, endorsed without restriction, made out to a fictitious payee, or otherwise in such form that title thereto passes upon delivery; incomplete instruments (including cheques, promissory notes and money orders) signed, but with the payee's name omitted.[25]

4. The term *currency* refers to banknotes and coins that are in circulation as a medium of exchange.

5. The term *physical cross-border transportation* refers to any in-bound or out-bound physical transportation of currency or bearer negotiable instruments from one country to another country. The term includes the following modes of transportation: (1) physical transportation by a natural person, or in that person's accompanying luggage or vehicle; (2) shipment of currency through containerised cargo or (3) the mailing of currency or bearer negotiable instruments by a natural or legal person.

6. The term *false declaration* refers to a misrepresentation of the value of currency or bearer negotiable instruments being transported, or a misrepresentation of other relevant data which is asked for in the declaration or otherwise requested by the authorities. This includes failing to make a declaration as required.

7. The term *false disclosure* refers to a misrepresentation of the value of currency or bearer negotiable instruments being transported, or a misrepresentation of other relevant data which is asked for in the disclosure or otherwise requested by the authorities. This includes failing to make a disclosure as required.

8. When the term *related to terrorist financing or money laundering* is used to describe currency or bearer negotiable instruments, it refers to currency or bearer negotiable instruments that are: (i) the proceeds of, or used in, or intended or allocated for use in, the financing of terrorism, terrorist acts or terrorist organisations; or (ii) laundered, proceeds from money laundering or predicate offences, or instrumentalities used in or intended for use in the commission of these offences.

The types of systems that may be implemented to address the issue of cash couriers

9. Countries may meet their obligations under Special Recommendation IX and this Interpretative Note by implementing one of the following types of systems; however, countries do not have to use the same type of system for incoming and outgoing cross-border transportation of currency or bearer negotiable instruments:

a) Declaration system: The key characteristics of a declaration system are as follows. All persons making a physical cross-border transportation of currency or bearer negotiable instruments, which are of a value exceeding a pre-set, maximum threshold of EUR/USD 15,000, are required to submit a truthful declaration to the designated competent authorities. Countries that implement a declaration system should ensure that the pre-set threshold is sufficiently low to meet the objectives of Special Recommendation IX.

b) Disclosure system: The key characteristics of a disclosure system are as follows. All persons making a physical cross-border transportation of currency or bearer negotiable instruments are required to make a truthful disclosure to the designated competent authorities upon request. Countries that implement a disclosure system should ensure that the designated competent authorities can make their inquiries on a targeted basis, based on intelligence or suspicion, or on a random basis.

---

[25] For the purposes of this Interpretative Note, gold, precious metals and precious stones are not included despite their high liquidity and use in certain situations as a means of exchange or transmitting value. These items may be otherwise covered under customs laws and regulations. If a country discovers an unusual cross-border movement of gold, precious metals or precious stones, it should consider notifying, as appropriate, the Customs Service or other competent authorities of the countries from which these items originated and/or to which they are destined, and should co-operate with a view toward establishing the source, destination, and purpose of the movement of such items and toward the taking of appropriate action.

Additional elements applicable to both systems

10. Whichever system is implemented, countries should ensure that their system incorporates the following elements:

a) The declaration/disclosure system should apply to both incoming and outgoing transportation of currency and bearer negotiable instruments.

b) Upon discovery of a false declaration/disclosure of currency or bearer negotiable instruments or a failure to declare/disclose them, designated competent authorities should have the authority to request and obtain further information from the carrier with regard to the origin of the currency or bearer negotiable instruments and their intended use.

c) Information obtained through the declaration/disclosure process should be available to the financial intelligence unit (FIU) either through a system whereby the FIU is notified about suspicious cross-border transportation incidents or by making the declaration/disclosure information directly available to the FIU in some other way.

d) At the domestic level, countries should ensure that there is adequate co-ordination among customs, immigration and other related authorities on issues related to the implementation of Special Recommendation IX.

e) In the following two cases, competent authorities should be able to stop or restrain cash or bearer negotiable instruments for a reasonable time in order to ascertain whether evidence of money laundering or terrorist financing may be found: (i) where there is a suspicion of money laundering or terrorist financing; or (ii) where there is a false declaration or false disclosure.

f) The declaration/disclosure system should allow for the greatest possible measure of international co-operation and assistance in accordance with Special Recommendation V and Recommendations 35 to 40. To facilitate such co-operation, in instances when: (i) a declaration or disclosure which exceeds the maximum threshold of EUR/USD 15,000 is made, or (ii) where there is a false declaration or false disclosure, or (iii) where there is a suspicion of money laundering or terrorist financing, this information shall be retained for use by the appropriate authorities. At a minimum, this information will cover: (i) the amount of currency or bearer negotiable instruments declared / disclosed or otherwise detected; and (ii) the identification data of the bearer(s).

Sanctions

11. Persons who make a false declaration or disclosure should be subject to effective, proportionate and dissuasive sanctions, whether criminal civil or administrative. Persons who are carrying out a physical cross-border transportation of currency or bearer negotiable instruments that are related to terrorist financing or money laundering should also be subject to effective, proportionate and dissuasive sanctions, whether criminal, civil or administrative, and should be subject to measures, including legislative ones consistent with Recommendation 3 and Special Recommendation III, which would enable the confiscation of such currency or bearer negotiable instruments.

APPENDIX 8

Useful Websites

Anti-money Laundering Professionals Forum

<http://www.amlpforum.com/>

The homepage of an organization of anti-money laundering professionals from within and outside financial services and the other regulated industries in the UK, Europe, and internationally.

Bank for International Settlements (BIS)

<http://www.bis.org/bcbs/>

This is the homepage of the Bank for International Settlements (BIS). The Bank for International Settlements (BIS) is an international organization which fosters international monetary and financial co-operation and serves as a bank for central banks.

The Basel Committee on Banking Supervision

<http://www.bis.org/bcbs/>

The Basel Committee on Banking Supervision provides a forum for regular co-operation on banking supervisory matters.

<http://www.bis.org/list/bcbs/tid_32/index.htm>

Refers to a link with regards to publications on money laundering and terrorist financing.

British Bankers' Association (BBA)

<http://www.bba.org.uk/>

This is the official homepage. The BBA is the leading trade association for the UK banking and financial services sector. They speak for over 200 member banks from 60 countries on the full range of UK and international banking issues.

<http://www.bba.org.uk/policy/money-laundering>

This link refers to the section 'Policy – Financial Crime' where you can find a link referring to money laundering issues.

Council of Europe

The Council of Europe website includes links to a number of its conventions, including the following:

<http://conventions.coe.int/treaty/en/treaties/html/141.htm>

Council of Europe Convention: Strasbourg 1990 (extracts regarding money laundering offences)

<http://conventions.coe.int/treaty/en/treaties/html/197.htm>

Council of Europe Convention: Warsaw 2005

Council of Europe—Committee of Experts on the Evaluation of Anti-money Laundering Measures and the Financing of Terrorism (MONEYVAL)

<http://www.coe.int/t/dghl/monitoring/moneyval/About/MONEYVAL_in_brief_en.asp>

This link refers to website Council of Europe—Committee of Experts on the Evaluation of Anti-money Laundering Measures and the Financing of Terrorism (MONEYVAL). The aim of MONEYVAL is to ensure that its member states have in place effective systems to counter money laundering and terrorist financing and comply with the relevant international standards in these fields.

Department for Business and Innovation & Skills (BIS)

<http://www.bis.gov.uk/policies/export-control-organisation>

The BIS website includes this page dealing with the Export Control Organisation, which is responsible for assessing and issuing export and trade licences for specific categories of 'controlled' goods. The page includes links to useful Notices for Exporters and other similar documents.

Egmont Group of Financial Intelligence Units

<http://www.egmontgroup.org/>

This link refers to official homepage of the Egmont Group (see Glossary).

EUR-Lex

<http://eur-lex.europa.eu/en/tools/about.htm>

This refers to the official homepage of Eur-lex. EUR-Lex provides free access to European Union law and other documents considered to be public, including the following:

<http://eur-lex.europa.eu/LexUriServ/LexUriServ.do?uri=CELEX:31991L0308:EN:HTML>

First EU Money Laundering Directive 1991

<http://eur-lex.europa.eu/smartapi/cgi/sga_doc?smartapi!celexplus!prod!CELEXnumdoc&numdoc=32001L0097&lg=EN>

Second EU Money Laundering Directive 2001

<http://eur-lex.europa.eu/LexUriServ/LexUriServ.do?uri=OJ:L:2005:309:0015:0036:EN:PDF>

Third EU Money Laundering Directive 2005

Financial Services Authority

<http://www.fsa.gov.uk/>

This is the official home page. The Financial Services Authority (FSA) is an independent non-governmental body, given statutory powers by the Financial Services and Markets Act 2000. The FSA is a company limited by guarantee and financed by the financial services industry.

<http://fsahandbook.info/FSA/index.jsp>

This is the link which relates to the FSA handbook which contains a section with regard to anti-money laundering dealing with the requirements for anti-money laundering systems and controls.

Financial Action Task Force (FATF)

http://www.fatf-gafi.org

This is the official homepage of the Financial Action Task Force (FATF). In addition to the 40 Recommendations and the 9 Special Recommendations, there are links on the site to FATF Mutual Evaluations and other relevant documents.

Her Majesty's Treasury

<http://www.hm-treasury.gov.uk/>

This is the official homepage. HM Treasury has responsibility for financial regulations and sanctions.

<http://www.hm-treasury.gov.uk/fin_money_index.htm>

This is the link to the 'Financial Services' section which leads to the 'Counter Illicit Finance Section' dealing with issues such as combating money laundering: guidance, consultation documents and details of the Money Laundering Advisory Committee

<http://www.hm-treasury.gov.uk/fin_sanctions_index.htm>

This is the link to the 'Financial Services' section which leads to the 'Financial Sanctions' section with regard to Asset Freezing Unit providing e.g. Asset Freezing List to download.

Home Office

<http://www.homeoffice.gov.uk/>

This is the official homepage.

<http://www.homeoffice.gov.uk/about-us/home-office-circulars/circulars-2005/053-2005/>

Home Office Circular 53/2005 'Money-Laundering: the Confidentiality and Sensitivity of Suspicious Activity Reports (Sars) and the Identity of those who make them'

<http://www.homeoffice.gov.uk/about-us/home-office-circulars/circulars-2008/029-2008/>

Home Office Circular on Consent (see also Annex A below)

457

<http://www.homeoffice.gov.uk/about-us/home-office-circulars/circulars-2008/029-2008/621959?view=Binary>

Annex A to the Home Office Circular on Consent

IBA Anti-money Laundering Forum

<http://www.anti-moneylaundering.org/>

This refers to the International Bar Association's Anti-money Laundering Forum website. The IBA Anti-money Laundering Forum, the lawyer's guide to legislation and compliance, is an internet-based network assisting lawyers in dealing with their current responsibilities in connection with new anti-money laundering legislation.

Institute of Chartered Accountants in England and Wales (ICAEW)

<http://ww.icaew.com>

This is the link to the official homepage.

<http://www.icaew.com/index.cfm/route/143703/icaew_ga/en/Members/Support/Professional_conduct/Members_Handbook/Members_Handbook>

This is the link to the members' handbook. Section 9 contains anti-money laundering guidance for the accountancy sector.

Institute of Money Laundering Prevention Officers (IMLPO)

<http://www.imlpo.com/>

This is the official homepage of the Institute of Money Laundering Prevention Officers and the link to the website 'About Institute of Money Laundering Prevention Officers'. IMLPO was established in 2001. It is a cross-representative forum of anti-money laundering professionals who share views, experiences and concerns of the day-to-day business of combating money laundering.

Joint Money Laundering Steering Group (JMLSG)

<http://www.jmlsg.org.uk/>

This refers to the home page of the Joint Money Laundering Steering Group website

The Joint Money Laundering Steering Group is made up of the leading UK trade associations in the financial services industry. Its aim is to promulgate good practice in countering money laundering and to give practical assistance in interpreting the UK Money Laundering Regulations. This is primarily achieved by the publication of industry guidance.

<http://www.jmlsg.org.uk/reporting-suspicions>

This link refers to the part of the section of their website dealing with 'Reporting suspicions as money laundering activities'.

The Law Society of England and Wales

The Law Society represents solicitors in England and Wales.

<http://www.lawsociety.org.uk/home.law>

This is the official homepage.

<http://www.lawsociety.org.uk/productsandservices/antimoneylaundering.page>

This is the home page for matters concerning money laundering, including a link to the AML Practice Note.

Office of Fair Trading

<http://www.oft.gov.uk/>

This is the official homepage. The OFT is the UK's consumer and competition authority. It is a designated authority with supervisory responsibilities under the Money Laundering Regulations. An easy link from the homepage leads to the anti-money laundering section of the site.

Serious Organised Crime Agency (SOCA)

<http://www.soca.gov.uk/>

This is the official homepage of SOCA. The UK FIU is now located within SOCA.

<http://www.soca.gov.uk/about-soca/the-uk-financial-intelligence-unit>

This link refers to the UK Financial Intelligence Unit—the part of SOCA that focuses on the proceeds of crime and terrorist financing.

Solicitors Regulation Authority

<http://www.sra.org.uk/solicitors/code-of-conduct/guidance/warningcards/Money-laundering.page>. This website relates to the Solicitors Regulation Authority (SRA), the regulatory body of the Law Society of England & Wales and in particular to the section dealing with money laundering.

See also The Law Society.

United Nations

The UN website includes links to a number of useful UN instruments, including:

<http://www.unodc.org/pdf/convention_1988_en.pdf>

UN Convention: Vienna 1988

<http://www.unodc.org/documents/treaties/UNTOC/Publications/TOC%20Convention/TOCebook-e.pdf>

UN Convention: Palermo 2000 (Articles 1–7 and Articles 11, 12, 15 are relevant)

<http://www.un.org/law/cod/finterr.htm>

International Convention on the Suppression of the financing of terrorism (1999)

<http://www.coe.int/t/e/legal_affairs/legal_co-operation/fight_against_terrorism/4_Theme_Files/UN%20SC%20Res%201373%20(2001)%20E.pdf>

UN Security Council Resolution 1373 (2001)

<http://www.ustreas.gov/offices/enforcement/pdf/unscr1452.pdf>

UN Security Council Resolution 1452 (2002)

<http://www.unodc.org/documents/treaties/UNCAC/Publications/Convention/08-50026_E.pdf>

UN Convention Against Corruption 2003. (Articles 14, 23 and 24 are relevant).

US Treasury Department

<http://www.ustreas.gov/topics/law-enforcement/index.shtml>

The website of the US Treasury Department includes much material that is important and useful in the field of money laundering and terrorist finance. This page includes (under the heading Related Offices) links to the Office of Terrorism and Financial Intelligence (TFI) and the Office of Terrorist Financing and Financial Crime (TFFC).

<http://www.ustreas.gov/offices/enforcement/ofac/>

This refers to the homepage of the Office of Foreign Assets Control (OFAC), which administers and enforces economic and trade sanctions based on US foreign policy and national security goals against targeted foreign countries and regimes, terrorists, international narcotics traffickers, those engaged in activities related to the proliferation of weapons of mass destruction, and other threats to the national security, foreign policy, or economy of the United States.

The Wolfsberg Group

<http://www.wolfsberg-principles.com/index.html>

This refers to official homepage of the Wolfsberg Group. The Wolfsberg Group is an association of 11 global banks, which aims to develop financial services industry standards, and related products, for Know Your Customer, Anti-money Laundering and Counter Terrorist Financing policies.

<http://www.wolfsberg-principles.com/diligence.html>

This useful link refers to the part of their website dealing with International Due Diligence Repository where you can find useful downloads regarding Due Diligence FAQS and an AML Questionnaire.

GLOSSARY

Accredited financial investigator   An accredited financial investigator is a civilian investigator who has been accredited by the National Policing Improvement Agency under section 3 of POCA. In order to exercise specified powers under the Act the accredited financial investigator will also have to fall within a description specified in an order made for the purposes of that provision by the Secretary of State under section 453 of POCA.

Authorised officer   Amendments to Part III of TA 2000 that came into force on 26 December 2007 brought with them a new term: 'authorised officer'. In sections 21ZA and 21ZB, authorised officer means a member of staff of SOCA 'authorised for the purposes of this section' by the Director General of SOCA.

Authorised disclosures   *See* Disclosures.

Beneficial owner   Where there is a beneficial owner who is not the customer, customer due diligence under Regulation 5(b) requires the relevant person to identify the beneficial owner and take adequate measures to satisfy himself that he knows who the beneficial owner is. Regulation 6 goes on to spell out what the phrase means in connection with a body corporate, a partnership, and a trust.

Cash   There are different definitions of cash, for different purposes, in Part 5 of POCA and in the Regulations.
- In connection with the seizure, detention, and forfeiture of cash in Part 5 of POCA 'cash' is given a broad interpretation to include, in addition to banknotes and coins in any currency, most forms of financial instrument. The definition is in section 289 of POCA.
- For the purposes of defining a high value dealer, a narrower interpretation is given to cash. In Regulation 2(1), 'cash' means notes, coins or traveller's cheques in any currency.

Commissioners of Revenue and Customs   *See* Supervisory authorities.

Competent authorities   The phrase 'competent authorities', extensively used in both the FATF Recommendations and in the Third Money Laundering Directive, is not defined in either document. The meaning of the phrase appears to vary according to the context. The Third Directive requires that all relevant persons are supervised by a 'competent authority'—a 'supervisory authority' under the Regulations.

Consent reports   SOCA uses the term 'consent reports' for disclosures about criminal property combined with a request for consent. [*See also* under Disclosures.]

Criminal conduct   The two key concepts in relation to money laundering are criminal conduct and criminal property. Both are defined in section 340 of POCA. Note that the full definition of money laundering occupies section 340(2) to (11):
340(2)
    Criminal conduct is conduct which—
        (a) constitutes an offence in any part of the United Kingdom, or
        (b) would constitute an offence in any part of the United Kingdom if it occurred there.

Criminal property   At the heart of the money laundering regime is the concept of criminal property, which is defined in section 340(3) of POCA. See also criminal conduct above.
340(3):

Property is criminal property if—
- (a) it constitutes a person's benefit from criminal conduct or it represents such a benefit (in whole or part and whether directly or indirectly), and
- (b) the alleged offender knows or suspects that it constitutes or represents such a benefit.

Customer due diligence (CDD)   Regulation 7 of the 2007 Regulations obliges relevant persons to apply customer due diligence measures in various circumstances, including establishing a business relationship. The definition of CDD is in Regulation 5 and includes, for example, verifying the identity of the customer and obtaining information on the purpose and intended nature of the business relationship. The CDD requirements are detailed and occupy the whole of Part 2: Regulations 5 to 18 inclusive. Applying the risk-based approach, the Regulations allow for *simplified* due diligence measures in some circumstances (set out in Regulation 13), and require *enhanced* due diligence measures in others (set out in Regulation 14).

Designated authority   A limited number of supervisory authorities are also designated authorities for the purposes of Part 5 of the 2007 Regulations, as set out below:
'designated authority' means—
- (a) the Authority;
- (b) the Commissioners;
- (c) the OFT; and
- (d) in relation to credit unions in Northern Ireland, DETI.

Designated non-financial businesses and professions (DNFBPs)   DNFBPs are designated non-financial businesses and professions which are included in the scope of the revised FATF Recommendations. The widening of the regulated sector to include DNFBPs such as accountants, estate agents, and legal professionals is reflected in the definition of relevant persons in the 2007 Regulations.

Disclosures   Part 7 of POCA makes provision for disclosures about suspected money laundering to be sent to the UK FIU at SOCA. The two main types of disclosure are *required disclosures* and *authorised disclosures*.

- Required disclosures: a person in the regulated sector who knows or suspects or has reasonable grounds to suspect that another person is engaged in money laundering is required to make a disclosure to SOCA.

- Authorised disclosures: an authorised disclosure is a disclosure about criminal property. The money laundering offences are widely drafted and authorised disclosures provide a means of avoiding potential liability for a money laundering offence. In most cases where an authorised disclosure has to be made, it will also be necessary to seek appropriate consent to deal in some way with the criminal property. (*See also* Consent reports).

Egmont Group   The Egmont Group is an informal group or network of FIUs, formed in 1995. For an FIU to become a member, it must comply with international standards and the criteria of the Egmont Group. These FIUs meet regularly to find ways to co-operate, especially in the areas of information exchange, training and the sharing of expertise.

Enhanced CDD   See Customer due diligence (CDD).

Equivalence   In the context of Reliance (q.v.), the concept of equivalence is used to limit the categories of person carrying out business in a non-EEA state on whom reliance can be placed to apply CDD measures. In order to limit the reliance provisions to persons in whom the same degree of confidence can be placed as on persons carrying on business in the UK or another EEA state, the provisions make use of the notion of equivalence. 'Equivalence' appears variously in the context of an equivalent institution, equivalent requirements, and equivalent supervision.

Financial Action Task Force (FATF)   The Financial Action Task Force was established at the G7 meeting in Paris in 1989. In the following year FATF issued its 40 Recommendations on money laundering.

Financial Intelligence Unit (FIU)   To comply with the FATF Recommendations, every country should establish an FIU. An FIU is defined by the Egmont Group (q.v.) as follows:

> A Financial Intelligence Unit (FIU) is a central, national agency responsible for receiving (and, as permitted, requesting), analyzing and disseminating to the competent authorities, disclosures of financial information: (i) concerning suspected proceeds of crime and potential financing of terrorism, or (ii) required by national legislation or regulation, in order to counter money laundering and terrorism financing.

The UK FIU which was formerly part of the National Criminal Intelligence Service (NCIS)) is now located within SOCA.

Financial Services Authority (FSA)   Under the Financial Services and Markets Act 2000, the FSA is the UK regulator for banks and financial services. One of its objectives is the reduction of financial crime. All or almost all persons in the financial services sector will be relevant persons under the 2007 Regulations and will be regulated for anti-money laundering and counter terrorist financing purposes by the FSA. In the 2007 Regulations, the FSA is referred to as 'the Authority'.

HM Revenue and Customs (HMRC)   *See* Designated authorities and Supervisory authorities. (Note that HMRC is referred to in the 2007 Regulations as 'the Commissioners'.)

Home Office Circular   The Home Office regularly publishes official guidance addressed to chief constables and other senior law enforcement officers, in the form of Home Office Circulars. Among those currently in force are one on the confidentiality and sensitivity of SARs and the identity of those who make them (circular 53/2005), and another on the consent regime for SARs, incorporating guidance on when consent should be given or refused (circular 029/2008). The latter circular should be read with the 'consent policy' in annex A, which is intended to be followed by all law enforcement agencies.

The Law Society of England and Wales   The Law Society is the representative body for solicitors in England and Wales. Its regulatory arm is the Solicitors Regulation Authority (*see* below). The Law Society has issued guidance to solicitors in its Anti-Money Laundering Practice Note.

Money Laundering Advisory Committee (MLAC)   MLAC is the UK government's high-level advisory committee on money laundering and the proceeds of crime.

Money laundering reporting officer (MLRO)   MLRO is the term generally used in the regulated sector for individuals given the responsibility to act as nominated officers (*see* below). MLROs often have other related responsibilities in connection with money laundering and terrorist financing, such as responsibility for anti-money laundering training.

National Criminal Intelligence Service (NCIS)   NCIS was a UK policing agency in which the UK FIU was located until April 2006. From that date, the Serious Organised Crime Agency (SOCA) took over responsibility for the UK FIU.

Nominated officer   A nominated officer is a person nominated by a discloser's employer to receive disclosures under various sections of Part 7 of POCA and Part III of TA 2000. The term 'nominated officer' is the one used in POCA 2002 and TA 2000; outside the confines of statute, nominated officers are usually called MLROs. (*See also* Money Laundering Reporting Officer).

Occasional transaction   'Occasional transaction' is a defined term (defined in Regulation 2) and means a transaction (carried out other than as part of a business relationship) amounting to 15,000 euros or more, whether the transaction is carried out in a single operation or several operations which appear to be linked. Accordingly, a relevant person does not need to apply customer due diligence measures when he carries out a transaction (whether carried out in a single operation or several linked operations) that is not part of a business relationship if it involves less than 15,000 euros.

Office of Fair Trading (OFT)   See Designated authorities and Supervisory authorities.

Outsourcing   The outsourcing of CDD measures is different from 'reliance' and is no more than a particular method by which a relevant person carries out the obligation to apply CDD to customers or clients. The use of commercial third party credit reference agencies to verify the identity of customers is widespread. To avoid confusion, Regulation 17(4) makes it clear that a relevant person can apply customer due diligence measures 'by means of an outsourcing service provider or agent'.

Palermo Convention   The United Nations Convention against Transnational Organized Crime (Palermo Convention) 2000. Article 6 of the Convention restated in wider terms the money laundering offences that had originally been set out in the Vienna Convention (q.v.).

Politically exposed persons   In summary, the term PEP refers to an individual who has a 'prominent public function' in a state other than the UK, a community institution or an international body, as well as an immediate family member or close associate of a PEP. The full definition is set out in Regulation 14(5) and paragraph 4 of Schedule 2 of POCA.

Protected disclosures   A protected disclosure is not really an additional category of disclosure but is a term that describes certain types of disclosure specified in section 337 and the protection given to disclosers who make any of those disclosures.

Recoverable property   Recoverable property is property obtained through unlawful conduct. Recoverable property is defined for the purposes of cash forfeiture proceedings in section 304(1) of POCA 2002.

The regulated sector   The 'regulated sector' is a term widely used to describe collectively the natural and legal persons who are subject to the requirements of the Money Laundering Regulations 2007. In the Regulations they are referred to as 'relevant persons'.

Relevant persons   A relevant person means a person, whether a legal person or an individual, who is subject to the requirements of the 2007 Regulations. (*See also* Regulated sector.)

Reliance   Regulation 17 makes provision to allow relevant persons—in limited and defined circumstances—to rely on another person to apply CDD measures. Reliance is confined to certain categories of person whose status is such that it is considered appropriate that they can be relied on for this purpose.

Reporting sector   The 'reporting sector' is not a term of art and is not used in the Regulations. It is, however, a term used in connection with the suspicious activity reporting regime. The reporting sector consists of a large number of private sector organizations, mainly but not wholly regulated bodies, across a wide variety of businesses and professions. The 'reporting sector' is wider than the 'regulated sector' because some required disclosures are made by MLROs in businesses outside the regulated sector and authorised disclosures may be made by anyone. The reporting sector, therefore, consists mainly of companies and professional firms, large and small, as well as unincorporated businesses and sole traders.

Required disclosures   *See* Disclosures.

The risk-based approach   The risk-based approach is now an essential feature of anti-money laundering regulation, with particular reference to the application of CDD measures.

It requires a relevant person to apply such measures '. . . on a risk sensitive basis depending on the type of customer, business relationship, product or transaction . . .' More generally, relevant persons must establish and maintain appropriate and risk sensitive policies and procedures relating to money laundering and terrorist financing.

SAR Online   SAR Online, which incorporates the SOCA preferred reporting form, is the facility provided by SOCA on its website for the submission of SARs to the UK FIU. SAR Online provides a convenient and practical way to report for anyone in the regulated sector and outside it. For the discloser, it also has the advantage that submission of the SAR Online form automatically generates a receipt by email which contains SOCA's allocated reference number for the report.

SARs (Suspicious Activity Reports)   In UK practice, 'Suspicious Activity Report' or 'SAR' is the generic term for disclosures used by the Financial Intelligence Unit (FIU) at SOCA, and by law enforcement, regulators and the regulated sector.

Serious Organised Crime Agency (SOCA)   SOCA is the national law enforcement agency responsible for proactive operations against serious and organized crime. When it was set up in 2006, it took over the functions of the National Criminal Intelligence Service (NCIS). The UK FIU is now part of SOCA.

Simplified CDD   *See* Disclosures.

Solicitors Regulation Authority (SRA)   The Solicitors Regulation Authority is responsible for the regulation of solicitors in England and Wales, including the supervision of solicitors for anti-money laundering purposes. The SRA is part of the Law Society for administrative and legal reasons, but operates separately and independently from the representative part of the Law Society. The SRA deals with all regulatory and disciplinary matters, and sets, monitors, and enforces standards for solicitors across England and Wales.

Supervisory authorities   The regulated sector now consists not only of the banks and financial institutions, but also of a range of other businesses and professions. (See DNFBPs.) Like the banks, most of these businesses and professions were already regulated for reasons of public interest that are separate from any concerns about money laundering and terrorist financing. For the most part, therefore, supervisory authorities under the 2007 Regulations are existing regulators and supervisors. There are, however, relevant persons such as money service businesses and high value dealers who were not previous regulated. Responsibility as a supervisory authority for previously unregulated businesses has been given to various bodies such as HMRC and the OFT.

Suspicious transaction report (STR)   In international documents and in UK statutes and regulations, a number of different words and terms are used for anti-money laundering and counter terrorist financing disclosure. FATF uses the term 'suspicious transaction report' (STR); the EC Third Directive refers to 'disclosures of information'. In POCA 2002 and in TA 2000, the word 'disclosure' is used.

Terrorist financing   Terrorist financing is widely defined in the 2007 Regulations to bring together the offences under TA 2000 and further offences under the ATCSA 2001 and the sanctions provisions in the orders implementing United Nations measures. The main offences of terrorist financing are those under the following sections of TA 2000: section 15 (fund-raising), section 16 (use and possession), section 17 (funding arrangements), section 18 (money laundering), and section 63 (terrorist finance: jurisdiction).

Terrorist property   Section 14(1) of the 2000 Act defines 'terrorist property' as:
   (a) money or other property which is likely to be used for the purposes of terrorism (including any resources of a prescribed organization);

(b) proceeds of the commission of acts of terrorism; and

(c) proceeds of acts carried out for the purposes of terrorism.

UK Financial Intelligence Unit (UK FIU) The UK FIU has national responsibility for receiving, analysing, and disseminating financial intelligence submitted through the SARs regime. The UK FIU was originally located in the National Criminal Intelligence Service (NCIS), but this body was abolished in 2006 and its functions were transferred to the then newly established Serious Organised Crime Agency. Since April 2006, the UK FIU has been part of SOCA.

Vienna Convention The United Nations Convention against Illicit Traffic in Narcotic Drugs and Psychotropic Substances (the Vienna Convention), 1988 and the United Nations Convention against Transnational Organized Crime (Palermo Convention), 2000 are the starting point for international recognition of the concept of money laundering and for the definition of anti-money laundering offences.

INDEX

Printed in Great Britain
by Amazon.co.uk, Ltd.,
Marston Gate.